Production Management Analysis

Second Edition

Production Management Analysis

Second Edition

Leonard J. Garrett

*Professor of Management and
Chairman of the Department of Information Sciences
Temple University*

Milton Silver

*Professor of Management and Operations Research and
Director of the Institute of Urban Management
Drexel Institute of Technology*

Harcourt Brace Jovanovich, Inc.
New York   Chicago   San Francisco   Atlanta

© 1966, 1973 by Harcourt Brace Jovanovich, Inc.

ISBN: 0-15-571991-2

Library of Congress Catalog Card Number: 73-1831

Printed in the United States of America

Preface

Over the last several years, production management has changed in three important ways. It has become more analytical, it has placed increased emphasis on the systems approach, and it has broadened its area of concern to encompass nonmanufacturing activities.

In preparing this second edition of *Production Management Analysis,* we have tried to reflect these changes and still maintain a balance between the descriptive and analytical approaches. Each chapter contains a brief synopsis of the institutional characteristics of the phase of production under discussion that acquaints the reader with the special problems encountered in that phase. This background enables the reader to evaluate the analytical techniques available. He is not led to believe that production management analysis is merely a collection of unrelated solution techniques, nor is he deluged with descriptive material that ignores the analytical tools available to production management.

Such modern tools of management science as linear programing, queueing theory, information systems, and simulation are introduced within the context of specific production problems. We emphasize that these are not abstract concepts but ways of solving real management problems.

To reflect the increasing emphasis on the systems approach to management analysis, we have reorganized our material to some extent. Part I presents an overview of the management process, including a brief historical survey of production management and an introduction to systems analysis and its applications to managerial decision making. To illustrate the systems approach, Chapter 1 discusses how the production system, as a subsystem of the firm, in turn comprises a number of smaller subsystems. In treating the problems of these smaller subsystems in individual chapters, we thus simplify our study of the production system as a whole.

Part II considers the product, material, capital, and labor inputs to the production process. The discussion of forecasting has been expanded and set apart in Chapter 14. In the section on labor, we have added Chapter 9 on the human factors to be considered in production—human physiological and psychological needs as they relate to the design of the working environment and work methods.

Part III deals with the production process itself. The topics here range from plant location to cost and quality control, acquainting the reader with the diversity of process-related problems and the methods of their solution. An important addition to this part of the book is the section in Chapter 21 on learning curves, which have been found to be a valuable aid in production planning.

The question and problem sections at the end of each chapter have been carefully revised and expanded to provide the instructor with ample material for testing the student's understanding of both concepts and techniques. Finally, the list of references appended to each chapter will help the instructor to expand upon subjects of particular interest to the class.

We wish to thank once again all those whose efforts and encouragement helped us publish the first edition of this work. In addition, we thank the many people who have helped us with the present volume. The efforts of the entire Harcourt staff have been invaluable. In particular, Robert Syron has been the source of much of the motivation for the work. Jo Satloff has been of immense help, editing the manuscript and staying on top of all the problems. Pam Goett's considerable efforts reduced the reviews of text and artwork to a bearable level.

Finally, we are indebted to Rolfe Garrett, who has helped immeasurably by reading and revising galleys and page proofs.

Leonard J. Garrett

Milton Silver

Contents

Introduction 1

PART I Management

Chapter 1   *The Production System*   7

History   7
The Systems Approach   9
Systems Flow Patterns   9
Comprehensive Systems Flow Diagrams   11
Subsystems   15
Comprehensive System Model   18
The Firm as a System   20
Text Organization   22

Chapter 2   *The Management Process*   28

A Definition of Management   29
Management Theories   29
The General Functions of Management   31
Planning   31
Organizing   37
Assembling Resources   44
Directing   45
Controlling   48
The Interrelation of Management Functions   51

Chapter 3   *Managerial Decision Making*   54

The Background of Decision Making   54
Decision Theory   56

The Scientific Method   60
Models as Decision Aids   62
Systems Approach to Decision Making   70
The Decision Process   70
Problem Types and Decision Approaches   73
The Management Task   82

PART II   Inputs

Chapter 4   *Product Design and Development*   87

The Innovation Cycle   88
The Role of Management   94
The PERT Concept   98

Chapter 5   *Product Reliability and Quality Assurance*   122

A Company View   124
Quality Assurance Programs   125
Product Effectiveness   130
Product Reliability   132

Chapter 6   *Product-Line Determination*   145

Evaluation of New Product Lines   145
Product Planning   154
Evaluation of the Existing Product Line   155
A Balanced Product Line   160

Chapter 7   *Capital Planning*   180

Demand for Capital   181
Supply of Capital   183
Capital Allocation   184
Evaluation of Specific Opportunities   188
Investment Decision Factors   192

Chapter 8   *Capital-Allocation Methods*   201

Methods of Evaluation   201
Summary of Basic Methods   214
Advanced Methods of Analysis   216
Noneconomic Investment Factors   227

Chapter 9   *Human Factors and the Design
of Work Conditions*   233

Man as a Physical System—Anatomical Factors   233
Working Conditions   234
Man as a Behavioral System   239

Chapter 10   *The Design of Work Methods*   250

Productivity and Efficiency   251
Identifying the Problem   253
Describing the Problem   254
Analyzing the Problem   259
Developing New Work Methods   271
Selecting the Best Method   272
Installing the New Method   280
Following Up the Installation of the New Method   281
Management's Role in Methods Study   281
Work Methods in Clerical Activities   281

Chapter 11   *The Development of Labor Standards*   285

Standards of Measurement   286
Approaches to Work Measurement   287

Chapter 12   *The Selection and Payment of a Labor Force*   328

Selection of Workers   328
Employee Selection   333
Personnel Training   335
Hiring   336
Wage and Salary Administration   337
Summary   352

Chapter 13   *Materials Management—
Purchasing and Inventory*   355

Historical Aspects of Materials Management   356
Materials Management   357
The Purchasing Function   361
The Purchasing Policy   371
The Inventory Problem   376
The Functions of Inventory   379

Chapter 14   *Demand Forecasts*   385

      Forecasting   387
      Forecasting Approaches   390

Chapter 15   *Inventory Control Systems*   417

      Inventory Costs in the Purchase of Goods   417
      Inventory Costs in the Supply of Goods   420
      Inventory Models   421
      Aggregate Inventory Concepts   432
      Inventory Models with Uncertainty   436
      Inventory Systems   440
      A Sample Inventory Problem   447
      The Overall Inventory Problem   450

PART III   Production Process

Chapter 16   *Plant Location Analysis*   459

      Location   459
      Measurement of Locational Factors   462
      The Location-Decision Process   470
      Current Location Trends   480

Chapter 17   *Plant Layout Analysis*   487

      Layout   487
      Classes of Layout   495
      Comparison of Layout Classes   498
      The Layout Compromise   499
      Service Considerations   510

Chapter 18   *Materials Handling Systems*   516

      Materials Handling Equipment   517
      Design of a Materials Handling System   522
      Operating Effectiveness   537

Chapter 19   *Production Planning and Control*
             I: Preproduction Planning   542

      The Production Environment   543
      Preproduction Activities   552
      Preproduction Planning   567

Chapter 20 *Production Planning and Control*
      II: The Production Process 572
    Routing 573
    Scheduling 577
    Activating 595
    Monitoring 596
    An Overview 601

Chapter 21 *Maintenance Analysis* 609
    The Concept of Maintenance 609
    Minimizing Total Maintenance Costs 613
    Balancing Preventive Maintenance and Breakdown
        Maintenance 613
    Repair Alternatives 615
    Crew Size Considerations 625
    Maintenance Information 637

Chapter 22 *Quality Control Systems* 642
    Manufacturing Quality Assurance 642
    Production Quality Assurance 646
    Acceptance Sampling 648
    Attribute Sampling 651
    Variable Sampling 662
    Control Charts 662

Chapter 23 *The Firm as a Cost System* 676
    Introduction 676
    The Setting of Cost Control Standards 680
    Comparative Evaluation of Actual Costs 688
    Use of Costs Standards 697
    The Firm as a Cost System 702
    Other Uses of Cost Standards 702
    An Overview of Cost Standards 705

Appendix

    Glossary of PERT Terms 709
    Table of Logarithms 711
    Present Value of $1.00 713
    Present Value of $1.00 Received Annually for x Years 714

Index 715

Introduction

A Working Definition

"Production" and "management" are general terms that have been defined in many ways. Dictionaries state broadly that production is "the act or process of producing," and management is "the art of managing." This is certainly true, but these definitions give us very little insight into the meaning of the subject of this book, "production management." The difficulties encountered in trying to obtain a meaningful definition of production management from the dictionary are typical. Within business, even within the production management field itself, there are only inadequate descriptions of the field. The reason for this dilemma is that, by its nature, production management is a difficult process to describe. As a consequence, in this book we will not attempt to construct a simple or concise definition. Instead, we will try to develop an understanding of production management by describing its characteristics.

The basis of production is the transformation of inputs into goods and services. Five input factors—information, management, materials and land, labor, and capital—are employed within a firm to create a mix of output goods and services. Figure I–1 is a graphical presentation of this process.

Production management, then, is the management of the transformation process. In general it is responsible for the performance of the following tasks:

1. *Specifying and accumulating the input resources required.*

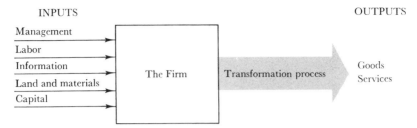

Figure I-1   A general diagram of the production process

2. *Designing and installing the assembly or conversion process that will be employed to transform input resources into output goods and services.*
3. *Coordinating and operating the production process so that the desired goods and services are made efficiently.*

The first of these tasks is concerned with providing the proper mix of production inputs needed to create the output goods or services; the others are devoted to the design and operation of the transformation process.

This listing is not meant to suggest that production management is not also involved in the design and specification of output goods and services. In fact, determining the quantity and type of output is the starting point for decisions regarding production inputs and processes. Moreover, this relationship is circular, since decisions about the nature of the outputs must reflect the capabilities of the transformation process in terms of cost, volume, and quality. However, the major responsibility for the determination of output characteristics and the performance of the distribution functions, including pricing and selling, is normally outside the scope of production management.

The Nature of Production/Operations Management

With this background, let us consider the nature of the production manager's job. Production management involves both theory and art. The theory portion is concerned with the methodology or approaches used in making managerial decisions. These range from simple diagrams such as flow charts and factory layouts to complex and abstract mathematical models.

The art portion of production management encompasses a mixture of intuition and judgment. As with all form of art, these aspects are difficult to place into a book or to teach. Consequently, in teaching production management we are primarily concerned with presenting the nature of the transformation process and the decision approaches that lead to an effective production system.

Such a presentation of production management can be independent of the specific transformation process involved. The basic production problems arise in all types of processes, and the decision approaches apply to all types of processes. That is why production management may be taught in school. If the problems and methodology were not general for all production systems, regardless of the particular technology involved, we would be forced to have an apprenticeship system where the student could acquire through experience not only the art but also the theory of production management.

The scope of this textbook encompasses the general concepts, problems, and methodologies of production management. Although the examples are drawn primarily from manufacturing, the text fits individuals who may enter such diverse fields as banking, transportation, communication, hospitals, mining, food processing, data processing, brokerage, and petroleum. Each of these industries is involved to some degree in a transformation process and thus encounters the problems of production management.

The breadth of the concept of production management and the fact that the production process is essential to nonprofit, profit, and governmental organizations have in recent years led to the use of the term *production/operations management* in place of production management. This term highlights the generality of the production function and its application to all types of organizations. In keeping with this, we will employ the term production/operations management wherever it will help to convey the breadth of the applications of the material under discussion.

The Objective of the Text

The aim of this book is to provide a broad view of production/operations management. We have tried to balance descriptive and analytical material. Descriptions of production areas and the problems involved are blended with analytical approaches that fit these problems so that the student can understand both the problem and the techniques of its solution; this method of presentation provides a sound framework for the teaching of production management.

Most of the illustrations presented in this book are drawn from large firms, but this is so only because of the accessibility of the material. The principles and concepts discussed are equally applicable to both large and small companies.

I

Management

In order properly to carry out the function of production/operations management, managers need to understand the nature of their task, the relationship of production management to the other functions of a firm, and their place in the management hierarchy. Part I provides the background information necessary to such an understanding.

Chapter 1, "The Production System," first presents a brief history of production/operations management, outlining the evolution of ideas and bringing the reader up to the current systems approach. Next it presents the general systems concepts that underlie production systems, focusing on the inputs, outputs, and conversion aspects of systems. These concepts of general systems are then applied in turn to the firm and to the production function. Finally, the organization of this book is detailed, using the systems approach.

Chapter 2, "The Management Process," treats the basic management jobs of planning, organizing, assembling resources, directing, and controlling. Since these tasks are common to all managers, they act as a link between production management and other managerial functions. In discussing these jobs, an effort is made to show how the organization and authority relationships in a firm will influence the production manager. The objective of this chapter is to show the student where and how production/operations management fits into the overall scheme of the firm and into the field of general management.

Chapter 3, "Managerial Decision Making," concludes Part I with a survey of the decision approaches used in the production field. The decision-making approaches are presented only briefly in this chapter, in order to lay the groundwork for their future use. In later chapters, detailed examples of each method will be used to solve specific production problems.

In sum, Part I is designed to give the readers enough background information on systems, the essential value of management, and the analytical methods used by managers in coping with problems that they may relate the discussions of specific problem areas, which follow, to the larger concept of the firm as a whole.

1

The Production System

History

It is quite obvious that production systems have existed since the earliest times. One has only to consider the Pyramids, the Great Wall of China, Greek and Roman temples, and ancient cities with hundreds of thousands of people to recognize that production activities have long been organized and coordinated.

During these early periods and through the Middle Ages the production process was largely powered by individual human efforts. With the introduction of the steam engine, this cottage-type industry was rapidly replaced by a factory system. Machines replaced muscle; semiskilled labor replaced artisans; and, above all, production facilities were concentrated around the source of power.

Through the nineteenth century the factory system developed into an efficient, if less than humane, means of production. Little consideration was given to the well-being of the worker. Production workers were equated to machinery. Men, women, and children worked up to 12 hours a day six days a week. Working conditions were unsafe, unsanitary, and generally unpleasant. Production was forced from the worker rather than elicited. However, despite this dismal background, the very nature of the factory system led to the formulation of new production concepts. Many of the approaches now followed in plant layout, division of labor, departmentalization of work, material flows, and incentives were conceived or refined during this time.

Early in the twentieth century, a group of men led by Frederick Winslow Taylor, often called the "father of scientific management," pioneered in developing production management as a science. Taylor was the founder of a school that included, among others, Carl Barth, Henry L. Gantt, and Harrington Emerson, as well as more contemporary followers such as Frank and Lillian Gilbreth. The writings of this scientific management school are primarily concerned with production operations. Present-day practices and techniques in such production management areas as labor simplification and measurement and plant scheduling are outgrowths of the ideas developed by the members of this school.

Perhaps the major contribution of Taylor and his followers was the introduction of the "scientific method of problem solving." This was an attempt to apply formalized scientific methods of inquiry to business problems. To further this effort, new ways of describing and analyzing managerial problems were developed. Charts were designed, for example, for use in analyzing manual factory operations. One of these charts, the "elemental breakdown form," is still applied to stopwatch time study, and another, the "left hand–right hand" chart, is still used in making motion studies of individual operators at work. The solution to a problem would be chosen only after the alternatives had been developed and evaluated. As will be seen throughout this book, modern managers still use many of these methods of analyzing difficult problems.

The impetus that Taylor and his followers gave to the search for sound managerial decision techniques led to the development of a great number of analytical approaches. Many of these, which fit specific functional areas of production management, will be presented in later chapters during the consideration of those functions.

In their studies, Taylor and his immediate followers adopted a mechanistic view of man. Workers were viewed primarily as machines of production; their behavioral characteristics were neglected. Later, in the 1920s, the behavioral aspects of workers began to be taken into consideration. The Hawthorne experiments conducted at Western Electric clearly indicated that psychological factors such as recognition and morale played an important part in productivity and were as important as working conditions and wages. Thus another dimension was added to the study of production systems.

The work of Walter Shewhart and Henry Ford added still other facets. Shewhart conceived the statistical control techniques that are the foundation of mass production with interchangeable parts. Ford took these techniques and developed them in his production facilities.

The most recent step of this evolution began during World War II. At that time considerable research was undertaken in military operations, which resulted in a knowledge of how to apply mathematical and other interdisciplinary scientific approaches to military operations and produced new mathematical approaches that could be used in the decision process. After the war these new procedures found their way into business. Over the past thirty years, their use has developed and changed, maturing into what is commonly termed the "systems approach." Although it is still in its embryonic state, the systems approach to production management is gaining increasing favor.

The Systems Approach

What Is a System?

We are surrounded by and live in many systems. In fact, we ourselves are each a system. Some systems are natural, such as the planetary system, animal systems, insect systems, and environmental systems. Others are man-made, such as social and business systems.

Before proceeding further, let us define what we shall mean here by the term *system*. In a general sense, it has been said that a system is any on-going process. However, since this definition would be of little help to us, we shall define a system as *a purposeful means for accomplishing an objective*. For our purposes, therefore, a system must have a specific set of objectives that it is expected to accomplish by means of precise methods and procedures. An integral part of any production process, for example, is a materials handling system. The objective of this system is to move production material through the process by utilizing established methods and procedures. There are, of course, virtually an infinite number of systems that could be established for this purpose. But a good materials handling system is one that can achieve this common objective (given the requirements of a particular company) at minimum cost.

The Objective of the Systems Approach

The objective of the systems approach is to provide management with an analytical framework with which it can identify, describe, and interrelate the processes and components that make up a particular system. Stated in another fashion, the systems approach allows a manager to maintain the perspective of the whole process while he analyzes its parts.

Systems Flow Patterns

Elementary Flow Patterns

Systems are most often viewed as flow charts or block diagrams. The most elementary presentation is shown in Figure 1–1. The major parts of a system are the input, conversion process, and output. The flow of the system is such that inputs are passed through a conversion process to produce outputs.

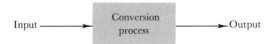

Figure 1–1 Elementary systems flow diagram

Inputs

The inputs to a system can be classified in a number of ways. For our purposes we will divide them into three kinds. The first will comprise the materials that flow through the conversion process. Work is performed on these materials, which are called the *systems load*. In a hospital, the systems load is the patients; in a beauty parlor or barber shop, the customers; in an insurance office, the policies, claims, and payments; in a factory, the materials that will be assembled into the final output—the parts and materials that will become an automobile, radio, or other product.

The second kind of input is the environment that affects the systems operations. The environment of a system will be discussed in detail later in the chapter; at this time let us merely identify it. The environment is composed of those influences on the system which constrain the system and over which the systems designers have no control. In a natural system the force of gravity is environmental; men working on rockets or airplanes cannot change gravity but must consider it in their systems design. In like fashion, the laws of the country and the general state of the economy are examples of environmental factors influencing a production system. The designer of a hospital, office, factory, or assembly plant rarely, if ever, can change these factors, but it is evident that they will materially influence the system with which he is concerned.

The third and final category covers the energy, capital, management, labor, land, and information inputs that combine to make up the conversion process itself. The design of the amount, placement, timing, and type of these inputs is in fact the design of the conversion facility—the hospital, factory, or office.

Conversion Process

The second basic part of a system is the conversion process, through which the inputs flow to produce the desired outputs. To be both effective and efficient, systems must be designed so that the correct process acts on the inputs at the proper time. Again using our previous examples, patients in a hospital flow (in a real or figurative sense) from one process to another, from X-ray to laboratory to operating room. Parts for automobiles must flow into the production line at the correct place and time to be properly ssembled into the finished automobile. Each step in the conversion process must perform the work assigned to it.

Output

The third and last of the major components of a system is the output. Output comprises the accomplishment of the system. In the automobile factory it is the number of completed cars of a desired quality produced within a specified time frame. It is not simply the number of cars, since without quality and timing criteria the number of cars in itself is not completely useful.

Every system must have a set of goals or objectives that it attempts to meet. Without them the nature of the output becomes meaningless. As in *Alice in Wonderland,* "If you don't know where you are going it doesn't matter how you get there." If goals are well defined and measurable, an evaluation of the effectiveness and efficiency of the system can be made. Without well-defined and measurable goals, systems evaluation becomes extremely difficult if not impossible. Consequently, output criteria are an important part of any system. In fact, the critical problem in the design of a system is to determine the inputs and the conversion process, with its capacity and flows, that will best meet the output measurement criteria.

Comprehensive Systems Flow Diagrams

We will now expand our general view of a system by adding control elements, by discussing the environment in detail, and by introducing the notion and role of information flows and subsystems. When this is done, we will be able to present a comprehensive view of a system.

Control

Just as goals or objectives are needed in the design of a system, control is required in its operation. The purpose of the control is to maintain the quality and quantity of the output so that it meets the goals of the system. In the ideal case the control would be self-regulating and thus hold the output at the desired level without outside intervention.

For a simple example of a self-regulating control, consider a heating thermostat. The device shown in Figure 1–2 is designed to keep the room temperature—the output of the heating system—between 68° and 72°F. Accordingly, we may consider this temperature range as the output standard. A measuring device inside the thermostat continuously monitors the room temperature. When it falls below 68°, a signal is fed back to the heating elements, ordering them to activate. Heat is then supplied to the room until the temperature is again up to 72°, at which time the feedback signal shuts the heat off. All the elements of any control system are present in this simple system:

1. *A well-defined objective*
2. *An output standard*
3. *A measuring device*
4. *A feedback signal*
5. *A corrective course of action*

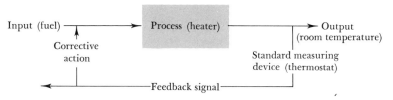

Figure 1–2   A simple control system

Moreover, in our example each element is so precisely defined that the system may operate automatically without the need for human intervention.

Unfortunately, in most management situations not all of the elements of control are present, or if they are, they are not precisely defined. Consider, for example, a production process in which a standard of ten units of output per hour has been established for a job. When the output from the process is monitored, however, it is found that eight units are being produced per hour. In this situation there is an objective, an output standard, a measuring device, and a feedback signal, but no corrective action has been specified. This break between feedback and correction is shown in Figure 1–3. Before corrective action can be taken, management must ascertain why the output standard is not being met. The reason could be faulty input material, a slow worker, incorrect methods, or a host of other factors. The corrective action is far from automatic. The absence of an automatic link between corrective action and the other four elements of control is one of the major reasons for the existence of a management hierarchy.

Gaps can also exist in the control process at the other points. The objective may be too vague; the output standard may be ill defined; the measuring device may not have the required accuracy, and the feedback signal may be missing. Regardless of the limitations of the control system, however, there must be a feedback of information, or else the control process cannot operate.

Environment

The concept of the environment was introduced in the discussion of systems inputs. At this time let us elaborate on that discussion.

A system's environment is composed of all activities outside of the system which if changed will affect the system, or which will be changed by the system.

In this context the general level of economic activity can be considered as environmental for most production activities, since changes in it will affect production levels. The interdependency of the system and its environment is also recognized by environmental conservationists, who are concerned with production processes because outputs from the processes, such as heat and wastes, may act upon the natural environment.

This raises the question, When is an activity that affects the system part of the system and when is it outside the system and thus in the system's environment?

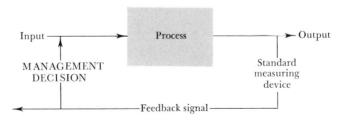

Figure 1–3   A control system with nonautomatic correction

If an activity can change the system, should it not be considered as part of the system? In practice, it is not easy to answer this question; it is never easy to separate the essential elements of a system from the nonessential.

Let us illustrate the problem by returning to the heating system example. On an every-day basis, an architect designing a city house does not consider the source of heating fuel in the design of the heating system. He will evaluate alternative types of fuel—electricity, gas, coal, oil—but he is not concerned with their source. If he selects electrical heat, the electricity will be available from the electrical company—he is not concerned with the power stations or lines carrying the electricity. Similarly, if he chooses oil, he is not concerned with the company that will supply it. For his purposes the availability of the fuel is outside his concern, outside his heating system, and therefore in the system's environment. Certainly, problems may occur with the fuel supply. Electrical blackouts happen; strikes prevent fuel oil delivery; but these events do not occur often enough to merit their inclusion in the design of the heating system.

In a hospital, however, where loss of power could be critical, the source of power is considered in the design of the electrical system. Lines from more than one power station may be run to the building, and gasoline generators may be installed. In this way the hospital can be assured of power regardless of what occurs. Thus we see that whether an element is included as part of the system or in its environment depends on the goal of the system.

When everything that is essential to the system is part of the system and controllable, the system is said to be a *closed system*. Such a system can be self-regulating. Environmental changes will not influence it. In the hospital, for example, power for lighting and life support systems would be available at all times. For practical purposes, the house heating system is also closed, even though on rare occasions it is really not.

Systems designers would like to have all systems closed and self-regulating since everything essential to the system would then be under their control. Most production systems, however, are open systems. This results from two causes. First, economic, political, and human elements exist that materially influence the systems, are not controllable in the system, and are thus environmental. Second, in many cases not enough is known about the process to specify everything necessary to the system. Such systems cannot be self-regulating but require management control action on a continual day-by-day basis.

Information Flow

As just noted, to effectively control a system, data relevant to the activity must be transmitted to the decision maker. This is true whether the system is self-regulating or requires management for decision making. In all cases a means of accumulating, storing, processing, and transmitting data must be an integral part of the system.

For analysis we can divide the systems data flow into three classes: operating data, control data, and planning data. These categories are not exclusive; the same item of information may fit into all three. The three types of data are identified simply to illustrate different aspects of the information flow.

Operating data   Operating data include all the routine information that must be generated within the system in order to keep it in motion. Some of the kinds of information that must be kept just to operate a business, for example, are receiving reports, purchase orders, and payroll records. The generation of operating data is a fairly routine activity. Because of this, companies generally computerize their operating activities first.

Control data   The second type of data is control (or feedback) information. Since systems are designed to achieve specific objectives, they must be monitored continuously to make sure that they are meeting those objectives satisfactorily. Thus, data reflecting the status of operations must be constantly reviewed. For example, in the production of an item, a specified number of labor hours are often allocated for each unit of production. In supervising the process, management wants to know if this standard is being met or if there is a significant deviation. Data conveying this information to management are called control information. The use of such data was illustrated in the discussion on systems control.

Planning data   The last type of data that should be available is planning data. This includes all the information that will be required by management to solve anticipated future problems. Problems do not remain the same; as soon as one problem is solved, another emerges. The management of a firm faces a continual inventory of problems as depicted in Figure 1–4. In the decision process, management uses both the information about the problem that it gets from the data flow and the knowledge it has gained through experience or schooling. Decisions and actions taken on problems breed new problems; and the consequence is that the exact nature of future problems cannot be known. Nonethe-

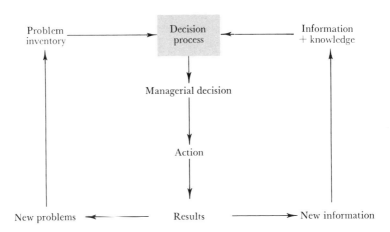

Figure 1–4   The problem-generation cycle

less, a manager must have information to work with. Since it is economically and technically impossible to collect data about everything, some limit must always be imposed on data accumulation; this forces managers to make a decision today about what information will be needed tomorrow.

The inability to predict exactly what information management will need has proved to be one of the most difficult problems encountered in the design of large-scale systems.

Subsystems

Because of the complexity of most real systems, it is extremely difficult to work with or to understand the entire system. In order to overcome this problem, systems are broken into smaller and smaller subsystems until the individual subsystems are understandable. In other words, we look at an overall system, such as a production system, as a group of subsystems in order to understand the overall system.

A total production system may be viewed as being composed of many subsystems, each of which possesses the characteristics shown in Figure 1–5. Here we see that each subsystem receives inputs that are fed into a conversion process that has its own feedback system for control purposes. The process is carried out, yielding outputs.

In the purchasing process shown in Figure 1–6, for example, requisitions are received in the purchasing department, where they are then processed, yielding purchase orders. All of this activity takes place within the purchasing department, under that department's control.

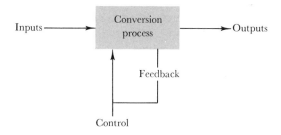

Figure 1–5   Basic subsystem

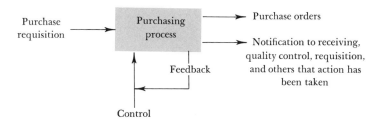

Figure 1–6   The purchasing subsystem

It is important to note that as long as the inputs to and outputs from the purchasing department remain stable, it does not matter to the requisitioner and other affected departments how purchasing does its work. Purchasing may change its internal system as often as it wishes without affecting the other departments. However, any change in the inputs to or the outputs from the purchasing department will necessitate changes in the purchasing system and in the other subsystems that are related to it. The stability of inputs and outputs is the basis of systems engineering, since it enables the designer merely to indicate the inputs and outputs without specifying the details of the process. Accordingly, the process is often depicted graphically as a black box, or magical square, in which inputs are transformed into the desired outputs. The actual way in which this conversion is performed is left to the subsequent design of the individual processes. By specifying only the inputs and outputs, a complicated system can be greatly simplified and reduced to manageable proportions for analysis of its interrelationships.

This concept of systems engineering is illustrated graphically in Figures 1–7 through 1–9. In Figure 1–7 we see an entire production system, composed of three subsystems, in which the output from one subsystem is the input for the next. This is an extremely simple system since there are few interrelationships among the subsystems. Many straight-line, product-oriented systems follow this pattern.

Figure 1–8 shows parallel subsystems. Here the outputs from three prior processes—A, B, and C—are combined with input D as inputs into process D. As in the serial case, the feedback and control functions are self-contained within each individual subsystem.

The final type of system involves the feedback of output information or physical product from a subsystem later in the process to one earlier in the process. This type of system, shown in Figure 1–9, is characteristic of more complicated systems such as those usually encountered in production management. Notice that it incorporates both serial and parallel subsystems. Far more important, however, is the fact that output information from process B is fed back to process A, where it is used to control process A. Likewise, there is a feedback from process D to process C. This means that the control information necessary to direct processes A and C is not entirely generated within those processes and that, as a consequence, they are intimately coupled with other processes.

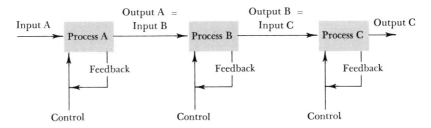

Figure 1–7 Serial subsystems

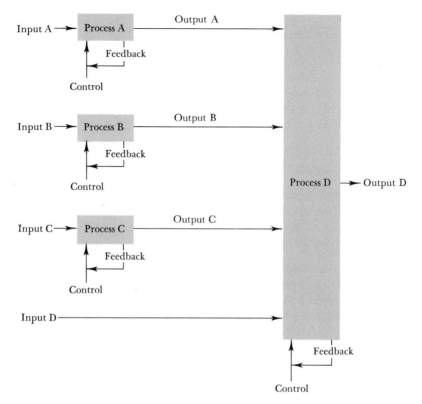

Figure 1–8   Parallel subsystems

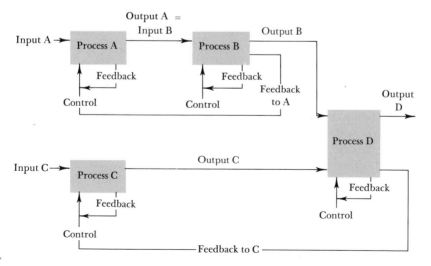

Figure 1–9   An integrated feedback system

This type of system can be illustrated by considering an extremely simple production line composed of a production operator and an inspector. The operator has the following inputs for his subsystem:

1. The required machine setup
2. The specifications for the output
3. The quantity of output needed
4. The raw materials to be processed

He sets up his machine and processes the materials. The operator's output is then given to an inspector whose inputs are:

1. The required work setup
2. The product test specifications
3. The quantity of output needed
4. The output from the operator

The inspector tests the output and passes on the good products. In addition, he has the output that the operator must rework and the feedback information on the causes of the rejects. This output is returned to the operator, where the rejects become material inputs and the feedback information serves as control information. This simple system is diagramed in Figure 1–10. It is a highly simplified case but quickly becomes more complex when we add such realistic details as the feedback of information on rejects from the inspector to the production foreman, to purchasing, and to engineering, for product redesign. In addition, each subsystem usually yields other outputs, information that is needed by various departments; for example, information about work hours on the job is needed by payroll, cost estimating, and the production foreman.

The operator–inspector system just described suggests the complexity of understanding any production system and why it is so difficult to discuss the entire production process. For this reason this book will concentrate on the separate subsystems of a production system.

Comprehensive System Model

Before completing the discussion of general systems concepts, let us look at a comprehensive model of a system that incorporates the ideas of our discussion. This model, illustrated in Figure 1–11, serves both for an overall system and for its subsystems. The figure shows three classes of inputs: the environment, materials to convert, and the resources that are used to produce the conversion process itself. These inputs are converted, and output goods or services are produced. The output is evaluated against the criteria of goal achievement. Where deviations exist, information is fed back to management, where the information is analyzed and a decision made. Action carrying out the decision is initiated, and changes in the inputs, conversion process, or measurement criteria are made when required.

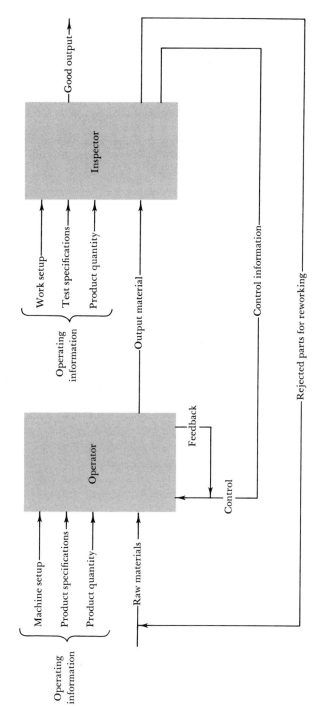

Figure 1–10 An operator–inspector subsystem

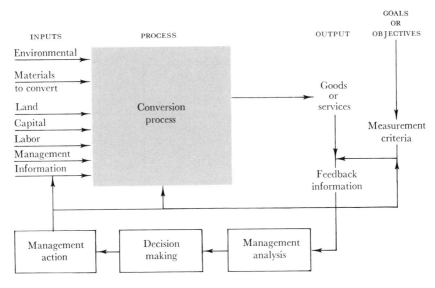

Figure 1–11 Comprehensive system model

The Firm as a System

We can now look at a firm as a system. Business firms and service organizations, be they manufacturing, sales, governmental, or hospital, are dynamic systems. A starting point in understanding them is to consider the needs or desires of their customers. Customer needs and desires represent market opportunities for firms that produce goods and services. Products are designed to meet these opportunities and are then produced in the conversion process. The finished goods or services are then marketed, fulfilling the needs and desires of the customers.

As can be seen in Figure 1–12, this system is dynamic. It operates continuously. Customer needs and desires undergo perpetual change; consequently, managements must constantly monitor their markets. When changes occur, the product, production, and marketing plans must be altered to meet the new situation. The faster the organization can react to the change, the greater the probability that it will survive and grow. Business, service, and governmental organizations are market oriented; they exist by meeting needs and desires, not by producing unwanted products. This does not mean that new products cannot in themselves create new desires. Style changes in clothing and automobiles, for example, are presented to the marketplace, and when they are acceptable they create demands. The cycle from needs and desires to needs and desires can be influenced at any point. Regardless of where the impetus for change originates, ultimately the firm must meet the market demands or cease to exist.

Production Systems

The production system is a subsystem of the firm system. In Figure 1–12 the production system includes all of the conversion process plus part of the product

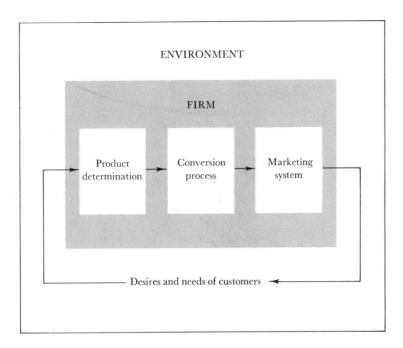

Figure 1–12 The firm as a system

determination. The task of deciding what product to make and when and how to produce it is a joint activity of marketing and production. The market desires and the conversion process available must both be considered and integrated.

Figure 1–13 represents an expanded view of the production system. It shows the major inputs to the production or conversion process. As in the earlier diagrams, the inputs are divided into three groups, environmental, resource, and material to convert. Environmental inputs include the legal, social, and environmental factors, which constrain and prescribe the production process, and the customer desires, needs, and reactions, which are an input to the product-planning activity. Resource inputs are the product information, capital, labor, and management inputs that shape and mold the conversion process. The final input is the materials to be converted in the production process. All three types of inputs play a part in the conversion process, whose outputs become inputs to the marketing system.

In order to look further into how a production system operates, let us make it more comprehensible by breaking it into subsystems. Figure 1–14 breaks down the system diagramed in Figure 1–13 into a number of subsystems. The subsystems shown here form the basis for the organization of material in this book. Each subsystem block corresponds to a chapter. This particular subsystems breakdown is by no means the only subsystem structure that could be designed for a production system. But it does represent a convenient way to organize a production system in order to analyze it, particularly for those readers who are studying production management for the first time.

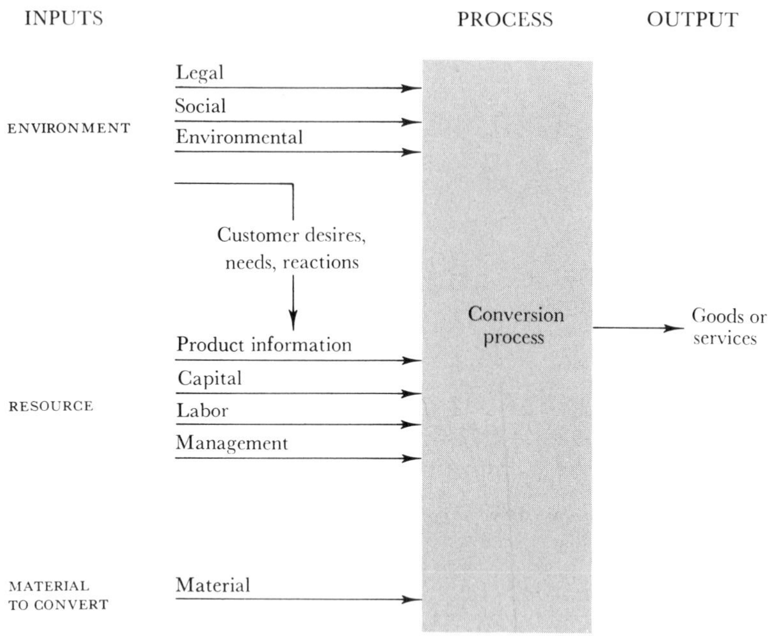

Figure 1–13   The production subsystem of a firm

When analyzing and studying anything as complex as a production system, it is not fruitful to look immediately at the overall system. The level of complexity is too great to be understood and only generates confusion. While it is conceptually nice to talk about studying the overall production system, it is not practical to do so. It is much better to break the system into subsystems. The institutional factors, decision processes, and system flows for each subsystem can be analyzed and understood. After that the interactions between the subsystems can be attacked, and with this comes understanding of the total production system.

Text Organization

This book is organized into three part to fit this systems approach: I, Management; II, Inputs; and III, Process.

Management

Part I consists of Chapters 1 through 3. This first chapter initially presented a brief history of the evolution of production management. With that as a base, the systems view of production management that is prevalent today was then treated in detail.

In the next two chapters the managerial inputs to the production process are examined in order to explain that part of the production manager's task which is shared by all other managers. The managerial inputs are divided into two sections, first the management process and second the concepts of managerial decision making. Although the presentation of these subjects is relatively brief, it will introduce the reader to the typical decision process and methodology used in production management. The management input is separated from the other inputs because the managerial process and decision making pervade every task of management and are thus central to it.

Inputs

Part II, Chapters 4 through 15, covers all the other inputs to the conversion process except the environmental inputs. Environmental considerations are scattered throughout the text to help convey the fact that they must be considered at every point in the system. For example, environmental constraints on managerial actions are discussed in the chapter on the management process, and specific environmental factors relating to the use of labor are analyzed in the chapter on human factors.

The study of the remaining inputs begins with an exploration of product planning. Product planning generates the specifications of the goods and services to be produced, thereby providing one of the bases for the design of the production system. In considering product planning, the areas in which production management is most involved are presented. They are product line determination, product design and development, and product reliability and quality assurance.

After this the capital inputs are discussed. The questions of how a firm budgets its capital resources and how production management can make the necessary economic decisions in the selection of facilities and equipment are analyzed in Chapters 7 and 8.

Four chapters are then devoted to labor. Chapter 9 considers the behavioral influences on workers' performance and attitudes. With this background information in hand, the subject of work methods is attacked in Chapter 10. The aim in presenting this chapter is to develop the methodology through which efficient man–machine systems can be designed. Chapter 11 deals with the problems and approaches of establishing output standards, while Chapter 12 analyzes the problems associated with acquiring, training, and paying a labor force.

The last three chapters on inputs are devoted to the management of input materials. "Materials" are broadly defined to include raw materials, supplies, work-in-process, and finished goods, in order to deal with inventory problems as a whole.

Process

The process tasks confronting the production manager begin with the determination of what kind of production plant will be needed. Aspects of the physical plant such as its location, layout, and materials movement have a strong effect on production costs and are therefore covered in the first three chapters of Part III.

INPUTS

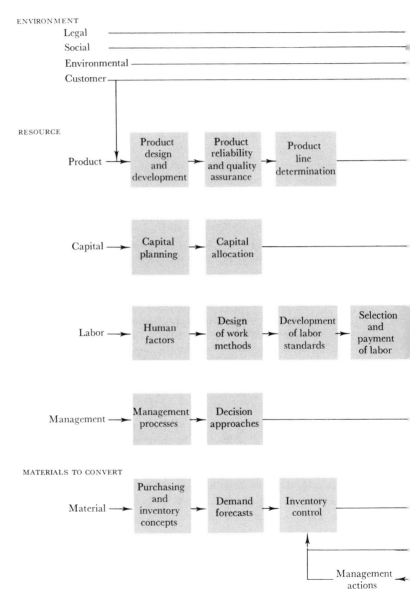

Figure 1–14   A subsystem structure of the production system

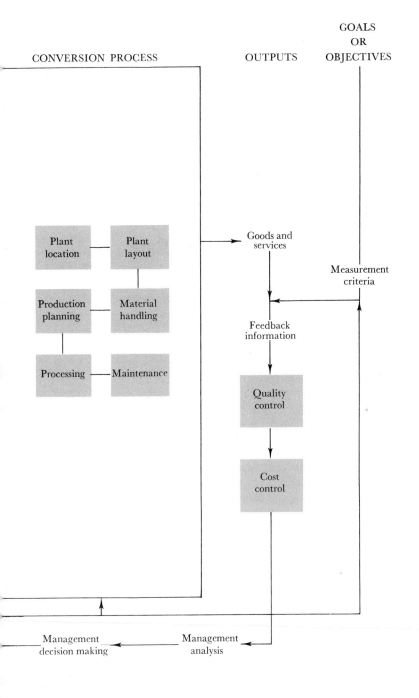

Following this, Chapters 19 and 20 discuss the task of synchronizing men, materials, and machines during the production process—the job of production planning and control. For each item manufactured, a schedule and route or path through the plant must be prescribed, and proper quantities and skills of labor must be assigned to the right equipment.

Chapter 21 considers the problems and decisions relevant to the maintenance of the production facility.

Throughout the production process it is important to ensure that the quality of output be maintained. From a long-range point of view, the ability of a firm to deliver products that consistently meet or exceed competitive performance standards will determine its reputation, its profits, and perhaps its survival. Quality control, broadly defined, is a function that begins with the setting of product and performance standards (as treated in the input chapters) and ends with the assurance that these standards have been met (as discussed in Chapter 22).

Ending the process section, Chapter 23 deals with the cost information systems needed to control production costs. Just as it is important to control the quality of the product if a firm is to be profitable, so too must production costs be controlled if the firm is to maintain its profit margin under competition.

Questions and Problems

1. Define production. Describe how the following can be considered as production activities.
   (a) Banks
   (b) Financial institutions
   (c) Farms
   (d) Hospitals
   (e) Universities
   (f) Wholesale organizations
   (g) Restaurants
   (h) Service companies
2. List the primary inputs, outputs, and conversion processes for three of the organizations in question 1.
3. Why do most text examples of production come from manufacturing? What justification exists for saying that production is not limited to manufacturing?
4. Why is the term *operations management* coming into use?
5. Trace the historical development of production/operations management.
6. What is a system? Why is it important to consider a firm as a dynamic system? as a set of subsystems?
7. Why is it important to consider a system's environment? How do systems and their environments interact?
8. What is a control system? What are the common elements of such systems?
9. What part does feedback play in a control system? What are the physical means of transmitting feedback? Do they differ among the organizations of question 1?
10. What determines the boundaries of a system? What problems arise when the boundaries are poorly drawn? Can you give real-life examples of these problems?
11. Describe an example of a self-regulating system. How is the feedback information generated? What measures of output are used? How is the control action taken?

12. Develop the information flows for two of the types of organizations listed in question 1. Include operating, control, and planning information. How is the information collected, stored, and transmitted? Why does it differ between examples?

References

Churchman, C. W., *Systems Approach,* Dell, New York, 1969.

Filipetti, G., *Industrial Management in Transition,* rev. ed., Irwin, Homewood, Ill., 1953.

Giffin, W. C., *Introduction to Operations Engineering,* Irwin, Homewood, Ill., 1971.

Hall, A. D., *A Methodology for Systems Engineering,* Van Nostrand, Princeton, N.J., 1962.

Hare, V. C., Jr., *Systems Analysis: A Diagnostic Approach,* Harcourt Brace Jovanovich, New York, 1967.

Hopeman, R., *Systems Analysis and Operations Management,* Charles E. Merrill, Columbus, Ohio, 1969.

Johnson, R. A., *et al., The Theory and Management of Systems,* 2nd ed., McGraw-Hill, New York, 1967.

Levin, R. I., *et al., Production/Operations Management,* McGraw-Hill, New York, 1972.

McDonough, A. M., *Information Economics and Management Systems,* McGraw-Hill, New York, 1963.

———, and Garrett, L. J., *Management Systems: Work Concepts and Practices,* Irwin, Homewood, Ill., 1965.

Optner, S. L., *Systems Analysis for Business and Industrial Problem Solving,* Prentice-Hall, Englewood Cliffs, N.J., 1965.

Rudwick, B. H., *Systems Analysis for Effective Planning: Principles and Cases,* Wiley, New York, 1969.

Schoderbek, P., and Schoderbek, C. G., *Management Systems,* 2nd ed., Wiley, New York, 1971.

Shewhart, W. A., *Economic Control of Quality of Manufactured Product,* Van Nostrand, Princeton, N.J., 1931.

Starr, M. K., "Evolving Concepts in Production Management," in Buffa, E. S. (ed.), *Readings in Production Operations Management,* Wiley, New York, 1966.

———, *System's Management of Operations,* Prentice-Hall, Englewood Cliffs, N.J., 1971.

Taylor, F. W., *Scientific Management,* Harper and Row, New York, 1947.

2

The Management Process

In Chapter 1 we developed the general concepts of a system and applied them to production systems. In this chapter we will look at the general practice of management as a prelude to analyzing the specific tasks of production management.[1]

Management is an extremely complex process. Consequently, any analysis of management requires abstractions from reality. Concepts thus derived should provide the basis for a general model of management. The general model can then be applied to specific areas such as production management.

The models of management practices that have been developed to date are commonly accepted as mixtures of art and science. Management can be viewed as analogous to the practice of medicine. In medicine, knowledge of how the body functions is needed. This knowledge comes from the scientific principles of biology, chemistry, physics, physiology, and psychology. In addition to mastering these principles, the successful practitioner needs the creativity and intuition to apply them to practical problems. This part of the practice of medicine is undoubtedly an art.

In management, effective production managers must understand the managerial and technical principles involved in their work and be skilled in the art of

---

[1] Ideally, students of specific areas of management, such as production management, should have had a prior course in general management. This chapter is included primarily for those who have not had such a course. It is a brief treatment of the subject to give such readers the background necessary to proceed through the text.

applying these principles to production problems. They must draw on principles of mathematics, engineering, the social and behavioral sciences, and economics.

A Definition of Management

Before proceeding with an analysis of general management, we will first define the term *management*. Frederick W. Taylor defined management as ". . . knowing exactly what you want to do and then seeing that they do it in the best and cheapest way." Later management practitioners have taken issue with Taylor's definition. They feel it overemphasizes the aspect of efficiency—"in the best and cheapest way"—and seemingly neglects the behavioral side of management. To overcome this shortcoming, they have defined management as getting things done through others. This definition emphasizes the accomplishment of goals by people and represents a swing from the economic to the behavioral. It highlights the personal aspects of management and seemingly underestimates the economic aspects.

By combining these two approaches we can develop a definition that we can use in this text: *Management is the practice of determining what has to be done and accomplishing this goal in the best fashion through other people.*

Management Theories

The task of presenting a general model of management, which forms a framework for production management, would be much simpler if there were a generally accepted model of management. Unfortunately this is not the case. People have puzzled over the process of management for years without coming to an agreement on one general model. No one model explains the entire process; each model has areas where it is strong and others where it is weak.

The fact that a single model (or theory) does not explain or predict everything in a complex process should not be startling. Many processes are so complex that we cannot—at least not initially and perhaps not ever—explain them with a single model. In these cases, theories are developed that explain a portion of the activity and are useful when working on that part of the problem. The physical sciences are replete with examples of theories that explain only a part of a phenomenon. At least three theories of electricity are in common use; they each give useful answers when applied within their scope but do not hold when applied generally to the phenomenon of electricity.

In like fashion, there are a number of theories of management. Each contributes to our understanding of the process but none is complete in itself. Management practitioners should be versed in all of the theories, selecting and applying those parts of each which pertain in a particular case.

There are three major management theories in use today. Each concentrates on a different aspect of management and explains a portion of the process that was not properly explained by the earlier approaches. The adherents of each sometimes consider their particular approach as a complete model of management and thus in conflict with any other model of management. In reality they are neither complete nor conflicting, they are complementary, and when considered together they give a better picture of the management process than can be obtained from any one of them alone.

Traditional Theory

The earliest of the three theories, which has come to be known as the traditional theory, concentrated on explaining management as a process. Adherents such as Fayol, Moody, and Urwick conceived of management as a series of functions such as planning, organizing, assembling resources, directing, and controlling. Together, these functions define the management process and are a model of management.

Since these functions are identifiable and are present in all management—manufacturing, sales, service, or governmental—it was held that managers could be trained in their workings and could apply them universally to any situation. As knowledge of the functions expanded, particular aspects became detailed to the point where they were defined as management principles.

Behavioral Theory

Chronologically, the second theory of management to mature was the behavioral theory. Because the traditional theory could not explain all of management and was particularly lacking in the human relations aspects, students of management began to study the influence of interpersonal relations in the managerial process. Starting with the so-called Hawthorne experiments of Roethelsberger and Dixon in the 1920s, work in the behavioral facet of management took on increasing importance. The resulting studies in interpersonal relationships and individual motivations and abilities have led to a better understanding of the role of individuals and groups in the management process. The work of behaviorists such as McGregor, Argyris, and Likert is now an accepted part of any study of management.

Decision-Making Theory

The most recent theory of management is concerned with the decision processes that determine managerial actions. Its adherents hope to improve the ability of managers to make correct decisions. To accomplish this, they are analyzing the manner in which problems are studied and solutions are selected and developed. Studies in this field deal with the mental decision processes of individual managers rather than with the process of management. The understanding of what is involved in particular problems, how decisions have been made, and how they can be improved adds another dimension to our understanding of management.

A Combined Approach

In this book we are concerned with how each of these theories can add to our understanding of production management. As stated earlier, we do not consider the theories competitive. We believe they are additive and together help explain more of management, and thus of production management, than each could do alone.

We will follow this concept throughout the book. In the remainder of this chapter we will discuss the traditional view of management. In Chapter 3 we will analyze the decision processes of production management. We will concentrate on the behavioral aspects of production management in Chapter 9, the first of the chapters related specifically to the work force. Throughout the rest of the book we have attempted to integrate the three theories of management by discussing problems from all three viewpoints.

The General Functions of Management

The general managerial functions may be summarized as follows:

1. *Planning*
2. *Organizing*
3. *Assembling resources*
4. *Directing*
5. *Controlling*

The exact mixture and degree of importance of these functions in any manager's job will depend upon his organizational level and technical area. However, their effective performance at all management levels is necessary to the achievement of a firm's goals.

Planning

Many managers believe that the most important task they perform is decision making. In traditional theory, decision making is the planning function. In presenting planning we are not concerned with decision-making tools, but rather with how the decision process is accomplished within an organization.

Planning involves the generation and identification of alternative courses of action and the selection of an optimum course of action from these alternatives. The choice of a particular alternative is dependent upon the knowledge of pertinent factors and issues and upon the selection criteria utilized. It has been said that effective management is based upon an ability to ask the right questions. It is not necessary to know all the right answers, but it is important to know what data are needed, how to obtain them, and how to use them. This is the key to sound planning and decision making.

Planning Time Frames

Management is chiefly concerned with planning the future operations of the firm. The past is useful only insofar as it provides historical data and thus gives insights into future activities. Management devotes considerable attention to the question of how far in advance a firm should plan. Obviously, the longer the planning cycle, the more unreliable the decision data become. Despite this handicap, however, there is widespread interest in long-range planning in the industrial world. Indeed, five- and ten-year plans are common. The reason for this is basic. It is summed up in the familiar business axiom: "A businessman must plan far enough ahead to recover his cost." Many fundamental production decisions such as plant location, design and development of a product line, and investment in operating technology involve a commitment of resources that may be irreversible for periods up to and exceeding ten years. In short, the firm must depend for its survival on the ability of its executives to make sound long-term decisions despite the fact that the information available is highly tenuous.

Thus, time is a significant factor in planning. Short-term decisions are also important; in fact, they often prescribe some of the boundaries within which the long-term decisions are made. Short-term decisions can generally be made with greater reliance on specifics than the long-term ones, however, and so they can be made in a more prescribed and routine fashion.

Some companies use time as a measure of the importance of the decisions and planning responsibilities that are assigned to specific managers. Thus, the longer a decision commits the company, the greater the importance of the decision. The level within the organization where decisions are made is directly related to the commitment time. Long-term decisions are normally made by top company executives, while lower levels of supervision have the authority to commit the company's resources only for short periods of time, such as a week or a day. Figure 2–1 shows the relationship between organizational rank and commitment time.

Decisions involving the daily scheduling of labor and equipment, for example, are normally made at the lowest level of management; weekly and monthly production schedules are formulated at the next higher level. Decisions as to what products should or should not be made, the location of plants, and the labor policy are most often made by the top company executives. This hierarchy of planning is typical, and it is found throughout the functional phases of production management.

Such an approach is consistent with the organizational concept of the vertical specialization of labor. The essence of this principle is that the level selected for decision authority should provide the greatest probability of success consistent with the economic utilization of available managerial resources. In practice it is applied by assigning decisions to the lowest supervisory level at which there is sufficient managerial capability. In so doing, routine and other decisions of lesser importance in terms of dollars and time are located lower in the organization than those of greater significance. Vertical specialization works best if the most

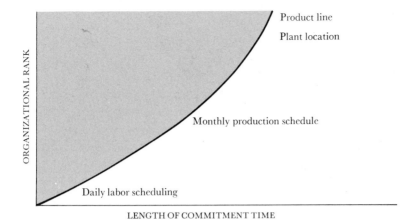

Figure 2-1 The general relationship between organizational rank and commitment time

capable managers hold the highest ranked positions. Unfortunately, this is not always the case; therefore, in many operating situations, decisions will in fact be made by those who demonstrate ability regardless of organizational rank.

A Planning Hierarchy

Planning is done at all levels of an organization and must be integrated in order to keep the organizational levels in tune with each other. The nature of the decisions varies at the different organizational levels. One way in which the differences can be categorized is by the latitude given the decision maker. The top of an organization has the greatest choice of alternatives. It determines the overall aims of the organization. Decisions made at the top limit the latitude given to the levels below and give direction to these levels so that their decisions can be kept in tune with the aims of the organization. Similarly, the decisions made at the second level further limit the levels below. In this fashion, as shown in Figure 2-2, the freedom of choice is progressively narrowed and focused at the overall aims.

A common terminology has developed to describe plans with varying degrees of latitude. The relationships among the different levels of plans comprise a planning hierarchy.

Goals At the top of the hierarchy are goals. Goals are the broadest group of managerial plans and set forth the aims of an enterprise. In a typical firm, top management, in concert with the board of directors,[2] formulates the overall purposes and objectives of the corporation and determines both the line of endeavor and the nature of the firm's participation. The degree of integration and the scale of operation are also decided at this level, along with related decisions dealing

---

[2] The corporate form of business enterprise is tacitly assumed.

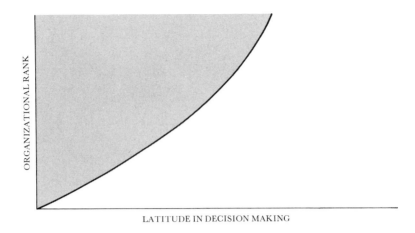

Figure 2–2 The general relationship between organizational rank and the
latitude of decision making

with financial, operational, and marketing objectives. These goals are, in effect,
the *raison d'être* of the corporation, so it is not surprising that these decisions are
made by top management.

Within the framework of the firm's overall goals, the individual managers have
to determine their own organizational aims. Thus, the goals of the total enterprise are divided to create goals for the major sections of the firm. These, in
turn, are subdivided to define the goals of lower organizational units. The process is repeated until goals are determined for all operating units, even those of
the lowest organizational rank. If properly performed, this process results in
a set of consistent goals that act to synchronize the efforts of the entire company.

To illustrate this, consider the case of a major electronics firm. At the corporate level, a goal of $1 billion of sales was set; this was approximately $150
million more than the firm had sold the preceding year. In order to achieve the
goal, subgoals were formulated for each of the firm's divisions. These goals were
further broken down by product line and so forth. In the end there was an
integrated system of goals and subgoals that pointed toward the achievement of
the corporate goal.

Policies Once the firm's objectives have been established, it is necessary to
formulate guidelines that will govern actions taken in pursuit of these objectives.
This is the purpose of policies. Policies are guidelines rather than rules; they
leave the decision maker some latitude to modify his decisions according to the
specific circumstances involved. Policies are used to set up criteria for decisions
concerning all of the functional areas of the enterprise. In purchasing, for example, policies must be formulated regarding such items as reciprocity, discounts, number of approved vendors, and annual contract buying. Many companies, it might be noted, have a policy that limits the amount of money that
may be spent without prior authorization at various managerial levels. Thus, a

department manager may be able to sign purchase orders only up to $500 without seeking higher authorization. As was true with respect to goals, a hierarchy of policies is necessary to insure the achievement of many targets.

Action plans With his policy guidelines, a manager has to determine appropriate courses of action. The action plan represents the operating route selected as the best way to achieve organizational goals according to the applicable company policy.

To illustrate the relationship of policies and action plans, consider a firm that has a policy of "paying its workers at the prevailing rate for the job in the area where the work is done." The manager who establishes wage rates under this policy must have a plan by which he can determine just what the prevailing wage is for a job. There are many ways he can do this. His task is to select the best way and to incorporate it into an action plan.

Procedures A precise delineation of the sequential steps that must be taken in the accomplishment of an action plan is called a procedure. Procedures are designed to cover the similar action patterns of recurring tasks. In this way we may obtain uniformity and consistency of action for specific situations and thus improve efficiency. Procedures therefore minimize the amount of management time needed for decision making by standardizing routine operations. In addition, they permit assignment of planning responsibility to lower operating levels, and thus, in keeping with the vertical specialization theme, higher level management can concentrate on significant and unusual problems. This delegation of routine, less important decisions to lower management is often referred to as "management by exception."

There are many procedures in the average company, encompassing actions in all functional areas. They usually include such routine tasks as the preparation of purchase requisitions, the processing of labor grievances, the maintenance of inventory records, and the making of an economy study. Procedures are followed at all levels of the organization, but they are most common at the lower levels because they limit freedom of action and keep the number of alternatives available to the decision maker to a minimum.

Rules In some areas of a firm's activities, no latitude in decision making is desired or allowed, and rules are formulated to enforce specific company policy. For example, safety regulations may prescribe a rule of "no smoking" in a production area. Because of safety needs, no latitude can be tolerated in interpreting this rule; it is either obeyed or violated. Because of the rigidity of rules, their use within business organizations is limited. Organizations that become rule-bound are inflexible and cannot react to changing conditions. It is precisely the need to react to change that fosters the use of guidelines, such as policy statements, in the decision process.

The range of alternatives and the degree of managerial freedom are increasingly smaller in scope the lower one moves in the organizational framework. This does not mean, however, that the upper management levels operate only

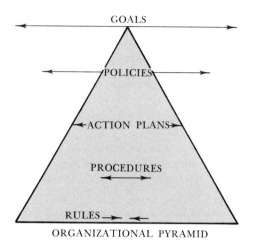

Figure 2–3 Managerial planning hierarchy

under policies and the lower levels only under rules. It does mean that the use of rules as an operating mode increases as one moves downward in an organization, and conversely, the use of policy increases as one moves upward. The general pattern of this condition is shown in Figure 2–3.

Programs Very often a firm finds it necessary to concentrate its resources on a specific major objective. This occurs in the automobile industry, for example, whenever a new model is introduced or, as now, when environmental protection and safety devices must be developed by a set date. In many industries, the receipt of a major contract can mean the mobilization of a substantial portion of a firm's resources for a particular task. When such mobilization is necessary, a program is initiated. The program, or project, constitutes a specific company goal with its own composite mixture of policies, plans, and procedures. It is not unusual for considerable variation to exist between normal company planning and that associated with a particular project. In fact, planning in many research-oriented firms is really a group of separate programs rather than a homogeneous entity.

Programs are created in order to marshal resources for a specific objective. There is, however, one important limitation with the program technique. Management must not allow individual programs to interfere with the pursuit of normal company objectives. All too often, firms weaken their effectiveness in normal business operations by using too many resources in a spotlighted, glamorous program. This leaves only below-average talents and facilities to conduct the regular affairs of the company. There is also the danger that the "crash" policies and procedures that were developed for a program may infiltrate into normal operations. This is one of the major reasons why companies such as General Electric and Boeing Aircraft have taken strong steps to insure a sharp, clear separation between defense and commercial operations. This separation is not only evident on the organization chart but is often reinforced by a physical separation of plants and facilities employed in the two business areas.

Organizing

The organization structure of a firm is really a formalized plan for the most efficient employment of personnel. It is important to remember that organizing is a planning function because it highlights the need for continual review and modification of the structure of the firm. Organizational plans are not sacrosanct; they should be changed whenever more effective alternatives exist. There are a great number of alternative organizational patterns.

In practice, of course, the dynamic personal interactions within an organization relegate its organization structure to the role of guide as to what is required. Day-to-day relations create the real organizational pattern. In short, management must monitor the operating characteristics of the company and be prepared to make organizational adjustments as they appear necessary.

Departmentation

The design of an organization begins with the basic objectives of the enterprise; the use of resources must be directed toward the achievement of these ends. Normally, the desired output is specified in terms of goods or services, and the role of the firm will thus be to provide a conversion process that will efficiently transform the factors of production into the desired products. In this conversion process, work is performed by management and labor in concert with capital, land, and materials; this work is the object of the organization. The total corporate task is subjected to successive subdivision until areas of work are created that can be performed by a single individual without the aid of subordinates. Such work blocs are then established as jobs.

The diagrams in Figure 2–4 depict the job-defining process. In diagram A the total corporate task is identified but not divided. The division process begins in diagram B, where the first cuts establish departmental sectors of work labeled production, finance, and sales. In diagram C the division process has been continued in the sales department; the jobs of field sales and order writing have been carved out of the total sales function.

As jobs are defined, they are grouped into administrative units. A hierarchy of supervision and management is constructed on top of the working base. There are many levels of management: operating employees must be supervised and their supervisors must be managed. Thus an organizational structure is created that links the presidential level with the lowest job-performing levels. The process of partitioning work into performance units and then grouping the units to facilitate management is called *departmentation*. Performance units are most frequently grouped into departments according to function, product, customer, geography, or numbers.

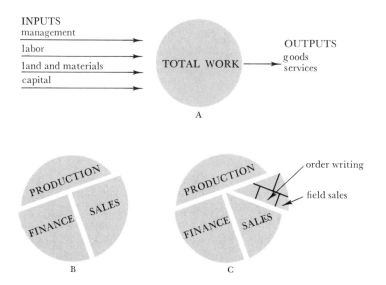

INPUTS
management
labor
land and materials
capital

TOTAL WORK

OUTPUTS
goods
services

A

PRODUCTION
FINANCE SALES

B

PRODUCTION
FINANCE SALES
order writing
field sales

C

Figure 2–4   Organization: The job-defining process

Span of Control

The number of subordinates that a manager can effectively supervise is determined by the particular organizational level, the complexity and importance of the activity, the training and skill of the subordinates and the supervisor, and the control techniques available. This concept is termed the *span of control* or the *span of management*.

The span of management is determined by asking a fundamental question: How much control is economically feasible in a given situation? Close supervision requires more managers and thus raises the firm's managerial expenses. Small spans also increase the number of managerial levels required in the organization. To illustrate this, consider Figure 2–5, which depicts an operation requiring 81 production operators. A span of three (lower diagram) results in 40 indirect supervisory or administrative personnel. The ratio of supervisory to operating personnel is approximately 1/2. By increasing the span to nine (upper diagram), the number of supervisory people will be reduced to ten, or about 10 percent of operating labor. The difference in cost is significant. Therefore, in structuring the organization of a firm, management must strike a balance between the advantages of close supervision and its associated cost. Smaller spans mean a greater number of organizational levels, and this produces problems in communication and coordination. The more levels communications must traverse, the slower the movement and the greater the chance for misunderstanding. On the other hand, there are definite limits to the number of people, processes, and activities that can be effectively supervised by one manager. However, certain improved control techniques and data processing equipment are able to increase management spans. Yet as our technology becomes more advanced it appears

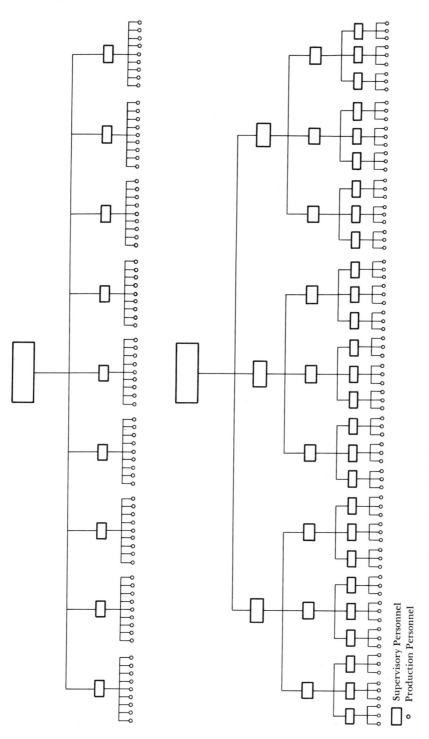

Supervisory Personnel
Production Personnel

Figure 2–5 The influence of span size on organization structure

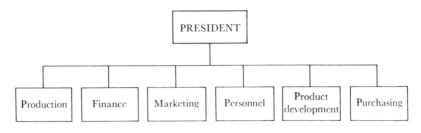

Figure 2–6   Departmentation of a firm by function

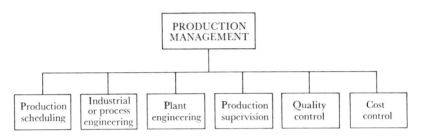

Figure 2–7   Functional organization of the production activity

that managers will be called upon to supervise increasingly diverse packages of skills and processes. Thus, a reverse trend may arise, tending to contract the span of management. In practice, spans often range from six to nine in the higher management areas, and as many as twenty to thirty at lower levels where production personnel are involved. The concept of span of management is reflected in the organizational design of any firm no matter how its performance units are departmentalized.

Function   One of the most common ways of grouping performance units into departments or administrative units is by function. Similar tasks are grouped together. This system follows the logic of specialization of labor and has gained widespread favor in industry. The organizational structure that results when this method is applied is shown in Figure 2–6.

Departmentation along functional lines may be applied in all activities and at all levels of the organization. Figure 2–7 shows a typical functional organization of the production activity. The functions shown are essentially self-descriptive and will be treated in detail in later chapters.

Product   Management may also use the end product as the focal point for clustering activities in an enterprise. In a sense, under this system, a separate company or operating entity is established for each product. Each one has its own resource inputs for performing the necessary business functions: production, marketing, engineering, and finance. This organizational form is depicted in Figure 2–8. This system has been successfully used by many companies, including General Motors. Essentially, it extends the principle of specialization of labor

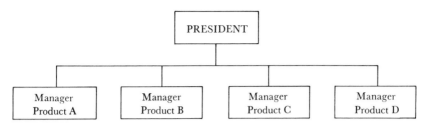

Figure 2–8 Departmentation by product

beyond the level attained in the functional approach. In fact, departmentation by function is very often introduced within each of the respective product divisions. Product departmentation is most often found at the higher management levels and at the lowest operating levels, where the use of a product layout in the plant is an extension of this concept. The approach is less often applied to middle management and administrative levels. One of the main advantages of product departmentation is that it provides a training arena for future executives. Unlike the functional mode, it gives lower level managers responsibilities that are multifunctional and therefore prepares them better for top executive posts. The major disadvantage of product departmentation is that duplicate functions and facilities are required within a firm for the different products. Each product must have its own production facility, for example. Unless the volume of work in each product area is sufficiently large to support its own production facilities, inefficiencies and underutilization of resources may result.

Customer Customer departmentation, shown in Figure 2–9, is quite similar to product departmentation. It has the same advantages and limitations. Here, again, function is often the secondary mode of departmentation. Customer organization has been effectively used by companies that are strongly sales-oriented; it has also been successful in the insurance and banking fields.

Geography It is often desirable to group activities according to physical location, or geography. Field salesmen are frequently organized on this basis, for example; so are floor walkers in department stores and concessionaires at sporting events. The principal advantage is the provision of timely, on-the-scene decision making. Figure 2–10 depicts a sales organization that is geographically

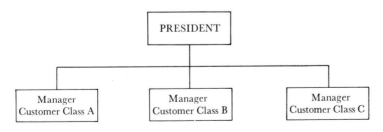

Figure 2–9 Departmentation by customer

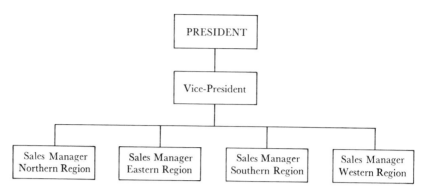

Figure 2–10   Geographic departmentation

organized. As one might expect, geographic departmentation is used principally in the sales sector of enterprises; however, many companies with nationally distributed products have set up manufacturing facilities in different parts of the country on this same principle.

Number   Numerical departmentation has been used successfully by the military, but industrial use has been largely restricted to lower operating levels. Workers are often assigned to production supervisors in quantitative terms. Frequently, the supervision of field salesmen in a given market area is determined largely by the number of men a supervisor already has assigned to him. In general, numerical departmentation is most effective when subordinates are relatively unskilled and do routine work that requires little coordination on the part of the supervisor.

Project   When firms enter into special activities, such as the development and manufacture of a new product, they sometimes give the responsibility for the project to one manager, who is therefore called a project manager. Generally, this is done when the projects are important because of their size, cost, impact on the firm, or technical complexity. If, for example, a company is going to develop a new product, top management may select someone, relieve him of his current duties, and assign him to coordinate all activities in the design and production of the new product. In this way a single project manager, or project office, is given the task of making the key decisions relating to the project. When the project is completed—in our example, when the product goes into routine production—the project office is disbanded and the project manager and his staff return to their normal activities.

Project management's activity cuts across the functional organizational units of production, finance, and marketing. This is shown in Figure 2–11, where the project manager is shown coordinating his product across the functional departmentation. Companies may have more than one project office at the same time. In this case the functional managers—production managers, for example— will have to work with a number of project managers at the same time. Minimiz-

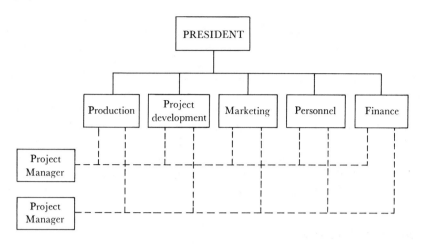

Figure 2-11 Project organization

ing the conflicts between the projects requires careful coordination if the advantages of project management are not to be lost.

While project organization is not new, its use is increasing because of the greater number of special and large-scale projects that confront modern management. Earlier in the chapter we mentioned that automobile companies had established project offices to speed the development of safety and environmental controls. Defense and research firms commonly organize this way to concentrate on specific programs. By using the project concept, they can keep more flexible and are able to respond more readily to varying product demands and new technical breakthroughs.

Matrix In recent years some firms have found that they are continuously faced with large projects and that these projects have become normal in their operation. They have therefore formalized project management as one means of organization. In recognition of its advantages, they maintain two-dimensional organizations. One dimension is made up of the normal functional departmentation; but overlaying it is another composed of projects. This dual departmentation is called a matrix organization.

General A single mode of departmentation need not be followed throughout a company. The organizer has complete freedom to use any and all systems in various operating areas. The organization of any firm should be a unique composite of approaches that best suits its peculiar needs. Thus it is quite conceivable that, in a single company, sales could be organized by customer or territory; production and engineering, by product; and finance, by function. In addition, because the operations of the company may vary over time, the nature of the organization structure may also vary. For this reason it is particularly important to review the structure periodically.

Once the organization structure has been decided upon, it must be implemented. Organization charts, as illustrated in the foregoing examples, are commonly used to facilitate the implementation. Generally an organization manual contains, in sequence, from the top of the company to the bottom, all of the firm's organization charts. The manual is, therefore, a summary of the work assignments made within the company. It is customary to supplement the organization charts in the manual with job descriptions that summarize the pertinent information about each position. The manual is useful not only in indoctrinating new employees but, for existing members of the organization, as a ready reference explaining "who does what." Thus, operational and jurisdictional disputes can often be avoided by referring to the manual. Furthermore, an organization manual is useful in locating sources of help when new or unusual problems arise.

Assembling Resources

The first two management functions—planning and organizing—were concerned with the establishment of objectives and the distribution of work for their achievement. Now we will examine how the resources that constitute the firm's input are accumulated. Management personnel, labor, land and materials, and capital facilities must be provided.

In later chapters, specific problems associated with the assembling of labor resources, land and materials, and capital will be analyzed in detail. At this point, however, we will examine the resource aspects of the managerial input in order to complete our general discussion of the management function.

Management

The experience and training required to produce a good manager has long been the subject of wide debate. It is a matter of critical importance, however, for management is a principal factor in the success of a company. In handling this problem, many companies have created executive-development programs, whose purpose is to identify the employees with potential for advancement and give them the mixture of experience and formal training that they will need as members of top management. Various approaches are used in these programs, including job rotation, in-house training programs, and special training at colleges and universities.

One characteristic of executive-development programs is worthy of special note: the relatively long cycle needed to prepare candidates for executive positions. Because management training may cover a period of ten years or more, action must be taken as soon as possible to develop the managerial talents that will be needed in the future. This means that executive development must dovetail with organizational development. Someone must constantly monitor the changing organization structure to determine what managerial skills will best fill the future needs of the firm. Often the personnel department assumes the responsibility for organizational and executive development. Typically the personnel department confines itself to identifying the managerial positions that must be filled, from the viewpoint of the present organization structure. The task of executive development is "dynamic"; placing capable managers in the optimum positions demands continual review. Most firms are convinced that they cannot depend upon the random availability of managerial manpower to satisfy their needs. While recruitment from external sources, including the pirating of proven executives from other firms, can be a short-run stopgap, long-run success depends largely upon carefully planned executive-development programs of one type or another.

The personnel department is also responsible for helping line management to secure and maintain a productive work force. The average supervisor or manager has neither the time nor, in many cases, the specialized skills needed to recruit and train large numbers of operators. However, line management is responsible for participating in this program. It defines the specifications of the men needed, designs some of the tests for applicant-screening, has the final responsibility for hiring, and helps develop training programs for satisfactory candidates. Automation and technological change have brought about rapid changes in required employee skills in recent years. This has made the task of obtaining needed manpower much more difficult. It is particularly important that close liaison be maintained between the production planning and control departments on the one hand and the industrial engineering department on the other. The former departments provide data regarding the quantities of labor needed, while the latter department has information on the manpower skills required for the processes used on the production line.

The personnel department also keeps a close watch on employee relations as an indicator of morale and is responsible for the development of both executive and labor compensation plans.

Directing

Directing is the fourth managerial function. A manager directs when he initiates actions needed to achieve goals and makes certain that the necessary tasks are performed as planned. Directing is the catalyst that starts the process, and organizational goals determine exactly what work is required. The work to be done is partitioned into jobs, which are then grouped into administrative units. An administrative unit, in the form of a work package, is assigned to a manager. A cornerstone principle of good management, the *parity principle*, requires that this individual have the authority commensurate with the work or duties for which he is responsible. When a manager assigns work to subordinates he should also delegate the authority needed to carry out the task. In turn, the subordinate is responsible to the manager for the performance of that work. It is important to note that whereas duties and authority can be assigned or delegated to subordinates, responsibility cannot. Responsibility is owed to the next higher echelon and is not transferable. A manager will not usually delegate all of the duties that are given to him. Delegating duties does not eliminate the manager's work altogether, of course; he must still supervise his subordinates. A possible superior–subordi-

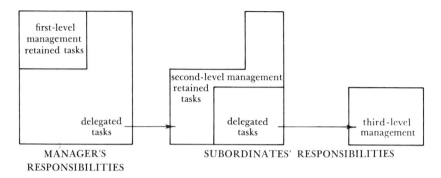

first-level
management
retained tasks

delegated
tasks

second-level management
retained
tasks

delegated
tasks

third-level
management

MANAGER'S
RESPONSIBILITIES

SUBORDINATES' RESPONSIBILITIES

Figure 2–12 Superior–subordinate relationship within an administrative unit

nate relationship resulting from the delegation of work is depicted as in Figure 2–12.

Types of Authority

The superior has authority over the subordinate because he exacts accountability from him. This type of authority is called *line authority*, and it is normally defined as the right to direct, to sanction good performance and to punish for bad performance. Line authority is action-oriented and may be delegated to subordinates in amounts commensurate with the duties that are delegated. Conversely, when a subordinate is given the task of preparing data for or advising management but is not given the authority to act, his work is called a *staff* job. A third type of authority is known as *functional authority*. A subordinate has functional authority if he may prescribe the manner in which a particular task is to be accomplished but does not have the authority to reward or punish its performance. Functional authority cuts across departmental lines and can transcend the echelons of the management hierarchy. It is employed principally to obtain full benefit of specialized skills or talents of specific individuals in the organization, or to assure consistency of action when that is desirable. Functional authority is often used in legal areas in large firms. The corporate legal officer may prescribe how others in the firm will act with respect to legal needs, but he normally does not have the right to enforce the regulations; that is left to the line managers. Since the legal officer can say how something is to be done, the entire firm gains from his special knowledge.

It is possible to illustrate these three superior–subordinate relationships visually. Line authority flows from the company president down through the vice-presidents and lower echelons of management to the employees at the operating level. The *scalar principle*, or chain, is the name given to the linking of the president to the lowest employee by the downward flow of line authority. This relationship is illustrated in Figure 2–13 by the bold line connecting the president to the lowest echelon. Staff authority is illustrated by the heavy dotted line; the relationship is advisory to the president of the firm. In this case the adviser is a

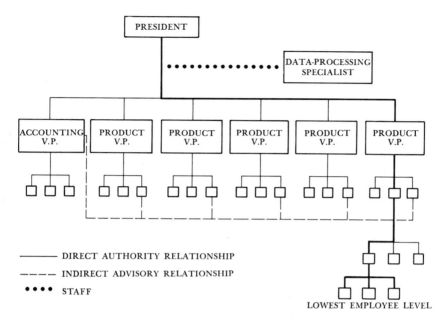

Figure 2–13 Superior–subordinate relationships

specialist in data processing. Functional authority is shown on the chart by a dashed line. It connects the firm's accounting vice-president with the chief accountants in product areas. The accounting vice-president has functional authority to state how the accounts will be kept but not to direct the keeping of the records.

The Source of Authority

Many of the early writers and practitioners insisted that all the authority in a firm flows from the president, who, in turn, obtains it from the owners. It was popular to state that the authority to manage was a natural right of the owners. In fact, at one time, the concept of line authority as a flow of authority from the property owners to the president and down through the company was a fairly realistic one. The superior had almost absolute power over his subordinates. The subordinates could be subjected to disciplinary layoff, pay cuts, or even dismissal without recourse. In such an environment, the directing function was completely authoritarian.

Many factors have helped to alter this relationship substantially, including: (1) increased separation of ownership and management, (2) increased scale and complexity of the business unit, (3) increased emphasis on human relations in management, (4) increased impact of labor unions, and (5) increased standards of education and living. The listing could be continued for several pages. The net result of these factors, however, is that management is no longer able to *compel;* today it can only *influence.* In fact, at present, any attempt to manage by compulsion would probably result in low morale and productivity; thus, it would be self-defeating. In short, the supervisor must use persuasion and reason to get orderly, prescribed performance from his subordinates.

There are some people today who claim that authority in our industries really flows from the subordinate to the superior. The exercise of authority, they contend, is accomplished only when the employee accepts the authority or directions of his superior. This concept is termed the *acceptance theory of authority*. While this may seem too radical a statement of the situation, it is clear that operating efficiency is to a large extent determined by the degree of subordinate acceptance enjoyed by the superior. While the acceptance theory of authority has met with a violent reaction in many quarters, a realistic manager will recognize the necessity of winning the support of his subordinates. The modern manager must know how to stimulate or motivate rather than push or drive. Motivating employees involves a whole spectrum of problems since all men are different and therefore respond differently to various managerial approaches. These individual differences should be recognized by the manager, who must tailor his approach to different employees accordingly. On the other hand, of course, a manager who does not treat all his subordinates alike is apt to be accused of favoritism. The solution to this dilemma is still unknown.

Controlling

The last function of management that we will mention in this general discussion is controlling. The previous functions were concerned with the establishment of objectives and the employment of resources to achieve those goals. After this has been done, the manager must check to make certain that the targets have been realized. This checking process is called controlling; it is a follow-up activity that seeks to compare actual with estimated results. Thus it involves status reports and progress assessments. If the firm's actual position can be determined relative to the planned targets, the manager has a basis on which to plan future action.

A diagram of this function appears in Figure 2–14, which illustrates the two principal categories of control.

Case A depicts a situation in which there is a predetermined input; the quantity and mix of resources are set. The *standard output* is the goods and services that are expected under these conditions. Controlling involves a comparison of the actual output and standard output. In this particular instance the quantity of the output is less than the standard. This information is fed back to the input phase of production so that corrective action can be taken. The feedback of output data is an integral part of the control process. Many alternative paths of corrective action are available, of course. The output standard may not have been realistic; perhaps the company was overly optimistic to expect this standard level of output considering the input utilized. There may have been unforeseen variations in the input mix or the operating conditions that invalidated the output standard as a fair level of achievement. On the other hand, the difference between the standard and actual may be attributed to poor performance; the

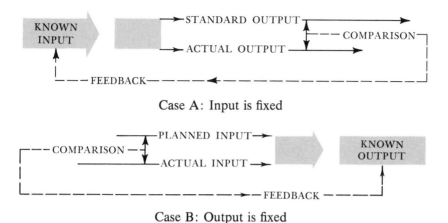

Case A: Input is fixed

Case B: Output is fixed

Figure 2–14 The control function

output standard may have been a reasonable expectation, but perhaps management or labor did not perform their jobs with reasonable effectiveness. Lastly, the materials may have been defective or not available in the proper quantities or at the proper time. There are many possible explanations for the unfavorable outcome. Thus, controlling does not stop with reporting a variance between actual and planned output; it must also determine the cause of that discrepancy. The more information that is available about the probable cause of a variance, the greater the possibility that management will be able to take remedial action. In fact, a sound control procedure will identify the man who should be given the specific responsibility for developing the corrective action. This is the feedback aspect of control depicted in Case A.

Case B illustrates a situation where a target output must be achieved. Inputs are fed into the conversion process until the desired quantity and quality of goods and services are produced. In this case, it is necessary to compare the actual input required with the planned input of resources. Therefore, feedback of information flows to the output side since the manager is interested in comparing planned input and actual input required to produce a fixed output. The cause of variation may lie in an unrealistic standard or poor performance by one or more of the resources employed. Management must develop the proper corrective action based upon the data obtained in the control process.

Controlling is often considered largely a measuring process. This is a helpful way to envision the control function since it highlights the need for sound yardsticks. Effective measurement depends upon the availability of suitable, understandable measures that can be easily applied. A great deal of time and effort have been spent on the problem of designing fair performance standards. The units most frequently employed are dollars and physical quantities, such as the number of man-hours of labor, pounds of material, and pieces finished. Such measuring units meet the criteria of being easily understood and readily applied. However, it is often quite difficult to set up a realistic relationship between input resources and the output of goods and services expressed in terms of these units. Such relationships, commonly referred to as *output standards,* are extremely important both for measuring and for planning the firm's operations.

The Universality of the Control Concept

Every manager within a given company must know the result that may reasonably be expected from the use of a given mix of resources. He must be able to estimate fairly accurately what input is needed to achieve a specified outcome. The planning, organizing, assembling of resources, and directing of work all depend upon intelligent estimation of this sort. The purchasing agent must have a reasonable expectation of the anticipated sales volume in order to be able to place the necessary volume of requisitions. When an emergency shipping invoice is received at the warehouse, the warehouse manager must be able to estimate the number of men, the number of forklift trucks, and the hours of work required to insure on-time delivery. To close the company's books on time, the controller must employ the proper number of accountants, clerks, and calculators; perhaps he may even need a computer. Such problems are part of the daily routine of any company's managers. Experience, intuition, and judgment are often the only sources of data. In specific cases, intuitive standards may be reasonable, accurate, and, therefore, effective. Frequently, however, this is not the case. Typically, a manager will seek to be safe by overstating his needs for resources. As a consequence, in many firms and departments the input resource costs are excessive, and this has an adverse impact on the company's profit and loss statement.

There are many ways in which a manager can improve his estimates. Factory supervision has long benefited from the contributions made by *work simplification, time and motion study,* and *work sampling.* In office work, the traditional application of industrial engineering to offices is called "systems and procedures," which is a form of methods analysis. The increasing mechanization of the clerical activities and the rising costs associated with offices will probably accelerate the development of measurement standards for office operations.

The Timing of Control

Many of the principal functions found in a model of a firm contain the word "control" in their titles: inventory control, production control, and quality control. This underscores the importance of controlling or measuring the firm's efforts in critical areas, not only by checking final results but by monitoring work in process. If a manager waits until all the results are in, there may not be time or resources available to prevent the disastrous consequences that could result if plans do not materialize. When difficulties or potential variances are identified early, the manager can make the necessary adjustments. Thus, the questions of *when* and *where* to exercise control are critical. In fact, the effectiveness of a control system depends to a large extent upon the proper choice of control points.

The sooner and oftener a process is checked, the greater the probability that the objectives will be achieved, because variations, or potential variations, will be identified before large amounts of unsuitable output are produced. In addition, there will be more time available for necessary remedial action. At each control point, it is necessary to have a *performance standard,* a technique for comparing actual output with standard output, and an information-feedback procedure. Because this costs money, a balance must be struck between the cost of exercising control and the cost of not exercising it. Fewer control points mean less cost but also an increased probability that variances will go undetected longer, thus permitting less time for correction.

Problems also exist when goals are being "overaccomplished." Such cases may result from too large a commitment of resources, for example. The overcommitted resources could perhaps have been used to better advantage elsewhere. Furthermore, the underestimation of productivity invariably leads to idleness and higher costs. Thus, even when variances are positive, it is important to diagnose the situation as soon as possible and initiate corrective action.

The Interrelation of Management Functions

We arbitrarily dissected the overall management function into five separate functions, which we then discussed in turn. Actually, all management functions interact, since they all involve planning, organizing, assembling resources, directing, and controlling. Management is a continuous, dynamic process. Production managers, like all other managers, continually face decisions in each of these functional areas. The following chapter will present the decision tools and concepts that production management uses in the technical areas. Together with the earlier discussion of systems and the foregoing description of the general functions of management, it will provide a background for the reader for an understanding of the specific problems of production management to be dealt with in the remainder of the book.

Questions and Problems

1. Can a business organization be considered and analyzed as a system?
2. Develop a statement of objectives for a firm. Given this statement, outline the steps to be taken to organize the firm.
3. What are the three main theories of management, and what are their weaknesses and strengths?
4. How would you define management? Does the definition differ among a factory, a hospital, and a department store? If so, why? If not, why not?
5. On what basis does a project manager's authority rest?
6. Since matrix organization violates the concept of unity of command, why do firms use it to organize? Doesn't it lead to conflicts over authority?
7. Managers are said to perform the same functions regardless of their place in the organization structure and regardless of the type of enterprise in which they are engaged.
   (a) What are the implications of this statement?
   (b) What limitations are inherent in this statement?

8. The vice-president in charge of sales of the ABC Company has four territorial sales managers reporting to him and for whom he establishes policies. Why doesn't the vice-president merely establish rules and procedures for these subordinates instead of policies?

9. Span of control is usually considered to be an important problem in organizations. However, it is remarkable to observe that the holder of functional authority seems to have no problem with the span of control; his functional authority simply blankets all appropriate departments, and he seems to be able to handle any span. What is the reason for this, or is this statement wrong?

10. The planning–controlling mechanism in management theory assumes (a) a set of objectives, (b) a method of achieving the objectives, and (c) a method of detecting deviations from the objectives.

    Contrast the problems in applying these concepts to a mass production industry, a hospital, and a city government.

11. It has been the observation of many modern social psychologists that groups tend naturally to select their own leaders, to devise roles for their members, and generally to structure themselves.
    (a) If this is so, why do we spend time on the problems of administrative organization?
    (b) Does the above statement imply that the "acceptance theory" of the source of authority is a valid theory?

12. A manufacturer of a variety of products sells them through retail grocery stores and to industrial and institutional users. Suggest three bases he could use for grouping the selling functions and illustrate each. Specify the circumstances under which he might select each basis.

13. "The use of a product basis for departmentation rather than a functional basis makes coordination and control much simpler." Do you agree or disagree? Why?

14. "Policies are merely rough techniques to limit the discretion of decision makers but are not specific enough to serve the control function." Discuss.

15. "Long-range plans are just window-dressing. It is easier to be on your toes and ready for a change than to be wrong." How would you argue against this proposition?

16. The president of a hospital is faced with the problem of coordinating his medical, nursing, and administrative staffs. Suggest alternative approaches that might be used to resolve this problem, citing the strengths and weaknesses of each.

17. The James Chemical Corporation has ten plants located in ten cities, and each plant has an employment manager. The president contends that each of these employment managers should report to his respective plant manager. The head of the personnel department in the central headquarters contends that employment is part of the personnel function; consequently, he feels that these employment managers should report to him. How would you resolve this difficulty?

18. Define the types of authority a staff unit might have. Draw a chart showing an example of a staff management structure in a university.

References

Argyris, C., *Interpersonal Competence and Organizational Effectiveness,* Irwin, Homewood, Ill., 1962.

Barnard, C. I., *The Functions of the Executive,* Harvard University Press, Cambridge, Mass., 1938.

Carzo, R., Jr., and Yanouzas, J. N., *Formal Organization: A Systems Approach,* Irwin, Homewood, Ill., 1967.

Cyert, R. M., and March J. G., *A Behavioral Theory of the Firm,* Prentice-Hall, Englewood Cliffs, N.J., 1963.

Drucker, P. F., *The Practice of Management,* Harper and Row, New York, 1954.

Etzioni, A., *Modern Organizations,* Prentice-Hall, Englewood Cliffs, N.J., 1964.

Haire, M., *Modern Organization Theory,* Wiley, New York, 1959.

Kast, F., and Rosenzweig, J., *Organization and Management: A Systems Approach,* McGraw-Hill, New York, 1970.

Koontz, H. D., and O'Donnell, C. J., *Principles of Management: An Analysis of Managerial Functions,* 3rd ed., McGraw-Hill, New York, 1972.

Litterer, J., *The Analysis of Organization,* Wiley, New York, 1965.

March, J. G., and Simon, H. A., *Organizations,* Wiley, New York, 1958.

McGregor, D., *The Human Side of Enterprise,* McGraw-Hill, New York, 1960.

Newman, W. H., Summer, C. E., Jr., and Warren, K., *The Process of Management,* 3rd ed., Prentice-Hall, Englewood Cliffs, N.J., 1972.

Starr, M. K., *Management: A Modern Approach,* Harcourt Brace Jovanovich, New York, 1971.

3

Managerial Decision Making

The daily administration of the affairs of any business enterprise requires an endless sequence of decisions. Some of them are routine and are guided by company practice or by procedures previously formulated. Others are unusual and demand management's attention. Varying degrees of importance are attached to these decisions; many are comparatively trivial, but some will have a profound impact on the future of the firm. In any case, certain characteristics are common to all business decisions. For example, all are concerned with the future—the goals and actions to be pursued by the company. Every business decision also involves a choice between many available alternatives.

As noted in Chapter 2, the study of managerial decision making, decision theory, is aimed at determining how "good" decisions can be made. To understand the decision process it is necessary to consider the background against which the decisions are made. The most important factors are the system's objectives, its environment and value system, and its constraints.

The Background of Decision Making

At one time, perhaps, it could have been said that profit maximization was the main objective of the firm and hence the theme underlying all decisions made by management. Decision making in such an environment was relatively simple, because profit was the primary consideration whenever a manager was confronted with a choice among possible plans of action or solutions to a problem.

Today's managers must consider many other interacting forces and objectives when making a decision. Profits continue to be a highly important criterion for decision making, but there has been a growing emphasis upon what might be termed the social and service objectives of the business enterprise. The changing environment of decision making is depicted in Figure 3–1. Social and service objectives are not new, of course; they have always influenced management decisions to some extent. The major change has been in their relative importance *vis-à-vis* profits. The principal factors that have helped to increase their importance are:

1. The increased regulation of business activity by the federal and local governments. This regulation has come about largely because of the "excesses" associated with profit maximization under *laissez faire.* The government has not only enacted specific legislation such as the Sherman and Clayton Acts, but has also shown increased willingness to participate actively in business decision making when it feels that the national or local interest warrants it. The direct intervention by the President in the labor disputes that threatened the railroad and steel industries during the early 1960s, the increasing activity of the regulatory agencies, and the establishment of wage and price controls are examples of this activist posture. Thus, it is becoming increasingly evident that managers today must give some thought to how any proposed plan of action may affect the well-being of the entire economy.

2. The growing separation of ownership and management in industry. With the continuing growth in the size and complexity of the typical business firm, an increasing number of owners now exert their influence on an increasing number of managers. This tends to make the owners' (stockholders') influence less direct and intense. Only if results are extremely poor does the modern manager need to fear direct intervention by the stockholders; satisfactory profits and growth result in managerial security. Hence modern managers are usually reluctant to take risks that might result in huge profits lest failure bring about owner intervention.

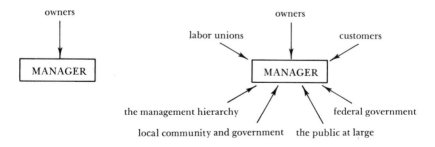

Yesterday
Profit maximization was the "single" objective of the firm

Today
Profit is joined by social and service objectives for the firm

Figure 3–1 The changing decision-making environment of the manager

Instead they seem to be aiming for the middle of the road in their decision making.

3. The steadily increasing importance of high-level education in top management. The intensive recruiting of men with graduate degrees in business administration is symptomatic of this trend. The cultural and educational environment from which these men come is partly responsible for their placing increased emphasis on human or social values in business. Interest in employee adjustment and morale, and a concern about the image of the firm and its managers, are reflections of this increased awareness of social values in business. Modern managers are increasingly concerned with balancing the needs of all the groups listed on the "today" side of Figure 3–1. Management's growing awareness of the social contributions it makes by providing employment and investment opportunities to the public has led many managers to try to avoid losses rather than to earn huge profits by taking dangerous risks.

4. The expansion of market areas cultivated by the typical firm because of improved transportation and communications. Local advantages are being minimized, which means increased competition for many industries. This, in turn, has helped to make managers more sensitive to the needs and desires of customers and suppliers. The ability to deal effectively with these groups can literally determine the success or failure of a company. Relations with customers is a marketing or sales function, but production management feels the influence of customer demands indirectly through product specifications, quality and reliability standards, and delivery schedules.

5. The growth of labor unions. Collective bargaining now exerts considerable influence on the decision making of managers, particularly in the production area of the firm, largely through the union–company contract. The influence of organized labor is also felt in other production management areas such as plant location, facilities acquisition, plant layout, materials handling, and production scheduling.

6. The growing social pressures. In the past ten years the influence exerted on managerial actions by a mobilized public has increased greatly. The pressures on business for greater safety measures, less pollution, and increased social concern in general have reawakened the regulatory agencies and have led to new laws regulating business activities. In addition to conforming to the new legal structure, managers have had to reevaluate their decisions in light of the changing structure of public values.

Decision Theory

The different approaches used for managerial decision making offer insights into a theory of decision making useful in production/operations management.

Two extreme approaches to managerial decision making exist. At one end of the spectrum, in the systems approach the entire decision process is formalized: the problem is carefully described and analyzed, possible alternatives are identified, sound decision criteria are formulated, and the data needed to implement the criteria are painstakingly gathered and then applied. At the other end, decisions may be based on experienced judgment and intuition without a conscious attempt to define the problem and identify all the alternatives. This pattern of decision making is characterized by intuition, trial-and-error, or follow-the-leader decision making. Generally, however, the decision approach chosen lies somewhere between these two extremes. The executive uses his formal training, judgment born of experience, his knowledge of outside forces that affect the enterprise, and his understanding of the fundamental nature of the firm's operations.

At this point we will look at the two extremes in some detail in order to develop further the concepts of decision making. First we will discuss the intuitive, trial-and-error, and follow-the-leader approaches. By looking at their weaknesses, we will be able to see why the systems approach has gained favor today.

Intuitive Decision Making

History records the accomplishments of a long line of specialized decision makers—tribal chiefs, medicine men, kings, generals, and priests. Early man looked to the heavens for guidance. He relied on a vast array of good omens and spirits to help him decide where to build his home, where to plant his crops and when to harvest, and how to plan a battle. Providence was kind enough to furnish devils or evil spirits, which gave him a convenient excuse for the outcome of decisions deemed poor in retrospect. Astrologists and fortunetellers, like the oracle at Delphi, acted as decision consultants for such famous ancients as Alexander the Great and Julius Caesar.

Such magical decision making is by no means a thing of the distant past, however. Early writings in the field of personnel management emphasized phrenology. It was suggested that applicants be screened on the basis of the number of bumps on their heads. A jutting jaw was thought to denote a strong, forceful personality, whereas a receding chin was taken as a sign of a retiring individual lacking in confidence. Even today, managers have been known to select subordinates by the way they shake hands; a firm handshake is considered good, whereas a "wet fish" is thought to indicate a passive individual lacking in drive and motivation. One's personal appearance strongly influences others—mustaches, beards, glasses, or baldness may have a decidedly adverse or favorable impact. Candidates are still selected because they have a confident bearing or "air" about them. Some managers may still rely on mental stereotypes that insist, for example, that successful salesmen are fast-talking extroverts and all creative engineers are unkempt introverts.

A discussion about the stock market would quickly convince one that intuition and hunches are still employed in the decision process. Of course, to the extent that hunches and intuition are based on the training and experience of the individual, they have a valid role as aids in a sound decision technique. They actually involve an unstructured gathering and classifying of historical data, which is followed by subjective evaluation based on decision criteria that are applied, somewhat subconsciously, to the problem situation.

Intuitive decision making can be dangerous, however. Most important decisions demand an organized collection and interpretation of data followed by cautious application that reflects an understanding of the limitations of the standards employed as criteria. An interesting illustration of the dangers inherent in the historical approach to decision making concerns the owner-manager of a small plumbing-fixture company. The ABC Company had been profitably engaged in defense subcontract work during World War I. At the close of this conflict the coffers of the company were filled with earnings derived from government contracts. The owner, who had been in the plumbing-fixture field for many years, decided that the firm should switch to the manufacture of bathtubs. The techniques of mass production learned during defense-contract days were applied to the manufacture of this product. Operations began in earnest in 1920, and a short while later this country experienced a slight recession. The labor surplus created by troops returning from the war was accentuated, and pay scales were driven to very low levels. Material costs were also depressed. Consequently, the time was ripe for the low-cost manufacture of bathtubs. Heavy cash reserves were available, so the program progressed despite the low level of sales. The company's warehouses were soon full of bathtubs, and additional space was leased in the local area. Then, near the end of 1923, there was a sharp rise in the number of houses constructed, and houses need bathtubs. The demand was accentuated by a trend toward two or more tubs in each house. Thus, the ABC Company was in an ideal position. It had plenty of low-cost units that were immediately available to supply the strong demand. As a consequence, its profits were enormous and, in the later 1920s, the company expanded its line to include the manufacture of all plumbing fixtures.

Then came the crash of 1929, and the country was plunged into a severe depression. The management of the company "knew" exactly what to do in a depression—namely, build bathtubs. Experience seemed to indicate that this was the route to large profits. Soon the company's warehouses were again filled with tubs. As before, additional space was leased and filled. Something went wrong this time, however, because the company ran out of money in 1932. Shortly thereafter it went bankrupt. The owner wondered what had gone wrong. Hindsight is better than foresight, of course, and it seems relatively easy to diagnose this case. The building of tubs during the depressed years of the early 1920s had not been the key to success. Instead, the profits had resulted from the sale of these units during the construction boom that followed immediately after. This same approach failed approximately ten years later because conditions had changed. No building boom came along to create a demand for the plentiful low-cost bathtubs that were lying in the warehouses. Thus, the outcome was a disaster for the company.

Trial-and-Error Decision Making

Trial-and-error decision making is an adaptation of intuitive decision making. It is probably the most widely used approach to decision making. In the trial-and-error approach a problem is subjectively isolated, defined, and analyzed, and a course of action is selected. The course of action may be selected intuitively or through the follow-the-leader approach that will be discussed next. In this process a number of alternatives may be developed and evaluated, or only one may be conceived and instituted. Once the decision is made and implemented, its results are monitored. If the results are favorable, management is satisfied and the decision is allowed to stand. In fact, in many cases when the decision works it becomes a prototype for future decisions. If the results are not satisfactory, the process is repeated and another decision is made, implemented, and monitored.

Since the trial-and-error approach incorporates the monitoring of the decision, it is better than the intuitive approach, which, as defined here, lacks this follow-up. The trial-and-error approach does, however, have the other weaknesses of intuitive decision making. Decisions that work have a tendency to become standard operating procedures and be used for problems where the environmental conditions may not apply, as was the case with the bathtubs. In addition, the development and selection of alternatives is haphazard. Thus, better alternatives may be neglected or put aside because the current approach to the problems is satisfactory. This condition is epitomized in the "don't rock the boat" attitude that often emerges when new approaches to old problems are suggested. Better alternatives are often put aside by the comment, "What we have works, why take a chance with something new? Besides, didn't we try something like that twenty years ago?"[1] Since new alternatives are not systematically evaluated, the presence of a working solution effectively stops the progress toward better solutions.

Follow-the-Leader Decision Making

The essence of the final judgment and experience approach is captured in the expression, "It worked for them, so why not for us?" In this approach, decisions are based on the decisions of other firms or organizations or on accepted trade practice. Pricing decisions are often made this way. In the automobile industry, for example, General Motors sets the pattern, and the other companies follow.

Justification for follow-the-leader decisions rests on the idea that such decisions minimize risk. The decisions are considered safe because they have been tried by others. This premise is not, however, necessarily true. Every company and organization is different. What may be a sound decision for one may be bad for another. Since environments differ between firms, so too generally must decisions differ. To neglect the differences over time by following the leader will invariably lead to trouble.

Evaluation of the Judgment Approaches

The intuitive, trial-and-error, and follow-the-leader approaches to decision making may be very effective. Their effectiveness depends almost totally on the ability of the individual making the decisions. If he has superior judgment, intuition, and knowledge, the results can be excellent. However, the probability that an organization will have a continuous stream of such men is small. More-

---

[1] These words are the authors' recollection of the comments made at a meeting called to consider a new inventory system in a large department store. They were persuasive enough to forestall the introduction of the new system. It was finally instituted several years later, but only after large inventory losses.

over, as conditions change, an individual may not adapt to the changes—a manager who was excellent at one point in time may be a failure at a later date.

The so-called judgment approaches maximize the art aspect of management. The availability of managers who have all of the necessary abilities for this type of decision making can be likened to the number of great artists or statesmen. In the long run, when decisions are left primarily to individual judgment, the result is a strong dose of mediocrity and a small dose of brilliance.

The Scientific Method

The systems approach to decision making had its beginnings in the depression of the 1930s. There were many business failures during this period, and many of the firms that did survive were severely shaken. Business owners and managers were deeply concerned and puzzled by this trend. What was wrong? Why were businesses failing? There had to be better ways of making decisions. The individualistic intuitive approach, based on experienced judgment, had proved to be quite uncertain and even dangerous. Confidence in business decision making could be restored only if better tools and techniques were discovered. Past business practices, experiences, and writings were reexamined in an effort to identify and classify the best decision-making approaches previously developed. There was also a keen interest in the formation of new ways of solving business problems. This interest was shared by industry and universities alike. Research was sponsored by both the government and business concerns. Many believe that it was during this period that the development of enterprise management as a professional science really began. The challenge confronting United States industry with the outbreak of World War II intensified efforts to design more effective management methods. In addition, profits reaped by business during this era provided the funds needed for research. The strong interest in this subject spawned by the exigencies of the depression and World War II has continued to this day, with a great acceleration in the development of improved managerial techniques.

Striving to find a better decision-making process, management turned to the scientific method. The scientific method is a process of analysis that has been used in the physical sciences for a hundred or more years. Students are taught it early in their educational training, and yet it still forms the foundation for doctoral dissertations. The method follows a four-step process.

1. Define the problem.
2. Develop a hypothesis.
3. Test the hypothesis.
4. Prove or disprove the hypothesis.

The process begins with the recognition of a problem. Data are collected about this problem until a hypothesis can be formulated. The hypothesis is a statement of an assumption about the problem that is to be tested. It sets the framework for the collection of additional data to be used to determine if the hypothesis is valid.

To accomplish this, experiments are conducted that yield primarily quantifiable data. Since the experiments are normally conducted under laboratory conditions, some variables can be held constant while others are allowed freedom to vary. Laboratory equipment is used that is able to measure minute changes in the variables. In this fashion, the influence of the individual variables can be ascertained. For example, in Boyle's famous experiments, the temperature of a gas was held constant to test the changes in volume brought about by changes in pressure.

When the experiments are completed, the results are analyzed to determine whether or not the hypothesis is valid. If it is upheld, a fundamental relationship is established that can be repeatedly demonstrated when desired. It is thus predictive of future events. It is an underlying truth that can be used alone or as a basis for the understanding of other problems.

In attempts to carry the scientific method over to managerial problems, a number of difficulties were encountered. Looking at these difficulties in the order of the steps in the scientific method, the first problem arises in the definition of the problem. Business problems are characterized by a multiplicity of symptoms. The causes of the problems are not easily recognized; consequently, the symptoms are often taken for the problem. Remedying the symptoms may give short-term relief, but it does not remove the problem, which often pops up again in a short time.

The second area of difficulty relates to the concept of a hypothesis. Science looks for truths. In business there are no universal truths. Situations change dramatically. What will produce a desired result today may not do so tomorrow. Solutions to business problems may not be repeatable and are rarely transferable. Furthermore, there generally is not "one" right answer but a group of acceptable solutions, and a choice must be made from among these solutions.

Two sets of problems arise during the testing of the hypothesis. In a laboratory a scientist has a controlled environment—a closed system. He can manipulate variables as he desires. A business manager rarely if ever has such control. The external environment and the organization within which he works are constantly undergoing change. He cannot stop many of these changes nor can he initiate others. As a consequence, he cannot totally control his experiments and thus cannot always accurately predict what effect changes will have.

The second type of problem having to do with testing hypotheses in business management arises from difficulties in measurement. Scientists can measure variables quantitatively with a high degree of accuracy. Managers can quantify only a portion of the factors involved in a problem and much of the time only with rough measures. Often the most important factors are qualitative, not quantitative; they cannot be measured in units but only in relative, subjective terms. Managers must therefore weigh the quantifiable factors against the nonquantifiable, with only their judgment to determine the relative weights.

The final area of difficulty pertains to the evaluation of the results. Since there is difficulty in stating the hypothesis, in developing experimental data, and in evaluating the data, it obviously is difficult to accurately evaluate the results of an experiment.

Because of these problems, the scientific method had to be adapted to better fit the managerial scene. Over time, techniques of measurement, of testing, and of analysis have been developed that make the method an excellent tool for managerial decision making. Central to this improved approach is the concept of a model. Therefore, before proceeding to the systems approach we will explore the notion of a model.

Models as Decision Aids

A *model* is a general term denoting any abstract representation of a real situation. Its objective is not to identify all aspects of the subject but rather to identify significant factors and interrelationships. A model can be a useful decision aid because it presents a simplified description of the problem at hand and thus facilitates the isolation and analysis of the issues that will have the greatest influence on the decision to be made. In this fashion, models provide an operating perspective that tends to improve the quality of the solution formulated. For these reasons considerable effort has been directed toward the design of various models as decision aids. The most common ones can be labeled *verbal, schematic, iconic, analog,* and *mathematical.*

Verbal Models

As the name implies, these models describe the problem and its constituent interrelated elements with words, and they are usually structured in essay form. This is the most common approach to problem solving. They are particularly well suited to simple day-to-day situations, where they are most frequently used. The advantages of this type of model include its low cost and ease of construction. Usually there is neither time nor money available for applying more sophisticated decision approaches to daily routine questions. Such expenditures could not be justified even if the resources were available.

The major limitations of verbal models stem from their reliance on verbal language; semantic difficulties and misunderstandings often arise when individuals communicate verbally. There is also the danger that the description will be incomplete or that it will place improper emphasis on certain factors.

Schematic Models

To avoid many of the weaknesses inherent in verbal models, schematic models have been developed. These models include all forms of diagrams, drawings, graphs, and charts, most of which are designed to deal with specific types of problems. By presenting significant factors and interrelationships in pictorial form, schematic models are able to indicate problems in a manner that facilitates analysis. A bar chart, for example, can be used effectively as a summary presen-

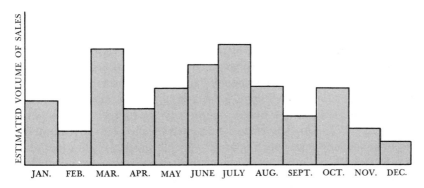

Figure 3–2 Forecast of monthly production of the ABC company

tation of a company's monthly production forecast, as illustrated in Figure 3–2. This schematic model shows more clearly than words or numbers that the estimated level of production is subject to wide and irregular fluctuation during the year.

Other frequently employed schematic models are listed together with the problem areas in which they are used in Table 3–1: They will be discussed in detail later in the text in conjunction with the problem areas to which they apply.

Like verbal models, schematic models are relatively inexpensive and can be quickly constructed whenever a problem arises. It is important that the manager know which type of schematic model is suited to his particular problem, however, for one of the major limitations of these devices is their relatively narrow area of application. Furthermore, with few exceptions, such as flow charts for computer programing, schematic models are not well suited to highly complex problems.

Table 3–1 Common schematic models and their uses

Schematic Model	*Problem Area*
Flow-process charts	Plant layout; process analysis
Operator charts; multiple-activity charts	Labor simplification
Elemental-analysis chart	Labor measurement
Break-even chart; sales-dollar analysis chart	Operation analysis and planning
Materials handling analysis chart	Materials handling analysis and planning
Quality control $\bar{x}$, $\bar{p}$, and $\bar{c}$ charts	Inspection and quality control
Gantt charts	Production scheduling
Routing and assembly diagrams	Production planning
Block diagrams	Multiple uses; e.g., information systems analysis
Organization charts	Organization planning
Flow charts	Information flow analysis; computer programing

Iconic or Physical Models

An *icon* is an image or likeness of something. Thus, *iconic models* are scaled physical operating replicas of a product or operation. They are extremely helpful tools in analyzing certain problems since they make possible a thorough, actual operational observation of the forces present. The range of management problem areas where these models can be used effectively is extremely narrow, however; it consists largely of those fields that are oriented toward engineering and science. In research and development, engineers have long used "mockups," or pilot models, to test the physical operation of theories and new products. The final design of many types of chemical plants is often based upon data derived from the testing of pilot plants. Similarly, scale models of new airplanes are placed in wind tunnels to test the performance of the craft under various wind patterns and environmental conditions. Only iconic models could simulate the actual performance of a product like an airplane for testing purposes, thereby avoiding the tremendous expense of designing full-scale experimental models; therefore, they make possible much more experimentation in product form.

Iconic models can be excellent decision aids, but by their nature they are generally costly and time-consuming tools to use. Consequently, iconic models have largely been limited to significant decision areas where the costs involved justify the expense of more elaborate and more accurate models.

Analog Models

Analog models are closely akin to iconic models; however, they are not replicas of problem situations. Rather, they are small physical systems that have characteristics similar to those of the problems. In operation, analog models seek to approximate the interaction of forces experienced in the environment under examination. Often the similarity between the model and the problem is confined to a single aspect. The objective is to gain by analogy an understanding of the issues and forces present in the real problem. This technique has been used primarily in the area of research. The flow of water through conduits under varying conditions of velocity and wall resistance was used as an analogy of electrical current in a wire, for example. The data and conclusions that were drawn from this experiment proved to be applicable to the real situation; they could not have been derived by observing the actual electrical current flow because our technology has not yet advanced to the point where such observations are feasible. A more sophisticated application of the analog model concept is the analog computer, in which an electrical system may be used to simulate complex systems, such as a manufacturing plant. In this way, proposed production plans, including machine assignments and the sequencing of different products and production operations, can be tested, and the feasibility of alternate plans can be compared. At present, analog models can be applied effectively to only a relatively narrow range of production problems, and they are costly and time-consuming to construct. It seems quite likely, however, that cheaper and more versatile ones will be developed in the future.

Mathematical Models

The major advantage of mathematical models stems from the precision of mathematics. These models permit a clear, unambiguous statement of the relationships that exist among the variables in a problem. An equation such as $a = b + 1$ means the same thing to anyone who reads it. Furthermore, it defines a direct and unique relationship between a, the dependent variable, and b, the independent variable—namely, that a is always one unit greater than b. Thus, when data concerning b are available, the value of a may easily be obtained by anyone who has read the formula. Because of the clarity and simplicity of expression in a mathematical model, complex relationships between large numbers of variables can be defined. Moreover, the rules of mathematics allow manipulations of the model to obtain a desired result. For these reasons there is a continuing effort in the industrial and academic worlds to develop mathematical models that are representative of business situations.

Deterministic models   There are two basic types of mathematical models—deterministic and probabilistic. Both are useful for managerial decision making.

In deterministic models, the variables and their relationships are stated exactly. Conditions of certainty exist, with definite relationships between the variables. The results obtained with the same data are always the same. As an example, consider the problem of determining the break-even volume—the volume where sales revenues equal costs—for a particular product.

The general form of the sales revenue line is determined by the equation

(1) $$R = (P)(V)$$

where R = revenue
P = unit price
V = number of units or volume

The shape of the total cost line results from

(2) $$\text{TC} = \text{FC} + (V)(C_v)$$

where   TC = total cost
FC = fixed cost
C_v = variable cost per unit

The break-even point occurs when

(3) $$\text{TC} = R$$

or from equations (1) and (2),

$$(P)(V) = \text{FC} + (V)(C_v)$$

Finally, the break-even volume can be determined by solving the equation

(4) $$V_{be} = \frac{\text{FC}}{P - C_v}$$

where V_{be} = break-even volume
$P - C_v$ = contribution per unit of sales

With a given set of data the answer will always be the same. If we take the unit sales price to be \$5.00; fixed costs, \$350,000; and variable costs, \$2.50 per unit; then the break-even volume will be

$$V_{be} = \frac{350,000}{5.00 - 2.50} = 140,000 \text{ units}$$

Probabilistic models   Probabilistic models come into use when there is uncertainty about variables or about their relationships. Because of this uncertainty, probablistic models do not yield the same answers each time. Since the variables or relationships change, the results must change.

Consider a firm that wishes to know how much inventory it should hold for a certain product. It must consider both its sales and the delivery times of its orders, and generally both of these factors are variable. To simplify their problem, management could assume that the variables have a particular relationship and construct a deterministic model. However, the result would not relate to real-life conditions.

Instead, they can treat the sales and delivery times probabilistically. For example, they could use data for a recent time period to develop frequency distributions of both sales and delivery times. Then, using the information gained from these, they could proceed to develop a series of answers based on various assumptions about future demand and delivery times. The selection of a particular answer would depend on which set of assumptions management thought best fit the situation.

For such an inventory problem, the solution will normally call for the maintenance of a safety inventory to take care of those instances when the demand exceeds the normal inventory or when delivery is later than usual. Safety inventory thus protects against the uncertainties; since we cannot predict with certainty, we must have a means of overcoming the undesirable aspects of uncertainty.

Simulation Models

A special class of mathematical models that is taking on increasing importance in management decision making comprises what are termed simulation models. Simulation is an experimental method used to study behavior over time. The process is similar to trial-and-error decision making. Instead of implementing the decision and seeing the results in the real world, a model is constructed and used to test the decision. In this way decisions can be evaluated without the risks inherent in actually implementing them.

A simulation model does not yield answers as do the other types of mathematical models. It is merely a vehicle with which ideas can be projected and their outcomes seen. The evaluation of the outcomes is generally not part of the model.

The question, then, is Why use a simulation model if it doesn't yield answers whereas other mathematical approaches do? The answer is that simulation models can be built for problems that are not amenable to other methods. In addition, in some cases simulation models are easier to design and use than other techniques. These reasons will be readily demonstrated by examples later in the text.

To illustrate the essential aspects of a simulation model, let us consider a very simplified example. A druggist wishes to know how many copies of the Sunday paper to get to make the most profit. The papers cost the druggist $0.25 each, and he sells them for $0.35 each. He cannot return papers nor can be obtain more than one delivery.

The druggist knows that in the past he has sold papers at the following rate:

Demand per Week	Percent of Weeks (relative frequency)
10	5
11	10
12	20
13	30
14	20
15	10
16	5

At the present time the druggist receives 16 papers each weekend, but he does not think that this gives him the maximum profit. He believes his best approach is to order the same number of papers for a given week as were demanded the previous weekend. That is, if the demand one week is 13, then he will order 13 papers the following weekend. Before trying that approach, though, he would like to test it. He therefore has taken 100 slips of paper and written on the slips the number of papers demanded according to their relative demand: five slips have 10 on them, ten slips have 11, twenty slips have 12, and so forth. He has then randomly drawn ten slips from the pile, replacing each in the pile after it was drawn. The values on the slips represent a simulated demand for ten weeks. Writing down the number on each slip as it was drawn, he has constructed the simulated demand table shown in Table 3–2.

Table 3–2 Simulated demand for papers

Week	Simulated Demand
1	12
2	16
3	12
4	10
5	11
6	13
7	14
8	13
9	15
10	13

Table 3–3 Profit when orders are constant

Week	Cost per Week[a]	Simulated Demand	×	Sales Price	=	Revenue	Profit
1	$4.00	12	×	$0.35	=	$4.20	$0.20
2	4.00	16	×	0.35	=	5.60	1.60
3	4.00	12	×	0.35	=	4.20	0.20
4	4.00	10	×	0.35	=	3.50	0.50
5	4.00	11	×	0.35	=	3.85	0.15
6	4.00	13	×	0.35	=	4.55	0.55
7	4.00	14	×	0.35	=	4.90	0.90
8	4.00	13	×	0.35	=	4.55	0.55
9	4.00	15	×	0.35	=	5.25	1.25
10	4.00	13	×	0.35	=	4.55	0.55
							$5.15

[a] Papers ordered × cost per paper = 16 × $0.25 = $4.00.

The druggist then constructs Table 3–3, which shows what his profit would be with this simulated demand if he were to follow his old pattern of ordering 16 papers a week. He finds that for the ten-week period his profit would be $5.15.

To determine what his profit would be if he let demand determine the following week's order, he draws an additional slip from the pile. This slip, with a demand of 13 papers, simulates the demand for the current week (week 0). Consequently, 13 papers should be ordered for the following week (week 1). According to his simulation model, during week 1 only 12 papers are demanded and sold, leaving one unsold. As a result, for the next week (week 2), only 12 papers are ordered. In week 2, 16 papers are asked for but only 12 are available to sell. He carries out the simulation in this manner for ten weeks. The results are given in Table 3–4. If he had followed his new idea, he would have had

Table 3–4 Profit when orders follow simulated demand

Week	Papers Ordered	×	Cost per Paper	=	Weekly Cost	Simu- lated Demand	Papers Sold	×	Price per Paper	=	Revenue	Profit
0						13						
1	13	×	$0.25	=	$3.25	12	12	×	$0.35		$4.20	$0.95
2	12	×	0.25	=	3.00	16	12	×	0.35	=	4.20	1.20
3	16	×	0.25	=	4.00	12	12	×	0.35	=	4.20	0.20
4	12	×	0.25	=	3.00	10	10	×	0.35	=	3.50	0.50
5	10	×	0.25	=	2.50	11	10	×	0.35	=	3.50	1.00
6	11	×	0.25	=	2.75	13	11	×	0.35	=	3.85	1.10
7	13	×	0.25	=	3.25	14	13	×	0.35	=	4.55	1.30
8	14	×	0.25	=	3.50	13	13	×	0.35	=	4.55	1.05
9	13	×	0.25	=	3.25	15	13	×	0.35	=	4.55	1.30
10	15	×	0.25	=	3.75	13	13	×	0.35	=	4.55	0.80
												$9.40

$9.40 in profit for the same demand that would yield $5.15 with his current ordering pattern.

The results could be quite different if a different set of simulated demands had been drawn. If we were to simulate this process in real life, we would want many more weeks of demand, enough that we could rid ourselves of any chance factors in the demand. A large number of iterations are needed to give high reliability for complicated systems. For this reason alone, most simulation models are computerized.

What we have done in the example is to test two alternatives, the new ordering rule and the old. There are many more alternatives that could be tested. We might consider a standing order of 13 papers, or 14, or 15, or any other number we wish. Simulation models do not indicate what the best answer is. What they do is project the results for whatever alternatives are tested. If the best alternative is not tried, the model cannot test it.

One more point to be made at this time is true of all models. In order to simplify the example, we omitted an important feature of the real-life situation. We did not consider the consequences of a customer not being able to purchase a paper. Will he go to another source? Will he perhaps stop coming to our druggist and go to the other store thereafter? Such questions are difficult to answer and even more difficult to quantify. Yet they play a part in management thinking. Management may assume that no harm is done when a customer is disappointed or, conversely, they may attach a high degree of importance to the consequences. In any case, the possible consequences should be considered; management must place a value on them. Once that is done, they can be incorporated into the model or omitted, depending on the assigned level of importance. Elements of a situation should be included only if they are important—i.e., will change the solution; however, they should not be left out just because they have been overlooked.

Model Limitations

In most real-life situations, with advantages come limitations. So too with models; models are abstractions of real life and should not be confused with reality. Indeed, very few business problems can be completely described by a mathematical model because of the great number of factors involved in a realistic problem, many of which are intangible. Some factors must of necessity be omitted from the model, and some intangible ones must be qualified. In order to do this, assumptions must be made about the importance and nature of these factors. Even if it were possible to construct a model that accurately included all factors, it would probably be too complex and unwieldy for business purposes. The manipulation needed to solve the problem would be burdensome and probably time-consuming and expensive. For these reasons the typical business model is simplified and thus incomplete. The amount of error introduced by the assumptions incorporated in the model will vary from problem to problem. Nonetheless, the decision data obtained from models can be extremely useful to the manager who understands the limitations of the model and of the input data used.

There is a danger of succumbing to the subtle lure of a model and becoming so involved with it that it becomes reality. The test of a model is not how well it looks but how well it performs predictively. The value of a model lies in the aid it provides in analyzing a situation. It should furnish a better understanding of the real world and enable a manager to develop predictions of what will occur with changes in the variables or in their relationships.

Systems Approach to Decision Making

The systems approach to decision making can be broken down to answering three fundamental questions.

1. *What is the problem?*
2. *What are the alternative solutions?*
3. *Which of the alternatives is best?*

While we will deal with each of these questions in detail later, it is important at this time to get a general overview of the process.

The most important phase of the process is the definition of the problem. If the wrong problem is selected, it doesn't matter how you solve it. Second in importance is the development of alternatives. If you overlook choices you may miss the best alternative.

This leaves the third phase, the selection of an alternative. It is only at this stage that the decision-making techniques, which some people incorrectly characterize as the systems approach, come into play. These techniques are used to evaluate alternatives. They can be effective only if the first two phases of the process are valid. We repeat, if you state the wrong problem and miss alternatives, it doesn't matter what solution you choose.

Finally, some uncertainty is unavoidable in the decision process. Some risk always exists. These risks should be acknowledged and handled openly by the manager making the decision. Facing uncertainty with managerial judgment is far less risky than attempting to ignore it.

The Decision Process

Let us now take a step-by-step look at the decision process. The formal decision process can be broken down into five steps.

1. *Defining the problem*
2. *Developing objectives or goals and their criteria of measurement*
3. *Model building*
4. *Generating alternatives*
5. *Testing and selecting an alternative*

Defining the Problem

In the systems approach, problems are viewed in a broad perspective. The entire firm is looked upon as a single operating system and is considered to be the appropriate arena for problem solving. When a problem arises, it is examined with respect to the total firm rather than just in terms of the sector that is apparently involved.

The objective of this approach is to identify all significant interactions between the problem area and the operation of the firm as a whole. Thus, it is hoped that decision making in any functional area, such as the production control department, will reflect what is best for the entire company. This is in sharp contrast to the earlier approach whereby a problem was isolated and solved in a particular area of a company. Under the earlier system, production problems would be considered only in terms of what was best for that department. This approach causes difficulty since it may lead to a solution that is not an optimum one for the total firm but only for a sector of it. This process of not optimizing the benefit to the overall firm is called suboptimization.

On the other hand, since the systems approach views the organization as a whole, it will often produce decisions that may be viewed as burdensome for a particular department, because optimization is desired at the firm level in order to produce the greatest overall net benefit.

Of course, the interrelated problems that may be uncovered with this broad approach cannot or need not all be solved at once. Management problems can be quite complex. In fact, the complexity is generally so great that while it is conceptually nice to conceive of developing a solution for all of the problem's ramifications, it is not operationally possible to do so. Typically, the most important aspects of the problem are attacked first. The significant fact is that when a problem area is studied, consideration is given to its interactions with other problems in the entire system. Those interactions which have important consequences are considered in arriving at the solution; the others are ignored. While this means that the decision may not yield an optimum solution, the solution arrived at is close enough for the purpose intended and is in fact the best that can be obtained.

To properly define a problem, a clear-cut statement of the problem must be developed, preferably in writing. This includes determination of the internal conditions and the environment associated with the problem. Together, the internal conditions and the environment define the area in which feasible solutions to the problem can be found.

Objective Criteria

Once the problem is defined, the next step is to develop a set of objectives, or goals, for the solution. Like the problem definition, the goals should be precisely stated, clearly relating what the solution is to accomplish. Often, during the definition of the problem and the determination of its goals, it becomes apparent that the problem is too large to treat as an entity and must be broken into sub-problems. Each subproblem is then attacked in the same manner as the overall problem, with its own set of goals. Each objective should have an associated set of measures that will indicate how well the objective is met. These measures, which are often called objective criteria, should wherever possible be quantitative. Good measures lead to good decisions, since they enable a sound selection of alternatives to be made. In the absence of valid measures, alternatives can be evaluated only by intuition.

Managers often find that there is a conflict between the different goals for a problem. Resolution of such conflicts is a prime management function. The matter may be further complicated by the unavailability of an agreed-upon measure for achievement of a goal. As an example of this, consider two of the general goals of higher education. One is to make higher education available to as many students as possible. Another is to improve the education each student receives. Conflict arises when resources must be allocated to these goals. The more that is spent on intensive and graduate education, the less that is available to handle additional students. The more allocated to increase the student body, the less available for intensive education. Complicating the problem is the difficulty of measuring educational quality. What is "good" educational training? How do you measure it? We could argue that point for many hours without arriving at a consensus. However, we need some measure or else we cannot properly evaluate alternatives.

Areas of uncertainty exist in most management decisions. Objective criteria cannot always be assigned to every goal. Being aware of where they do not exist and openly facing the problem leads to better decisions. Moreover, over time, as more insight into the problem is gained, the reliability of the measures can be increased.

In our educational example, educational management must determine what constitutes a good education, how it can be measured, and what the tradeoff between intensive education and more students is worth. While these judgments may be quite subjective, they provide a means to evaluate alternatives. Without them, it doesn't matter what alternatives you choose since there is no way to rationally distinguish one from another.

Model Building and Alternative Testing

With the problem defined, its goals stated, and measures of effectiveness developed, the next step is to generate the alternative solutions to the problem. Alternative courses of action are not always obvious. It is at this point that a model enters into the process. Construction of a model forces a systematic approach. It pinpoints what is and is not known about the situation. Thus, it highlights the relationship between elements of the problem and leads the decision maker to alternatives.

Once completed, the model is the vehicle to test alternatives. Since answers to business problems lie in the future, the models provide a means of predicting the future. They are not aimed at providing truths. They give the decision maker a means of projecting some assumptions into the future and predicting what the outcome will be providing the assumptions hold. The results are transitory.

Problem Types and Decision Approaches

Virtually all of the problems encountered in production/operations management can be viewed through the systems approach. For ease of discussion and understanding, we will divide the problems into eight categories and will present them in a broad perspective. The eight categories we will consider are *inventory, allocation, queuing, sequencing, routing, replacement, competitive,* and *search.*

Inventory Problems

An inventory may be defined generally as the commitment of resources—manpower, materials, or facilities—in anticipation of future use. Since these resources will remain idle until used, the firm is forfeiting possible gains that could be earned if these resources were used in another way. Thus, the main problem in inventory management is how large an inventory to maintain. Optimum inventory size may be determined by balancing two kinds of costs:

Class 1 costs increase as the size of the inventory increases. Included in this category are those costs associated with maintaining the inventory, such as the interest on the tied-up funds and inventory spoilage.

Class 2 costs decrease as the size of the inventory increases. The costs of acquisition and those incurred by running out of the inventory fall into this category.

Thus, the cost curves of a typical inventory are illustrated by the simple model in Figure 3–3. The objective of cost balancing is to determine the minimum total

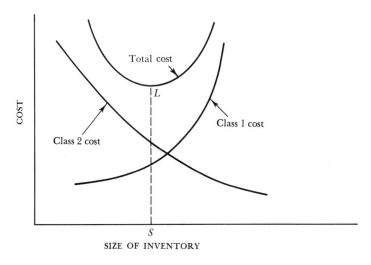

Figure 3–3 A model of inventory problems

cost for a particular inventory. This is at the lowest point (L) on the total cost curve, which comprises Class 1 and Class 2 costs. Optimum inventory volume, therefore, would be quantity S. The mathematical techniques for balancing these costs are well developed. They depend principally upon the use of calculus and probability theory. For very complex cases where precise mathematical solutions cannot be obtained, simulation models can be constructed to determine approximate answers.

The inventory type of problem is not restricted to finished goods, raw materials, and work-in-process inventories. It has wider applications. Suppose, for example, that the horizontal axis of Figure 3–3 was relabeled to denote the cost of a maintenance program including maintenance crews and spare parts. Then Class 1 costs would represent resources committed to the performance of maintenance work, and Class 2 costs would represent losses due to machine downtime, including production delays, idle men and machines, and dissatisfied customers. The germ of the problem is the same as that in the finished goods, raw materials, or work-in-process case: how to balance the two types of conflicting costs to obtain the minimum total cost.

As another example of the general nature of the inventory type of problem, suppose we let the horizontal axis of Figure 3–3 represent the amount of quality control inspection within a firm. Class 1 costs would then relate to the size of the inspection crews and the characteristics of the inspection process. The greater the number of inspection points and the more intensive the inspection routines, the larger the costs. Class 2 costs would represent costs incurred by passing on bad units. They include further work on those units, possible harm to workmen, possible loss of goodwill, and field repair.

Problems regarding the capacity that factory facilities or materials handling equipment should have may also be approached in this fashion. If too great a capacity is provided, the resources committed will stand idle until the demand catches up. On the other hand, if there is insufficient capacity the firm incurs costs as a result of inefficient methods and an inability to satisfy demand. The same is true of capital budgeting problems. If the funds set aside for investment in the firm exceed the firm's requirements, other potentially profitable uses for these funds have been passed up. Conversely, insufficient funds may result in Class 2 costs arising from lost investment opportunities or the need to borrow at unfavorable terms. In short, the inventory type of problem is quite common in the business world.

Allocation Problems

Allocation problems involve matching available resources to tasks that must be performed in order to minimize total cost or maximize total profit. The nature of allocation problems can best be shown by considering the input–output chart shown in Table 3-5. In order to fulfill the required production output, 600 labor hours are needed for task 1, 395 for task 2, 365 for task 3, and 270 for task 4. The labor is available from four departments, A through D. Department A, for

Table 3–5 A model of the allocation process

Tasks	Resources (*in labor hours*)				Total Labor Hours Needed
	Depart-ment A	Depart-ment B	Depart-ment C	Depart-ment D	
1	100	150	350		600
2	75	100	90	130	395
3		270		95	365
4	105		75	90	270
Total department labor hours used	280	522	515	315	
Total department labor available	400	700	600	700	

instance, has 400 labor hours that can be allocated to the tasks. The question is how available labor from the various departments should be allocated to the tasks. One possibility is shown in the table, but it is obvious that there are many others. The allocation selected must therefore depend on some special factor. If, for example, we introduce different department labor costs to this problem, the best allocation would minimize the total costs.

There are many variations of allocation problems. In the simplest cases any of the resources could perform all of the tasks (albeit not with the same efficiency), and the amount of resources available would exactly equal that required. In more complicated cases the performance of all tasks requires more resources than are available, and various combinations and sequences of resources must be applied to accomplish the individual tasks. These problems are commonly solved by using some form of mathematical programing—linear, nonlinear, stochastic, parametric, or dynamic. Usually, the amount of computation required in the typical case is formidable, and an electronic computer is required. Fortunately, computer programs are now readily available for this task.

Many different management problems may be approached as allocation problems—for example, the location of a new production plant for a multiplant firm. The problem in locating the new plant is to decide where it would be least costly in the overall firm distribution system. To determine the optimum distribution system, the networks created by alternative new plant locations must be tested. One way this can be done is by using the transportation method of linear programing.

Other common examples of allocation problems are the assignment of students to classrooms at a university, patients to hospital facilities, and delivery trucks with different load-carrying capacities to delivery service, and the product mix problem in the chemical and petroleum industries. In the latter case there is a known demand for a wide range of products that cannot be made at the same time because of their nature and the facilities required. Therefore the question becomes: What combination of products should be made, given the available resources, so as to yield the greatest profit to the firm?

Queuing Problems

The diagram in Figure 3–4 illustrates the basic nature of a queuing problem. Jobs or tasks, regardless of their nature, are referred to as "customers." These customers arrive at a "service facility" and form a "queue," or line, to await processing. Jobs are performed at the service facility. If more than one task can be performed simultaneously, there are multiple service "channels," as in Figure 3–4, where two customers can be "satisfied" at the same time. A service channel may consist of a line, a sequence of service points or operations, or only one point. The order in which customers leave the queue for service is referred to as the queue "discipline." After the required tasks are performed, satisfied customers leave the service facility.

Queuing problems in business generally result in waiting customers and idle service facilities in the form of men, materials, and machines. Both of these factors create costs for a firm: waiting customers can mean lost business, and unused service facilities result in idleness costs for the resources involved. Therefore, the chief objective in a queuing problem is to minimize delay and thereby reduce costs. It is interesting to note here a certain similarity between some queuing and inventory problems. A stock of finished goods, for example, can be considered an idle service facility awaiting customers. The demand for stock is the customer, and queues (or outages) result when the stock (or service facility) is inadequate to satisfy the demand.

The mathematics used to solve queuing problems is highly developed. Sophisticated use is made of probability theory and differential and integral equations. In many cases the mathematical expression of the problem is so complex that it is almost insoluble; however, simulation can be used to obtain meaningful answers.

Queuing problems are common in production management. An example can be drawn from the maintenance function. If the customers are the machines that require maintenance, then the service facility is the maintenance personnel; the question becomes: What size maintenance force will balance the maintenance and downtime costs? A problem of this type is presented and solved later in the book.

If the customers are job lots that are being processed through a job order machine shop, then the service facility would be the materials handling equip-

Figure 3–4   Representation of a queuing problem

ment that moves the lots from operation to operation. Other service facilities within the typical manufacturing operation include tool stockrooms, coffee-break areas, lavatories, cafeterias, and exits to the company parking lot.

Sequencing Problems

Sequencing problems differ from queuing problems in one important respect—the matter of queue discipline. In queuing problems, a sequence for processing customers is generally given or assumed. By contrast, the objective of sequencing problems is to develop the queue disciplne (the order in which the jobs are taken) that will yield the best results and satisfy the customers within the shortest possible time. For example, consider a firm whose customers place orders that involve promised due dates and specified penalties for tardy delivery. The sequencing problem is to reflect these priorities in the sequence for processing the orders, so that costs measured in purchaser goodwill, company reputation, and penalty costs are at a minimum.

The essence of a sequencing problem may be illustrated by a simple case. Suppose that a factory has received orders for two products, A and B, which are both manufactured in a definite two-step process. The first operation is performed on a lathe and the second on a milling machine. Unfortunately, only one of each of these machines is available for use. Consequently, we must determine how to process both orders within the shortest possible time cycle. See the data in Table 3–6, which pertain to this example. Since operation 1 must precede operation 2, only two production sequences are possible. Either Product A is processed first, or B is processed first. Figure 3–5 dipicts graphically the relative

Table 3–6   Machine processing times

Order	Operation 1 Time on lathe (in hours)	Operation 2 Time on milling machine (in hours)
Product A	4	12
Product B	8	6

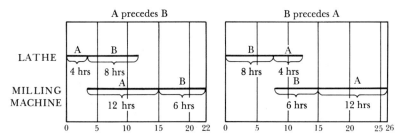

Figure 3–5   Graph of a sequencing problem

apportionment of time under each production sequence. Here it can be seen that if A precedes B the total time required for processing will be 22 hours, whereas if B precedes A the total time becomes 26 hours. Clearly it would be preferable to process A before B.

Application of this graphic method of analysis is limited to relatively simple problems, however. If the number of products to be made were increased to ten, for example, and all of them had to be processed through operations 1 and 2, the number of possible sequences rises rapidly. It would be economically unsound to graph every possibility in order to obtain the best sequence.

Unfortunately, mathematical analysis also is feasible for only relatively simple sequencing problems of this type. To obtain more than an intuitive solution, for almost all real problems it is necessary to resort to computer simulation. In most cases, however, even simulation requires considerable work although the solutions derived are only approximate. Despite this fact, certain production operations have been successfully simulated. In these cases, alternate sequences for running production orders are put into a computer for processing through a simulated factory; the sequence that requires the least amount of time is deemed best.

One type of sequencing problem does lend itself to mathematical analysis. This type of problem is concerned only with the order in which tasks are performed and not with scheduling them on particular pieces of equipment. In the construction industry, for example, management may want to know what sequence of building operations will enable them to complete a structure in the minimum time. The building sequence is limited only by what is termed "precedence"—when specific operations can be performed only after others have been completed. Plumbing, for example, can be put into a building only after a certain portion of the structure has been completed.

Today the most commonly used approaches for this type of sequencing problem are PERT and PERT/COST.[2] PERT and PERT/COST give management a systematic means for creating a scheduling sequence that best meets a set of test criteria. For small problems, PERT networks can be constructed graphically, whereas for large problems computers are used. The principal industrial application has been in the planning and control of research and development programs; however, its use as a tool to design production facilities has been increasing rapidly.

Routing Problems

The traveling salesman faces another common type of problem, the routing problem, as illustrated in Figure 3–6. The salesman is located in the home city at the center of this diagram. He must call on customers in cities A through H, which are in his territory. The cost in time and money for traveling between any two cities can be calculated. The problem is how to design a path that will take

---

[2] PERT is an acronym for Program Evaluation and Review Technique.

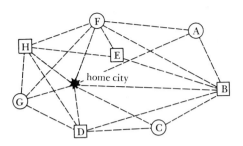

Figure 3–6 A typical routing problem

him to all the cities so that he may return home with a minimum expenditure of time and money. If the salesman must visit only two cities, A and B, and then return home, there are only two possible routes: A → B → home or B → A → home. If, however, there are eight cities that must be visited, there are more than 40,000 possible routes. If the time or cost of traveling between two cities in one direction is different from the time or cost associated with a trip in the opposite direction between the same two cities (as it might well be), the number of alternatives is further increased. Notice that this problem is closely allied to sequencing problems, particularly for production of the job shop variety. The sequence in which production operations are performed influences the route established for the manufacture of the product and, therefore, the time and distance traveled by the product through the plant. Both factors are directly translatable into factory costs.

Another problem area in which routing analysis is helpful is plant layout. In the manufacture of many different products involving many different sequences of operations, the problem is to locate production centers so that the total distance traveled in the manufacture of all products is at a minimum.

Replacement Problems

Replacement problems may be divided into two general categories. First, there are items that deteriorate with the passage of time, such as trucks, machines, motors, and tools. Second, there are items that provide a constant level of output until they fail after a certain amount of use or a certain passage of time, such as light bulbs, transistors, and tires. As a rule the items in the former category are larger and more expensive than those in the latter.

Let us first examine replacement problems of the first type, which usually involve large, costly equipment. The amount of maintenance required to keep up the efficiency of a machine typically increases with use and the passage of time. After a certain point the maintenance cost becomes so high that the machinery must be replaced. On the other hand, if the equipment is replaced too frequently, investment costs will rise. Thus, the objective of replacement analysis is to balance the costs of acquiring new equipment against the maintenance cost of sustaining the old equipment so that total cost is at a minimum. Procedures for evaluating the feasibility of investing in a new piece of equipment are usually lumped under the title of "project economy studies." In Chapter 8 there is a detailed discussion of various methods of making project economy studies and how the results obtained are interpreted by management.

Replacement of items that provide a relatively constant level of output up to a certain amount of use may be carried out in several ways:

1. Replace each item as it fails.
2. When an item fails, replace all items that have had an equivalent amount of use, despite the fact that many have not yet failed.
3. Replace items before they fail, singly or in groups, according to the time that they were put in use. This technique seeks to avoid any failures in actual operation.

The relative costs of each of these strategies depend upon the cost of a failure to the overall system of which the item is a part and the costs of acquiring and inserting the replacement item itself. It may seem comparatively easy to select the least costly alternative, but it can require the use of probability theory and sophisticated mathematical methods of analysis.

Competitive Problems

Competitive problems are situations in which the decisions made by one manager are influenced by those made by one or more other managers in other firms. This interaction between decision makers may be either cooperative or competitive. Very little attention has been given to the analysis of cooperative interaction, however, because of the competitive nature of our economy. On the other hand, competitive interaction between decision makers has been the subject of considerable study. Businessmen are well aware of the importance of considering probable competitive reaction when making decisions.

Competitive problems may be categorized most conveniently according to the degree of knowledge of the competitors' strategy, as follows:

1. *Competitor reaction can be accurately predicted in advance.* In some industries the price policies of the major competitors are well known. A price cut by one will result in a corresponding action by the others in the industry.
2. *Competitor action can be predicted on the basis of past actions.* A high level of accuracy in prediction can sometimes be achieved this way. In bidding for government contracts in the aerospace and electronics industries, for example, past-performance data have been used effectively to develop estimates of the prices that will be quoted by certain competitors on future contract opportunities.
3. *Competitor reaction cannot be predicted with a reasonable level of confidence.* This is often the case when a firm launches a brand new product, or when it introduces a new product line or enters a new marketplace.

Competitive problems can also be classified according to the duration of the competitive influence. "One-shot competition," as in the bidding for defense subcontracts, presents very different types of problems than continuing competition, as in the marketplace for standardized products. Competitive problem situations may also be classified according to the number of active competitors involved and whether or not the government is the customer.

Competitive problems influence production management, but only indirectly. Decisions regarding products and their features, their form, their quality, and their prices are affected by competition. These decisions, in turn, influence the design and operation of the firm's production process, including such areas as capital acquisitions, plant layout, and materials handling. Product delivery schedules, for example, are often a direct reflection of competitive pressure. Similarly, many of the inventory decisions made by management, including whether the company will carry an inventory of finished goods or produce to order, are based in large part on an analysis of demand and competition.

Because the principal impact of competition, when viewed by the firm's production management, is on the product itself, the discussion of the influence of competition is concentrated on product-line determination and research and development.

Search Problems

As the name implies, search problems are situations in which management is looking for something. Activities such as auditing, forecasting, and estimating fit into this broad category. Typically, there are two kinds of errors that may be encountered in search problems:

1. Failure to find the object of the search because the search is not sufficiently intensive.
2. Failure to find the object of the search (despite an adequately intense search) because of faulty observation.

Within the field of production management, search problems invariably involve an application of statistical methods, particularly sample theory. The first type of error described, for example, is a type of sampling error, while the second represents an observational error. The larger the size of the sample and the more meticulous the care exercised in observation, the greater the likelihood that the search will produce accurate results. Since search costs rise in direct proportion to these factors, the objective is to reach a compromise between effectiveness and cost.

Search theory is directly applicable to the design of inspection and quality control systems for monitoring the quality of purchased materials as well as of work in process and outgoing products. The design of such systems is the subject of considerable discussion in Chapter 20.

The Management Task

Business problems in general and production/operations management problems in particular do not fit neatly into the categories presented; most actual problems cut across many categories. Sound decision making, therefore, must rest upon the ability of managers to apply combinations of these approaches to the elements of a specific problem in a particular firm. To illustrate this point, consider a production control problem that is faced in many plants. The first decision that must be made is the quantity of each of the company's products that will be manufactured during a given period. This is primarily an inventory problem. Then the desired product quantities must be scheduled and routed through the plant as efficiently as possible, and the necessary resources must be assembled. This is a combination routing and sequencing problem. Resources may also have to be allocated if they are in short supply—another type of problem. Furthermore, not all of the time available on the different machines may be used because of unexpected delays or breakdowns. At this point, a queuing problem can arise as the different products compete for machine time. Keeping the machinery in working order may make it necessary to deal with the replacement problem. Finally, production management might have to solve a search problem in order to design systems that could effectively monitor the quality of the products manufactured.

This illustration highlights another fact about decision making; problems typically occur in clusters. This is particularly true if the firm is systems oriented. As we mentioned previously, the entire chain of problems frequently cannot be resolved simultaneously; time and cost factors militate against it. Nonetheless, the solution of any problem in the cluster must be reached with an awareness of the effects it will have on the other problems.

In presenting the problem areas as we have, it should be apparent that what we have done is to focus on another aspect of the task of production/operations management. Throughout the rest of this book, production/operations management is discussed from a functional point of view. The decision techniques applicable to each functional area are included in chapters devoted to those areas. Here we have focused on the decision approaches themselves in order to give the reader an overall appreciation of these techniques and to show that their use transcends functional boundaries.

Questions and Problems

1. What are the major environmental factors that influence the decision process? How would you expect the relative weights to change in the future?
2. Can a business firm serve society if it does not make a profit?
3. Are the societal aims of a business firm, a governmental unit, or a hospital or other nonprofit organization the same?
4. In the structure of decision making, what is the importance of goals, objective criteria, and alternatives?
5. What is the role of models in decision making? What are their advantages and

limitations, and how do you measure their effectiveness—that is, what is the ultimate test of a model?

6. What types of models are used in production/operations problems? Are they applicable to nonprofit organizations as well as to profit-making activities?
7. Are the intuition and judgmental decision approaches ever valid?
8. What relationship exists between the level of management and the planning and decision-making period?
9. What are the steps in the scientific method? Why are they altered in the systems approach? What are the steps in the systems approach?
10. The objective of the systems approach to decision making is to optimize the use of all resources in a business enterprise.
    (a) Define the concepts *optimization* and *suboptimization.*
    (b) How does decentralization of authority conflict with the concept of optimization?
11. What role does a model play in contemporary decision making?
12. What are the advantages and disadvantages for production problems of (a) verbal models, (b) iconic models, and (c) mathematical models?
13. What is the general nature of queuing problems? In what areas of management are queuing models useful?
14. What are the limitations of graphic models in sequencing problems? Do mathematical models remove all of these limitations?
15. A major problem in business decision making is the identification of alternatives. What part do models play in the identification of alternatives?
16. To what extent, in your opinion, should management decision making in a company be quantified and integrated? Give your reasons.
17. Discuss the general rationale and requirements for the development of mathematical models as a major aid to business problem solving. What are the alternatives? When are the alternatives advisable? Give examples.

References

Ackoff, R. L., and Sasieni, M. W., *Fundamentals of Operations Research,* Wiley, New York, 1968.

Beer, S., *Management Science: The Business Use of Operations Research,* Doubleday, Garden City, N.Y., 1968.

Bowman, E. H., and Fetter, R. B., *Analysis for Production and Operations Management,* 3rd ed., Irwin, Homewood, Ill., 1967.

Brinckloe, W. D., *Managerial Operations Research,* McGraw-Hill, New York, 1969.

Bross, I. D., *Design for Decision,* Free Press, New York, 1965.

Forrester, J. W., *Industrial Dynamics,* MIT Press, Cambridge, Mass., 1961.

Hopeman, R., *Systems Analysis and Operations Management,* Charles E. Merrill, Columbus, Ohio, 1969.

Horowitz, I., *Decision Making and the Theory of the Firm,* Holt, Rinehart and Winston, New York, 1970.

Howell, J. E., and Teichroew, D., *Mathematical Analysis for Business Decisions,* Irwin, Homewood, Ill., 1963.

Jedamus, P., and Frame, R., *Business Decision Theory,* McGraw-Hill, New York, 1969.

Kemeny, J. G., *et al., Finite Mathematics with Business Applications,* Prentice-Hall, Englewood Cliffs, N.J., 1962.

Levin, R. I., and Kirkpatrick, C. A., *Quantitative Approaches to Management,* 2nd ed., McGraw-Hill, New York, 1971.

McMillan, C., and Gonzalez, R. F., *Systems Analysis,* rev. ed., Irwin, Homewood, Ill., 1968.

Miller, D. W., and Starr, M. K., *Executive Decisions and Operations Research,* 2nd ed., Prentice-Hall, Englewood Cliffs, N.J., 1969.

Simon, H. A., *The New Science of Management Decision,* Harper and Row, New York, 1960.

Thierauf, R. J., *Decision Making Through Operations Research,* Wiley, New York, 1970.

II

Inputs

The introductory chapters examined the basic functions of management and the managerial decision process; we will now consider the various problems associated with the *inputs* of the production process.

For the purpose of the text the inputs to the production function are divided into four categories: product, capital, labor, and materials. Since the decision processes involved differ from one category to another, the inputs will be discussed individually.

The type of product that a firm produces provides an important input to production management. In a sense the production process begins with product design and development, since the specifications that the production process must meet are developed at that time. Production management must be involved in product decisions in order to merge production considerations into the product design. To accomplish this in a satisfactory fashion, production management should have an understanding of product design.

Capital investment decisions are long-term decisions requiring relatively large sums of money. They are usually of a "one time" nature, and, as a consequence, firms spend considerable time and effort on their solution. The purchase of a new piece of machinery, for example, usually necessitates the commitment of funds for two or more years, during which time it is expected that the equipment will be in constant use. Thus, many of the factors involved in capital allocation should be subjected to careful economic analysis.

The utilization of labor is a dynamic process. The quantity and quality of labor needed, its costs, and the results achieved fluctuate widely. Production management is principally concerned with the supply, cost, productivity, and efficiency of labor, which require determination of the quantity and quality of the labor inputs needed. These characteristics may be measured by various techniques such as time study, motion study, and work sampling. The amount of labor used depends on its productivity, which in turn depends on the relative efficiency of the work process itself. Thus, in determining labor inputs, management must consider production methods.

Materials include raw inputs, purchased components, and finished goods. Management's task is to acquire the correct quality and quantity of material at a competitive price at the right time. The arrival of materials must be carefully synchronized with the planned use of labor and capital. Problems involving the quality and source of the purchase are examined in the chapters dealing with procurement. Timing the purchase and production of materials is discussed in the chapters dealing with inventory management. This division is particularly important since the decision-making factors in the two areas are different.

In summary, Part II discusses management problems related to inputs and the approaches necessary to determine what inputs are needed for the transformation process and how these inputs can be accumulated.

4 Product Design and Development

The nature of the production process within a company reflects the state of production technology and the type of products manufactured by the firm. Changes in these areas take place at a rapid pace; new production techniques and new products are continually coming into being. As might be expected, production managers are deeply involved in the process of keeping their firm's production facilities up to date. Managers also play an important part in the design and development of the firm's products, since, in the broad sense, product design and development include the design of production facilities. In fact, the production process begins with product design and development, because it is here that the specifications that the production process must meet are determined. Furthermore, the characteristics of the production process in turn influence the final design of a product.

In the case of a new company or an entirely new product, the entire production process may have to be designed and built from scratch. In a going concern, the introduction of new products may require only modification of the present production facilities and processes. In either case it is essential for production managers to understand product design and development. With this in mind, the present chapter will give a broad view of product design and development and the managerial approaches used in planning and controlling this function. In Chapters 5 and 6, the frame of reference will narrow to a consideration of the problem of selecting the firm's product line.

The Innovation Cycle

Product design and development can be approached in many ways, but in this chapter we have chosen to take a broad view of the field, defining design and development to encompass all of the activities that are incorporated in the innovation cycle.

The *innovation cycle* is that portion of the life of a product that precedes its manufacture on a full scale. This cycle may be divided into six segments: pure research, applied research, product configuration, market research, pilot run, and production process (see Figure 4–1). In actual practice, the boundaries of the divisions are not so clearly marked, however. It is often difficult, for example, to determine where pure research ends and applied research begins. Nevertheless, this breakdown does provide a convenient framework for an analysis of the field.

The basic idea for a new product may arise in a number of different ways. The sales force may see an opportunity for a new product and recommend that it be developed or, at the opposite end of the process, the product may be conceived in the laboratory as the result of a breakthrough in pure research. To simplify our discussion, we will concentrate on tracing the evolution of a product created in pure research. Once the idea for a new product has been conceived, the company must transform it into a physical entity. This initial transformation process is usually called applied research. At this point in the development of the product its configuration is, at best, tentative. Market research on the sales potential of the product may lead to many modifications, and others may arise in the design of an appropriate production process. Most of the production changes come about during the pilot-run stage, when the product and the manufacturing process are "shaken down." Once this has been accomplished, the product design becomes definite, and a "permanent" production process is assembled so that the item can be manufactured and marketed on a full scale.[1]

[1] In Chapter 5 we will examine the market research segment of the innovation cycle, while confining ourselves in this chapter to the remaining five segments.

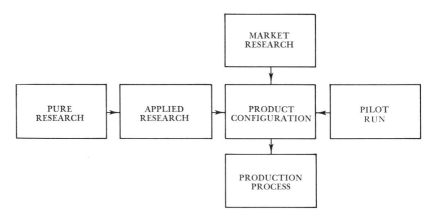

Figure 4–1   The innovation cycle

Pure Research

One common method of classifying research work is to distinguish between *pure* and *applied* research. Whether research is pure or applied depends upon its purpose. *Pure research* is concerned with the study of the basic laws of nature; its objective is to contribute to man's general knowledge of his environment by clarifying the cause-and-effect relationships in natural phenomena. It attempts to explain why things happen or to achieve hitherto unknown results by mixing new combinations of events and materials. To the pure researcher, the practical application of findings is not often a significant factor. Thus, it is not surprising that pure research very often results in ideas with little or no commercial application, at least at the time of discovery. *Applied research*, by way of contrast, is concerned almost entirely with practical application and the solution of practical problems. In the industrial world its objective is the design of a product or process that will have some economic value.

Industrial experience indicates that many pure research projects produce little of commercial value. Dupont reports that approximately one-third of its chemical research projects are "laboratory flops" and that a high percentage of the remainder prove to be impractical in production.[2] Engineering management at the Radio Corporation of America estimates that more than 90 percent of its research ideas prove to be useless. In view of statistics such as these, one may well ask why companies invest so heavily in pure research. One answer is that the rare successes pay for both themselves and the failures many times over. At RCA, about 85 percent of its sales come from products that originate in its research program. Similarly, one-third of General Electric's sales come from products that were nonexistent twenty years ago, and Standard Oil of New Jersey claims that every dollar spent on research has returned itself five times in sales revenue.

Another reason for the research expenditure is the competitive pressure for more and better products. New products are needed to support company stability and growth. To fall behind the innovation rate of others in the industry is to face the risk of considerable loss and perhaps failure as new items in the field reduce the marketability and profitability of the older products.

The conduct of pure research is not restricted to the efforts of industrial concerns, of course. It is also carried on by colleges and universities, trade associations, research institutes, independent consulting laboratories, and numerous agencies of national, state, and local government.[3] The significant findings of these agencies often prove extremely useful to industry, and many of them are available at little or no cost. Thus, an alert management will keep itself informed about the research being done by outside agencies in the company's fields of interest, for by so doing it can usually get more mileage out of its limited funds for pure research.

[2] "The Age of Research," *The New York Times*, July 9, 1956, p. 74.
[3] It is interesting to note that for these agencies, pure research, with or without the other activities in the innovation cycle, is a final *product*.

Pure research is ordinarily conducted in a single centralized department of a company. This guards against the danger that the needs of a single product line or division of the company might dominate the efforts of the company's research facility. More important, perhaps, is the fact that pure research is best performed in a location that is isolated from the pressures of daily operations. Nonetheless, the research group is often called upon to assist in the solution of product problems. Although pure and applied research are different activities, in many companies the same men or engineering groups are assigned both responsibilities, particularly in small companies.

Applied Research

We have said that the role of applied research is to translate potentially profitable product ideas into marketable goods in order to strengthen the company's product line and thus its competitive position. It is possible to identify four main categories of applied research projects:

1. The design of new products
2. The redesign of existing products
3. The identification of new uses for existing products
4. The improvement of the packaging of existing products

New product design   Diversification of a company's product line can be accomplished in two ways: new products can be integrated into the current product line, or they can supplement the current line or be entirely unrelated to it. This is a useful distinction to make, because the risk associated with making products outside the current product line are generally greater than those associated with incorporating new products into the existing line. Launching an entirely new and different type of product usually requires different kinds of skill in product design, production, and marketing; inexperience in any of these areas can be a serious handicap. To offset this problem, companies that wish to enter a different product area often acquire or merge with firms with product lines in that area, thus acquiring all the skills required for the development and launching of that new product. Mergers and acquisitions are not without their own pitfalls, however. The inability to cope with organizational problems created by such mergers has adversely affected the operations of many companies.

Another method of entering new product areas is to purchase the design and development efforts of other companies. This is often done by marketing finished products made by other firms under the purchasing company's own label or trademark. The private line of Sears, Roebuck and Company is a well-known example of this technique, and the air conditioners marketed by RCA were for a long time designed and produced by other firms. By following this course of action the purchaser hopes to minimize product design and development risks; but the purchasing company also relinquishes the possibility of earning spectacular returns from a technological breakthrough resulting from its research.

Still another way of expanding a company's product line into a new area without incurring the full weight of design and development costs is to purchase a license to manufacture the products of another firm. For a fee, or royalty, the right to market (or manufacture and market) patented items created by other firms can be obtained. This technique has been used in such industries as chemicals, automobiles, and aircraft, and for such electronics products as color television and digital computer equipment.

Product redesign   The redesign of existing products is undertaken for many reasons. One is to extend the market for the product by effecting greater consumer appeal and acceptance. To accomplish this objective, new features can be added, or the packaging or form of the product can be adapted to new styling trends. The mere presence of competitive items on the market makes it mandatory that products be updated periodically; this is certainly the case in the automobile industry where new models are introduced each year. Even in industrial markets, styling has become an important factor; digital computers are now being offered in many colors so they will blend with the customer's office décor.

Another important reason for redesigning a product is to reduce its production cost. As a product moves through its life cycle, there is increasing emphasis on reducing costs, and redesigning the product is one way of accomplishing the reduction. Product changes initiated for this purpose enable the firm to utilize more efficient tools and methods of production. Examining product costs does not stop with an appraisal of the producer's cost; there is a growing awareness of the need to consider the purchaser's costs as well. In addition to the price, or acquisition cost, a purchaser also faces operating, maintenance, and reliability costs. Operating costs have always been deemed a significant factor in the choice of equipment, but recently there has been a growing interest in maintenance and reliability costs as well. Accordingly, a company that can demonstrate the superior performance of its product in these customer cost areas will have a distinct competitive advantage. With these factors in mind, many products such as machine tools have been redesigned to make service and maintenance easier and less expensive. Companies have also tried to reduce the failure rate of certain machines to lower the overall purchaser's costs.

New product uses   The exploration of new uses for existing products is another common objective of a company's applied research work. Here, too, the research is becoming increasingly user-oriented; the researcher tries to devise ways in which the present product, or a slightly modified version of it, can be adapted to new markets or can provide additional service to current users. Thus, the chemical industry is constantly seeking new uses for its chemicals and their by-products, and the textile industry is spending a great deal of time and money trying to find new uses for fabrics and yarns. The objective of all of the applied research work discussed so far is to provide the firm with the capability for satisfying the greatest possible number of needs of its existing and potential customers.

New product packaging   More and more, buyers are seeking products that are pleasing to the eye as well as utilitarian, so that a product's form is now a

Shipping/dispensing pouch for wine is designed to replace glass jugs and cut transportation costs. Made of complex lamination in 1- or 5-gallon sizes, pouch fits reusable barrel-like dispenser. Courtesy of *Modern Packaging*

principal determinant of its salability. Consequently, the art of packaging goods has become a highly specialized field, and many firms hire full-time specialists for this purpose. Just as styling can be an effective means of accomplishing product differentiation, so can packaging, although to a lesser extent. Eye-appealing packaging materials or those that can be used again for another purpose can help to differentiate one firm's product from another's.

Another reason for seeking to improve the packaging of a product is to be able to offer greater convenience in using it and thus enlarge its market. Packaging in this sense means changing the shape, size, layout, or other external characteristics of a product without changing its purpose. In the machine tool and electronics industries, for example, great strides have been taken in making equipment controls and adjustment mechanisms more readily accessible to the operator. The miniaturization of products in both industrial and commercial fields proved to be an effective means of enlarging many markets. Large, bulky, and unattractive products such as television sets, radios, and computers have been reduced to smaller, more convenient, and often more attractive sizes by the use of miniaturized components, and their sales have risen sharply in recent years. Considerable research is now being done on the miniaturization of existing systems and subsystems in many other fields. Future advancement in the aerospace industry, for example, will depend to a large extent upon progress in this area.

Product Configuration

The immediate result of applied research work is the creation of a physical model of the product demonstrating that the ideas underlying the product are practical. Rough prototypes made for this purpose normally bear little physical resemblance to the final product that will eventually be marketed, but they do help management visualize the proposed operating characteristics of the product.

Evaluation of the prototype greatly facilitates decisions regarding the finished product.

The process of establishing the characteristics of the final product is usually called the product configuration phase of the innovation cycle. Although it is true that product specifications are generally established to guide applied research, they must be further refined before the product is marketed. The information on which the final specifications are based comes primarily from two sources: market research and performance tests using the prototype models. At this stage such factors as production cost, packaging, quality level, reliability, operating features, marketing plan, and competition are considered. Each of these factors, in turn, comprises many important subfactors: the production cost will be affected by design specifications, projected sales volume, and production technology, among other things. Furthermore, these factors often conflict. High quality and reliability levels may raise the production costs to uncompetitive levels. Similarly, if all the desirable operating features were incorporated, the cost and the appearance of the product might suffer.

Compromise among all these configuration factors is therefore essential. One way to effect this compromise is to establish a committee composed of representatives of all the interested departments, including market, finance, engineering, and manufacturing, to help ensure that no one factor will be given undue weight. To aid the decision process the committee should have access to market research and economic feasibility data,[4] and it should have the authority to make special cost studies to show the impact of specific factors such as quality or style on the marketability of the product or its production cost.[5]

Pilot Run

Now the product is at a stage where it can be manufactured. Products that require major production innovations or the installation of new processes are normally begun on a trial run, or pilot run, basis. A *pilot run* is simply the manufacture of a new product under simulated factory conditions. Generally a small quantity of it is manufactured in order to "shake down" the new process and thus uncover any product defects or process inefficiencies that may still exist. Defects can be in the product itself, or they can stem from manufacturing problems encountered in trying to make the item according to the specifications. Incorrect dimensions or tolerances that are too strict for the existing technology are often found at this stage. Thus, close engineering liaison is needed to ensure that the real problem is properly identified. The speed with which a solution is found often depends upon the degree to which alternative product characteristics may be tested at the point of manufacture. For this reason, many companies place the responsibility for supervising pilot run operations in the hands of their industrial engineering departments.

The pilot run also affords management the opportunity of testing the channel

[4] The precise nature of these data will be discussed in Chapter 6.
[5] The area of product reliability and quality will be explored in detail in Chapter 5.

of distribution selected for the product. Similarly, advertising and sales promotion ideas may be checked in small selected marketing areas by observing the reactions of distributors and customers. This can help identify the need for further product changes as well as changes in advertising, promotion, and distribution.

At the completion of the pilot stage, the product configuration and the production process should have crystallized into final form. At this point, then, it should be possible to refine still further the cost estimates prepared for the product. Once the internal production process is established, costs can be estimated from projected sales and manufacturing volumes; on this basis, pricing and general marketing strategy can be determined.

Production Process

As a rule, only a limited production facility is developed during the pilot run; therefore, one must be created that will be sufficient for the manufacture of the product in the quantities projected. This means that sufficient plant space must be allocated and that facilities must be acquired and set up in the plant. Necessary support activities, such as tool cribs, rest rooms and cafeterias, and a materials handling system must also be designed or redesigned to accommodate the new production operation. A plan for controlling the inventories and production activities of the new process must be formulated, and a system for maintaining the quality level of the outgoing product must be created. In short, decisions regarding all phases of production must be made at this stage.

The development of a manufacturing process is complex, but an inefficient manufacturing process may have a dire effect on the firm. Therefore, to guard against inefficiencies, some companies assign manufacturing engineers to products while they are still in the applied research stage. These men are encouraged to participate in the design and development of the item to make certain that its features will not create costly problems in the future manufacturing process. They have an intimate knowledge of the specifics of the product design that enables them to anticipate and thus circumvent possible production problems by the proper choice of processes and tools. A close manufacturing–engineering liaison of this nature can greatly accelerate the flow of a new item through its innovation cycle.

The Role of Management

As far as management is concerned, the main problems arising in connection with the design and development of a product are:

1. *The speed with which new products can be placed upon the market and the need for coordinating the various departments that participate in the innovation cycle*
2. *The allocation of resources for pure and applied research and the planning involved in product development*
3. *The control of efforts expended during the innovation cycle*

Timing

One of the most important factors determining the success or failure of a new or improved product is the timeliness of its entry into the marketplace. The company that first brings out a successful item or a popular style usually has a distinct advantage over its competitors; tardy entry usually means an uphill fight to secure a share of the market. The reason for this becomes apparent when we refer to the product-life S-shaped curve in Figure 4–2. Three phases of a product's life are shown on the curve. Phase 1 covers the introduction and testing of the product; during this phase, sales are at a low level and are not growing rapidly. Phase 2 takes place when the product is accepted in the marketplace and sales accelerate rapidly as the product comes into general use. In Phase 3 the product is in general use, and sales are to new users and to the replacement market.[6] Ideally a product should be offered to the market in time to ride the crest of rapidly increasing sales that characterizes Phase 2 of the life curve. Management is often faced with the likelihood that the planned date for the release of a new product is later than the ideal date. One solution to this problem is to subcontract one or two stages of the innovation cycle to accelerate the process. While time can be saved in this manner, much depends upon the degree of coordination and control that can be achieved with the outside vendors; good communication and cooperation are essential. Without them the procured unit may fall below company standards, or it may turn out to be a mismatch in the overall system.

Another way of improving the launching date of a new product is to utilize

[6] The subject of product-life curves will be expanded in Chapter 5.

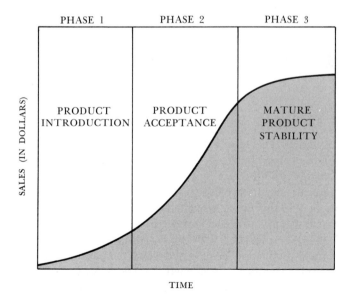

Figure **4–2**   Product-life curve

resources more intensively. The work week may be extended and overtime operations may be employed to speed up the innovation cycle. This approach has proved successful for short periods of time, but protracted use generally results in a productivity decline, largely offsetting any benefit that might be derived from the added working hours. After a time the personnel will consciously or unconsciously pace themselves and thus reduce the level of productivity.

An all-out effort to reduce the time required for the innovation cycle is usually called a *crash program;* it calls for resources to be intensively applied up to the limit of human endurance and financial means. In addition, tasks that are normally performed serially or in sequence are usually done simultaneously wherever possible. Thus, instead of waiting for the completion and "checkout" of a preceding activity, the next task is started as soon as possible. Obviously this increases the possibility of errors and their resultant costs, so that crash programs tend to be expensive and extremely wasteful of resources. However, some time can usually be saved if a firm is willing to pay the price. During the Korean crisis and both world wars, for example, most firms found that the need to save time transcended the extra costs incurred, since the government was willing to pay the bill. In normal commercial operations, however, the technique has been limited to a few highly selective cases where the cost and time factors are balanced.

Large companies with huge engineering, marketing, and manufacturing staffs tend to move slowly in the development of new products; apparently the sheer weight of numbers complicates the coordination and communications needed to bring out a new product. Smaller companies enjoy a natural advantage in this respect; they are usually able to get a new product on the market sooner and thus enjoy large early sales. To offset this inherent disadvantage, large companies frequently organize on a product-line basis in the belief that by creating many small "companies" within the parent firm they will enjoy the cycle speed and specialization of their smaller competitors. General Motors, General Electric, and Westinghouse are among the large firms that have pioneered in this direction.

Resource Allocation

The funds needed to support product design and development work come from a company's capital budget.[7] This means that each project must pass some type of economic feasibility test in every firm. From a financial viewpoint, the anticipated return from the project must exceed the lowest return that the company will accept, and this lowest acceptable return is termed the *capital rejection rate*. In calculating the anticipated return from a project, an estimate must be made of all the costs associated with the design and development as well as the projected normal production cost. To develop an accurate estimate of these costs, a project plan should be formulated that stipulates the specific assignments of manpower and other required resources and the projected costs of these re-

---

[7] This aspect of the capital budget is discussed at length in Chapter 7.

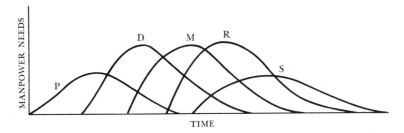

Planning. Define objectives and set preliminary product specifications.
Design. Design prototype and furnish associated documents.
Model. Build and test prototype and release final specifications.
Release. Engineering follow-through on units in pilot run.
Support. Support of production and sales.

Figure 4-3   Engineering manpower needs during phases of the
innovation cycle

SOURCE: Adapted from Peter V. Norden, "Resource Usage and Network Planning Techniques," in *Operations Research in Research and Development,* Dean Burton, Ed. (New York: Wiley, 1963), p. 160.

quirements. Revenue estimates based upon market expectations are also needed. Then, by comparing cost and revenue data, a projection of the *return on investment* can be made.

The planning of design and development work, because of its very nebulous nature, is a difficult task, but one that must be done nonetheless. Technical skills as well as capital funds must be allocated among various research projects. Scientific and engineering manpower is a scarce resource, and this scarcity has the dimensions of both quantity and quality. Thus, it is important that both the proper number of men and the correct skills be utilized. Although it is difficult to generalize, some insights into recent developments in the proper use of personnel during the innovation cycle are now available. It appears that engineering personnel are often used in patterns that are independent of the nature of the project. Five manpower phases may be identified in most projects: planning, design, model, release, and support; and for each of these phases typical manpower-utilization curves may be drawn.[8] One common flow pattern for manpower needs is shown in Figure 4-3. Although manpower-utilization curves do not apply to the whole innovation cycle and are still in an experimental stage, they do show promise of reducing the amount of personnel resources wasted in making work assignments during the innovation cycle.

Over- or understaffing projects with people who possess specialized skills is wasteful.[9] In either case, costs and cycle times may be adversely affected. Waste-

[8] Peter V. Norden, "Resource Usage and Network Planning Techniques," in *Operations Research in Research and Development,* Dean Burton, Ed. (New York: Wiley, 1963), pp. 149-69.
[9] It is common practice to classify engineering and scientific manpower according to experience or creativity.

ful manpower practices may also limit the number of projects that a firm can afford to undertake, thus depriving it of many new product opportunities or delaying the development of its projects so that returns are significantly reduced.

To help avoid these pitfalls and to strengthen management's control, some type of output standards are usually formulated for design and development work. Realistic standards can help to improve the effectiveness of resource allocation among projects; they can also provide a basis for more effective project control. The difficulty, however, is to develop valid standards; at present, more often than not, firms are forced to rely solely on the unstructured judgment of participating engineers. In an attempt to increase the accuracy of such standards, many firms have established programs to accumulate and classify experience data for use as guidelines.[10]

Project Control

Effective project control demands realistic, equitable standards and depends upon information systems that can produce data that permit comparisons between actual performance and established standards. The information fed back for this purpose should be accurate, timely, and properly spaced. Problem areas in the project should be subject to frequent reporting, whereas the status of more routine work can be reviewed less frequently. The important thing is for management to receive information in time to take effective remedial action when necessary. These objectives must be tempered, of course, by the expense of the reporting itself. A compromise must be struck between the cost of an unreported problem and the cost of reporting for each project. In many firms, management is becoming increasingly desirous that projects be designed with an awareness of control needs. There are many methods of tackling this problem, including one referred to as PERT, which has received much favorable comment in recent years.[11] Admittedly this technique is not perfect, but it is one of the better means available today for strengthening managerial control of design and development work as well as other production activities.

The PERT Concept[12]

PERT is an acronym formed from the first letters of Program Evaluation and Review Technique; it is an approach to planning, coordinating, and controlling the work efforts required to accomplish an established goal. PERT can be applied to projects of any size in any field of endeavor, but it has proved particularly useful in analyzing situations in which widely diversified activities con-

---

[10] This highlights the importance of research efforts such as Norden's.

[11] Other similar approaches are CPM (Critical Path Method) and PEP (Program Evaluation Procedure).

[12] A glossary of PERT terms is presented in the Appendix. For a complete treatment of PERT, the reader is referred to the "PERT Time and Cost Guide" issued by the National Aeronautics and Space Administration or to one of the many texts in the field; for example, J. Moder and C. Phillips, *Project Management with CPM and PERT* (New York: Reinhold, 1964).

tribute in a predetermined sequence to the completion of a program according to a definite time schedule. PERT has also been applied to the development of new products and processes, construction of plants, building of information systems, and analysis of work on government contracts.

PERT has provided management with a sound solution to a long-standing problem—the planning and control of complex activities. The government became acutely aware of this industrial problem during the late 1950s, when military procurement increasingly centered on research and development. The government's experience with contracts for products that required any research and development work was almost universally bad. Delivery dates for new weapons systems were often missed, and substantial differences frequently arose between planned and actual costs. As a result, the government found it extremely difficult to plan and control its defense budget properly. To help resolve this problem, the PERT system was developed by the special projects office of the U.S. Department of the Navy.[13] It was first used in the management of the Polaris missile program. Here, and in other programs, the technique built up a record of gradual, although not spectacular, improvement in estimating the time and cost of research and development efforts. Today, PERT has an established reputation and is held in such high esteem by the U.S. Department of Defense that on June 1, 1962 a memorandum was issued endorsing its adoption by all government procurement agencies. Defense subcontractors were subsequently informed that utilization of PERT would be mandatory on all contracts awarded after January 1, 1964.

Companies now find themselves in a position where a PERT capability is essential for bidding on government contracts; these contracts, of course, constitute a significant percentage of the market in the aerospace and electronics industries and related fields. Although they were initially government-oriented tools, PERT and similar approaches are being increasingly applied to the analysis of commercial design and development programs. The Critical Path Method,[14] for example, is now extensively used in the construction industry.

The PERT Technique

The main objective of PERT is to *furnish information* for managerial purposes. PERT is not a decision-making process; it simply generates useful information for planning and control. Thus, at the beginning of a new project, PERT focuses attention on

1. The tasks that must be done in order to complete the job
2. The sequence, timing, and, in some cases, the costs of performing the tasks

When the project reaches the development stage, PERT begins to generate control information concerning

[13] The consulting firm of Booz, Allen & Hamilton, Inc. was the principal agent.
[14] CPM was being developed by E. I. du Pont de Nemours & Company and the Univac Division of Sperry Rand Corporation at the same time as PERT.

1. The status of task performance

2. The available alternatives to compensate for missed schedules

Finally, when changes are to be made in the product sequence or plan, PERT provides a way for management to test the proposed changes.

To utilize this technique effectively, a manager must have a basic understanding of the principles on which it operates and the appropriate method of application. He must also know the nature of the data that PERT furnishes and how they can be used in making project decisions. Therefore, the remainder of this chapter is devoted to providing an understanding of this most useful tool.

The PERT Network

The first step in the PERT process is to define the particular goal, or target, of the program under consideration. Then a *network*—a schematic model depicting a sequential work plan to accomplish the established target—is constructed. This network, or model, traces the major performance milestones, or *events* as they are called, and the activities that connect them. The basic relationship between events and activities is shown in Figure 4–4.

An *event* is a meaningful specific accomplishment (physical or intellectual) in the program plan, recognizable at a particular instant in time. Events do not consume time or resources and are normally represented in the network by circles. An activity represents the work or expenditure of resources necessary to move the project from one event to the next. In Figure 4–4, for example, the activity $1 \rightarrow 2$ might represent the total work or time required by specific engineers on a new product-development program.

When designing a PERT network, the analyst should bear in mind the following cardinal rules:

1. Events must take place in a logical order.

2. The work and time it takes to get from one event to another is denoted by activity.

3. No event can be reached until all the activities leading to it are completed.

4. No activity can be completed until the event preceding it has occurred.

To demonstrate the network-construction process, let us see how one might set up a simple PERT network for the work required to bring a new Broadway show to its opening night performance. A list of major milestones in this process may be drawn up as follows:

1. Writing of the play started
2. Final dress rehearsal completed
3. Advertisement of the play started
4. Opening of show on Broadway (target)
5. Auditions completed
6. Writing of the play completed
7. Cast changes completed
8. First rehearsal started.

Event 1   Event 2

Figure 4–4 Diagramatic relationship between events and activities in a
PERT system

9. Scenery completed
10. Advance sale of tickets completed

It is at once obvious that these events are not in any logical sequence, a condition that is typical in the field of industrial design and development. In practice, lists of events are developed from informational inputs received from more than one source at more than one time; in gathering the information for the list, the principal concern is usually to make certain that no events are omitted. If **PERT** is to be effective, all events must be included in the network; the failure to report events leads to incorrect schedules and inaccurate resource estimates.

Once the list of events is complete, a network connecting the various tasks in logical sequence can be constructed. Figure 4–5 represents *one* network that can be developed from the list drawn up for putting on a Broadway show; it is important to note, however, that this is *not* the only network or plan that can achieve the objective.

Network Time Estimates

If the network is to be useful for scheduling purposes, a reasonably good estimate of the time required for the performance of each event must be added to the diagram; this estimate is designated[15]

$$t_e = \text{expected time to complete an event}$$

[15] Often t_{en} is used, when n is the identifying number of the event.

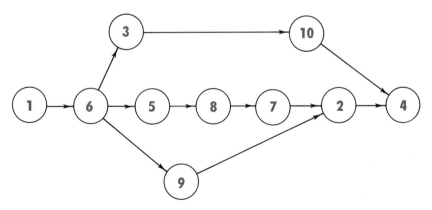

Figure 4–5 PERT network for putting on a Broadway show

Currently, the most widely used procedure for determining t_e makes use of three distinct time estimates for each event.[16] The estimates are made by individuals who are familiar with the activity; after these estimates are analyzed, three of them are chosen to represent (1) an optimistic time a, (2) a most likely time m, and (3) a pessimistic time b. These estimates are usually stated in periods of days, weeks, or months. Once made, they are considered firm and are not usually altered unless a significant change takes place in the scope of the work or the assignment of resources. The three time estimates are then combined to yield an expected "elapsed time" for the event; one common formula for determining elapsed time is[17]

$$t_e = \frac{a + 4m + b}{6}$$

Many individuals think that more reliable results can be obtained by combining estimates in this fashion than by using a single estimate. But some PERT users prefer to employ only a single estimate. Since these estimates can readily be checked against historical data, it should be possible to select the most appropriate approach for a particular company or type of project.

Once the project-time estimate t_e has been determined, the analyst may also wish to attach a numerical value to the relative uncertainty of that estimate to facilitate comparison between alternative networks. Assuming that the beta distribution was used to calculate t_e, the variance or uncertainty associated with t_e may be computed with the formula:

$$\sigma^2 = \left(\frac{b - a}{6}\right)^2$$

If this variance is large, there is much uncertainty about the time that it will take to perform a particular activity. If, however, the variance is small, it means that the optimistic and pessimistic estimates are not very different and so the completion time can be known quite precisely. To illustrate, consider two events with the same t_e values but different variances:

$$t_{e1} = \frac{3 + (4 \times 4) + 5}{6} = 4 \qquad \begin{array}{l} a = 3 \\ m = 4 \\ b = 5 \end{array} \qquad \sigma_1^2 = \left(\frac{5 - 3}{6}\right)^2 = 0.111$$

$$t_{e2} = \frac{1 + (4 \times 2) + 15}{6} = 4 \qquad \begin{array}{l} a = 1 \\ m = 2 \\ b = 15 \end{array} \qquad \sigma_2^2 = \left(\frac{15 - 1}{6}\right)^2 = 4.43$$

Figure 4–6 illustrates graphically the relationships between a, m, b, t_e, and σ^2 values. Notice that for t_{e1}, the variance is small and thus the uncertainty of the t_e estimate is correspondingly small. Since the variance for t_{e2} is large, however, the uncertainty of the t_e estimate is also large.

[16] For other approaches, see for example, Martin K. Starr, *Production Management* (Englewood Cliffs, N.J.: Prentice-Hall, 1964), pp. 123–24.

[17] This equation follows the beta distribution, which is used primarily because of its ease of calculation.

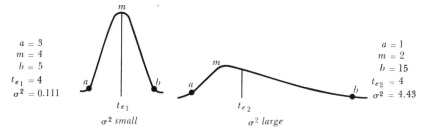

$$a = 3$$
$$m = 4$$
$$b = 5$$
$$t_{e_1} = 4$$
$$\sigma^2 = 0.111$$

$$t_{e_1}$$
$$\sigma^2 \text{ small}$$

$$a = 1$$
$$m = 2$$
$$b = 15$$
$$t_{e_2} = 4$$
$$\sigma^2 = 4.43$$

$$t_{e_2}$$
$$\sigma^2 \text{ large}$$

Figure 4–6   PERT value relationships

Notice also that in the second case t_e was 4 and yet the best estimate of when the task would be finished was 2. This disparity highlights the fact that the computed t_e value for a particular event may be distorted by the range between estimates. Over a complex network, however, these variations will probably balance out, and so the sum of the t_e values will usually furnish a rather accurate estimate of the time required to complete a project.

An example   To illustrate and summarize the calculations required to compute the t_e and σ^2 values of a PERT network, let us consider a specific case involving the establishment of a microwave radio relay station at a field site. Table 4–1 is an activity–event schedule for the project. Notice that for each activity, three time estimates $(a, m, \text{ and } b)$ are shown. The respective t_e's and σ^2's were worked out on the basis of these data. The calculations for computing the values for the activity connecting Events 1 and 2 are given below the table as samples. Figure 4–7 shows the PERT network for the task and the $a, m, b,$ and t_e values for each step of the project. For this project the training of field service engineers, which took place between Events 3 and 5, was estimated to be the most time-consuming $(t_e = 23.7$ weeks) activity. The greatest uncertainty $(\sigma^2 = 1.8)$ pertained to the checkout of the system between Events 2 and 5.

PERT Network Time

A completed PERT network provides a great deal of useful information for the supervising manager of a project. To begin with, it enables him to prepare a work-performance schedule for the project, listing the expected starting and completion time for each activity. To do this, Event 1 (or "project start") is set at zero on the time axis. The expected time (T_E) at which each event or milestone will be reached is measured cumulatively from that point. Thus, the T_E for any event is the *largest sum* of the t_e's on any activity path leading to that event. The T_E's applicable to the microwave radio relay example are shown in Figure 4–8. Here, the T_E for Event 1 is 0. The activity that connects Event 1 with Event 2 has a t_e of 9.8, so the expected time required to reach this milestone is 9.8 weeks. Similar analysis yields the T_E's applicable to Events 3 and 4. Events 5 and 6 pose a slightly different problem, however, since each can be approached along more than one activity route. Event 5 can be reached by route

Table 4–1 Activity–event schedule for microwave radio relay station[a]

Activity	Prede-cessor Event	Suc-cessor Event	a (weeks)	m (weeks)	b (weeks)	t_e (weeks)	σ^2
Assembly of system components $(1 \to 2)$	1 → 2		7	10	12	9.8	0.7
Recruiting of field service personnel $(1 \to 3)$	1 → 3		16	18	20	18.0	0.4
Survey of installation site $(1 \to 4)$	1 → 4		7	8	9	8.0	0.1
Test and checkout of system components $(2 \to 5)$	2 → 5		9	12	17	12.3	1.8
Training of field service engineers $(3 \to 5)$	3 → 5		20	24	26	23.7	1.0
Construction of site housing units $(4 \to 6)$	4 → 6		14	18	20	17.7	0.1
Preparation of operation manuals and accumulation of spare parts $(5 \to 6)$	5 → 6		2	3	7	3.5	0.7

Sample calculations for activity $(1 \to 2)$:

$$t_e = \frac{a + 4m + b}{6} = \frac{7 + 40 + 12}{6} = \frac{59}{6} = 9.8$$

$$\sigma^2 = \left(\frac{b - a}{6}\right)^2 = \left(\frac{12 - 7}{6}\right)^2 = \left(\frac{5}{6}\right)^2 = 0.7$$

[a] The PERT network designed for this project appears in Figure 4–7.

$1 \to 2 \to 5$ or $1 \to 3 \to 5$. Therefore, the most time-consuming path represents the earliest possible time for reaching this milestone because an activity that is initiated by an event, say Event 5, cannot begin until *all* previous activities have been completed. Thus, the T_E for Event 5 is determined by route $1 \to 3 \to 5$ and is 41.7. Similarly, the T_E for Event 6 (route $1 \to 3 \to 5 \to 6$) is 45.2.

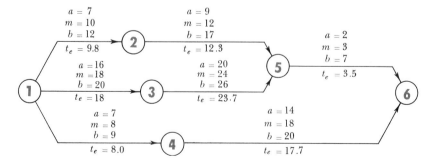

Figure 4–7 PERT network for microwave radio relay station

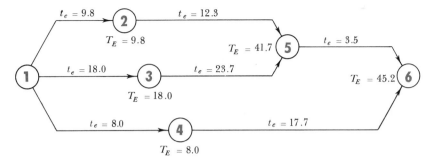

Figure 4–8 PERT time schedule for microwave radio relay station

Slack Analysis

The T_E determined for the last, or target, event (in this case Event 6) represents the expected overall cycle time required for the project. Having determined this figure, the analyst will want to know whether the project will be completed on schedule. The *schedule date* is generally arrived at independently of the PERT network and is given the symbol T_S. Suppose, for purposes of illustration, that we have a T_S of 42.0 weeks on the microwave radio relay station project under study. Looking again at Figure 4–8, we see that if this PERT network is followed, the program will be finished 3.2 weeks behind schedule. How do we solve this problem? To gain an insight into the factors causing the schedule discrepancy, a "slack analysis" will be performed and a "critical path" determined. When completed, these studies should indicate the optimum course of remedial action.

Slack analysis is useful not only for behind-schedule projects but also for those that are on or ahead of schedule, since it helps provide a basis for effective resource allocation and cost reduction. For example, slack analysis of several projects may alert management to the possibility that by shifting attention from a program that is ahead of schedule to one that is in trouble, both may be completed on time without the need of costly overtime.

Slack analysis starts with a determination of the T_L for each event. T_L is defined as *the latest time by which an event must be completed in order to keep the project on schedule*. The method used to compute this figure is the exact opposite of that used in computing T_E. The target event is the starting point, and the analysis proceeds backward to the first event. To compute the T_L for a given event, the value of t_e is subtracted from the value of T_L for the following event. If more than one activity path leads to an event, there are alternate T_L's for that event, and the smallest value is selected. In Figure 4–9 the T_L's have been calculated for the microwave radio relay station example, and the PERT network has been redrawn to show this additional information.

To illustrate how these figures are computed, notice that the T_L for Event 5 represents the difference between the T_L of its successor (Event 6) and the t_e applicable to the activity linking these two events. Thus we have

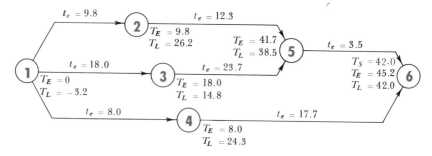

Figure 4–9 PERT network for microwave radio relay station. Slack analysis.

$$T_L 5 = T_L 6 - t_e$$
$$= 42.0 - 3.5 = 38.5$$

The T_L's for Events 4, 3, and 2 are computed in a similar fashion. The T_L for Event 1 cannot be computed so easily, however, since it can be approached from three directions—from Events 2, 3, or 4. Applying the rule that the lowest resultant T_L is the governing one, we choose route 3 → 1.

Having computed the T_L for each event we can determine the *slack* for each according to the formula:

$$\text{Slack} = T_L - T_E$$

It is obvious that the value of slack can be either positive, negative, or zero, depending upon the relationship between T_L and T_E. Positive slack indicates that the project is ahead of schedule; the greater the slack, the greater the margin of safety will be. If here is no slack at all, the project is probably on schedule, but this situation is usually considered a potential problem by project managers. If any difficulty arises, the project is likely to fall behind schedule. Finally, negative slack indicates that the project is behind schedule; corrective action must be planned for it immediately. Here again, the larger the negative number, the more serious the problem is.

Table 4–2 is a slack table summarizing the status of the microwave project. One glance at this table will indicate that the microwave project is having trouble

Table 4–2 PERT slack table for microwave radio relay station

Event	T_E	T_L	Slack
1	0	−3.2	−3.2
2	9.8	26.2	+16.4
3	18.0	14.8	−3.2
4	8.0	24.3	+16.3
5	41.7	38.5	−3.2
6	45.2	42.0	−3.2

staying on schedule. The significant amount of positive slack for Events 2 and 4 is a hopeful sign, however. Management should consider the possibility of delaying the start of these events or of shifting some of the resources allocated to them to the four negative-slack events, where management might also try to reduce performance times. Additional resources might even be obtained from outside the project for Events 1, 3, 5, and 6, if necessary. Still another common method of increasing the resources allocated to a project is to use overtime operations. To enable itself to select the optimum combination of changes in resources allocation, management may conduct a *cost trade-off analysis*. The name of this technique is derived from its objective—trading resources for time—which requires that the cost of the shift or addition of resources be weighed against the possible gains in time that could be realized.

The Critical Path

Many paths lead from the initial to the terminal event. The path that requires the longest amount of elapsed time is termed the *critical path*. Thus, in our example, the critical path is $1 \rightarrow 3 \rightarrow 5 \rightarrow 6$, the sum of whose t_e's is 45.2.[18] The slack along the critical path may be positive, negative, or zero. It will be zero when the completion goal is equal to the length of the critical path. Where the completion goal falls on an earlier date than the terminus of the critical path (as in the example), the slack will be negative. Conversely, if the completion goal is further away in time than the terminus of the critical path, the slack will be positive.

Determination of the critical path is of crucial importance; it should be the focal point of the analysis, even if the critical path has positive slack, as it will in some projects. Since the critical path is the series of events requiring the most time to perform in moving from Event 1 to the end of the project, any event along this route that is delayed will cause the final event, project completion, to slip by the same amount of time. Also, if it is decided that performance times must be reduced in order to meet the scheduled project completion date, remedial action should be focused on activities along the critical path. In determining which activities along the critical path are most amenable to acceleration, one guide that is often used is the presence of high variance in time estimates for any of the activities. In the microwave example, the critical path $(1 \rightarrow 3 \rightarrow 5 \rightarrow 6)$ has a negative slack of 3.2 at each event, meaning that 3.2 weeks must be squeezed out of the activities somewhere along this route. It would be difficult to reduce the t_e of each of the three activities by 1.1 week. By referring back to the variance (σ^2) calculations summarized in Table 4–1, however, it can be seen that the highest variance value along the critical path ($\sigma^2 = 1.0$) applies to the activity $3 \rightarrow 5$. Therefore, this should be the first activity analyzed for possible acceleration.

---

[18] The different paths are *not* really *alternative* paths. *All* must be completed; therefore management seeks to focus its time-saving efforts on the most time-consuming one.

Probability of Success

These analytical tools—the critical path, variances, and slack analysis—also serve another purpose: they provide an indication of the probability of finishing the job within the scheduled time.

Although it is important to know the probability of being able to finish a single event within the estimated time, it is of even greater significance to know the probability of completing the entire project within the anticipated time, T_S. The probability of meeting T_S is denoted by P_r. The numerical value of P_r is determined by a two-step process. The first step is to evaluate the probability factor, Z, where

$$Z = \frac{T_S - T_E}{\sqrt{\Sigma \sigma^2}}$$

The numerator of Z is obtained by subtracting the expected time for the performance of the event, T_E, from the scheduled completion date, T_S. The denominator is the square root of the sum of all the variances of activities along the critical path.

Once the value of Z has been found, P_r is determined by referring to a statistical table of values for the standard normal distribution function, such as Table 4–3.

To illustrate the process, let us assume that the scheduled completion date of the microwave project is $T_S = 47.0$ weeks. We know that for the critical path, $1 \rightarrow 3 \rightarrow 5 \rightarrow 6$, $T_E = 45.2$ and, from Table 4–1, that the variances for $1 \rightarrow 3$, $3 \rightarrow 5$, and $5 \rightarrow 6$ are 0.4, 1.0, and 0.7, respectively. Therefore, the probability factor is

$$Z = \frac{T_S - T_E}{\sqrt{\Sigma \sigma^2}} = \frac{47.0 - 45.2}{\sqrt{0.4 + 1.0 + 0.7}} = \frac{1.8}{1.46} = 1.24$$

Referring to Table 4–3, we see that a Z of 1.24 yields a probability P_r of 0.8922. In other words, there is an 89.22 percent chance of meeting the scheduled date of 47 weeks.

Implementation of PERT

The actual projects to which PERT is applied in industry are usually far more complicated than the example we have used in the preceding discussion. As a consequence, their PERT networks are highly complex and involve a great number of events. For example, the network developed to supervise the design of guidance electronics for a guided missile project was composed of more than 20,000 events. To develop PERT networks of such magnitude, the work is divided into homogeneous subsytems. These, in turn, can be subdivided into sub-subsystems and the process continued until manageable units called "work packages" emerge. It is interesting to note the similarity between this process and the division of work to facilitate the measurement of factory jobs by direct time study or predetermined time values. The PERT network constructed for each

Table 4–3 Values of the standard normal
distribution function

Z	P_r	Z	P_r
0	0.5000	−3.0	0.0013
0.1	0.5398	−2.9	0.0019
0.2	0.5793	−2.8	0.0026
0.3	0.6179	−2.7	0.0035
0.4	0.6554	−2.6	0.0047
0.5	0.6915	−2.5	0.0062
0.6	0.7257	−2.4	0.0082
0.7	0.7580	−2.3	0.0107
0.8	0.7881	−2.2	0.0139
0.9	0.8159	−2.1	0.0179
1.0	0.8413	−2.0	0.0228
1.1	0.8643	−1.9	0.0287
1.2	0.8849	−1.8	0.0359
1.3	0.9032	−1.7	0.0446
1.4	0.9192	−1.6	0.0548
1.5	0.9332	−1.5	0.0668
1.6	0.9452	−1.4	0.0808
1.7	0.9554	−1.3	0.0968
1.8	0.9641	−1.2	0.1151
1.9	0.9713	−1.1	0.1357
2.0	0.9772	−1.0	0.1587
2.1	0.9821	−0.9	0.1841
2.2	0.9861	−0.8	0.2119
2.3	0.9893	−0.7	0.2420
2.4	0.9918	−0.6	0.2743
2.5	0.9938	−0.5	0.3085
2.6	0.9953	−0.4	0.3446
2.7	0.9965	−0.3	0.3821
2.8	0.9974	−0.2	0.4207
2.9	0.9981	−0.1	0.4602
3.0	0.9987		

work package can be compared to the design of a method, or standard practice, for each operation in a manufacturing process. In this sense, the network may be conceived of as a method of doing the work, or achieving the target, as defined by the work-package subsystem. The PERT network for the entire project is a cumulative total. The work-package networks are added together, forming sub-subsystem networks, which in turn are united in subsystem networks. The process is repeated until the whole project is integrated. Each time networks are added together to form a larger unit, it is said that a *summary level* has been created. Indeed, one measure of the complexity and size of a project network is the number of summary levels that exist within the system.

Small networks composed of fewer than 200 events can be set up and analyzed manually. An analyst equipped with a desk calculator can prepare such a network in about eight hours. For more complex projects, computers are required, and the leading computer manufacturers have developed programs for this purpose. To use these programs the analyst identifies the events to be performed, the sequence in which they must be done, and the time estimates for the activities connecting them. These data are fed into the computer, and a PERT network with all of the time and variance measures is printed out by the computer.

PERT/COST

To increase the usefulness of the PERT technique, many companies have expanded the information presented on the networks. The PERT approach described so far in this chapter is called PERT/TIME, because time is the common denominator and the only measuring unit. Other approaches are designed to reflect the application of resources as well. Of particular interest are approaches that relate the cost and time aspects of a network. Numerous systems have been developed to optimize time factors and minimize costs;[20] the one we will present is called PERT/COST.

In PERT/COST, a network is constructed in the same fashion as in PERT/TIME except that two sets of estimates are required at each step:

1. *A minimum cost estimate for the path with its completion time*
2. *A minimum completion time for the path with its cost estimate*

First the critical path is determined by the minimum cost estimates, yielding a completion date based on minimizing costs. As might be expected, the time needed to complete a project under these conditions may be too great, since, as a rule, research and development tasks are less costly when they proceed slowly. Therefore, the analyst will substitute alternative times that are faster and generally more costly along the critical path. In this way, the time requirements of the critical path can gradually be shortened until the path meets the schedule requirements or until another path becomes critical.

To illustrate this approach, consider the network shown in Figure 4–10, where

[20] For examples see Modre, J. J., and Phillips, C. R., *Project Management with CPM and PERT* (New York: Reinhold, 1964), Chapter 7.

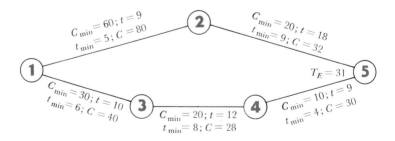

Figure 4–10 An illustration of PERT/COST network

costs are in thousands of dollars. For minimum costs, the critical path is $1 \rightarrow 3 \rightarrow 4 \rightarrow 5$ with $T_E = 31$ weeks. If the time allotted for the task were 31 or more weeks, the least-cost network would be usable. However, suppose only 28 weeks were available to do the work or, alternatively, that management wanted to know what the added costs would be to complete the work in 28 weeks.

In order to reduce the time most economically, the activity along $1 \rightarrow 3 \rightarrow 4 \rightarrow 5$ that has the lowest cost increase per decrease in units of time should be selected. The changes in cost per unit of time $(\Delta C/\Delta t)$ for the activities are[21]

$$1 \rightarrow 3: \quad \frac{40 - 30}{10 - 6} = \$2,500$$

$$3 \rightarrow 4: \quad \frac{28 - 20}{12 - 8} = \$2,000$$

$$4 \rightarrow 5: \quad \frac{30 - 10}{9 - 4} = \$4,000$$

The least cost is encountered by reducing the time on segment $3 \rightarrow 4$. To reduce the time by 3 weeks would cost $6,000. The final network is shown in Figure 4–11.

A budget for the project can now be developed. As would be expected, the budgeted costs fall between the minimum cost budget and the minimum time budget. The budgets for the various alternatives are shown in Figure 4–12. The smallest cost budget that meets the schedule requirement of 28 weeks would be used as the project budget.

PERT Dynamics

To this point we have considered the means of planning a project to optimize the time–cost relationship. The remainder of the discussion will consider the use of PERT and PERT/COST to control the progress and cost of the project over time.

Effective management of a project by means of network analysis demands

[21] In the illustrated example, the relationship between the times and costs were assumed to be linear, each unit reduction in time yielding the same increase in cost. In many cases this assumption is not valid. Because of this, the procedures and calculations involved in PERT/COST can become quite complex.

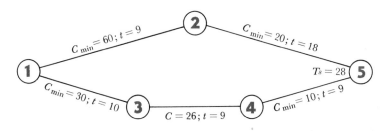

Figure 4–11   Minimum cost network to meet time schedule

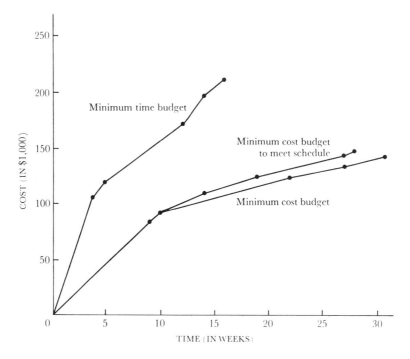

Figure 4–12 Project budgets

periodic reviews of progress. Actual performance must continually be compared with estimates for the network plan, which must then be revised. The actual progress to date plus the estimated time and cost required to complete the project constitute the latest PERT network and operating plan available to the company. Any required corrective action may be obtained by following the analytic routine—slack analysis, critical path, and trade-off studies—previously discussed. In PERT/COST systems, these study procedures evaluate specific resources in great detail. The information generated is often so specific that a trade-off study, for example, might suggest the shift of one junior mechanical engineer from an activity of positive slack to one of negative slack for a period of three weeks.

Project Reports

Computer programs have been developed that generate reports on the actual and projected utilization of every type of resource. Particularly useful are reports that spell out the quantities and grades of engineers, draftsmen, technicians, and other specialists that should be utilized on a project.

In general, these reports provide information to answer such questions as

1. What is the progress on the project to date?
2. What are the costs to date?

3. How do the actual costs and progress compare to the planned positions?
4. By how much time and cost will the project overrun or underrun?
5. How do questions 1 through 4 apply to activities, groups of activities, or specific resources such as manpower?

As the project progresses, the expenditures, labor hours, and progress made are recorded. These input data are then processed and the cost relationships developed. Numerous means of presenting this information are in use; only one is shown here.

The project summary report   The aim of the project summary report is to show the schedule and cost status of the project and of the major activities of the project. In doing so, it attempts to highlight the problem areas so that management can focus its attention on them. This report shows schedule slippage, cost over- or underruns to date, and the projected over- or underrun to complete the project.

To illustrate its use, consider that management has opted to proceed with the minimum cost schedule projects in Figure 4–11. After 14 weeks of work, the project status is as shown in Figure 4–13. From this report, management could see that time slippage has occurred. Activity $3 \rightarrow 4$, which started early, is now expected to be completed one week late, delaying the project. To counteract this, management can either add resources to it or revise its plans for activity $4 \rightarrow 5$ to cut its time.

The project cost overrun is currently $3,100, and the estimated overrun at completion is $6,000. If more funds are required to speed up activities $3 \rightarrow 4$ or $4 \rightarrow 5$, the overrun will be even greater.

The critical area at this time is activity $3 \rightarrow 4$, which has both cost and time overruns.

The budget report   The purpose of the budget report is to show the budget cost for the work, the actual costs to date, the estimated cost for the work performed to date, and the estimate of the cost at the completion of the project. Figure 4–14 is a budget report for the project in our example.

The data for the budget report come from the project summary report and from the original project budget (Figure 4–12). From the project summary we can see that the actual costs were $107,200 and the estimated value of the work done to date is $104,100. Thus the cost overrun for the work performed to date is $3,100. This means that the cost of the work performed to date has been $3,100 greater than estimated. Furthermore, from the original budget report, the expenditures at the end of the fourteenth week should have been $106,000. The actual expenditures have been $1,200 greater than the budget expense for that date. In other words, the expenditures are higher than budgeted, and the work less than estimated.

Finally, the latest estimate of the cost to complete the project on the project summary is $152,000, and the time to complete the project is 29 weeks. A comparison of these to the original budget figure of $146,000 and time schedule of

Project summary report week 14

Cost of work (in $1,000) Schedule progress (weeks)

Activity	Performed to Date			Totals To Completion			Scheduled Starting Date	Actual Starting Date	Estimated Time To Complete	Scheduled Completion Date	Estimated Completion Date	Completion Date	Slack (Critical activities only)
	Original Estimate	Actual Costs	(Overrun) Underrun	Original Estimate	Latest Estimate	(Overrun) Underrun							
Overall	104.1	107.2	(3.1)	146	152	(6)	1	1	15	28	29		−1
1 → 2	60	58	2	60	58	2	1	1		9		10	
1 → 3	30	34	(4)	30	34	(4)	1	1		10		9	
2 → 5	5.5	6.2	(0.7)	20	22	(2)	10	11		28	28		+1
3 → 4	8.6	9.0	(0.4)	26	28	(2)	10	9	6	19	20		−1
4 → 5				10	10	0	19		9	28	29		−1

Figure 4-13 PERT/COST project summary report

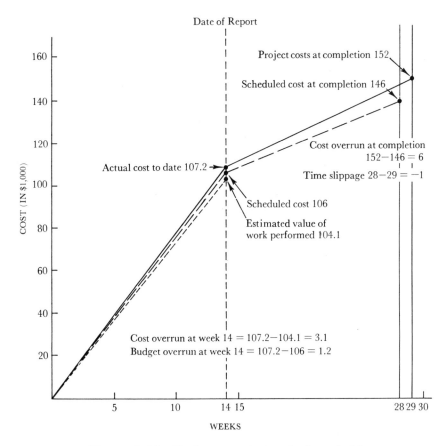

Figure 4–14 Budget report at end of week 14

28 weeks indicates a slippage of one week and an overrun of $6,000 unless changes are made.

Schedule outlook report The schedule outlook report (Figure 4–15) shows the weekly history of the project progress. The project has been reasonably on schedule. During the sixth and seventh weeks it was ahead of schedule but it has since slipped. By looking at the trend and relating it to actions taken to remedy the problems, the management can determine if the actions they took to control the situation were successful.

Cost outlook report The historical picture presented by the cost outlook report (Figure 4–16) is not as encouraging as the schedule report. The cost overrun has been continually increasing and has increased at an increasing rate over the past four weeks. If management has taken steps to control this overrun, they have not worked. If nothing has been done to stop the trend, efforts to reverse or contain it are in order.

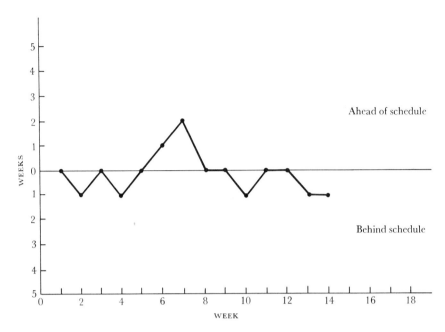

Figure 4–15 Schedule outlook report

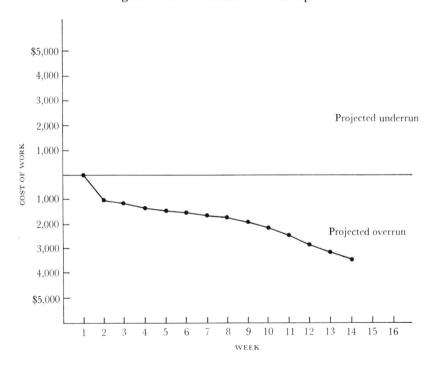

Figure 4–16 Cost outlook report

Manpower loading reports   The final set of reports to be illustrated deal with manpower requirements. Manpower loading reports are normally prepared for critical labor skills needed in the project, to furnish management the information it needs to reschedule work, increase or reduce the labor force, or schedule overtime work.

The overall picture of the manpower requirements for skill "A" for our example is shown in Figure 4–17. It indicates that the need for skill "A" is not regular during the course of the project. To smooth the pattern, management will probably have to consider overtime.

The heaviest loading falls between weeks 12 and 18. During this period, activities $2 \to 5$ and $3 \to 4$ are in progress. The question arises of how the load is to be split between the two activities. The information to answer this type of question is found in the Manpower Loading Report, Figure 4–18, which presents the planned distribution of the labor skill per week to each activity. During week 14, 75 hours were used on activity $2 \to 5$ and 25 on $3 \to 5$. The schedule for weeks 15 through 18 calls for a shift of 5 man-hours from activity $2 \to 5$ to activity $3 \to 5$. Since $2 \to 5$ has positive slack, it may be possible to shift additional skill "A" labor from $2 \to 5$ to $3 \to 5$. Management should investigate this opportunity.

Additional shift in skill "A" labor will have to be made if activity $3 \to 5$ is not brought back to schedule. Only 20 hours are scheduled during week 19, and they are for activity $2 \to 5$. If $3 \to 5$ is still in progress, labor will be needed for it.

By highlighting these conditions, manpower reports alert management and thus enable timely consideration of the loading problems.

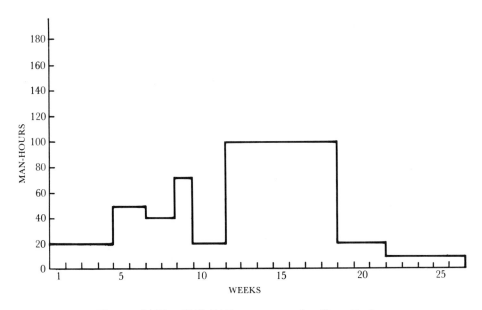

Figure 4–17   Skill "A" manpower loading display

			End of Week _14_
Week	Activity	Estimated Man-Hours	Activity Slack (weeks)
14	2→5	75	+1
	3→4	25	-1
15	2→5	70	+1
	3→4	30	-1
16	2→5	70	+1
	3→4	30	-1
17	2→5	70	+1
	3→4	30	-1
18	2→5	70	+1
	3→4	30	-1
19	2→5	20	+1
20	2→5	20	+1
21	2→5	20	+1
22	2→5	10	+1
23	2→5	10	+1
24	2→5	10	+1
25	2→5	10	+1
26	2→5	10	+1

Figure 4–18 Skill "A" manpower loading report

PERT/COST Dynamics

The PERT/COST approach, as shown in previous pages, offers management a means of dynamically linking costs to work progress. As the project progresses, the costs and performance will usually vary from schedule. The availability of up-to-date information on what has happened as well as PERT/COST's extrapolation of the work progress into the future make it an invaluable tool.

Questions and Problems

1. What is an innovation cycle? How many segments does it comprise?
2. Differentiate between pure and applied research. Of what importance is pure research to a commercial firm?

3. Why can't product design be solely the function of the marketing department?
4. Of what use are pilot runs? Considering the cost of such activities, why are they used?
5. Should a business that offers a service be concerned with the design of its output? State whether product design enters into the consideration of each of the following.
    (a) Medical services
    (b) Government
    (c) Vacation sites
    (d) Dental services
    (e) Appliance repair services
6. What managerial problems does a network analysis such as PERT seek to overcome?
7. What is a PERT network? What part does precedence play in the design of a network?
8. In what ways may "times" be estimated in network analysis? Why are three time estimates used? Why are statistical estimating techniques used?
9. What is network slack, and how is it related to the critical path?
10. What measures can determine the probability of success of a particular network?
11. Does the amount of detail required to build a valid PERT or PERT/COST network and the amount of data flow needed to keep it up to date make its use uneconomical except for extremely large projects?
12. What is PERT/COST? What advantages does it have over PERT?
13. Explain the elements of PERT/COST, and discuss the prerequisites for using this approach.
14. PERT and PERT/COST are used in the planning and administration of projects. How are they used to increase the effectiveness of a project?
15. What is the critical path in a PERT network? How is it used?
16. How are PERT and PERT/COST used in management control?
17. The following data were obtained from a study of the time required to train sales personnel.

TIME (IN DAYS)

ACTIVITY	a	m	b
$1 \rightarrow 2$	5	6	13
$1 \rightarrow 3$	2	7	12
$2 \rightarrow 4$	1.5	2	2.5
$4 \rightarrow 5$	1	3	5
$3 \rightarrow 5$	4	5	6

    (a) Schematically diagram the PERT network from the tabulated information, showing the expected performance times for each activity.
    (b) What is the overall cycle time, and what is the critical path?
    (c) What activities should receive the greatest attention in order to assure scheduled completion?
18. Your company has just received an order for a construction project that is made up of the following jobs.

JOB NUMBER	IMMEDIATE PREDECESSOR JOBS	TIME ESTIMATES (IN DAYS)		
		Optimistic	Most likely	Pessimistic
1	—	1	3	5
2	1	3	4	11
3	1	2	4	6
4	1	1	2	3
5	2	1	2	3
6	3	1	2	9
7	4	2	3	4
8	6,7	3	5	13
9	5,8	1	2	3
10	9	1	1	1

(a) Draw the appropriate network diagram.
(b) Calculate the expected completion time (in days).
(c) Calculate the standard deviation of the expected completion time.
(d) Find the critical path.
(e) Suppose that each day the completion date can be shortened is worth $1,000 to you. If you have your choice of (1), (2), or (3), below, each of which would cost $2,500, which, if any, would you choose?
    (1) t_e for job 2 can be shortened by 3 days.
    (2) t_e for job 3 can be shortened by 3 days.
    (3) t_e for job 8 can be shortened by 3 days.

19. The PERT network in Figure 4–19 has been prepared for the design of a new product.
    (a) Determine the estimated time for each event.
    (b) Which activity has the most precise estimated performance time? Which one has the most uncertain performance time?
    (c) The design of the new product is scheduled for completion in 20 weeks ($T_S = 20$). Do you think this target will be met?
        (1) Support your conclusions with a slack table.
        (2) Identify the critical path, and discuss what possible action could be taken to increase the chance of success.
        (3) Indicate how the probability of achieving the end date could be estimated.

20. The ABC City Hospital has decided to provide new operating facilities for a new surgical procedure that promises to reduce surgical complications significantly. The hospital administrator has been asked to set up a plan to get the facilities

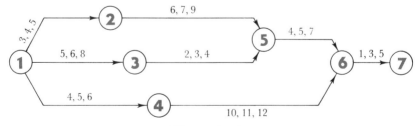

Figure 4–19

into operation as rapidly as possible but not to exceed an expenditure of $57,500. To accomplish this he has developed the following PERT/COST data.

ACTIVITY		LEAST TIME (WEEKS)	LEAST TIME COST	LEAST COST TIME (WEEKS)	LEAST COST
Design facilities	$1 \rightarrow 2$	6	$ 9,000	9	5,000
Select & order equipment	$2 \rightarrow 4$	3	1,000	4	850
Select staff	$1 \rightarrow 3$	2	500	3	400
Train staff	$3 \rightarrow 6$	4	8,000	8	3,000
Prepare facility	$2 \rightarrow 5$	4	12,000	12	7,000
Receive equipment	$4 \rightarrow 5$	4	28,000	6	22,000
Install equipment	$5 \rightarrow 6$	3	2,000	4	1,500
Test staff & facility	$6 \rightarrow 7$	3	7,000	3	7,000

(a) Construct the PERT/COST diagrams.
(b) Determine the critical path for least time.
(c) Determine the critical path for least time meeting the cost considerations.
(d) How much time is traded from the least-time solution to the cost-contained solution?

References

Archibald, R. D., and Villoria, R., *Network-Based Management Systems,* Wiley, New York, 1967.

Asimow, M., *Introduction to Design,* Prentice-Hall, Englewood Cliffs, N.J., 1962.

Dean, B. V., *Operations Research in Research and Development,* Wiley, New York, 1963.

Dreyfuss, H., *Designing for People,* Simon and Schuster, New York, 1958.

Evarts, H. F., *Introduction to PERT,* Allyn and Bacon, Boston, Mass., 1964.

Iannone, A. L., *Management Program Planning and Control with PERT, MOST and LOB,* Prentice-Hall, Englewood Cliffs, N.J., 1967.

Kaufmann, A., and Desbazeille, G., *The Critical Path Method,* Gordon and Breach, New York, 1969.

Levin, R. I., and Kirkpatrick, C. A., *Planning and Control with PERT/CPM,* McGraw-Hill, New York, 1966.

Lowe, C. W., *Critical Path Analysis by Bar Chart,* 2nd ed., Business Books, London, 1969.

Moder, J. I., and Phillips, C. R., *Project Management with CPM and PERT,* Van Nostrand-Reinhold, New York, 1964.

Niebel, B. W., and Baldwin, E. N., *Designing for Production,* rev. ed., Irwin, Homewood, Ill., 1963.

Newton, N., *An Approach to Design,* Addison-Wesley, Cambridge, Mass., 1951.

Riggs, J., and Heath, C., *Guide to Cost Reduction Through Critical Path Scheduling,* Prentice-Hall, Englewood Cliffs, N.J., 1966.

Starr, M. K., *Product Design and Decision Theory,* Prentice-Hall, Englewood Cliffs, N.J., 1963.

Wiest, J. D., and Levy F. K., *A Management Guide to PERT/CPM,* Prentice-Hall, Englewood Cliffs, N.J., 1969.

5

Product Reliability and Quality Assurance

In Chapter 4 we discussed and analyzed the broad managerial problems that arise in the design and development of new products. In this chapter we will treat one aspect of this process—product reliability and quality—in detail, because of its increasing importance in the production function.

When a consumer speaks of a "quality product" he generally means a high-priced item such as a Rolls Royce or the most expensive model of a washer, dryer, or refrigerator. Most consumers cannot afford to purchase Rolls Royces and deluxe appliances, however, so they are willing to settle for products that have satisfactory quality, which simply means the highest quality they can get for the price they are willing to pay. When consumers, in their search for satisfactory quality, take into consideration the expenses of use and maintenance as well as the purchase cost, they are said to be appraising "product effectiveness."

A manufacturer wants his products to be of the finest quality possible, yet priced so that he can sell them. Thus, like the consumer, he is balancing the cost of quality against the benefits (increased sales, in this case) to be derived from the product's effectiveness. By making the cost, delivery date, and quality of his product attractive, a manufacturer is able to enjoy large sales and good customer relations. Consequently, during the production and design phases he must keep close watch on his costs and delivery schedules, for these factors affect the customer's purchase decision.

Since a product's quality and overall effectiveness are generally not discernible at the time of purchase, a customer often has difficulty equating the costs and delivery date of a product with its relative quality. When the customer begins to use the product he has just purchased, he may discover that it does not meet his quality standards and therefore does not represent a fair value. Local service agencies and reputable retail outlets sometimes act as buffers between disgruntled customers and the manufacturer as, for example, in the appliance and automotive fields. Faulty goods are repaired or replaced, but only at a cost to the producer and customers. The monetary cost of product support and repair operations in the United States now stands at over $7 billion annually, and the figure is still growing.

Selling goods of low quality is not in the producer's best interest because funds the customer must spend for maintaining and repairing existing items cannot be used to purchase new items. Defense spending, for example, has been seriously curtailed by the high cost of maintaining current equipment. Automobile manufacturers, intent on encouraging an increase in the number of multiple-car families, have recently recognized this fact; therefore, they are putting more emphasis on the quality of their products, hoping thereby to free customers' funds for purchasing additional autos.

In defense of low-quality products, manufacturers often claim that the customer would not pay the additional price that they would have to charge in order to manufacture a more reliable product that would perform satisfactorily, meet advertised specifications, and fulfill the customer's expectations regarding (acceptable) product quality and reliability. Paradoxically, experience indicates that, in most cases, the extra cost required to raise a submarginal product to a competitively acceptable quality level is small; often it is no more than 10 percent of the original production cost. This is a small investment for what could be a large payoff in an improved company reputation and repeat sales. Indeed, in many cases no extra cost is required at all in raising the quality level of a product to a competitively acceptable level, and the production cost may actually decline if one considers the indirect cost of product warranty and repair.[1] In short, in most instances it is extremely short-sighted to make a product that cannot meet acceptable quality limits.

To highlight this fact we will approach the topic of quality assurance from the customer's viewpoint rather than the manufacturer's. Thus, the objective will be to ensure that a product's specifications give maximum value for its price and that, compared with other offerings of a similar nature, it is the "best buy." Customer-oriented quality assurance also seeks to ensure that the specifications established for the product are actually met. In this sense quality assurance may sound like a form of altruism, but it is really just sound business practice. The payoff in satisfied customers, low warranty costs, and good company reputation more than offsets the cost of achieving it.

---

[1] Consider the high costs incurred by automotive companies in recent years to call back and repair badly designed or produced parts plus the numerous lawsuits.

A Company View

To understand better what is involved in customer-oriented quality assurance, let us turn to Figure 5–1, which depicts the high level of interdependence that exists among the various stages in the life cycle of a product, stretching from its design and production to its installation and use. Decisions regarding factors that pertain to each stage in the cycle can affect costs at the other stages. When the product is still in the design stage, for example, producers must consider the costs that the consumer will encounter when he uses it; product configuration will have a direct bearing on installation costs, including the cost of training operators. In the past, quality-assurance efforts tended to be concentrated in the areas labeled "producer" in Figure 5–1. The main objective used to be simply to get out a product that met the specifications established by the manufacturer; warranty costs were about the only factor that was considered on the "consumer" side of the diagram. Only when warranty costs were high or isolated because of specific component failures did the manufacturer take any corrective action. But even this remedial action was too often taken after the fact and could repair only some of the damage done to the company's image. While it is certainly to a firm's advantage to have a reputation for standing behind its product, too many "repair trips" by the customer are likely to undermine that advantage.

Today, manufacturers still strive to meet product specifications, but those specifications now reflect consumer interests to a greater extent. This significant change in approach has been stimulated by three major factors. First, defense subcontracting has become increasingly important during the last decade. The government is a single customer who pays directly for all the work required over the life cycle of sophisticated military systems. To reduce the overall costs to the government, therefore, the concept of "trade-off" was introduced, which meant that purchases were made only if a favorable response could be given to the following question: Could an increase in the design or production costs required to achieve greater reliability and ease of use result in operating savings that would justify them? Studies of this type have been called *cost effectiveness studies* because they are reminiscent of product-effectiveness studies made in the consumer market, where a typical question might be: Would higher product-acquisition costs (including the expenses of installation and personnel training) be offset by lower operating costs, greater reliability, and longer useful life? Because customers are concerned about such matters, manufacturers have found

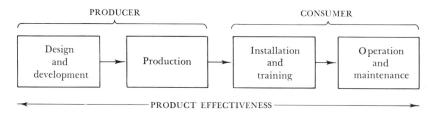

Figure 5–1   Product life cycle

that it is good business to be able to demonstrate the effectiveness of their product as part of their sales pitch.

The second factor is the growing concern of the consuming public over product quality. During the past years, consumers have gained increased strength through legislation, consumer groups, and new governmental bodies. These efforts have in general increased the producer's liability for his products' safety and quality.

A third impetus toward greater consumer orientation has been the trend to leasing equipment rather than buying it, particularly in the computer and automotive fields. This trend has forced manufacturers to come to grips with the cost, or product effectiveness, concept, since all expenses over the entire life cycle of a product are borne by the manufacturing firm, and hence they all have a direct bearing on the firm's competitive position and profits. This trend has also given manufacturers an opportunity to see what it is like to be a user of their own products. The insights gained from this new perspective have caused the manufacturers to join the more enlightened customers—both government and commercial—in demanding that decisions regarding product configuration be made in terms of the entire life cycle of the product. The coordination of the chain of decisions that must be made in many separate functional areas of the firm is called *quality assurance.*

Quality Assurance Programs

There are many aspects in designing a sound quality assurance program, but for purposes of analysis they can be grouped into three stages: reliability engineering, manufacturing quality assurance, and usage.

Reliability Engineering

Reliability engineering refers to the process of determining, in the initial product-planning stage, the appropriate quality level for product components, including specifications, tolerance limits, and workmanship. This must be a joint decision; marketing, production, and engineering aspects of the configuration must all be considered, and the importance of each will vary among different industries and products.

Firms frequently sell the same product in markets that are to all outward appearances differentiated only by price. Tires of the same size, for example, are sold at many prices ranging from $15.00 to $50.00, yet in most respects the outward characteristics of the tires are the same. They have essentially the same wheel diameters and tread design; they may even use the same type of rubber and tire cord. The differences lie only in the design specifications: the amount of rubber, the ply of tire cord, and the weight and tensile strength of the tire are different. In the more expensive tire lines, the design specifications relating to performance are aimed at higher product effectiveness. In other words, the quality level of a product is directly related to its engineering specifications; different levels of quality are achieved by varying those specifications.

In some cases, only one quality level can be produced. Some pharmaceuticals, for instance, are compounds that cannot be changed. Aspirin is aspirin, provided, of course, that proper levels of compound purity and workplace cleanliness are maintained according to legal requirements. By the same token, certain defense products are so experimental that performance specifications for components are at the limit of design capabilities. In a more typical case, however, several quality levels can be created through engineering design; machines capable of performing the same tasks can be built at many quality levels. Home laundry equipment, for instance, is not designed for the same quality and performance levels as commercial equipment.

Today, most manufacturers recognize that, although production must have some voice in determining the product's quality level, first consideration should be given to the needs of the customer as reported by the marketing department; this is particularly true of firms that are in highly competitive industries. This means that the production process must meet the specification stipulated by the marketplace, within the limits imposed by technology. Interestingly, improvements in the production process often result from the need to meet tough specifications and tolerances.

Manufacturing Quality Assurance

Once the design specifications for the product have been decided upon, production can begin. At this stage, input materials that meet the desired quality levels are procured, and the production process is monitored to see that it achieves the projected overall quality level. All activities pertaining to meeting the design specifications during the production process are referred to as *manufacturing quality assurance.*

Quality assurance includes more than just meeting the design specifications; the efficiency of all operations in meeting those specifications must also be considered. The desired quality levels can be achieved in many ways and at varying costs, but the production objective must be to achieve them at the minimum overall cost.

Production variation   In any production process in which the product is expected to conform to measurable specifications, variations may be expected. This is true even if costly and automated machine tools are utilized. Most product specifications, such as the depth of a cut or the location and diameter of a hole, vary slightly with each unit of output. There are many possible causes of variations: the input materials may not be perfectly homogeneous, the cutting tools may have become worn, an operator may tire and make slight errors, and the machine tool itself may not be operating consistently due to wear and tear. Individually and collectively, all of these variations will appear in outputs.

The existence of variations is the reason most production specifications include plus or minus ($\pm$) tolerances. Some chance variations are expected in all outputs; they are normal and can never be eliminated. As long as they are confined to a range that is acceptable, the production system is under control and stable.

For instance, to drill a hole a machine operator must first locate the center of the hole. Although he will not hit the precise center of each hole he drills, he can control the deviations from the precise center within an acceptable range.

If, in the process of drilling these holes, the tool becomes dull or the operator tires and becomes careless, variations resulting from causes other than chance will enter into the operation. As a result, the holes may be drilled outside the range expected from chance variation. When variations that are not attributable to chance, such as operator fatigue and carelessness, creep into the picture, the production system is considered out of control. It will be turning out products that are outside the allowable tolerances—defective parts—and they must be located and weeded out. Sometimes they can be reworked, but in other situations they must be scrapped. In either case, the result is added costs of production.

Production efficiency   Knowing this, many people rush to the conclusion that the least costly production process is one that will yield no defects and will always be under control. There are two reasons why this is not true, however. First, it is virtually impossible to construct a process that will not yield some defective parts. Second, since management's objective should be to achieve the lowest possible unit cost of production, the cost of preventing rejects must be compared with the cost of having the rejects. This analysis may indicate that the most economical output would actually result from a process in which there was a high level of rejects, since redesigning the system to attain fewer rejects might be more costly than accepting the high levels of rejects.

Figure 5–2 depicts this cost relationship. For any given level of output, the total cost is equal to the sum of the production systems costs and the costs asso-

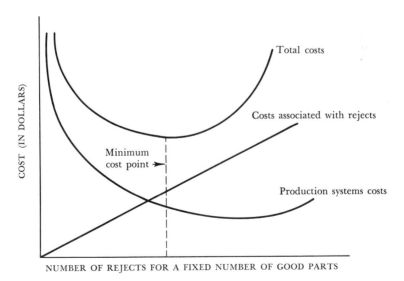

NUMBER OF REJECTS FOR A FIXED NUMBER OF GOOD PARTS

Figure 5–2   Total systems costs

ciated with rejects, including the expense of inspection, rework, scrapping, and customer relations.

In this hypothetical situation it is quite obvious that the least costly production system is not the one that yields no rejects. Once the most economic production system is selected, however, efficient operation requires that it be controlled, that is, that the level of rejects produced be satisfactory.

Usage

Management's interest in the quality of its product does not end once the product has been made and sold. The quality history that evolves during the product's use will tell management whether its design and production quality decisions have been good.

In an attempt to anticipate usage problems, many products are field-tested under conditions that approximate normal use or that are more demanding than normal. In this fashion, some quality problems can be located and corrected before the product is marketed, but other deficiencies are not found until the product is actually used. As service facilities report product failures, these failures should be analyzed, and then corrective designs and production methods should be developed.

Over time, the quality characteristics of a product will change, and, of course, quality affects costs. Figure 5–3 shows changes in three cost factors of television sets that have taken place over a period of years: purchase cost, service costs, and operating costs. This chart was compiled by averaging the costs for TV sets produced during a calendar year over an expected set life of ten years. Notice that, interestingly, the cost showing the greatest reduction is the service cost.

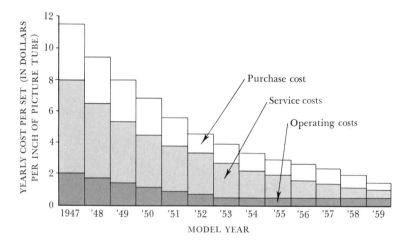

Figure 5–3   Television factor costs

SOURCE: This table was adapted from R. R. Landers, *Reliability and Product Assurance* (Englewood Cliffs, N. J.: Prentice-Hall, 1963), p. 256.

This reflects the fact that there was a significant improvement in the quality of TV sets during the given period. This is not an uncommon pattern; the quality of many products improves gradually over time, principally because of the development of experience and competence in the design and manufacturing phases.

Interaction among Quality Functions

Overall quality planning requires an understanding of the interrelationships among the three major quality phases. For example, when a company decides to manufacture a new product, quality specifications at the initial design phase usually pertain to an ideal product. As the product is redesigned, produced, and used, it undergoes changes that reduce the level of its quality specifications, and lower quality specifications mean lower product effectiveness.

This situation is illustrated in Figure 5–4, where the product, as originally conceived, is shown to have ideal specifications and thus an effectiveness of 100 percent. This does not mean that the product is perfect; the 100 percent value is used simply to denote what the manufacturer considers maximum specifications. In the later stages of product design, these specifications will be relaxed

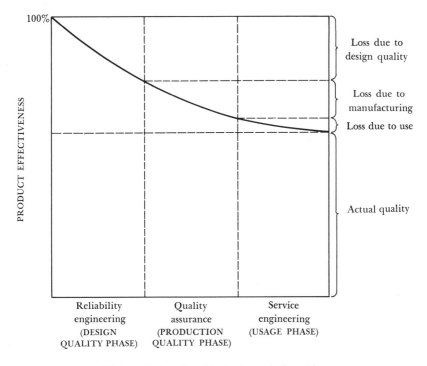

Figure 5–4 Quality factor relationships

SOURCE: This table was adapted from R. R. Landers, *Reliability and Product Assurance* (Englewood Cliffs, N. J.: Prentice-Hall, 1963).

due to the designer's inability to convert all of his ideas into workable specifications, or to the unavailability of ideally made parts, or to engineering compromises made to facilitate production, or to compromises caused by tight schedules. For reasons such as these, the product's ultimate effectiveness, as measured in Figure 5–4, falls below the level set by the original specifications. During the production cycle, the product's effectiveness declines still further because of production errors that are not detected, the use of materials that are not as good or as uniform as expected, or the inability to meet established tolerances. Finally, in the usage stage, further reductions take place in the product's effectiveness because of product misuse, improper service, and damage that occurs during installation and shipping.

It is important for management to watch closely the reduction of effectiveness that inevitably accompanies the introduction of a new product. Minimum levels of acceptability should be established by a firm, and slippage from the ideal should be constantly monitored by its quality assurance function. Here experience is still the best guide when the problem arises of trading off costs against desired characteristics. It is important to note in this regard that no matter how diligent the efforts of production quality control may be, quality assurance efforts during the manufacturing phase cannot raise the quality level above the inherent design specifications; at best, production quality control may be able to keep the quality at that level. To improve a product's overall quality, one must consider the interaction of all three quality phases. It may be far easier and cheaper, for example, to improve quality through product redesign than through closer manufacturing control.

Product Effectiveness

To differentiate this new concept of quality control (which focuses on the interaction among reliability engineering, production quality control, and the impact of the product's quality at the usage stage) from the more traditional approach, the term *product effectiveness* is used. The term implies that to provide the level of quality required by increasing customer demands, control must begin at the product-design stage and continue through the usage stage. To do this, the marketing department performs the necessary consumer research and reports the minimum quality that the consumer will accept in the market where the product is to be sold. The engineering department then tries to convert the marketing evaluation into design specifications; the purchasing department then secures the materials needed to meet the design specifications, and the production department tries to manufacture the product with these materials according to specifications. Finally, the shipping and installation functions, together with all other service activities, feed back failure reports to marketing, production, and engineering so that product effectiveness may be continually reevaluated.

The Evolution of Product Effectiveness

Before the early 1900s, most factory production workers were skilled craftsmen. A product was made by one worker or, at most, by a small group of workers. Consequently, the quality of a product was logically considered the responsibility of individual craftsmen.

Then, in the early 1900s, the factory system as we know it today came into being. Large groups of semiskilled workers, each doing the same or similar tasks, were placed under the supervision of a foreman, who was held responsible for the quality of the group's output. The foreman was also responsible for the design of work methods to achieve product specifications and meet the daily production quota. Thus, to the worker, company authority—as expressed through policies and work standards—emanated from the foreman.

As the industrial process became more complex and production units became larger, companies began using full-time quality inspectors. By the late 1930s, specialist inspectors had become so common that inspection became a separate activity altogether. During World War II, the pressure to increase production efficiency led to the introduction of statistical means of inspection, which greatly increased the efficiency and reliability of inspection.

Finally, in the early 1950s, management began to realize that it was not enough to prevent defective goods from being shipped to customers; it was also important to appraise the quality of the products from the customer's point of view as they were being used.

Product Characteristics

When the effectiveness of a product is being assessed, not all of the specifications or characteristics of the product are of equal importance. Some are critical, but others have a lesser effect. A critical specification, in this sense, is one that must be precisely met lest it lead to product failures and customer displeasure or to difficulties in the later stages of production.

Many critical characteristics can affect the usefulness of a product; these are usually operating or external product characteristics. Others, which are of no concern to a customer, are critical to production; for example, a component that is slightly oversized may not allow the spatial clearance needed for subsequent production operations. A few characteristics are critical from both the consumer's and producer's points of view.

Even a relatively simple product has hundreds of characteristics, and management clearly cannot attempt to control all of them. It must concentrate on the critical ones. Fortunately, many characteristics that are critical for both production and consumption are not difficult to control; the production process itself will be able to keep many of them under control. For example, complex radio transmitters for aircraft have over 1,000 parts; almost all of them are critical from the consumer's point of view, and most of them are critical from the producer's point of view, yet many of these parts are not critical in terms of control since they virtually always meet standard specifications and thus do not have to be checked closely. They may be sampled periodically or not at all. Other parts may consistently have difficulty meeting production standards; since they are critical for control purposes, each unit may have to be tested and possibly redesigned.

Product Reliability

The amount of time and money spent on the reliability phase of product effectiveness has been increasing significantly in recent years for two reasons. The first is that a growing number of automated products and integrated processes and systems are being put to use. With older manual operations, an individual worker was "on hand" who could exert control over the operations, but on automated equipment this control factor is gone. For instance, on manually operated washing machines the housewife started and stopped the machine herself and thus had control over the wash as it moved through the washing cycle. On an automatic washer, the housewife is replaced by a timer and a control system. If either unit fails it is difficult to operate the machine manually. Therefore, the reliability of the timer and the control system are of critical importance. Moreover, improved reliability has a definite monetary value to the housewife because of convenience and eliminated repair costs and to the manufacturer because of avoided warranty and reputation costs. The need for increased reliability is becoming more important for many products. Greater machine complexity increases the amount of time and money required for repair; this in turn makes users less and less willing to pay the costs of downtime. As a consequence, the amount of money that producers are willing to invest in reliability engineering and manufacturing quality assurance has steadily risen.

The second reason for the increasing importance of product reliability is that as any product becomes more complex, its very complexity tends to make it less reliable. The greater the number of parts, or components, in a machine, the greater the probability that one of them will fail and cause the machine to break down.

As a result of these two factors, the emphasis on product reliability is bound to increase in the future.

Reliability: A Working Definition

The increased importance of product reliability has led to a search for quantitative systems for measuring reliability. In this sense, reliability is usually defined as a measure of the probability that a product will operate over its designed life under normal operating conditions.

In practice, the operating life of similar products usually varies quite a bit; some have a long life while others have quite a short life. With sufficient historical data, a frequency distribution of product failures can be developed; using this distribution, a probability prediction of the life of a product can then be made. Expressed as a probability value, the reliability of a product may be anything between 0 (indicating certainty of failure) and 1 (indicating certainty of operation).

To obtain a valid probability measure of reliability for a product, certain operating characteristics must be standardized. Because every product is designed for specific applications, its reliability should be tested when it is being properly used. A washing machine, for example, is designed to wash a certain weight of laundry, but if the weight greatly exceeds this limit, the washer will not clean properly and may even fail. Such results would clearly not represent the washer's reliability.

No product will last forever, so reliability must also be measured in terms of time. Here we are interested in determining the probability of a product performing its function properly over a given period of time—its *normal life expectancy*.

Finally, environmental conditions determine the level of external stress to which a product is exposed, and this factor will also affect the product's operating performance. For example, the lubrication system of washing machine motors is not designed for cold weather performance, and if the machine is operated outdoors in cold weather, the motor is likely to fail. Failures of this sort clearly should not be regarded as indicative of the reliability of the washer for normal home operation.

Product Failures

The basic unit of measure for reliability is the product failure rate (FR) or its reciprocal, the mean time between failures (MTBF). As the name suggests, the failure rate measures the frequency of failure during a period of time by means of the following ratio:

$$FR = \frac{\text{Number of failures in the evaluation period}}{\text{Number of operating hours in the evaluation period}}$$

The mean time between failures is the reciprocal of the failure rate and yields the average time between equipment failures.

$$MTBF = \frac{\text{Evaluation time period}}{\text{Number of failures in the evaluation period}}$$

A great deal of research has been done to try to determine product failure rates over time. Most of these attempts have been hindered by the fact that, in many instances, failures can only be defined subjectively. There is, as yet, no precise universal definition that will describe what is or is not a failure. If a television tube fails after ten years of operation, for example, the owner of the television set may regard this as a failure, yet to the manufacturer a ten-year performance record may seem a "success." For purposes of this discussion, let us define a failure as an event that denotes a change from an operational to a nonoperational status.

Many products have published failure rates. These rates must not be accepted without close scrutiny, however. Failure rates for a product or a component measured in isolation may vary greatly from the rate recorded when the item is tested within a system with other components. Many television tubes tested individually prove to have very long lives, yet in a television set they may be failures.

The importance of calculating failure rates for products and components in the environment where they are used points up the importance of selecting appropriate quality specifications for components. Since a system's reliability is no better than its most unreliable part, it is false reliability and an unnecessary expense to design components for a system that have reliabilities far beyond the requirements of the system.

Reliability Measurement Considerations

The statistical measure of reliability denotes how reliable a product is. A statistical comparison of two brands of firecrackers showed that 75 out of 100 of one brand exploded, whereas only 56 out of 100 of another brand exploded. The statistical failure rates for the two brands were thus:

$$FR_1 = \frac{25}{100} = 0.25$$

$$FR_2 = \frac{44}{100} = 0.44$$

The tests suggested, in other words, that 25 percent of the first brand could be expected to fail in normal use, whereas 44 percent of the second brand could be expected to fail.

Most products cannot be measured this simply, however. For a single-use item like a firecracker, only two conditions exist—either the firecracker works or it does not work. It cannot operate 75 percent of the time or 56 percent of the time. This is also true of products that operate continuously. Of every 100 light bulbs produced, for example, two may fail in the first 100 hours of use, but if a single bulb were tested, it would either operate or fail. Thus, it is not enough to say that a light bulb is 98 percent reliable; further elaboration is necessary.

In a strict statistical sense, use of the term *reliability measure* is incorrect even when applied to a product class, for reliability measure denotes the probability of an event occurring in the future, whereas measurement connotes counting something that has occurred and thus is an historical fact. Reliability measure, therefore, actually refers to a measure of the demonstrated reliability in the past. The firecrackers tested had a demonstrated reliability of 0.75 and 0.56. For practical purposes, however, we refer to the demonstrated reliability as a reliability measure.

Reliability measurement   To illustrate the use of failure rates and the mean time between failures, let us consider a test that was conducted to determine the reliability of a transistor that had been designed to operate for 900 hours. One thousand transistors were tested and their failure times noted; a frequency diagram of the operating lives of these transistors is given in Figure 5–5.

A failure pattern   As can be seen in Figure 5–5, 60 transistors failed during the first 50 hours of operation and 40 failed during the next 50 hours of operation. Such early failures are often termed *infant mortalities* and are common to most products. They are primarily due to factors such as inferior material or poor workmanship and are of a nonrandom nature. Although failures of this type are relatively numerous, they generally end within a period of 100 hours or less. Then we see that for the next 800 hours of operation about 23 transistors failed per 100 hours; this rate of failure is fairly constant. Finally, from 900

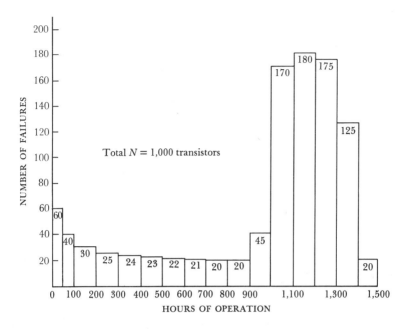

Figure 5–5 Transistor failures

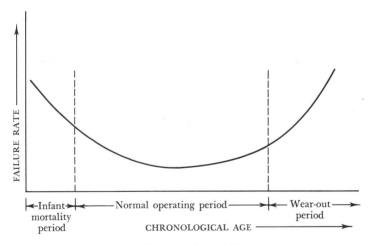

Figure 5–6 Characteristic failure rate curve

hours on, the number of failures per 100 operating hours increased sharply until all transistors failed.

A generalized version of this type of failure pattern is shown in Figure 5–6. This is a typical pattern and applies not only to many types of equipment but to human mortality as well. It is colloquially known as a "bathtub" curve. The life cycle of products that follow this pattern can be divided into three distinct periods. The first is the infant mortality period, where failures have assignable causes. The second is the normal operating period, in which failures are primarily due to chance factors. Finally there is the third, the wear-out period, in which the rate of failures goes up until all products fail.

Product mortality   On the basis of this characteristic failure rate curve, we can establish a normal operating age at which a given product will fail. In the transistor example, we can assume that a transistor that has been operating for 1,000 hours has a greater probability of operating 1,100 hours than one that has been operating for only 100 hours. However, the transistor that has been operating for 100 hours has a greater probability of operating for another 100 hours than the one that has been operating 1,000 hours. Once a product has passed the infant mortality stage, the longer it has been in operation the greater the probability that it will fail; this movement toward failure with age is termed the *force of mortality*.

The mortality force may also be divided into three patterns. First the force decreases with time during the infant mortality period, when a product's tendency to fail lessens. Then the force remains constant during the normal operating period. Finally, it increases as the product ages during the wear-out period.

If one has no specific information about the age of a product, it is usually safest to assume that the mortality force is constant. However, if it is known that the product is in the increasing or decreasing mortality phase, the results can be interpreted accordingly. Suppose, for example, that a manager wants to know how many spare parts he should maintain for a product. If the product is still in the infant mortality stage, he knows that the number of failures that occur will be greater than during the normal operating phase. Therefore, he should carry fewer spares than would otherwise be indicated by the present failure rate. On the other hand, if the product is known to be in the wear-out stage, more spares than normal are required.

Reliability Calculations

The calculations for determining failure rates and the mean time between failures for the transistor example reflect the frequency diagram of Figure 5–5. For instance, the failure rate of transistors with up to 50 hours of operation is calculated as[2]

$$FR_{0-50} = \frac{\text{Number of failures}}{\text{Total hours of operation} - \text{Non-operating time of the failures}}$$

$$= \frac{60}{\left[1000 \times 50 - \left(\frac{50}{2} \times 60\right)\right]} = \frac{60}{50\left(1000 - \frac{60}{2}\right)}$$

$$= .00121 \text{ failure per hour}$$

[2] It is assumed that failures are distributed at random throughout the time of a frequency class.

The mean time between failures is

$$\text{MTBF}_{0-50} = \frac{1}{\text{FR}_{0-50}}$$

$$= \frac{1}{.00121}$$

$$= 825 \text{ hours between failures}$$

The failure rates and the mean time between failures calculated for the entire operating range are listed in Table 5–1.

The average MTBF over the entire possible life of the transistors is 939 hours. Notice that this is longer than the MTBF for the infant mortality period, which was only 825 hours. This difference underscores the caution that must be exercised in extrapolating overall reliability from data recorded during the introductory period when equipment is first put into use. The wear-out period shows an even greater difference from the average MTBF. From 1,000 hours of use on, the mean time between failures is one-third or less than the average mean time between failures. Here again we see the necessity of studying a product's entire life cycle.

Constant Failure Rates

In practice, of course, transistors would be replaced after failure. When this is done the failure rate for the first 1,500 hours would be nearly the same as if there were no replacement. New replacement transistors would show the same failure pattern as the original transistors and would yield the same probabilities. At about 1,100 hours of operation there would be a peaking in failures as the majority of the original transistors failed. Another peak would occur at about 2,200 hours, as the bulk of the replacements failed. This later peak would be

Table 5–1 FR and MTBF for the transistor test

Frequency Classes (in hours)	Number of Failures	Number Remaining	Operating Hours	FR	MTBF (in hours)
0–50	60	940	48,500	0.00121	825
50–100	40	900	46,000	.00871	1,149
100–200	30	870	88,500	.000345	2,950
200–900	155	715	554,750	.000281	3,580
900–1,000	45	670	69,250	.000652	1,540
1,000–1,100	170	500	58,500	.00292	344
1,100–1,200	180	320	41,000	.00439	228
1,200–1,300	175	145	23,250	.00752	133
1,300–1,400	125	20	8,250	.0152	66
1,400–1,500	20	0	1,000	.020	50
	1,000	0	939,000		939

smaller than the one at 1,100 hours, however, since all of the replacement transistors did not begin operating at the same time. Continuing in this fashion we find progressively smaller failure peaks at 3,300 and 4,400 hours. At the end of six or seven cycles, there would no longer be a failure peak since a constant rate of failure would have been established.

Once a constant failure rate has been achieved, failures occur on a purely random basis so that the chance of one occurring at any particular point in time is equal to the chance of one occurring at any other point; this is illustrated in Figure 5–7.

Constant failure rates are most often encountered during the normal operating period of the lives of complex parts and equipment. To illustrate this, let us take a closer look at the normal operating period shown in Figure 5–5, covering the transistors' operating history between 200 and 900 hours. This information is repeated in Figure 5–8. If we divide the number of failures in a time period by the number of transistors operating at the start of the period, we see that the result is approximately the same: $25/870 = 0.0287$, $24/845 = 0.0284$, and $20/735 = 0.0272$; this is clear evidence of a constant failure rate.

If the transistors were tested over a long period (say, 5,000 hours), their number increased, and the size of the class intervals reduced, a continuous curve relating the hours of operation and the transistors' reliability could be drawn. This curve (shown in Figure 5–9) is described by the formula:

$$R_t = e^{-t/\text{MTBF}}$$

where R is the probability of operating until t time without a failure and MTBF is the average mean time between failures, which is the constant failure rate.[3]

[3] The letter e represents the Napierian base of natural logarithms and is equal to 2.7183.

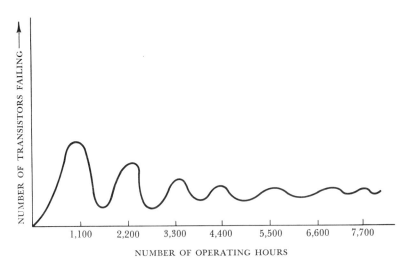

Figure 5–7 Evolution of a random-failure rate

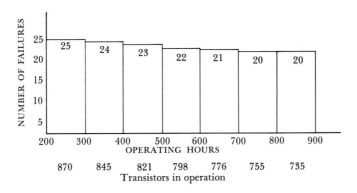

Figure 5–8 Transistor failures 200–900 hours

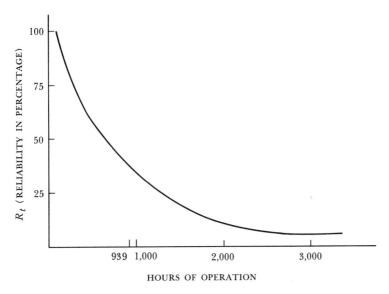

Figure 5–9 Exponential reliability curve

Thus, the probability of a transistor operating for a designed life of 939 hours can be calculated from the formula as follows:

$$R_{939} = e^{-t/\text{MTBF}}$$

$$= e^{-939/939} = e^{-1} = \frac{1}{e} = \frac{1}{2.7183}$$

$$= 0.37 = 37 \text{ percent}$$

Thus, if we are looking for a transistor with a high probability of operating for at least its intended lifetime, the ratio of the failure-free operating time to the MTBF must be small. In other words, the MTBF must be many times greater than the period over which the failure-free operation is desired. For example, to assure a 90 percent probability that a transistor will operate perfectly during an intended life span of 939 hours:

$$0.90 = e^{-939/\text{MTBF}}$$

$$0.90 = \frac{1}{2.7183^{939/\text{MTBF}}}$$

$$\text{MTBF} = 3{,}240 \text{ hours}$$

Notice that the MTBF is over three times the length of the designed lifetime.

Combined Reliability

So far we have confined our discussion to methods of measuring the reliability of a single part or component. In practice, however, a final product is usually made up of many parts, or components, and each one has its own rate of reliability.

To measure the reliability of products in which a failure of any part causes the entire assembly to be inoperative, we simply find the product of the individual reliabilities as follows:

$$R_S = R_{t_1} \times R_{t_2} \times R_{t_3} \times \cdots \times R_{t_n}$$

where R_S = system reliability

   R_{t_1} = reliability of component 1, etc.

This method could be used to measure the reliability of a product such as the one depicted in Figure 5–10.

Where there are enough data available on product performance so that management can tell that individual parts are failing at a constant rate, overall product reliability may be computed according to the formula:

$$R_S = (e^{-t/\text{MTBF}_1})(e^{-t/\text{MTBF}_2}) \cdots (e^{-t/\text{MTBF}_n})$$

If the failure rate (FR) is substituted for the MTBF, the equation becomes:

$$R_S = (e^{-(t)\text{FR}_1})(e^{-(t)\text{FR}_2}) \cdots (e^{-(t)\text{FR}_n})$$

and it can be expressed in a shorter form as follows:

$$R_S = e^{-t(\text{FR}_1 + \text{FR}_2 + \cdots + \text{FR}_n)}$$

To illustrate the effect that the number of component parts has on a product's reliability, let us consider hypothetical products composed of 1, 10, 100, 1,000, and 10,000 experimental transistors. We know that the designed lifetime for tran-

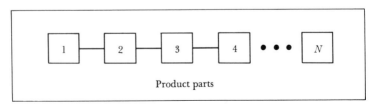

Product parts

Overall product

Figure 5–10   A series-designed product

sistors is 939 hours and that the average failure rate is 1/939, or 0.001065. To determine the reliability of these various hypothetical products over 500 hours of operation, we simply solve the following equations:

$$R_S(1) = e^{-500(0.001065)} = e^{-.533} = 58.4 \text{ percent}$$
$$R_S(10) = e^{-500(10 \times 0.001065)} = e^{-5.33} = 0.456 \text{ percent}$$
$$R_S(100) = e^{-500(100 \times 0.001065)} = e^{-53.3} = \text{less than } 0.00001 \text{ percent}$$
$$R_S(1,000) = e^{-500(1,000 \times 0.001065)} = e^{-533} = \text{less than } 0.00001 \text{ percent}$$
$$R_S(10,000) = e^{-500(10,000 \times 0.001065)} = e^{-5,330} = \text{less than } 0.00001 \text{ percent}$$

This example indicates that the reliability of a piece of equipment drops off quickly as the number of component parts is increased. Figure 5–11 illustrates graphically the rapid reduction in reliability that typically accompanies an increase in the number of parts in a product; this is true even though the individual parts have a high reliability. In addition, notice that there is a significant drop in the overall product reliability when there is a small decrease in component reliability—in this case from 99.9 to 99.0 percent.

Safety Margins

The most common engineering method of attaining design reliability is the use of safety margins. Bridges are usually constructed to carry three, four, or even ten times the normal expected load as a safety factor to overcome any possible design shortcomings and to compensate for any unforeseen stresses. This safety factor also helps to allow for the inevitable variations in construction material, which cause the true capacity of a bridge to differ somewhat from its designed strength. Figure 5–12 depicts the distribution of stresses and strength of a typical bridge member. Here we see that the mean expected stress is 10,000 pounds per square inch. Having established this fact, the engineer designed the member to withstand a load of 30,000 pounds per square inch. Notice that even with this safety margin there is some overlap of stress and strength in which failures could occur.

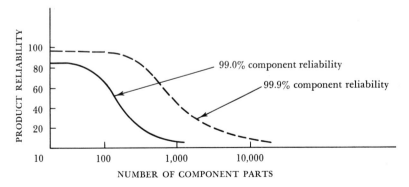

Figure 5–11 Reliability and product complexity

SOURCE: This table is adapted from R. R. Landers, *Reliability and Product Assurance* (Englewood Cliffs, N. J.: Prentice-Hall, 1963), p. 340.

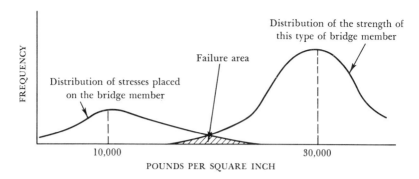

FREQUENCY

Distribution of the strength of
this type of bridge member

Failure area

Distribution of stresses placed
on the bridge member

10,000　　　　　　　　　　30,000

POUNDS PER SQUARE INCH

Figure 5–12 Product stress and strength distributions. The curve at the right shows the distribution of loads at which test girders of this type failed.

In the manufacture of other products where failure is considered particularly costly, the safety margin will often be set from five to twelve standard deviations above the mean expected stress. Here again a tradeoff is involved—the "costs" of failure are balanced against the costs of increasing the reliability or minimizing the chance of failure. In some instances, the margin of safety reflects what is termed the *state of the art*. Current technology in the field of electrical resistors and capacitors makes high safety margins for normal stress in such products as television sets an easily and economically attainable objective. However, to set comparable safety margins for the tubes and transistors in the same TV sets would, at present, be quite costly.

Derating

Another way of providing a quality safety margin is to derate parts, which is the process of assigning a simple task to a part that is designed for a more difficult job. If, for example, a power supply that was originally designed to operate at a temperature of 75°C were used on jobs where the operating temperature was only 50°C, it would be derated. Since less stress is put on the equipment, the net effect is a decrease in failures.

Redundancy

Product reliability can also be increased by building into the design of the product alternate means of producing the output. This is done so that if one path fails, another can accomplish the job; alternate facilities are called *redundant*. For example, hospitals usually have redundant power sources so that if the ordinary source fails, an emergency supply is available which can keep the hospital running. Military rockets often have several "standby units," and many automobiles now have dual braking systems for the same reason.

Either redundant parts may serve a purely standby function (as in the hospital example), or they may be kept in operation at a reduced capacity. When they are kept in operation, they are referred to as *parallel facilities*. Figure 5–13 is a simplified schematic diagram of a motor assembly with parallel power

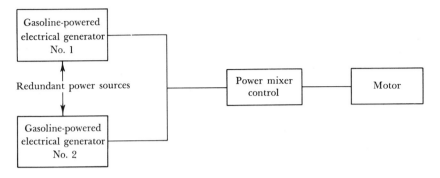

Figure 5–13   Redundant design

sources. Under normal conditions each works at half capacity; in effect, these power sources are derated. If one does fail, the other is capable of picking up the slack immediately.

This approach is often used to launch new production or information systems. Before a new system takes over completely, it is run parallel to the existing one so that if there are still defects in the design of the new system, the output of the existing one can be used until the defects are remedied.

As a rule, redundant paths are employed only when other means of achieving reliability do not work. The reason is, of course, that it can be extremely expensive to have this productive capacity sitting idle. For instance, in a rocket, redundant power supplies raise both the cost and the weight of the rocket.

Production Interaction

Once management has decided upon a suitable product design, it goes to production. Design models are built in a model shop by skilled craftsmen to guide the semiskilled workers on the production line. Between the mass-produced item and the prototype model there is often some slippage in reliability. To guard against this slippage, either the design specifications are changed, or the production effectiveness is raised, or both. In Chapter 21 we will examine the role of production in product effectiveness and the function of production quality control.

Questions and Problems

1. What is meant by product quality?
2. What are management's responsibilities with respect to the quality of a company's product?
3. What is reliability engineering?
4. What costs are involved in quality-assurance considerations?
5. How is product reliability measured?
6. What is a failure rate?
7. How does "infant mortality" enter into quality considerations?
8. In what ways can a product's reliability be increased?
9. "Quality control encompasses specifications, production of quality work, and in-

spection; all of these functions ideally should be the task of the direct worker and line supervisors." Comment on this statement.

10. How do the number of components in a product affect its reliability?
11. Should management strive for the same quality level in all parts that go into a product?
12. "Quality is designed in a product, not manufactured into it." Comment on this statement.
13. How are reliability engineering, quality assurance, and usage related in setting a product's total quality?
14. Is product quality a production responsibility?
15. How does reliability measure quality with respect to:
    (a) automobile tires
    (b) a fire alarm system
    (c) a patent medicine
    (d) a toaster
    (e) steel bridge girders
    (f) a lathe
16. Can you differentiate between design quality and manufacturing quality?

References

Bazovsky, I., *Reliability: Theory and Practice,* Prentice-Hall, Englewood Cliffs, N.J., 1961.

Caplen, R. H., *A Practical Approach to Quality Control,* Auerbach, Princeton, N.J., 1970.

Duncan, A. J., *Quality Control and Industrial Statistics,* 3rd ed., Irwin, Homewood, Ill., 1965.

Enrick, N. L., *Quality Control and Reliability,* Textile Book Service, Metuchen, N.J., 1969.

Feigenbaum, A. V., *Total Quality Control,* McGraw-Hill, New York, 1961.

Fuchs, I., "Product Failures: Causes and Prevention," *Mechanical Engineering,* Vol. 86, No. 2, Feb. 1964, pp. 36–39.

Gilmore, H. L., and Schwartz, H. C., *Integrated Product Testing and Evaluation,* Wiley, New York, 1969.

Grant, E. L., *Statistical Quality Control,* 3rd ed., McGraw-Hill, New York, 1964.

Haddon, M., "Guaranteed Reliability, Part 1," *Industrial Quality Control,* Vol. 21, No. 8, Feb. 1965, pp. 390–392.

Hansen, B., *Quality Control,* Prentice-Hall, Englewood Cliffs, N.J., 1963.

Harris, D. H., and Chaney, F. B., *Human Factors in Quality Assurance,* Wiley, New York, 1969.

Kuehn, A., and Day, R., "Strategy of Product Quality," *Harvard Business Review,* Vol. 40, No. 6, Nov. 1962.

Landers, R. R., *Reliability and Product Assurance,* Prentice-Hall, Englewood Cliffs, N.J., 1963.

Shewhart, W. A., *Economic Control of Quality of Manufactured Product,* Van Nostrand, Princeton, N.J., 1931.

Smith, C. S., *Quality and Reliability,* Pitman, New York, 1969.

Starr, M. K., *Product Design and Decision Theory,* Prentice-Hall, Englewood Cliffs, N.J., 1963.

6

Product-Line Determination

Chapters 4 and 5 presented the broad managerial aspects of product design and development. This chapter narrows the perspective to the problem of determining specifically *what* products or services a company should produce and market. Almost every aspect of a company's operations is affected by the nature of its output. The revenues derived from marketing the product line must cover input and operating costs, and they must allow for profits. This means that decisions regarding plant scale and location, selection and layout of facilities, and design of a materials handling system must all reflect the conditions established by the company's product line. Similarly, the size and composition of the labor force and the quantity and kinds of materials purchased are directly related to the end product. In short, all management decisions specifying the products that are to be manufactured will influence *all* of the firm's production activities.

Evaluation of New Product Lines

A product line is not fixed or static; it is always undergoing change. Thus, decision making in this area must be a continuous process, for to maintain an existing family of products without change over time, whether by default or design, amounts to a decision not to alter the company's offerings to its market. Since the market itself is in flux, the firm's offerings must keep pace; so management has to continually make decisions on proposed additions, modifications, and deletions in its product line, as well as deciding when and how these changes should be made. Although these problems may be stated simply, they do not lend themselves to simple, clear-cut solutions. In this chapter we will attempt to outline a very general decision approach that includes many techniques; for discussion purposes we will divide these techniques into two categories: *market research* and *economic feasibility.*

Market research—the study of external factors that may affect a company's product line—deals with marketplace forces that are hard to define and measure, and over which any one firm can usually exercise only minimal control. Economic feasibility, on the other hand, deals with the operating specifics of an individual firm that affect its product line. Data of this type are more readily available and can be measured more precisely; furthermore, management can exert a greater degree of influence or control in this area.

Market Research

In capsule form, the basic approach used by market research when gauging the salability of an item is to ask the man who knows—the consumer. One widely used method of market research is the questionnaire survey. Here, a list of carefully phrased questions is used either to guide a personal interview or to elicit the desired information on a written questionnaire. But designing a questionnaire that can provide useful, unbiased information with a minimum of questions is an art that few people possess. Because of this and because special skills are also required to conduct interviews and to interpret accumulated data, market research is dominated by specialists. As a result, the cost of these services is high; surveys to test the market for industrial products may range from $100 to $200 per interview, for example.

In the performance of a study, statistical methods are generally employed. The potential market, or "universe," is normally so large that it can only be investigated by a sampling process. Many methods of statistical sampling have been developed to insure that the data obtained are representative and meaningful. Even with these techniques, however, interpreting the material can be difficult if the problems and data are unique. Care must be taken in interpretation to avoid biasing the results with preconceived ideas about the outcome of the study; it is all too easy to make statistical evidence fit a predetermined pattern.

The information developed by means of a market survey should indicate the dimensions of a potential market in quantities over time for alternate product characteristics, alternate prices, and alternate distribution of sales in the marketplace. In addition, predictable fluctuations such as seasonal variations, if significant, should be delineated. Clearly, this type of information can be extremely useful, not only for selecting new products, but for evaluating existing ones and for guiding product development programs already in progress. Without such guidelines it is extremely difficult to distinguish between laboratory curiosities and products with sound commercial potentialities. On the other hand, given complete freedom, a research program can run far afield from the study of market demand, and few firms can afford to let that happen. Product research involves substantial operating costs, and launching the new product itself (including the expense of advertising, distribution, and production) represents even greater costs. Even major companies have acknowledged their inability to launch all of the potentially salable new product ideas developed in their research laboratories; at present only about two out of every five of these ideas actually become salable products. The reason, as we have said, is that the costs of developing and marketing a new product are quite high and the required time cycle can extend over many years. Therefore, a high premium is placed on selecting the best sales opportunities; even well-conceived products can miss the mark in terms of consumer acceptance.

Product timing In addition to its use in evaluation of product characteristics and prices, market research can also help determine when a product should be launched. This is an important contribution because the time at which a product is introduced can be crucial to its success. Many believe that a classic example of this point was the Edsel automobile, introduced by the Ford Motor Company just in time to be caught by the recession of 1957. This competitively designed and priced automobile never recovered from its initial inability to sell in a market that was not in a buying mood. Thus, in considering the feasibility of alternative products, management must evaluate their respective time cycles; on occasion it may be necessary to abandon internal development in favor of buying and marketing another company's products in order to reach the market at the proper time. In other words, the make-or-buy decision, which is generally associated with finished products and components, also applies to the design and development of new products and subassemblies.

So far we have confined our discussion of market research to its uses in evaluating a company's own products. In addition to this, however, market research can assess new competitive products and the market position of competitive firms; information on a competitor's position is invaluable in product planning.

Other sources of market information It should not be concluded, however, that the consumer is the only source of product-line information; there are a number of readily available sources of secondary data that can be tapped at relatively low cost. The most important of these sources are publications such as *Thomas' Register, Moody's Industrial Manual, Standard & Poor's Corporation Records*, and *Dun's Review & Modern Industry*, all of which contain up-to-date information on new products and company plans.

In addition to these external sources of market data, a company may refer to its own records of past sales. The computer now makes it possible for companies to build *simulation models* of the marketing areas in which they propose to sell their product. These mathematical models attempt to describe as realistically as possible the characteristics of the marketplace and the probable reactions of customers and competitive firms therein. The possible results of alternative courses of action may then be tested by simulation. Building models of this sort is a very complex process because of the vast number of factors involved; even the most sophisticated models are still gross simplifications of reality. The results are not truly predictive of reality, but they do enable a firm to obtain general information about the marketplace and to make approximate forecasts of demand.

Economic Feasibility

Once a firm has gathered all the information it can on the degree of market acceptability for its product, it must consider the economics involved. Since considerable money is required to design, develop, and launch a product, most firms allocate funds separately at each stage of product development. Frequently a fixed percentage of income, say 5 percent, is earmarked for the introduction of new products. Since this is only a gross allocation, the funds must then be assigned to individual projects. Generally, products with the greatest expected return on investment are given priority. To determine a product's profitability, management must first estimate the product's funding requirements and then balance these against its anticipated revenues. Initially this entails a projection of the costs for the design and development of the new product.

Product-development expenditure   The expenditures for the launching of a new product normally take the form of the curve depicted in Figure 6–1. Here, we see that heavy expenditures are made during the design and development phases and in the establishment of an appropriate marketing structure. The expenditure rate drops thereafter as the firm confines its efforts to normal product improvements and to making adjustments in marketing. In other words, the bulk of the costs are incurred before a product reaches the marketplace. This means that errors in judgment on product-line changes can be extremely costly, and it underscores the importance of reliable marketing information.

Product revenues   The sales revenues that will accrue from a new product tend to follow an S-shaped curve as shown in Figure 6–2. The returns during the pilot and early production stages are relatively low because the product has usually not yet gained acceptance, and there are still production and marketing

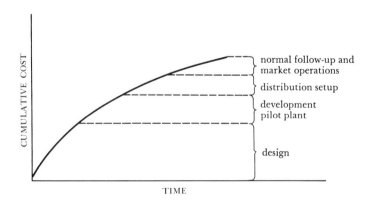

Figure 6–1   Product-launching costs over time

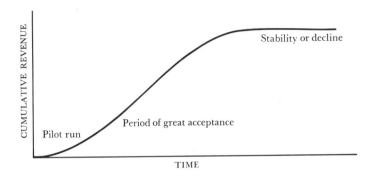

Figure 6–2   Product revenue over time

problems to be resolved. Once the product is established, however, and has been recognized and accepted, the revenue stream accelerates rapidly. In fact, increased sales volumes may generate an interest in developing more efficient manufacturing methods to earn even greater profits. The period of rapid acceleration then tapers off as the market becomes saturated and sales stabilize or decline. At this point replacement sales become important, and competition from new or substitute products increases.

Product financial plans   By plotting the investment and revenue curves on the same graph, management may construct an overall product financial plan, as illustrated in Figure 6–3. The shaded area represents a drain from the company's capital budget. The break-even point indicates both the length of time needed before the product breaks even and the amount of sales dollars at which it will break even. The area labeled "Profit" shows the size of the positive returns.

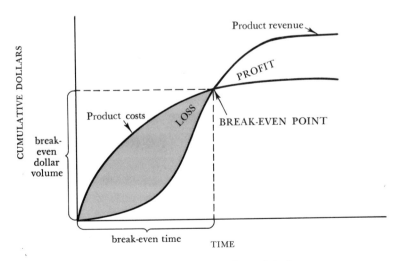

Figure 6–3   Product financial plan

Break-even Charts

The product financial plan shown in Figure 6–3 illustrates one use of a commonly used managerial tool of analysis called the break-even chart. Because of the widespread use of break-even charts and their contribution to managerial decision making, a detailed analysis of the technique will now be presented.

A break-even chart graphically presents the relationship between the volume of production and sales and the amount of income and expenditure. It can be prepared on the basis of historical data or on the basis of figures budgeted for the future. The chief advantage of using a break-even chart is that it enables one to reduce to a single sheet of paper significant information regarding past, present, or future operations.

The typical break-even chart is illustrated in Figure 6–4. Theoretically we know that the break-even point occurs when sales revenue (R) is exactly equal to the total operating cost $(FC + VC)$. Thus, in Figure 6–4 we see that the break-even point is located at the intersection of R and $FC + VC$. As the cost and revenue lines shift, the break-even point will also shift. Thus, the break-even chart shows the impact of changing costs and prices on the break-even volume and on the total profit or loss.

The chart is constructed with the horizontal axis measuring units of output or sales (volume) and the vertical axis representing dollars of cost or revenue.

Frequently it is difficult to choose a unit of volume for the horizontal axis. Sometimes a simple unit such as tons of steel, cases of soda, and number of guest days (hospital or motel) can be used. However, when the variety of prod-

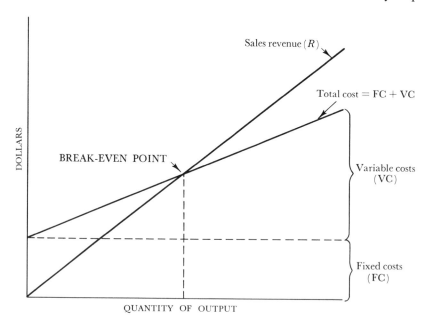

Figure 6–4   The break-even chart

ucts is great, indirect measures of volume are often employed. For example, a printing shop might use man-hours of labor, and a fabrication shop might use machine-hours.

In Figure 6–4 we have assumed that the price will remain constant over the entire period studied. Often this is not the case. Depending upon the elasticity of demand facing a given firm, significant price cuts may be necessary at certain times in order to achieve a given volume of sales. In such cases the revenue line would be a curve rather than a straight line; it would increase at a decreasing rate. Furthermore, it is often impractical to segregate the firm's costs into "fixed" and "variable" categories as indicated on the chart. It should also be noted that variable costs here are assumed to have no value when there is no production and to remain constant per unit over the entire operating range. This is the only way in which we can produce a straight line for variable costs. However, it would be difficult indeed to find a company with operating costs that behave exactly in this manner. Direct labor and direct material are often cited as variable costs, for example, yet such factors as setup costs[1] and learning[2] prevent labor from following a straight line in actual practice. Other factors, such as quantity discounts, make material costs really nonlinear. Similarly, the number of purely fixed costs is small, too. Costs such as supervision, maintenance, and plant safety are commonly considered fixed, yet they will be subject to some variation as the level of activity in the plant is altered. In short, although the concept of the break-even chart is a simple one, the effective use of this tool requires extreme care lest the results produced be unrealistic and consequently of little value.

To illustrate how the break-even chart may be effectively used, consider the annual budget data for a medium-sized manufacturer of bicycles presented in Table 6–1.

The break-even chart that appears in Figure 6–5 was drawn from the data in this table. Plotting the revenue line was relatively easy, since it is assumed that the price received for bicycles is independent of the quantity sold. This is a realistic assumption because of the highly developed market for low-price bicycles. Because of the problems previously discussed, however, the lines representing costs are not so easily drawn. The most realistic approach is to draw a line showing the magnitude and variation of each cost element by plotting and connecting the respective costs for the two different volumes indicated in Table 6–1—in this case 60,000 and 160,000 bicycles. The two volumes chosen should be far enough apart to assure the validity of the resulting slopes; if 60,000 and 70,000 units had been selected, not enough variation would have been shown. If data for more than two volumes are available, the accuracy of the cost slopes can be increased. One important proviso should be noted, however. The operat-

---

[1] Setup costs occur at the start of production and do not vary with output volume. They are thus more of a fixed than a variable cost.

[2] An employee who starts work on a new product does not reach his true output level until he has gone through a learning period. Thus, in the early stages of production, labor costs per unit are higher than in later stages of production.

Table 6–1 O.K. Bicycle Company operating budget for 197–

Budget, Year 197–	Low Volume	High Volume
Number of units	60,000	160,000
Income (sales price $6 per unit)	$360,000	$960,000
Fixed charges	$200,000	$200,000
Labor	60,000	120,000
Material	60,000	160,000
Other manufacturing costs	80,000	120,000
Total manufacturing cost	$400,000	$600,000
Selling and administrative costs	100,000	150,000
Total cost	$500,000	$750,000

ing volumes considered must be based on the same price and cost. If the data stretch over successive years, and changes in prices and labor rates occur during this period, it will be necessary to adjust prices and costs to a consistent operating level.

The first item usually drawn on a break-even chart is the fixed charges. This cost line is horizontal because "fixed costs" are the same for both volumes. Then

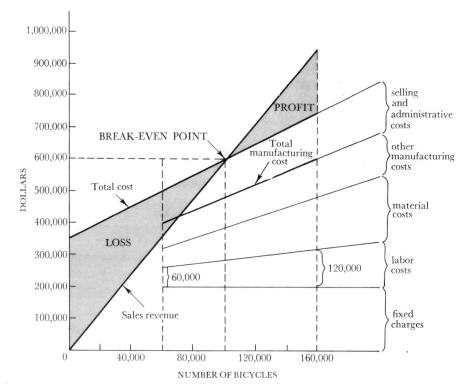

Figure 6–5 O.K. Bicycle Company break-even chart for 197–

the labor line is constructed. This is done by adding the labor costs at the 60,000- and 160,000-unit output levels to the fixed costs at these points. The resultant values—$260,000 and $320,000—determine the labor line. Material costs, other manufacturing costs, and selling and administrative costs are plotted in a similar fashion.

This approach avoids the knotty problem of subdividing each cost element into its fixed and variable components, assuming that the high and low volumes selected delimit the total area of the break-even point and the firm's predicted level of operation. In a break-even analysis it is the magnitude of each cost element that is important, not its composition. If it were necessary to analyze in detail the operating characteristics of the firm at very low volumes, it would probably be necessary to subdivide each cost element into its fixed and variable components so that a suitable break-even chart could be drawn.

It should be noted in this chart that the cost lines extend only between the volumes for which data were available. The assumption is that for any cost element, such as labor, all fixed-cost components have already been accounted for and are reflected in the cost at the lower volume. Hence only purely variable labor costs fluctuate in the operating region between the high and low volume. The difference between high- and low-volume costs is due entirely to the accumulation of variable costs. "Fixed charges" are assumed to be the same at both ends of the operating range. How realistic this assumption is must be assessed in terms of the operating characteristics of each specific case. As a rule, however, the proper selection of the two operating volumes will result in a chart that is accurate within a sufficiently large operating area to eliminate the need for extrapolation of the cost lines in either direction. Such extrapolation is usually risky and difficult to interpret.

The important part of the chart is the region surrounding the break-even point where the total revenue and total cost lines intersect. To the right of this point is an area between revenue and cost lines called the *profit wedge;* to the left of the point the company experiences losses. The size of the profit or loss wedge at a particular output volume indicates the amount of profit or loss the firm will experience at that volume.

Use of the break-even chart   Usually a break-even chart covers a one-year period, but charts can also be constructed for shorter intervals. Because the chart shows the impact of various volumes of output upon profits at a given average price, it answers such important questions as: (1) If unit prices are reduced, by how much must the company increase output in order to keep profits at their present level? (2) If unit prices are increased, how much of a reduction in volume can occur before profits are adversely affected? The break-even chart does not show demand elasticity, so the manager must look to marketing research for this data. However, by indicating how possible price changes can alter a company's break-even point, the break-even chart can show the impact of changes in price and volume on the firm's projection of profit or loss.

This type of chart is also useful in analyzing costs. Depicting the relative significance of each type of cost helps focus cost-reduction efforts in the appropriate areas. Break-even charts show the impact that various volumes have on each type of cost and depict the proportion of total cost that is fixed and variable. Where there is great cost variability with volume, cost-reduction efforts can be fruitful. On the other hand, if a large percentage of costs is fixed, it would be best for a company to focus on sales promotion, since with high fixed costs the best route to large profits is increased volume.

When a break-even chart is used in connection with a cost-reduction program, it is customary to plot the cost in question just under the total cost line in order to facilitate visualization of the impact of cost reduction on the break-even point and profit wedge.

The break-even chart may also be used to portray the company budget. It is often a useful way of providing a meaningful, readily understood summation of all revenue and cost budgets for the planning period in question. Budgetary planning for a wide range of volumes can be indicated on a single break-even chart. Operating profits or losses can thus be visualized at various levels so that management can more readily determine what measures to take.

Finally, this chart may be used to examine proposals for expansion or contraction of company operations. The abandonment of, or additions to, a company's facilities, for example, can have a far-reaching effect on its financial equilibrium, and the break-even chart can provide management with an accurate estimate of this change. Thus, these charts are very helpful when technological changes are introduced, when products are added to or deleted from a firm's line, or whenever a horizontal or vertical merger is contemplated. For example, if the purchase of another company is being considered, a composite break-even chart may reflect such high fixed charges that the break-even point is raised dangerously high, thus indicating that this purchase would be undesirable. On the other hand, it may indicate a significantly wide profit wedge, thus making company prospects very attractive in an expanding market.

In short, the break-even chart is a very useful device for obtaining a simple yet comprehensive view of the operations of an enterprise; as such, it is an aid to decision making. It does not render decision making automatic, however. In examining a break-even chart the executive must take into account the limitations of the cost data presented; only the available cost data can be included. Therefore, predictions and estimates derived from break-even charts must be used with a full recognition of the possible errors in such data. Intangibles, such as the actions of customers and employees and the reactions of competitors, cannot be forecast with any degree of accuracy. Yet such factors can be of great importance. Thus, in the final decision process, the executive must take into account the inevitable inaccuracies in the data stemming from unpredictable factors.

Product Planning

Clearly, accurate predictions of future revenues and expenditures are vital in making a reliable evaluation of a product's potential or in evaluating the relative merits of alternative projects. It is not surprising, therefore, to find that a great deal of industrial research has been directed toward the formulation of more accurate cost and revenue models. Complex equations are often employed to simulate the flow of funds required for a project. These models may then be manipulated to test alternative design, development, and marketing strategies.

Despite the assistance of these models in decisions on product-line changes, past experience is still employed most frequently. Yet the dangers inherent in reliance on historical data can be demonstrated by analyzing one major firm's approach to the launching of color TV sets. This company seemed to base all of its plans and forecasts for the project on its experience with the production and marketing of black-and-white TV. As a result, the color TV expenditure curve proved to be very accurate, but there was little similarity between the revenue curves of black-and white TV and those of color TV sets. Figure 6–6 gives some idea of the size and nature of the disparity. As this company learned to its chagrin, the rate of growth for black-and-white TV was much more rapid than for color TV. Thus, the revenue gap between actual and expected returns placed a heavy burden on the company's financial planning until the sales volume rose to a satisfactory level.

This example also underscores the need for follow-up planning. As product sales figures come in, it is important that the data from the actual experience be fed back into the planning process to improve the accuracy of forecasts. Models, equations, and general predictions must be modified to reflect this market information. In the color TV example, product and market development plans were drastically altered when returns proved to be significantly below expectations. The revised plans enabled the company to distribute the cash flow deficit from the color TV launching over a longer, more realistic time frame so that the financial burden could more easily be carried by the company.

Evaluation of the Existing Product Line

The selection and development of innovative products is a dynamic, and often spectacular, area of product-line planning that receives a great deal of attention. For the going concern, however, planning for the existing product line is of equal

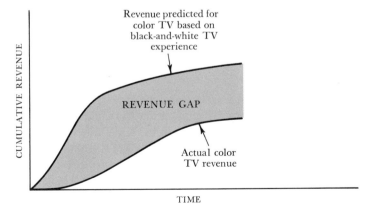

Figure 6–6 Actual and predicted revenue curves for color TV

or greater importance. Indeed, the profitability of current operations is largely determined by this more routine aspect of product planning—the evaluation of existing line items and the design of actions to maximize the company's profit potential.

One of the most perplexing product-line problems facing management is the determination of the optimum degree of product variety; too much variety raises costs, while too little may retard sales.

Product Simplification

One way of coping with this dilemma is to remove those items from the product line that offer unnecessary variety and immaterial differences. This process is generally referred to as *product-line simplification*. The principal impetus for such a program is the desire for increased efficiency and economical production. Too much variety also places a burden upon the advertising and marketing functions, and it makes the record-keeping task of the accounting department unnecessarily complicated. In short, unnecessary products cause waste in all phases of the company's operations.

Product-line simplification can bring impressive savings. For example, before initiating a simplification program, one company was manufacturing 2,000 standard varieties of writing paper; another firm was producing hospital beds of 33 different lengths, 34 different widths, and 44 different heights; and a milk company was using 49 different types of milk bottles. After simplification the number of standard types of writing paper was reduced to less than 300, 8 standard varieties of hospital beds were made, and the number of different types of milk bottles was reduced to 12. These examples were chosen from among hundreds of illustrative cases to show that even in industries where style is *not* an outstanding factor, product lines can be too broad and therefore uneconomical.

When examining a particular product line from this perspective, management must determine if the existing variety is warranted in terms of market demand or if it is simply the result of loose product planning. In making its decision, management should consider four basic criteria, all of which offer sound arguments *in favor* of variety.

1. *Nature of the demand*
2. *Stability of sales and production*
3. *Profit stability*
4. *Utilization of by-products*

Demand   Change and diversity are the essence of fashion. In industries where style is a strong factor, for example, product-line simplification must be sublimated to the need for competitive offerings. In the apparel field, custom tailoring to fit the needs of individual customers can be a very profitable approach; in high-fashion women's clothing, "originals" are a mark of distinction and bring a high price. Similarly, in the home furnishings field, many decorators find that the uniqueness of tables and chairs made to order for the homeowner is a major selling point.

In addition, variety is demanded in certain product lines because the consumer simply cannot find satisfactory substitutes. Thus, although it might be highly economical for a firm to manufacture only one size of metal pipe—say, a pipe that is two inches in diameter—it would be uneconomical for the consumer to use a pipe of this size if a half-inch one would do the job. Component manufacturers in particular are faced with the problem of maintaining a large variety in certain product lines; they must be able to satisfy the specifications established by the makers of the final products. Consider the producers of automobile tires and spark plugs who must make an endless variety to meet the specifications of automobile manufacturers.

Another common reason for continuing an "unnecessary" degree of product variety stems from the fact that customers often seem to prefer to do business with a company that can supply them with a "full line." Companies that offer a more economical, but limited, variety of products may thus be at a competitive disadvantage. This is particularly true in the appliance field, where consumers seem to become attached to a brand name and prefer to buy a full range of appliances of that brand. The same is true in grocery supermarkets and department stores; many supermarket chains give their store managers authority to stock small amounts of special items to satisfy customers even when money is lost on these products. In department stores, the stationery department will often stock such things as 5-cent erasers, at a loss, to maintain a full range of stationery products.

Stability of sales and production Although it may seem paradoxical, many industries diversify their product lines to promote stability. Most companies would like the demand for their products to be constant throughout the year, since this would enable them to plan a stable and economical factory operation. However, they must usually face the problem of some degree of seasonal demand, and diversification is one way of overcoming this obstacle. In past years, ice companies sold coal in the winter to balance the summer ice production. A modern example is a sporting goods firm which produced fiberglass fishing rods and the accompanying reels. As could be expected, their sales were concentrated in the summer months. To balance the seasonality, they looked for a product for the winter months, concentrating their search in the sporting world where their production and marketing know-how rested. They now produce ski equipment and have smoothed their production problems greatly.

Excess or idle capacity in off-season periods has provided a great impetus for diversification programs. The result can be interesting. For example, many companies not previously in the subcontracting business have actively sought out opportunities to turn out components and subassemblies for other companies as a means of balancing their own work load. A prominent producer of canned goods acts as a printing house for other canning companies in the off-season simply because it cannot keep its label-printing shop busy with company work throughout the year. Thus, during the company's own peak period the printing shop does only internal work, but during the slack season it does outside work as well. Frequently the products or services resulting from diversification are offered at attractive low prices in order to obtain the work load required to liquidate overhead costs. These products may not yield much profit, but as long as they contribute to the overhead—that is, cover their own variable costs with something left to pay the costs of the main production facility—they fulfill their purpose.

This same reason for diversification may be applied to the sales field. For example, many companies think that their unit selling expenses can be reduced if their salesmen have a larger line to sell. This thought frequently prompts the addition of products for which existing customers represent a potential market. There are pitfalls to be avoided in this approach, of course. Products with which a firm has neither production nor sales experience should be added only after a very thorough analysis of the dangers involved. Consider, for example, the fate of many firms (previously classified as airframe, chemical, and agricultural) who rushed headlong into the electronics business and, to their dismay, encountered staggering entry costs. In some cases the companies' survival was jeopardized because of the addition of this new product line.

Profit stability Still another factor encouraging product diversification is the possibility of attaining greater profit stability. By diversifying its product line, a company hopes that it may protect itself against a decline in the demand for a single product or the loss of a major customer. To achieve this objective, management should give careful thought to the cyclical aspects of the economy in its product planning. Depression and prosperity, the two cyclical extremes, will produce quite different market potentials for "necessary" goods as against luxury items. Similarly, the impact of cyclical fluctuations will vary depending upon whether a particular product is a consumer good or a capital good. This approach to profit stability can be quite successful, however. Dupont, for example, has been able to achieve a relatively stable profit and loss statement by marketing a wide range of products, including rayon, cellophane, paints, chemicals, and dyes, to many different groups of customers.

Utilization of by-products Finally, the nature of a company's raw materials and production processes can lead to a broad product line. Certain processes lead naturally to the development of profitable by-products, which enlarge the product line. A prime example is the meat-packing industry, where it is said that there is a market for every part of a pig except the oink and that this item is being studied. The petroleum industry also derives a good portion of its profits from by-products. Although primarily interested in the production and distribution of gasoline and oil, most petroleum companies also include cleaning fluids, chemicals, waxes, insect sprays, and leather dressings in their product lines. By-product diversification depends for its success in large part upon the imagination of the marketing and engineering personnel.

Product-Line Standardization

The question then arises: How can a firm achieve the benefits of a broad product line and at the same time enjoy the fruits of simplification? One partial

Courtesy of Motorola, Inc.

This television set with "works in the drawer" has ten plug-in circuits that can be individually removed and replaced when necessary. The use of modules cuts production costs for the company as well as repair costs for the consumer.

solution is the *modular design* concept, which involves the development of component "building blocks" that can be assembled in many different combinations and configurations in order to provide the variety of products desired. The automobile industry began to enjoy great success, for example, when it discovered that a great many automobile models could be produced by varying the combination of modules. To differentiate the automobiles still further, the industry found that it had tremendous potential in simply varying the trim items. The same approach has been employed with success in the home appliance and machine tool industries.

For a company that does not have a building-block approach, the development of a modular product is a long-term project. A large investment is required, primarily during the design and development phases. First, management must carefully review the designs of current-line items to determine to what extent they may be divided into standard modules. Then these modules must be designed and developed, which generally means that the production process must be redesigned to some extent. These expenditures must be carefully weighed against possible savings that might be derived. To make certain that this is done, many companies have adopted the policy of applying the modular concept to products on a selective, piecemeal basis.

The modular concept can best be applied to new product lines when product planning is done in terms of a family of products that will be offered for sale. In this way standard components can be utilized in a wide variety of products, and the added engineering costs can easily be recouped from production efficiencies. This is not to say that every variety of product must be developed and introduced to the market at the same time. In fact, it is common practice to add and delete products over an extended period of time. This practice tends to fulfill the customer's desire for diversity as well as to maximize the sales volume derived from the product family. It also means that the high initial design and development costs can be spread over a large base, thus, as a rule, permitting greater profits.

Many advocates of standardization claim that it yields the best results when confined to the component level. The electronics industry, for example, for years has used standard 19-inch chassis and racks on which to mount communications equipment. Doors, windows, and cinder blocks are some of the standardized components that are used in construction. Indeed, in the manufacture of many products, standardization of components is not just desirable; it is almost essential. If such things as bolts, nuts, screw and pipe threads, and fittings were not standardized, the manufacture and repair of equipment containing these items would be considerably more complicated and expensive.

It might be asked why the standardization of components is not more widespread. The answer lies in the fact that proposed standard sizes and shapes must be approved by both the makers and users, both of whom have been dependent upon their ability to be different, or unique, in order to survive. Professional societies and trade associations, which have tried for many years to introduce greater industrial standardization, report slow progress because of these factors.

A Balanced Product Line

Simplification, diversification, and standardization *each* contribute to stability and profitability if properly applied. They are *not* mutually exclusive approaches. A sound product line can be developed only by creating a mixture of these three factors that is best suited to a particular company's product design, productive capability, channel of distribution, and market. These factors are dynamic and vary constantly, so periodic assessment is required in order to frame policies and operations that will be tailored to changing needs. For example, a drop in the market demand for a particular product may encourage diversification as a means of recouping lost revenue. Interest in simplification is apt to arise when multiple products create excessive downtime for production machinery and equipment, or when the sales force has been so overloaded and confused by the variety of products that it is unable to sell and service them all properly, or when the controller decides that working-capital requirements are excessive because of slow inventory turnover. The push toward standardization, in turn, may result from the desire to lower production cost.

The challenge confronting management is to create a competitive and profitable product line. The achievement of this objective depends to a large extent upon management's ability and imagination in determining the company's unique blend of the techniques of standardization, simplification, and diversification. Fortunately, there are many proved decision approaches available to management that will help in analyzing a product line; three of these will be discussed in the remainder of this chapter.

Percentage of Sales Volume

The first step in attempting to achieve a balanced product line is to attach a relative value to the individual products within a company's product line. One method of doing this is to analyze the sales volume according to the percentage of revenue that is attributable to each product. Usually this is done not only for the current time period but also for some specified past period. The amount of sales data included depends upon the stability of the product line. For products that sell well for many years and have stable sales histories, data going back five or more years may be used. Other products lose their marketability after a matter of months, and thus historical data are of little use. In other cases the availability of past data is the determining factor in their use; despite the fact that the product may have sold well for a number of years, reliable data may exist for only a short period. This emphasizes the fact that the accumulation of historical data is often necessary for effective product planning and that where data are unobtainable a plan for their future accumulation should be made.

To illustrate, sales data are presented for a hypothetical ball bearing manufacturer. Table 6–2 summarizes the percentage of sales revenue applicable to various types of bearings for the past year. Figure 6–7 depicts graphically the sales history of one particular bearing, Model ABC, over the past five years.

Table 6–2 tells us that Model ABC ball bearing provided 3.3 percent of the annual sales volume during the past year, and Figure 6–7 shows that its sales have dropped from a high of 2,800 units five years ago to only 1,000 units this past year. Since the overall company sales have been fairly stable during the five-year period, it is apparent that there has been a decrease in the relative importance of this model in terms of its contribution to profits. Furthermore, it seems likely that management can expect a continuation of the downward trend unless a shift occurs in the market demand or in the company's distribution strategy.

Presenting the data in this fashion highlights the need to reassess the marketing approach followed for this product, but additional information is required for the assessment. The company's history can be compared with the industry pattern, for example. If the product's downward trend for the ABC Company

Table 6–2 ABC Ball Bearing Company.
Product percentage sales summary, 197–

Product	Units Sold	Average Price	Total Sales	Percentage of Total Company Sales
Model ABC	1,000	$2.00	$ 2,000	3.3
Model DEF	10,000	1.50	15,000	24.4
Model GHI	20,000	1.75	35,000	56.9
Model JKL	2,000	2.50	5,000	8.1
Model MNO	1,500	3.00	4,500	7.3
			$61,500	100.0

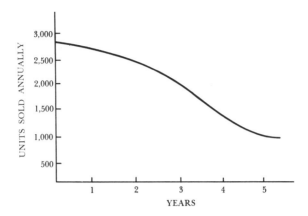

Figure 6–7 ABC Ball Bearing Company. Model ABC sales trend summary

has occurred during a period of expanding industry sales for this type of bearing, management can be relatively sure that its approach is at fault. On the other hand, if total industry sales of this type of bearing are declining, then the company's trend can be considered normal. The sales data could also be augmented by profit information. If the firm is earning a low profit on sales of the bearing, its production might be stopped altogether and these funds diverted to more profitable products in an effort to maintain the firm's share of the market.

There are many other ways of analyzing sales data, of course. Formal presentation of the data merely serves as a springboard toward developing meaningful information for management.

Product Contribution

Another method of appraising a product line is to develop a *contribution ratio* for each product. The contribution ratio is designed to measure the impact of management decisions concerning volume, cost reduction, and selling price on the company's profit potential.

Contribution, C, is defined as the difference between unit sales price and unit variable costs:

(1) $$C = I_s - C_v$$

where I_s = unit sales price
C_v = unit variable cost

Using this equation, management can compute the contribution made by a single unit of product, by a whole product line, or by an entire company. Suppose, for example, that a firm manufactured a product with the following cost and sales characteristics:

> Sales price per unit = \$8.00
> Total variable cost per unit = \$3.00
> Fixed cost for the operating range = \$20,000

According to equation (1), the contribution per unit of sales would be

$$C = I_s - C_v$$
$$= \$8.00 - \$3.00 = \$5.00$$

Like the break-even point, contribution is affected by changes in the selling price and variable expenses, but not by changes in the fixed operating costs. Thus, the relationship between contribution and the break-even point for the firm is a direct and simple one. When the total contribution, which is equal to the sales volume times the contribution per unit, equals the total fixed costs, the firm breaks even. To liquidate its fixed costs, therefore, the firm must produce and sell the break-even number of units:

$$\text{Break-even volume} = \frac{FC}{C}$$
$$= \frac{\$20,000}{\$5.00} = 4,000 \text{ units}$$

The values calculated for the contribution and the break-even volume tell the firm that for each unit over 4,000 that is produced and sold, the firm will make $5.00 profit.

The *contribution ratio,* CR, represents contribution as a percentage of net sales income. It is expressed mathematically as

$$CR = \frac{I_s - C_v}{I_s}$$

For our example, the contribution ratio is found to be

$$CR = \frac{\$8.00 - \$3.00}{\$8.00} = 0.625$$

The interpretation of this value is that 62.5 percent of each sales dollar is available to liquidate fixed costs and to furnish a profit.

Use of the contribution ratio The contribution ratio is a helpful guide to top management in its formulation of general company policy. When this ratio is high, it is usually best to pursue a strong sales promotion campaign, because in such a situation a relatively small increase in sales volume can produce a large increase in profits. Conversely, a small decrease in sales volume can have a heavy impact on the firm's profits. On the other hand, when the contribution ratio is low, the impact of volume changes in either direction is relatively small. Therefore, substantial increases in sales would be necessary before profits could rise significantly. In such a situation, profits would probably be improved far more by a successful cost-reduction program.

Imagine, for example, a small cabinet-making company with a contribution ratio of approximately 15 percent. In a recent fiscal year this company was just able to break even on its share of the market. An examination of this problem revealed that the best way to increase profits was to improve the contribution ratio. Intense competition militated against capturing a much larger share of the market, and the relative inelasticity of demand for this product made price decreases unwise. Therefore, the company chose to reduce variable operating costs. This was done by investing in new machinery. As capital was substituted for labor, the magnitude of fixed costs rose but variable costs dropped. This in turn raised the company's contribution ratio to 24 percent and, more important, lowered the break-even point by 18 percent. In this way the firm was able to show a profit of approximately 5 percent even though it had the same sales volume as the preceding year.

The contribution ratio is also helpful in assessing the relative earning power of different company products. This tool, in conjunction with the break-even chart (which can be drawn for individual products), can guide managerial decisions on selling price, volume, cost reduction, and allocation of fixed costs among the several products. Consider the example of a manufacturer of automobile tires. The company distributes 70 percent of its tires through a large chain of auto supply stores and markets the remaining 30 percent through its own franchised dealers. To maintain its relationship with the chain, the company reduced the price of the largest-selling tire by 15 percent. This tire represented approximately 50 percent of the firm's sales volume. As a result of this price decrease, the firm's break-even point rose from $4,200,000 to $5,300,000. This change was extremely significant since the company's plant capacity can only support annual sales of approximately $5,500,000. If management had examined the probable impact of this change in selling price on its contribution ratios, it is doubtful that it would have acted as it did. Before the price decrease the ratio for dealer sales was 25 percent and for chain-store operations 15 percent. The contribution ratio for the whole company was 18 percent. After the price decrease, these three ratios were 25 percent, 10 percent, and 14.5 percent, respectively. These figures indicated that the company should seek a substantial increase in sales volume. Unfortunately, however, such action would have been inconsistent with existing plant capacity, and so the company was forced to reappraise its operating policies.

The contribution ratio can also be used to assess the relative profitability of specific company products. When management is contemplating the addition of new items to the product mix or the deletion of old ones, the contribution ratio can help them appraise product performance accurately.

Finally, in the planning of production operations it is frequently necessary to assign manufacturing priorities for specific products because there is just not enough capacity to make all of the different products ordered. This is particularly true for companies that manufacture a large number of small-volume products. By ranking products according to their contribution, a manager can gain considerable insight into the desirability of producing or not producing particular items.

Profit–Volume (P-V) Analysis

Since the contribution ratio relates the rate of change of a product's contribution to profits and its sales volume, it is often called a profit–volume, or P-V, ratio. Products with a relatively high P-V ratio provide large profits when the break-even volume has been surpassed; conversely, they inflict a large negative impact on a company's profit and loss statement when sales are below the break-even volume.

To facilitate analysis of the P-V ratio, data are usually assembled in a chart that is basically an alternative version of the break-even chart. Figure 6–8 is a P-V chart for the Model 110 ball bearing, based on the following financial data for the previous year.

Sales of 20,000 units @ $10.00/unit	$200,000
Profit	24,000
Fixed costs	66,000

The slope of the P-V ratio line is

$$\text{P-V slope} = \frac{\text{Profit} + \text{Fixed costs}}{\text{Sales dollars}} = \frac{24,000 + 66,000}{200,000} = 0.45$$

The slope of the line may also be determined as follows:

$$\text{P-V slope} = 1 - \frac{\text{Variable costs}}{\text{Sales dollars}} = 1 - \frac{110,000}{200,000} = 0.45$$

By either method the slope of the P-V line indicates the amount of contribution to cost recovery, or profits, that will result from each additional dollar of sales. In the example, for every dollar of sales there is 45 cents of contribution. The break-even point, in terms of number of units sold, is therefore

$$\text{Break-even volume} = \frac{\text{Fixed costs}}{\text{P-V ratio} \times \text{Sales price in dollars}}$$

$$= \frac{66,000}{0.45 \times 10} = 14,667 \text{ units}$$

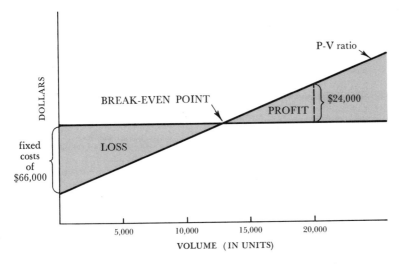

Figure 6–8 P-V analysis—Model 110 ball bearing

The P-V chart is an effective tool for gauging the profit–cost interactions between members of the same product family. Suppose, for example, that the identical production facilities used to manufacture the Model 110 ball bearings are also used to produce other bearings. In that case the question facing management would not be whether the 110 bearing itself was profitable or ought to be discontinued, but rather, what effect would a discontinuation of the bearing have on the cost structure of the entire product line? To analyze this problem, management should examine the operating characteristics of the entire line on a multiproduct P-V chart such as the one shown in Figure 6–9. Notice that in this example the fixed costs remain the same regardless of whether a product is added or dropped from the line. The equipment and labor are on hand and must be paid for whether they are used or not.

To form this multiproduct line, a P-V line is plotted for each of the products under consideration. The P-V line for Product A starts below the horizontal axis at a distance equal to the total fixed costs, which in this case are $66,000. The slope of this segment of the P-V line is equal to the product's contribution ratio, and its length corresponds to the product's production volume as measured along the horizontal axis. The P-V line for Product B then starts where Product A's line ends; Product C's P-V line starts where B's ends, and so forth. If the feasibility of dropping an item from the firm's product line is under consideration, its P-V line is plotted last, thus facilitating identification of the profit that would be forgone if the product were discontinued. A decision to drop the product would move the total profit to that point of the P-V line at which the deleted product began. This occurs because the fixed costs that were formerly covered by this item must now be absorbed by the other products.

The example shown in Figure 6–9 is a simple case. In a more typical situation, each product would have its own fixed costs, and the graph drawn for multiproduct P-V analysis would look like the one in Figure 6–10. The P-V line for

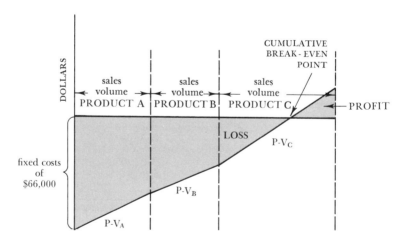

Figure 6–9   Multiproduct P-V analysis

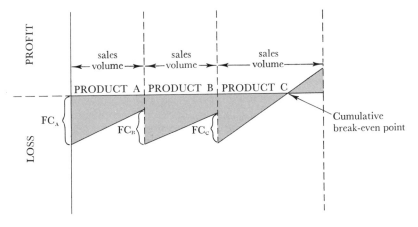

Figure 6–10 Multiproduct P-V analysis with product fixed costs

Product A begins on the vertical axis at the point of the product's fixed costs, and it runs until the dollar sales volume for Product A is reached. At that point the fixed costs are plotted for Product B and then its own P-V line is drawn. In like fashion the fixed costs and P-V lines are drawn for all products. The resulting graph is analyzed in the same way as it was for Figure 6–9.[3]

Margin of safety ratio The P-V analysis can be expanded for the purpose of developing a margin of safety, or MS, ratio. The MS ratio is simply a device for measuring the magnitude of the sales decline that can occur before the firm begins to take a loss on a product. The ratio is calculated as

$$MS = \frac{\text{Net profit}}{\text{Net profit} + \text{Fixed costs}}$$

Thus, in terms of the data applicable to the ball bearing illustration in Figure 6–7, the MS ratio would be

$$MS = \frac{24{,}000}{24{,}000 + 66{,}000} = 26.7\%$$

This calculation means that sales would have to decline 26.7 percent in order to eliminate all of the profits now enjoyed. If the MS ratio for a product turns out to be low, the firm has three possible remedies at its disposal: it may attempt to increase the P-V ratio by increasing the price of the product, it may attempt to increase the sales volume, or it may attempt to decrease the fixed costs. There is no fixed value of the MS ratio that could be called the point at which remedial action should start; this decision must be based on such factors as company experience and economic conditions. As a general rule, however, MS ratios of at least 15 to 25 percent are considered desirable.

[3] This approach can easily be extended to cover cases that have some fixed costs attributable to all products (as in Figure 6-9) and other fixed costs assigned by product (as in Figure 6-10).

Profit Maximization via Linear Programing

The final technique for appraising a product line that we will consider is the application of *simplex linear programing.*

To illustrate this approach we will begin by considering a hypothetical problem. Let us suppose that a manufacturer has been making four different products with one production facility. Each product requires different amounts of inputs, which may be labeled Materials E_1, E_2, and E_3. It takes a fixed amount of inputs to make each unit of output. For example, to make one unit of Product A_1 requires one unit of Material E_1, six units of Material E_2, and three units of Material E_3. These input–output relationships are tabulated as follows:

	Product			
	A_1	A_2	A_3	A_4
Material E_1	1	2	1	2
Material E_2	6	5	3	2
Material E_3	3	4	9	12

The amount of each of these input materials available per week is fixed since the raw materials are a by-product of the company's main production process. Thus, each week there are available

20 units of Material E_1
100 units of Material E_2
75 units of Material E_3

The revenues from each product vary; they are

Product	*Units of Revenue per Unit of Output*
A_1	6
A_2	4
A_3	7
A_4	5

The demand for the products is greater than the company can satisfy. Therefore, the company wishes to determine what product mix will maximize its revenue; that is, it wishes to maximize the equation

$$\text{Revenue} = 6A_1 + 4A_2 + 7A_3 + 5A_4$$

The solution, of course, will be subject to the constraints imposed by the limited supply of inputs. These limitations are listed in the following equations. We see that up to 20 units of Material E_1, 100 units of Material E_2, and 75 units of Material E_3 are available for allocation among Products A_1 through A_4.[4]

---

[4] The symbol $\leq$ stands for "less than or equal to." Thus, in the first equation, for example, it signifies that less than 20 or 20 units of E_1 can be used.

$$1A_1 + 2A_2 + 1A_3 + 2A_4 \leq 20 \, E_1$$
$$6A_1 + 5A_2 + 3A_3 + 2A_4 \leq 100 \, E_2$$
$$3A_1 + 4A_2 + 9A_3 + 12A_4 \leq 75 \, E_3$$

Stated in this manner, the data may be analyzed by means of a linear programing model in order to determine the optimum product mix.

Formulating the matrix The first step in preparing data for linear programing is to set up the equations in matrix form. Each row in the matrix represents an equation; each column represents the variables in the equations. Thus, in our example, we would construct the matrix shown in Figure 6–11.

A_1	A_2	A_3	A_4	B	
1	2	1	2	20	E_1
6	5	3	2	100	E_2
3	4	9	12	75	E_3

Figure 6–11 The inequalities matrix

The equations in a matrix are inequalities.[5] For example, the equation

$$1A_1 + 2A_2 + 1A_3 + 2A_4 \leq 20 \, E_1$$

tells us that up to 20 units of E_1 can be used to manufacture products at the rate of one unit of E_1 for every unit of A_1 produced, two units of E_1 for every unit of A_2 produced, and so forth. The amount of each input used can be either equal to or less than the limiting quantity. Algebra does not lend itself readily to working with inequalities, so we must change the equations to equalities. To do this without changing the sense of the equations, we simply introduce a new variable, called a "slack variable," to each equation. The slack variable represents the amount of material needed to make the equation an equality; that is, the sum of the real variables (A_1 through A_4) times their coefficients plus the slack variable equals the total amount of material available. For example, the original constraint for Material E_1 was

$$A_1 + 2A_2 + A_3 + 2A_4 \leq 20$$

Adding the slack variable A_5 it becomes

$$A_1 + 2A_2 + A_3 + 2A_4 + A_5 = 20$$

The same is done for the other equations using slack variables A_6 and A_7. With the addition of these three slack variables, a new matrix can be constructed as shown in Figure 6–12.

The use of slack variables in each equation means that the number of linear equations is always less than the number of variables in the problem. In the

---

[5] In some linear programing texts, these inequalities are not considered as equations but rather as restrictions.

A₁	A₂	A₃	A₄	A₅	A₆	A₇	B	
1	2	1	2	1	0	0	20	E₁
6	5	3	2	0	1	0	100	E₂
3	4	9	12	0	0	1	75	E₃

REAL VARIABLES SLACK VARIABLES

Figure 6–12   The equalities matrix

illustration there are three equations and seven variables; therefore, instead of one solution, there are a large number of solutions to the equations. To illustrate this, consider the following two simple equations:

$$x + 2y = 10$$

$$2x + 3y = 18$$

Here one set of values for x and y ($x = 6$ and $y = 2$) solves the equations; no other set of values will do. Let us now expand the equations by adding a z variable as follows:

$$z + x + 2y = 10$$

$$z + 2x + 3y = 18$$

Here we find no unique answer to the equations: one set of values that will satisfy the equations is $z = 0$, $x = 6$, and $y = 2$. Another set of values that will also satisfy the equations is $z = 1$, $x = 7$, $y = 1$. Many other sets of values could equally well be used. The same is true with the linear programing matrix; a great number of sets of values for the variables will satisfy the equations. What we want to determine is *which* set of values will enable us to maximize our profit. To do this, we use what is called an *objective function*. Since our objective is profit, the objective function is composed of the coefficients of profit that relate to the individual final products. In our earlier example this equation was

$$6A_1 + 4A_2 + 7A_3 + 5A_4 = C_{profit}$$

These values are then added to the matrix, with their signs changed as shown in Figure 6–13.[6]

Solving the matrix   All methods of linear programing are designed to select from a large number of possible solutions the optimum one that makes the objective function the largest. This is done by trial and error, but it is not a random procedure; it follows a definite course leading to the solution with the highest value objective function. Such a procedure is termed an *algorithm*, and the individual trials are called *iterations*.

---

[6] The reason for the change in signs will be explained during the solution procedure.

A_1	A_2	A_3	A_4	A_5	A_6	A_7	B	
1	2	1	2	1	0	0	20	E_1
6	5	3	2	0	1	0	100	E_2
3	4	9	12	0	0	1	75	E_3
−6	−4	−7	−5	0	0	0		C

Figure 6–13 The complete matrix

There are four steps in the simplex[7] system of optimizing a linear matrix. The first is to find that column of the matrix which, when changed, will lead to the greatest increase in value in the objective function. The second is to determine which value in the selected product column will limit the amount of change that can be made without violating the limitations of the matrix. Once this limiting value is introduced into the matrix, the third step is to update the matrix to reflect the new value. The fourth is to check the matrix to determine if further changes will increase the value of the objective function. If they will, then steps one through three are repeated; if not, the problem is solved.

This process is depicted graphically in Figure 6–14. For further illustration we will apply this technique, step by step, to the solution of our hypothetical optimization problem, showing the rationale behind the method.

First iteration

Step 1 The first step in the process is to determine what products should be in the solution. Looking at the original matrix in Figure 6–13, we see that in the revenue equation, the product with the most negative C value (−7) is A_3. This tells us that we will incur the greatest opportunity cost if we omit A_3 from the final solution; stated another way, Product A_3 returns the most profit per unit of output. Consequently, we want as many units of A_3 in the final solution as possible.

Step 2 But how many units of A_3 can be in the final solution? We can have 20 units of A_3 and still satisfy the E_1 equation, since each unit of A_3 produced only takes one unit of E_1 and there are 20 units of E_1. To make 20 units of A_3, 60 units of E_2 are needed (3 × 20). Since there are 100 units of E_2 available, nothing at this point prevents the production of 20 units of A_3. However, to produce 20 units of A_3, 180 units (9 × 20) of E_3 are required; but only 75 units of E_3 are available, so only 75/9 or 8.33 units of A_3 can be made. This means that the number 9 in column A_3 is the limiting value.

---

[7] There are many modifications of the original simplex approach, which have been formulated primarily to take advantage of computer characteristics. Some of these methods are the modified simplex, the modified revised simplex, the network approach, the product inverse, and the symmetric method. The way in which the numbers are manipulated varies in each method, but the basic arithmetic is essentially the same.

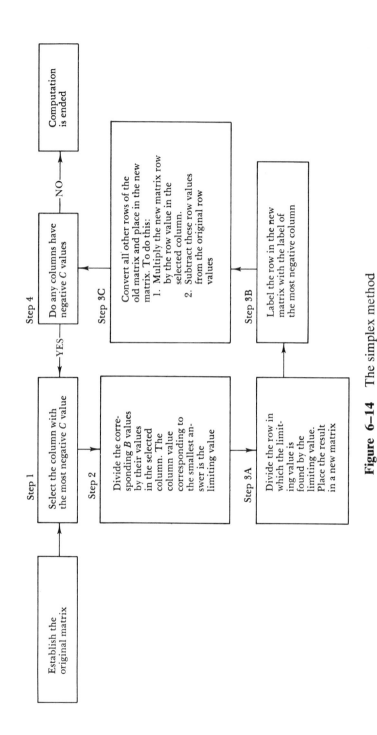

Figure 6–14   The simplex method

A_1	A_2	A_3	A_4	A_5	A_6	A_7	B	
1	2	1	2	1	0	0	20	E_1
6	5	3	2	0	1	0	100	E_2
3	4	⑨	12	0	0	1	75	E_3
−6	−4	−7	−5	0	0	0		C

Figure 6–15   The original matrix with the selected column and limiting value

The process of finding the limiting value can be done in a routine manner by dividing each value in the selected column into its corresponding B value. In the example this yields values of 20, $33\frac{1}{3}$, and $8\frac{1}{3}$. Because the smallest value is $8\frac{1}{3}$, 9 is the limiting value; it is circled in Figure 6–15.

Steps 3A and 3B   Once the limiting value has been found, the original matrix is manipulated in order to construct a new matrix that will reflect the decision to manufacture Product A_3.[8] The initial operation in constructing the new matrix is to divide the row containing the limiting value by the limiting value itself. The resulting figures are placed in the new matrix, and the row is labeled with the title of the selected column as shown in Figure 6–16.

A_1	A_2	A_3	A_4	A_5	A_6	A_7	B	
								E_1
								E_2
3/9	4/9	1	12/9	0	0	1/9	75/9	A_3
								C

Figure 6–16   Partial first iteration matrix

Step 3C   The next step in constructing the new matrix is to multiply the new matrix row (as shown in Figure 6–16) by each value in the selected column of Figure 6–15. For example, the value in row E_2 of the selected column is 3. Multiplying the A_3 row in the new matrix by this number gives values of

$$3(3/9, 4/9, 1, 12/9, 0, 0, 1/9, 75/9) = 1, 12/9, 3, 4, 0, 0, 3/9, 25$$

These values are then subtracted from the old row values and the resulting values are placed in the new matrix. Continuing with the example of the E_2 row, the row values from Figure 6–15 are

	6,	5,	3,	2,	0,	1,	0,	100	
subtracting	1,	12/9,	3,	4,	0,	0,	3/9,	25	from above
gives	5,	33/9,	0,	−2,	0,	1,	−3/9,	75	

[8] These manipulations are basic matrix operations.

A_1	A_2	A_3	A_4	A_5	A_6	A_7	B	
								E_1
5	33/9	0	−2	0	1	−3/9	75	E_2
3/9	4/9	1	12/9	0	0	1/9	75/9	A_3
								C

Figure 6–17 Partial first iteration matrix with new E_2 row

These values are then placed in row E_2 of the new matrix as shown in Figure 6–17. Following the same procedure for rows E_1 and C, we obtain the matrix illustrated in Figure 6–18.

A_1	A_2	A_3	A_4	A_5	A_6	A_7	B	
6/9	14/9	0	6/9	1	0	−1/9	105/9	E_1
⑤	33/9	0	−2	0	1	−3/9	75	E_2
3/9	4/9	1	12/9	0	0	1/9	75/9	A_3
−33/9	−8/9	0	39/9	0	0	7/9	175/3	C

Figure 6–18 First iteration matrix

Step 4 The final step in the first iteration is to see if we have reached the optimum solution, which means that there must be no negative C values. If there are negative C values, omission of the product with the negative C value will represent an opportunity cost, or a loss of profit that could be obtained from the product. In the example there are negative C values for Products A_1 and A_2, so the process must be repeated (the second iteration) from Step 1.

Second iteration

Step 1 The most negative C value is −33/9; therefore the selected column is A_1, as indicated by the tinting in Figure 6–18.

Step 2 Dividing the selected column values into the B values gives 105/6, 15, and 25. The smallest value is 15, making 5 the limiting value; it is circled in Figure 6–18.

Steps 3A and 3B The limiting value is divided into its row, and the results are placed in the new matrix; it is labeled as shown in Figure 6–19.

Step 3C The rest of the matrix is then calculated. The final matrix is shown in Figure 6–20.

A₁	A₂	A₃	A₄	A₅	A₆	A₇	B	
								E_1
1	11/15	0	−2/5	0	1/5	−1/15	15	A_1
								A_3
								C

Figure 6–19 Partial second iteration matrix

A₁	A₂	A₃	A₄	A₅	A₆	A₇	B		
0	16/15	0	14/15	1	−2/15	−1/15	5/3	E_1	
1	11/15	0	−2/5	0	1/5	−1/15	15	A_1	Maximum values
0	1/5	1	22/15	0	−1/15	2/15	10/3	A_3	
0	9/5	0	43/15	0	11/15	8/15	340/3	C	

Shadow prices

Figure 6–20 Second iteration matrix

Step 4 Since there are no negative C values, the problem is solved, as follows:

15 units of Product A_1
10/3 units of Product A_3
5/3 units of unused Material E_1

The profit, or revenue, is equal to

$$R = 6(15) + 4(0) + 7(3.33) + 5(0)$$
$$= 340/3 = 113.33$$

Interpreting the results Solutions to linear programs may be designed to yield three types of information. The first is a set of coefficients and variables that will satisfy the constraints and maximize the objective function. The values for the variables will tell you how much of each will be found in the optimal solution; thus, in the foregoing example, the optimal production solution has 15 units of A_1 and 3.33 units of A_3. This solution leaves 1.66 units of Material E_1 unused and yields a profit of $113.33.

The second type of information provided by linear programing solutions is termed *shadow prices*. They represent the projected loss in revenue that would occur if the variables that are not in the optimum solution were introduced. Thus, in terms of the values in the final matrix (Figure 6–20), for each unit of A_2 produced, revenue would drop 1.8 (9/5) units, and for each unit of A_4 produced, the drop would be 2.86 (43/15) units. The shadow prices attached to slack variables indicate the drop in revenue that would occur for every unit of input that was not used. Thus, if one unit of E_2 was removed from the process,

0.733 (11/15) units of revenue would be lost, and for each unit of E_3 omitted the loss would be 0.533 (8/15) units. Shadow prices are a valuable aid since they tell management what it would cost to manufacture a product that is not in the optimum solution. This information will help management evaluate the cost of manufacturing a product when, for example, it is considering whether to carry a full line or whether to meet a customer's demand for the product. In the case of input materials, shadow prices tell management how much will be lost by not having the inputs available.

The third type of information provided by linear programing solutions concerns the sensitivity of the solution to changes in profit from the products and to changes in the values of the constraints. Although the calculation of these values is beyond the scope of this book, the meaning and use of the data are not. The sensitivity of a variable to profit shows the range of profit over which a variable may be changed without changing the optimality of the solution. That is, the sensitivity factor tells management how much a product's profit can be changed before it would be preferable to replace one product with another. Since a product's profit can be both raised and lowered, the sensitivity range will normally be for values both above and below the one used in the solution. For example, the profit ranges for the products in the solution of the sample problem are

	Range 1	*Range 2*
A_1	−2.45	7.16
A_3	−1.95	10.99

Thus, the revenue gained by manufacturing a unit of Product A_1 must drop to less than $6 - 2.45 = 3.55$ before it would affect the optimality of the solution. If this occurred, revenue could then be maximized by manufacturing a product other than A_1. If the revenue gained by producing a unit of A_1 rose to greater than $6 + 7.16 = 13.16$, the optimality of the solution would again be affected. This time, to maximize the revenue, more of Product A_1 and less of others should be made. This type of product information is extremely valuable to management in determining the effect of price and cost changes on the firm's profit position.

The sensitivity of the solution to changes in the value of the constraints is somewhat more difficult to visualize. This type of sensitivity indicates how much the values of the constraints can be varied before the solution becomes unfeasible, and it is calculated for slack variables. Like the cost sensitivity range, it is both plus and minus. For the sample problem the ranges are

	Range 1	*Range 2*
E_2	−12.49	74.99
E_3	−24.99	24.99

What this means is that the constraint in which E_2 appears can be changed negatively by −12.49 or positively by 74.99 before the feasibility of the whole model is destroyed. $6A_1 + 5A_2 + 3A_3 + 2A_4$ can range between $100 + 74.99$ and

100 − 12.49. This sensitivity measures the reaction of the model to changes in the values of the constraints.

Questions and Problems

1. What role do production managers play in the market research for a new product?
2. "Inasmuch as acquiring new and changed products has survival value for an enterprise, every firm should make product development one of its major departments or functional activities." Comment on this statement.
3. What is the major function of market research? Are market research and sales forecasting the same?
4. Is there a distinction between the break-even point and the complete recovery point for a new product?
5. If the sales and profits of a company making Product A are increasing, why might the company find product diversification not only desirable but necessary?
6. How do simplification and diversification contribute to the stabilization of a going concern?
7. Outline the variety of methods that can be used to get new products for revitalizing the product line of a company. Which of your suggestions would be helpful to a commercial bank? an accident insurance company? a department store? It is possible, of course, that these enterprises have no product-line problem.
8. What is the significance of the assumption of linearity that is used in so many management techniques?
9. Should a company that is operating below its break-even point in sales volume try to solve its problem by product-line diversification?
10. "In general, product simplification reduces production costs, and diversification facilitates marketing, but there are no real benefits to the manufacturer in diversification." Comment on this statement.
11. Discuss the relationship between functional design and production design in arriving at a product design that will meet functional requirements, cost considerations, and the limitations of available processes. Why is product design so important in many concerns and quite unimportant in others?
12. A firm has a monthly sales volume of $192,000 for two products. The cost pattern for manufacturing the product is

PRODUCT	FIXED COSTS	BREAK-EVEN POINT	PROFIT
A	$32,000	$80,000	$ 24,000
B	68,000	76,000	−12,000

Should the manufacture of Product B be discontinued? What positive and negative factors are involved?

13. Draw a P-V chart for a product which has a fixed cost of $5,000, a sales income of $20,000, and a profit of $3,000.
14. Draw a P-V chart for the following products:

PRODUCT	FIXED COST	SALES INCOME	PROFIT
A	$10,000	$75,000	$30,000
B	15,000	35,000	5,000
C	5,000	20,000	10,000

What happens to the analysis if a fourth product, E, which shares fixed costs with Product B, is introduced? The new fixed cost for Products B and E is $17,000; the sales income for E is $20,000 and the profit is $10,000.

15. The XYZ Company is a manufacturer of printed circuit boards. The process can be simplified by identifying three operations: assembly, soldering, and inspection. The company has been operating at a constant volume, but a technological breakthrough has placed an unlimited demand for two types of printed circuit boards— 100 and 101—on the plant. Since the plant capacity could not immediately be increased, it was decided to devote the second shift exclusively to the manufacture of these two boards. The capacity of this shift to perform the operations involved is set forth as follows:

PRINTED CIRCUIT TYPE	ASSEMBLY	SOLDERING	INSPECTION
100	8,000	12,000	7,000
101	6,000	5,000	14,000

(a) How should the existing capacity be allocated to the two types of boards?

(b) If the contribution for type 100 is $6.00 per unit and for type 101, $4.50 per unit, what will be the total contribution to profit and overhead under the proposed production plan?

16. What is an algorithm?

17. What is a shadow price? How is this value used?

18. Why are we concerned with the sensitivity of a linear programing solution?

19. The Brown Company produces two types of locks. Each requires four process operations. The demand for the locks is so great that the company will be able to sell all it can produce. Since the number of each type of lock that can be processed at the several production steps varies and the profit from the locks is different, the company wants to know what mixture of locks it should produce.

The profit per unit from lock 1 is $0.30 and from lock 2, $0.34, and the number of locks that can be produced per week at each stage is

	LOCK 1	LOCK 2
Forging	1,000	1,000
Milling	1,500	800
Stamping	900	700
Assembly	1,000	1,100

20. The Tempest Instrument Company makes four sizes of industrial scales. They want to reduce their line to three scale sizes. The financial data for each are as follows:

	1/4 TON	1/2 TON	1 TON	3 TON
Sales	$100,000	$200,000	$75,000	$150,000
Variable costs	75,000	150,000	60,000	140,000
Fixed costs	30,000	25,000	5,000	5,000

(a) Which scale size should the company discard on a purely financial basis? Justify your answer.

(b) What other factors should be taken into consideration?

21. What is a contribution ratio? How does it help in management decision making?

22. The ABC Company is a manufacturer of electric clocks. It is currently formulating plans for the following year's operations. The president of the company wants to establish "break-even" as the firm's sales objective.

   (a) From the projected operating data below, determine the target volume for the following year.

   | | Unit sales price | $8.00 | |
   | | Fixed operating charges | $175,000.00 | |

	VOLUME 1	VOLUME 2
Units produced	60,000	150,000
Material costs	$120,000	$300,000
Direct labor costs	90,000	180,000
Other manufacturing expenses	75,000	120,000
Total manufacturing costs	$285,000	$600,000
Selling and general administrative expenses	$100,000	$154,000

   (b) If the projection of a sales volume of 110,000 units for the following year is realized, what profit or loss can be projected for the year?

References

Ackoff, R. L., and Sasieni, M. W., *Fundamentals of Operations Research*, Wiley, New York, 1968.

Barish, N. N., *Economic Analysis for Engineering and Managerial Decision-Making*, McGraw-Hill, New York, 1962.

Baumol, W. J., *Economic Theory and Operations Analysis*, 2nd ed., Prentice-Hall, Englewood Cliffs, N.J., 1965.

Bowman, E. H., and Fetter, R. B., *Analysis of Industrial Operations*, rev. ed., Irwin, Homewood, Ill., 1961.

Buffa, E. S., *Operations Management Problems and Models*, 2nd ed., Wiley, New York, 1968.

Dantzig, G. B., *Linear Programming and Extensions*, Princeton University Press, Princeton, N.J., 1963.

Di Roccaferrera, G. F., *Introduction to Linear Programming Processes*, South-Western, Cincinnati, Ohio, 1967.

Driebeek, N. J., *Applied Linear Programming*, Addison-Wesley, Reading, Mass., 1969.

Gass, S. I., *Linear Programming*, 3rd ed., McGraw-Hill, New York, 1969.

Grant, E. L., and Ireson, W. G., *Principles of Engineering Economy*, 5th ed., Ronald Press, New York, 1970.

Hadley, G., *Linear Programming*, Addison-Wesley, Reading, Mass., 1963.

Kemeny, J. G., *et al.*, *Finite Mathematics with Business Applications*, Prentice-Hall, Englewood Cliffs, N.J., 1962.

Levin, R. I., and Lamone, R. P., *Linear Programming for Management Decisions*, Irwin, Homewood, Ill., 1969.

Schuchman, A., *Scientific Decision-Making in Business*, Holt, Rinehart and Winston, New York, 1963.

7

Capital Planning

Among the most vital input decisions that a production manager makes are those involving capital acquisitions. The importance of these decisions varies according to the amount of money involved and the length of time for which the firm's funds are committed. Typically, capital-acquisition decisions are long-term commitments that will affect the firm for two years or more; the quantity of money spent is often measured in the millions. Hence, these decisions play a crucial role in determining the company's future course of action. They are a particularly difficult type of decision to make, however, because of the comparative inaccuracy of the forecasts on which they must be based.

Capital allocations are made when future anticipated returns are large enough to take the risk of commiting funds in the present, with the expectation of recovering the expense in the future. A going concern makes capital allocations under two sets of conditions: expansion and replacement of existing facilities. Since the vital, dynamic companies in our economy must continue to develop over time, they must modify or add to their scale of operations from time to time. Profitable firms periodically change their capacity, enter into new areas, and change their product mix. In the long run, no company can continue to exist if it attempts to market exactly the same product line to the same market in the same quantity. New items must be developed and produced to meet the ever-changing demand, and capital to develop, manufacture, and market these goods or services must be allocated well in advance—at the planning stage.

The physical plant and the machinery of any industrial firm gradually become obsolete over time. As the pace of our economy increases, capital goods become obsolescent at an increasingly rapid pace. Machinery that will function satisfactorily for years is frequently rendered practically worthless because of technological advances long before it has failed mechanically.

This continual need for expansion and replacement capital, and for intelligent capital-allocation decisions, applies to *all* economic activities. Actually, any decision involving a present commitment of funds based on estimated future costs and returns falls into this category. Thus, in financial institutions the decision to commit funds to stocks and bonds is much like the decision to buy new machinery in a factory; they both require an economic choice between future alternative uses of funds.

The basic economic problem of capital management may be summarized as How to achieve the optimum return on invested capital. In pursuit of this goal, a firm must find answers to the following fundamental questions:

1. *How much money will be needed for capital expenditures on necessary projects for the period under consideration?*
2. *How much money can be made available for this purpose? How will the funds be obtained, and what will the costs be?*
3. *How should the available funds be allocated among the project opportunities available?*

A plan that coordinates the solutions to these questions is often referred to as a firm's *financial plan*. The formulation of such a plan requires the establishment of a reference time frame. Industrial planning periods usually run from five to ten years, which is consistent with the belief that a firm must plan far enough ahead to determine how it will recover its investment. Within the framework of this long-term plan, a company will normally set up a group of short-range plans for the first two to three years to estimate the cash-flow characteristics of specific projects. These plans usually state explicitly the amount of money allocated for each project and the proposed source of these funds. Such a description of capital expenditure plans for the immediate future is called a firm's *capital budget*.

Demand for Capital

One way to determine a firm's overall need for capital is to construct a comprehensive inventory of possible capital expenditure projects. The inventory should include all proposals that would require capital investment for additional facilities, equipment replacement, equipment and process design, product research and development, and other alternatives. One of management's major responsibilities is to ensure that there is always a backlog of highly desirable investment plans that may be studied as alternatives at any time. In terms of the production function, the industrial engineering department is usually assigned the responsibility for determining how to reduce costs (or to increase profits) by utilizing new equipment and new processes. Similarly, a product-planning department would be primarily responsible for identifying the need for new-product research and development. To ensure that investment ideas generated anywhere in the organization receive the appropriate amount of executive attention, many firms establish a standard proposal format that enumerates the data required to evaluate projects. Usually, these data include the amount of funds needed, the timing of the expenditure, and the projected return on the capital invested. The use of such a format has two major advantages: it facilitates an examination of the data presented, and it places all projects on the same basis, thus permitting comparisons between projects. Because of the vital importance of investment decisions, it is not unusual for a committee of high organizational rank to pass on the merits of each project submitted for decision.

The Demand Curve

A demand schedule may be constructed as a tool to assist management in examining the proposals for capital expenditure. Table 7–1, for example, lists the amount of money required for each project, the projected rate of return, the dollars of return per year, and the number of years during which the return will exist. In addition, the table notes the total amount demanded and whether the project is a new or a continuing effort. Although the fact that a project has already begun does not necessarily mean that it must automatically be carried forward, inclusion of this information alerts management to the fact that the past history of the project must be considered. Once all of the information for a schedule is obtained, the projects are listed in descending order according to their expected rates of return.

On the basis of the projected rate of return and the estimated cumulative demand for capital shown in the table, a capital demand curve (as in Figure 7–1) may be drawn for the firm. The curve shows the amount of money that can be invested at various rates of return. According to Figure 7–1, the firm could invest $550,000 in available projects having a return of 15 percent or better, assuming that 15 percent was the desired return on investment. The higher the desired return, the fewer the projects that can meet the criteria. This means that as the rate of return requirement is raised, less money can be invested. At an 18 percent rate of return, for example, this firm could invest only $250,000. The

Table 7–1   Project demand schedule

Project	Value of Investment	Life (years)	New or Con- tinued	Investment during Budget Period	Projected Rate of Return (percent)	Cumulative Demand during Budget Period
1001	$400,000	1	C	$200,000	20	$ 200,000
1000	100,000	3	N	50,000	18	250,000
1008	300,000	2	N	300,000	15	550,000
1003	500,000	3	N	300,000	13	850,000
1002	90,000	3	N	150,000	12	1,000,000

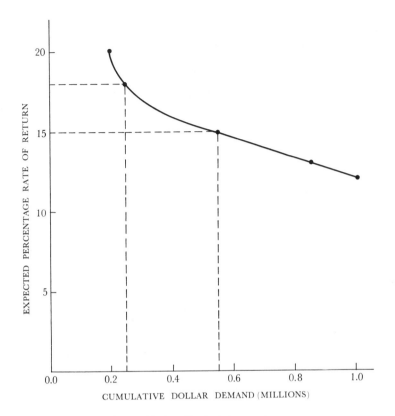

Figure 7-1 Capital demand curve

minimum acceptable rate of return is determined by many factors, one of which is the availability of capital for investment, which will be considered next.

Supply of Capital

Internal Sources

The funds available to a firm for investment are derived from many sources, both internal and external. A firm can generate investment funds internally in two ways: through retained earnings and through depreciation. Retained earnings are that portion of net operating profit[1] that is not distributed to the owners, or stockholders. Deciding how much profit to pay out in the form of dividends can be a difficult problem. Such factors as company policy and reputation, investment needs, and the mood of the stockholders enter into this decision. Most stockholders, however, realize how important it is for a company to keep abreast of technological changes in the industry. Moreover, since a corporation's tax

[1] This is profit after the payment of fixed debt obligations, management compensation. and taxes.

obligation on capital gains (which often result from heavy reinvestment of retained earnings) is generally lower than the average investor's income tax, more and more firms are financing capital expenditures out of retained earnings.

The other internal source of capital is depreciation. Most fixed assets have a limit to their useful life. The original cost of an asset is, therefore, treated as an expense for the period during which it is used. The portion of the cost that may be charged in any given accounting period is fixed by law. The accounting procedure that handles the gradual conversion of a fixed asset to an expense is termed *depreciation*. Thus, the depreciation process acts to "create" funds because, although it is an expense that reduces stated profits, it is not an "out-of-pocket" cost. Consequently, the funds reserved for depreciation remain within the company and can be used for investment purposes.

External Sources

External sources of capital, as the name implies, include the money market and its several institutions. Thus, a firm may obtain funds externally by issuing more stock, by offering bonds for sale, or by seeking loans. The issuance of stock has the advantage of avoiding fixed debt commitments, thereby maintaining a maximum of operating flexibility. On the other hand, this method tends to dilute the control of the corporation exercised by existing stockholders; therefore, they are often given first option when a new stock issue is floated. Bonds and loans, on the other hand, do not normally dilute stockholder equity. The need to meet interest and retirement payments, however, introduces an element of rigidity into the capital budget that restricts management action, so most methods of *funding* utilize a composite of stocks, bonds, and loans.

Funding decisions are based upon the condition of the money market at a particular time as well as upon company policies, financial structure, and projected operating characteristics. The final plan will reflect the cost of obtaining the needed money, such as the effective interest rate on bonds or loans, or else the dividend rate will reflect the price obtained for stock. The external cost of money is an important criterion for decisions on the funding of available projects. For this reason many companies try to keep a finger on the pulse of the money market, even though borrowing may not be contemplated at the time.

Capital Allocation

The equilibrium point for the supply and demand of capital is determined by establishing a minimum acceptable rate of return for projects. This minimum rate is called the *capital rejection rate*. Only those alternative investment projects that offer a projected return equal to or greater than the rejection rate are considered for funding. Thus, the rejection rate identifies the effective demand for capital. This process is illustrated in Figure 7–2, where a rejection rate of 10 percent was used; at this rate there is $2 million of effective demand.

Determination of the rejection rate is a critically important process. The two

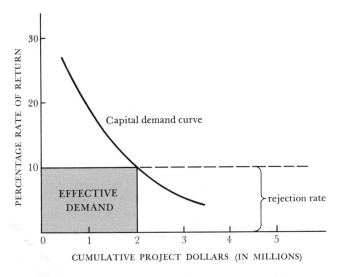

Figure 7–2 Effective demand for capital

common approaches to the calculation of this rate employed by industry are *fluctuating effective rates* and *long-term minimum rates.*

Fluctuating Effective Rates

This method of setting a rejection rate is based on the belief that the rate should reflect immediate short-run expectations. Thus, the expected rate of return on capital presently used either in a firm or on outside investments serves as the rejection rate. This is basically an "opportunity cost" approach.

Opportunity costs are the additional gains or returns that could have resulted from the investment of capital in other opportunities. Investment in one alternative deprives the company of the opportunity of utilizing these funds elsewhere. Possible gains that could have been enjoyed by selecting other projects are lost, and this loss is considered a cost of selecting a particular project. To illustrate this concept, imagine a company with the following investment opportunities and sufficient capital to invest in only one of the projects listed. For this company

Project Number	Funds Required	Projected Return (est.)	
1000	$100,000	12%	
1001	90,000	15	←Maximum return
1002	85,000	13	
1003	100,000	10	
1004	95,000	9	

the best expectation of return from available projects is 15 percent. Only Project 1001 can meet this standard, so it would be the logical investment choice. All other projects would involve opportunity costs because the money could earn more if invested elsewhere. For example, the opportunity cost for Project 1000 would be 3 percent (15 percent − 12 percent) of the invested funds, or $3,000. Opportunity costs only involve the economic side of an investment. Therefore, a project that does not yield 15 percent return might be chosen for many intangible reasons, such as the desire to maintain a leadership position in the field or to enhance customer goodwill. If this should happen, the opportunity cost incurred would never appear in the profit and loss statement or in any other accounting document; it would merely be an aid to managerial decision making.

The concept of opportunity cost can also be useful in allocating resources other than capital. Consider, for example, an office typist who has time during the day to read magazines and manicure her nails. An analysis of her work pattern might reveal that, on the average, this typist has two hours of free time during the day. In such a case, assigning her two additional hours of filing work would involve no additional real labor cost, since she would otherwise be idle. It does, however, involve an opportunity cost, which is the difference between the value of her performing a higher skilled job as opposed to filing. If no higher skilled job can be found for her to perform, the fact that an opportunity cost is involved should not deter a manager from assigning her to the filing job.

Similarly, imagine a computer that is totally occupied doing routine data processing. A task may arise that has a high payoff value to management, but because the computer is fully loaded, it cannot be processed. In this case an opportunity cost is incurred: the loss in value to the company resulting from processing the routine jobs instead of the high-value problem.

Long-Term Minimum Rates

The other method stresses long-run expectations and attempts to formulate a rejection rate that will represent a reasonable average return for the entire business cycle. Statistics reflecting a firm's accomplishments and industry-wide experience are used to determine this long-term minimum rate. One advantage of this method is that it eliminates the necessity of investing in relatively low-return projects in times of plentiful money and having to curtail investment plans when interest rates are high. Thus, the impact of business conditions on the firm's investment policy is minimized.

General Investment Considerations

In the investment process, forces other than the rejection rate must also be considered when specific opportunities are examined. For example, *balance* is often thought to be an important investment objective. Many companies attempt to spread the risk by investing in several different projects rather than conform strictly to rate-of-return criteria and invest all their funds in one high-yield opportunity. For this reason, petroleum companies seek a balance between domestic and foreign investments and also between drilling, refining, and distribution operations.

In the service industries, the need to maintain a good *public image* is an important factor. Public transportation, utilities, and telephone companies usually tailor their investment decisions toward this end despite what is, in many cases, at obvious variance with a high rate of return.

Some investment decisions are made primarily for *strategic* purposes, including capital expenditures for cafeterias, parking lots, and other personnel services, where the return can be measured only in better employee relations. The need to carry a full line of products to meet customer expectations or the desire to prevent a competitor from gaining a foothold in a market may also dictate investments that cannot be justified on the basis of individual project returns. In such cases the impact of the investment on the total profitability of a firm is considered to be sufficient justification, and it illustrates the importance of evaluating the effect of strategic investments on the firm's overall situation.

Postponability is another criterion that may be applied during the selection of an investment project. Thus, priority is given to projects that cannot be delayed, and those that can wait are postponed until the next budget-planning period. In this process the rate of return is often played down, and greater importance is placed on other aspects of the projects.

Finally, the *absolute return* from a project can be the deciding factor. Some projects with high rates of return may yield little total profit, whereas others with lower rates of return may offer the opportunity of netting large sums of money. A project with a 25 percent rate of return may only offer the opportunity for $10,000 of profit because of its limited scope. Another much larger project may have a rate of return of only 15 percent and yet lead to $1 million of profit. Therefore, it is important to consider the absolute return from investments in making investment decisions.

The Supply of Funds

Once the rejection rate has been established and the effective demand for capital identified, management can turn its attention to the supply of investment funds. The supply of funds can be either greater or smaller than the effective demand. These situations are respectively labeled Case 1 (supply > demand) and Case 2 (supply < demand) in Figure 7–3.

In Case 1 a decision must be made regarding the disposition of the excess supply of funds. There are many possibilities. The funds may be "stored" until the next budget-planning period, when there may be more suitable opportunities. Storage of excess funds is often accomplished by investing in short-term government securities or "blue chip" stocks so that a firm may obtain a return on its capital and still retain a good portion of its liquidity. Another means of reducing an excess supply of funds is to increase the dividend rate, a technique that has merit if future investment opportunities within a company appear to be limited. Assuming that the stockholders will reinvest these funds elsewhere, it also has the effect of diverting capital toward industries that can better employ it, which is a form of capital allocation on a national scale. Rather than leave the invest-

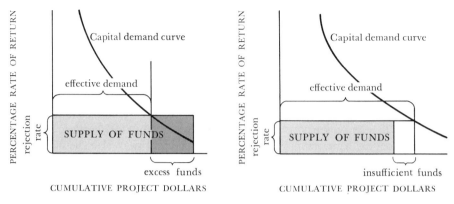

Case 1: Supply greater than demand   Case 2: Supply less than demand

Figure 7–3   Supply of funds in relation to demand

ment decision to the shareholders, however, many companies have chosen to look for possible uses for capital outside the firm. The Ford Motor Company purchased Philco because it felt that investment opportunities in the electronics industry held great promise, and Dupont invested in General Motors, prompted by the same line of reasoning.[2]

Case 2 represents a diametrically opposed problem: a company needs additional funds to permit implementation of projects it considers necessary. Postponability could be used as a compromise criterion in such cases; however, the most common solution is to borrow the needed funds.[3]

Evaluation of Specific Opportunities

Now let us examine those factors that must be considered in the assessment of individual projects. For the remainder of this chapter, we will discuss income streams, expense streams, and depreciation policy, since capital-budgeting decisions must be based on an understanding of these factors. In Chapter 8, we will examine the methodology employed in choosing among alternative investment opportunities.

Income Streams

In making capital-allocation decisions, very often it is not enough to consider the total amount of profit that a project returns, because the timing of the returns may greatly affect the true value of the revenue, as illustrated by the following example.

    [2] It is interesting to note that relatively few companies contemplate a substantial lowering of the rejection rate in order to accommodate an excess in the supply of funds.
    [3] It is assumed here that the rejection rate is *greater than* the cost of capital. If this were not true, the company would naturally limit its borrowing to those projects that offered a return greater than the cost of the money.

Table 7–2   Income streams

Years	Investment A	Investment B
1	$ 200	
2	200	
3	200	
4	200	$ 200
5	200	800
Total revenue	$1,000	$1,000

Imagine two lump-sum investments of equivalent size in machinery or bonds, which will both return a total of $1,000 in revenue after five years. Investment A returns $200 over expenses for each of the five years. Investment B returns $200 over expenses at the end of the fourth year, and $800 at the end of the fifth year. These "income streams" are shown in Table 7–2.

A cursory glance at these two sets of figures might lead one to the conclusion that the investments have equal promise since both return $1,000 of profit at the end of the five-year period. When the _timing_ of the revenue is considered, however, Investment A emerges as the better alternative; its time stream of revenue makes the funds available sooner and more consistently than alternative B, thus permitting the early application of returns to the funding of new investment opportunities. It is clear that the timing of the returns is of great importance, because a dollar returned today is more useful, and therefore more valuable, than a dollar returned a year from now.

One method of comparing various time streams of revenue is to give them "present values" by transforming them into present-day-equivalent dollars. Studies that employ this approach have gained increased favor, particularly in cases where the alternate investments have substantially different income and expense streams. This approach tends to be more complicated than other kinds of studies; also, it generally requires a great deal of mathematical computation. However, since computers have materially reduced the cost and time involved in the calculations, present value approaches are becoming increasingly popular.

As an introduction to the present-value approach, let us recall for a moment the concept of compound interest. A hundred dollars placed in a bank account that pays 4 percent interest annually is worth $104 at the end of one year; at the end of the second year it is worth $108.16. This sum is obtained by multiplying the annual interest rate of 4 percent times the sum accumulated at the end of the first year.

$$\$104 + (0.04 \times \$104) = \$108.16$$

If the interest rate remains constant, the initial $100 will have grown to $148.01 at the end of ten years. Expressed mathematically this is

$$S = 100(1 + 0.04)_1(1 + 0.04)_2(1 + 0.04)_3 \cdots (1 + 0.04)_{10}$$
$$= \$148.01$$

where S equals the sum of money accumulated at the end of ten years, and the subscripts denote year 1, year 2, and so on. The subscripted factors $(1 + 0.04)$ indicate the application of interest in the year denoted by the subscript to a sum that is increasing because of interest earned in previous years. From this mathematical expression, we can derive a general formula for compound interest sums.

(1) $$S = X(1 + i)^n$$

where $\quad n =$ number of years
$\quad\quad\quad i =$ interest rate
$\quad\quad\quad X =$ sum to be compounded
$\quad\quad\quad S =$ future worth of present sum

Thus, in the example cited, for a ten-year period this formula becomes

$$S = 100(1 + 0.04)^{10} = \$148.01$$

If we solve equation (1) for X, we can tell how much a sum of money S received n years from now would be worth today. Thus, \$148.01 received in a lump sum ten years from now would have a value of only \$100 today. This is the essence of the present-value approach, enabling one to look at future sums of money and calculate their present worth. The conversion process relating future sums to their present value is called *discounting*. Hence, \$100 received ten years from now, if discounted at 4 percent, would be worth only \$67.60 today. This is simply the reverse of saying that \$67.60 invested at 4 percent per year would have a value of \$100 in ten years. To compute the value for discounting, the following formula is used:[4]

(2) $$\text{Discounted value} = \frac{1}{(1 + i)^n} X$$

where $\quad n =$ the number of years of discounting
$\quad\quad\quad i =$ the interest rate (or discount rate) to be used for discounting purposes
$\quad\quad\quad X =$ sum to be discounted

The income streams listed in Table 7–2 can now be reevaluated. To calculate discounted values we must first determine the interest rate, or cost of capital. The higher the interest, or discount, rate, the more profitable it becomes to get early returns. This important principle will become increasingly clear in the subsequent discussion. For the present, let us evaluate the returns in Table 7–2 in terms of equation (2), using 4 percent and 10 percent rates. The results of these calculations are shown in Table 7–3.

Using the 4 percent discount figure, Investment A is worth \$62 more than alternative B; at the 10 percent discount level, A is worth \$124.60 more than B. In short, the discounting approach provides a common denominator for evaluat-

---

[4] It should be noted that in this formula the sum to be discounted is multiplied by the reciprocal of the compounding factor of equation (1).

Table 7–3 Discounted revenue streams

Year	Investment A			Investment B		
	Revenue	*4%*	*10%*	*Revenue*	*4%*	*10%*
1	$ 200	$192.40	$181.80			
2	200	185.00	165.20			
3	200	177.80	150.20			
4	200	171.00	136.60	$ 200	$171.00	$136.60
5	200	164.40	124.20	800	657.60	496.80
Totals	$1,000	$890.60	$758.00	$1,000	$828.60	$633.40

ing investment alternatives; "today's dollars" is an effective measure of the worth of different revenue streams.

The effect of changes in discount rates on the present value of the money is also illustrated in Table 7–3. An increase from 4 percent to 10 percent reduces the present value of the $1,000 in Investment A by $132.60 and in Investment B by $195.20. Thus, the discounting approach also facilitates numerical comparisons of differing income streams at various discount rates.

Expense Streams

Timing is as important a factor in planning expenses as it is in planning revenue. In neither case can the manager afford to think only of total amounts; both require consideration of present values. The "real" monetary cost of expenses depends upon *when* they will occur over time. This factor is especially important since the manager must arrange to have sufficient funds available at the time they are needed. The total cash requirements of two programs may be equal, but the timing may make a significant difference to the firm. Suppose, for example, that Investment C requires a $20,000 capital investment and $5,000 yearly for operating expenses to obtain $7,000 in annual revenue[5] for five years. Investment D, on the other hand, requires a $10,000 capital investment and $7,000 per year for operating expenses; it yields $5,000 in annual revenue. Table 7–4 shows the two expense streams. Each project returns $15,000 over the life of the investment, but the initial outlays and the operating expenses vary. Investment C has a greater initial outlay and smaller operating expenses.

These statistics could be analyzed in many ways. At this point, however, we will confine ourselves to an examination of the differences in initial capital outlay and operating expenses. The additional capital requirement of $10,000 for Investment C might, under some circumstances, be sufficient to dictate the choice of Investment D. Conversely, the initial outlay might be of less concern than the higher yearly operating expenses and lower revenue of Investment D. This would lead to the selection of Investment C. In any case, the specifics of the firm's operations will provide the criteria needed to make the final decision.

[5] Revenue = Income − Expenses.

Table 7–4   Expense streams

	Investment C	Investment D
Capital outlay	$20,000	$10,000
Expense per year	5,000	7,000
Income per year	12,000	12,000
Revenue per year	7,000	5,000
Total revenue	$35,000	$25,000
Profit	$15,000	$15,000

Investment Decision Factors

From the foregoing discussion it should be clear that a sound, comparative evaluation of alternative investment projects rests primarily upon a consideration of three sets of data:

1. *The magnitude of the investments*
2. *The projected revenue stream calculated on an annual basis*
3. *The time period over which the revenues will occur*

Now let us look at these categories of data in more detail from the firm's point of view to see *what* specific information is needed and *why*.

Investment

The term *investment* as it applies to capital-allocation decisions is broadly defined to include all the differential, or incremental, costs that are involved in a prospective expenditure, including all those required to undertake a project as opposed to not undertaking it. The size of an investment, therefore, reflects more than just the simple cost of new equipment. Such "one-shot" expenses as those needed for survey and feasibility, site preparation, installation, and, in many cases, labor training and retraining must also be taken into account. The total sum is generally far greater than the simple purchase price of the equipment. Labor costs have become increasingly important, for example, because owing to the growth of automation, large sums of money are required to train or retrain employees in new skills.

Because investment, as it is defined here, includes many items not usually classified as such for accounting purposes, the required data cannot generally be obtained directly from company statements and records. Instead, it must be secured by an organized investigation and information-gathering effort.

Cost Information

As just mentioned, management's capital-allocation decisions require *relevant costs*, those costs that will influence the decision in question, yet the firm's accounting records are often not established to reflect this. This problem can be illustrated by considering a class of costs called sunk costs.

Sunk costs are resource expenditures that have already been made and are therefore *not retrievable*. Since decisions made in the past are in a sense irrevocable, they should not have an undue influence on decisions being made today. Resources available now, including investment dollars, should be committed where they can earn the best return for the company. Thus, it would be unwise to continue to fund a project or hold on to a facility simply because large sums were consumed in that area in the past. If better opportunities are available, the best course of action might be to abandon completely the old project and all of its sunk costs.

To illustrate this point, consider the dilemma faced by the management of a medium-sized firm that makes metal specialties. It has a particular piece of equipment for which it has no future use. The book value of the machine (initial cost less depreciation) is $25,000. The company has the opportunity to sell it for $6,000 (its current market value) and apply the funds toward the purchase of a sorely needed automatic lathe. Clearly the firm should sell the machine, despite the fact that its stockholders may be upset by the apparent loss on a special purpose machine of $19,000 (book value minus market value). This loss is really the result of poor decisions in the past. Perhaps there was an incorrect forecast of demand for the machine's output or an unsound depreciation policy. Whatever the mistake was, the loss is now irretrievable. The sunk cost on the machine should not prevent management from selling it and using the money to buy an automatic lathe, if that is deemed the most profitable course of action.

Or suppose a firm desires to purchase a machine that sells for $15,000 to replace a piece of equipment purchased five years before. The old machine cost $10,000 and now has a *book value* of $5,000—that is, it has been depreciated $5,000 for accounting purposes. Its *resale value* in the marketplace, however, is only $2,000. Thus, the actual capital outlay required is $15,000 − $2,000, or $13,000; this is the real cost to the firm of buying the new equipment. The fact that the accounting records carry the value of the old equipment at $5,000 has no meaning in *this* calculation.[6]

The foregoing examples highlight the importance of incremental costs for capital-allocation decisions. In this case the *incremental cost* is the purchase price less the trade-in, or resale, value. This type of cost actually determines the expenditures needed for the future. To the manager making the purchase decision, what has occurred in the past is of no value except as it may be able to provide insight for the future. It is not worthwhile, for example, to look at the $3,000 difference between the $5,000 book value and the $2,000 resale value in the case just cited. This loss has already occurred, and no action in the future will be able to change that fact. To illustrate this idea further, consider a final example. A firm has been exploring the possibility of using an automated machine to do a minor production job. To date it has expended $40,000 in research for the project and feels that it is now in a position to build the machine for $20,000. The $40,000 has already been spent; it is a past expense and as such should be

_____

[6] For tax and other purposes, however, it has *considerable* meaning.

reflected in the accounting records. The $20,000 is in the future; it is the cost that should be considered in the allocation decision made at this point in time.

Expected Earnings

The second category of information needed for capital-allocation decisions is the expected earnings stream. Since the expected earnings stream is the difference between the income and expense streams, as mentioned previously, it is necessary to obtain a detailed forecast of future sales. The preparation of such a forecast is normally a function of the firm's sales or marketing department.

The expense stream is composed primarily of the operations of the production facility, and they are usually broken down into four classes: depreciation costs, the cost of capital (or interest), direct project costs, and indirect (or overhead) costs.

Depreciation costs   The production capacity created by an investment of capital will decrease in effectiveness as it is utilized over time. It will also experience a corresponding decrease in value as an asset of the firm. This decline in usefulness and worth is termed *depreciation*. Depreciation expense is a charge to the firm that generally represents this decline. It is a legitimate operating expense and is an important factor in the planning for capital investment. Depreciation thus involves (1) a decline in usefulness or worth and (2) a plan to recoup the capital invested.

To illustrate these two aspects of depreciation, consider a man who invested $3,250 in an automobile to use as a taxi. For four years the car was used to provide his income. During the last year the car was in continual need of repair, which led the owner to sell it. He received $50 for its scrap value. The car had depreciated $3,200 in worth. An appropriate depreciation plan would have developed

$$\frac{\$3{,}250 - \$50}{4} = \$800/\text{yr}$$

of depreciation charges against each year's revenue. Then when the car was worn out, the owner would have been able to replace it.

The unpredictable nature of depreciation makes it very difficult to develop an exact depreciation plan. The Internal Revenue Service has suggested plans and life limits for various types of investment. These plans set the legal background; management philosophy makes the actual selection.

The best depreciation method provides a realistic cost pattern. It recovers all of the investment, taking advantage of any tax considerations that are involved.

Many different methods of calculating depreciation are in use today. The most common is the *straight-line method;* it is the easiest to calculate and use because it assumes a constant rate of decline during an asset's life. The formula for straight-line depreciation is as follows:

$$D = \frac{F - S}{N}$$

where D = annual depreciation expense
F = investment cost
S = estimated salvage value[7]
N = estimated life of investment

As a hedge against uncertainty resulting from future technological change or the advent of new products, many businessmen prefer to depreciate an asset as quickly as possible. Depreciation methods such as the *sum of the digits* and the *declining balance* were developed by accountants primarily for this purpose. Another reason for the popularity of these methods is the tax benefits that accrue to the firm during the early years of an investment project.[8]

In the *declining-balance method* of depreciation, a fixed percentage is applied to the declining book value (or balance) of the assets. This percentage is applied year after year to the asset value that remains after deducting the depreciation of previous periods. Table 7–5 illustrates how this approach could be used to depreciate an investment of $2,000 at a fixed rate of 20 percent. The percentage rate by which the declining book value is depreciated each year is arbitrarily selected, except for one important limitation. Income tax regulations stipulate that the *maximum* percentage that can be used is double the percentage that would be used under the straight-line method if there were no salvage value involved. This restriction may be expressed mathematically as

$$D \text{ percent} = \frac{2.0 \times F}{N}$$

Therefore, in practice, the D percent for the declining-balance method is geared

Table 7–5 Declining-balance depreciation

Year	Book Value	Annual Amount of Depreciation
0	$2,000	
1	1,600	$400
2	1,280	320
3	1,024	256
4	819.20	204.80
5	655.36	163.84

[7] This is the estimated resale value of the investment at the end of the depreciation period.

[8] Accelerated depreciation increases a firm's expenses for tax purposes during the early years of an investment. As a result, the taxable profits are decreased and the firm's tax burden is lowered. This gives the firm extra cash early, and, considering the present value of money, the practice is most worthwhile.

to depreciate the asset to a specified salvage value by the end of its estimated life.[9]

In the *sum-of-the-digits method,* all of the digits for the depreciation period are added together to form the denominator of a varying fractional depreciation rate. Thus, for an asset with a depreciation period of ten years, the sum is

$$10 + 9 + 8 + 7 + 6 + 5 + 4 + 3 + 2 + 1 = 55$$

Accordingly, after the first year of use the asset would be depreciated by 10/55 of its initial value. The second year's depreciation of the original value would be 9/55, and the third year's depreciation would be 8/55. In this fashion, at the end of ten years the asset would be fully depreciated since

$$\frac{10}{55} + \frac{9}{55} + \frac{8}{55} + \frac{7}{55} + \frac{6}{55} + \frac{5}{55} + \frac{4}{55} + \frac{3}{55} + \frac{2}{55} + \frac{1}{55} = \frac{55}{55}$$

The greatest amount of depreciation takes place during the first years of ownership just as it does in the declining-balance method.

Interest costs   Interest, or the cost of capital, constitutes the second type of expense associated with the production function. Like depreciation expense, interest charges are also incurred over the life of an investment. This factor constitutes another break with traditional cost-accounting practice; whereas depreciation expense is normally included in cost accounting, interest charges are not, unless an annual interest payment is required. This means that "opportunity-cost" interest charges are scarcely ever included in cost-accounting records. Such expenses must be considered for any capital-allocation decision, however, since the commitment of funds to any project must reflect the cost of forgoing other investments. No investor will invest unless he can get back his original investment plus the highest possible profit at a given risk level. The same principle applies here: management must not only recover its original investment but must also earn profits greater than could be obtained through other investment opportunities. Thus, the rate of interest charged against a project must reflect the alternative uses of the capital and the cost of obtaining the capital for the project.

Direct and overhead costs   The last two types of production expenses, direct costs and overhead costs, may be discussed together, since the same principles apply to both concerning the costs that should be included in an economy study. Only those expenses that would be incurred if the project were undertaken (differential costs) need to be considered; others that would be largely unaffected by the investment decision need not be evaluated. This means that such overhead costs as executive salaries, supervision, plant security, heat, and light would not normally be included in the study. Of course, certain projects could

---

[9] The formula used for this purpose is

$$D \text{ percent} = 100 - 100 \sqrt[N]{\frac{S}{F}}$$

have a great impact on some of these indirect costs, as for example, if a project required special heating or air conditioning. In the electronics industry, exacting product specifications often require the creation of tightly controlled temperature conditions, and these indirect costs *should* be considered since they will be *directly* affected by the project. In summary, unless a cost element is directly changed by the project being considered, it should not be included in the economy study. Therefore, maintenance, power, fuel, and materials-handling costs may or may not be included, depending on the nature of the projects. Direct labor and insurance, on the other hand, are examples of direct costs that should normally be part of the study.

Frequently, an investment decision involves a choice between alternate methods of implementing the same project. This occurs, for example, when two different machines can do the same job. In such cases an economy study should concentrate on the direct and overhead costs associated with each alternative. Management is looking for a cost advantage, and if the operating expense is the same for both alternatives, this alone will not tell management what the real cost differences are.

Time Periods

The last type of data needed to evaluate investment projects is the estimated life of the investment. The time over which the equipment will be productive can be considered from many perspectives, but the most significant are its

1. *Accounting life*
2. *Machine life*
3. *Economic and technological life*

Accounting life The *accounting life cycle* of an investment is determined by the method of depreciation selected for that investment. The method, in turn, is often prescribed or influenced by government tax regulations. As mentioned previously, however, the depreciation rate and the book value seldom apply directly to managerial capital-allocation decisions since the rate of depreciation rarely coincides with the actual decline in the usefulness of the equipment. Furthermore, the book value and the actual market value are rarely the same. For these reasons, accounting life is not often used to project the actual life of an investment for the purposes of an economy study.

Machine life The *machine life cycle* of an investment is an estimate of the length of time that the machine, or asset, will be able to perform its function. Metal-working equipment and buildings can remain usable over remarkably long periods of time, but the durability of buildings and such machines as turret lathes and drill presses can be deceptive. The economic feasibility of using these assets may disappear long before they are functionally inoperable; it may increase production costs to utilize such outmoded equipment even though it is in perfectly sound working order.

A good illustration of this problem is in the electronic computer field. New and improved computers are continually replacing older ones because the older computers, although they are still operational, soon become uneconomical to operate—the newer machines can do more work at a lower price. Thus, to continue operating the older equipment would simply penalize the company.

Economic and technological life   For the purposes of an economy study, the most logical time frame is the *economic life* of an asset. It is simply an estimate of the length of time over which an asset will be *economically* productive; such estimates are difficult to make, however. When does a machine or a building cease to be economical? It is hard to say. Periodic comparisons of existing equipment and possible innovations using the economy-study technique are perhaps the only ways of estimating an asset's economic life. In such cases possible savings in operating costs become the principal criteria in determining whether a replacement investment is wise.

An interesting statistical solution to the question of economic feasibility is offered by the MAPI technique, which is discussed in Chapter 8. Using this approach, historical data on the operation of large samples of various types of machines over their respective lives are accumulated and analyzed. The result is a series of typical operating curves, cost curves, and graphical decision rules that can be used to estimate economic life.

The preceding discussion of capital facilities is primarily oriented toward the cost of production. In our rapidly expanding economy, the major determinant of costs and, in turn, of economic life is the applicable level of technology or "state of the art." The pace of technological change is the critical factor in determining the economic life of capital assets. Equipment that is still usable can quickly become an economic burden because of technological improvements. These improvements can be either new, less costly processes or systems that eliminate the need for an old process; both types of improvements may lead to the destruction of capital tied up in an asset. The pace of change is ever increasing. Equipment, products, buildings, and most other capital assets have been losing their economic value faster and faster in recent years, which means that returns from investments must be recovered sooner: this is the heart of the challenge facing the management of capital today.

Questions and Problems

1. If a business has bought an asset for $25,000, would it be sensible for the business to refuse to sell it for anything less "because this would involve a loss"? Would your answer be the same if adjustments had been made for depreciation and taxes?
2. A company official proposed the following policy: "Each year, purchase plant equipment in an amount equal to its depreciation charge." Discuss the merits of this policy.
3. What steps should a company take in order to make the best use of its capital funds?
4. In what way does time enter into an analysis of income and expense funds?

5. "The capital-budgeting procedure is often unrealistic because it frequently rules out the allocation of funds to projects that are vital to the life of the firm." Discuss.
6. In capital budgeting, a demand curve is constructed from the inventory of project opportunities available to the firm. Evaluate the "cost of capital" as the rejection rate that should be applied to all projects in the capital-rationing process.
7. What are the differences between direct, indirect, fixed, and variable costs?
8. What is sunk cost? Why is it irrelevant in evaluating investment opportunities? What are relevant costs?
9. What are the meanings of economic life, technological life, accounting life, and machine life?
10. What is the discounting factor? How do you calculate the present value of money?
11. Does the economic life of an asset equal its machine life?
12. What are the purposes of depreciation?
13. Why do firms normally use accelerated methods of depreciation even though these methods cause the profit picture to be lower in the early life of the asset?
14. Is it rational to retain an asset because it has a large sunk cost? Explain.
15. How should a firm determine its minimum acceptable rate of return on capital expenditures?
16. What are the available sources of funds for capital investment? What are the advantages and limitations of these sources?
17. Calculate the present value of a new investment whose income stream is tabulated below, assuming the discount factor is 9%.

YEAR	REVENUE
1	387,000
2	490,000
3	1,250,000
4	3,200,000
5	1,100,000
6	700,000
7	600,000

18. An investment opportunity will require three equal payments of $100,000. The first payment is due at the start of the project and the other two in two and five years, respectively. What is the present value of money needed for the project if the discount rate is 7 percent?
19. Compare the declining-balance, straight-line, and sum-of-the-digits depreciation approaches for an initial investment of $40,000. The investment is to be depreciated for 20 years and the interest rate for the declining balances is 10 percent. Do any of the methods leave a salvage value?
20. What are opportunity costs? How do they influence capital decisions?
21. A company is reviewing a proposed project that will require an investment of $100,000 and that will return the profits listed below over the next five years.

YEAR	ESTIMATED PROFIT
1	30,000
2	40,000
3	40,000
4	20,000
5	10,000

What is the net present value of the project if the discount rate is 10 percent? How much would it change if the salvage value of the investment after 5 years were $10,000?

References

Anthony, R. N., *Management Accounting Practices,* rev. ed., Irwin, Homewood, Ill., 1969.

Barish, N. N., *Economic Analysis for Engineering and Managerial Decision Making,* McGraw-Hill, New York, 1962.

Bradley, J. F., *Administrative Financial Management,* 2nd ed., Holt, Rinehart and Winston, New York, 1969.

Colberg, M. R., Bradford, W. C., and Alt, R. M., *Business Economics: Principles and Cases,* 4th ed., Irwin, Homewood, Ill., 1970.

Dean, J., *Capital Budgeting,* Columbia University Press, New York, 1951.

————, *Managerial Economics,* Prentice-Hall, Englewood Cliffs, N.J., 1951.

De Garmo, E. P., *Engineering Economy,* 4th ed., Macmillan, New York, 1967.

Eckstein, O., *Water-Resource Development: The Economics of Project Evaluation,* Harvard University Press, Cambridge, Mass., 1958.

Gardner, F. V., *Profit Management and Control,* McGraw-Hill, New York, 1955.

Gillis, F. E., *Managerial Economics: Decision Making under Uncertainty for Business and Engineering,* Addison-Wesley, New York, 1969.

Grant, E. L., and Ireson, W. G., *Principles of Engineering Economy,* 5th ed., Ronald Press, New York, 1970.

Hanssmann, F., *Operations Research Techniques for Capital Investment,* Wiley, New York, 1968.

Levin, R. I., and Kirkpatrick, C. A., *Quantitative Approaches to Management,* 2nd ed., McGraw-Hill, New York, 1971.

Riggs, J. L., *Economic Decision Models for Engineers and Managers,* McGraw-Hill, New York, 1968.

Solomon, E. (ed.), *The Management of Corporate Capital,* The Free Press, New York, 1959.

Taylor, G. A., *Managerial and Engineering Economy: Economic Decision-Making,* Van Nostrand-Reinhold, Princeton, N. J., 1964.

Thuesen, H. G., and Fabrycky, W., *Engineering Economy,* 3rd ed., Prentice-Hall, Englewood Cliffs, N. J., 1964.

8

Capital-Allocation Methods

Chapter 7 presented the background information relevant to capital-allocation decisions. In this chapter we will analyze the various approaches to capital-allocation decisions and pinpoint their strengths and weaknesses. In order for sound decisions to be made in the allocation of capital to specific projects, differences between the alternatives must be expressed in common units. Yardsticks must be formulated that can deal adequately with the time value of money, the rate of return, the size of investment, and the impact of risks such as obsolescence.

Methods of Evaluation

The most common methods of analyzing data on various alternative investments may be divided into three general categories:

1. *Annual-cost approaches*
   (a) Payback period
   (b) Average value, or equivalent uniform annual cost
2. *Present-value approaches*
   (a) Present-value total cost
   (b) Present-value average cost
   (c) Discounted cash flow
3. *Empirical approaches*
   (a) MAPI

In the first group of methods, investment and operating costs are distributed over the life of the asset involved. Regardless of when they occur and whether they are "lump sum" or "annual stream" in nature, a single average annual cost is set up as being representative of all costs. In theory it is assumed that all project expenses can be spread uniformly over the time period under consideration and that this "average" cost is the approximate annual cost to the firm of undertaking the investment. In contrast, present-value approaches relate all costs and revenues to their present-day value on the assumption that all expenses, regardless of time or form, should be expressed in terms of today's dollars. In a sense, this second group of methods expresses the problem by envisioning a single, hypothetical pool of capital, existing now, from which all project expenses during the period under consideration will be defrayed. The differences between these two types of economy studies are depicted in Figure 8–1.

Diagram (a) represents the typical cost pattern for an acquisition with operating costs that will occur during a five-year life span. Diagram (b) illustrates how the present-value methods would treat this project's costs. All expenses would be discounted in terms of today's dollars, and a single pool of these dollars would be created in an amount equal to the total of these costs. In diagram (c), on the other hand, an average annual cost is created by distributing the project's total costs evenly over the life of the project.[1]

The final category of economy-study methods is typified by the MAPI technique, which involves an empirical weighting of data that have been statistically accumulated and analyzed in order to create an average-machine operating profile.

Now let us take a closer look at each of the methods within the three categories.

Payback Period

One method of evaluating investment opportunities is to calculate the payback period of each alternative. *Payback period* may be simply defined as *the time it takes to recover an investment.* A comparison of this figure with the estimated economic life of the investment will provide one criterion for assessing the merits of a particular project. The analysis is based upon a representative, or average, year's activity. In mathematical terms, payback period is calculated as follows:

$$PB = \frac{I}{Z}$$

where   PB = payback period in years
         I = investment in dollars
         Z = either the yearly net cost savings or the yearly net profit resulting from the investment

---

[1] How these conversions are performed will be explained shortly, during the discussion of these methods.

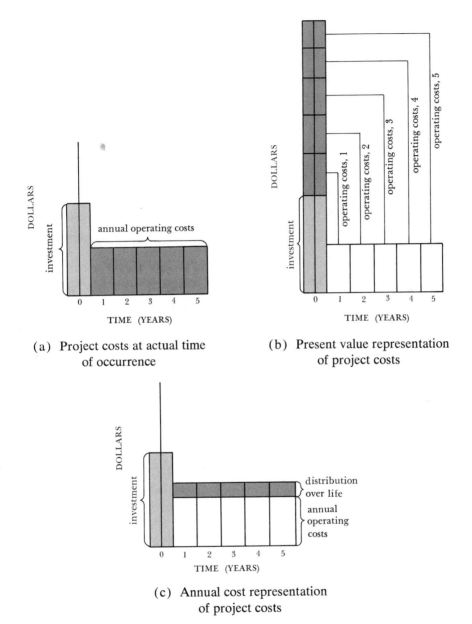

(a) Project costs at actual time of occurrence

(b) Present value representation of project costs

(c) Annual cost representation of project costs

Figure 8–1 Analyzing costs in terms of annual cost and present value

If the salvage value is significant, I should be changed to $I - S$, where S is the expected salvage value of the equipment. Where one piece of equipment is considered as a replacement for another with no change in output, Z represents the net cost savings, or the difference between the annual costs of operating the new equipment and continuing to operate the old. In this context the payback period is the time it takes for the cost savings to equal the actual investment. Where the output is affected, Z is the average annual net profit from the investment. If a machine is purchased to produce a new product, for example, the average annual net profit is the difference between revenue and expenses, and the payback period is the time required for the profit from the project to equal the investment.

This approach stresses the importance of determining the length of time needed by an investment to pay for itself. In our rapidly changing business environment, it is vitally important to determine if an asset will become obsolete before its cost can be recovered. Although payback measures how fast the original investment will be returned, it does not measure the life of the investment or the overall return. Thus, payback alone is not a sufficient measure of an investment. Imagine two alternate investments, A and B. A's payback period is two years; B's is three years. However, A's economic life is only three years, whereas B's is nine years. Payback alone would suggest that alternative A should be selected, yet when overall return on investment is considered, B would seem to be the wiser investment.

Nevertheless, in our fast-paced economy, it is extremely important to pinpoint the speed with which capital assets will become obsolete. It has been found reasonably accurate to set up arbitrary, approximate payback periods of two to three years for small equipment investments. This may seem rather short, but the period of economic life for such assets is also short. For larger equipment, however, the payback period is generally longer, and extreme care must be taken to establish accurately the length of time over which the firm's funds will be tied up in the investment.

Here, many managers fall prey to a common mistake. Too often they become overly concerned with the accuracy and validity of the techniques used to calculate the payback period applicable to a particular investment. The major problem is deciding what will be an acceptable payback period; once established, this number (say, two years for small equipment) will act as a "go–no go" gauge for potential investment. The importance of establishing an accurate gauge can be illustrated by the experience of a well-known electronics manufacturer. In response to an apparent high rate of obsolescence in the electronics industry, this firm established a payback limit of 1.25 years. Although such a relatively low figure might have been desirable if applied to *some* investment categories, its application to the company's metal fabrication plant proved disastrous. The short payback cycle forced the firm to acquire machines at relatively low prices. This equipment required large numbers of highly skilled, expensive labor. To achieve the operating volumes needed to generate sufficiently large savings, the equipment had to be general purpose in nature and was not, therefore, precisely suited to economical manufacture of any of the firm's products. The results were paradoxical. The plant's facilities paid for themselves in short order, but management soon discovered that the company's operating cost structure was becoming increasingly uncompetitive. At length, the company recognized the need to rethink the payback criteria applied to investment in machines for its plant.

Some pieces of equipment have no meaningful payback period. This occurs, for example, if the life of the equipment is shorter than what the payback period would be. This may seem unlikely, yet in many complex processes, units will wear out before they have paid for themselves. Peripheral gear for computer installations, such as tape stations and printers, sometimes fall into this category. They are integral parts of the overall system, and no alternative selections exist. In such cases the concept of economic life is completely unrelated to economic usefulness; therefore, the objective becomes to minimize loss, and payback does not contribute to this analysis.

Average Value, or Equivalent Uniform Annual Cost

A second method used to evaluate investment opportunities is the *average-value method*. The basic assumption underlying this approach is that investments in capital assets are made in order to obtain production over a number of years. Therefore, it is thought that decreases in the value of an asset due to wear and age, and the cost of interest charges, should be spread uniformly over the projected life of the asset. In effect, both the decrease in the value of the asset and the interest charges are treated as a *cost of producing the final product*. This results in a common denominator that may be used to compare alternative investments even though their economic lives are different. Any uniform time period may be used to calculate the costs and earnings. Normally, a one-year period is used, since this is consistent with the accounting practices of most firms. Thus, the making of cost and earnings estimates is simplified, and the interpretation of the results is easier.

The average-value approach is normally used to evaluate alternatives with the same income stream in order to isolate cost patterns as the deciding factor—for example, to evaluate two or more ways of accomplishing the same goal, such as choosing between two machines, either of which could make the same part.

Suppose that an executive has to decide whether or not to purchase a new type of machine to replace an existing piece of equipment. At present he is using a machine that was purchased and installed at a cost of $20,000; it is six years old and has been depreciated at 10 percent a year, using the straight-line method. Thus, its current book value is $8,000; its resale value is only $4,400, however. A new set of expense estimates for the *future* use of the equipment has been developed, as shown in Table 8–1. Expense estimates for the proposed new equipment, which would cost $16,000 after installation, also appear in Table 8–1. Notice that only differential, or incremental, cost items are listed on this expense schedule. It is tacitly assumed that all other expenses, such as supervision, would be the same regardless of the machine chosen. Hence, these other expenses do not have a meaningful bearing on the selection decision; they are not relevant.

The economy study analyzing these statistics is shown in Table 8–2. The format used is a common one; it is designed to facilitate comparative evaluation of the two alternatives.

Calculation of the annual operating expenses, such as labor and indirect manu-

Table 8–1   Comparative expense and installation costs

	Present Equipment	*Proposed Equipment*
Investment	$20,000	$16,000
Original rate of depreciation	10%	
Current book value	$ 8,000	
Salvage value	$ 4,400	
Expense estimates		
Interest	8%	8%
Depreciation (straight line)	25%	10%
Taxes and insurance	10%	10%
Social security and workmen's compensation	7%	7%
Direct labor	$ 7,200	$ 3,800
Indirect costs (power, etc.)	$ 850	$ 420

Table 8–2   Comparison of alternatives. Average-value method of economy study (approximate method)

	Present		*Proposed*	
Fixed Expenses (1 year)				
Interest (8% × average value)[a]	0.08($2,750) = $	220	0.08($8,800) = $	704
Depreciation (depreciation rate × investment)[a]	0.25($4,400) =	1,100	0.10($16,000) =	1,600
Taxes + insurance (10% × average value)	0.10($2,750) =	275	0.10($8,800) =	880
Subtotal		1,595		3,184
Operating Expenses (1 year)				
Direct labor		7,200		3,800
Social security + workmen's compensation (7% of direct labor)	0.07($7,200) =	504	0.07($3,800) =	226
Indirect costs		850		420
Subtotal		8,554		4,486
Total		$10,049		$7,570

Net yearly savings   = $10,049 − $7,570 = $2,479
Net capital investment = $16,000 − $4,400 = $11,600
Payback period   = 11,600/2,479   = 4.6 years

[a] These values are calculated by the approximate method.

facturing costs, is a routine matter. These data can be easily derived from the firm's accounting records. Annual taxes and insurance expenses, which are part of the projected fixed expenses, are calculated by applying a percentage to the average value of the investment. The problem is how to determine the average investment value; a simple formula used for calculating this is

$$I_{avg} = I\left(\frac{N+1}{2N}\right)$$

where I = current real (or market) value of the investment

N = number of years over which the investment is depreciated, or its economic life

Applying this formula to the hypothetical case cited in Table 8–1, we have an average investment value for the proposed machine of

$$I_{avg} = 16,000\left(\frac{10+1}{2 \times 10}\right) = 16,000\left(\frac{11}{20}\right) = 8,800$$

This figure was used in the calculations for Table 8–2.

Transforming the original investment into a uniform annual cost is a bit more complex. This annual charge must provide for the recovery of the investment (the depreciation) plus the interest on it. Obtaining an average value is further complicated by the fact that the investment is steadily declining in value during the period under consideration. One may arrive at an approximate solution to the problem by treating the investment and the interest charges separately, thus handling investment simply as annual depreciation. The annual interest charge is determined by applying the interest percentage to the average investment value. In this case, 8 percent interest was applied to the $8,800 average investment that we just calculated for the proposed machine, resulting in an average annual charge of $704. This approximate method of computing average cost understates the true cost, however. The amount of error becomes greater as the interest rate and the economic life of the asset increase. Occasionally, accuracy is of critical importance, and when it is, the average-value method should be bypassed in favor of a more exact method that we will describe in a moment. However, if only a rough comparison of the costs is required (as is usually the case), the approach described above will serve the purpose.

Using a more exact method, one may calculate the average depreciation and interest charges simultaneously. A single annual compounding factor, commonly called the *capital-recovery factor,* is used. The mathematical expression for this factor is

$$CRF = \frac{i(1+i)^n}{(1+i)^n - 1}$$

where CRF = capital-recovery factor

i = interest rate

n = economic life of the asset

Inserting the data for the proposed equipment into the formula, we have

$$CRF_{proposed.} = \frac{0.08(1+0.08)^{10}}{(1+0.08)^{10} - 1} = 0.149$$

The annual charge for interest and depreciation is the product of the CRF and the amount invested. For the proposed machine it is

Annual interest and depreciation charge = $16,000 \times 0.149 = \$2,384$

The economy study presented in Table 8–3 has been prepared using this more precise method of computing investment recovery and interest. Notice that all the other terms are the same as in the approximate method shown in Table 8–2. Notice, also, that the difference between the interest, tax, and investment costs is not very great. For the proposed machine the difference is only $80 ($2,384 − [$1,600 + $704]).

While the average-value method is simple to use and compares alternatives on the basis of annual costs (a practice quite familiar to management), it has several major limitations. In the hypothetical case just discussed, the income streams for both present and proposed equipment were assumed to be the same. Therefore, the only comparison necessary was on the cost side. However, the proposed equipment has a projected economic life of ten years as opposed to only four more years for the present equipment. If the average-value method is to be valid, the alternatives must be compared over the same length of time; otherwise, the income streams will differ and thus negate the pure-cost approach. A four-year period was used in the example to keep the income streams equal. Thus, only 4/10 of the cost of the new equipment (four years of depreciation based upon a projected ten-year economic life) was considered. It must be assumed, of course, that the remaining 6/10 of the cost will be recovered from the resale of the equipment at the end of the four years. Whether or not this would be so is

Table 8–3   Comparison of alternatives. Average-value method economy study (exact method)

	Present		*Proposed*	
Fixed Expenses (1 year)				
Depreciation and interest[a] (CRF × *I*)	0.301($4,400) =	$ 1,324	0.149($16,000) =	$2,384
Taxes + insurance (10% × average value)	0.10($2,750) =	275	0.10($8,800) =	880
Subtotal		1,599		3,264
Operating Expenses (1 year)				
Direct labor		7,200		3,800
Social security + workmen's compensation (7% of direct labor)	0.07($7,200) =	504	0.07($3,800)	266
Indirect costs		850		420
Subtotal		8,554		4,486
Total		$10,153		$7,750

Net yearly savings   = $10,153 − $7,750 = $2,403
Net capital investment = $16,000 − $4,400 = $11,600
Payback period   = 11,600/2,403   = 4.8 years

[a] These values are calculated by the exact method.

questionable; therefore, the inclusion of this assumption in the average-cost approach lessens the value of the approach somewhat. How much it is reduced depends on how much confidence management has in the resale assumption.

The second limitation is implicit in the method itself. In the average-cost method, all expenses are considered equal regardless of when they arise in time. Therefore, in the example, expenses that occur during the fourth year are equal to those that occur during the first year. The fallacy in this approach should be apparent from our previous discussion of the present value of money.

Present-Value Total Cost

Present-value total cost, as the name implies, is an economy-study method that relates all project expenses to their dollar value at the time of investment. The basic assumption of this approach is that the best investment among possible alternatives is the one that requires the least funding of today's dollars. This approach and others like it are particularly useful in cases where conservation of capital is of primary importance.

The objective of this method is thus to compare investment possibilities in terms of present-dollar cost rather than in terms of the "real-dollar" cost arising over future periods. Unlike the average-cost approaches, the period of time during which the expenses associated with an alternative are computed under this method is the economic life of the equipment. Thus, for each year of operation, the annual costs must be discounted back to the time of the original investment so that all costs can be expressed in present dollars. Depreciation of the equipment is not considered, because its total cost at the time of purchase is included in the study; adding depreciation would simply mean double counting. Other criteria, such as risk of obsolescence or rate of return, are not directly considered; this is one of the major difficulties in using present-value methods.

In our previous example comparing two machines, the old machine had an economic life expectancy of four years, while the proposed one had a life expectancy of ten years. The difficulty of comparing total costs for these two alternatives under the present-value method is readily apparent. To establish comparability for the purpose of determining which investment requires the least funding of present dollars, the manager must do one of the following:

1. Assume that the new equipment will wear out in four years
2. Compare the equipment over four years and subtract the estimated resale value of the new equipment from the total costs
3. Assume that the old equipment will last ten years
4. Assume a common denominator for the two alternatives, which, in this case, would be twenty years.

Table 8–4 shows the calculations involved if the manager chooses the first alternative. The present values used in these and subsequent calculations are contained in the Appendix. In terms of this analysis, it would be unwise to purchase the new equipment since savings would be virtually nonexistent. This re-

Table 8–4   Present-value total cost (equipment life: four years)[a]

	Present		*Proposed*	
Equipment		$ 4,400		$16,000
Taxes and insurance on equipment				
Year 1	$ 275 (0.9259) = $	254	$ 880 (0.9259) = $	814
Year 2	275 (0.8573) =	235	880 (0.8573) =	754
Year 3	275 (0.7938) =	218	880 (0.7938) =	699
Year 4	275 (0.7350) =	202	880 (0.7350) =	646
Operating expenses				
Year 1	$8,554 (0.9259) = $	7,910	$4,486 (0.9259) = $	4,150
Year 2	8,554 (0.8573) =	7,330	4,486 (0.8573) =	3,840
Year 3	8,554 (0.7938) =	6,780	4,486 (0.7938) =	3,570
Year 4	8,554 (0.7350) =	6,290	4,486 (0.7350) =	3,290
		$33,619		$33,763

[a] Costs are figured here with an 8 percent discount factor.

sult is due to the fact that we have assumed that the total cost of the new equipment must be absorbed in four years. In contrast, under annual-cost methods, only 4/10 of the cost of the new equipment would be considered at the end of four years.

Using the second alternative, the salvage value of the new equipment is subtracted from its purchase price. Thus, if we assume that the market value corresponds to the depreciated book value, using straight-line depreciation we could subtract the projected book value at the end of four years from the total cost of the new method to determine present cost. Of course, these figures would have to be discounted back to present dollars. Thus, under this method the discounted resale value is

$$\frac{6}{10}(\$16,000) \times 0.7350 = \$6,356$$

Subtracting this amount from the cost of the new method, we have

$$\$33,763 - \$6,356 = \$27,407$$

Subtracting the present cost of the proposed equipment from the present cost of existing equipment, we find that there is a potential saving of $6,212, which is still considerably less than the one shown in the average-value approach. The reason for this is that the major costs of the new method are incurred at once with the purchase of the equipment, so these dollars are not discounted. On the other hand, the major costs shown for the old method are actually operating costs that occur over time and are thus discounted. In short, the discounting process operates to put stress on the cost of initial investments.

A third way of equalizing equipment life for purposes of comparison would be to assume that the old equipment will last for ten years. This assumption would clearly be meaningless if an accurate estimate of the life of the old equipment is believed to be four years. For this reason few firms use the third alternative.

Finally, one could assume a period of time that would be exactly divisible by the estimated lives of both alternatives. In the example we have been using, this "least common multiple" would be twenty years. The basis for this assumption is that in twenty years, five of the old machines and two of the new machines would be purchased and utilized. This is a highly tenuous basis for analysis, particularly as the length of time grows. It would be extremely unusual in our dynamic economy if the same type of equipment could be profitably utilized with the same operating characteristics for twenty years. Where the common multiple in years is under five, however, the method has greater validity.

An example of this "least-common-multiple" approach is shown in Table 8–5. Note that it is assumed that the price for machines purchased in the future will be the same as for machines purchased today. This is a highly suspect assumption, considering our experience of rising price levels. However, it does permit a relatively easy calculation of future equipment purchases. Present costs of proposed equipment are simply multiplied by a discount factor, DF, based upon the interest rate and number of years involved.

The common-multiple approach further assumes that annual operating costs such as direct labor and expenses such as taxes and insurance will remain constant throughout each year of the period under consideration. This makes it pos-

Table 8–5 Comparison of alternatives. Present-value total cost: common-multiple economy study

Present Machine

Investment: Acquisition of machine	
Today	$ 4,400
4 years later, $4,400 \times DF_4$ (or 0.7350) =	3,234
8 years later, $4,400 \times DF_8$ (or 0.5403) =	2,377
12 years later, $4,400 \times DF_{12}$ (or 0.3971) =	1,747
16 years later, $4,400 \times DF_{16}$ (or 0.2919) =	1,284
Annual operating costs, taxes, and insurance	
$C_A \times PWF_{20} = \$8,829 \times 9.818$	$ 88,600
Total present worth	$101,642

Proposed Machine

Investment: Acquisition of machine	
Today	$16,000
10 years later $= 16,000 \times DF_{10}$ (or 0.4632)	7,411
Annual operating costs, taxes, and insurance	
$C_A \times PWF_{20} = \$5,366 \times 9.818$	52,700
Total present worth	$76,111
Net savings $= \$101,642 - \$76,111 =$	$25,531

sible to use a single multiplier, often called the *present-worth factor* (PWF), to obtain present-day-equivalent dollars for the operating costs that will be incurred over the span of the common multiple, in this case the next twenty years. The mathematical expression of this factor is

$$\text{PWF} = \frac{(1 + i)^n - 1}{i(1 + i)^n}$$

where   PWF = present-worth factor
i = interest rate
n = length of study period

The size of the present fund needed to cover projected costs is equal to

$$F_p = C_A \times \text{PWF}$$

where F_p = present fund
C_A = annual cost to be funded

It is interesting to note that PWF is actually the reciprocal of the capital-recovery factor (CRF) used in the annual-cost economy study. This is not surprising when we consider that PWF measures how much money must be set aside today at a known rate of interest in order that a specified sum can be paid out annually over a fixed period.

The results obtained from the "common-multiple" present-value analysis are often difficult to evaluate. For example, a "net saving" of $25,531 was attributed to the proposed machine in our hypothetical case, yet a manager would be hard-pressed to put his finger on this saving. Actually a "safer" interpretation would be that the proposed machine represents a good investment, but even this "safe" interpretation is suspect when one considers that entirely different results would be obtained if the study period were reduced from twenty to four years. Once again the manager must be warned against relying too heavily on the mathematical precision of these approaches. Because a certain amount of error is built into the assumptions that are present in each method, the results must be considered very carefully. It usually requires a manager with experienced judgment to relate these figures and assumptions to operating reality.

Present-Value Average Cost

The present-value average-cost approach is, in essence, a combination of the present-value total cost and the average-value approaches. Like the latter methods, it considers only the cost side of the investment. The fundamental objective of the present-value average-cost method is to use the discounting approach to depict "financial reality" and yet present costs on an annual basis to facilitate interpretation of the operating characteristics of alternatives.

The present value of all costs that will be generated over the entire life of a project is calculated by using the appropriate discount and present-worth factors

Table 8-6 Comparison of alternatives. Present-value average cost[a]

Investment	Present		Proposed	
Equipment cost		$ 4,400		$16,000
Operating costs, taxes, and insurance	$8,829(3.312) =	29,400	$5,366(6.709) =	36,000
Total		$33,800		$52,000
Average cost per year	$33,800/4 =	$ 8,450	$52,000/10 =	$ 5,200

Savings per year = $8,450 − $5,200 = $3,250
Payback period = 11,600/3,250 = 3.5 years

[a] Costs are figured here with an 8 percent discount factor.

just discussed. The total present value of an investment is then divided by its projected economic life to obtain an average annual cost. Although it is possible to present investment data on the basis of an average year, the problems inherent in comparing alternatives with different life spans persist. In particular, the manager is faced with the problem of how to treat the income stream, but usually it is simply assumed that income will "continue as before."

The application of the present-value average-cost method to our hypothetical case is depicted in the economy study shown in Table 8–6. For both the present and proposed alternatives, the current market value of acquisition is listed as the investment cost. The operating costs, taxes, and insurance for the present machine are held constant over the predicted economic life of four years. A PWF based upon four years and 8 percent interest was used to determine the present value of the existing machine's cost stream. Similarly, a PWF based upon ten years of economic life and 8 percent interest was used to determine the present value of the proposed machine's projected annual cost stream. The average costs for the two alternatives were compared, and it was found that a "saving" of $3,250 per year would be earned if the proposed equipment were purchased. The time required to pay back the differential investment of $11,600 was estimated at 3.5 years.

As with the present-value, total-cost approach, it is possible to derive more realistic figures by comparing both alternatives over a four-year span and then estimating the resale value of the new equipment. From the calculations made previously, we know that the resale value in present dollars would be $6,356 at the end of four years. Incorporation of this item as a reduction in investment cost for the proposed equipment is illustrated in Table 8–7.

Using a standard four-year time frame for both alternatives has a sharp impact on the resulting figures. The estimated payback period is now 7.3 years, which is definitely not attractive. Once again it is apparent that the validity and usefulness of these economy studies depend upon how well management can tailor assumptions and methodology to the particular case; no one approach will give accurate answers under all circumstances.

Table 8–7 Comparison of alternatives.
Present-value average cost with resale value[a]

Investment	Present	Proposed
Equipment cost	$ 4,400	($16,000 − $6,356) = $ 9,644
Operating costs, taxes, and insurance	$8,829(3.312) = 29,400	$5,366(3.312) = 17,700
Total	$33,800	$27,344
Average cost per year	$33,800/4 = $ 8,450	$27,344/4 = $ 6,836

Savings per year = $8,450 − $6,836 = $1,614
Payback period = 11,600/1,614 = 7.3 years

[a] Costs are figured here with an 8 percent discount factor.

Summary of Basic Methods

Before examining the last two approaches, let us summarize the most common problems encountered in the methods already presented, since the last two approaches are designed to overcome some of these limitations.

Uneven Economic Lives

The economy-study methods already presented usually assumed that the economic lives of alternatives were equal. This assumption was often made even when comparing old and new equipment, and this was clearly inaccurate. When the projected economic life of one alternative is shorter than that of another, some way must be found to make the periods comparable.

In the approaches already considered, the solution was generally to use the shorter life as the basis for comparison. This obviously permitted a direct comparison of the two alternatives over the shorter time span, but it did not take into consideration either the salvage value of the longer proposal or its economic worth during the period when the shorter-lived alternative was not operable.

For example, consider two alternative methods, one with an economic life of ten years and the other with an economic life of five years. During the first five years, the methods can readily be compared, but problems arise in the sixth year. If the alternative with the ten-year life were selected, there would be no need for an additional outlay; if the other alternative were chosen, there would be. To solve this dilemma, the discounted resale value of the longer-lived machine should be subtracted from its costs, as was done in several earlier examples. This is a very tenuous cost estimate, however, since predictions about technological and price-level changes are very risky if made far in advance. Furthermore, it still does not take into account the income stream of the longer-lived alternative after the fifth year; this is a major weakness. The replacement of machinery or investments is normally not a one-time phenomenon. Generally, there should be a chain of replacements[2] over time because this better reflects the dynamics of

[2] This concept is explained further in the discussion of the MAPI approach.

technological development. Proper analysis, therefore, should be based on a comparison of the chains themselves rather than on a comparison of discrete units. The first four methods of economy study presented in this chapter do not allow for this type of analysis, however.

Unequal Annual Earnings

Another assumption that both annual-cost and present-value methods must make is that the earnings stream is the same for all alternatives. In reality, this is rarely the case since costs and incomes vary. For example, maintenance costs ordinarily increase as equipment ages; thus, even if income remained the same, revenue from the investment would decrease over time. Although one could average the different yearly revenues, this would not be a satisfactory answer because the *timing* of the earnings stream is such an important factor.

For a large class of capital-allocation problems, however, one can make the assumption that the revenues are identical. These are generally machine-replacement problems where the replacement affects only the cost stream, not the income stream. In these cases, as in the examples already discussed, the income stream can safely be ignored because it is indeed the same for all alternatives.

Consider, however, two alternative investments—a typewriter plant and a computer plant. The income and cost streams will vary greatly in these two alternatives; none of the economy-study approaches discussed so far can easily cope with a problem of this sort.

Salvage Value

The question of how to handle the salvage value of investments is closely allied to the problem of unequal economic lives. In the methods discussed so far, as well as in the more advanced ones, salvage value is treated awkwardly as an allowance for resale. When the salvage value is small in comparison to the size of the investment, no difficulties are encountered using this technique. But when the salvage value is significant, it is difficult to get accurate results in this fashion. The reason for this is that salvage value must reflect the rate of technological development and therefore it is difficult to predict.

The usual procedure followed for any method is to subtract the resale, or salvage, value from the purchase price. This is a valid procedure in cases where there is already a salvage value at the time of installation, since the marketplace itself established the value. But when the salvage value does not arise until after a certain period of time has elapsed, an estimated value must be subtracted from the cost stream, and this estimate must be based on the level of technology that would be expected to exist at that time. As we have mentioned previously, the more distant the projection, the more difficult it is to make a valid estimate. This is particularly true if management wants the results to be expressed in present dollars, because then the discounting factor must be estimated as well.

Although the problem of handling salvage value is thorny, its impact on the final investment decision is normally not nearly so great as the problems of obsolescence, risk, sunk costs, and uneven lives; although the estimates and methods for salvage value are uncertain, they can be useful if properly interpreted.

This review of the limitations of the basic methods of economy-study analysis is not meant to imply that these methods are worthless; it is simply an attempt to delineate where the basic approaches will be useful and where alternative study methods should be utilized.

Advanced Methods of Analysis

The following alternative methods of economy-study analysis have been designed to overcome some of the limitations of the basic approaches.

Discounted Cash Flow for Investments

The *discounted-cash-flow method* can be used in difficult cases where annual earnings cannot be treated as constant, where resale values are significant, where investment is incremental, and where the lives of the investments are uneven. This is essentially a trial-and-error approach. The expected earnings for each year are listed, and various discount rates are tried until one is found that will make the present value of the earnings stream equal to the required investment. This procedure is followed for all alternative investments, and the one with the highest discount rate is chosen.

This approach plays down all other factors and focuses on opportunity costs. If a particular investment alternative has a discount rate of 10 percent, the opportunity to obtain the same rate would be considered when evaluating other alternatives; obviously another project with an 8 percent discount rate would not be judged as good.

Consider the case of two alternative investment opportunities that are designed to serve the same purpose and have the same projected economic lives. One alternative's revenue stream equals the investment when discounted at 10 percent; the other's revenue stream equals its investment at 8 percent. The earnings that are discounted at 10 percent are judged preferable to those discounted at 8 percent in this case, because if the earnings of the 10 percent alternative were discounted into present dollars at 8 percent there would be a surplus of earnings over investment and profits would rise. Thus, the 10 percent alternative would repay the investment faster. Furthermore, it has what amounts to a 2 percent safety margin over the 8 percent alternative in the event that earnings estimates prove overly optimistic.

The mechanics of the discounted-cash-flow method are somewhat complicated, as can be shown by a simple example. Suppose a manager receives a proposal that will require an initial $10,000 investment, and he chooses the discounted-cash-flow method to evaluate it. In the first two years, the projected earnings are $2,000 each year; in the third and fourth years, $4,000 each; and in the fifth and sixth years, $1,000 each. This revenue stream is shown in Table 8–8. To evaluate the relative profitability of this proposal, the manager first assumes a

Table 8–8 Comparison of alternatives. Discounted cash flow

Year	Earnings Estimates	Discount Rate				
		25%	*20%*	*15%*	*10%*	*12%*
1	$2,000	$1,600	$1,666	$1,740	$ 1,818	$1,786
2	2,000	1,280	1,390	1,512	1,652	1,596
3	4,000	2,048	2,312	2,628	3,004	2,848
4	4,000	1,640	1,732	2,288	2,732	2,544
5	1,000	327	402	497	621	566
6	1,000	262	335	432	564	507
Present value		$7,157	$7,837	$9,097	$10,391	$9,845

discount rate and then uses it to determine the present value of the projected earnings. Suppose he first selects a 25 percent discount rate. At this rate the earnings stream shows a present value of $7,157. This is below $10,000, the amount of the investment, so a smaller discount rate must be selected. Moving down to a 20 percent rate, the present value of earnings is $7,837. This is still too low; so is the $9,097 yield at a 15 percent rate. At a discount rate of 10 percent, however, the yield is $10,391, which indicates that a greater discount rate can be used. A 12 percent rate gives a present value of $9,845, which is just too low. Thus a discount factor of 11 percent appears "correct" for this hypothetical situation.

The usual expression of the equation for this method is based on increments that reflect the intervals at which business data are normally collected.

$$I = \sum_{t=1}^{T} \frac{Rt - Et}{(1 + i)^t} + \frac{S(T)}{(1 + i)^T}$$

where
I = investment in dollars
T = economic life in years
t = time increments
Rt = revenue for a given period
Et = expenses for a given period
$S(T)$ = scrap value at end of the economic life
i = discount rate

Various alternative investments can also be compared using this approach. Earnings vary not only from year to year but also from alternative to alternative. If the investment is incremental, the added investment can be handled either as an expense in the year it occurs or as an addition to the original investment. Adding it to the original investment means that it must be discounted to its present value, which in turn means that a projected discount rate must be posited. Since this rate is difficult to estimate accurately, the expense approach is commonly used. It is important to make a distinction between the discounting procedure used in the discounted-cash-flow method and in the present-value, average-cost, and total-cost methods. In the latter cases, it is necessary to estimate the discount rate that will actually exist. In the discounted-cash-flow method, however, it is not. This is another reason for the popularity of the discounted-cash-flow method among contemporary managers.

The problems posed by investment alternatives having different economic lives can also be handled by the discounted-cash-flow method, since the basis for comparison is the discount rate, which equates projected earnings with investment cost. This rate can be obtained for any alternative regardless of its economic life.

The case for using the discounted-cash-flow method is not quite so strong as the preceding discussion may seem to suggest, however. A vast amount of calculation is involved in a realistic study; furthermore, the repetitive trial-and-error process often takes a great deal of time. For these reasons the discounted-cash-flow method is generally thought to be a very expensive technique, although the use of electronic computers can reduce the required time and cost considerably. Nonetheless, the discounted-cash-flow method has been used principally to evaluate investments of considerable magnitude where the computation costs involved can be justified.

There are several other problems in using the discounted-cash-flow method. This approach does indicate which *rate of return* is greatest, but it does not specify the size of the investment, and this information is often of critical importance in the final evaluation of alternatives. A $10,000 investment opportunity may have a discount rate of 15 percent while a $20,000 opportunity may have one of 25 percent, yet the added investment of $10,000 would not be taken into consideration under this method.[3]

Closely allied to the problem of investment size is the question of repayment. Alternatives with higher discount rates tend to repay an investment faster than those with lower rates, yet the discounted-cash-flow method can provide no data for use in timing repayments. Furthermore, alternatives with higher discount rates may yield less profit in absolute terms than those with lower rates.

Like simpler methods, the discounted-cash-flow method depends upon an accurate estimate of the salvage values of alternatives at the end of their economic lives. As previously noted, these values are difficult to predict. The salvage value must be discounted to present value and subtracted from the original investment, or from the operating costs, at the time of the sale. This is the same general procedure followed in the simpler methods, and it is subject to the same shortcomings.

Although the discounted-cash-flow method clearly has many limitations, it also has an impressive list of advantages. As we mentioned earlier, selection of a method is contingent on the type of problem to be solved, and many problems can best be evaluated by the discounted-cash-flow approach. In practice this approach is chiefly used in evaluating new product opportunities, where the flow

---

[3] This is a universal problem which is confronted when using any one single indicator to measure an activity. Rate of return, return on sales, and other similar measures have the same failing.

of revenue is important for comparison purposes. Since firms are continually evaluating new products or variations in older products, this method is important because it helps management make these investment decisions.

Discounted Cash Flow for Equipment Replacement

The discounted cash flow concept can also be adapted to the problem of the chain of replacements involved in a continuing equipment-replacement program. If a firm is to continue in business it must periodically replace worn or economically unsound equipment. The problem is to decide when to replace it— should it be now, next year, or ten years from now?

In this situation the earnings are considered to be the same for the new equipment as for the old. The problem then resolves to the question of what replacement program will yield the lowest costs. The equation for the present worth of a future cost pattern is

$$PW = \left[I - \frac{S_t}{(1+i)^t} + \sum_{t=1}^{T} \frac{C_t}{(1+i)^t} \right] \frac{(1+i)^t}{(1+i)^t - 1}$$

where
I = investment
T = economic life
i = interest rate
S = salvage value
C = cost of operation and maintenance
PW = present worth of cost stream
t = time increment

The equipment should be replaced when the present worth of its cost stream (PW) is a minimum.

When a series of alternative replacement plans and alternative equipment plans are available, each of the alternative PW values should be calculated; the alternative with the least PW is the best investment. The procedure for doing this is iterative, as will be shown in the following example.

Consider the problem of the owner of a taxicab. Since he intends to stay in business for many years, his question is when should he replace his cab. The cost pattern is as follows.

Purchase price of cab	$3,250
Interest costs	10%
Operating costs per year	$400
Maintenance (where t = years of operation)	$250t$
Estimated salvage value	
1st year	$2,500
2nd year	2,000
3rd year	1,400
4th year	1,000
5th year	700

Table 8–9   Present worth calculations

T (in years)	I	St	$\dfrac{1}{(1+i)^t}$	$\dfrac{St}{(1+i)^t}$	Ct
1	3250	2500	.91	2275	650
2	3250	2000	.83	1660	900
3	3250	1400	.75	1050	1150
4	3250	1000	.68	680	1400
5	3250	700	.62	434	1650

$$^{\text{a}}\left[I - \frac{St}{(1+i)^t} + \sum_{t=1}^{T} \frac{Ct}{(1+i)^t} \right].$$

The task is to solve the formula for PW using successive *T*'s until the minimum value of PW is found. This is done in Table 8–9. As can be seen from the table, the lowest PW value occurs when the cab is replaced after two years. Omitting other considerations, replacement at that time will result in the best investment policy.

This approach to equipment replacement suffers from the same shortcomings as the iterative procedure used for evaluating alternative investments. The primary problem lies in predicting the values needed for the equation. These include estimates of future salvage value, interest rates, and operating and maintenance costs. A secondary problem is the cost and time involved in the calculations.

In general, when reliable estimates of costs are available, this approach is the best solution to the continuing replacement problem. Where cost cannot be predicted with the desired reliability, another approach must be used.

MAPI

One way to make such an analysis is to use the MAPI method developed by George Terborgh.[4] It is specifically designed to evaluate alternatives when estimates of the future stream of costs are not obtainable, as is frequently the case with replacement chains. Suppose, for instance, that a manufacturer wants to replace an old model of computer with a newer model and that the present piece of equipment has been in use for two years. New and more efficient models of computers are continually coming on the market. If the manufacturer purchases a new computer now, it will probably be economically unsound to purchase a more efficient model that *may* come on the market next year. Thus, in replacing a computer a firm must consider not only the economics of purchasing a new model but also how such a purchase will probably influence the future stream of purchases. Although little is known about opportunities that may arise

[4] The initials stand for Machinery and Allied Products Institute. The method is presented in George Terborgh's *Business Investment Policies* (Washington, D.C.: MAPI, 1958), and *Business Investment Management* (Washington: MAPI, 1967). The calculation methods are somewhat different in the two books and yield slightly different answers. The method presented here is the most recent MAPI version, which is discussed in the 1967 book.

for taxicab replacement

$\dfrac{Ct}{(1+i)^t}$	$\displaystyle\sum_{t=1}^{T} \dfrac{Ct}{(1+i)^t}$	[ ]^a	$\dfrac{(1+i)^t}{(1+i)^t-1}$	PW
591	591	1566	11.00	17226
747	1338	2928	5.76	16865
862	2200	4400	4.03	17732
952	3152	5722	3.17	18138
1023	4175	6991	2.64	18456

in the future, some means must be employed that will measure empirically the soundness of alternative investments. To accomplish this, the MAPI method tries to establish a relative rate of return for alternatives. For each alternative, a tax-adjusted rate of return on investment for the next year is calculated. In early versions of the MAPI method, this was called an *urgency rating,* and the term is still in common use. The urgency rating attempts to measure the difference between investing in an opportunity now or deferring it for a period of time, by comparing the rate of return for the incremental, or net, investment with the rate of return if the company did not make the investment. It is assumed that the higher the urgency rating, the greater the opportunity of profit associated with making the change.

This approach differs from the methods discussed earlier in two basic ways:[5]

1. *The MAPI method does not rely upon average costs per year or upon total costs over the life of an investment.* Instead, it concentrates on the initial rate of return for the next period or, as it is commonly referred to, "one more year."
2. *MAPI includes income taxes in its calculations.* Since most businessmen treat these taxes as a cost of doing business, their inclusion is generally considered valid and useful.

Four elements are used in the calculations to determine the urgency rating.

Element 1: Next-year operating advantage. This is the algebraic sum of the total increase or decrease in operating costs and revenues for the next year. It reflects the changes in operating costs and revenues for all items except capital costs and income taxes. With the purchase of a new piece of equipment, operating costs usually decline; its increased efficiency typically reduces the cost of

---

[5] The 1958 version also differed in a third way. It used three different methods to evaluate the residual value of an alternative—by three separate obsolescence schedules. The standard schedule posited a uniform decline over the economic life of the asset; the other schedules assumed an accelerated and a decelerated reduction in the usefulness of the equipment during the early years of the predicted economic life. This feature was dropped in the 1967 version since in practice it was little used and did not significantly change the ratings.

labor, maintenance, and materials. On the revenue side, the introduction of new machinery usually increases production output and thus leads to increased revenue.

Element 2: Initial net investment. This is the installed cost of the alternative less any investment avoided or released by it. "Released investment" is the salvage, or resale, value of the present equipment; "avoided investment" represents any capital additions that would have been required if it had been decided to continue using the present equipment. To return for a moment to the computer purchase example, the difference between the cost of the new computer and the resale value of the present one would be the installed cost of the investment. Any repair or maintenance work that would have been needed to keep the present computer in operation would be avoided investment, and thus it would be subtracted from the installed cost to give the net investment.

Element 3: Terminal net investment. This is the projected retention value of the new equipment at the end of the year less the resale value of the old equipment if kept until then. To find the retention value of new equipment at the end of the year, MAPI has developed an accurate and simple method using charts. One of these charts is illustrated in Figure 8–2. The values on the chart are derived from a complex formula that gives a realistic and useful estimate of capital depletion on the basis of such factors as economic life, salvage value, expense stream, income tax rate, depreciation, interest, and overhaul costs.[6]

Element 4: Next-year income tax adjustment. This is the *net* change in income taxes that will be expected as a result of an investment. A firm undertakes an investment to increase its profits by reducing costs and raising revenues, but increased profits change the income tax liability of the firm; not all of the profits can be retained. Therefore, it is usually quite important to study the impact of projected tax changes.

The urgency rating can be computed on the basis of these four elements, as follows:

$$\text{Relative rate of return} \atop \text{(urgency rating)} = \frac{(1) - (4) - [(2) - (3)]}{[(2) + (3)]/2} \times 100$$

or

$$\text{Urgency rating} = \frac{\begin{matrix}\text{Operating} \\ \text{advantage}\end{matrix} - \begin{matrix}\text{Increase in} \\ \text{income tax}\end{matrix} - \begin{matrix}\text{Capital} \\ \text{consumed}\end{matrix}}{\text{Average investment}} \times 100$$

The numerator is a measure of a project's return on investment, while the denominator represents its cost. The result is an empirical rating by which alternative investments for a company can be ranked. It is a valid measure only for the next year, however, and should not be taken as a measure for future years.

MAPI calculations   To illustrate the use of the MAPI approach, let us trace

[6] For a detailed explanation of the formula, see G. Terborgh, *Business Investment Management* (Washington: MAPI, 1967), Appendix D, and Edward H. Bowman and Robert B. Fetter, *Analysis for Production Management* (Homewood, Ill.: Irwin, 1957), pp. 375–81.

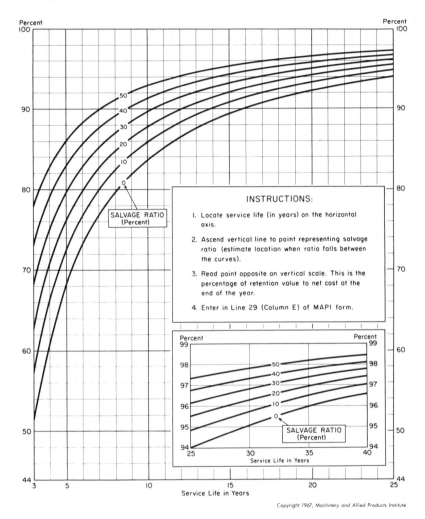

MAPI CHART No. 1A

(ONE-YEAR COMPARISON PERIOD AND SUM-OF-DIGITS TAX DEPRECIATION)

INSTRUCTIONS:

1. Locate service life (in years) on the horizontal axis.

2. Ascend vertical line to point representing salvage ratio (estimate location when ratio falls between the curves).

3. Read point opposite on vertical scale. This is the percentage of retention value to net cost at the end of the year.

4. Enter in Line 29 (Column E) of MAPI form.

SALVAGE RATIO (Percent)

Service Life in Years

Figure 8–2   MAPI calculation chart

its use in a particular replacement problem: we wish to investigate the feasibility of replacing our current equipment with a new machine. To do this, we will calculate an after-tax return, or urgency rating, for the new equipment, using the MAPI Summary Form shown in Figure 8–3. This rating can then be compared with similar ratings obtained for alternative projects. Those projects with the highest ratings are considered to be the best economic investments.

Our project is the replacement of machine 1203 with a new piece of equipment, machine 1307. We shall make the comparison for a period of one year, as

MAPI SUMMARY FORM

(AVERAGING SHORTCUT)

PROJECT _Replacement of Current Machine #1203_

ALTERNATIVE _Machine 1307_

COMPARISON PERIOD (YEARS)   (P) _1 year_

ASSUMED OPERATING RATE OF PROJECT (HOURS PER YEAR)   _3430_

I. OPERATING ADVANTAGE

(NEXT-YEAR FOR A 1-YEAR COMPARISON PERIOD,* ANNUAL AVERAGES FOR LONGER PERIODS)

A. EFFECT OF PROJECT ON REVENUE

		INCREASE	DECREASE	
1	FROM CHANGE IN QUALITY OF PRODUCTS	$ 10,000	$	1
2	FROM CHANGE IN VOLUME OF OUTPUT	15,000		2
3	TOTAL	$ 25,000 X	$ Y	3

B. EFFECT ON OPERATING COSTS

		INCREASE	DECREASE	
4	DIRECT LABOR	$	$ 10,000	4
5	INDIRECT LABOR	1,500		5
6	FRINGE BENEFITS		2,600	6
7	MAINTENANCE		3,000	7
8	TOOLING	500		8
9	MATERIALS AND SUPPLIES		1,000	9
10	INSPECTION		3,000	10
11	ASSEMBLY			11
12	SCRAP AND REWORK		1,000	12
13	DOWN TIME		1,000	13
14	POWER		500	14
15	FLOOR SPACE	1,500		15
16	PROPERTY TAXES AND INSURANCE	500		16
17	SUBCONTRACTING			17
18	INVENTORY			18
19	SAFETY			19
20	FLEXIBILITY			20
21	OTHER			21
22	TOTAL	$ 4,000 Y	$ 22,100 X	22

C. COMBINED EFFECT

23	NET INCREASE IN REVENUE (3X−3Y)	$ 25,000	23
24	NET DECREASE IN OPERATING COSTS (22X−22Y)	$ 18,100	24
25	ANNUAL OPERATING ADVANTAGE (23+24)	$ 43,100	25

* Next year means the first year of project operation. For projects with a significant break-in period, use performance after break-in.

in the majority of MAPI evaluations. The machine is used for two shifts of 35 operating hours each per week. Since the plant shuts down for two weeks of vacation and one week of holidays per year, the operating rate of the equipment is assumed to be 49 × 70, or 3430, hours per year. This information is entered as shown at the top of the MAPI Summary Form.

NEXT-YEAR OPERATING ADVANTAGE   The remainder of Sheet 1 of the form

II. INVESTMENT AND RETURN

A. INITIAL INVESTMENT

26	INSTALLED COST OF PROJECT	$250,000		
	MINUS INITIAL TAX BENEFIT OF	$ ———	(Net Cost)	$250,000 26
27	INVESTMENT IN ALTERNATIVE	$ ———		
	CAPITAL ADDITIONS MINUS INITIAL TAX BENEFIT			
	PLUS: DISPOSAL VALUE OF ASSETS RETIRED			
	BY PROJECT *	$50,000	$ 50,000 27	
28	INITIAL NET INVESTMENT (26—27)		$200,000 28	

B. TERMINAL INVESTMENT

29 RETENTION VALUE OF PROJECT AT END OF COMPARISON PERIOD
(ESTIMATE FOR ASSETS, IF ANY, THAT CANNOT BE DEPRECIATED OR EXPENSED. FOR OTHERS, ESTIMATE OR USE MAPI CHARTS.)

Item or Group	Installed Cost, Minus Initial Tax Benefit (Net Cost)	Service Life (Years)	Disposal Value, End of Life (Percent of Net Cost)	MAPI Chart Number	Chart Percentage	Retention Value $\left(\frac{A \times E}{100}\right)$
	A	B	C	D	E	F
Machine 1307 Sum-of-the-digits depreciation	$250,000	9	10	1A	84.2	$210,500

	ESTIMATED FROM CHARTS (TOTAL OF COL. F)	$210,500		
	PLUS: OTHERWISE ESTIMATED	$ ———	$210,500	29
30	DISPOSAL VALUE OF ALTERNATIVE AT END OF PERIOD *		$ 35,000	30
31	TERMINAL NET INVESTMENT (29—30)		$175,500	31

C. RETURN

32	AVERAGE NET CAPITAL CONSUMPTION $\left(\frac{28-31}{P}\right)$	$ 24,500	32
33	AVERAGE NET INVESTMENT $\left(\frac{28+31}{2}\right)$	$187,750	33
34	BEFORE-TAX RETURN $\left(\frac{25-32}{33} \times 100\right)$	% 9.9	34
35	INCREASE IN DEPRECIATION AND INTEREST DEDUCTIONS	$ 36,265	35
36	TAXABLE OPERATING ADVANTAGE (25—35)	$ 6,835	36
37	INCREASE IN INCOME TAX (36×TAX RATE)	$ 3,417	37
38	AFTER-TAX OPERATING ADVANTAGE (25—37)	$ 39,683	38
39	AVAILABLE FOR RETURN ON INVESTMENT (38—32)	$ 15,183	39
40	AFTER-TAX RETURN $\left(\frac{39}{33} \times 100\right)$	% 8.1	40

* After terminal tax adjustments.

Figure 8–3 MAPI summary of analysis form

shows the calculations of next year's operating advantage to be gained by investing in the new equipment. (This corresponds to calculation element 1 mentioned earlier.) Lines 1–3 determine the new equipment's effect on revenue. We know that the new machine will produce the same volume of output as the old equipment and thus will not influence revenue in this way. However, it is expected to hold tolerances better, so it will produce fewer rejects. The additional usable output is expected to yield $15,000 in added revenue. In addition, the improvement in quality is estimated to be worth $10,000 per year, giving a total increase in revenue (line 3) of $25,000.

Lines 4 through 22 help to calculate the effect of the new equipment on operating costs. For example, direct labor costs are calculated to decrease by $10,000 and indirect labor costs to increase by $1,500. Concomitant with the drop in direct labor costs is an expected drop in fringe benefits amounting to $2,600. Maintenance costs will be $3,000 less with the new machine, but tooling will be $500 more. Lines 9 through 21 are filled in with data arrived at in a like fashion. Line 22 shows the total increase and decrease in costs. The net decrease is then entered in line 24. Adding the increase in revenue (line 3) to the decrease in operating costs (line 24), we obtain the annual operating advantage of the project (line 25).

Turning to sheet 2 of the summary form, we proceed to calculation elements 2, 3, and 4. Section II of the form, Investment and Return, is divided into three parts. A, Initial Investment, corresponds to element 2; B, Terminal Investment, to element 3; and C, Return, incorporates element 4—tax adjustment—to arrive at the urgency rating, here called the *after-tax return*.

INITIAL NET INVESTMENT   Our data show that the new equipment will cost $250,000 to install. It will do all the work required in the next year without additional capital expenditures. The current resale value of the machine now in use is $50,000; therefore the initial net investment for the project is $200,000, which is entered on line 28.

TERMINAL NET INVESTMENT   The calculations carried out for lines 29 and 30 give us the terminal net investment to be entered on line 31. The table under line 29 is completed with the aid of one of the MAPI charts. We will use sum-of-the-digits depreciation and therefore we refer to MAPI Chart 1A (Figure 8–2). Under the column heading "Item or Group" we enter the machine number and the depreciation method to be followed and in column D we write the chart number. The installed cost of the equipment is $250,000; its estimated service life is 9 years, and at the end of that time it has an estimated salvage value of $25,000 or 10 percent of its cost. This information is entered into columns A, B, and C.

To find the entry for column E we enter Chart 1A (Figure 8–2) at 9 years on the horizontal axis and move upward to the curve relating to a salvage value of 10 percent. Moving left to the vertical axis, we obtain a percentage figure of 84.2, which we enter in column E of line 29 in the summary form. Finally, for column F we calculate

$$\frac{\$250,000 \times 84.2}{100} = \$210,500$$

This is the final entry for line 29, the retention value of the project at the end of the comparison period.

If replacement of the present machine is delayed another year, its salvage value will decrease by $15,000, so its resale value at that time will be $50,000

— $15,000 or $35,000, which is entered on line 30. Subtracting this amount from the retention value, we obtain terminal net investment of $175,500 for line 31.

URGENCY RATING   To compute the rate of return or urgency rating, we must first find the before-tax return as directed in lines 32 through 34. Next we must calculate the project's effect on income tax (element 4). The profits to be taxed will be reduced by additional depreciation and interest deductions. Our added net investment for the year (line 33) will be $187,750; at 6 percent, there will be additional interest charges of $11,265. Depreciation during the year for the new equipment will be $9/45 \times \$200,000$, or $40,000. As noted earlier, the old equipment would depreciate an additional $15,000 during that time, so the increase in depreciation if the new machine is purchased will be $25,000. The sum of the interest deductions and depreciation, $36,265, is entered in line 35.

For tax purposes, the taxable advantage is the difference between lines 25 and 35, $6,835, which is entered in line 36. Since the company is taxed at the rate of 50 percent, the increase in income tax will be half the taxable operating advantage, or $3,417 (line 37). Completing lines 38 through 40, we find that our project has an urgency rating or after-tax return of

$$\frac{15,183}{187,750} \times 100 = 8.1 \text{ percent}$$

This figure presents the first-year tax advantage as a percentage of investment. The selection or rejection of this project will depend not only on the ratings of alternative projects relative to this but also on the availability of capital.

MAPI summary   In essence, MAPI simply offers a tax-adjusted first-year rate of return. If numerous proposals are competing for the same funds, however, the MAPI method can pick out those that should have priority for the funds. Thus, it may be used to make periodic tests of a firm's capital equipment status and investment opportunities and thus help management make sound investment plans.

The MAPI method, in its latest form, makes it possible to apply complicated calculations to investment analysis in a simple fashion. When used by competent personnel, it yields realistic approximate data for investments whose income and expense streams cannot be estimated. As noted, the major weakness of the method is that it evaluates alternatives only one year in advance. With certain modifications, the MAPI approach can be utilized for new product opportunities. As a rule, however, it is used only for equipment-replacement studies, because it does not examine future earning streams.

Noneconomic Investment Factors

In concluding this discussion of capital inputs, it is important to repeat that methods of evaluating capital acquisition deal primarily with the economic factors of an investment. Very little formal consideration is given to risk or other important investment intangibles. It should also be stressed again that the selection of a particular analysis approach is of tremendous importance. Since all approaches incorporate different assumptions and have individual strengths and weaknesses, the one that best fits the characteristics of a particular investment decision should be selected. No one method fits all conditions. Since it is possible to get completely opposite information by applying different approaches, a firm should be particularly careful in selecting its analysis approach.

Questions and Problems

1. Which of the following two guidelines would you prefer in choosing between various proposed capital-expenditure projects, discounted dollars or payback period? Explain.
2. Identify the conditions under which you would prefer each of the following methods in evaluating capital allocation:
    (a) Payback period
    (b) Average value on annual cost basis
    (c) Present value of total costs
3. The newly formed Alpha Manufacturing Company is in the market for new machinery. An investigation of available equipment has narrowed the choice to the two machines described below.

	MACHINE A	MACHINE B
Type of equipment	General purpose	Special purpose
Installed cost	$8,000	$13,000
Salvage value	800	3,000
Annual labor cost	6,000	3,600
Estimated life	10 years	4 years
Annual taxes, insurance, etc.	2.5 percent of initial cost	

Assume an interest rate of 8 percent. Which machine would you recommend on the basis of (a) annual cost; (b) present value? State and discuss all assumptions.

4. The XYZ Company is a manufacturer of metal furniture. It is currently considering updating its technology and is focusing its attention on its turrent lathes. Six lathes are used in the production process, and the operating data are presented below:

Initial cost	$7,200 each
Estimated salvage (at the end of 10 years)	200 each
Estimated salvage now—the machines are six years old	1,200 each
Annual labor cost	6,500 each
Economic life	10 years each
Annual taxes, insurance, etc.	2 percent of initial value

The company is considering the purchase of six new labor-saving machines. Their characteristics are as follows:

Initial cost	$11,000 each
Estimated salvage at the end of life	2,000 each
Annual labor cost	4,200 each
Economic life	6 years each
Annual taxes, insurance, etc.	2 percent of initial value

Assuming an interest rate of 10 percent, should the present machines be replaced? Your answer should be developed using (a) annual cost; (b) present value. What would your answer be if the company's payback period were three years? Discuss.

5. The DEF Investment Corporation has purchased an office building in the center of town. The present financial characteristics of this building are summarized as follows:

12 stories tall	
Total investment	$16,000,000
Total income	1,675,000 per year
Total fixed and operating expenses	775,000 per year

The corporation is considering the addition of eight more floors to this building. If this were done its financial characteristics would be:

20 stories tall	
Total investment	$19,500,000
Total income	2,950,000 per year
Total fixed and operating expenses	1,200,000 per year

If the rule of this corporation is to have all investments earn a minimum of 12 percent, would you recommend the expansion of this building? Support your position.

6. The Longhand Motor Freight Company is considering the purchase of a new fleet of trucks. The cost data are as follows:

	OLD	NEW
Original installed cost	$100,000	$140,000
Reserve for depreciation	60,000	—
Overhead costs (less depreciation)	7,500	10,000
Operating costs	150,000	110,000
Present market value	60,000	—
Estimated future life	4 years	10 years
Rates of interest		
Bank	5 percent	
Rate of return	20 percent	

Should a new fleet be purchased?

7. Why are sunk costs omitted from economy studies?

8. What part do opportunity costs play in economy studies? Which methods use opportunity cost concepts?

9. The Acme Company currently has three punch presses in its machine shop. It is considering the sale of these presses and the purchase of two automatic presses that could provide the needed "punching capacity." The pertinent data are presented below. Develop a recommendation regarding this purchase based upon a present-worth analysis. If the purchase is made, what will be the magnitude of the sunk costs incurred? Explain how the present-worth approach can provide useful data for capital-budgeting purposes.

PRESENT: PUNCH PRESSES

Installed cost	$12,000 each
Salvage value now (the presses are three years old)	2,000 each
Disposal value	5,000 each
Annual labor cost	6,500 each
Annual power, fuel, and supplies	700 each
Original depreciation (sum of the digits)	8 years
Estimated future life	4 years
Annual insurance, taxes, etc.	2.5 percent

PROPOSED: AUTOMATIC PRESSES

Installed cost	$20,000 each
Salvage value	3,000 each
Annual labor cost	4,200 each
Annual power, fuel, and supplies	800 each
Estimated life	5 years
Annual insurance, taxes, etc.	2.5 percent

10. The Day Company is contemplating the purchase of a new piece of equipment to be used in its machine shop. The two machines described below will meet this company's requirements.

   Machine G. This is a general-purpose machine that can perform many different operations. It has an estimated productive life of 15 years. Its first cost will be $9,000 installed; the salvage value at the end of 15 years is estimated at 10 percent or $900. The machine utilizes semiskilled labor at a probable annual cost of $6,000.

   Machine S. This is a special-purpose machine that will perform the operations required immediately, but is less flexible and can be purchased for $17,000 installed. Future uncertainties make it necessary to calculate the machine's productive life conservatively at 6 years. At that time, its salvage value is estimated to be $2,500. The annual labor cost to provide the same volume of product as machine G would probably be $3,600, since unskilled labor will be employed.

   Assume that taxes and insurance will be 2.75 percent per year of the initial investment and that the "interest rate" is 9 percent. For all other factors the two machines are identical. Decide which machine to buy on the basis of annual cost alone.

11. Should depreciation and interest costs be included as relevant costs in the present value methods of analysis?

12. What are relevant costs? Are they the same for all methods of analysis?

13. Since different methods of capital analysis lead to different answers, how can you be certain which method and answer is correct?

14. A hospital is evaluating the purchase of two alternative machines to use in the analysis of blood samples. One unit is more expensive than the other, but because of its high degree of automation it has a lower labor cost. Both machines meet the hospital's needs. Which should they purchase?

	UNIT 1	UNIT 2
Purchase cost	$15,000	$22,000
Installation	4,000	5,000

Economic life	8 years	8 years
Labor costs per year	14,000	9,000
Maintenance costs		
First year	$500	$ 1,000
Increase per year (after first year)	50	150

15. The administration of ABC Insurance Co. is considering the purchase of a new copying machine. The machine will cost $8,300. It will lead to the saving of $0.025 per copy. Currently 12,000 copies are run per month. The machine is estimated to have an economic life of 4 years. The depreciation is 10 years straight line, and the firm evaluates its opportunity costs at 10%. What rate of return will the company get if it purchases the new copier?

16. What effect on the MAPI problem illustrated in Figure 8–4 and discussed in the text would each of the following have?

    (a) A change in the estimated service life to 12 years.
    (b) The use of declining balance depreciation.
    (c) A drop in the tax rate to 35%.

17. A company that repairs appliances is considering opening a new centralized facility to replace two smaller repair centers. The investments for land, building, and equipment are $7,000, $180,000, and $70,000, respectively. Because of the location and newer equipment, labor costs will decline $60,000 a year. In addition, the company will save $25,000 in yearly rental costs paid for the old facilities. Cost increases will occur in insurance, maintenance, real estate taxes, income taxes, travel, and heating and lighting. The sum of these estimated increases is $38,000. The centralized facility will decline in value uniformly for 30 years with an expected salvage value of $20,000. The equipment will decline in value uniformly for 8 years with no expected salvage value. The facility will be used 2,000 hours a year; tax depreciation is declining balance, and the tax rate is 50%. What is the MAPI urgency rate for the new facility?

18. A company wants to determine the MAPI urgency rate to see if an old piece of equipment should be replaced by a new machine. To carry out the analysis, management has developed these estimates.

Cost of new equipment	$17,000
Installation cost	3,000
Salvage value of present equipment	3,000
Reduction in direct labor	5,000
Reduction in maintenance cost	1,500
New tooling costs	700
Service life of new equipment	10 years
Salvage value of new equipment	$700
Income tax rate	50%
Capital costs avoided by new equipment	$ 900
Increase in revenue due to increased quantity of output	2,300
Decrease in revenue due to lowering of quality	1,500

What is the MAPI urgency rating for this project? Using it, would you go ahead with the project?

References

Anthony, R. N., *Management Accounting Principles,* rev. ed., Irwin, Homewood, Ill., 1970.

Barish, N. N., *Economic Analysis for Engineering and Managerial Decision-Making,* McGraw-Hill, New York, 1962.

Baumol, W. J., *Economic Theory and Operations Analysis,* 2nd ed., Prentice-Hall, Englewood Cliffs, N. J., 1965.

Bowman, E. H., and Fetter, R. B., *Analysis for Production Management,* rev. ed., Irwin, Homewood, Ill., 1961.

Buffa, E. S., *Models for Production and Operations Management,* Wiley, New York, 1963.

Colberg, M. R., Bradford, W. C., and Alt, R. M., *Business Economics: Principles and Cases,* 4th ed., Irwin, Homewood, Ill., 1970.

Dean, J., *Capital Budgeting,* Columbia University Press, New York, 1951.

———, *Managerial Economics,* Prentice-Hall, Englewood Cliffs, N. J., 1951.

De Garmo, E. P., *Engineering Economy,* 4th ed., Macmillan, New York, 1967.

Gillis, F. E., *Managerial Economics: Decision Making under Uncertainty for Business and Engineering,* Addison-Wesley, New York, 1969.

Grant, E. L., and Ireson, W. G., *Principles of Engineering Economy,* 5th ed., Ronald Press, New York, 1970.

Masse, P., *Optimal Investment Decisions, Rules for Action and Criteria for Choice,* Prentice-Hall, Englewood Cliffs, N. J., 1962.

Riggs, J. L., *Economic Decision Models for Engineers and Managers,* McGraw-Hill, New York, 1968.

Swalm, R., "Economics of Machine Selection and Replacement—A Bibliography," *The Engineering Economist,* Vol. 6., No. 3, Spring 1961, pp. 51–57.

Terborgh, G., *Business Investment Policies,* Machinery and Allied Products Institute, Washington, D.C., 1958.

———, *Dynamic Equipment Policy,* McGraw-Hill, New York, 1949.

Thuesen, H. G., and Fabrycky, W. J., *Engineering Economy,* 3rd ed., Prentice-Hall, Englewood Cliffs, N. J., 1964.

9

Human Factors and the Design of Work Conditions

Man is an integral part of every production system. In a highly manual system, he is a vital part of the conversion function. In a highly automated production system, his intervention is necessary to control unpredictable events. The degree to which man is part of the system is a function of the economic and technical characteristics of the system. In considering these factors, it is easy to overlook the fact that man himself is an extremely complex system. He has many talents, but also many limitations. If a production system is to be efficient, man as an element in it must function efficiently. This means that systems designers must understand the way man functions in order to properly design his job, his work area, and the tools he uses. They must also understand his interpersonal relationships, his motivations, and numerous other psychological factors that bear on his performance.

In recent years the study of man as it relates to systems has come to be given the title Human Factors. In our investigation of human factors, we will develop some generalizations about human participation in a production system. In dealing with people, no set of precise rules can be followed. Man is too diversified. However, an awareness of the generalities of behavior will help to develop approaches for analyzing man's role in a production system.

Man as a Physical System—Anatomical Factors

One of the prime concerns in designing man into a production system is the consideration of man as a physical system. People differ physically in many ways; they differ in size, shape, strength, and endurance. Before we can design an efficient production system involving workers, machines, work areas, and production flows, we must have statistics that describe man's physical or anatomical characteristics.

The facilities people use should be in tune with both their function and the anatomy of the user. Hospital beds are functionally different from beds used in a home. In addition, hospital beds in a general hospital are larger than those in a children's hospital because of the differences in the users' physical characteristics. Secretarial desks and chairs are different from those used by managers in both functional design and size. Work areas highly efficient for one sex may be totally inadequate for the other. While flexibility is the key word in the design of any work area, it is often impossible to create efficient work places for the whole range of physical differences. If women are to be exclusively employed for the job, work areas conforming to female anatomical averages should be designed. The design should also incorporate enough flexibility to cover the physical variations within the group.

Consider the problem of designing a work position on an automobile production line. Numerous questions relating to man's physical characteristics arise, such as: How high off the ground should the assembly area be? How heavy should the tools be, and what shapes should they have? How fast should the line move? How much strength should the assembly worker be expected to need?

To help in answering such questions, numerous anatomical models have been developed. A sample is shown in Figure 9–1. When the information from such models is used and additional data are developed where needed, a working environment can be designed to fit the average worker's physical characteristics.

Indeed, just as man's anatomical characteristics should be considered in the design of a work area, they should also be considered in product design. How many different shoe sizes should be made in each style? How far should the brake and clutch pedals be from the seat of an automobile?[1] Anatomical models play an important part in the design of successful products and production facilities.

Working Conditions

Man's performance in a production system is also influenced by his reaction to his working environment. A good working environment is one that tends to increase motivation, whereas a poor environment suppresses it. In a bad environment, efficient production may be impossible.

Today it is generally recognized that good working conditions are essential, that poor working conditions are unsound both socially and economically. Some of the environmental conditions that influence performance are obvious. For example, typists need good lighting, and a photographic laboratory should have adequate ventilation. Other factors are more subtle. Designers of modern fac-

---

[1] The author vividly remembers having to have extenders welded to the clutch and brake pedals of a new sports car so that his wife could drive it.

tories, for example, consider the psychological effects of color and music in their architectural plans, since these factors affect workers' moods, fatigue, and alertness.

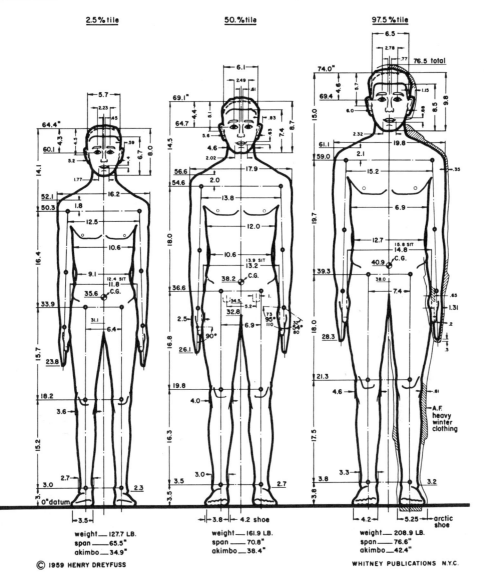

Figure 9–1 Anthropometric data—standing adult male (accommodating 95% of U.S. adult male population)

SOURCE *The Measure of Man,* copyright 1959 by Henry Dreyfuss, published by Whitney Library of Design, New York

Table 9–1   Level of illumination for various tasks[a]

Work Conditions	Minimum Foot-candles	Type of Task
Precise work of great accuracy	1,000	Extremely fine machine and assembly work. Most difficult inspections
	500	Difficult inspection and fine machine and assembly work
Fine detail work	200	Drafting, dental work, and close inspection
	150	Accounting, tabulating, business machine operation
	100	Regular office work. Ordinary assembly and machine work
Ordinary work	70	Intermittent filing and reading
	50	Ordinary inspection
Tasks not requiring prolonged viewing	30	Interviewing, washrooms, shipping
	20	Stairwells, elevators

[a] Data from *IES Lighting Handbook*, 4th ed., Illuminating Engineering Society, New York, 1966.

Lighting

The level of illumination that is required in a work area varies according to the particular job and the individual performing the task. Some jobs and some workers require more light than others. Jobs requiring exacting discrimination, such as wiring of computer memories, require more light than standard office jobs, for instance. The design of lighting systems is normally left to experts. The general approach is to establish the average level of illumination for the task, and then to provide some means for the individual worker to alter the intensity in his work space to suit his needs.

Standards of average illumination for various tasks have been developed by the Illuminating Engineering Society; a sample of their data is presented in Table 9–1. However, the variation in illumination desired by individuals will range broadly about these averages. An indication of the range of this variation is shown in Figure 9–2, which shows the dispersion of lighting intensities desired by individuals for reading an ordinary telephone book. From Table 9–1 we would expect to find the illumination between 70 foot-candles for intermittent reading and 100 for office work. Figure 9–2 indicates that when individuals are able to adjust their own lighting, the spread is extended upwards significantly.

Noise

Another important environmental consideration is the effect of noise, where noise is defined as unwanted sound. Two effects of noise concern us. One is the damage to the ear caused by high noise levels, which at the extreme can result in a loss of hearing. The other is the lowering of production efficiency resulting from nuisance levels of noise.

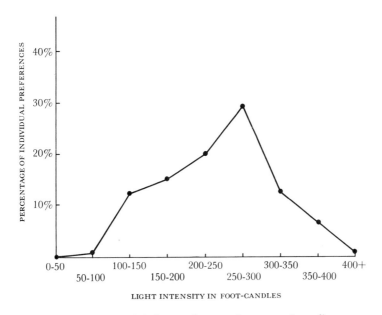

Figure 9–2   Lighting preference for normal reading

SOURCE   Data from Martin K. Starr, *Production Management Systems and Synthesis,* Prentice-Hall, Englewood Cliffs, N.J., 1964, p. 152.

Evidence piled up over many years shows that prolonged or sudden high noise levels can lead to hearing loss. Although debate still takes place over what noise level is enough to cause problems, most experts agree that noise levels over 100 dB will cause damage.[2] For this reason, aircraft ground personnel wear protective devices when working near jet engines, which produce a noise level of 130 dB as far away as 50 feet.

Noise levels can be well below the 100 dB limit and still be decided nuisances, with high-pitched sound being particularly aggravating. The average factory noise level of 80 dB falls into this category. Workers react to nuisance noise levels by increasing their muscle tension, which in turn increases their expenditure of energy and tends to bring about tiredness, irritability, and nervousness. Over time, people seem to accommodate to nuisance noise levels; however, there is considerable debate as to the costs involved. Many experts claim that even with accommodation there is a reduction in productive output and noticeable impairment of the emotional fitness of the worker. There is no question that work environments with high noise levels are unattractive, thereby diminishing a company's ability to obtain and keep better workers.

[2] The standard unit of measurement of sound is the decibel (dB). The measure is expressed as the logarithmic ratio of a particular sound to the threshold of audible sound, which is taken as 1 dB. For example, 100 db is 10^{10} times as great a sound as the audible level, or 10^2 times as great as 80 dB.

Management can control noise in three ways:

1. They can eliminate or lessen the noise by keeping equipment in good repair and by redesigning equipment to overcome noise problems.
2. Baffles can be erected to isolate the noise, protective equipment can be worn, or the source can be moved to a remote area.
3. Acoustical equipment can be installed to absorb or dampen the sound.

Some of these steps, such as keeping equipment in good repair, can be accomplished by management action. However, coping with the design of baffles, acoustic absorption equipment, or new machines is the task of an acoustical engineer.

Atmospheric Conditions

Atmospheric conditions also have a major effect on worker productivity and health. Great improvements have been made in the last twenty years in controlling the temperature, humidity, odor, and purity of the work atmosphere. Most offices and many factories are now air conditioned. Where special problems occur, such as when noxious and toxic fumes are emitted in metal plating or painting processes, protective clothing and air barriers or special exhaust systems are used.

The problems of creating and maintaining suitable atmospheric conditions can be dealt with at two levels. Harmful agents in the atmosphere must be controlled or kept from contacting workers.[3] This may require redesign of equipment and provision of protective clothing. In some cases elaborate warning systems are utilized: radioactivity-sensing badges are worn, and toxic gas warning systems are installed.

Secondly, an environment must be created that will be socially and productively beneficial. Hot, stuffy, poorly ventilated offices are undesirable; a comfortable air-conditioned environment will enhance productivity and increase social well-being.

Safety

The safety of workers must be an overriding factor in design of the work environment. Safety relates to all aspects of the physical work environment. We cannot, however, speak of absolute safety; it does not exist. Consequently, we must strive for acceptable degrees of safety. What is an acceptable level of safety? How do you evaluate an acceptable level of safety in an atomic power plant? How do you measure the value of a life, an arm, of hearing or sight? If they were held of infinite value, the cost of any processes would be too great to allow to exist. Yet certainly we do not want to undervalue them.

Consider the problem of a school district in which most of the children walk to school. To obtain an exceptionally high degree of safety, we might consider

---

[3] This will be discussed further in the section on safety.

having a police escort for each student. From a cost basis, this solution is obviously untenable. We might consider an adult crossing guard at each intersection, but this too will normally be too costly. So we probably end up with adult crossing guards at dangerous intersections and student patrols at others. We arrive at a socially acceptable level of safety consistent with an acceptable cost. The level of safety that is acceptable is continuously changing, continuously moving closer to absolute safety. At any point in time it represents a compromise between social and economic values.

Safety is undoubtedly a managerial problem. Management therefore should work to minimize accident rates and the consequences of accidents. Machines must assure reasonable safety levels, and so must processes and work areas. When management reduces accidents, it achieves both social and economic gains. The indirect and direct costs of accidents are considerable. To the employee, a reduced rate of accidents means less physical and mental pain and less financial loss. The employer benefits from a reduction in insurance and compensation costs, from less need to hire and train new workers or replace destroyed equipment, and in addition attains a safety reputation that attracts labor.

The causes of accidents can be divided into two categories: unsafe acts by workers, such as driving too fast, and unsafe work conditions, such as a poorly designed machine or a slippery floor. Studies have shown that in over 80 percent of industrial accidents both causes are present. A good accident prevention plan will thus attack both causes. One part of the plan should be aimed at eliminating bad practice by properly training workers and continually checking to see that they follow the prescribed methods. The other part of the plan will aim at improving the work conditions that can either cause accidents or heighten the severity of the accidents. In the automobile industry, for example, models have been recalled to replace defective parts, and special safety devices, such as seat belts, padded dash boards, and collapsible steering columns, have been installed to reduce the effect of accidents.

Man as a Behavioral System

Motivation

Up to now we have considered the physical aspects of man in a production system. Man in this sense is a factor of production. He produces output and is paid for his physical and mental effort. In dealing with man as a behavioral system, we will first investigate why and how well man puts forth this effort.

Human behavior is the result of a complex, interacting, often conflicting structure of cause and effect. Management's task would be quite simple if we could say that man works (the effect) for money alone (the cause)—that the more you pay him the harder he works. However, such a statement is a gross oversimplification, true only under certain conditions.

Then what does motivate man to work? Theories about this have gone through

Safety measures can take many forms. The rabbits in the upper picture are part of a warning system that detects leaks of a highly poisonous gas. The rabbits live only 30 seconds after exposure to the gas, thus giving workers time to sound the alarm and evacuate the area. Although the plant has a complex mechanical warning system, the workers place more faith in the rabbits. The lower photo shows a network of safety nets strung over a construction site to protect workers below from falling objects.

many changes and continue to evolve. Even as recently as fifty years ago, the working man was deemed to be incapable of even moderate social aspirations. He was thought to be concerned only with his subsistence, working only enough to sustain himself. Management "motivated" him by means of dictatorial, bullying practices. The first major change in this attitude was led by Frederick W. Taylor in the 1920s. Taylor expanded the subsistence theory. He believed that workers wanted more physical comfort than mere subsistence and consequently that the way to obtain greater worker productivity was to offer the worker incentive compensation.

During the 1930s, the vision of what motivates workers was broadened to include behavioral factors. It was observed that employees produced more if their psychological need to belong was satisfied. Ball teams, country clubs, bowling leagues, and employee associations were begun to bring the worker closer to the company—to give him a sense of belonging.[4]

Today we recognize that each of these ideas is but a small piece of the whole of human motivation. We view every individual as having his own pattern of wants, each of which influences his behavior. The strength of each factor varies with the individual and the particular set of circumstances. Sometimes financial wants will be paramount. At other times a desire for recognition may reign. Some wants will push the worker toward higher productivity, some toward maintaining the status quo, and others toward lower productivity. The managerial task of motivation is to increase satisfaction of the workers' productive wants within the accepted social structure.

Physiological Needs

Employees who are paid reasonable wages generally report to work. How well they perform depends on how well the job and the work environment meet their needs and desires. Human wants derive from two sources—physiological and psychological. The physiological needs, which form the primary want level, relate to the physical feeling of well-being. They include, among others, the need for food, water, sleep, exercise, and shelter. They are generally grouped by psychologists into three classes.[5]

1. *Positive or supply motives.* These result from deficiency and produce seeking and consumption of needed substance (hunger, thirst).
2. *Negative or avoidance motives.* These result from the presence of harmful or potentially harmful stimulation and produce flight or avoidance (pain, fear).
3. *Species-maintaining motives.* These result from the nature of the reproductive system and produce mating, child-bearing, and nurturant behavior (sex, love).

---

[4] This was one result of the Hawthorne experiments noted in Chapter 1.
[5] Berelson, B., and Steiner, G. A., *Human Behavior,* Harcourt Brace Jovanovich, Inc., New York, 1964, p. 242.

Psychological Needs

Until the physiological needs are reasonably well satisfied, they are generally the primary motivating force. In our society, the minimum physiological wants of workers are usually satisfied. Very little of a worker's day-to-day behavior is directly related to satisfying his physical needs. Working to buy an automobile, saving to take a vacation or to send a child to college, and working to "get ahead" are far removed from physiological needs. These activities are, however, goal related. They reflect psychological needs. These wants are secondary to the physiological needs, coming into play after the primary physiological needs are satisfied.

For purposes of analysis, human psychological wants can be separated into three areas—social needs, security needs, and achievement needs.

Social needs   The social needs encompass man's need for social contact and his need to belong. People in general want to be part of a group. They want to be considered in deliberations affecting the group, and in its gossip. They desire status within the group and want to be respected by outsiders for their membership in it. Some occupations are generally accorded higher status than others. A professional is normally held in higher esteem than a construction worker, even though an engineer may earn less than a plumber. Companies also differ in status—a trucking company generally is not as appealing as a space research firm.

Security needs   Man's security needs have two facets, economic security and job security. A great deal of attention has been given to economic security— steady employment; medical, disability, and other insurance plans; and provisions for old age. Government programs like medicare, social security, unemployment insurance, and workmen's compensation, and industrial pensions and insurance programs are all aimed at economic security. These programs are not generally under the control of production management.

The worker's need for job security, however, does lie within the realm of the production manager's concern. This need generates within the worker worries about his ability to meet future job requirements, to deal with his supervisors, and to cope with technological, organizational, and managerial changes. The average worker becomes anxious when he must learn new habits and forget old patterns. He must be helped to develop confidence so he can respond to new conditions.

Achievement needs   The final area of psychological wants covers man's need for achievement. Does his job allow him to do what he likes? Does it allow him to assert himself? Does it help or enable him to grow?

Few people put forth their best efforts unless they obtain a degree of satisfaction, personal and public, from their work. Furthermore, most people aspire to progress and grow in their work; they are rarely content to remain fixed. If progress or variety in their jobs is limited, workers tend to produce indifferently.

A Hierarchy of Needs

The totality of wants at this point may seem overwhelming, particularly if the interactions and conflicts between them are considered. Despite this, and despite the differences in individual responses, generalities can be drawn about need satisfaction.

Man has a hierarchical need pattern. The satisfaction of physiological needs is primary. To give an extreme example, in a desert the need for water is supreme. Once that is satisfied, the primary desire may be for a four-wheeled vehicle to replace the camel, or some other relatively less important satisfaction.

As the basic or primary physiological needs are satisfied, the psychological needs come into play. The ability to satisfy these needs depends on a person's aspiration level. An individual's image of himself establishes the level of fulfillment required to satisfy his psychological needs. A worker who believes he is the best worker will put forth great effort to maintain his position, especially if he feels that he is properly appreciated. Certainly he will work harder than an individual who perceives himself as a mediocre worker or who does not obtain satisfaction from the accomplishment of his work.[6]

Workers generally look for improvement over time. Continued improvement in status, responsibility, and pay is often extremely important. Most people are realistic, however. They recognize that there are tasks connected with any job that are onerous and unappealing. They generally will perform such work as long as it is a minor part of the total job. These odious tasks in themselves do not have to contribute to the want satisfaction as long as the overall mixture of work provides means for fulfillment.

Means of Want Satisfaction

In our analysis of human wants, we have concentrated on the wants that can be satisfied in whole or in part by work.[7] Work provides want satisfaction both directly and indirectly. Direct satisfaction can come from the work itself, the working environment, and interactions with other workers and management. Indirectly, work provides satisfaction through a reward structure that includes pay, vacations, pensions, and insurance.

Until recently, most studies and writings have concentrated on indirect want satisfaction. The importance of direct want satisfaction has come into prominence only through the recent work of behavioral scientists. Table 9–2 presents a structure of needs and the manner in which their satisfaction is obtained.

[6] The reverse may also take place. People may have aspiration levels far out of reach of their abilities. Repeated failure may bring the aspiration level down to reality; if it doesn't, the individual becomes frustrated and his productive capacity lowered.

[7] We have not discussed wants that are primarily outside the work area. These include social, religious, family, and other involvements. These wants play an active and important part in need satisfaction. They are omitted only to maintain our focus on the work environment.

Table 9–2 Work satisfaction of human needs

Need	Direct Satisfaction (*from work itself*)	Indirect Satisfaction (*from work rewards*)
Physiological	Working conditions and environment	Money to purchase necessities
Psychological		
Social	Belonging; company status; social contact	Money to use for achieving social status; status from position and nature of company
Security	Psychological	Economic security
Achievement	Achievement; self-assertion; growth	Money and time to engage in desirable activities and hobbies

Examples of Need Satisfaction

The job and the environment in which it is performed define the work environment in which workers live for about eight hours a day. This environment can help satisfy their wants or it can deter or block such satisfaction. Consequently, the work environment is an important factor in the achievement of good productivity.

In the succeeding chapters, means for designing the technical part of a job and work area will be analyzed. The intent of this chapter is to give the reader an overview of the behavioral considerations that enter into the design of jobs and the work environment.

To highlight the importance of the behavioral considerations, two pairs of examples will follow that show how proper attention to behavioral factors can contribute to worker satisfaction and productivity.

Job enlargement   The first two examples cover what is commonly called job enlargement. Job enlargement has application in many areas. We will discuss two applications; one clerical, the other a manufacturing assembly operation.

The clerical example took place in an insurance company. As a part of the processing of policy applications, the company had about one hundred women working in one large open room. The women were grouped into sections with about five women in each section, with each section doing a small part of the total checking of an application. As might be expected, the work was repetitive and monotonous. The women had no sense of pride or accomplishment in their work. Their social groups were not oriented with their work, and there were no feelings of belonging.

After studying the situation, the company moved the women into small rooms with five or six women to each room, where, instead of checking one part of the application, each woman reviewed the entire application. Over a period of time the social groups became more work oriented. In the smaller rooms the women gained a sense of belonging. Furthermore, the enlarged scope of the job enabled them to realize the value of their work and to take pride in it.

By making these changes in the work environment, the company had helped the women satisfy some of their psychological needs. The women were happier and the company benefited from higher productivity and a marked decrease in absenteeism.

The concept of job enlargment that was introduced in this illustration also lies at the heart of the second example. Industrial workers doing small, highly specialized jobs on production lines find little satisfaction in their work. They are unable to gain any sense of achievement and normally regard their work as menial and boring.[8] When the jobs are enlarged to encompass an entire unit of identifiable product, they become challenging, a sense of responsibility for the task is initiated, and a sense of achievement in its completion is available.

One of the authors witnessed a marked example of this in an electronics firm. Cables were wired by groups of workers, each of whom placed four or five wires on the cable wiring board. The productivity of the group was low and, even more important, substantial numbers of the cables were found to be wired incorrectly when they were tested.

In an attempt to overcome these problems, the company changed the production method. Each worker was retrained to produce an entire cable assembly. After the learning process, the output of the group was 40 percent higher than before. The number of defective cables was down dramatically. The company also achieved another benefit. It realized (and the workers did also) that the work force had a high degree of responsibility and capability. Furthermore, the work force had shown that it was well prepared to undertake additional tasks.

Participation After reviewing the positive results of the job enlargement in cable production, the management of the electronics firm looked for other ways to increase productivity. One of their persistent problems was overcoming the resistance to change caused by new production methods. The company's product line was highly volatile. There were constant changes in products and hence in the production process. Resistance to these changes had led to increasingly poor productivity.

The normal procedure for introducing new products or production changes was to have the production line and work areas designed by methods engineers. When the new facilities were constructed, the workers were trained and the process started. The workers viewed the changes as a threat to their job security and, because of this, cooperation was extremely poor.

As an experiment, the management decided to have the next new production line designed jointly by the methods engineers and the workers who were to operate the line. The work force spent two days reviewing the layout, work areas, and methods designed by the engineers. Numerous changes were suggested, de-

---

[8] This situation is the cause of General Motors' labor problems at its Vega plant. A series of strikes have occurred which have their roots in the repetitive, small tasks which have been assigned to workers. Volvo, in Sweden, is experimenting with having a small team of workers assemble an entire car in the hope that this will give the sense of satisfaction that leads to responsible, well-motivated workers.

Production workers at Raytheon are being trained to wire complex cables. In the past, each worker wired only one cable; today one person is responsible for wiring the entire cable board. This procedure not only speeds training, but also raises performance levels because of increased work satisfaction.

bated, and in many instances initiated. When production started, the results were dramatic. Output was far ahead of expectation. Rejects were low, and the constant bickering that generally went with the introduction of a new production line was absent.

In reviewing the situation, the methods engineers could point to numerous instances where the tools, work flow, and methods employed could be improved. In fact, some of the changes the workers made had led to these conditions. The final production line, from a technical aspect, was not as good as others that had had far less success. It was quite evident that the increased cooperation and productivity was due to the psychological satisfaction of the workers and not to superior work methods. Group participation had overcome the fear of change and the threat to job security that arose from it.

One last situation highlighting the effect of participation will conclude our examples. A large hospital in Philadelphia had determined that it needed a new medical information system. The nurses were spending so much of their time on paper work that little time was available for the patients. Two years of effort by the best computer and systems people the hospital could hire were spent designing the new system. Outside groups were hired to evaluate the system; except for minor changes, which were made, it was found to be highly effective. When the system was installed on a trial basis on two hospital floors, the results were disastrous. Some nurses refused to use the new input terminals and forms despite the fact that they simplified the reporting work. Those who tried the new system consistently made errors.

To overcome these problems, additional training was instituted and talk sessions were held between nurses and administration. Some improvement resulted, but not enough. The new system was abandoned. The resistance to change was too great.

Several months after these events, another hospital's administrators looked at the system and decided it met their needs. Having learned from the first hospital's experience, they did not try to impose the system on their staff but instead presented the new system as a starting point for change. The nursing staff was asked to select two nurses to work with the medical staff and the administration to review this system and develop an even better one.

The two nurses who were selected—by consensus of the entire staff—became a communication link between the systems people and the nurses. They kept the nurses up to date, relayed suggestions, and were an active part of the analysis team. Changes were suggested and evaluated. A number were introduced but none had a material effect on the system.

When the system was approved, two training stations were established. Nurse training was conducted by the two nurses who had worked on the system. Little resistance was encountered.

When the system was finally made operational, it worked amazingly well. Even in instances where problems cropped up they were overcome quickly. The nurses felt that this was their system and that they would make it work.

The differences in the two situations are obvious. In one case, participation had elicited the help of the nurses; in the other, its lack had engendered hostility.

All of these illustrations show how productivity can be increased through the knowledge and satisfaction of human needs. Productivity achieved at the expense of well-being is in the end self-defeating.

Questions and Problems

1. What behavioral factors should be considered in the design of work stations?
2. In designing a production function, when and for what purposes, if any, should a mechanistic view of man be taken?
3. What motivational factors make people want to perform well on a job? What factors hinder their performance?
4. Since profit is the central concern of firms in a free enterprise system, why should companies consider the welfare of their workers?
5. What factors attract workers to a job? What factors motivate against taking a job?

6. What changes have taken place in management philosophy as a result of better insights into the satisfaction of worker wants?
7. How do anthropometric data help in the design of work stations and jobs?
8. With increasing degrees of automation and mechanization, what changes are brought about in the relative weights of workers' needs?
9. What environmental conditions should be considered in the design of work stations?
10. How do noise, temperature, and lighting influence a worker's performance?
11. Outline the wants that influence performance. What structure or hierarchy exists among these wants? Is this hierarchy constant, or does it shift over time?
12. In your view, which of man's wants are most important to
    (a) production workers
    (b) clerks
    (c) sales personnel
    (d) executives
    (e) professional men such as teachers, doctors, and lawyers
    If the importance of a particular need differs between jobs, why is it so?
13. What is the aim of job enlargement?
14. Why do workers often resist change? How would you gain acceptance for change? How can you provide for the social and psychological needs during change?
15. Can both organizational goals and human needs be satisfied at the same time?
16. To what extent do financial rewards meet an employee's needs?
17. Is it true that the more workers are satisfied the more they will produce?

References

Bennett, E., *et al.* (eds.), *Human Factors in Technology,* McGraw-Hill, New York, 1963.

Berelson, B., and Steiner, G. A., *Human Behavior,* Harcourt Brace Jovanovich, New York, 1964.

Cummings, L. L., and Scott, W. E. (eds.), *Readings in Organizational Behavior and Human Performance,* Irwin, Homewood, Ill., 1969.

Fogel, L. J., *Biotechnology: Concepts and Applications,* Prentice-Hall, Englewood Cliffs, N.J., 1962.

Foulkes, F. K., *Creating More Meaningful Work,* American Management Association, New York, 1969.

Hersey, P., and Blanchard, K. H., *Management of Organizational Behavior,* 2nd ed., Prentice-Hall, Englewood Cliffs, N.J., 1972.

Lawless, D. J., *Effective Management: Social Psychological Approach,* Prentice-Hall, Englewood Cliffs, N.J., 1972.

Likert, R., *The Human Organization: Its Management and Value,* McGraw-Hill, New York, 1967.

McCormick, E. J., *Human Factors Engineering,* 2nd ed., McGraw-Hill, New York, 1964.

McGregor, D., *Human Side of Enterprise,* McGraw-Hill, New York, 1960.

Roethlisberger, F., and Dickson, W. J., *Management and the Worker,* Harvard University Press, Cambridge, Mass., 1939.

Sayles, L. R., *Behavior of Industrial Work Groups,* Wiley, New York, 1958.

Schein, E. H., *Organizational Psychology,* 2nd ed., Prentice-Hall, Englewood Cliffs, N.J., 1970.

Simon, H. A., *Models of Man,* Wiley, New York, 1957.

Tannenbaum, A., *Social Psychology of the Work Organization,* Wadsworth, Belmont, Calif., 1966.

Vroom, V. H., *Work and Motivation,* Wiley, New York, 1964.

Whyte, W. F., *Organizational Behavior: Theory and Applications,* Irwin, Homewood, Ill., 1969.

Woodson, W. W., and Conover, D. W., *Human Engineering Guide for Equipment Designers,* 2nd rev. ed., University of California Press, Berkeley, Calif., 1964.

10

The Design of Work Methods

Before the management of a company establishes work standards and hires a labor force to man its production facilities, it must decide what *work methods* will be used in the production process. Its main objective in selecting work methods is to maximize labor productivity and efficiency. To do this, management must begin by deciding what is the most efficient mix of input resources for the production process in terms of the firm's operating environment, and this in turn requires determination of which operations are most efficiently performed manually and which are best performed mechanically.

The decision on the mix of input resources, which is primarily economic, coordinates capital investment with the utilization of labor. Once this decision has been made, management tries to determine the best way to perform each task in the production process. These methods are then incorporated into standards for the performance of each job. Ideally, such standards approximate the highest reasonable expectation of labor productivity for each task in the production process.

Once performance standards have been established, labor output standards can be calculated; the latter serve as a measure for evaluating the performance of employees and as a means for determining how much labor is required. In this latter capacity, they also provide a standard for production planning and scheduling. If output standards are to be effective measures of employee performance and required inputs, they must be based on sound work methods. Time standards drawn up from imperfect procedural standards are bound to lead to unrealistic performance standards. Accordingly, in this chapter we will examine the establishment of work methods, and in Chapter 11 we will discuss output standards based on these work methods.

Finally, after the work methods have been designed and the output standards set, production management must acquire and pay a labor force. The quantity and quality of workers needed and the means of payment should depend upon the work methods and output standards that have been chosen. Chapter 12 will deal with the problem of acquiring and paying a work force.

Productivity and Efficiency

In order to analyze the basic managerial problems of using labor in the production function, we must first understand the meaning of two important terms that are prevalent in this field: *productivity* and *efficiency*. Essentially, productivity is a measure of how much input is required to achieve a given output, so it focuses on the relationship between these particular quantities.

$$\text{Productivity} = \frac{\text{Output}}{\text{Input}}$$

Efficiency, on the other hand, pertains to how well the input resources are utilized in the production process. Thus, it compares the *actual* output achieved with the *expected* output that should have resulted from the employment of given resources.[1]

$$\text{Efficiency} = \frac{\text{Actual output}}{\text{Normal, or expected, output}}$$

It is often difficult to know precisely what portion of output produced can be attributed to a specific input. Rarely is the output of goods and services dependent solely upon the quantity of any one resource; instead, it is influenced by the relative quantities of inputs in the resource mix and their quality. Nevertheless, labor productivity is commonly defined as the total output resulting from the use of a given quantity of labor.

$$\text{Labor productivity} = \frac{\text{Quantity of output}}{\text{Quantity of labor}}$$

This is obviously an oversimplification, since the resource mix has a profound impact on the quantity of output produced. An increase in capital in the form of new equipment will generally raise the output level, for example, and this will distort the measure of productivity in the formula. In spite of this limitation, measuring labor productivity can be useful if it is employed for comparative, rather than absolute, measurement.

---

[1] While the discussion at this point is focused on labor productivity and labor efficiency, these productivity and efficiency measures may be applied to any of the other inputs in the production process—materials, capital, or management.

Similar problems are encountered with common measures of labor efficiency. In assessing how well labor is used in the total productive process, the resource mix is again an important factor. The same increase in capital, in the form of new equipment, that raises the output level per unit of labor will also raise the efficiency of labor, as it is commonly measured.

$$\text{Efficiency} = \frac{\text{Actual output per unit of labor}}{\text{Standard output per unit of labor}}$$

If such measures of efficiency are to be meaningful, therefore, either the resource mix must be kept constant or the output standard per unit of labor must be changed simultaneously with each change in the resource mix.[2]

Thus, it can be seen that it is difficult to measure precisely the productivity or efficiency of any of the factors of production because changes are constantly taking place in all of them. Hence, the results of any measure are subject to wide interpretation concerning what portion of a change may be attributable to any specific input factor. The measures do, however, point up the relationship between the factors and can be used effectively for relative comparisons.

Production management, therefore, is not so interested in the absolute amounts of labor or capital costs as it is in the relationship between output and total costs. High labor costs per unit of output are not necessarily a vice, and low unit labor costs are not necessarily a virtue. Labor costs may represent a high proportion of the total, and yet the total cost per unit may be low; this may reflect the inefficiency of labor or the high efficiency in the other factors of production. Production management's task with regard to work methods is not simply to obtain low unit labor costs but to maximize overall efficiency. This is a clear example of the problem of optimization and suboptimization that was discussed in the section on systems analysis. The systems approach attacks the overall problem and not just a part of the problem. Concentrating on minimizing labor costs would be a classic case of suboptimization.

Although there are very few formal principles that apply to the establishment of work methods, there is a well-established seven-step procedural approach. The individual steps of the approach will not automatically yield good results, of course, but they do offer a tested means of analyzing and evaluating methods systematically. This approach can be described as the basic scientific method of problem solving; the steps are

1. *Identify the problem.*
2. *Describe the problem (give the present work method).*
3. *Analyze the problem.*
4. *Develop new work methods.*

[2] The efficiency measure can also be used to test the results of changes in other elements of the resource mix. This is done by studying the changes in labor efficiency resulting from changes in any of the factors in the resource mix except labor. This approach is often used to measure the effectiveness of management and to analyze the relative worth of different materials.

5. *Select the best method.*
6. *Install the new method.*
7. *Follow up the installation of the new method.*

Identifying the Problem

Organizational Aspects

To develop and maintain a competitive production process, management must constantly evaluate it and seek ways to improve it. To do this requires periodic reviews of the production technology and the work methods used. In our rapidly changing modern economy, the need to be informed about technological innovations that could be gainfully used by a particular enterprise is acute. Therefore, an important part of management's job in the average company should be the study of capital investment opportunities and work methods. Its failure to realize the importance of this responsibility can lead to uncompetitive plants and unprofitable operations. The use of new tools, materials, and machines almost always necessitates changes in work methods. Very often, however, a production process becomes uncompetitive, not because of a failure to utilize a spectacular technological innovation, but because of a failure to keep up with the unspectacular developments in hand tools, materials, and other production aids. The status of production methods deserves full-time attention. Even without changes in the input mix, output performance may be increased by improving the methods of work performance.

In many organizations, the responsibility for developing efficient methods of production is assigned to an industrial engineering department or, as it is sometimes called, a systems department. This department studies tasks whose performance is considered to be inefficient. The tasks to be studied may be selected because of preliminary cost studies or because their study has been requested by operating managers.

The number of requests for job reviews normally exceeds the capacity of the industrial engineering department. Thus, it is usually necessary to assign priorities, but this is not an easy matter. The operating manager is responsible for the production process. He must meet the production schedules and must keep the production costs within their assigned limits. Inefficiencies in the production process lower his ability to meet these standards. By the same token, the manager of the industrial engineering department is responsible for its productivity, and he wants to work on projects that will bring his group the most reward. At times these objectives may not be compatible, especially when the engineering group services a number of production centers.

A simple analogy provides a helpful guideline for assigning priorities in job studies. If a sponge is immersed in water and withdrawn brimming full, it is relatively easy to squeeze a great deal of water out of it. Subsequent attempts to squeeze out water require an increasing amount of effort for a diminishing quantity of water. So it is with the study of work methods. A previously unstudied task normally provides the greatest opportunity for "squeezing out" inefficiencies, thereby producing savings. Subsequent reviews of the same task require an increasing investment of time but produce a decreasing amount of savings. Thus, industrial engineering departments find that they can obtain a maximum return by focusing attention on previously unstudied jobs and methods, and so priorities are assigned accordingly. Naturally, sudden "bottlenecks" can occur, creating urgent priorities that must be promptly honored, but the sponge analogy should be applied to the normal routine.

A Problem Classification

Once a problem is received by an industrial engineering department, the first step is to identify its basic nature. Past experience and experimentation have provided a general classification system for methods problems, which greatly facilitates formulation of workable solutions. The first phase of classification is to decide whether the problem involves work performed at a single work station in the process or whether it concerns interrelationships among several work stations. If it involves a single work station only, the problem is classified as "INTRA work station"; if it concerns more than one station, the problem is classified as "INTER work station."

INTER-station problems include the movement, or flow, of a product from one operating element to another. The researcher approaches this type of problem by taking a bird's-eye view, or "big picture" perspective, of the production process. He concentrates on the work flow between process steps and on the process capacity that must be established. This overall review will usually indicate which individual work stations need closer study, and then the appropriate INTRA-station study can be initiated. INTRA-station problems include the movement of men and machines in performing a task at a single station. Here the analysis is highly detailed and concerned with the most minute aspects of the task. Thus, it can be seen that the INTER and INTRA approaches are complementary, and together they provide a meaningful way of dissecting a production activity for study and improvement.

Describing the Problem

For both INTER- and INTRA-station problems, a series of standardized approaches and supporting forms have been developed over the years that provide a simple but effective way of describing the problems. The forms are designed to help focus attention on data that are pertinent to the analysis of a given problem and the formulation of a solution. They also summarize all information pertaining to the work method being studied to facilitate analysis.

Describing INTRA-Station Problems

In the description and analysis of INTRA-station problems, the work methods are often divided into three general categories:

1. *Single operator, using only hand tools*
2. *Single operator, using a single machine*
3. *More than one operator or more than one machine (where the tasks involve combinations of men and machines)*

For each of these categories there is a separate approach, but all three approaches are actually variations on the same theme. All provide a means for delineating the sequence in which elements of work are accomplished by each "significant work performer" under study. In the case of the single operator using hand tools, the significant work performers are his two hands. Consequently, a chart designed for the first category listed above would include a vertical column describing the activity of each hand. This type of chart is in common use in various forms, each with slight modifications, and is usually called either an *operator chart* or a *left- and right-hand chart*. Figure 10–1 shows a typical left- and right-hand chart that was used to analyze an existing method of assembling a selenium rectifier (a component found in many electrical devices). Notice that there is a central coordinating axis to ensure that elements of work performed by each hand are recorded in their proper sequence and relationship. This is necessary for subsequent analysis of the method employed. A brief verbal and symbolic description of each operation is also included, together with sketches of the parts being made and the physical layout of the operation. Finally, in the upper left-hand corner, the researcher has filled out a summary of the types of operations performed. Everything that is needed to define the task completely is included.

In the second category of INTRA-station problem (involving a single operator and a single machine), the significant work performers are the operator himself and the machine. Accordingly, the appropriate chart is called a *man–machine chart*. Like the left- and right-hand chart, it has a central coordinating axis and vertical columns that describe each element of work performed by the man and the machine. In special cases, where a closer look at the man–machine relationship is needed, the "man" side of the chart may be further subdivided into left- and right-hand columns. Figure 10–2 is a man–machine chart, showing a milling operation. The basic difference between this chart and the left- and right-hand chart in Figure 10–1 is that it relates the operator's activities to those of the machine rather than relating the activities of the operator's left and right hands. Aside from this distinction, the features of the two charts are basically the same.

The third type of INTRA-station problem comprises tasks that require the combined efforts of a number of men and machines. A chart for this type of problem provides a vertical column for each man or machine and a coordinating, sequential axis. This chart is simply an extension of the man–machine chart and is called a *multiple-activity analysis form*. The one shown in Figure 10–3 could be used when studying any work station where one man operates two machines. The task shown in Figure 10–3 is the same as in Figure 10–2—the milling of the end of a metal shaft. However, in Figure 10–3 the operator runs two milling machines instead of one. Any number of variations of this analysis form are

SUMMARY *Per Piece*

	PRESENT		PROPOSED		DIFF.	
	LH	RH	LH	RH	LH	RH
○ OPERATIONS	1	23				
▷ TRANS.	1	15				
▽ HOLDS	34	0				
D DELAYS	4	2				
Total	40	40				

OPERATION *Assembly of Selenium Rectifier*

METHOD ~~PRESENT~~ ~~PROPOSED~~ DATE *6-29*

OPERATOR *J.P.S.* ANALYST *M.J.P.*

LAYOUT

Finished parts — Eyelet — Insulator sleeve — Terminal — Plate — Spacer — Plate — Stake (with automatic riveting mechanism) — Riveting button

PART SKETCH

Spacer — Eyelet — Insulator sleeve — Terminal — Plates — Selenium rectifier

LEFT HAND	OPER	TRANS	HOLD	DELAY		OPER	TRANS	HOLD	DELAY	RIGHT HAND
Idle				●	1		▶			Reach to eyelet bin
				●	2	●				Grasp eyelet
				●	3		▶			Move eyelet to stake
				●	4	●				Position eyelet to stake
Hold			▼		5	●				Release eyelet
			▼		6		▶			Reach to insulator bin
			▼		7	●				Grasp insulator
			▼		8		▶			Move insulator to stake
			▼		9	●				Position insulator to stake
			▼		10	●				Release insulator
			▼		11		▶			Reach to terminal bin
			▼		12	●				Grasp terminal
			▼		13		▶			Move terminal to stake
			▼		14	●				Position terminal to stake
			▼		15	●				Release terminal
			▼		16		▶			Reach to plate bin
			▼		17	●				Grasp plate
			▼		18		▶			Move plate to stake
			▼		19	●				Position plate to stake
			▼		20	●				Release plate
			▼		21		▶			Reach to spacer bin
			▼		22	●				Grasp spacer
			▼		23		▶			Move spacer to stake
			▼		24	●				Position spacer to stake
			▼		25	●				Release spacer
			▼		26		▶			Reach to plate bin
			▼		27	●				Grasp plate
			▼		28		▶			Move plate to stake
			▼		29	●				Position plate to stake

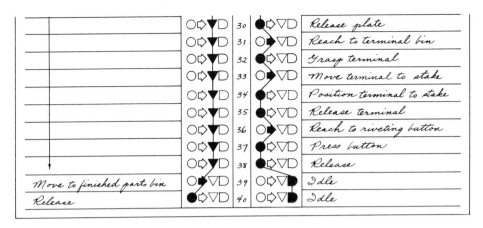

Figure 10–1 Left- and right-hand chart for assembly of selenium rectifier (present method)

possible; the precise mixture of men and machine columns depends on the operation to be studied.

Describing INTER-Station Problems

For INTER-station problems, the appropriate descriptive form is usually called a *process chart* because it attempts to present a picture of the overall production process used. To accomplish this, each step of the process under consideration is classified as one of five standard categories and designated by a standard symbol.

○ *Operation.* The work performed in manufacturing the product. This task has usually been assigned to a single work station.

▷ *Transportation.* The movement of the product, or any of its parts, among various locations that represent different phases of the production process.

▽ *Storage.* Intervals during which the product, or any part of it, waits or is at rest. Often the symbol ▽T distinguishes "temporary storage," when the product waits before and after the performance of a specific operation, from "permanent storage" ▽P , when it may wait in a storage facility for more than a day or two.

☐ *Inspection.* All activities that are performed to verify that the product has the required mechanical, dimensional, and operational characteristics.

D *Delay.* Another term for temporary storage before or after a production operation. Where the temporary storage symbol ▽T is used, this category is often omitted.

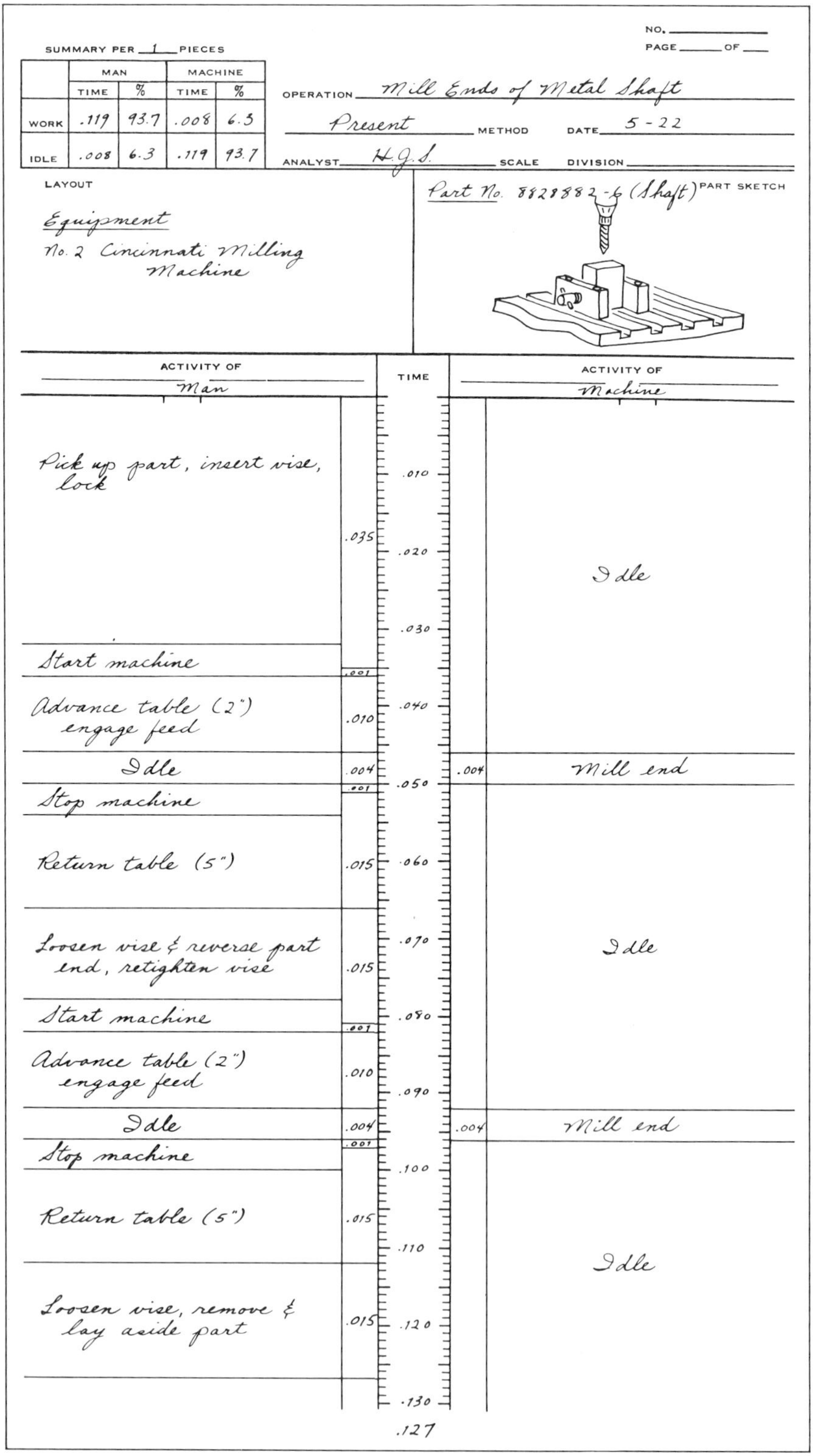

	MAN		MACHINE	
	TIME	%	TIME	%
WORK	.119	93.7	.008	6.3
IDLE	.008	6.3	.119	93.7

SUMMARY PER __1__ PIECES

NO. _____
PAGE _____ OF ____

OPERATION Mill Ends of Metal Shaft
Present METHOD DATE 5-22
ANALYST H.G.S. SCALE DIVISION

LAYOUT

Equipment
No. 2 Cincinnati Milling
Machine

Part No. 8828882-6 (Shaft) PART SKETCH

ACTIVITY OF Man	TIME	ACTIVITY OF Machine
Pick up part, insert vise, lock	.035	
	.010	
	.020	Idle
	.030	
Start machine	.001	
Advance table (2") engage feed	.010	.040
Idle	.004	.004 Mill end
Stop machine	.001	.050
Return table (5")	.015	.060
Loosen vise & reverse part end, retighten vise	.015	.070 Idle
Start machine	.001	.080
Advance table (2") engage feed	.010	.090
Idle	.004	.004 Mill end
Stop machine	.001	.100
Return table (5")	.015	.110
		Idle
Loosen vise, remove & lay aside part	.015	.120
		.130

.127

Figure 10–2   Man–machine chart

Figure 10–4 is a typical flow-process chart, describing the existing method for assembling a power transformer in the production department of a manufacturing firm. The form provides a vertical column for listing, in sequence, the steps in which the process is performed. Beside each step the analyst marks the symbol designating the classification of that step. If it is an operation, the time required to perform the work is also recorded; if it is a transportation, the number of feet to be traveled is indicated. During the analysis the researcher uses the time specified for the operation to determine the number of work stations needed at each phase to cope with production requirements. An analysis of this sort is usually the starting point for deciding the amount of capital facilities required. For each transportation and storage step, the analyst examines the adequacy of facilities for moving and storing. Thus, this chart provides the information needed to appraise the materials handling system that supports the production process. The layout of the plant facilities is often affected by the sequence of operations indicated on a process chart. When management is principally concerned with layout, an alternate form of the flow-process chart (Figure 10–5) is used. It more clearly depicts the materials flow and interrelationships among operations in assembling the power transformer. Note how the operational interdependencies revealed in the flow-process chart have been reflected in the arrangement of the production facilties in Figure 10–6. Using data from a flow-process chart, an industrial engineer might be able to design an alternative layout minimizing the distance traveled and the time consumed in the manufacturing process. Thus, it can be seen that a flow-process chart provides data that have many useful applications. Here we are concentrating on the work performed on a product using a company's present equipment and its existing plant layout in order to determine the most efficient process that could be used. Frequently, however, a methods study of this type will trigger a series of changes in plant layout or impel a search for improved technology.

Describing Standard Practice

At the beginning of this chapter we stressed the fact that, in order to be fair, performance standards must be based on sound work methods. Time standards, for example, are meaningful only when they can be applied to a particular procedural standard. The task description written on both INTER and INTRA forms provides the most efficient method of defining a standard work method, or, as it is usually termed, a *standard practice*. Thus, these forms can serve as a link between work methods and labor measurement; if there is a link, the time standards furnish a valid criterion for identifying an alternative work method that may be superior to existing standard practice.

Analyzing the Problem

After a problem has been identified and described, it must be analyzed. The analysis of work methods has been simplified by the development of a group of

SUMMARY PER **2** PIECES

	MAN		MACHINE			
	TIME	%	TIME		%	
			1	2	1	2
WORK	.226	100	.009 .008		2.7 2.7	
IDLE	0	0	.216 .216		97.3 97.3	

OPERATION _Mill Ends of (2) Metal Shafts_

Present METHOD _____ DATE 5-29

ANALYST _H.G.S._ SCALE _____ DIVISION _____

LAYOUT

Equipment

Mach. 1   No. 2 Cincinnati Milling Machine

Mach. 2   No. 2 Cincinnati Milling Machine

Part No. 8828882-6 (_Shaft_) PART SKETCH

ACTIVITY OF Man	TIME	ACTIVITY OF Mach. No. 1	Mach. No. 2
Pick up part, insert vise, lock .035	.010 .020 .030		
Start machine .001			
Advance table (2") engage feed .010	.040		
Walk to #2 miller .002		.004 Mill end	
Stop machine .001	.050		
Return table (5") .015	.060		
Loosen vise, reverse part end, tighten vise .015	.070		
Start machine .001	.080		
Advance table (2") engage feed .010			
Walk to #1 miller .002	.090		.004 Mill end
Stop machine .001			
Return table (5") .015	.100		
Loosen vise, reverse part end, tighten vise .015	.110		
Start machine .001	.120		
Advance table (2") engage feed .010	.130		

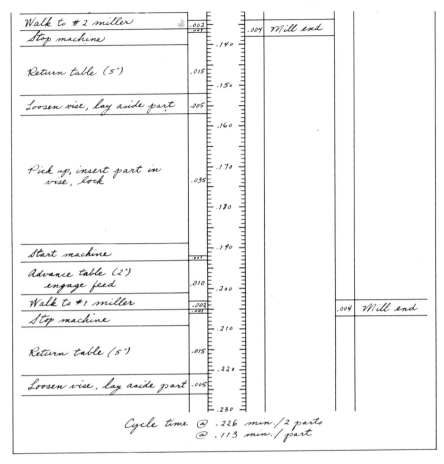

Figure 10–3 Multiple-activity analysis form

tested techniques for dissecting existing methods and identifying their inherent weaknesses and strengths.

The first (and perhaps the most important) of these analytical tools has been called the "questioning attitude." This "attitude" simply means that nothing should be taken for granted and that every aspect of work performance should be scrutinized in terms of the following four queries:

1. *Can it be eliminated?*
2. *Can it be combined?*
3. *Can it be simplified?*
4. *Can the sequence be changed?*

These questions are designed to weed out unnecessary work immediately or,

SUMMARY

	PRESENT NO. TIME	PROPOSED NO. TIME	DIFF. NO. TIME
◯ OPERATIONS	12	2.14				
⇨ TRANS.	13					
☐ INSPECTIONS	1					
D DELAYS	13					
▽ STORAGES	1					
DIST. TRAVELED	94 FT.		FT.		FT.	

JOB _Assembly of Power Transformer_
Quantity of One

☐ MAN OR ☒ MATERIAL
CHART BEGINS ____ _Operation 1_
CHART ENDS ____ _Operation 8_
CHARTED BY ____ HJ ____ DATE ____ 3-26

	DETAILS OF (PRESENT / PROPOSED) METHOD	OPERATION / TRANSPORT / INSPECTION / DELAY / STORAGE	DISTANCE IN FEET	QUANTITY	TIME	POSSIBILITIES — ELIMINATE / COMBINE / SEQUENCE / PLACE / PERSON / CHANGE / IMPROVE	NOTES
1	Wind core	●⇨☐D▽			.10		(0 - 1)
2	Post Operation 1 temporary storage	◯⇨☐D▽					
3	Transport to Operation 2	◯⬤☐D▽	8				
4	Pick 4 leads from coil	●⇨☐D▽			.20		(0 - 2)
5	Post Operation 2 temporary storage	◯⇨☐D▽					
6	Transport to Operation 3	◯⬤☐D▽	4				
7	Cut to length / Strip 4 leads	●⇨☐D▽			.32		(0 - 3)
8	Post Operation 3 temporary storage	◯⇨☐D▽					
9	Transport to Operation 4	◯⬤☐D▽	4				
10	Cut to length / Thread sleeving on 4 leads	●⇨☐D▽			.32		(0 - 4)
11	Post Operation 4 temporary storage	◯⇨☐D▽					
12	Transport to Operation 5	◯⬤☐D▽	4				
13	Punch "E" laminations	●⇨☐D▽			.10		(0 - 100)
14	Post Operation 100 temporary storage	◯⇨☐D▽					
15	Transport to Operation 101	◯⬤☐D▽	15				
16	Stack "E" laminations	●⇨☐D▽			.15		(0 - 101)
17	Post Operation 101 temporary storage	◯⇨☐D▽					
18	Transport to Operation 5	◯⬤☐D▽	4				
19	Assembly of "E" laminations	●⇨☐D▽			.15		(0 - 5)
20	Post Operation 5 temporary storage	◯⇨☐D▽					
21	Transport to Operation 6	◯⬤☐D▽	4				
22	Punch "I" laminations	●⇨☐D▽			.10		(0 - 200)
23	Post Operation 200 temporary storage	◯⇨☐D▽					
24	Transport to Operation 201	◯⬤☐D▽	15				
25	Stack "I" laminations	●⇨☐D▽			.15		(0 - 201)
26	Post Operation 201 temporary storage	◯⇨☐D▽					
27	Transport to Operation 6	◯⬤☐D▽	4				
28	Assembly of "I" laminations	●⇨☐D▽			.15		
29	Post Operation 6 temporary storage	◯⇨☐D▽					
30	Transport to Operation 7	◯⬤☐D▽	4				
31	Assembly of core and frame	●⇨☐D▽			.15		(0 - 7)
32	Post Operation 7 temporary storage	◯⇨☐D▽					
33	Transport to inspection & test-1	◯⬤☐D▽	4				
34	Inspection and test (I & I-1)	◯⇨■D▽					

#	Description	Symbols	Dist/Time	Notes
35	Post inspection temporary storage	○◇□▽		
36	Transport to packing (Operation 8)	○●□▽	4	
37	Pack for shipment	●◇□▽	.25	(0 - 8)
38	Post Operation 8 temporary storage	○◇■▽		
39	Transport to stock	○●□▽	20	
40	In stock	○◇□▼		
41				
42	Summary			
43		○◇□▽	1	
44		12 13 1 13 1 94	2.14	

Figure 10–4 Flow-process chart for assembly of power transformer (present method)

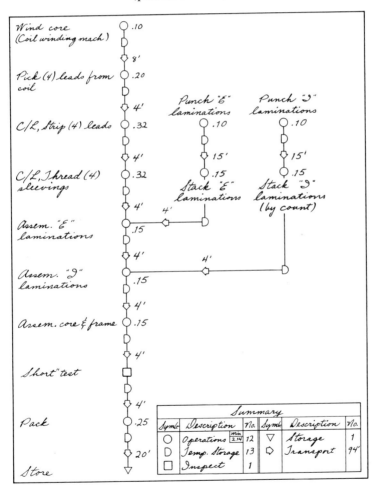

Figure 10–5 Alternate flow-process chart for assembly of power transformer (present method)

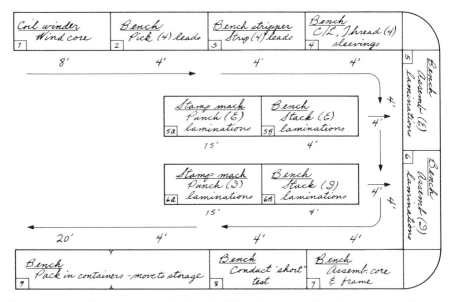

Figure 10–6 Layout of production facilities for assembly of power transformer (present method)

where elimination is impossible, to combine, simplify, or change the sequence of techniques in order to reduce the time and effort required to accomplish a task.[4]

A second technique that often increases the effectiveness of the questioning approach is a check list commonly referred to as "The Principles of Motion Economy." Based upon the fruits of considerable past experience and experimentation, these principles are derived both from practices that have increased efficiency and from practices that have slowed production and reduced efficiency. Thus, by comparing elements of a particular work method with the check list of principles, the researcher may get a better idea of where a problem lies.

The Principles of Motion Economy[5]

1. Both hands should preferably begin their motions at the same time.
2. Both hands should preferably complete their motions at the same instant.
3. Both hands should not be idle at the same instant except during rest periods.

---

[4] A more detailed list of questions might be obtained by using the six honest serving men identified by Rudyard Kipling:

> I keep six honest serving-men
> (They taught me all I knew);
> Their names are What and Why and When
> And How and Where and Who.
> —*The Elephant's Child*

[5] There are many lists of motion principles. Most of them take their basic ideas from Frank and Lillian Gilbreth.

4. Motions of the arms should be in opposite and symmetrical directions instead of in the same direction, and they should be made at the same time.

5. Hesitation should be analyzed and studied, and its cause should be accounted for and, if possible, eliminated.

6. The shortest time demonstrated in one part of a study should be used as a goal to attain, and the reasons for longer times required in other parts of the study should be known.

7. The number of motions required to do a job should be counted, for the best way is almost always a sequence of the fewest motions.

8. The best sequence of motions in any one kind of work is useful in suggesting the best sequence in other kinds of work.

9. Every instance where a delay occurs suggests the advisability of providing some optional work that will permit utilizing that time, if so desired, or making a fatigue study of the interval.

10. The lack of coordination among various parts of the body should be studied and corrected.

11. Wherever possible, all materials and tools should be located within the range of normal grasp.

12. Movements should be confined to the lowest possible classification (in order to reduce fatigue) according to the list below, which gives the least fatiguing and most economical first.
    (a) Finger movements
    (b) Finger and wrist movements
    (c) Finger, wrist, and elbow movements
    (d) Finger, wrist, elbow, and shoulder movements
    (e) Finger, wrist, elbow, shoulder, and hip movements

13. Tools and materials should be so located as to permit the proper sequence of motions. The part required at the beginning of a cycle should be located next to the point of release of the finished piece from the preceding cycle.

14. The sequence of motions should be arranged to build rhythm and smoothness into the operation.

15. The hands should be relieved of all work that can be done by the feet or other parts of the body.

16. Tools and materials should be prepositioned as much as possible in order to reduce the motions of searching, finding, and selecting.

17. Gravity-feed containers, which are used to take goods to the delivery point, should be near the height at which parts are assembled in order to eliminate any lifting or change in direction in carrying the parts.

18. Containers for holding supplies should preferably be arranged at an angle of about 22 degrees from the perpendicular so that parts may be taken from them easily.

19. Materials and tools should be located at a height slightly above the work-

ing point, and the working point should be so located that the operator's hand may easily reach that point in a more or less relaxed manner, with the arms at a comfortable angle.

20. Ejectors should be used to remove the finished part.

21. Use "drop delivery" by means of which an operator may deliver the finished article (by releasing it in the position in which it was completed) without moving to dispose of it.

22. Levers, crossbars, and hand wheels should be located so that an operator can manipulate them with the least change in body position and with the greatest mechanical advantage.

23. The height of the workplace and the chair should preferably be arranged so that alternate sitting and standing at work is easily possible.

24. A chair of the proper type and height to permit good posture should be provided for every worker.

25. When arranging the workplace, the comfort of the operator should always be considered. Provision for him to be seated should be made whenever practicable; also proper lighting, heating, and ventilation should be maintained.

These principles are little more than a summary of what common sense should dictate. They are helpful as guidelines, but the researcher must be careful lest any technique of analyzing work methods come to dominate his thinking too rigidly. Common sense and imagination led to the development of these tools, and they will continue to be responsible for new instruments used in methods analysis.

To illustrate the importance of imagination in methods analysis, consider the following example:[6] A restaurant manager wishes to determine the best way to toast three slices of bread in an old-fashioned toaster of the type shown in Figure 10–7. This machine can toast one side of two pieces of bread at the same time, but it takes two hands to insert or remove each slice of bread. To turn a slice of bread to toast the other side, the operator only has to push the toaster door down and allow a spring to bring it back; this operation requires only one

Figure 10–7   Old-fashioned toaster

---

[6] While this example is simple, it clearly illustrates the type of ingenuity needed in methods work.

hand. Therefore, two pieces of bread can be turned at the same time. The time needed to toast two pieces of bread on both sides using this method is

Minutes Exactly

Toasting (one side)	=	0.50
Turning time	=	0.02
Toasting (other side)	=	0.50
Removing time	=	0.05
Insertion time	=	0.05

The restaurant manager drew up a process chart describing the existing method of toasting three pieces of bread on this machine, as illustrated in Figure 10–8; he found that it took 2.29 minutes to accomplish this task. Since one side of the toaster remained idle while the third piece of bread was being toasted, there seemed to be room for improvement. Changing the sequence of toasting to that depicted in Figure 10–9, he found that the time needed to prepare the toast could be reduced significantly without introducing any new tools. This change in work methods was simply the product of common sense and imagination.

Micromotion Study

More sophisticated tools, many of which involve the motion picture camera, are also used in methods analysis. The two principal areas of application for these instruments are called *micromotion study* and *memomotion study*.

When rapid, short-cycle operations lasting two minutes or less are being studied, the researcher may use a constant high-speed camera capable of photographing at speeds of up to 960 or 1,000 frames per minute. Sometimes a microchronometer[7] is positioned so that it may be photographed along with the operator, thus providing precise time data that can be related to each work motion performed. The information needed to prepare a man–machine chart may be obtained from these films by running them in slow motion—at a speed of only 60 frames per minute or slower. In this fashion the films can be studied and restudied in order to scrutinize even the smallest details.

The advantage of micromotion study is that it can slow down a high-speed operation so that it can be dissected and described for purposes of analysis; moreover, the analysis can be done away from the production operations. Because the analyst can run the same film over and over again, he is less likely to miss any details of the process. The films also provide a permanent record of what standard practices look like and therefore can be used to help teach these

[7] This is a high-speed clock that is calibrated to read in 1/1,000ths of a minute. When the performance films are reviewed, the time for the motion elements is obtained from the readings of the microchronometer at the beginning and end of each element. The "winkcounter" that is calibrated in 1/2,000ths of a minute has also been used for this purpose. These timing devices were more necessary in the past when constant-speed cameras were subject to wide variations in speed. Now the accuracy of photographic devices is such that time values can be obtained by directly counting frames in the film.

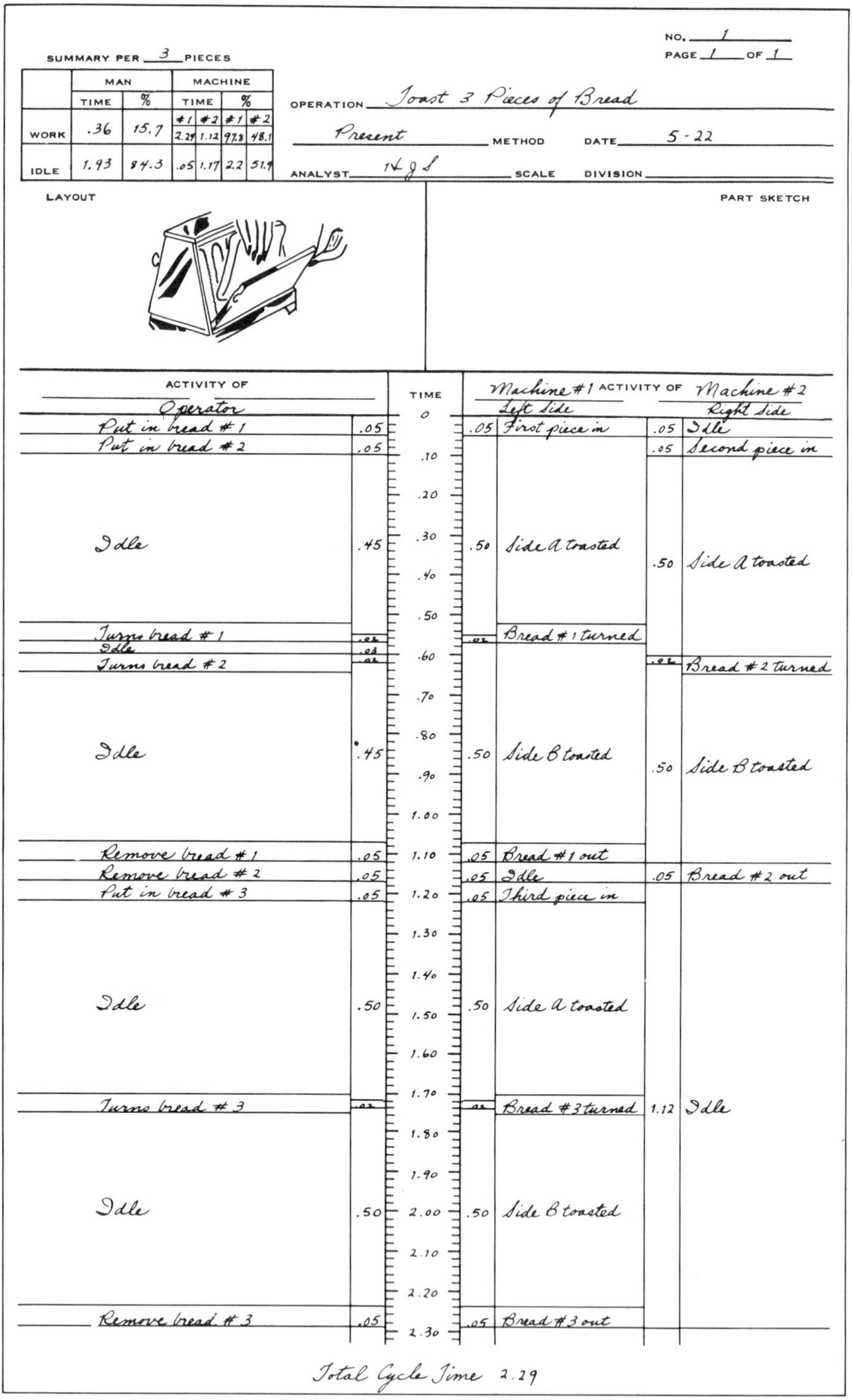

SUMMARY PER __3__ PIECES

	MAN		MACHINE			OPERATION	Toast 3 Pieces of Bread
	TIME	%	TIME	%			
			#1	#2	#1	#2	
WORK	.36	15.7	2.29	1.12	97.8	48.1	Present METHOD DATE 5-22
IDLE	1.93	84.3	.05	1.17	2.2	51.9	ANALYST H.J.S. SCALE DIVISION

LAYOUT

PART SKETCH

ACTIVITY OF Operator	TIME	Machine #1 ACTIVITY OF Machine #2
		Left Side / Right Side
Put in bread #1	.05	0 / .05 First piece in / .05 Idle
Put in bread #2	.05	.05 Second piece in
	.10	
	.20	
Idle	.45	.30 / .50 Side A toasted
	.40	.50 Side A toasted
	.50	
Turns bread #1	.02	.02 Bread #1 turned
Idle	.01	
Turns bread #2	.02	.60 / .02 Bread #2 turned
	.70	
Idle	.45	.80 / .50 Side B toasted
	.90	.50 Side B toasted
	1.00	
Remove bread #1	.05	1.10 / .05 Bread #1 out
Remove bread #2	.05	.05 Idle / .05 Bread #2 out
Put in bread #3	.05	1.20 / .05 Third piece in
	1.30	
	1.40	
Idle	.50	1.50 / .50 Side A toasted
	1.60	
	1.70	
Turns bread #3	.02	.02 Bread #3 turned / 1.12 Idle
	1.80	
	1.90	
Idle	.50	2.00 / .50 Side B toasted
	2.10	
	2.20	
Remove bread #3	.05	2.30 / .05 Bread #3 out

Total Cycle Time 2.29

Figure 10–8 Multiple-activity chart for toaster operation (present method)

practices to employees. The high cost of acquiring the necessary equipment has limited the use of micromotion study techniques in industry, however. Even where equipment is available, the amount of time and money required to use it restricts its application to large-volume, short-cycle operations.

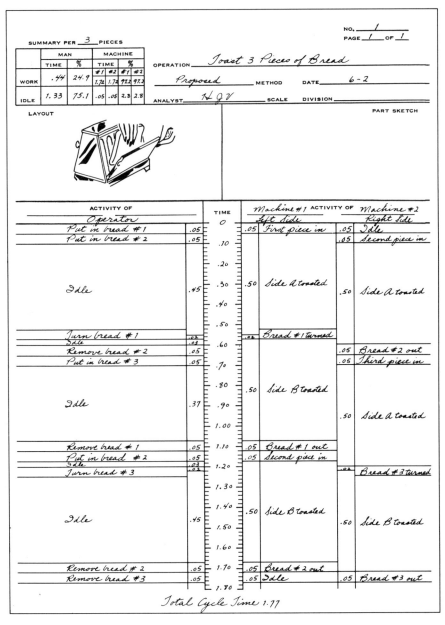

NO.			
PAGE 1 OF 1			

SUMMARY PER **3** PIECES

	MAN		MACHINE			
	TIME	%	TIME	%		
			#1	#2	#1	#2
WORK	.44	24.9	1.72	1.72	97.2	97.2
IDLE	1.33	75.1	.05	.05	2.8	2.8

OPERATION *Toast 3 Pieces of Bread*

METHOD *Proposed* DATE *6-2*

ANALYST *H.Q.V.* SCALE DIVISION

LAYOUT

PART SKETCH

ACTIVITY OF Operator	TIME 0	Machine #1 ACTIVITY OF Left Side		Machine #2 Right Side	
Put in bread #1	.05	.05	First piece in	.05	Idle
Put in bread #2	.05 .10			.05	Second piece in
	.20				
Idle	.45 .30	.50	Side A toasted	.50	Side A toasted
	.40				
	.50				
Turn bread #1	.02	.02	Bread #1 turned		
Idle	.03 .60				
Remove bread #2	.05			.05	Bread #2 out
Put in bread #3	.05 .70			.05	Third piece in
	.80	.50	Side B toasted		
Idle	.37 .90				
	1.00			.50	Side A toasted
Remove bread #1	.05 1.10	.05	Bread #1 out		
Put in bread #2	.05	.05	Second piece in		
Idle	.03				
Turn bread #3	.02 1.20			.02	Bread #3 turned
	1.30				
	1.40	.50	Side B toasted		
Idle	.45 1.50			.50	Side B toasted
	1.60				
Remove bread #2	.05 1.70	.05	Bread #2 out		
Remove bread #3	.05	.05	Idle	.05	Bread #3 out
	1.80				

Total Cycle Time 1.77

Figure 10–9 Multiple-activity chart for toaster operation (proposed method)

Memomotion Study

In contrast to micromotion study, memomotion techniques make use of a slow, constant camera speed of approximately 60 frames per minute. Slow-speed cameras are well suited to the study of long-cycle tasks. Indeed, crew activities extending over periods of time as long as a day may be analyzed by memomotion study. The films obtained are run at high speed to give the analyst a better idea of the whole operation. Although this high speed makes the motions appear choppy, it presents all of the details of the task in a more intelligible sequence. The chief advantage of memomotion studies is that they can give an analyst an overall perspective of a long-cycle task in a short amount of time. The films can also provide source data for use in preparing the appropriate descriptive form, which can then be used to analyze the particular task.

Like micromotion study films, memomotion films constitute a permanent record of work practices that can be used to settle labor disputes over work methods and to help train employees.[8] Cost has also limited the use of this technique, however.

Cyclegraph

The most unusual use of cameras in the field of motion study is a technique known as *cyclegraph*. Flashing light bulbs are attached to an operator's fingers and hands, and he is photographed at work by a single, long time exposure of highly sensitive film. The photographic print reveals light smears of varying intensity that trace the motion paths followed by the worker's hands. These paths are studied to identify efficient or inefficient work methods. To illustrate how effective this approach can be, Figure 10–10 depicts the "before" and "after" motion paths used to operate a photocopier; a cursory glance at these pictures is enough to show the improvement.

The cyclegraph is also an expensive procedure, and technical limitations of the photographic process further restrict its use. Hence, in practice, it is employed only when a refined analysis of methods used in high-volume production is needed. The cyclegraph is the only known method of recording accurately the actual motion paths in work performance, and in appropriate situations it can be an extremely effective tool.

Employee Reaction to Camera Studies

There is, however, one problem in using the camera in methods analysis—the employees' reactions. Employees often become hostile and suspicious when attempts are made to take motion pictures to gather information that could be used to improve their job performance. Even a usually cooperative worker tends to become nervous and uneasy when he is being photographed. Although new types of film have removed the need for lighting equipment and have thereby

---

[8] The same approach is used to help improve the performance of athletes.

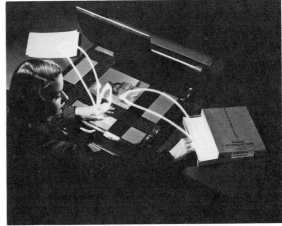

) A cyclegraph study showing the motions
uired to operate an old-style photocopier

(b) A cyclegraph study showing the motions
required to operate a new-style photocopier

Figure 10–10

lessened the discomfort somewhat, there are still serious problems. For studies
on the cyclegraph, the necessity of placing lights on the operator's hands seems
to increase the possibility of fear and hostility. Here, as in other aspects of industrial engineering work, it is extremely important to encourage employee
cooperation.

Developing New Work Methods

The analysis of existing work methods provides a starting point for a synthesis
of suggested improvements in task performance. Inefficient work motions should
be eliminated and replaced with methods that are consistent with the principles
of motion economy. In order to obtain a smooth motion pattern, some modifications of efficient methods may be necessary. This is justified since the overall
objective is the design of a system of work methods that contain no inefficient
motions. If the complex of efficient motions cannot work together as an efficient
method, the new method will clearly be no improvement.

New methods often result from, and require, the design of simple new fixtures.
A special holding vise may be designed, for example, that will eliminate the need
for using the hand as a holding device. Such improvements in work methods result from industrial engineering experience, imagination, and a thorough understanding of production practices. The contributions that can be made by the man
on the job should not be overlooked in this field. Employees have a vast reservoir
of know-how concerning their own work. The most efficient results usually come

from blending this know-how with the engineer's technical knowledge. Toward this end, many companies encourage employee participation in methods improvement by offering rewards for ideas that lead to cost savings.

Suggestion Programs

A formal suggestion program may be established to facilitate the submission and evaluation of new ideas. The reward offered for suggestions is normally a percentage of the first year's savings, except that it cannot exceed a fixed amount for any one reward. Thus, the company makes a minimum investment in return for ideas of tested value; in computing this investment, the cost of administering the suggestion program must be included, of course. It has been found that a relatively small reward is usually a sufficient stimulus to obtain many sound methods improvements, provided that the program is well administered. Experience indicates that for a program to be successful, it is essential to give submitted ideas prompt consideration and fair evaluation; it is also important to determine and pay the reward as soon as possible.[9]

Many companies even provide elementary courses in methods simplification to improve the quality and quantity of the improvements suggested. They justify the expenditure of the necessary time and money mathematically as follows. A typical firm that employs 1,000 direct-labor operators might also have 100 supervisory men and 15 industrial engineering men on the payroll. If methods improvement were the exclusive province of the industrial engineering group, only 1.5 percent of the firm's employees would be concerned with the problem. Admittedly they are by far the best qualified for the job and would have the most time to spend on it. If supervisory personnel also participate, however, 11.5 percent of the payroll is involved; if all direct-labor operators participate as well, the limit is 100 percent. Certainly the amount of participation from these last two groups will not be at a maximum, if only because their efforts in methods improvement can only involve a small portion of their time and because they are not fully trained in methods-study techniques. The percentage of suggestions received that have any practical value may be quite low. Nonetheless, there is a strong probability that there will be many useful suggestions and that there will be a significant increase in the effective percentage of employees who are concerned with methods improvement.

Selecting the Best Method

When improvements in work methods have been suggested, it is up to management to select the best alternative. The primary criterion for selecting the best method of performing a task is *cost*. Proposed work methods and patterns of motions should be compared in this respect; the possibility that the presently

[9] Methods of work performance have traditionally been considered the responsibility of supervisory personnel. Accordingly, many suggestion programs offer management employees a lesser reward (perhaps 2 percent of the first year's savings) to encourage them to suggest improvements.

used method may be the least costly should not be ignored. Frequently, only a cursory evaluation of the alternatives will be necessary to indicate which method is the cheapest; this is likely to be the case if there is a substantial methods change resulting from the introduction of new equipment[10] or if obvious inefficiencies can be eliminated from work methods with a nominal investment.

In many cases, however, the decision is not easy; the information needed to make a detailed cost comparison may not be readily available. In those cases, it is often advantageous to avoid the costs of computing accurate cost data if it is possible to make the decision without it. What is needed are decision criteria that provide *good* approximations of cost; fortunately, such criteria are available. Those outlined below have evolved pragmatically from past experience in this field.

INTRA: The Single Operator

1. *Time.* The time required for the operating cycle can be used to decide among alternative methods. As a rule, the shorter method is best.
2. *Number of operations.* The method that involves the fewest number of work motions is usually the least costly.
3. *Balance of work.* The method that provides for the most efficient utilization of both hands is normally best. (*Note:* To determine this, the percentage of the operating cycle that each hand works is calculated. Idle and holding operations are considered "not working" for this purpose.)

In a typical case, an individual analyst may use one or all of these indirect indices in making a selection from among alternative work methods. For example, consider again the problem of assembling a selenium rectifier, which was presented earlier in the chapter as Figure 10–1. No times were recorded for the task. However, the number of each type of activity—operation, transport, hold, and delay—is recorded in the summary at the top of the form. Figure 10–11 describes a new approach to performing the same task. It, too, has a summary of each type of activity. Looking at the two summaries, notice that in the new method both hands are moving symmetrically and that the holding operations have been reduced from 34 to 6. As a result, the new method has balanced the operations between the hands. The 24 necessary operations are now assigned with 13 to the right hand and 11 to the left hand. Moreover, the total number of steps in the process has been reduced almost 25 percent from 40 to 31. It is fairly obvious, without actually comparing time and cost data, that the proposed method is more efficient.

INTRA: Man and Machine

1. *Time.* The shortest overall operating cycle in time will normally be the best among alternative methods.
2. *Percentage of utilization.* During what percentage of the operating cycle

[10] An economy study to determine the feasibility of acquiring new equipment will normally contain data indicating cost savings that should result from using the new equipment.

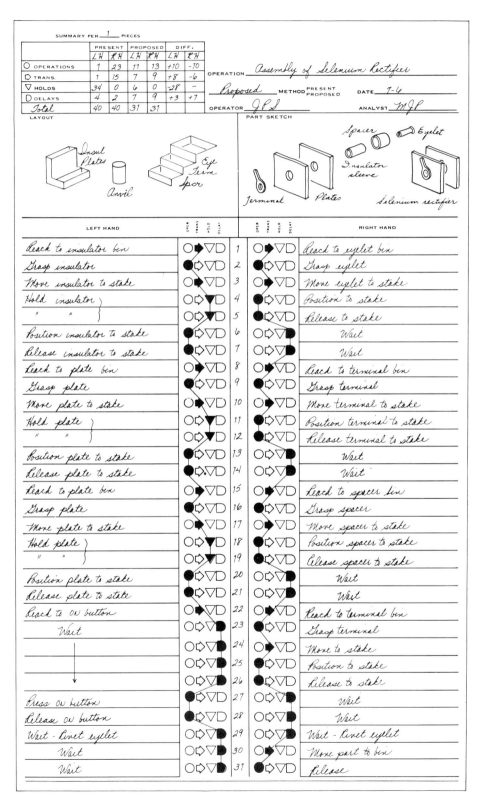

Figure 10–11 Left- and right-hand chart for assembly of selenium rectifier (improved method)

is the machine being utilized, and during what percentage is the operator working? The most complete utilization of both is normally associated with the most efficient overall method, but the ideal of 100 percent utilization of both man and machine is rarely attainable. Usually, a greater utilization of the machine can be obtained only by increasing the operator's idle time, or vice versa. The analyst can easily figure out the approximate relative costs of man and machine times, and this ratio will provide a rough measure of the percentage to which both the operator and the machine should be utilized in order to maximize the efficiency of the work process. For example, if light machinery is involved, as in the garment industry, man time is far more expensive than machine time. Consequently, fuller utilization of the operator's time is desirable. In the steel industry, where high-cost equipment is involved, however, the emphasis is on full-time use of machines.

To illustrate how this concept works, consider the simple operation shown in Figure 10–12. Here the man and machine are both operating at only half their capacity. If the machine is expensive, this idle time is costly, so it would be advantageous to figure out some way to keep the machine running more of the time. Suppose that the supervisor who is faced with this problem hires another man to handle the "put away" operation. As shown in Figure 10–13, we now have only 33 percent operator utilization, but the machine is being used 66 percent of the time. By adding the helper we have increased both machine utilization and output, but at the expense of the operator's time.

If instead of adding a helper, we can devise some technique whereby the "put away" operation can be accomplished while the machine is performing the "do" operation, both the machine's and the operator's utilization can be improved, as is shown in Figure 10–14. Now we have a method that more fully utilizes both the operator and machine time. Clearly, if we can develop a method to accom-

OPERATOR	MACHINE
Make ready (2 minutes)	Idle
Idle	Do (4 minutes)
Put away (2 minutes)	Idle

Total cycle time ("Make ready" + "Do" + "Put away")	8 minutes
Total man time ("Make ready" + "Put away")	4 minutes
Total machine time ("Do")	4 minutes
Machine utilization (machine time divided by cycle time)	50 percent
Operator utilization (man time divided by cycle time)	50 percent

Figure 10–12 Present method—operator and machine utilization

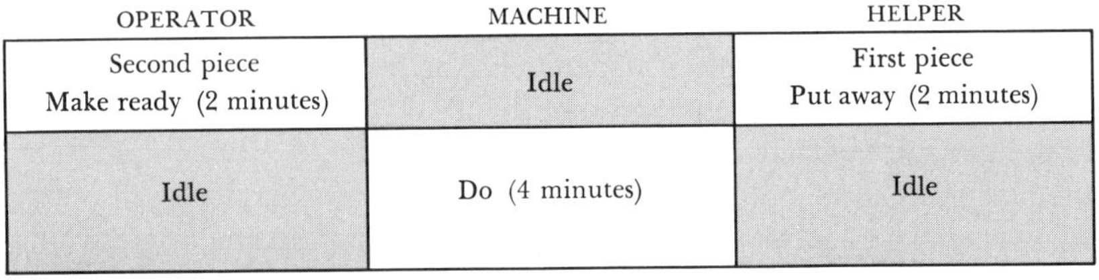

OPERATOR	MACHINE	HELPER
Second piece Make ready (2 minutes)	Idle	First piece Put away (2 minutes)
Idle	Do (4 minutes)	Idle

Total cycle time	6 minutes
Total man time	2 minutes
Total helper time	2 minutes
Total machine time	4 minutes
Machine utilization	66 percent
Operator utilization	33 percent
Helper utilization	33 percent

Figure 10–13   Proposed method 1—operator and machine utilization

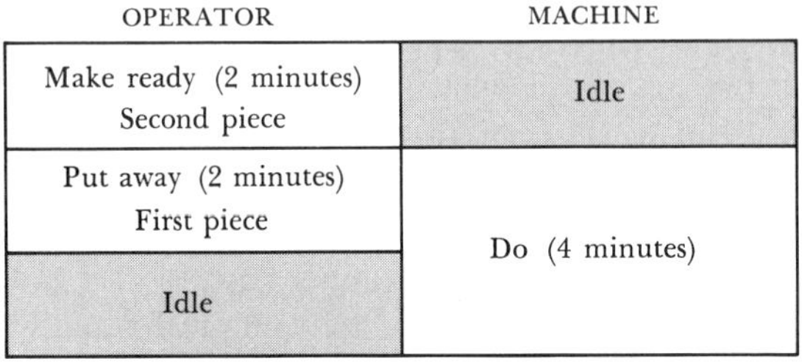

OPERATOR	MACHINE
Make ready (2 minutes) Second piece	Idle
Put away (2 minutes) First piece	Do (4 minutes)
Idle	

Total cycle time	6 minutes
Total man time	4 minutes
Total machine time	4 minutes
Machine utilization	66 percent
Operator utilization	66 percent

Figure 10–14   Proposed method 2—operator and machine utilization

plish greater utilization of both the operator's and the machine's time that does not involve costly machine changes, that method should be adopted. There is no need to develop expensive cost data to show that this should be done.[11]

INTRA: Multiple-Activity Analysis

This type of analysis is really an extension of the man and machine situation described above. The approximate criteria are the same: the time required for the production cycle and the percentage utilization of all of the men and machines involved. Here, too, it is important to consider the relative cost differen-

[11] An actual example of this type of analysis can be seen in Figures 10–2 and 10–3, where two methods of milling a metal shaft were shown. The first method utilized one operator and one machine, whereas the second method utilized one operator and two machines.

tials between men and equipment in evaluating alternatives that involve less than 100 percent utilization of all factors.

INTER: Process Analysis

The most meaningful approximate measure of cost that can be used for comparative evaluation of alternative processes is the number of separate operations ($\bigcirc$), transportations ($\Rightarrow$), inspections ($\square$), storages (∇), and delays (D) involved. A box score summary may be prepared that will record the number of occurrences of each of these activities in the processes being studied. A sample box score summary appears in Figure 10–15, showing in this case how a proposed method for assembling a power transformer would reduce the number of occurrences of each activity; such a reduction often indicates the superiority of a new method.

A proposed method for assembling a power transformer is shown in Figure 10–16. (The present method of assembling the transformer was depicted in Figure 10–4). The alternative type of flow-process chart for the proposed method is illustrated in Figure 10–17, and the layout that accompanies the method is shown in Figure 10–18.

In the proposed method, six operations are eliminated, reducing the overall assembly time from 2.14 minutes to 1.44 minutes. The reduction is accomplished by

1. Eliminating one operation through the use of a new type of insulated wire.
2. Redesigning a punching die so that it can perform two operations simultaneously.
3. Eliminating the need for the operator to count the number of transformer core plates being assembled; this is done by using a new index tool.

The distance the material moved was also reduced from 94 to 59 feet.

The number of occurrences of each activity in the box score summary do not tell the whole story, however. An analyst should also record the standard times (or estimates thereof) for each operation and inspection in the alternative method being studied. Similarly, the distances traveled in each transportation activity should also be recorded. In this fashion, the box score summary can be expanded to include a comparison of total manufacturing time and distance moved for each alternative method; this added information will lend weight and perspective to the numbers previously determined.

Activity	Old method	Proposed method	Saving
OPERATION $\bigcirc$	12	6	6
TRANSPORTATION $\triangleright$	13	7	6
INSPECTION $\square$	1	1	0
STORAGE ∇	1	1	0
DELAYS D	13	7	6

Figure 10–15 Box score summary for assembly of power transformer

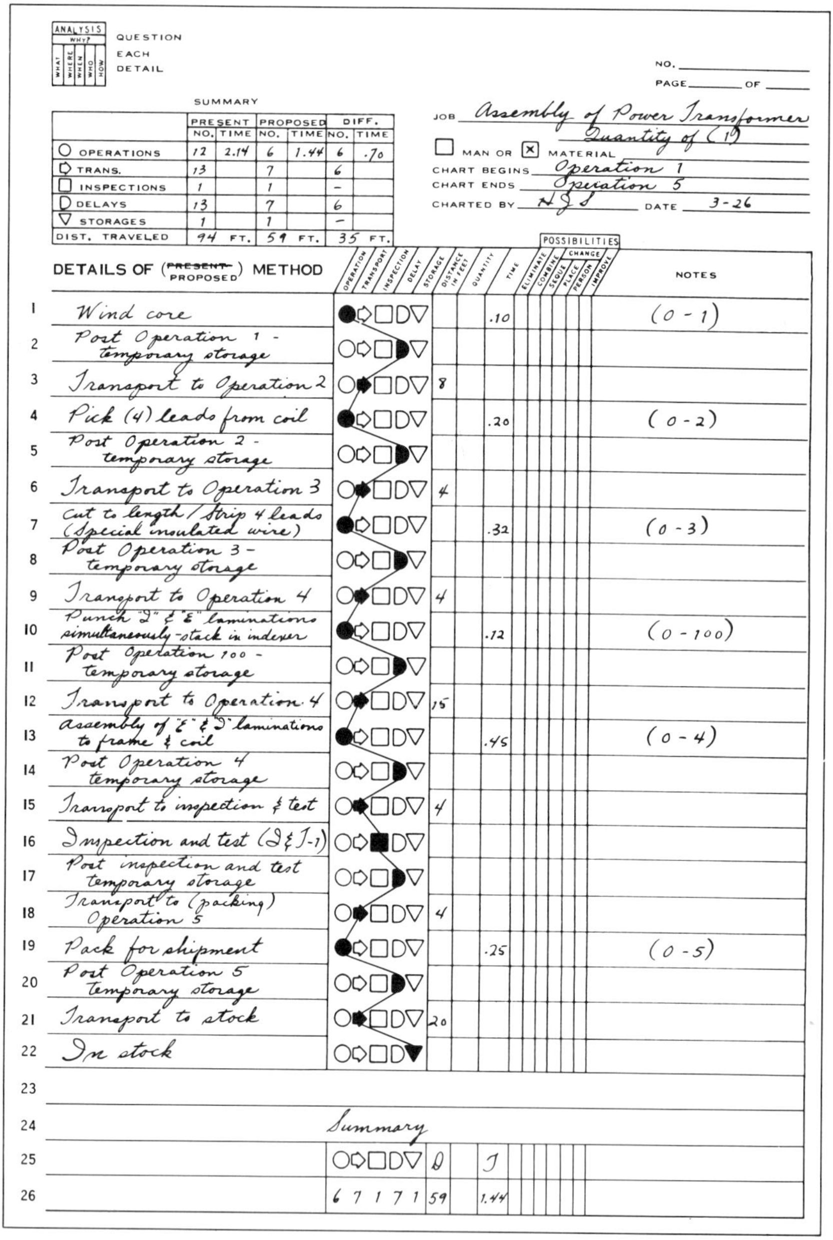

ANALYSIS WHY? WHAT WHERE WHEN WHO HOW — QUESTION EACH DETAIL

NO. ______ PAGE ______ OF ______

SUMMARY

	PRESENT NO.	PRESENT TIME	PROPOSED NO.	PROPOSED TIME	DIFF. NO.	DIFF. TIME
OPERATIONS	12	2.14	6	1.44	6	.70
TRANS.	13		7		6	
INSPECTIONS	1		1		–	
DELAYS	13		7		6	
STORAGES	1		1		–	
DIST. TRAVELED	94 FT.		59 FT.		35 FT.	

JOB Assembly of Power Transformer Quantity of (1)

MAN OR [x] MATERIAL

CHART BEGINS Operation 1

CHART ENDS Operation 5

CHARTED BY H J S DATE 3-26

	DETAILS OF (~~PRESENT~~ PROPOSED) METHOD	DISTANCE IN FEET	QUANTITY	TIME	NOTES
1	Wind core			.10	(0-1)
2	Post Operation 1 - temporary storage				
3	Transport to Operation 2	8			
4	Pick (4) leads from coil			.20	(0-2)
5	Post Operation 2 - temporary storage				
6	Transport to Operation 3	4			
7	Cut to length / Strip 4 leads (Special insulated wire)			.32	(0-3)
8	Post Operation 3 - temporary storage				
9	Transport to Operation 4	4			
10	Punch "I" & "E" laminations simultaneously - stack in indexer			.12	(0-100)
11	Post Operation 100 - temporary storage				
12	Transport to Operation 4	15			
13	assembly of "E" & "I" laminations to frame & coil			.45	(0-4)
14	Post Operation 4 temporary storage				
15	Transport to inspection & test	4			
16	Inspection and test (I & T-1)				
17	Post inspection and test temporary storage				
18	Transport to (packing) Operation 5	4			
19	Pack for shipment			.25	(0-5)
20	Post Operation 5 temporary storage				
21	Transport to stock	20			
22	In stock				
23					
24	Summary				
25		D		T	
26	6 7 1 7 1	59		1.44	

Figure 10–16 Flow-process chart for assembly of power transformer (proposed method)

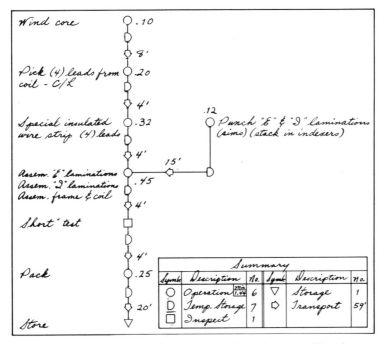

Figure 10–17 Alternate flow-process chart for assembly of power transformer (proposed method)

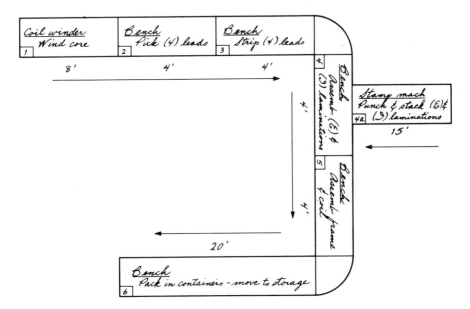

Figure 10–18 Layout of production facilities for assembly of power transformer (proposed method)

Installing the New Method

Once the analyst has selected what appears to him to be the most efficient alternative method, he will submit to management a proposal containing all pertinent information that demonstrates the superiority of the new method. This proposal should include a description of the problem, a discussion of alternative solutions, and an indication of the criteria used to demonstrate the superiority of the proposed solution. A detailed cost analysis should also be submitted if the project seems sufficiently important to justify the effort.[12] The new method must be explained and "sold" not only to top management but also to the line supervisors in charge of the activities that will be affected by the proposed change. The time and cost of installing the method and any investment in new facilities that prove necessary must be justified. Resistance to change may be encountered within the hierarchy of management as well as in the ranks of labor. Determining how a job should be done and instructing workers have traditionally been supervisory functions, and line managers may feel that industrial engineers are usurping their work. Furthermore, introducing a new method may be interpreted as an implied criticism of a supervisor and the methods presently used by employees under his direction. Hostility or defensive cooperation from a foreman can make the introduction and use of new work procedures infinitely more difficult. Workers may sense their supervisor's opposition to the new method and take a defensive attitude toward the method and the men who developed it.

Cooperation from both supervisors and workers is absolutely essential to the success of any labor simplification program. Indeed, the fate of all industrial engineering projects depends upon the ability of the analyst to gain the respect, confidence, and support of operating management and employees. The key man is the supervisor; to win his support, the industrial engineer must never forget that he (the engineer) is a staff man and "works for" the supervisor. All changes in work methods must be funneled through the supervisor, who in turn will instruct the workers. If the supervisor is allowed to be the "changer of methods" and the "answerer of all questions," the traditional supervisor–subordinate relationship will be maintained and even enhanced. This approach maximizes the chances that a new method will be successfully introduced, and it removes from the industrial engineer the burden of explaining and selling the new method to the employees, which can be a tedious and frustrating task.

As a further means of reducing resistance to change, many organizations have found it helpful to train line supervisors in the techniques of methods study. It has been found that this training facilitates the transfer of information between the industrial engineer and the supervisor because there is a common understanding of the language and principles involved; this training helps to ensure that the methods changes will be installed and used as designed. In addition, the supervisor tends to become more methods-conscious and thus more receptive to

---

[12] Such cost data are particularly important when the new method requires purchasing new capital facilities; in those cases, cost data are usually presented in an economy study, such as the type discussed in earlier chapters.

the idea of change. Indeed, this training is often reflected in the introduction of new methods developed by supervisors.

Following Up the Installation of the New Method

After line management has accepted the task of incorporating the method change, there should be some type of informal follow-up by the industrial engineer to see that the new worth method is, in fact, being used as designed and that the results are as expected. Deviations from expectations can result from two distinct causes. First, there may be a misinterpretation of the new method; in that case, further explanation to the supervisor should clear up the misunderstanding. Secondly, the new method, which seemed satisfactory in the development stage, may prove to have operational deficiencies. A performance detail may have been overlooked; in that case, the method itself can be adjusted by the industrial engineer. Even if the new method has been properly installed and is operating as smoothly as designed, a follow-up examination by the engineer is advisable because it will add the new process to the existing inventory of methods projects that may later be considered for improvement. Subsequent periodic audits of work methods are also necessary to ensure the maintenance of high operating efficiency.

Management's Role in Methods Study

Management's role in labor simplification is largely one of stimulating and maintaining an interest in methods improvement among the work force. The need to increase operating efficiency by designing improved work methods must be continually stressed. Management is also responsible for providing the necessary capital to finance any methods changes, since it will be necessary to purchase new machinery and tools from time to time. Furthermore, it costs money to establish a fully staffed engineering department with adequate laboratory facilities. It is crucial that this department receive the well-publicized backing of management and that there be adequate funds available to investigate the profitability of new work methods.

Finally, top management should periodically review the projects studied and the results achieved by the industrial engineering department. It must also assess the performance of the engineering department by subjecting its activities to periodic planning and measurement.

Work Methods in Clerical Activities

One further point seems worthy of comment. Most of the forms and techniques of methods analysis have been developed for manufacturing activities. Their application to office operations has been neglected until recently, but all of these approaches may be used for clerical operations as well, with only minor changes. Since clerical activities are increasing at a rapid pace in this age of automation, the application of methods-study techniques to this area is receiving more and more attention.

Questions and Problems

1. Evaluate the principles of motion economy from the standpoint of their usefulness in (a) job design and (b) increasing worker productivity.
2. How does the seven-step motion-study approach relate to scientific management?
3. Of what value are the INTRA and INTER work station classifications in methods studies?
4. Why are formal means of describing problems used in methods studies? What is the difference between those used for INTER- and INTRA-station problems?
5. How do micromotion and memomotion studies differ from traditional motion studies? What are the advantages and limitations of these techniques?
6. What measures besides total time can be used to evaluate alternative motion patterns?
7. Construct a man–machine chart for a simple task such as assembling a ballpoint pen.
8. A company produces metal stampings on machines that operate automatically. The machines only need to be filled with input materials. It takes an operator 2.10 minutes to load a machine and 0.12 minute to move to the next machine. The machine uses up a load of metal every 0.14 minute. Machine costs far outweigh labor costs on this task. How many machines should an operator service?
9. Why should methods work be as nearly complete as possible before attempting to set time standards?
10. (a) Develop a motion-study (SIMO) chart for shaving.
    (b) Identify and describe four basic hand motions that occur in shaving.
    (c) List four principles of motion economy and indicate how they can be used in developing the best method for shaving.
11. "An operator who has learned to do work in the wrong way would rather continue in the wrong way than try to overcome formed habits."
    (a) Assuming that the above statement is correct, what are its implications for methods improvements?
    (b) When the worker is faced with a methods change, what are the various "pulls" on him both toward and against the change, and how should the methods man deal with them?
12. "In making a micromotion study, it is wise to study either the best, or, preferably, the best two operators. This is fundamental for a number of reasons: the proficient employee is usually a dexterous individual who will instinctively follow the laws of motion study related to the use of the human body; this type of operator is usually cooperative and willing to be photographed; extra effort put forth by this operator will show greater results than when a similar effort is made by a mediocre person." Discuss.
13. What are the "tools" used for methods improvement? Give an example of the application of each.

14. Draw a process chart for the manufacture of a claw hammer from the information given below.

PURCHASED MATERIAL

Wood for handle
Head (forged to finished shape)
Wedge (to put in top of handle to hold head)

OPERATIONS TO BE PERFORMED (NOT IN ORDER)

Painting
Sanding handle smooth
Nailing wedge in top of handle
Final inspection
Assembling head to handle
Cutting shape of handle on lathe
Labeling
Packing for shipping
Degreasing
Cutting off wood for handle on saw

15. Would training in methods analysis benefit the following? If so, how?
    (a) Hospital administrators
    (b) Insurance management
    (c) Computer center managers
    (d) Production managers

16. (a) What conditions would lead you to use a memomotion study over a micromotion study?
    (b) Does the principle of diminishing returns apply to motion studies?
    (c) Can micromotion studies be used to train workers?
    (d) Why do unions generally try to require management to get their approval before taking micromotion studies?

17. The Simple Machine Company produces small machined parts. One process involves 10 semi-automated machines. The machines take 22.5 minutes to finish the part. It takes the operator

    2.0 minutes to load the machine
    1.5 minutes to unload the machine
    1.3 minutes to inspect the finished part
    2.0 minutes to pack the finished part
    0.5 minutes to move from machine to machine

    (a) How many machines can one man operate?
    (b) If machine time costs $20 per hour and the operator $5 per hour, does your answer to (a) still hold?

18. Fraser Volpe Company makes and sells optical devices. One of their products, a special lens, is purchased in lots of 100. Fraser Volpe repacks the lenses in cartons of 10 for sales. The lenses are taken from their purchase cartons, inspected, wrapped in tissue, and placed in the sales carton. The carton is then sealed with a pressure-sticking tape.
    (a) Analyze the job and develop a process flow.
    (b) Use an operations chart to indicate the work steps.

19. A hospital laundry is considering adding equipment. At present the process is

WASHING

Load	3 minutes
Run (automatic)	21 minutes
Unload	3 minutes

DRYING

Load	2 minutes
Run	35 minutes
Unload	2 minutes

(a) What is the present cycle time?

(b) What percentage of time are the washer, dryer, and operator now idle?

(c) What changes in idle time would occur if a second washer were purchased?

References

Abruzzi, A., *Work, Workers and Work Measurement,* Columbia University Press, New York, 1956.

Barnes, R. M., *Motion and Time Study,* 6th ed., Wiley, New York, 1968.

Currie, R., *Work Study,* Pitman, London, 1961.

Fogel, L. J., *Biotechnology: Concepts and Applications,* Prentice-Hall, Englewood Cliffs, N.J., 1962.

Gilbreth, F., and Gilbreth, L., *Fatigue Study,* 2nd ed., Macmillan, New York, 1919.

Hopeman, R., *Production: Concepts-Analysis-Control,* 2nd ed., Charles E. Merrill, Columbus, Ohio, 1971.

Krick, E. V., *Methods Engineering,* Wiley, New York, 1962.

Mayer, R. R., *Production Management,* 2nd ed., McGraw-Hill, New York, 1968.

Maynard, H. B., and Stegemerten, G. J., *Guide to Methods Improvement,* McGraw-Hill, New York, 1944.

Maynard, H. B., Stegemerten, G. J., and Schwab, J., *Methods-Time Measurement,* McGraw-Hill, New York, 1948.

McCormick, E. J., *Human Factors Engineering,* 2nd ed., McGraw-Hill, New York, 1964.

Mundel, M. E., *Motion and Time Study: Principles and Practice,* 3rd ed., Prentice-Hall, Englewood Cliffs, N.J., 1960.

Nadler, G., *Work Design,* Irwin, Homewood, Ill., 1963.

Niebel, B. W., *Motion and Time Study,* 4th ed., Irwin, Homewood, Ill., 1962.

11 The Development of Labor Standards

In Chapter 10 we said that if production management is to utilize labor inputs efficiently it must formulate "standard" methods of work performance. Then, on the basis of these methods, management can develop labor output standards, providing yardsticks for measuring labor efficiency and assessing the effectiveness of the production process. Less than 100 percent labor efficiency means that, according to the output standards set by management, resources are being wasted and higher than normal product costs are being incurred. Performances at or above 100 percent efficiency, on the other hand, produce a cost level that (in management's opinion) is "as good as" or better than could reasonably be expected for the production process being utilized. Management also uses labor output standards as a basis for

1. *Planning manpower requirements, including the number and types of labor skills needed*
2. *Comparing and evaluating alternative work methods and processes*
3. *Developing efficient plant layouts*
4. *Planning and scheduling product deliveries*
5. *Determining plant capacity and planning the utilization of that capacity*
6. *Formulating labor incentive plans*
7. *Making purchase decisions when facilities are acquired and alternative equipment is available*
8. *Formulating labor budgets*

9. *Formulating standard costs*
10. *Cost estimating and pricing*

In this chapter we will examine the various methods presently being used to determine these output standards.

Standards of Measurement

The many uses of labor output standards increase the importance of selecting an appropriate unit of measure. It is essential that the unit chosen be an accurate, realistic indication of labor output, that it be easily understood and generally applicable to the solution of the ten management problem areas just listed, and that it be easily determined for a specific task. It is also important that the means of formulating the standard be economical.

These requirements can usually be met by expressing output standards in terms of labor inputs per unit of production. Since the time required to accomplish a specific task will vary among different workers, labor inputs must not reflect the output of the fastest or the slowest worker but rather of an "average," or "normal," worker. The output rate of the normal worker is taken to be the mean time of *all* workers. This is expressed in Figure 11–1, which depicts the variation in output rate that usually occurs when large numbers of workers are assigned to the same task. Using the normal worker rate of output as a standard is generally an equitable and effective measure of performance, provided that each worker knows the task and possesses the skill required to perform it and that each employee can maintain the required expenditure of energy for an entire working day without undue or harmful fatigue. Thus, a more precise definition of the customary unit of measure for labor output standards might be: *the time required per task for the normal worker working with normal effort and skill.*

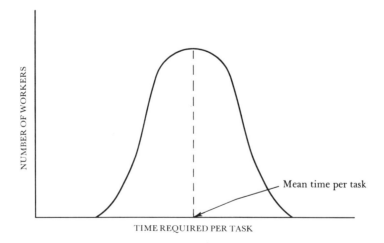

Figure 11–1   Output rate of the normal worker

Approaches to Work Measurement

Now that we have determined the appropriate unit of measure for labor output standards, we must examine how this unit of measure is applied to specific tasks. In practice there are four principal methods of setting output standards:

1. *The historical data approach*
2. *The direct time study approach*
3. *The predetermined time standards approach*
4. *The work sampling approach*

It is clearly impossible to determine the task performance rate of an average worker by training an entire potential labor force to do a particular job, timing them at their normal pace, and then computing the mean performance rate from the data so derived. What is needed is a method of estimating normal performance with only a modest expenditure of time and money from performance data that can be obtained easily and practically from a typical operating situation. Although there are substantial differences among the four approaches just listed, *all* are applications of sampling techniques.

Historical Data Approach

The oldest approach to setting time standards includes a wide variety of techniques using data from past performances, that is, historical data. The most unscientific and unstructured of these techniques is the use of *unsupported judgments,* whereby the average task performance rate is estimated by an individual who is familiar with the task. In a small machine shop, for example, a veteran machinist might be called upon to estimate the average length of time required for a new job. Frequently, the experienced judgment of the estimator is reinforced by written records that summarize analogous past performances. Many companies accumulate written performance data in an organized manner to ensure their ready availability for estimating performance rates. Needless to say, however, when tasks change or new tasks are introduced, past experience must be supplemented by the intuition and judgment of the estimator.

The weaknesses of the historical data approach are obvious; some of its principal limitations are:

1. Errors are introduced by the estimator's natural inability to remember exactly what occurred previously. In addition, unscientific, subjective interpretation and extrapolation of past experience will often result in predictions that are both inconsistent and inaccurate.
2. Since new jobs rarely, if ever, exactly duplicate past conditions, subjective adjustment of available data is almost always necessary. An extreme case would be a new job for which there was no analogous past experience; in that case estimates must be highly subjective and the possibility of error great.

3. The approach assumes that past performances were normal, or average, but this is probably not true. Thus, if previous operations are deemed atypical, the data must be adjusted further to obtain an estimate of normal output, and this must be done subjectively by the estimator.[1]

On the other hand, the historical data approach has a number of operating advantages:

1. Capable estimators can develop rough results that are sufficiently accurate on a short-term basis for some applications, such as labor budgeting and pricing.
2. Output standards can be drawn up in advance of the actual performance of a particular task; this can be extremely important for functions such as manpower planning and production scheduling.
3. The standards are obtained quickly and relatively inexpensively.
4. The approach can identify trends that may be used as a base for relative measures. Present performance can be compared with past achievements, and any improvement or deterioration in operating effectiveness can be assessed.

Many small companies use the historical data approach when estimating labor standards, and they have enjoyed profitable operations. Indeed, subsequent auditing of their output standards often reveals surprising accuracy and consistency, especially where their operations are characterized by small job lots and long operating cycles.

The historical data approach is also used in certain kinds of work situations such as the processing of invoices in a warehouse or the typing of letters in a typing pool. These jobs have a number of significant common characteristics. Typically there are great variations in the quantity of work assigned, and, although the basic method of doing the work remains essentially the same from unit to unit, the actual task to be performed varies. Invoices may contain few or many items, and letters may be long or short. In brief, certain jobs are not constant in magnitude or the time required to perform them, thus making it difficult to obtain a precise output measure.[2]

To overcome some of these problems and maximize the benefits that can be obtained from this approach, data are normally gathered over a long period of time, often as long as a year. The principal reason for the extended sample time (and the consequent large volume of data) is to determine the characteristics of an average work unit. It is hoped that the large sample will include, in representative proportion, most of the variations that can occur in the work content and in the flow of work units. The mean performance rate of this average work unit will give at least some standard for planning and measuring performance.

The performance rate developed in this manner is accurate if it is used to

---

[1] As an indication of the possible error in this approach, companies that have changed from historical standards to measured standards find that the normal output estimated by the former method is about 60 percent less than that computed by other approaches.

[2] These very characteristics make certain jobs prime targets for the use of *work sampling,* as we shall discuss later in this chapter.

measure labor performance over long periods of time. But when planning and performance measurement deal with only short periods—a week, for example—the fairness of the standard must be evaluated carefully in view of the content of the actual work flow. Any differences between the actual distribution of units of work processed and the distribution found in the sample would have to be reconciled by managerial judgment.

Direct Time Study Approach

Direct, or "stopwatch," time study is the approach most frequently employed to set labor output standards. Its use dates back to the scientific management movement, the beginning of which is generally associated with the writings of Frederick W. Taylor. He and others used time studies to set labor output standards in an attempt to achieve "a fair day's pay for a fair day's work." Numerous improvements have been made since then, yet the accuracy of standards set by the time study method still provokes considerable comment as it has done throughout the years.

The rationale for using direct time studies rests on the assumption that a valid output standard can be estimated by observing a single worker perform a particular task, provided, of course, that he has sufficient skill to perform the task and that he works according to the standard method. An outline of this approach is presented in Figure 11–2.

Data collection The first step in preparing a direct time study standard is to record the *work conditions* associated with the task. This information usually consists of a sketch of the workplace layout and a detailed description of the *work method* being used, including all tools, fixtures, and materials. This description of how and under what conditions a task is performed is called a *standard practice*. As we mentioned in Chapter 10, there must be a standard practice for performing a task before a meaningful time standard can be developed.

Once the standard practice is recorded, the task must be analyzed into the units of motion involved in the work performance; these units are commonly called *elements*. Task performance analysis is required in order to identify the component parts for timing purposes; the following guidelines are helpful in breaking jobs down into elements:

1. Nonrepetitive work elements should be separated from those that are repeated every cycle. If this is not done, the time needed to perform the

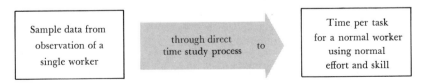

Figure 11–2 The essence of direct time study

nonrepetitive elements (such as setup time) would be included in the cycle time even though they were not performed in every cycle. If the nonrepetitive elements were included in the element breakdown, the resulting time would consequently be an overstatement of the time actually needed to complete a cycle of the task.

2. Accidental operations not normally involved in the task should be identified and separated from the repetitive work. Again, if this is not done, the observed time will overstate the amount actually needed to perform the task.
3. Machine-controlled or machine-paced elements should be identified and separated from operator-controlled or operator-paced elements.
4. The elements selected should have definite stopping and starting points in the sequence of movement to facilitate taking clock readings.
5. Elements of less than 0.03-minute duration are difficult to time and should be avoided.
6. In general, an elemental analysis should not be made until a skilled worker has learned the standard method and is performing it smoothly in a standard work environment.

In dividing a job into elements it is crucial that the entire task be included in the analysis. A sound knowledge of shop practices and a careful study of the job itself are necessary to ensure that all aspects of the task, including irregular and nonrepetitive elements, are reflected in the analysis. When completed, the elemental analysis and the information on which it was based (see Figures 11–3, 11–4, and 11–5) constitute a detailed description of the task. Figure 11–3 shows the elemental analysis for assembling a mounting case for the power section of a television receiver. Together with Figures 11–4, which is a diagram of the workplace for the job, and 11–5, a drawing of the assembly, it gives a complete and concise description of the work to be performed. One hidden benefit of this analysis is that it uncovers any gross inefficiencies that may exist in the method presently used and permits corrections to be made before the study is made and the output standards are actually established.

Once all of the elements have been identified and recorded, the analyst can then note the time it takes the worker selected for observation to perform each element. In Figure 11–6, where the times for the operations are recorded, the watch is allowed to run continuously, and readings are taken after the completion of each element. Thus, at the end of the first element of the first cycle the reading was 0.08 minute, at the end of the second element, 0.12 minute, and at the end of the third element, 0.14 minute. The actual *times* for these elements, however, were 0.08, 0.04, and 0.02, respectively. The number of operating cycles timed depends, as a rule, on the length of the cycle. Generally, an average performance time can be obtained for each element by observing from five to twenty successive cycles. In Figure 11–6, eight cycles were timed and recorded.

Obtaining select times   After the elements have all been timed in a sufficient number of cycles, the analyst must decide what a representative time is for each element of the given task. To do this he simply computes the arithmetic mean of

	Left Hand					Right Hand	
No.	Elemental Description	Elem. Time	Cumulative Time	Cumulative Time	Elem. Time	Elemental Description	No.
1	Plu fiber washer	0.0120	0.0120	0.0120	0.0120	Plu eyelet	1
2	TL to stake pin	0.0085		0.0205	0.0085	TL to pin	2
3	wait		0.0251	0.0251	0.0046	Ins eyelet	3
4	Insert fiber washer	0.0046	0.0297	0.0297		wait	4
5	Plu selium plate	0.0116	0.0413	0.0413	0.0116	Plu terminal	5
6	TL to pin	0.0078	0.0491	0.0491	0.0078	TL to pin	6
7	wait		0.0537	0.0537	0.0046	Ins terminal	7
8	Insert plate	0.0046	0.0583	0.0583		wait	8
9	Plu contact	0.0109	0.0692	0.0692	0.0109	Plu fiber washer	9
10	TL to pin	0.0070	0.0762	0.0762	0.0070	TL to pin	10
11	wait		0.0808	0.0808	0.0046	Ins to pin	11
12	Ins to pin	0.0046	0.0854	0.0854		wait	12
13	Plu fiber washer					Plu terminal	13
14	TL to pin				0.0240	TL to pin	14
15	wait		0.1094	0.1094	0.0046	Ins to pin	15
16	Ins to pin	0.0046	0.1140	0.1140		wait	16
17	wait				0.0235	Plu metal washer	17
18	wait					TL to pin	18
19			0.1375	0.1375		Ins to pin	19
20	Press safety sw	0.0076		0.1451	0.0076	Press safety sw	20
21	Machine cycle	0.0075		0.1526	0.0075	Machine cycle	21
22	wait			0.1616	0.0090	Plu assg-remove fro pin	22
23	wait		0.1674	0.1674	0.0058	Drop in slot	23

Figure 11–3 Task performance analysis for assembly of a mounting case for TV receiver

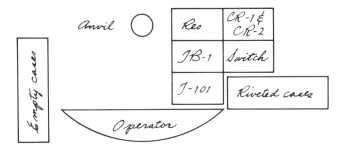

Figure 11–4 Workplace layout for assembly of a mounting case for TV receiver

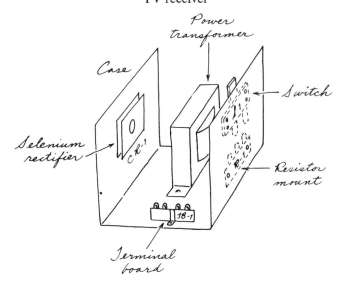

Figure 11–5 Mounting case assembly for TV rectifier

the times recorded for each element, and the answer is the *average observed time* for that particular element.

Before calculating average observed time, the data recorded for each element should be closely evaluated. If the worker is skilled and follows the standard method under standard working conditions, the differences in the time required for each element should vary only slightly from cycle to cycle. Wide variations in time values may mean that the operator either does not know the method or is intentionally not performing the task smoothly, or that the process has great inherent variability. The first cause of variance can be avoided by selecting a trained, experienced worker for observation. If the worker is intentionally varying his performance to distort the findings of the analyst, this would probably indicate a breakdown in labor–management relations, and the problem would be one of winning employee cooperation. If, however, the process seems to have great inherent variability, then the number of cycles timed must be increased until some consistency is obtained for the data pertaining to the particular elements. Enough cycles must be timed until a definite central tendency appears; then the mean value of the data can be considered a fair performance average. The question of how fair, or representative, an average is for variable data of this sort is difficult to answer. Operations that have great inherent variability are often excluded from labor incentive programs for this reason.

Frequently, a review of the sample data will reveal a single, isolated time recorded for an element that differs greatly from the other times recorded for the same element. When this happens, the cause of the variation should be investigated. For the most part these unusual times are the result of "irregular occurrences" such as dropped tools, bad materials, broken tools, or machine jams and should not be considered part of normal job performance.[3] Since allowances for irregularities will be built into the time standard later, these irregular times should be circled in red and deleted. The average observed time for each element is then recomputed without these "red-circled" times, and the new mean is called the *select time*. The process of computing a select time for an element can be expressed mathematically as follows:

Elemental average observed time (AOT_e):

$$AOT_e = \frac{\Sigma t}{N} \left(\frac{\text{Times recorded for performance of element}}{\text{Number of cycles studied}}\right)$$

Elemental select time (ST_e):

$$ST_e = \frac{\Sigma t}{N} \left(\frac{\text{Representative times recorded only}}{\text{Number of representative elemental times}}\right)$$

The select time for an entire task may then be computed by finding the sum of the select times for all the elements of the task. This will give the average time required by the observed employee to complete the task during the study. Mathematically expressed, we have

Task select time (ST):

$$ST = \Sigma \, ST_e \quad \text{(Sum of all elemental select times)}$$

Thus, in our example, the AOT for the first element is

$$AOT_1 = \frac{0.08 + 0.08 + 0.09 + 0.08 + 0.07 + 0.08 + 0.09 + 0.07}{8}$$

$$= \frac{0.64}{8} = 0.08 \text{ minute}$$

In this case the elemental select time is the same as the AOT because there are no unrepresentative times recorded. The elemental select time, therefore, is also 0.08 minute.

During the last cycle of the twentieth element, the riveting machine jammed, and a time of 0.13 minute was recorded for this element. Since this is an unrep-

---

[3] If this is not true and the exceptional times are inherent in the job, the analyst is faced with the problem just discussed in the preceding paragraph.

TIMESTUDY ENGINEERING

PART NAME: Assembly of Mounting Case for JV Receiver
SHEET NO. 1 OF 2   SECT. NO.   PART NO.   SUB.   OPERATION NO.

Description of Operation: Rivet the following to case. (1) Resistor Mount (2) Selenium Rectifier (3) Terminal Board (4) Switch (5) Transformer

Remarks

Material   Mat. Size   Order No.   Quantity   Equipment   Tools   Fin. No.   Misc.

RATE   Temp. ☐   Perm. ☐

	1 Sub.	1 Cont.	2 Sub.	2 Cont.	3 Sub.	3 Cont.	4 Sub.	4 Cont.	5 Sub.	5 Cont.	6 Sub.	6 Cont.	7 Sub.	7 Cont.	8 Sub.	8 Cont.	9 Sub.	9 Cont.	10 Sub.	10 Cont.	11 Sub.	11 Cont.	12 Sub.	12 Cont.
1	08	08	04	12	02	14	02	16	02	18	04	22	02	24	04	28	02	30	05	35	02	37	03	40
2		81	05	86	02	88	03	91	02	93	04	97	02	99	04	103	03	106	04	110	02	112	02	114
3		152	04	156	02	158	03	161	03	164	03	167	02	169	05	174	02	176	04	180	02	182	02	184
4		221	05	226	03	229	03	232	03	235	03	238	03	241	03	244	03	247	03	250	03	253	03	256
5		294	04	298	02	300	02	302	02	304	05	309	02	311	04	315	02	317	05	322	03	325	03	328
6		367	05	372	02	375	02	377	03	380	03	383	03	386	03	389	02	391	05	396	03	399	03	402
7		437	05	442	02	444	03	447	02	449	05	454	03	457	03	460	03	463	04	467	02	469	02	471
8		508	04	512	03	515	02	517	02	519	05	524	02	526	05	531	02	533	03	536	02	538	03	541
O-T		.64		.36		.19		.20		.19		.32		.19		.31		.19		.33		.19		.21
O-C		8		8		8		8		8		8		8		8		8		8		8		8
S-T		.090		.045		.022		.025		.024		.040		.024		.039		.024		.041		.024		.026
R-F		100		100		100		110		100		110		100		115		100		110		100		110
R-T		.080		.045		.022		.028		.024		.044		.024		.045		.024		.045		.024		.029

Min./Pc.   Pcs./Hr.   Select Time   Rating Factors   Total Rated Time   Multiplier   B.R.   R. & D.

22036

TIMESTUDY ENGINEER: H.G.I.   DATE 3-22   OPERATOR M.G.P.   CLOCK NO. 42719

Element descriptions:
1. Pick up case & position pattern
2. Pick up case & position pattern
3. Pick up 12 rivets to case. Line up hole to case. (Resistor)
4. Rivet 1st hole first hold (Resistor)
5. Line up washer to 2nd hold
6. Rivet 2nd hold case (Resistor)
7. Pick up (R.R.) position pattern to case
8. Rivet (R.R.) pattern to case
9. Position case to anvil
10. Rivet 15-16 case
11. Pick up switch (L.H.) position pattern
12. Line up 2 in hold case

PART NAME Assembly of Mounting Case for TV Receiver

SHEET NO. 2 OF 2 **TIMESTUDY ENGINEERING** SECT. NO. | PART NO. | SUB. | OPERATION NO.

Description of Operation

Remarks

Element descriptions (handwritten):
- Rivet 2nd hole to cover
- Position 3rd hole to cover & rivet
- Position 4th hole
- Rivet
- P.U. up 7-101. Position case to cover.
- Rivet 7-101. Position case to case.
- Rivet 7-101 1st hole
- Position Case to rivet 2nd hole
- Rivet 2 nd hole to cover
- Remove case from assembly. Lay aside in box.

	1		2		3		4		5		6		7		8		9		10		11		12	
	Sub.	Cont.	Sub.	Cont.	Sub.	Cont.	Sub.	Cont.	Sub.	Cont.	Sub.	Cont.	Sub.	Cont.	Sub.	Cont.	Sub.	Cont.	Sub.	Cont.	Sub.	Cont.	Sub.	Cont.
1	02	47	03	50	02	52	03	55	06	61	03	64	05	69	02	71	02	73						
2	02	116	02	118	03	121	02	123	07	130	03	133	04	137	03	140	03	143						
3	02	186	02	188	02	190	03	193	06	199	02	201	04	205	03	208	03	211						
4	03	259	03	262	02	264	02	266	08	274	02	276	05	281	02	283	04	287						
5	03	331	03	334	03	337	02	339	07	346	03	349	03	352	03	355	04	359						
6	03	405	03	408	02	410	02	412	06	416	02	418	05	423	02	425	03	428						
7	04	473	04	477	03	480	03	483	06	489	02	491	04	495	03	498	03	501						
8	03	543	03	546	03	549	02	551	09	560	03	563	04	567	(13)	580	05	585						
T-O-T	.19		.23		.20		.20		.55		.20		.34		.19		.27							
C-Y-C	8		8		8		8		8		8		8		7		7							
S T	.024		.029		.025		.025		.069		.025		.042		.026		.034							
R F	100		110		100		100		105		100		90		100		115							
R T	.024		.032		.025		.025		.072		.025		.038		.026		.039							

Misc. — Fin. No. — Tools — Equipment

Material — Mat. Size — Order No. — Quantity

RATE Temp. □ Perm. □ Pcs. □

Min./Pc.

Pcs./Hr.

Select Time 0.713

Rating Factors

Total Rated Time 0.740

Multiplier B.R. R. & D.

22D36

TIMESTUDY ENGINEER DATE OPERATOR CLOCK NO.

Figure 11–6 Time study data for mounting case assembly

resentative time, the time for the element would be biased if it were included. The average observed time for the twentieth element (including the unrepresentative time) is

$$AOT_{20} = \frac{0.31}{8} = 0.039 \text{ minute}$$

The select time for the element is

$$ST_{20} = \frac{0.18}{7} = 0.026 \text{ minute}$$

Thus, if the unrepresentative time were included, the time value for the element would be 50 percent greater than it should be.

Following through in this same manner for the rest of the elements, we obtain the task select time.

$$ST = 0.080 + 0.045 + 0.022 + 0.025 + 0.024 + 0.040$$
$$+ 0.024 + 0.039 + 0.024 + 0.041 + 0.024 + 0.026$$
$$+ 0.024 + 0.029 + 0.025 + 0.025 + 0.069 + 0.025$$
$$+ 0.042 + 0.026 + 0.034$$
$$= 0.713 \text{ minute}$$

Since direct time study is a sampling process, the question of sampling error naturally arises. How many cycles must be observed in order to reduce the probable sampling error to an acceptable level? Statistical theory suggests that this error varies inversely with the sample size. The larger the sample, the greater the "accuracy" it is thought to possess. There is no point, however, in attempting to achieve a higher degree of accuracy in the sample mean than it is possible to achieve in the overall time study process. Practitioners agree that an acceptable overall error range for work measurement standards is ±10 percent and that the sample size should be large enough to give at least 95 percent confidence that the mean is within these limits.

There are three ways of determining the necessary sample size in any particular case. The first method is to calculate the mean and standard deviations that apply either to the total cycle time or to representative elements within the cycle. Calculating the deviations applicable to representative work elements requires more work, but it provides an opportunity for testing the accuracy of the elemental times that show the greatest variability. In fact, many practitioners advise that only the element with the greatest variability should be analyzed, in the belief that if it passes the accuracy test, then the total select time will also be acceptable. After the mean and standard deviations for the most variable element have been determined, the standard error of the mean is calculated by traditional statistical methods. The limits prescribed by the 95 percent confidence level are calculated, and the "percent deviation" from the mean will determine if the sample is large enough. The same formula can then be manipulated to reveal the size of the sample needed. A simplified formula that gives directly the number of cycles needed when a 95 percent confidence level and an accuracy of ± 10 percent is desired is

$$\text{Number of cycles needed} = \left(\frac{20 \sqrt{N \Sigma X^2 - (\Sigma X)^2}}{\Sigma X}\right)^2$$

where X = individual elemental times
N = number of cycles observed

Thus, for the element with the greatest variation in the example given on page 295 (element 7), we have

$$\text{Number of cycles needed} = \left(\frac{20 \sqrt{8 \times 148 - (34)^2}}{34}\right)^2$$

$$= \left(\frac{20 \sqrt{1184 - 1166}}{34}\right)^2$$

$$= \left(\frac{20 \sqrt{18}}{34}\right)^2$$

$$= 6 \text{ (approximately)}$$

The second method of determining the necessary sample size is more easily applied. It is the use of standardized tables that relate sample range, sample size, and the estimated standard error of the mean. When these tables are available and applicable, they make the job of calculating the standard error of the mean much easier for the analyst. He merely obtains the figure from the table and then calculates the percent deviation associated with the 95 percent confidence limits.

The third method of determining the necessary sample size uses an approximation method and can safely be used provided that there are no red-circle events in the task elements. This method utilizes charts giving the approximate number of cycles required for varying lengths of operating cycle time. Table 11–1 is an example of this type of chart; its chief advantage is that it is ex-

Table 11–1 Number of cycles in
relation to the time of cycle[a]

Cycle Time	Number of Cycles Required
0.10	200
0.25	100
0.50	60
0.75	40
1.0	30
2.0	20
5.0	15
10.0	10
20.0	8
40.0	5
80.0	3

[a] These figures apply for a confidence level of 95 percent and an accuracy of ± 10 percent.

tremely simple to use. Once the analyst has computed the elemental or task select time, he can determine the approximate number of cycles required by simply reading them off the chart. Such charts are generally conservative and include enough cycles to be safe. In our example the task select time is 0.713 minute; the chart indicates that for this time just over 40 cycles are required, which is considerably larger than the number calculated by the first method.

Rating, or leveling, theory   Once the select time for the performance of a particular task has been calculated, the analyst must decide whether the worker studied was, in fact, an *average* worker. Was he producing more or less than could reasonably be expected from the average worker? If so, an adjustment must be made; Figure 11–7 summarizes this problem. The select time of the observed worker must be adjusted so that it will reflect the efforts of the average worker. To do this, a *transformation factor* is required; it is actually a multiplier that, when applied to the task select time, yields a time numerically equal to that required by the average worker for the task performance. This multiplier is called a *rating, or leveling, factor* (RF), and its function can be stated mathematically as follows:

$$\text{ST}_t \times \text{RF} = \bar{T}$$

where ST_t = task select time
        RF = rating factor
        $\bar{T}$ = output standard

The function of this factor is to convert the recorded performance of the worker observed to the expected performance of an average worker who is working with average effort and skill. Therefore, to determine the rating factor, the effort and skill exerted during the observed performance must be appraised, or rated, in some fashion. This is an extremely difficult feat; the factors comprising effort

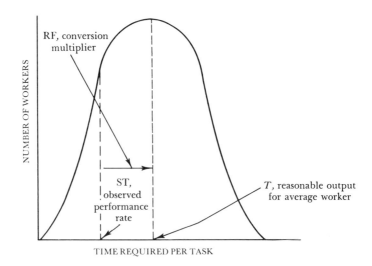

Figure 11–7   Adjusting the time per task to reflect the average worker

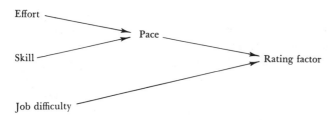

Figure 11–8   Factors influencing the rating factor

and skill are highly complex and not easily measured. Therefore, the analyst approaches the problem by what is called *first approximation,* whereby the pace, or speed, of performance is considered a measure of the effort and skill applied. Thus, "other things being equal," the greater the effort exerted by a skilled worker, the faster his performance pace will be. Similarly, the more skilled a worker is, the faster his performance is likely to be. Therefore, it should be possible to estimate a work pace that represents the normal employee working with normal effort and skill.

One other factor must be considered in this regard, however—the nature of the task performed. Can this estimated normal pace be maintained by the average worker for a typical work day without undue fatigue? The relative difficulty of a job must be taken into consideration before a normal pace is established. In short, the rating factor in a specific case must coordinate the pace and difficulty of the task, as illustrated in Figure 11–8.

Subjective rating   While he is recording the direct time study data obtained by observing the performance of a selected worker, the analyst should bear in mind the need to formulate a rating factor. This means that the actual pace of the worker and difficulty of the task must be evaluated in terms of what the analyst believes is "normal."

Rating methods that delegate the decision regarding what is normal to the individual analyst are referred to as "subjective" methods. Using judgment based upon numerous observations of work performance, the analyst attempts to "conjure up" a mental image of normal performance for the task as he is making his study; for his purpose, the rating factor attempts to quantify the measurement process.

$$\text{Rating factor (in percentage)} = \frac{\text{Actual performance pace of the task}}{\text{Image of normal performance pace of the task}} \times 100$$

The subjective rating factor is expressed as a percentage and acts as a simultaneous measure of skill, effort, and job difficulty.

For a long time, subjective methods were the only means of establishing rating factors, and many people considered this the chief drawback of time study. Although it is possible to develop a fair and equitable conversion factor in this fashion, the results were far from ideal in actual practice. A concept of what is normal naturally reflects the experiences, attitudes, and biases of the individual analyst; consequently, there were often great variations in this concept among the different industrial engineers employed by a single company. In fact, it was found that there was a significant variation in the concept as applied by the same analyst in moving from task to task—either because of his limited knowledge of different kinds of tasks or because of changes in his emotional tone. Many industrial engineers earned reputations of being "tight" or "loose" in their rating factors. In many instances, workers and union officials tried to have a particular analyst assigned to a job because of the supposed "looseness" of his rating factors, whereas the results developed by another time study engineer were attacked on the basis that "this man is known to be tight."

The very nature of subjective rating seriously limits management's defense against any complaint that a specific rating factor is in error. Therefore, collective bargaining tends to become the principal determinant of a rating factor, and persuasiveness and argumentative ability replace pace and difficulty as the key factors.[4]

Objective rating   The problems encountered in using subjective rating made it necessary to develop a more objective approach. Detailed study, including shop experience and laboratory experimentation, resulted in the development of so-called "objective" rating methods.[5] Two important innovations distinguish this class of methods from the subjective approach: the separate, individual treatment of both the operator's pace (skill and effort) and the task difficulty, and a common definition of "normal pace" that is approved by both management and labor. Industry- and company-wide conferences were convened to consider the matter of defining "normal pace." After much discussion and debate, it was agreed that "normal" could be defined as a pace that could be attained and maintained by an average worker during a normal work day consisting of "eight nominal hours" without undue fatigue.[6] The pace established as normal for a given task was then recorded on films for ready reference in case of dispute. The initial agreement included:

1. For walking on a smooth, level surface on a clear day, a normal pace would be 3 mph.
2. For light hand-assembly operations, a normal pace would be the ability to deal a deck of 52 cards into four equal piles in 0.50 minute.

Subsequent agreement then applied this normal pace to specific industries and specific machine tasks. In each case, motion picture films of normal pace were made. The significance of this breakthrough must not be underestimated; with an established normal pace considered as 100 percent, it then became possible, using trained operators paced by metronomes, to obtain films of paces varying from 50 to 200 percent of normal. Reference libraries could then be developed

---

[4] It should be noted that many experienced analysts have gained the confidence and respect of management, the workers, and their unions; these men can and do use subjective rating effectively.

[5] Actually, it would ˌbe more accurate to call these approaches "more objective" because, although far superior to the subjective method, they are still not entirely objective.

[6] This resulted in the widespread use of *fatigue allowances,* which will be discussed later in this chapter.

for representative tasks containing various paces in increments of 5 or 10 percent. This made it possible to rate the pace of a particular worker's performance objectively by taking a motion picture of his performance and then comparing it with the standard films. The comparison is made by running the motion picture of the employee beside a variety of standard films on the same screen. The appropriate rating percentage is determined by the standard film closest in pace to the observed performance level.

Taking motion picture studies to support each and every time study is impractical, of course, because of cost and operational factors. Therefore, standard films are typically used to train time study engineers and to resolve disputes. Films of men working at various paces can effectively improve pace rating; after this type of training, many companies report improved accuracy and consistency among most industrial engineers.

To increase the objectivity of task difficulty rating, many attempts have been made to identify the factors that limit the pace an average worker can attain and maintain for a normal work day. The extent to which each factor reduces the pace of a normal worker has also been carefully studied, resulting in tables (such as Table 11–2) to facilitate calculation of an "adjustment factor" in those cases where the intensity and duration of each factor can be determined.

Thus the performance rating process is divided into two steps: pace rating and job difficulty rating. The rating factor for job difficulty is often called a *secondary rating adjustment*.[7] With these two rates, the analyst can readily transform the select time of the worker who was studied into a *standard,* or *rated, time* for the task, as follows:

$$ST \times RF_p \times RF_d = RT$$

where ST = select time
RF_p = rating factor: pace
RF_d = rating factor: job difficulty
RT = rated time

To illustrate this process, consider a task that requires a worker to solder two wires to a delicate transistor. The work material is so minute that the worker must continuously look through a magnifying glass while soldering. The select time, calculated from a clock study, is 1.13 minutes. The operator was pace rated at 90 percent of normal. In Table 11–2, the secondary rating adjustment for eye–hand coordination of this type (reference letter M) is given as 10 percent. The rated time is

$$
\begin{aligned}
RT &= ST \times RF_p \times RF_d \\
&= 1.13 \times 0.9 \times 1.10 \\
&= 1.12 \text{ minutes}
\end{aligned}
$$

---

[7] The term *secondary rating adjustment* signifies that it is applied after the pace adjustments have been made. Most analysts have always made the adjustment for pace; because the adjustment for job difficulty is relatively new, it is often considered a secondary adjustment.

Table 11–2 Secondary rating adjustments

Category	Description	Reference Letter	Condition	Percentage Adjustment	Explanation
1	Amount of body used	A	Fingers used loosely	0	
		B	Wrist and fingers	1	
		C	Elbow, wrist, and fingers	2	
		D	Arm, etc.	5	
		E	Trunk, etc.	8	
		E2	Lift with legs from floor	10	
2	Foot pedals	F	No pedals or one pedal with fulcrum under foot	0	
		G	Pedal or pedals with fulcrum outside of foot	5	
3	Bimanualism	H	Hands help each other or alternate	0	
		H2	Hands work simultaneously doing same work on duplicate parts	18	Parts are "identical" in respect to work requirements
4	Eye–hand coordination	I	Rough work, mainly feel	0	Do not need to look other than casually
		J	Moderate vision	2	Occasional need for peripheral vision
		K	Constant but not close	4	Constant peripheral vision
		L	Watchful, fairly close	7	Foveal vision
		M	Within 1/64 inch	10	Close hand sewing
5	Handling requirements	N	Can be handled roughly	0	No need to consciously control muscular forces
		O	Only gross control	1	Can squeeze or bang objects
		P	Must be controlled, may be squeezed	2	Objects must not be banged
		Q	Handle carefully	3	Parts could be damaged by handling or pressure
		R	Fragile	5	Parts readily damaged
6	Weight	W	Use table		

This two-step objective rating procedure should yield a rated time that is based upon the accepted normal pace and reflects differences in job difficulty. This means that the rated time for any task in a plant should be equally difficult (or equally easy) to attain and maintain. Thus, it is hoped that the same level of performance will be required to achieve the normal output on each and every job so rated.

Allowances   Rated time is a fair measure of production output but not for actual operations, for reasons that are external to the job itself; these external factors must be handled separately by means of "allowances."

If a worker had the opportunity to work at his assigned task for the full 480 minutes in the normal eight-hour work day, the performance level defined by the rated time would, by definition, be a fair measuring rod. He does not, and cannot, work 480 minutes per day, however. A number of factors external to the task prevent him from performing at certain times during the day; these include *personal time, irregular occurrences, fatigue,* and *miscellaneous machine factors.*

PERSONAL TIME   This is the time allowed because of the physical needs of the worker. Normal bodily requirements create a need for a break periodically in the production routine. This is true in every working environment, and time periods of about fifteen minutes, both morning and afternoon, are usually allotted for this purpose.[8] Under abnormal or unusual working conditions, of course, the personal needs of the worker are correspondingly increased.

Initially, intuition and collective bargaining were the key factors used to set personal time allowances, and the customs and traditions of the industry, company, or occupation were reflected in the allowances. In an effort to improve the meaningfulness of these allowances, however, the relationship between various external factors and the needs of the workers have been analyzed in recent years; the results of these studies have been summarized in tables such as Table 11–3, which indicates various percentage allowances that should be used under specific external conditions. Five percent, or 23 minutes per day, seems to be the average allowance for personal time under normal conditions. However, un-

Table 11–3   Typical allowance table for personal time

Condition	Reference Letter	Daily Allowance for Personal Time[a] (in minutes)
Comfortable	S	23
Warm, or slightly disagreeable	T	30
Hot, dusty, noisy, etc.	U	50
Special, or unusual	SP	As required

[a] For an eight-hour day.

[8] Experience shows that daily production levels are increased, not decreased, by such allowances for time off.

usual allowances of 50 percent, or 240 minutes, have been negotiated for tasks that must be performed under particularly adverse conditions; for example, some blast furnace operators receive 30 minutes off each hour.

IRREGULAR OCCURRENCES   These are occurrences over which the employee has no control but which curtail production output and occur at various times during the day. Broken tools, defective materials, delayed receipt of materials, jammed machines, and power failures are common events that belong in this category. That such events occur and that they prevent the worker from performing his assigned task are not questioned. The frequency of these occurrences and the amount of time lost per day because of them have been the subject of much controversy, however. As a consequence, the amount of time allowed for irregular occurrences is set primarily through collective bargaining; typical allowances range from 3 to 7 percent.[9]

FATIGUE   There is universal agreement that operating conditions justify granting allowances for personal time and irregular occurrences. Allowances for fatigue are also widely used. However, more and more managers are beginning to question the validity of fatigue allowances. Those who *favor* them argue that a worker gradually becomes mentally and physically tired as a result of performing his assigned task. Fatigue, they claim, is accompanied by a steady decline in his ability to attain and maintain a normal pace. The *opportunity* to attain the normal production rate will also decline correspondingly, since the fatigued worker does not have the same performance "opportunity" that a fresh worker enjoys. Therefore, the argument concludes, allowance must be made to compensate for the decline in performance "opportunity" resulting from fatigue.

The case *against* the use of fatigue allowances is gaining favor. Here, the argument is that fatigue does not cause a worker's production ability to deteriorate gradually because there is little, if any, change in output levels until fatigue reaches serious proportions. At that point there is a sharp drop in ability because the employee is actually collapsing under the cumulative work load. Therefore, it is argued, if normal pace is carefully defined as the pace at which no undue or harmful fatigue effects will occur, and if this pace is actually implemented in the firm's output standards, then there will be no decline in output rates resulting from fatigue because the "opportunity" to achieve normal production levels will not be adversely affected by fatigue.

The increasing use of job difficulty factors (RF_d) in the rating system reinforces this argument because these factors adjust the pace demanded of the worker where conditions limit his ability to attain and maintain the normal pace. Therefore, the physical causes of fatigue are taken into consideration at this point, and, as a result, the output demands placed on the worker should not cause a fatigue breakdown during a typical work day.

Finally, personal time allowances that reflect a careful evaluation of the employee's needs and the external working environment also provide an oppor-

---

[9] A more accurate way of determining the average length of these occurrences is by means of *work sampling,* which we shall discuss later in this chapter.

tunity for the worker to relax and rebuild his stamina, thus preventing a fatigue breakdown during the work day.

In spite of these apparently valid arguments against the use of fatigue allowances, however, they are still widely used today. Where fatigue allowances are most widely used, they are ordinarily set by collective bargaining. Past practices and experienced judgment provide the basis for negotiating a percentage; a 5 percent allowance for fatigue is typical.

MACHINE ALLOWANCES Machine allowances can be subdivided for convenience into three basic categories. The first type arises when one operator runs more than one machine; there will of necessity be periods when a machine is idle while the operator is servicing another. The more machines that are assigned to an operator, the greater the amount of unavoidable machine idle time will be. Thus, the actual amount of idleness is a function of the number of machines operated, the distribution of service time, the relationship between service time and running time, and the length of the running time. In this type of situation, machine allowances are clearly necessary and must be figured out to meet the needs of each job. The most common approach is to use man–machine charts of the type discussed in Chapter 10. Work sampling, which will be discussed later in this chapter, can also be used.

The second type of machine allowance is machine maintenance. For much equipment it is normal to schedule time during each work day for cleaning, oiling, and other maintenance work. In most instances this work is done at certain fixed times.

The final type of machine allowance includes situations in which machine operations are erratic; this can be due to poorly designed or poorly maintained equipment or it can be the result of the overall technology of the process.

In practice, machine allowances are handled fairly well. Since they only apply to special tasks, no general rules of thumb have been developed; each case is considered individually. Therefore, the validity of any machine allowance depends to a large extent upon the skill of the particular analyst who sets the allowance.

OVERALL ALLOWANCES The total allowance permitted on a particular task is the sum of the time of each applicable individual allowance; for a specific task it might be computed as follows:

Personal time	5%
Irregular occurrences	4
Fatigue	5
Machine	3
Total task allowance	17%

Sometimes allowances are expressed in minutes. Many labor contracts, for example, call for personal time allowances of 20 minutes and irregular occurrence allowances of 15 minutes. In such cases, the minutes must be converted to percentages so that they can be incorporated into a time standard for the job.

$$\text{Allowance percentage} = \frac{A + B}{480 - (A + B)} \times 100$$

where A = personal time
       B = irregular occurrence time
       480 = minutes in a normal work day

To convert the 20-minute personal and 15-minute irregular allowance times to percentages, then, the formula is

$$\text{Allowance percentage} = \frac{20 + 15}{480 - (20 + 15)} \times 100$$

$$= \frac{35}{445} \times 100$$

$$= 7.8\%$$

Notice that the denominator of this equation includes only that part of the day during which the employee can be expected to work. This highlights an important characteristic of allowances—it is not expected that they will be used in every cycle. Rather, the time, as a percentage of each cycle, accumulates like deposits in a bank, and the sum total is used when there is an irregular occurrence or when personal time is taken.

Standard time   To obtain an overall time standard that will apply to any timed job in a firm, the rated time is adjusted by allowance percentages to yield a *normal allowed time* or, as it is often called, a *standard time.*

Normal allowed time (NAT) = RT + (Allowance percentage $\times$ RT)

= (1 + Allowance percentage)RT

This may also be expressed as

Standard time = Observed time $\times$ Rating factors $\times$ Allowance factors

The standard time is an attempt to record the total work opportunity available to an employee who is maintaining a normal pace. It is hoped that such a time will be reasonable both in terms of the effort and skill demanded of the employee and in terms of the losses in working time typically encountered because of factors external to the work process itself. If this is so, then standard time will indeed be a fair standard for planning and measuring labor performance, and the objectives of the direct time study procedure will be realized.

Let us now apply these procedures to the example shown in Figure 11–6.

1. ST (task select time) = 0.713
2. *Rating.* Each element was rated because a large number of them were machine controlled. Machine-controlled elements are by definition rated at 100 percent. The rating factor for each element is shown in Figure 11–6, where the multiplications are done. Therefore, to obtain the rated time, we add the individually rated elements.

$$RT = 0.80 + 0.045 + 0.022 + 0.028 + 0.024$$
$$+ 0.044 + 0.024 + 0.045 + 0.024 + 0.045$$
$$+ 0.024 + 0.029 + 0.024 + 0.032 + 0.025$$
$$+ 0.025 + 0.072 + 0.025 + 0.038 + 0.026$$
$$+ 0.039$$
$$= 0.740 \text{ minute}$$

3. In calculating the normal allowed time (standard time), an allowance of 17 percent was used.

$$NAT = 1.17 \times 0.740 = 0.866 \text{ minute}$$

Therefore, the standard time allowed for the task described in Figure 11–6 is 0.866 minute.

Despite the apparent logic of this procedure, direct time study has come under considerable attack, as we mentioned earlier. Now that the process has been explained, let us examine these attacks and evaluate the advantages and disadvantages of the process at each phase.

ELEMENTAL ANALYSIS   The chief danger in the initial phase of direct time study is that an incorrect description of the task may be formulated. If this happens, all of the elements that pertain to the job will not be included. Even an experienced industrial engineer may fail to include nonrepetitive elements in his analysis because he is not familiar with shop methods. Such errors can be minimized by providing the analyst with a brief training period during which he can familiarize himself with shop practices and techniques. On the whole, however, an experienced, knowledgeable analyst will rarely make the mistake of incorrectly defining the elements of a specific task.

TAKING THE STUDY   The use of the stopwatch is an art. Accurate data can be obtained in this manner only if the analyst has had sufficient practice and experience. With trained analysts, the data collected by using a stopwatch can show remarkable consistency, but with untrained personnel, considerable error can be introduced.

SELECT TIME   Adjusting observed times in order to eliminate nonrepresentative elemental times can also lead to error. Unusual times may result from flaws in the production process itself or from irrelevant chance happenings. Whether to include such data in the analysis is a subjective decision. Precise task definitions make it easier to identify accidental elements and irregular performances that should not be included in the sample data, however, and trained analysts can usually make the necessary adjustments to the satisfaction of all parties.

RATED TIME   The rating process can easily be abused and thereby produce results that are merely "guesstimates." Much of the criticism heaped upon direct time study as a whole can be traced to the subjective errors at this phase of the process; we have already discussed the lack of accuracy and consistency inherent in subjective rating.

The two-step objective rating procedure and the use of standard films for training can usually raise the consistency and accuracy of pace rating to acceptable levels. In practice, however, the full advantages of objective rating are often not obtained because companies do not have film libraries of various standard paces[10] and because they do not invest the time and money necessary to train analysts in the proper use of standard pace and job difficulty ratings. As a consequence, the rating phase of direct time study continues to be a large source of error.

ALLOWANCES   The standard time for a task may include allowances as high as 15 percent. With such an allowance level, the accuracy carefully attained in the previous phases of direct time study can be dissipated unless the allowances are also accurately estimated. Where they are determined by collective bargaining, errors often creep in; fortunately, however, collective bargaining as the chief determinant of allowances is disappearing. The trend now is toward an accurate and fair estimation. Since work sampling and other techniques can provide an accurate determination of the percentage of irregular occurrences, the errors previously found at this phase are now being minimized.

On the whole, therefore, it may be said that the time study process is continually being improved. Most of the potential errors in its techniques can now be eliminated or at least minimized if analysts are properly trained. Similarly, most of the criticisms leveled at guesstimates are no longer valid because of improvements already made in the whole process.

Time study still has a bad reputation, however, because of past shortcomings both in the process itself and in the analysts who used it; unfortunately, its past reputation was justified. Modern users of improved time study techniques must make a concerted effort to win the confidence and respect of the workers and supervisors who are involved in the use of time standards, but this can be a difficult task. In the long run, only improved performance can earn a better reputation for these techniques.

One other serious problem in using this approach is the fact that direct time study can only be used *after* a task has been learned and performed; this is a serious limitation. Data for planning purposes in such activities as budgeting and pricing are needed before, and not after, the task has been performed.

Because of the deficiencies and limitations in the historical data and direct time study approaches, other means of determining time standards were investigated. Two methods have been developed that correct or mitigate some of these disadvantages. The first, chronologically, is termed *predetermined time standards* and consists of synthetic and formula standards; the second method is called *work sampling*.

Predetermined Time Standards Approach

Systems for calculating predetermined time standards were developed to overcome three of the deficiencies of direct time studies that we have just discussed. First, predetermined standards can be ready *before* the task is actually per-

---

[10] Companies that cannot afford to maintain film libraries can often obtain these films for short periods from local universities or other educational facilities.

formed so that they are available for planning labor requirements, machine needs, and fulfillment schedules. Second, no pace rating is required; a standard pace is incorporated into the predetermined time values. Finally, the study can be carried out in a laboratory environment and thus will not upset normal production activities as direct time study does.

Conceptual basis of synthetic standards   The fundamental theory on which predetermined time studies are based is that all manual work can be subdivided into basic motion units. These units, much smaller in scope than the elements we have already discussed in direct time study, are called *therbligs*.[11] Listed below are seventeen commonly used therbligs from which it is possible to build up or synthesize almost any work motion necessary to perform a manual task.

Therblig Name	Symbol
1. Search	S
2. Select	SE
3. Grasp	G
4. Position	P
5. Preposition	PP
6. Use	U
7. Assemble	A
8. Disassemble	DA
9. Release load	RL
10. Reach	R
11. Move	M
12. Hold	H
13. Unavoidable delay	UD
14. Avoidable delay	AD
15. Rest	RT
16. Plan	PN
17. Inspect	I

It is only necessary to add the time factor to a therblig breakdown of a task in order to provide a means for establishing standard task time. The sum of the times it takes to perform each individual therblig equals the total time required to perform the task. The fact that time standards developed in this fashion are built up or synthesized has led many practitioners to refer to this approach as a "synthesis" or as "synthetic time values."

Development of time values   Once the basic theory of this approach had been accepted, it was necessary to formulate a means for assigning time values to therbligs. Should therblig time be expressed as select time, rated time, or standard time? After much study it was decided that the best results would be obtained if very large samples were used and time data were expressed as rated time. The reasoning behind this decision can be summarized as follows:

[11] The word *therblig* is the name of the inventor, Gilbreth, spelled backwards. It is a small tribute to the many valuable contributions of Frank and Lillian Gilbreth to the field of time and motion study.

1. Dissatisfaction with subjective ratings had been universal, and, to avoid similar difficulties in the new systems, it was decided to use samples so large in size that their means could not be questioned, thus making rating of any kind unnecessary. Gathering and analyzing the data for such large samples is, of course, very expensive; it is clearly impractical, therefore, to use this approach to develop an output standard for only one task. However, because the number of therbligs was relatively small and because it was hoped that the data obtained would have universal applicability, it was decided to invest the necessary time and money. The costs incurred would, in effect, be liquidated across literally millions of task studies, thereby reducing the effective cost to a nominal level.

Accordingly, large samples of approximately 10,000 workers each were examined, and time study data were recorded for each of the seventeen therbligs. The mean of these samples was then assumed to be the "universal mean" and thus also the pace-rated standard time. The magnitude of this undertaking should not be underestimated; although there are only seventeen basic hand motions, each is subject to a great number of variations. Consider, for example, "reach (R)," the therblig describing a simple hand movement. The distance moved and the nature of the target will have a significant impact on the performance time.

Studies could not be performed on every possible variation for every therblig, of course. Instead, key values were recorded and the balance of the values were derived by interpolation or extrapolation from the curves plotted for the available data. In the case of "reach to fixed location," for example, the time required for 1-inch, 5-inch, and 20-inch movements provided a curve that yielded mean times for the intermediate distances. Carefully and painstakingly, a comprehensive set of pace-rated time values was compiled, and these values are now the backbone of the predetermined time system.

2. The inclusion of any allowance percentage (as required for a standard time) would limit the direct use of the data to tasks where that allowance percentage applied. Using the predetermined times where other allowance percentages existed would require using a conversion factor to change the built-in allowances to those in actual use; this would clearly complicate the situation.

The same reasoning also led to the omission of any job difficulty adjustments. Thus, pace-rated time was selected because it is the most universally applicable time.

Installation program   Since the cost of developing this type of time data is so great, companies interested in using this method normally purchase a standardized predetermined time value (PTV) system.[12] Typical installation programs include training sessions for the analysts who are to apply the PTV data. Industrial engineers are taught how to use therbligs as a tool of analysis and how to identify various classes of motion. Certain specific therblig sequences are ineffective, because a worker cannot perform them in a smooth, rhythmic manner;

[12] The two most commonly used systems are Work Factor and Methods Time Measurement; these systems are sold by consulting firms of the same name.

therefore, allowance must be made for jerky movements in the study of the task. Finally, proper use of PTV data and methods requires a sound understanding of the techniques and practices used in a particular shop; analysts must study many representative tasks in order to obtain the experienced judgment necessary for effective use of PTV. Once mastered, however, PTV provides an accurate means of establishing labor output standards prior to the performance of a task. The procedure has been compared to baking a cake by following a well-defined recipe:

1. A particular task must be studied and a standard practice established. Here, as in other measurement approaches, the output standard can be fair and meaningful only if it is tied to a standard practice.
2. The standard practice is then analyzed into its constituent therbligs on a SIMO chart,[13] where each therblig is completely described, including such information as its class and the distance traveled.
3. The appropriate pace-rated times are then obtained from the PTV standards and entered on the SIMO chart. The times of all the therbligs are then totaled to give the standard length of the entire task cycle. Since the therbligs performed by each hand are entered on the SIMO chart in proper time juxtaposition to one another, the task cycle represents the time expended from the first therblig to the last, regardless of which hand performed it.
4. Since the time value obtained is assumed to be pace rated, the remaining steps require adding the job difficulty adjustment, if used, and allowances; both of these steps can readily be performed:

   (a) PTV = pace-rated time
   (b) PTV $\times$ RF$_d$ = rated time with difficulty adjustment
   (c) RT + (allowance percentage $\times$ RT) = standard time

ILLUSTRATIVE EXAMPLES   A portion of the data included in one of the predetermined time standard systems, Methods Time Measurement, is presented in Figure 11–9. Notice that the therbligs are descriptively named and that different classes of movement are identified for each therblig. All of the tables express time values in TMU's (time measurement units), which may be converted to decimal seconds or minutes by the use of simple conversion factors. A TMU is 0.0006 minute, and thus the time values are larger and easier to handle than minutes or even seconds would be.

The use of MTM data   To illustrate the use of the table in Figure 11–9, let us reexamine a simple assembly operation—the assembly of a selenium rectifier. The MTM data are applied to the assembly operation by means of a SIMO chart, Figure 11–10, and a workplace layout, Figure 11–4. On the SIMO chart, each therblig is described and designated by an appropriate symbol. The analyst

---

[13] This chart is used primarily for methods analysis. It is similar to the man–machine and multiple activity charts introduced in Chapter 10.

TABLE I—REACH—R

Distance Moved Inches	Time TMU				Hand in Motion		CASE AND DESCRIPTION
	A	B	C or D	E	A	B	
3/4 or less	2.0	2.0	2.0	2.0	1.6	1.6	A Reach to object in fixed location, or to object in other hand or on which other hand rests.
1	2.5	2.5	3.6	2.4	2.3	2.3	
2	4.0	4.0	5.9	3.8	3.5	2.7	
3	5.3	5.3	7.3	5.3	4.5	3.6	B Reach to single object in location which may vary slightly from cycle to cycle.
4	6.1	6.4	8.4	6.8	4.9	4.3	
5	6.5	7.8	9.4	7.4	6.3	5.0	
6	7.0	8.6	10.1	8.0	5.7	5.7	
7	7.4	9.3	10.8	8.7	6.1	6.5	
8	7.9	10.1	11.5	9.3	6.5	7.2	C Reach to object jumbled with other objects in a group so that search and select occur.
9	8.3	10.8	12.2	9.9	6.9	7.9	
10	8.7	11.5	12.9	10.5	7.3	8.6	
12	9.6	12.9	14.2	11.8	8.1	10.1	
14	10.5	14.4	15.6	13.0	8.9	11.5	
16	11.4	15.8	17.0	14.2	9.7	12.9	D Reach to a very small object or where accurate grasp is required.
18	12.3	17.2	18.4	15.5	10.5	14.4	
20	13.1	18.6	19.8	16.7	11.3	15.8	
22	14.0	20.1	21.2	18.0	12.1	17.3	
24	14.9	21.5	22.5	19.2	12.9	18.8	E Reach to indefinite location to get hand in position for body balance or next motion or out of way.
26	15.8	22.9	23.9	20.4	13.7	20.2	
28	16.7	24.4	25.3	21.7	14.5	21.7	
30	17.5	25.8	26.7	22.9	15.3	23.2	

TABLE II—MOVE—M

Distance Moved Inches	Time TMU			Hand In Motion B	Wt. Allowance			CASE AND DESCRIPTION
	A	B	C		Wt. (lb.) Up to	Factor	Constant TMU	
3/4 or less	2.0	2.0	2.0	1.7	2.5	1.00	0	
1	2.5	2.9	3.4	2.3				
2	3.6	4.6	5.2	2.9	7.5	1.06	2.2	A Move object to other hand or against stop.
3	4.9	5.7	6.7	3.6				
4	6.1	6.9	8.0	4.3				
5	7.3	8.0	9.2	5.0	12.5	1.11	3.9	
6	8.1	8.9	10.3	5.7				
7	8.9	9.7	11.1	6.5	17.5	1.17	5.6	
8	9.7	10.6	11.8	7.2				
9	10.5	11.5	12.7	7.9	22.5	1.22	7.4	B Move object to approximate or indefinite location.
10	11.3	12.2	13.5	8.6				
12	12.9	13.4	15.2	10.0	27.5	1.28	9.1	
14	14.4	14.6	16.9	11.4				
16	16.0	15.8	18.7	12.8	32.5	1.33	10.8	
18	17.6	17.0	20.4	14.2				
20	19.2	18.2	22.1	15.6	37.5	1.39	12.5	
22	20.8	19.4	23.8	17.0				C Move object to exact location.
24	22.4	20.6	25.5	18.4	42.5	1.44	14.3	
26	24.0	21.8	27.3	19.8				
28	25.5	23.1	29.0	21.2	47.5	1.50	16.0	
30	27.1	24.3	30.7	22.7				

TABLE III—TURN AND APPLY PRESSURE—T AND AP

Weight	Time TMU for Degrees Turned										
	30°	45°	60°	75°	90°	105°	120°	135°	150°	165°	180°
Small— 0 to 2 Pounds	2.8	3.5	4.1	4.8	5.4	6.1	6.8	7.4	8.1	8.7	9.4
Medium—2.1 to 10 Pounds	4.4	5.5	6.5	7.5	8.5	9.6	10.6	11.6	12.7	13.7	14.8
Large— 10.1 to 35 Pounds	8.4	10.5	12.3	14.4	16.2	18.3	20.4	22.2	24.3	26.1	28.2

APPLY PRESSURE CASE 1—16.2 TMU.   APPLY PRESSURE CASE 2—10.6 TMU

TABLE IV—GRASP—G

Case	Time TMU	DESCRIPTION
1A	2.0	Pick Up Grasp—Small, medium or large object by itself, easily grasped.
1B	3.5	Very small object or object lying close against a flat surface.
1C1	7.3	Interference with grasp on bottom and one side of nearly cylindrical object. Diameter larger than 1/2".
1C2	8.7	Interference with grasp on bottom and one side of nearly cylindrical object. Diameter 1/4" to 1/2".
1C3	10.8	Interference with grasp on bottom and one side of nearly cylindrical object. Diameter less than 1/4".
2	5.6	Regrasp.
3	5.6	Transfer Grasp.
4A	7.3	Object jumbled with other objects so search and select occur. Larger than 1" x 1" x 1".
4B	9.1	Object jumbled with other objects so search and select occur. 1/4" x 1/4" x 1/8" to 1" x 1" x 1".
4C	12.9	Object jumbled with other objects so search and select occur. Smaller than 1/4" x 1/4" x 1/8".
5	0	Contact, sliding or hook grasp.

TABLE V—POSITION*—P

CLASS OF FIT		Symmetry	Easy To Handle	Difficult To Handle
1—Loose	No pressure required	S	5.6	11.2
		SS	9.1	14.7
		NS	10.4	16.0
2—Close	Light pressure required	S	16.2	21.8
		SS	19.7	25.3
		NS	21.0	26.6
3—Exact	Heavy pressure required.	S	43.0	48.6
		SS	46.5	52.1
		NS	47.8	53.4

*Distance moved to engage—1" or less.

TABLE VI—RELEASE—RL

Case	Time TMU	DESCRIPTION
1	2.0	Normal release performed by opening fingers as independent motion.
2	0	Contact Release.

TABLE VII—DISENGAGE—D

CLASS OF FIT	Easy to Handle	Difficult to Handle
1—Loose—Very slight effort, blends with subsequent move.	4.0	5.7
2—Close—Normal effort, slight recoil.	7.5	11.8
3—Tight—Considerable effort, hand recoils markedly.	22.9	34.7

TABLE VIII—EYE TRAVEL TIME AND EYE FOCUS—ET AND EF

Eye Travel Time $= 15.2 \times \frac{T}{D}$ TMU, with a maximum value of 20 TMU.

where $T=$ the distance between points from and to which the eye travels.

$D=$ the perpendicular distance from the eye to the line of travel T.

Eye Focus Time $= 7.3$ TMU.

Figure 11–9 Predetermined time data tables for the methods time measurement system (Time data are in TMU's; 1 TMU = 0.0006 minute.)

refers to the tables in Figure 11–9 to obtain the appropriate TMU value for each therblig in terms of distance traveled and other characteristics of the specific movement. Then he adds the various therblig pace-rated times together to obtain the task pace-rated time. By performing the time study in this fashion, a rated time of 0.700 minute was obtained. The corresponding value (rated time) obtained by stopwatch study was 0.740 minute. The difference of 0.40 (or approximately 5.4 percent) is principally due to "stopwatch study limitations"—the reaction time of the watch and the use of different rating standards. By and large, the synthesis (as compared with time study) accuracy is satisfactory for work measurement purposes.

Advantages and limitations of PTV The elimination of potential sources of error in pace rating and the ability to produce output standards in advance are the major advantages of predetermined time value systems over direct time study methods. PTV systems can also reduce the investment of industrial engineering time and effort needed to develop output standards. One additional significant advantage is that this approach has been accepted by the trade union movement. The objectivity and consistency of the data developed by unbiased outsiders is a strong selling point when dealing with employee objections, and it is a fact that PTV has produced fair and equitable results. As a consequence, in many plants there is not the hostility that previously accompanied the use of direct time study. PTV effectively reduces employee complaints and offers an excellent means of quickly resolving the few that do arise. This in turn permits supervisors and union officials to spend their time to better advantage dealing with other important issues.

The need for a stopwatch is not completely eliminated by PTV, but it is generally minimized. The stopwatch time study must still be employed when a task is not sufficiently well defined to permit effective application of PTV. The stopwatch is also called back into service when grievances regarding the fairness of an output standard arise; in that case, management will usually take a stopwatch time study to decide if the standard set by PTV was justified. If PTV has been used correctly, the answer will generally be that the employee who raised the complaint was, in fact, able to accomplish the established normal output level. These uses of the stopwatch are relatively few and far between. In practice, a very small percentage of the labor standards in a typical plant whose standards are set by PTV are influenced by direct time study.

There is, however, one important danger in using PTV that can seriously distort the results—the process is almost too easy. There is a tendency to turn loose in the plant analysts who are not sufficiently familiar with the system; as a result, they generally produce standards that are too tight because they miss various subtle operating characteristics of the plant's production process. Great harm can thus result, for the system becomes suspect and industrial relations deteriorate.

Basic data   Some companies make use of a further refinement of PTV in order to reduce the cost of obtaining output standards. The establishment of therbligs was motivated by a desire to create motion "building blocks" that would be universally applicable. As a result, however, the building blocks are so minute that synthesis of the motions included in any task is often tedious and time-consuming. This can readily be seen by glancing at the SIMO chart in Figure 11–10. The long-drawn-out synthesizing process also provides many opportunities for error because of lost or missing therbligs. To circumvent these problems, many companies have developed a "reference book" of what are called *grouped data*. This book, or manual, contains groups of motions that are larger than therbligs and similar to the elements that would be used in direct time studies. For each of these motions a pace-rated time value is established by synthesis. The formulation of each time value for this grouped data is located in the reference book. If the time value of each motion is carefully reviewed to ensure correctness before it is entered into the book of grouped data, this technique can be almost as accurate as therblig analysis. With the passage of time the book will become quite complete, and most of the motions included in it can

Left Hand Elemental Description	Motion	Tmu	Culm Tmu		Culm Tmu	Tmu	Motion	Right Hand Elemental Description
Reach for case	{R16C 1300}	19.8			69.0			Wait
Grasp case	G1C	8.7						
Move case to anvil	{M16B 130}	18.6	69.0	50				
Position case to anvil	P2NL	21.9		69.0				
					17.0	R16C	Reach to resistor
					8.7	G1C	Grasp resistor
Hold entire cycle				100	63.4	15.8	M16B	Move resistor to case
				132.4		21.9	P2NL	Position resistor to case
				150	50.0			Rivet first hole to case
				182.4				
						5.7	M3B	Move case to 2nd hole
				200	19.8	14.1	P2SS	Position 2nd hole to anvil
				202.2				
				250	50.0			Rivet 2nd hole
				252.2				
						10.6	M8B	Move case to next position
						21.9	P2NL	Position case to anvil
				300	95.9	17.0	R16C	Reach for CR-1
						8.7	G1C	Grasp CR-1
						15.8	M16B	Move CR-1 to case
				348.1		21.9	P2NL	Position CR-1 to case
				350	50.0			Rivet CR-1
				398.7				
				400		8.9	M6B	Move case to next position
						21.9	P2NL	Position case to anvil
				450	94.2	17.0	R16C	Move case to next position
						8.7	G4	Grasp JB-1
						15.8	M16B	Move JB-1 to case
				492.3		21.9	P2NL	Position JB-1 to case
				500	50.0			Rivet JB-1
				542.3				
				550		10.6	M8B	Move case to next position
						21.9	P2NL	Position case to next position
					95.9	17.0	R16C	Reach for switch
				600		8.7	G1C	Grasp switch

Left Hand Elemental Description	Motion	TMU	Cumm TMU		Cumm TMU	TMU	Motion	Right Hand Elemental Description
						15.8	M16B	Move switch to case
					95.9	21.9	P2NSD	Position switch to case
			638.2					
			650			50.0		Rivet 1st hole to case
			700			14.1	P2SD	Position 2nd hole to anvil
						50.0		Rivet 2nd hole to case
			750		242.3	14.1	P2SD	Position 3rd hole to anvil
			800			50.0		Rivet 3rd hole to case
						14.1	P2SD	Position 4th hole to anvil
			850			50.0		Rivet 4th hole to case
			880.5			6.9	M4B	Move case to next position
			900			21.9	P2NSD	Position case to anvil
					92.5	17.0	R16C	Reach for J-101
						8.7	91C	Grasp J-101
			950			16.1	M16BW	Move J101 to case
			973.0			21.9	P2NSD	Position 1st hole J101 to case
			1000			50.0		Rivet 1st hole to case
			1025.0					
					19.8	5.7	M3B	Move J101 2nd hole to anvil
			1042.8			14.1	P2SD	Position 2nd hole to anvil
			1050			50.0		Rivet 2nd hole to case
			1092.8			5.6	92	Regrasp case
			1100			10.6	M3B	Move case to box
					4.99	21.9	P2NSD	Position case to box
			1142.7			11.8	RL2D	Release case in box
			1150					
			1200					

Total time = 1142.7 which is approximately .700 minutes of rated time

Figure 11–10   SIMO chart—MTM values for TV mount display

be used to describe the major portion of tasks within the company. To determine standard time by using grouped data, the analyst breaks a task down into its component motions, derives a time value from the grouped data book for each motion, and then synthesizes a pace-rated task time. To illustrate the use of basic data. Figure 11–11 presents a rough synthesis for the assembly of a mounting case. The rated time from this method is 0.722 minute as compared with 0.740 minute from the stopwatch study; this indicates the relative accuracy of rough synthesis where the basic data have been carefully prepared. The fine synthesis (MTM) had a value of 0.700 minute. The rough synthesis value is normally greater than the fine synthesis since it does not include as much detail.

The use of grouped data accelerates the process of synthesizing time standards. Much duplicate analysis is eliminated, and industrial engineering time is freed for use on other projects. The use of larger "building blocks" also tends to make the synthesizing process more consistent as well as more accurate, because the analyst has fewer decisions to make on classifying motions and therefore errors due to tedium are significantly reduced.

Predetermined time values: formula Another approach that helps to accelerate the establishment of output standards makes use of mathematical formulas. These formulas may be developed on the basis of either PTV data or direct time studies, and they usually reflect the relationship between the time required to perform a work assignment and the nature and number of tasks to be accomplished. To use a relatively simple example:

$$T_n = N \times W_t$$

where T_n = standard time required to manufacture N number of units
N = number of units included in the work assignment
W_t = standard time needed to make one unit

This formula merely states that the time needed to manufacture N units of output is equal to N multiplied by the time needed to make one unit. Such a formula is easily constructed, understood, and used, but its range of applicability is quite narrow. The limiting prerequisites for using this formula are illustrated in Figure 11–12. Here it can be seen that the average time per piece is unaffected by the manufacturing quantity, which simply means that the identical production process must be used on every unit made. Any carryover time required for setup or other operations from one piece to the next will invalidate the results. In essence, there must be a complete standardization of both product design and manufacturing methods, but only relatively simple assembly and manufacturing operations can meet these prerequisites.

Construction of a formula It is possible to design formulas that can be used under more realistic production conditions; the usual procedure is

1. Analyze the product(s) and process(es) to determine the appropriate form of the equation.

Left Hand Description	Sym-bol	TMU	Time TMU Cumul.	TMU	Sym-bol	Right Hand Description
Reach for case. Grasp, move to anvil & position.		134	50 / 100	134		Wait
Hold case to anvil		10790	150 / 200	75		Reach to resistor. Move to case. Position to case.
				36		Rivet 1st hole to case
			250	46		Position to 2nd hole
			300	40		Rivet 2nd hole to case
			350 / 400	73		Reach for CR-1. Grasp, move to case & position.
				40		Rivet CR-1 to case
			450 / 500	75		Reach for JB-1. Grasp & move to case. Position to case.
			550	40		Rivet JB-1 to case
			600	75		Reach for switch. Grasp & move to case. Position to case.
			650	40		Rivet 1st hole to case
			700	32		Position 2nd hole to case
				40		Rivet 2nd hole to case
			750	10		Position 3rd hole to anvil
				43		Position 3rd hole to anvil
			800	41		Position 4th hole to anvil
			850	41		Rivet 4th hole to case
			900 / 950	120		Reach for J-101. Grasp & move to anvil. Position to case.
			1000	41		Rivet 1st hole to case
			1050	63		Position 2nd hole to case
			1100	43		Rivet 2nd hole to case
			1150 / 1200	65		Move case to box. Position & release in box.
			1250			

Total TMU = 1213 = .722 min. rated time

Figure 11–11 SIMO chart—Rough synthesis for assembly of mounting case for TV rectifier

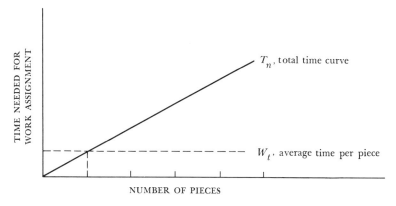

Figure 11–12 Illustration of a simple labor time formula ($T_n = N \times W_t$)

2. Draw up a master list of elements, including all the work that is and can be performed on the product(s) to be covered by the formula.
3. Classify these elements as to whether they are repetitively performed for each unit of output or whether they are done once (as in adjusting a machine—setting it up—to make a particular product).
4. Develop a standard time value for each element by using PTV, direct time study, or grouped data. The general nature of the equation will be as follows:

$$T_n = (W_1 + W_2 + W_3 + \cdots + W_n)N + (V_1 + V_2 + V_3 + \cdots + V_n)$$

where $W_1 + \cdots + W_n$ = standard time required to perform the repetitive work elements

N = number of units to be made

$V_1 + \cdots + V_n$ = standard time required to perform the nonrepetitive work elements

T_n = standard time required to produce N units of output

After a formula has been constructed, its results must be tested. Times obtained by formula for specific products and specific quantities should be compared with PTV studies, direct time studies, or even past production records to ensure that the mathematical model fairly represents the operating situation. The production process used and the design characteristics of the unit manufactured should also be checked periodically; if there are any changes, it will be necessary to recompute the parameters of the formula.

Work Sampling[14] Approach

The last method of developing output standards that we shall discuss is *work sampling;* this approach obtains results without using a stopwatch, and so it is radically different from the other major methods of setting output standards.

[14] The term *labor sampling* is often used as a substitute for *work sampling.*

Table 11–4   Work-sampling analysis of typing pool output

	Observations	*Percent*
Typing	160	$160/800 = 0.20 = 20\%$
Not typing	640	$640/800 = 0.80 = 80\%$
Total observations	800	
Average time spent typing	0.20×8 hours $= 1.6$ typing hours	

Work sampling is the newest of the measuring systems;[15] it was introduced after World War II and has been employed by an increasing number of firms since then. Work sampling is based upon a fundamental statistical sampling technique that has long been used for a variety of purposes; to illustrate how it may be applied to work standards, let us consider a typical office problem. Suppose an office manager wishes to know what portion of the day the girls in his typing pool are actually typing. He could determine this by a simple estimate, or by clocking the time they are working (which would be a prohibitively time-consuming task), or by work sampling. Using sampling methods, he would make random observations of his typists, noting each time how many girls were typing. The ratio of the total number who were observed to be typing to the total number of typists observed may then be considered a measure of the percentage of time each girl is typing per work day. The assumption is that the time spent typing is directly proportional to the number of instances in which girls are observed typing. Thus, to calculate the average amount of typing done by each typist, the office manager merely multiplies this percentage by the number of work hours as illustrated in Table 11–4.

Accuracy—number of observations   The accuracy of work sampling depends on three factors: the number of observations taken, the precision of the sampling process, and the precision of the definitions of the activities to be measured. It is axiomatic that the accuracy of the sampling process will increase in direct proportion to the size of the sample taken. The practical problem, however, is to decide how large the sample must be in order to yield only the accuracy required; a sample size that produces a greater accuracy merely increases the costs without effectively changing the value of the results.

One way to decide how many observations are needed to yield the desired accuracy is to follow standard statistical methods of working with distributions for proportions. The formula for the standard deviation of a proportion is

$$\sigma_P = \sqrt{\frac{P(1 - P)}{n}}$$

where $P = \dfrac{x}{n} = \dfrac{\text{Number of observations evidencing a condition}}{\text{Total number of observations}}$

n = number of observations

[15] Pioneering work was done by L. Tippet in the British textile industry during the 1930s.

Solving this equation for n, the number of observations required is

$$n = \frac{P(1 - P)}{\sigma_P^2}$$

In order to use this equation, the analysts must decide upon a preliminary value for P; this is usually done by taking a small sample of, say, 50 observations and using the P so obtained as an estimate of the true P. Management can then set an acceptable value for σ_P, and consequently for σ_P^2. Since P helps to define the confidence limits that pertain to the estimated P, many companies using this technique set $\pm 2\sigma_P$ at ± 10 percent of the estimated P. In such cases σ_P is equal to 5 percent of the estimated P. The value of n so derived will then define a sample size that will provide assurance that in 95 percent of the cases the true value of P will not deviate from the estimated value by more than 10 percent above or below. In the equation for n, with a given value of P, the greater the desired precision of the estimate, the smaller the assigned value of σ_P must be. Consequently, as the precision increases, the size of the sample must also increase.

Since the trial value of n found in the sample of 50 observations may not be exact, a further refinement is necessary in situations requiring a high degree of accuracy. One approach is to recalculate n after each set of observations has been made. For example, after 100 more observations, the n (sample size) calculated for 100 observations would be compared with the n found for 150 observations. This process would then be continued until the n obtained was the same for both sample sizes.

Another way of deciding how many observations are needed is to plot the cumulative values of P obtained as the sample size increases; when the value of P stabilizes, a sufficient sample has been taken. The main advantage of this method is that the user doesn't need any knowledge of statistics; he simply calculates a percentage value. In Table 11–5, the data are presented in groups of 100 observations for the typing pool example. Figure 11–13 shows the P values plotted on a chart.

Table 11–5   Observation data for typing pool example

(1) Cumulative Number of Observations	(2) Number of Typing Observations	(3) Cumulative Typing Observations	(4) Overall P Values[a]
100	35	35	0.35
200	10	45	0.22
300	10	55	0.18
400	25	80	0.20
500	28	108	0.21
600	9	117	0.19
700	21	138	0.19
800	26	154	0.20

[a] These values are calculated by dividing column (3) by column (1).

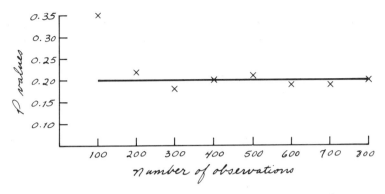

Figure 11–13 Plotted data for typing pool example

The value of P stabilizes at about 0.20 after roughly 800 observations. Notice that if we had stopped anywhere after 400 observations, the error in the P value would have been 1 percent. Further, if we had taken another 100 observations (a total of 900), there would have been no assurance that the P value would remain at 0.20. However, it is obvious that it had stabilized somewhere close to 0.20. Thus, while this method of determining the number of observations is not quite as precise as the statistical approach, it is generally accurate enough.[16]

Accuracy—sampling process and definition   In addition to the number of observations taken, the timing and descriptive accuracy of the observations will also influence the results of labor sampling. If the sampling technique is to yield valid results, the times at which the observations are taken must be truly random.

The descriptions of particular task elements must also be precise enough to allow an observer to make accurate observations, which means that he must study an activity long enough to get a basic understanding of it. To illustrate, let us go back to the typing pool example for a moment. The activities there were defined as typing and not typing. An observer can quickly and accurately determine which activity is occurring. Suppose, however, that the definitions had been simply working and not working. An observer who sees a typist in conversation with another might classify this activity either as working or as not working. Trained analysts who were shown a film of office operations and given definitions comparable to working and not working produced results that varied by as much as 50 percent. When the task elements were more precisely defined, the results were virtually the same among all analysts; precise definitions can therefore make the difference between valid and invalid results.

[16] A final method of determining the necessary sample size is through the use of families of curves, which, for estimates of P and σ_P, give the sample size required for various levels of accuracy. The reader who is interested in pursuing this further will find examples of these curves in Ralph M. Barnes, *Motion and Time Study*, 6th ed. (New York: Wiley, 1968).

Work sampling to set allowances   One common use of work sampling is to set the amount of time that is usually taken for personal allowances and the amount of time that should be allotted for unavoidable delays. This information is then used in calculating the standard time for a task.

To illustrate this use of work sampling, let us consider the management of a firm that wishes to determine the amount of time that should be allowed for personal allowances and machine delays at a particular production station. It has decided to use work sampling to figure out the allowances and the statistical approach to calculate the number of observations required. It wants the number of observations to be large enough so that 95 percent of the time the value calculated for the allowances will not deviate from the true value by more than about 10 percent.

As a preliminary study, 100 random observations were taken during a typical work day; they were classified as follows:

Actual time working	77 observations
Machine and other unavoidable delays plus personal time	23 observations

It was then necessary to decide what size sample should be taken. The first step in doing this is to determine the value of σ_P to insert in the equation for n. As discussed previously, σ_P is set at 5 percent of the preliminary P values. Thus, for working time,

$$\sigma_P = 0.05 \times 0.77 = 0.0385$$

and for machine and other unavoidable delays plus personal time,

$$\sigma_P = 0.05 \times 0.23 = 0.0115$$

Inserting the first value into the equation for n, the sample size needed to yield the required accuracy for working time is found to be

$$n = \frac{P(1 - P)}{\sigma_P^2}$$

$$= \frac{0.77 \times 0.23}{(.0385)^2} = \frac{0.1771}{0.001482}$$

$$= 119+ \text{ or } 120 \text{ observations}$$

The sample size needed for setting accurate allowances is

$$n = \frac{0.23 \times 0.77}{(.0115)^2} = \frac{0.1771}{0.00013225}$$

$$= 1,340+ \text{ observations}$$

It was decided to spread the study over 10 days, so 134 readings per day were required. The timing of the readings was determined from a table of four-digit random numbers. The first digit gave the day of the reading (1 indicated the first day, 2 the second, and so forth). The remaining three digits gave the time during the day to take the observation. The number 000 indicated a reading at 8 A.M., 060 at 9 A.M., and 480 at 5 P.M. Values above 480 were discarded. In this fashion the timing of the 134 readings to be taken each day was determined.

Then the observer was trained so that he would recognize the task elements, a tally sheet was designed, and the physical position of the observer while taking the reading was decided. This last procedure was arranged so that the observation could be made without the worker seeing the observer; this protected against the possibility that the worker might change her activities while the observation was being made.

After the preliminaries were finished, the study began. The consistency of the data was checked by graphing the *P* values as in Figure 11–13. Since these values stabilized by the sixth day, the sample size was deemed sufficiently large; the work, delay, and personal time percentages were calculated as follows:

Work	79%
Machine and other unavoidable delays plus personal time	21%

Management was then in a position to move forward and determine the standard time for the task.

Work sampling to develop output standards   It is possible to carry the technique of work sampling further and use it to develop output standards. In order to do so, we need two additional pieces of information about the job: the amount of product manufactured during the study and the performance rating for the task. Ordinarily, performance ratings are obtained for each observation and then averaged. To use work sampling to obtain a time standard, we make the following calculations:

$$\text{Observed time} = \frac{(\text{Total study time}) \times (\% \text{ time working})}{\text{Product manufactured}}$$

$$\text{Normal time} = (\text{Observed time}) \times (\text{Average performance rating})$$

$$\text{Standard time} = \text{Normal time} + \text{Allowances}$$

Thus, work sampling is easily extended from the setting of allowances to developing output standards.

Advantages and limitations   The most startling aspect of work sampling is that it permits the establishment of output standards without a stopwatch yet with an accuracy comparable to direct time study. Because the psychological aspect of being clocked by a watch generally has a pronounced negative influence on workers, an accurate means of establishing standards without clocking is a major advantage.

Another significant advantage of work sampling is that it can be used in nonrepetitive tasks where time study is of little use. In many jobs the sequence of tasks is not predictable—for example, the job of a stockroom worker in a retail store. He may stock the shelves, receive and unpack goods, clean up the stockroom, stamp goods with the date and price, and perform many other tasks. Here clock studies would be impractical, but work sampling can be used to determine the time allocated to each task and its expected output.

On behalf of work sampling, it should also be pointed out that it is the cheapest method of establishing a standard, the collection of results over many days balances out day-by-day fluctuations, operators prefer it to clock studies, and there is less chance for a worker to bias the study since he is observed over a longer and intermittent period.

Unlike predetermined standards, work sampling utilizes the leveling, or rating, process to set output standards. In this respect, therefore, it has all of the limitations of direct time study. Furthermore, because the observers used in work sampling do not have to be as highly trained as time study engineers, their leveling factors are probably more suspect.

Some of its other disadvantages are that work sampling is uneconomical if the study covers only one worker, the tasks analyzed can be broken down into finer elements by time studies, and the simplicity of the approach has led to improper statistical procedures.

Questions and Problems

1. Effort rating and leveling are considered to be highly subjective processes. It has been argued that the use of either can be avoided if an adequate (representative) sample of observations is used in making a time study. Do you agree with the above statement? Explain your position.
2. As a local union steward, what particular factors might be used as a basis for challenging the accuracy of a company's time study results?
3. A company has two plants. Can the results of a time study made in one plant be used in setting standards for the others? Explain.
4. John Doe wove 210 yards of cloth on his loom in 40 hours of actual work. State in exact quantitative form how good (efficient) his performance was. Calculate your answer from the following scrambled and simplified data:
   Job was originally time studied for 16 continuous hours (adequate). Overall effort rating: 95 percent (adjusted to machine–man working ratio).
   Avoidable delays during study: 120 minutes
   Use of fatigue allowance: 5 percent of total standard time
   Operating conditions: standard
   Use of allowance for unavoidable interferences and delays: 5 percent of total standard time
   Use of personal-delay allowance: 5 percent of total standard time
   Production during time study: 77.7 yards
5. Specify the elements of a standards system derived through time study that you would use for making labor cost estimates in connection with the bidding for government contracts. Assume that you will have to produce to governmental specifications.

6. What methods are available to decide how many cycles of work are needed for an accurate time study?
7. To what uses are time standards put?
8. How does work sampling differ from clock time studies? Is the accuracy of the two methods equal?
9. Outline the major steps in making a stopwatch time study.
10. Can time standards be applied to clerical tasks?
11. A stopwatch time study was made of an assembly task that involved four elements:
    (a) Calculate the normal task time.
    (b) Calculate the standard time.
    (c) What should be done with cycle 2, element 3 in the study?
    (d) Are enough cycles timed for an accurate study? If not, how many are needed?

			CYCLE			
ELEMENT	1	2	3	4	5	RATING
1	0.04	0.04	0.03	0.03	0.04	100
2	.12	.10	.09	.10	.10	90
3	.16	.24	.15	.16	.16	115
4	.13	.13	.12	.14	.14	120

Allowances are 15 percent of normal time.

12. The Ohm Electric Company has made a direct time study of a manual assembly operation; the observed data are summarized below. The employee observed was subjectively rated at 125 percent efficiency. Work-sampling procedures were used to derive a delay allowance for material shortage, the only significant factor that should prevent normal operation. From 1,200 observations taken at random, there were 60 observed occurrences of employees waiting for material. No personal allowances are granted other than two 10-minute coffee breaks plus a 10-minute washup time at the end of the day.

ELEMENT TIME (IN MINUTES)

CYCLE	1	2	3	4	5
1	0.08	0.20	0.30	0.40	0.20
2	.07	.21	.30	.38	.23
3	.09	.22	.29	.39	.22
4	.09	.18	.29	.41	.25
5	.08	.19	.31	.42	.22
6	.08	.20	.30	.39	.22
7	.07	.20	.30	.41	.10
8	.20	.20	.30	.40	.20
9	.08	.19	.31	.40	.22
10	.08	.21	.10	.40	.22

(a) Determine the standard time (allowed time).
(b) At the request of the union, the company tested the above time study by work sampling the operation. Over a period of two weeks (80 hours), the entire crew of 10 employees was randomly observed. It was agreed that

there would be no performance rating. Out of 2,500 observations, there were 125 observed occurrences of employees waiting for material and 2,375 observed occurrences of employees working. During the period, approximately 28,500 assemblies were produced. Does the work sampling verify the results achieved by direct study?

13. Assume that after the application of appropriate work-simplification techniques, you have taken a direct time study, and after subtraction, you get the following results.

ELEMENT TIME (IN MINUTES)

CYCLE	1	2	3	4	5
1	0.15	0.62	0.33	0.51	0.23
2	.14	.58	.20	.50	.26
3	.13	.59	.36	.55	.24
4	.18	.61	.37	.49	.25
5	.22	.60	.34	.45	.27

(a) Elements 2 and 4 are machine paced.

(b) You have a decision rule that states that any reading that varies by more than 25 percent from the average of all readings for an element will be considered "abnormal."

(c) The operator is rated at 120 percent.

(d) Allowances have been set (for an 8-hour shift) at:
Personal time: 30 minutes
Unavoidable delay: 26 minutes
Fatigue: 5 percent

(e) The operator, who is paid on a straight piece rate, receives $3.00 per hour.

(f) Material costs are $0.15 per piece.

(g) Overhead costs are calculated at 80 percent of the sum of direct labor and direct material costs.

How many pieces per shift should each operator produce, and what is the prodution cost per piece?

14. Defend or rebut the following statements:

(a) "The use of predetermined time values for the establishment of output standards eliminates the subjective errors found in direct time study."

(b) "For the establishment of time standards in indirect labor areas, two methods are available: historical sampling and work sampling. They are two different techniques that can furnish the analyst with the same information."

(c) "Direct time study is an imprecise tool that lends itself to easy abuse; the results produced are merely guesstimates."

(d) "The use of a historical sample provides the best way of estimating the standard time required to perform a specific task."

15. How, if at all, are human relations factors reconciled with timed production standards?

16. "The operator, not the operation, determines the extent to which personal-delay time is utilized." Is this statement valid?

17. Implementing the theory of work sampling for methods analysis, discuss the application of this technique with respect to:

    (a) Accuracy, randomness, and the number of observations.

    (b) The demands upon the analyst's time as compared with similar demands under direct time study.

    (c) Acceptance by the employees and the union.

18. Define normal times, performance rating, standard times, and allowances.

19. List the advantages and disadvantages of work sampling and stopwatch studies in setting standards. What type of activities lend themselves to each method?

20. An insurance company wishes to determine the percent of time its clerks are working and idle. They want to use work sampling, and their initial estimate is that the clerks are idle 30 percent of the time. How many observations do they need to take to be 95 percent confident that the results will not vary from the true result by more than 10 percent?

21. A work-sampling study has yielded the following results. What is the standard time for the task?

Units produced	320
Idle time	15 percent
Performance rating	120 percent
Allowance time	12 percent

22. Develop a work-sampling program to determine how the nurses on a hospital floor spend their time.

References

Abruzzi, A., *Work Measurement, New Principles and Procedures,* Columbia University Press, New York, 1952.

Bailey, G. B., and Presgrave, R., *Basic Motion Timestudy,* McGraw-Hill, New York, 1958.

Barnes, R. M., *Motion and Time Study,* 6th ed., Wiley, New York, 1968.

————, *Work Sampling,* 2nd ed., Wiley, New York, 1957.

Gomberg, W., *A Trade Union Analysis of Time Study,* 2nd ed., Prentice-Hall, Englewood Cliffs, N.J., 1955.

Hansen, B. L., *Work Sampling for Modern Management,* Prentice-Hall, Englewood Cliffs, N.J., 1960.

Heiland, R., and Richardson, W. J., *Work Sampling,* McGraw-Hill, New York, 1948.

Krick, E., *Methods Engineering,* Wiley, New York, 1962.

Maynard, H. B., Stegemerten, G. J., and Schwab, J., *Methods Time Measurement,* McGraw-Hill, New York, 1948.

Mundel, M. E., *Motion and Time Study, Principles and Practice,* 3rd ed., Prentice-Hall, Englewood Cliffs, N.J., 1960.

Nadler, G., *Work Design,* Irwin, Homewood, Ill., 1963.

Niebel, B., *Motion and Time Study,* 3rd ed., Irwin, Homewood, Ill., 1962.

Quick, J. H., *et al., Worker-Factor Time Standards,* McGraw-Hill, New York, 1962.

12

The Selection and Payment of a Labor Force

The preceding two chapters discussed the design of the work methods to be used in the production process and the development of output standards for these jobs. Using this information, production managers can determine the number of workers required to meet production levels and the exact nature of the work to be performed. The problems of acquiring and paying a labor force are discussed and analyzed in this chapter.[1]

Selection of Workers

It is obvious that, as a general rule, personnel must be assigned to jobs that match their skills in order to optimize work performance. Therefore, the first step in obtaining a worker for a specific job is to decide what skills are required. To do this, a complete study of the job should be made; all available information regarding the duties, responsibilities, conditions of work performance, further job opportunities, and privileges associated with the job should be noted. This process of dissecting a job and describing it in detail is called *job analysis*.

---

[1] Many of the activities discussed in this chapter are the responsibility of the firm's personnel department. Since these activities are so vitally intertwined with production activities, however, production managers should be conversant with them.

Job Analysis

There are many ways of making a job analysis. One approach is the *directed conference* in which a trained interviewer either asks an employee questions about the job he is performing or, if it is a new job, asks the production manager questions about it. The information received is then compiled by the interviewer into a preliminary job description. It is then reviewed with the employee, his supervisor, and the supervisor's manager; modifications are made as required, and the final job description is signed by the participating supervisor and manager.

A typical job description appears in Figure 12–1. Notice that the duties and responsibilities encompassed by the job are precisely defined.[2] The specific areas covered include: *administration,* where the appropriate job title, number, base rate, and so forth, are delineated; *work performed,* where the nature of the work done by the employee is described—for example, "the employee must construct, alter, and repair wooden pattern equipment"; *equipment and responsibility,* where the type of equipment that will be used is specified, for example, "power saws, planers, joiners, . . ., and a wide variety of hand tools"; and *working conditions,* where any special conditions that pertain to the work area will be noted, for example, "infrequent job assignments may involve working in the foundry for brief periods."

Although the directed conference method has been used effectively, it has some serious limitations. The employee or manager interviewed is interrupted from his normal routine, thus delaying his work performance. Furthermore, the employee is often reluctant to discuss the specifics of his job with the interviewer, who is usually considered an "outsider," but this problem can be minimized by explaining to the employee the purposes and methods of the job study. There remains, however, the inherent inability of the average worker to describe the details of his job accurately; many facts are likely to be omitted. To try to remedy this situation, the interviewer must hold time-consuming and costly review sessions with the worker, his supervisor, and the manager. But since the managers are rarely aware of the fine points of their subordinates' jobs, the final job descriptions, even with the reviews, are often incomplete and inaccurate.

Another common method of collecting data for a job description is by *observation;* an observer watches an employee perform his job and asks informal questions to clarify specific details. At the conclusion of this study the observer prepares a job description. As in the conference method, the description must be approved by the two levels of management directly above the operating employee. To obtain the information needed for accurate job descriptions by this method requires highly skilled observers. Furthermore, because the observation approach usually requires relatively long periods of time per job, it tends to be expensive. As with the conference method, it disrupts the normal operating routine of the employee being interviewed and is dependent on the employees'

---

[2] As will be discussed later in this chapter, job descriptions are often used for the purpose of assigning monetary value to a job.

Job title:	Pattern maker—wood	Job number: 504-101
Alternate title:	None	Department: Foundry #540
Base rate per hour:	$5.00 min., $5.30 mid-range, $5.60 max.	Date: January 15, 197__
Incentive:	None	
Analyst:	Harvey Middleman	

WORK PERFORMED

This job involves the use of decimals, fractions, and geometry. The incumbent must work from complex drawings. He must have a thorough knowledge of the pattern-making trade, including basic design and construction of pattern equipment, use of hand and power woodworking tools, knowledge of foundry and machine shop practice.

This job involves highly diversified work. The employee must construct, alter and repair wooden pattern equipment that is used to produce large castings of complicated design. He must possess a high degree of judgment, initiative, and ingenuity to convert engineers' casting specifications into layouts and models; make allowances for coremaking, molding, cleaning, and machining operations; construct all pattern, core box, and related equipment necessary to produce a rough casting of desired size and shape.

This job requires concentrated mental and visual attention necessary to work out problems involving the design construction, alteration, and repairing of complicated pattern equipment. The employee must be able to visualize pattern construction, core assembly, mold construction, and casting.

Light physical effort is required to use hand tools. Power woodworking operations may involve handling of average weight boards or pattern sections for short periods of time.

EQUIPMENT AND RESPONSIBILITY

The equipment used consists of power saws, planers, joiners, shapers, hole shooter, drill press, lathe, and a wide variety of hand tools. Probable damage is seldom over $50.

Probable damage to materials due to errors in construction seldom is over $100. Pattern-checkers follow the job from start to finish.

Compliance with standard safety precautions necessary as careless use of hand or power tools, improper handling or positioning of patterns or lumber may result in injury to others.

The employee is responsible only for his own work.

WORKING CONDITIONS

Some wood dust contaminates the air during sanding or turning operations. Infrequent job assignments may involve working in foundry for brief periods.

There is a possibility of hand or arm injury while using power woodworking equipment or sharp edged hand tools. Improper handling or positioning of lumber or patterns by others may result in injury.

Figure 12–1   Job description: pattern maker—wood

cooperation with the "outside" interviewer. Finally, it is impossible to use this approach for new jobs since there is no work to observe.

Sometimes a *combination* of the conference and observation methods is used, but a combined approach rarely yields significantly better job descriptions, for it has many of the disadvantages of both methods. Interestingly enough, however, a combined approach does improve employee acceptance of the program. Increased employee participation and cooperation result from conferences between the observer and the employee, possibly because the latter feels that the former has demonstrated his interest in the job and can better appreciate its fine points.

The last method to be discussed here is called *self-analysis*. Using this method the employee is asked to fill out a questionnaire concerning the duties he performs. The data gathered are then used to formulate the job description, which must be approved by the next two higher levels of management. The primary weakness of this approach is that most employees seem to be unable to give clear, straightforward, unbiased responses to the questions on these forms. For this reason, a well-designed form is essential; the problem is also minimized if employees are given prior training in using standard language and in filling out the form. In some cases, editing the questionnaires has proved helpful.

The proponents of the self-analysis method cite many advantages on its behalf. The main argument is the improved motivation of the worker, which often results because of his high degree of participation in the program. This, in turn, is reflected in better overall performance. Self-analysis provides an opportunity for superior–subordinate discussion of job content, which helps clear up any misunderstandings regarding work assignments and responsibility relationships. Another advantage of this approach is that it minimizes the need for, and therefore the cost of, outside professional help. It also permits the simultaneous study of all jobs, thus reducing the time required to complete the analysis of all jobs in the firm.

All the methods we have discussed have limitations. They are representative of the methods currently used, however, and they have been successful in industry. Of course, some data-gathering methods are better suited to particular types of work than others. For example, experience indicates that the observation method is most effective in studying assembly line and low-skill occupations, whereas other methods seem better suited to more complex clerical and manufacturing tasks and to managerial positions.

Job Specifications

After the detailed job description has been completed, the next step in the hiring process can begin. While the description tells what work has to be done under what conditions, it does not specify what skills are needed to perform the work. Consequently, the next step in the process is to draw up a list of significant factors that will affect an employee's ability to perform the particular task; lists of this type are called *job specifications*.

The specifications for the job described in Figure 12–1 are presented in

Job title:	Pattern maker—wood	Job number: 504-101
Alternate title:	None	Department: Foundry #540
Base rate per hour:	$5.00 min., $5.30 mid-range, $5.60 max.	Date: January 15, 197__
Incentive:	None	
Analyst:	Harvey Middleman	

EDUCATIONAL REQUIREMENTS

High school, trade school, or equivalent
Knowledge of decimals, fractions, and geometry
Ability to work from complex drawings

EXPERIENCE AND SKILL

Minimum of 3 years pattern-making experience
Knowledge of foundry and machine shop practice in the design and construction of pattern-making equipment
Ability to design, construct, alter, and repair complicated pattern equipment

PHYSICAL REQUIREMENTS

Capacity for light physical effort involved in using tools

RESPONSIBILITIES

Performance of *only* his own work
Compliance with standard safety precautions relating to foundry operation and use of hand power tools

WORKING CONDITIONS

Regular working day: 7:30 A.M. to 4:00 P.M.
Some wood dust contaminates the air during sanding or turning operations
Some danger from improper use of tools and patterns

Figure 12–2   Job specification: pattern maker—wood

Figure 12–2. Notice that the description of the job is converted into specifications for the individual who will hold the job; the factors identified include: administrative and wage data, education, experience and skill, physical requirements, responsibility, and working conditions. For the wood pattern maker, a high school or equivalent diploma plus a minimum of three years of experience are required. The employee is responsible for his own work only. Finally, the normal shift runs from 7:30 A.M. to 4:00 P.M., and the minimum starting wage is $5.00 per hour.

Job Standardization and Titles

The data obtained by means of job analysis and job specifications can also provide a basis for standardizing job content. It is usually possible to stipulate in the job description the tools, equipment, methods, and working conditions that shall apply to the performance of specific types of work. This makes it possible to eliminate unnecessary jobs and to increase the flexibility with which employees having specific skills can be used throughout the company. A closely related problem that is in many ways symptomatic of a lack of standardization is a multiplicity of job titles. Often there are many different jobs, each with its own title, and yet the work performed is substantially identical and requires the same basic skills. As a consequence many of these job titles are ambiguous and do not convey the nature of the work performed. Establishing standard job descriptions provides an opportunity to correct this problem by formulating standard titles. One common example of title standardization is the distinction between managers, supervisors, and administrators: a "manager" is one who has men reporting to him who supervise their own subordinates, a "supervisor" is one who has authority over operating employees only, and an "administrator" is a member of the management hierarchy who discharges his duties without the aid of direct subordinates.

Employee Selection

Once job specifications are available, employees can be hired who have the appropriate skills and other requirements. Many factors make it necessary to hire new employees, including turnover, expansion, promotion, and death. The relative importance of the recruiting and selection function is shown by industrywide statistics, which reveal that a typical firm experiences approximately a 31 percent turnover in manpower during an average year; this means that the average company must process a substantial number of new employees each year.

Recruiting the Applicants

There are many sources from which suitable job candidates may be recruited: educational institutions, commercial employment agencies, public employment agencies, classified advertisements, trade unions, trade and professional associations, and within the company itself. Each source, of course, has its strong and weak points. Educational institutions, for example, are excellent sources of job applicants with known educational and technical backgrounds. Many high schools, trade schools, and universities have placement services that can perform the initial screening of applicants if furnished sufficient data. In addition, these placement bureaus will often provide interviewing rooms and set up convenient interview schedules. These services save the recruiting company time and money. Only occasionally, however, can individuals who are highly proficient in specialized areas be secured through such services; ordinarily, these individuals must be obtained internally or by some other means.

Interviewing the Applicants

Normally, an individual who wishes to be considered for a job must fill out an application form. The completed form usually contains a brief factual record of the applicant's personal history and summarizes his physical, educational, and vocational status. These data may then be compared with the job specifications as a screening device.

After this initial screening, the usual practice is to interview all remaining candidates in order to identify and reject those who do not seem to be suitable for the particular job. Conducting these interviews is normally a function of the personnel department.

Testing the Applicants

To increase the effectiveness of the selection process, written tests are being used more and more to supplement interviews. Because of the growing interest in tests in recent years, many new types have been designed; at present three distinct types of tests are in use: psychological tests, performance tests, and physical tests.

Psychological tests Psychological tests are designed to measure the candidate's personality, attitudes, interests, and temperament. The objective, of course, is to assess his compatibility with the job requirements as expressed on the job description sheet. Results to date have been rather disappointing, however. There are widespread differences of opinion regarding the psychological characteristics required to perform a particular job effectively. Many attempts have been made to relate specific personality traits such as aggressiveness or self-confidence to effective job performance, but none has successfully uncovered any meaningful relationship. Even if such a relationship could be shown, there is much disagreement about how to measure the extent to which a particular candidate possesses the trait in question. Although it is generally agreed that a candidate who is thought to have a severe psychological disorder should not be accepted, it does not follow that a "perfect personality" is a valid basis for acceptance. Instead, the criterion usually applied is whether the candidate has a personality that might prevent him from effectively performing his assigned duties, including working with other employees when necessary. In short, the principal use of psychological tests today is to screen out candidates who have severe emotional problems or seem psychologically ill-suited to the job in question.

Performance tests Performance tests give the candidate an opportunity to demonstrate that he can do what his application claims. It is possible, for example, to check the ability of a machinist to read and understand blueprints, or the ability of an electronics technician to understand circuit schematics, or the ability of a quality control inspector to use control charts. For office jobs, it is possible to test a candidate's knowledge of accounting principles and practices or of commercial law. In fact, for most positions requiring specific knowledge or skills, tests may be used to evaluate the candidate's ability to perform.

Another type of performance test that has been successfully used is an on-the-job test whereby the candidate is taken to an actual or simulated job site and given a typical assignment. A typist, for example, would be given a letter to type, an IBM keypunch operator would be required to keypunch information on some cards, and a lathe operator would be assigned a typical lathe operation. For relatively unskilled jobs, simple dexterity tests have been used effectively. Many companies emphasize on-the-job performance tests, believing that they provide a clear demonstration of whether a candidate can or cannot do the work, and this, they believe, is the best criterion for deciding whether the candidate should be hired.

Physical tests In most firms, a physical examination of the job applicant by a company doctor is now almost a routine part of the selection process. The examination acts as a "go–no go" type of screening operation. The thoroughness of the examination is governed by the characteristics of the particular job. Sometimes a quick once-over is sufficient to make sure that the candidate doesn't have an organic ailment that could adversely affect his own work performance or that of other employees. For positions requiring heavy physical work, such as blast furnace puddlers, the examination is likely to be quite thorough.

Companies try to screen out the physically unfit for many reasons. Many of the life, accident, and health insurance plans call for adjustment of company premiums to reflect actual experience. In addition, companies make an investment in the orientation and training of their employees, and this investment is expected to yield a return in the form of effective employee performance, yet poor health can prevent them from performing at their full capabilities. For this reason many companies continue to examine their employees periodically after they have been hired; early detection and diagnosis can reduce the work time lost because of a serious ailment.

Personnel Training

Frequently even the best candidates available do not meet the job specifications. Companies are continually seeking new skills and new combinations of skills since rapid technological change has made many of the old skills obsolete. Consequently, the selection process is increasingly trying to secure employees who have the *potential* to satisfy the specifications for a particular job, rather than searching for employees who could perform immediately. This trend places a great emphasis on training.

There are many types of training programs. An employee who meets the job specifications may need some training to acquaint him with the company's operating procedures. *Orientation programs* are of great assistance to the new employee during his initial adjustment period; they can also benefit the company by reducing the amount of time needed to orient the new employee and the losses in time and material that result from learning by trial and error. If the new employee does not possess all of the necessary skills for effective job performance, the company's orientation should be supplemented by instruction in the specific phases of the work to be assigned. Even long-time employees occasionally need this type of training, because job requirements are continually changing; to retain efficiency the workers must learn new skills. Wherever possible, management should try to anticipate such changes in job skills; an innovation that will change work methods should ideally trigger a program to develop the necessary new skills.

Training programs can also be designed to enlarge the capabilities of specific workers in the hope that the tasks assigned to them can be increased and that the added flexibility of their increased versatility will be reflected in greater labor productivity.

Training to Meet Anticipated Requirements

There is a strong need to coordinate recruiting and employee training programs with production and organization planning. Production plans have specific manpower requirements that should be reflected in recruiting and training programs. Both internal and external sources of labor must be cultivated in time to ensure the availability of required labor skills to support the achievement of future goals; the company should not have to depend upon the random availability of necessary skills. Planned changes in plant technology, in office technology and systems (such as the introduction of electronic data-processing equipment), in operating philosophy (such as the decision to strive for greater decentralization), and new production programs must be anticipated by the employee recruiters if the manpower needs of the firm are to be met satisfactorily.

Training Methods

There is a multitude of different training methods, including lectures, conferences, on-the-job training, business games, courses offered by local universities, and trade or professional programs. In selecting the appropriate method for a particular program, the starting point is the job specification sheet. The duties to be performed determine the skills required and, hence, the subjects that must be learned. This in turn affects the selection of training methods. For any particular job the choice is difficult, and there is a considerable difference of opinion— even among professionals—as to how this problem should be approached. It is agreed, however, that the supervisor or manager of the functional area involved should have the major voice in deciding what materials and methods will be used to train his subordinates. His knowledge of job details and his experience with previous employees make him an invaluable source of information. Furthermore, since the training of subordinates has long been a fundamental role of the manager, any on-the-job training is usually handled by him. It should not be inferred from this, however, that the *administration* of the training program should be delegated to the line supervisor; the planning and coordinating of the program calls for specialized skills that are normally found in the personnel department.

Hiring

Whereas the recruiting, interviewing, and testing portions of the selection process are generally done by the personnel department, hiring is almost always a line function. Since the line manager is responsible for the performance of his em-

A chemical/metallurgical laboratory specialist, left, at IBM's Poughkeepsie, N.Y. manufacturing plant, evaluates analysis work performed by a student technician.

ployees, it is thought that he should make the final selection of candidates. To do otherwise would be to give the line manager all the responsibility for work performance and only part of the authority needed to control it. Consequently, the personnel department usually sends the candidates who have survived the screening process to the manager who would be responsible for their work, and the final selection and hiring are left to him.

So far in our discussion we have focused on the determination of labor requirements in terms of skills and on the recruitment and training of personnel to meet these needs. In the remainder of this chapter we will examine the problem of how to pay the labor force.

Wage and Salary Administration

Most people would agree that the primary reason for working is to earn money. However, when surveys are made to determine the relative significance of various factors that are generally considered important to job satisfaction, surprisingly, they usually rank money fifth or sixth among the factors identified. But a brief review of labor history would reveal that this was not always so. Indeed, wages were once the principal concern of the working man; the early labor union movement rallied around the idea of a "living wage." The present deemphasis of money is due in large part to the fact that wages have risen above the minimum subsistence level. It is also evidence of the success of most companies in establishing sound wage structures. However, in jobs where wages are still low (such as in municipal hospitals), money continues to be highly important to the worker. This is also true if workers feel that the wage structure of their firm is inequitable.

External Balance in Wage Policy

A number of policy decisions must be made by management in order to provide a frame of reference for the development of a sound wage and salary structure. Such policy decisions should include, first, a statement of the company's position with regard to the level of wages that will be offered. This involves a careful examination of two significant wage averages: the average base rate paid for specific labor skills by other firms in the same industry (the *industry average*), and the prevailing base rate offered within the labor market from which needed skills must be obtained (the *geographic average*). The industry average is often used as a convenient ceiling when deciding what wage levels can be offered. Thus, it is argued, to go above this level would have an adverse effect on unit labor costs, unless labor productivity could be raised above the industry level or unless other cost savings could be made. Conversely, the geographic average is often used as a convenient floor for decisions regarding the company's wage level on the assumption that it would be difficult to attract the necessary labor skills if the firm's base rates were substantially below those offered by other companies in the area. If the geographic average is above the industry average, the firm is in an undesirable position with respect to labor costs; therefore, it should make every effort to increase labor productivity in order to bring unit labor costs down at least to the industry average. On the other hand, when the industry average is above the geographic average, the firm is in a desirable position because it has greater operating flexibility. This consideration was one of the factors that stimulated the shift of textile firms from New England to the South, where low wage rates prevailed.

In order to attract and keep the type of worker it desires, a company's wage structure must be geared to the external demand for labor. This means that it is usually forced to meet the geographic average in order to ensure its ability to attract and hold a labor force. A firm that consistently offered wages below the geographic average would end up with a labor force that was capable of only marginal performance; this, in turn, would mean low labor productivity. In short, the "savings" associated with lower base rates are often illusory; indeed, unit labor costs might actually be higher than "average" in that case.

There are exceptions to the rule, of course. In some areas the supply of labor skills is sufficiently large to enable firms offering wage rates below the geographic average to hold better than marginal workers. Similarly, if a company's labor requirements called for a large proportion of unskilled or semiskilled workers, there would be less of a problem in having workers with only marginal ability. Even where highly skilled labor is required, job security and favorable working conditions may often be traded successfully for higher wages.

The argument in favor of setting wages above the geographic average stresses the advantages of having a stable work force with above-average capability. Such a policy usually attracts and holds good workers and minimizes the costs associated with labor disputes and high turnover. In turn, the high productivity of a well-trained and experienced work force often results in below-average unit labor costs despite the relatively high base rates.

Internal Balance in Wage Policy

To many a worker, the relative size of his pay in comparison with that received by people in other jobs within the company is a more important factor than the absolute amount received. As wages have risen above subsistence level, labor has become increasingly concerned with the fairness of the pay received for various jobs performed within a company. Every worker has his own conception of what the relationship should be between his pay and that received by others. Skilled workers, such as electricians or machinists, expect wages that are considerably higher than those paid to unskilled workers. Real or alleged wage inequities between various occupations can cause considerable friction among employees. The situation is even worse if employees who perform the same, or substantially similar, duties receive different pay. In short, wage differences that cannot be justified or explained in terms of the skill or responsibility required are likely to produce a working environment in which motivating and directing employees is extremely difficult. Consequently, in setting wage levels, management must consider both external balance and internal balance among the many jobs done within the company.

Establishing a Wage Structure by Job Evaluation

In order to satisfy the external and internal balance problems, many different approaches to setting wages have been used; we will discuss a few of the more common ones.

Ranking The first formal attempts to create an equitable wage structure were by ranking occupations within a company according to importance. The assumption was that wage rates should vary in direct proportion to the relative importance of a job. A rank card was prepared for each occupation in the firm, including the title of the job and brief notes on the duties performed, as illustrated in Figure 12–3. The information on the cards was then used to rank the

---

OCCUPATION TITLE

Machine operator, first class

DUTIES PERFORMED

Can operate milling machine, engine lathe, turret lathe, drill press, etc. with minimum of instructions. Can read blueprints. Can maintain tight tolerances.

Figure 12–3 Sample rank card

occupations. This highly subjective procedure proved unsatisfactory because of inaccuracies stemming from the ranker's limited knowledge of the various jobs and his personal biases toward them. Nonstandardized terminology and incomplete information also hindered the ranking procedure.

It was found that, at best, this technique could place occupational wage rates in ascending order, but it could not provide a sound basis for establishing the size of wage differentials among various occupations. Because of these important limitations, the ranking procedure is seldom used today.

Grading of occupations   Experience with the weaknesses of ranking led to the development of *occupation grading*. In this approach, a detailed occupational description is prepared for all jobs in question. This description includes the occupational title, information on education and experience required, and the particular duties assigned. Then, from the total number of occupations under study, certain "key occupations" are selected. The objective here is to choose representative jobs that range from the least important to the most important in sharply defined gradations. A median wage level is then established for each of the key occupations based upon industrial and geographic averages. This gives management a wage range tied to specific occupational levels, which extends at each level from perhaps 33 percent below the median wage to 33 percent above it.

The wage ranges thus created are assigned occupation grade numbers rising in ascending order from the lowest pay grade to the highest. All of the jobs being analyzed are then compared with the representative occupations and assigned the grade number and corresponding salary range of the one they most closely approximate.

This approach makes it unnecessary to assign a different rank and, therefore, a different wage to each separate job, and thus eliminates many artificial distinctions. The existence of a wage range also provides flexibility for recruiting new employees, because the wages offered can reflect the economics of the marketplace. Another advantage of wage ranges is that they make it possible to reward employees who have performed well without making real or imaginary changes in their assignments. Thus, rate distinctions can be made according to merit among employees performing the same occupation. These advantages are the primary reason why the more sophisticated job evaluation systems feature wage ranges.

The major weaknesses of the grading system stem from the necessity of subjectively deciding what grade should be assigned to a particular occupation. Lack of experience and knowledge and the personal biases of the evaluator can all combine to distort the results obtained.[3]

Factor comparison   Key occupations are also selected when the factor comparison method is used, and wage rates are likewise established for each category on the basis of geographical and industry-wide averages. The main difference

---

[3] It should be noted, in passing, that the U.S. Civil Service Commission is the principal user of the occupational grading system, but it modifies the system by using points to assign a grade number to particular occupations.

between grading and factor comparison is in the job description. The factor comparison method uses standard descriptions for the key factors in all jobs; a simple five-factor categorization might include:

1. Mental requirements
2. Skill requirements
3. Physical requirements
4. Responsibility
5. Working conditions

The first step in using this method is to construct a scale for each of the key factors so that individual jobs can be compared and rated. To do this, the wage rates for key occupations are set in accordance with the external labor market. Next, the payment assigned to each key occupation is divided into the five factors so that the monetary value assigned to each factor reflects its relative importance within the occupation. The sum of the money assigned to each of the factors equals the total wage of the occupation. Then, on the basis of monetary rates and factor descriptions for the key jobs, a scale relating dollars and factor descriptions may be constructed. Opposite each gradation on the monetary scale is a written description of the commensurate factor. This is illustrated in Table 12–1, which shows a comparison scale for three factors. In practice, at least five factors are used to rate a job.

Table 12–1   Factor comparison scale for three factors

Factors	Monetary Value
1. Educational requirements	
(a) Less than high school	$10
(b) Two years high school	20
(c) High school graduate	40
(d) Two years college	50
(e) College graduate	70
(f) Graduate degree	80
2. Experience requirements	
(a) Beginner—less than six months	10
(b) Six months to one year	20
(c) One to two years	30
(d) Two to three years	40
(e) Three to five years	60
(f) Over five years	80
3. Physical requirements	
(a) No requirements	10
(b) Some movement required and casual use of eyes	20
(c) Considerable movement and frequent use of eyes, ears, and other physical parts	30
(d) Use of all faculties required and considerable physical effort	40
(e) Full use of all faculties—no physical disability permitted	60

To establish a wage standard for a particular job, the manager selects a description of each of the job's constituent factors from the list under each factor on the scale. Then he obtains the corresponding monetary value for the selected description under each factor. The wage rate for the occupation will be the sum of the monetary values for each of the factors. This process is illustrated in Table 12–2, where the weekly base rates attributable to the three factors of Table 12–1 are shown for three jobs. The wage rate for these jobs is the sum of dollars from these three factors and from the other factors used to rate the jobs. After a wage rate has been developed, an occupational wage range is created by establishing limits such as 25 percent above and below the rate.

The factor comparison method is an improvement over the grading approach because it forces the evaluator to be more objective. It does not, however, remove all subjectivity in determining relative occupational grades and therefore is not free from error.

Table 12–2 Factor comparison by monetary scale

Factors	Monetary Value	Cost clerk	Messenger	Chief clerk
1. Educational requirements				
(a) Less than high school	$10			
(b) Two years high school	20		→$20	
(c) High school graduate	40	→$40		
(d) Two years college	50			
(e) College graduate	70			→$70
(f) Graduate degree	80			
2. Experience requirements				
(a) Beginner—less than six months	10		→ 10	
(b) Six months to one year	20			
(c) One to two years	30	→ 30		
(d) Two to three years	40			
(e) Three to five years	60			→ 60
(f) Over five years	80			
3. Physical requirements				
(a) No requirements	10			
(b) Some movement required and casual use of eyes	20			
(c) Considerable movement and frequent use of eyes, ears, and other physical parts	30	→ 30	→ 30	→ 30
(d) Use of all faculties required and considerable physical effort	40		→ 40	
(e) Full use of all faculties—no physical disability permitted	60			
Contribution to weekly base rate from these three factors		$100	$70	$160

Point plan The *point plan* is probably the most sophisticated approach to job evaluation; it is also the most widely used technique in industry today. Using this method, eleven factors are examined to determine the wage level of an occupation in a typical factory.

Skill
1. Experience
2. Education
3. Initiative and ingenuity

Effort
4. Physical demand
5. Mental demand

Responsibility
6. Equipment and process
7. Safety
8. Material
9. Work of others

Working Conditions
10. Physical environment
11. Health hazards

For each of the eleven factors, a maximum point value is assigned, but these values are not the same for all factors. For example, experience may be worth a maximum of 100 points, whereas health hazards may be given a top score of only 25 points; this limitation thus weights the factors in relation to one other. A table is then prepared for each factor, listing five degrees of importance. The fifth (and most important) degree is valued at the maximum point score, and each successively lower degree is reduced by 20 percent so that only 20 percent of the maximum point score is assigned to the first degree. A standard definition is prepared for each degree. A sample table is shown in Table 12–3.

Next, using a standard form that has eleven factors, factor descriptions are prepared for key occupations.[4] Standardized wording is used to describe the degree of applicability of each factor to a particular occupation. When the description is completed, the manager making the evaluation assigns points to each factor using the factor table. The sum of the points applicable to each factor is considered to be the score of the occupation. Next, a survey of the job market is made to establish wage rates for the key jobs in order to bring them into external balance. The job points and wage rates are then plotted on a scatter chart; Figure 12–4 shows a scatter chart for fifteen key jobs (*A* through *O*).

A representative line is then fitted to the scatter chart. Either the line is drawn freehand, or a regression line is fitted by the method of least squares. Figure 12–5 shows a line fitted by the least squares method to the points plotted in Figure 12–4. The slope of the line ($0.40/30 points) indicates the relationship between money and points that will be used to assign wage rates to occupations.

----

[4] The job descriptions used for hiring frequently provide the data needed to write factor descriptions.

Table 12-3   Points assigned to factors

	Points				
Factor	1st degree	2nd degree	3rd degree	4th degree	5th degree
Skill					
1. Experience	20	40	60	80	100
2. Education	16	32	48	64	80
3. Initiative and ingenuity	14	28	42	56	70
Effort					
4. Physical demand	10	20	30	40	50
5. Mental demand	6	12	18	24	30
Responsibility					
6. Equipment and process	5	10	15	20	25
7. Safety	5	10	15	20	25
8. Material	6	12	18	24	30
9. Work of others	5	10	15	20	25
Working Conditions					
10. Physical environment	12	24	36	48	60
11. Health hazard	5	10	15	20	25

For each point scored for a job, 1.33 cents will be added to the hourly base pay.

While the regression line gives a base rate for the job, if all workers were paid at this rate it would mean that all would receive the same pay regardless of their skill, experience, and time with the company. To overcome this problem, wage ranges are established for each job. The ranges usually cover an equal number of points for each job. For example, in our illustration the highest paid job has 270 points and the lowest 130. The difference is 140 points. It was divided by 10 to establish a point spread or interval[5] of 14 points for each job. The interval for job N, as shown in Figure 12-6, is from 200 points to 214 points. The minimum wage is usually fixed at about 10 percent below the dollar value of the regression line at its minimum point score within the interval. The maximum wage is usually set at about 15 percent above the dollar value of the regression line at its maximum point score within the interval. This process of establishing wage ranges is illustrated in Figure 12-6.

Once the point score for a job other than a key one is determined and the job is placed on the scatter chart, two types of deviation may occur; the job may be positioned below the wage range minimum or above the wage range maximum. In the former case the practice has generally been to raise the wage rate up to the minimum. It is difficult to initiate a program of job evaluation and then refuse to make adjustments when clear-cut inequities such as this are discovered. On the other hand, when a job carries a wage rate above the maximum wage range

[5] These intervals are often referred to as *classifications* or *grades*.

level, corrective action is much more difficult. Attempts to introduce wage cuts, however justified in theory, are generally received with great hostility and thus tend to undermine the entire program.

A common solution to the problem of above-normal wage rates is the establishment of "red-circle rates." This compromise calls for a continuation of above-normal wages to employees who have the job at the time the program is initiated. All new employees, however, are hired at the lower wages set by the new wage range. The red-circle rates eventually disappear because of the death, turnover, or retirement of employees. In addition, many companies attempt to speed up the process by training "red-circle employees" for other jobs with sufficient points to justify the higher wages paid.

Point plans do not eliminate all the subjective errors in job evaluation, but they do represent the best approach presently available for designing a sound and equitable wage structure within a company.

Point plans are most effective for measuring a limited range of similar jobs. To construct a single point plan that would cover all jobs within a firm would

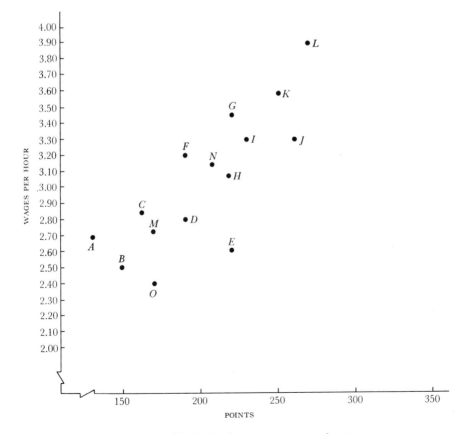

Figure 12–4 Point plan scatter chart

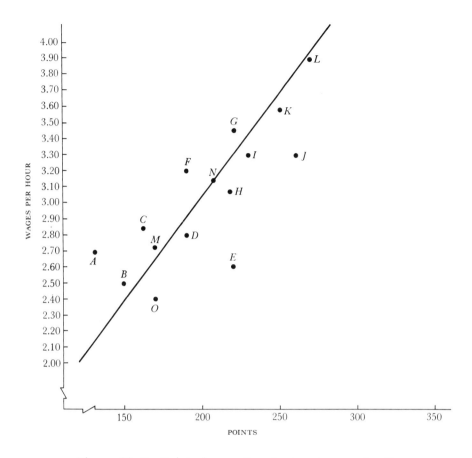

Figure 12–5   Point plan scatter chart and regression line

mean considerably increasing the number of factors and their relative degrees, which would tend to overcomplicate the program and make it unwieldly. The impact of collectively bargained wage increases on a wage structure established by means of a point plan must also be noted. Negotiated wage increases are normally expressed as percentage increases or as an increase of a given amount. A "flat increase"—an equal raise for all jobs—tends to distort the wage-level relationships between jobs. Since the flat sums are a larger percentage of wages received at the lower end of the scale than at the higher end, flat-sum increases diminish the relative differences between jobs. For example, consider two workers A and B at opposite ends of the wage scale. A receives $2.00 per hour while B receives $4.00 per hour. A's pay is 2.00/4.00 or 50% of B's. If a flat increase of $0.50/hour is given, the relationship between the two pays will change. It will now be $2.50/$4.50 or 56%. In such fashion, continued flat-sum increases remove much of the pay differentials between skilled and unskilled workers. Conversely, a fixed percentage increase for all occupations sharpens the slope of the regression line, making it more nearly vertical; this distorts the wage balance

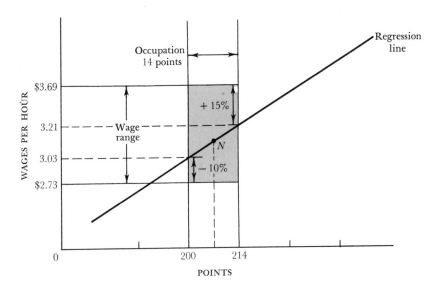

Figure 12–6 Establishing a wage range on a regression line

in the opposite direction. The best approach would be for any negotiated wage increases to reflect the established wage differentials so that all wage increases would be in direct proportion to the point scores of the various occupational categories.

Labor Incentives

In many production activities the cost of labor is affected by another major factor—the use of *incentive wage payment systems*. Incentive wage plans were one of the first techniques employed by management to increase the output of labor; this technique was particularly emphasized during the "scientific management" movement of the early 1900s.[6] Time study measures of labor productivity were developed in response to the need for establishing production levels on which to base an incentive system. A normal day's work (an average level of output as determined by time study) was considered as 100 percent of output, and any output that exceeded this level was rewarded according to a predetermined scale.

Incentive plans Incentive plans have become more sophisticated, but regardless of their complexity or nature, the following principles apply:

1. The output standards used in designing a plan should be accurate, equitable, and consistent.
2. The plan should be simple and easily understood by both management and

---

[6] The founders of the scientific management movement such as F. W. Taylor, H. L. Gantt, and H. Emerson all advocated the use of financial incentives.

labor. The performance levels and their associated rewards should be expressed in easily understood and easily measured units.[7]

3. There should be a direct, observable relationship between effort, output, and reward.

4. The worker must have an opportunity to earn an incentive bonus. This means that delays caused by mechanical failures must be minimized by effective management. Few things have so disastrous an impact on an incentive plan as depriving a worker of the opportunity to work and earn a bonus. Experience shows that a worker must feel that it is within his power to achieve a financial bonus, or else the edge of the incentive will be dulled.

The many types of incentive plans in use today may be broadly classified according to the incentive performance level and the magnitude of the reward. Thus, plans may be either "low task" or "high task," and they may provide either a constant reward or one that varies with effort.

In *low-task incentive plans,* financial rewards above the base wage rate start at some fraction of normal output, such as 80 percent. Normally this type of plan is used in manufacturing operations where either unskilled or semiskilled operators are used or where the labor unit cost is a small percentage of the total unit cost. In these cases the added unit costs of incentive payments are generally more than offset by the gains made in the output level. As in all incentive plans, this offset occurs because the fixed costs of manufacturing are spread over an increased output base, thus lowering the total unit cost of the product; this effect is shown graphically in Figure 12–7.

Implicit in this analysis is the assumption that output is not increased beyond the point where it would be necessary to change the basic mode of production.[8] The diagram is simply intended to illustrate that up to a point the total unit cost declines as the volume rises. The increase in unit labor cost is counteracted by the steady decrease in fixed cost per unit that comes from higher production levels.

Practically all incentive plans currently in use guarantee a worker a minimum of eight hours of straight-time pay per day.[9] If a worker's output is above normal, however, his wages increase as illustrated in Figure 12–8. Thus, a worker's wages are constant until the level of production defined by the output standard is reached; for production beyond the standard, wages increase at a fixed rate. A new form of incentive that is gaining in popularity is the "accelerated incen-

[7] Some of the early plans were purposely expressed in terms of fictitious production units, and the reward was based upon complicated mathematical formulas to prevent workers from figuring them out. It is interesting to note, however, that employees with a second-grade education were able to set up their own schedule of dollar-per-piece equivalents for these plans. Thus, the plans were complicated and hard to administer but did not fool the workers; indeed, all the activities, plans, designs, and operations could claim only employee suspicion and hostility in return.

[8] Thus, it is implied that there is no need to resort to such practices as increasing the number of shifts, using old or obsolete equipment, employing labor of marginal ability, or increasing the number of workers beyond the point of diminishing returns.

[9] Straight-time pay is the base pay rate without any incentive increment.

tive system," which is illustrated in Figure 12–9. According to this plan, straight-time wages are paid up to 80 percent of standard output; above this point a small "bonus per unit" is paid until 100 percent of standard output is reached; above this output level the bonus reward is increased sharply.

While, as noted above, virtually all industrial and clerical incentive systems guarantee eight hours of straight-time pay per day, there are still areas where straight piece-work (or piece-rate) plans are in use. Farm harvest workers and other contract laborers are still paid by the piece-rate system, though these workers are exerting a great effort to change this. Piece-rate payment is a constant payment per unit of output. Earning are calculated as

Earning = Number of units produced × Rate per unit

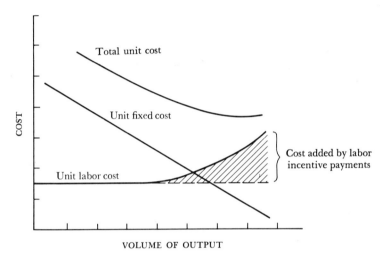

Figure 12–7   The impact of incentive plans on a firm's cost structure

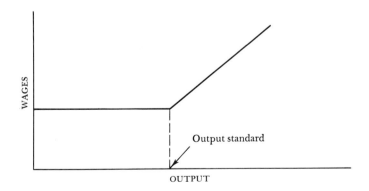

Figure 12–8   Wages received under an incentive system

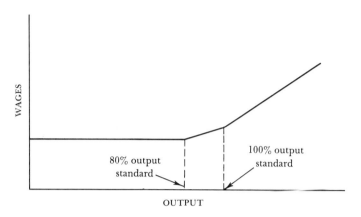

Figure 12-9 Wages received under an accelerated incentive system

and are depicted graphically in Figure 12–10. If the rate per unit is high enough to assure the average worker an equitable wage for work done at the normal pace, piece-rate plans can motivate workers. Where the piece rates are low, they tend to cause dissatisfaction.

In *high-task incentive plans,* a financial reward is not paid until the output produced exceeds 100 percent of the standard output level. In contrast to low-task incentive plans, these plans are most likely to be successful where both required labor skills and base rates are high, and where there is an emphasis upon superior quality as well as quantity in production. Under these conditions a premium is placed on having all employees attain the standard rate of production. When this output level is not achieved, it is necessary to pay an increased amount at the high base rate to complete the required production. In practice, a minimum level of acceptability is usually set at approximately 90 percent of average output. The worker's output is measured on a weekly or monthly basis, which permits him to have an occasional off-day without prejudicing his chances of turning out a standard quantity of output.

Under this type of plan the output per employee will generally range from a minimum of 90 percent to approximately 115 percent of standard. The output is usually limited to this range because of occupational practices, social mores, and the fact that the incentive reward may not be great enough to stimulate all-out employee efforts. The output produced under a high-task incentive system is pictured in Figure 12–11. Notice that the output of the great majority of workers falls into the narrow band between 90 and 115 percent of standard. Comparatively few workers produce below the 90 percent level; those who do receive straight-time pay but are generally encouraged to increase their output. If they fail to do so, management will seek either to transfer or to replace them.

A high-task incentive system, therefore, is really a means of assuring a fair day's work from all workers. In many cases it has replaced the measured day work (MDW) system, whereby the employees are paid a straight base rate each day with no reward for additional output. In return for this wage, a fair day's work is expected. Under the MDW system, management has often had great difficulty keeping the average output up to the standard. Even if the acceptable output were set as low as 75 percent of standard, the average output tended to gravitate to this minimum acceptable level. A strong management could demand and get standard production rates, of course, but this would usually require constant pressure and would result in a hostile, difficult-to-manage work force. Many companies, therefore, favor the high-task incentive approach to maintaining a standard output level.

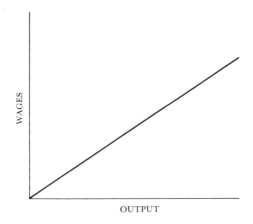

Figure 12–10   Piece-rate incentive system

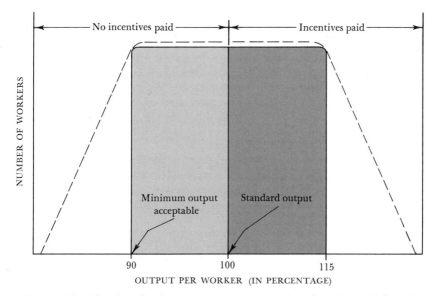

Figure 12–11   Standard output measures employed under a high-task incentive system

Summary

At this point we have concluded our discussion of labor as an input of the production process. Four general problems concerning the use of labor were analyzed: the first treated the design of jobs in the production process; the second, the establishment of labor output standards; and the final two, the acquisition and payment of a labor force.

Throughout our presentation, a broad managerial view was taken in order to make the reader aware of the important role labor plays in the production process. While recruiting and screening of employers may be considered to be outside the scope of production management, the effect of these activities on the production process, and hence on production management, is great. For this reason, production managers must understand as much as possible about recruiting and screening so that they can coordinate their own activities with those of the managers of other functional areas.

Questions and Problems

1. In what ways is a 100 percent bonus (standard hour, standard minute, or 100 percent premium) wage-payment plan similar to straight piece-work?
2. How is a regression line used in job evaluation?
3. In job evaluation, what is meant by internal balance and external balance?
4. Should a company have a wage policy? If so, who should participate in its formulation? Explain.
5. The union is demanding an extra 10-cent hourly wage increase for all hourly employees on jobs without incentive plans, because "their relative earnings have suffered as a result of the bonus earnings of the piece workers." The company is aware that there has been a great deal of grumbling about the fact that lesser skilled production workers are beginning to get pay checks almost equal to those of skilled maintenance workers. However, management can also argue that these increased earnings are a result of increased effort on the part of production workers. Furthermore, maintenance workers have vigorously opposed suggestions that their jobs be subjected to a time study for the purpose of establishing an incentive plan.
    (a) How important is this complaint?
    (b) Why have maintenance workers resisted switching to an incentive plan?
6. What part do individual differences among workers play in an incentive system?
7. Enumerate the various approaches to job evaluation, and specify their differences.
8. How is the information obtained on which job evaluations are based?
9. What are red-circle jobs?
10. What are the advantages and hazards to management of incentive pay systems?
11. What factors influence the worth of a particular job?
12. Using the context of a small manufacturing firm, describe the planning and control necessary for developing (a) base rates, (b) output standards, and (c) incentive systems. How are these three areas interrelated? Organizationally, how would you provide coordination among them?
13. How are job methods, work measurement, and job evaluation related?

14. Discuss the prerequisites for installing a financial incentive system that would give the company constant unit-labor costs.
15. What is the effect on the workers' wages and the unit production costs when output rises from 100 percent to 115 percent under
    (a) A piece rate system
    (b) Incentive system where workers get 50 percent incentive for output over 100 percent
    (c) Hourly wage
16. Managerial jobs cannot be time measured because they involve primarily mental output. In spite of this, some managerial positions have incentive pay. What basis can the incentive payments have? Should they be paid?
17. Using the discussion of human behavior in Chapter 9, discuss the concepts and relationships of incentive plans, work measurement, methods studies, and wages.
18. What are the advantages and limitations of establishing relative job payments by
    (a) Ranking
    (b) Classifications
    (c) Point systems
    (d) Factor comparison
19. A small company uses an incentive system with a guaranteed base wage. For output over 100 percent, the worker gains 50 percent. One worker has a base rate of $3.00 per hour. His standard time to produce a unit of output is 3 minutes of of a 480-minute day. Yesterday his output was 200 units. What was his pay? What would it have been if the incentive had been 100 percent rather than 50 percent?
20. The point values and wage rates associated with ten key jobs from an area job study are:

JOB	POINT VALUE	JOB RATES
1	40	3.50
2	48	4.20
3	50	4.55
4	53	4.80
5	57	5.70
6	62	5.25
7	69	5.60
8	71	5.95
9	82	6.30
10	91	8.05

(a) Draw a freehand wage trend line. (After Chapter 14 has been studied, a least squares line can be drawn.)
(b) Develop a wage plan for your firm from the data.
(c) What if some jobs are red-circle jobs?

References

Backman, J., *Wage Determination: An Analysis of Wage Criteria,* Van Nostrand-Reinhold, Princeton, N.J., 1960.

Belcher, D. W., *Wage and Salary Administration,* 2nd ed., Prentice-Hall, Englewood Cliffs, N.J., 1962.

Brennan, C. W., *Wage Administration: Plans, Practices, and Principles,* rev. ed., Irwin, Homewood, Ill., 1963.

Carroll, P., *Better Wage Incentives,* McGraw-Hill, New York, 1957.

Cartter, A. M., *Theory of Wages and Employment,* Irwin, Homewood, Ill., 1959.

Gilmour, R. W., *Industrial Wage and Salary Control,* Wiley, New York, 1956.

Jacques, E., *Equitable Payment,* Wiley, New York, 1961.

Lanham, E., *Administration of Wages and Salaries,* Harper and Row, New York, 1963.

Lovejoy, L. C., *Wage and Salary Administration,* Ronald Press, New York, 1959.

Louden, J. K., and Deegan, J. W., *Wage Incentives,* 2nd ed., Wiley, New York, 1959.

Lytle, C. W., *Job Evaluation Methods,* 2nd ed., Ronald Press, New York, 1954.

Otis, J. L., and Leukart, R. H., *Job Evaluation,* 2nd ed., Prentice-Hall, Englewood Cliffs, N.J., 1964.

Patton, J. A., Littlefield, C., and Self, S., *Job Evaluation,* 3rd ed., Irwin, Homewood, Ill., 1963.

Tolles, N. A., and Yoder, D., *Origins of Modern Wage Theories,* Prentice-Hall, Englewood Cliffs, N.J., 1964.

Yoder, D., *Personnel Management and Industrial Relations,* 5th ed., Prentice-Hall, Englewood Cliffs, N.J., 1962.

13

Materials Management— Purchasing and Inventory

The average manufacturing company spends over half of its sales income on purchased parts, components, raw materials, and services; but some firms spend considerably more than this. Material costs absorb approximately 70 percent of sales income in the container industry, for example, and for certain food processors the cost is even higher than that. Conversely, other firms such as pharmaceutical houses, mining companies, and oil producers spend 25 percent or less of their sales dollar on material purchases. On the average, however, manufacturers of goods like automobiles, household appliances, and electronics spend about 50 percent of their sales dollar for material inputs.

In contrast, typical manufacturing profits amount to only 9 percent of sales. Thus, it is easy to see that even slight changes in material costs will exert a great influence on a firm's profit picture. For example, a 2 percent decrease in material costs will usually result in an increase of 1 percent in the profit margin, which in turn will produce a relative increase in profits of over 10 percent. In other words, every dollar saved by reducing material costs has the same impact on profits as $10 in increased sales. Suppose, for example, that a company has a sales income of $100 million and spends about $50 million on materials. A 1 percent, or $0.5 million, reduction in this $50 million material cost will result in a profit increase of $500,000. To achieve this same increase through additional sales, the firm would have to boost sales by $5.5 million! These relationships are illustrated graphically in Figure 13–1. Because material costs exert a

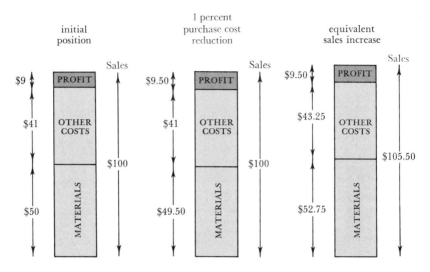

Figure 13–1 Cutting material costs versus boosting sales income

tremendous leverage on profits, companies can make or lose large sums depending upon how efficient they are in purchasing and controlling materials.

Historical Aspects of Materials Management

Because of the magnitude of the expenditures required in acquiring and controlling materials and their resultant leverage on profits, companies devote a great deal of attention to the efficiency of their materials management operations. A brief look at the historical evolution of the materials function will give us a fuller appreciation of the current situation. Up until the time of F. W. Taylor, the production foreman was to all intents and purposes in complete control of the production activity. He hired, fired, and promoted; he purchased the necessary raw materials, scheduled production, and handled individually almost all of the other aspects of production. If the operation was profitable, the foreman was subjected to little or no interference from top management. The principal criterion of his success, or managerial effectiveness, was profits.

The Development of the Purchasing Function

As the complexity of industrial activity increased, many of the activities performed by the foreman were gradually taken over by specialists; among these was the purchasing function. It was found that by transferring purchasing to a specialist, the firm could usually obtain greater economies of scale in purchasing and take advantage of specialized skills as well. A trained buyer who was familiar with the details of a large number of supplies could usually do a better job than a foreman who had many other duties to discharge. With the continued increase in both the size and complexity of manufacturing operations, it soon became a full-time task for the foreman just to direct the activities of the work force.

Meanwhile, the manufacturing process itself was also changing considerably. Companies became more specialized and produced fewer and fewer of the parts for their finished products. Some firms became pure assembly operations, producing virtually none of the components for their products. This change in manufacturing operations helped to raise the dollar value of materials purchased by the firm. Purchases no longer consisted primarily of raw materials but rather of complex components and subassembly units. Thus, whereas early buyers of raw materials needed only limited skills (since they were buying substantially the same product over and over again), later buyers needed far more preparation in order to cope with the complexities of the purchased materials. They needed some knowledge of engineering, production, finance, and marketing, and an overall familiarity with the workings of the entire firm.

As a result, today many firms reject a passive definition of the purchasing function as merely an order-placing activity. More and more firms feel that a purchasing agent should be interested in the efficiency of the firm's suppliers, the quality of their output, and their ability to meet delivery schedules. To this end, some large firms may even perform quality inspection in the supplier's plant or (for new products that they have developed) furnish engineers to help the supplier tool and plan the production process. The firms' aim is to establish highly competent suppliers and thus reduce their own costs for internal inspection and rework. Indeed, in many cases a supplier is considered as a continuation of a firm's own production facilities. In government subcontracting this is virtually always the case, since the prime contractor is responsible not only for the subcontractor's product and design but also for his fulfillment of the legal requirements.

Materials Management

The modern approach to the purchasing function is the all-encompassing concept of *materials management*. Whereas only one or two major firms subscribed to this approach in the early 1950s, by the mid-1960s several hundred had adopted it, and today it is in general use.

Materials management takes a broad view of the basic purchasing task, including in it all aspects of purchasing and supplying goods:

1. *Purchasing.* The procurement of materials as authorized in requisitions from production departments.
2. *The control of supply items.* The procurement and inventory control of standard, nonproduction goods, including office supplies, tools, maintenance equipment, and other operating goods.
3. *Inventory control of production items.* The determination of inventory levels and purchase quantities required to meet production schedules; also

the maintenance of physical inventories and their associated inventory records.

4. *Receiving.* The receipt, inspection, identification, and movement of incoming materials.

5. *Traffic.* The determination of the means of shipment for both incoming and outgoing materials.

6. *Shipping.* The packaging and labeling of finished goods.

Some firms have also included the production-control function under materials management. This has been done principally in cases where the manufacturing operation is short cycle and relatively simple so that the "value added" is comparatively small. In such instances, the head of materials management is responsible not only for the movement of materials to meet the production schedule but also for the determination of the schedule itself.

Materials Management Organization

When defined in this fashion, the materials management function of a firm plays as vital a role as production, marketing, or finance. Some companies recognize this by establishing the position of materials manager at the highest executive level, on a par with managers of manufacturing, marketing, and finance. This seems reasonable in light of the pivotal position that material costs play in the firm's profit picture. Purchasing activities and the handling of all expenditures associated with materials management must be coordinated with finance because the money spent constitutes a significant portion of the firm's budget for working capital. The interaction between marketing and materials management is also important. Delivery promises made to customers by marketing men must reflect the planned availability of purchased items, and the magnitude and diversity of those purchases are determined to a large extent by the customers' demands for quantities and types of products as measured by the marketing department. Manufacturing, in turn, relies upon the materials management function for the quantity and quality of input materials it uses. In addition, the delivery of purchased goods and the status of inventories of needed supplies play an important role in the formulation of manufacturing schedules and operating plans. Therefore, in order to obtain close coordination between these activities, many companies feel that top-level interaction is required.

Divided Materials Management Structure

More often, however, the men responsible for materials management are not on the same organizational level as those in manufacturing, marketing, or finance. In the typical organization, the heads of marketing, finance, and manufacturing report directly to the chief executive, and if there is a materials manager he usually reports to the vice-president of manufacturing. Thus, despite the fact that conceptually the materials management function is as important (in terms of dollars, anyway) as finance, manufacturing, and marketing, the typical organization does not reflect this.

To make matters worse, in many companies the materials management function is not unified under one man. Instead, it is divided as shown in Figure 13–2. There, materials management is not only subordinate to the other organizational functions, but is crippled as well by being split among them. Another common arrangement is to establish purchasing as a top-level activity and leave the other materials management functions as shown in Figure 13–2. This is frequently done in firms that have heavy purchasing requirements.

It is a commonly accepted principle of organization that it is most efficient to assign a single individual overall control and responsibility for any given function. Thus, the vice-president of finance usually has budgeting, payroll, receivables, payables, auditing, and accounting under his jurisdiction. The individuals who plan, carry out, and control these activities all report to him, so that he is in a central position to direct all aspects of finance in the organization. Thus, one man is responsible for all financial activities and has the authority necessary to control them.

Now let us consider the status of the materials manager shown in Figure 13–2 in light of this principle of organization. He has no control over the availability of materials. Control is spread throughout the organization; marketing is responsible for finished-goods inventories, finance for purchases, and other parts of the production function are responsible for purchased-goods inventories and production scheduling. The materials manager only controls the in-process inventory— the flow of materials already in the firm; he is not in complete control of the

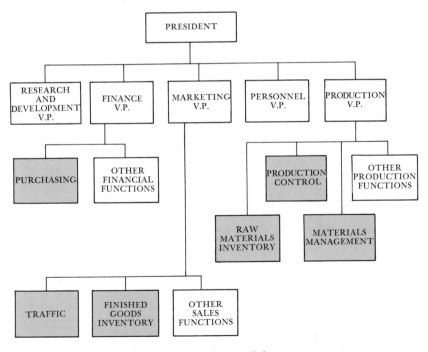

Figure 13–2 Divided materials management

materials function. Since this function is fragmented, it is often difficult to determine who should be held responsible for getting things done.

Centralized Materials Management Structure

To overcome this crippling split in responsibilities, some firms centralize the entire materials management function under a materials manager who is given responsibility for the total flow of materials and has a staff to direct this activity. An abbreviated version of this type of organization is shown in Figure 13–3.

Organizational Side Effects

These differences in organizational structure have some important side effects. In the divided organization (Figure 13–2), materials management activities are broken up among other functional areas and are low in organizational rank and status. Moreover, they are not integral activities of the departments that control them. Purchasing is not a "natural" or fundamental function of the finance department. Similarly, finished-goods inventory management is different from all other activities in the marketing department, although it can it can be argued that there is a natural bond between selling and ensuring that products will be available for sale. If the materials management function is fragmented, there is a tendency to look upon its component activities as merely paper-work jobs dealing with petty details. As a consequence, good personnel will tend to shy away from these jobs, since their chances for advancement within the parent functional areas may be hurt and the lowly status of these jobs probably means poor remuneration. These effects exaggerate the existing inefficiencies in the

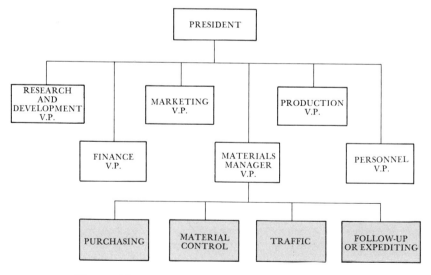

Figure 13–3 Centralized materials management

divided structure, since the level of performance in materials management is below that of the operating departments.

This problem became acute in the armed services during World War II, when men who were considered inadequate for combat duty were weeded out and transferred to supply work because logistic functions were not thought to be as important as other war work. As a result, the procurement and acquisition function proved to be tremendously inefficient. A major feature of the reorganization of the armed services after World War II was the raising of the level of personnel assigned to logistics functions. Indeed, use of the word "logistics" was a part of the campaign to upgrade the status of the work and the people involved. These activities now attract good men and are becoming increasingly productive.

Conclusions about Organizational Trends

Although the trend seems to be toward centralizing materials activities and raising the organizational status of the materials manager, these activities are still divided organizationally in the majority of firms today. The importance of the materials management function, in terms of its impact on a firm's cost and profit picture, is indisputable, and production management is intimately connected with it. Consequently, no matter where materials management activities may be performed in a firm, production managers should be knowledgeable about them. We will not discuss the traffic function in detail, since it is a highly specialized activity and beyond the scope of a book on production management. Materials movement activities are described throughout the book, however, since they are an integral part of all production activities.

The Purchasing Function

If the materials manager is held responsible for all aspects of the flow of materials through his firm, then purchasing is the first phase in the process for which he is responsible. The primary function of a purchasing department is to secure all material inputs needed for the production process. In this capacity it usually administers more than one-half of the firm's total expenditures.

The Purchasing Cycle

The placing of a purchase order is only the beginning of the process. To run quickly through the entire process, the purchasing department first reviews requisitions placed by other functional areas of the firm to ascertain if they are authorized. If they are, purchasing checks to see if each needed item is properly described and if available cheaper material could do the job. Before writing the orders, however, purchasing must select suppliers on the basis of price and the quality and delivery schedule of their products. Purchasing then records the suppliers' acknowledgements of receipt of orders and confirms the shipping dates. When the material is received, purchasing records its arrival and checks to see if there are shortages or defects in it. It checks purchase invoices and forwards them to accounting with an authorization for payment. Note that throughout this cycle, purchasing either performs the task or records its performance, as illustrated in Figure 13–4.

Note also that the purchasing cycle stretches from a decision to order the material to the point at which it is available for use by the requisitioner. Too often, purchasing agents consider their job done when the supplier has shipped the material, or when it has been received by the firm. This is not the case, however; only after the material has been checked and accepted by the requisitioner can the cycle be considered complete. A whole series of exchanges between the supplier and the purchasing agent may be required, for example, if material is delivered that does not meet the specifications.

The time that elapses between the receipt of a requisition for material and its actual delivery is also significant. This is generally called the "lead time" by the purchasing department. As one would expect, the lead time for any specific

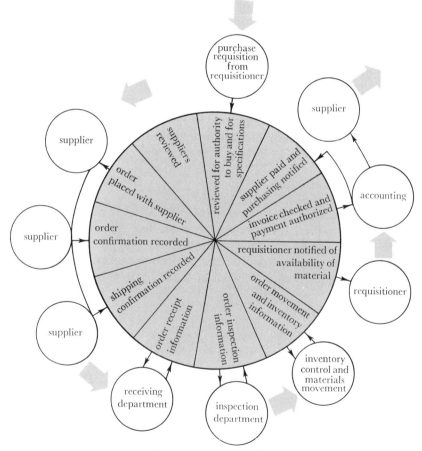

Figure 13–4   The purchasing cycle

order is influenced by many factors, including the nature of the item and whether it has been purchased before. The department requesting the material must allow sufficient time for the purchasing department to locate a suitable supplier before placing the order and for that supplier to manufacture the item. If there is insufficient time, the price paid for the item and its quality may both suffer. Therefore, purchasing departments strongly urge requisitioners to anticipate their needs well in advance in order to allow enough time for effective procurement. To give requisitioners an idea of how much lead time to allow, many purchasing agents periodically provide all departments with *lead-time charts* that delineate the average purchasing cycle times for different classes of items used within the firm. In the electronics industry, for example, standard resistors have a minimum lead time of one week, whereas for large transformers it is fourteen weeks.

The Purchasing Information Cycle

A complex information network is required to support the purchasing cycle. Figure 13–4 is a simplified flow chart showing the major exchanges of information that take place during the purchasing process. These exchanges are independent of processing methods and can be performed manually or with equipment as sophisticated as electronic computers. Some of the information flow is designed to support purchasing operations, such as the flows from the requisitioner to purchasing, and from purchasing to receiving. This information alerts the various departments that materials are coming and thus allows them to schedule their operations accordingly. Other phases of the information flow are designed to yield information useful for managerial planning and control, such as the flow of data from receiving and inspection to purchasing. This information provides management with a means of assessing the quality of the purchased material and the ability of the supplier to meet his schedule. The same information also serves as a record to answer questions from other areas of the firm concerning the current status of the order and the history of the transaction.

It is interesting to note that some information systems are organized primarily for the purpose of reporting exception data. These systems often trigger exception reports internally when delivery falls behind schedule, and periodically they scan the records of suppliers and report those who do not meet the firm's quality requirements or are consistently late in delivery. Systems have even been designed that can scan purchase requisition descriptions and point out functional similarities, thus promoting increased standardization.

The type of purchasing information system used in a firm is, for the most part, a reflection of the capabilities of the management and of the importance of the information in the firm's scheme of operations. In any system, however, the basic functions portrayed in Figure 13–5 will be found.

Some aspects of the purchasing cycle merit closer study because of their relative importance. The first of these is known as *value analysis*.

Value analysis Value analysis is the generic term commonly given to studies conducted by purchasing to determine if the materials to be bought will be ap-

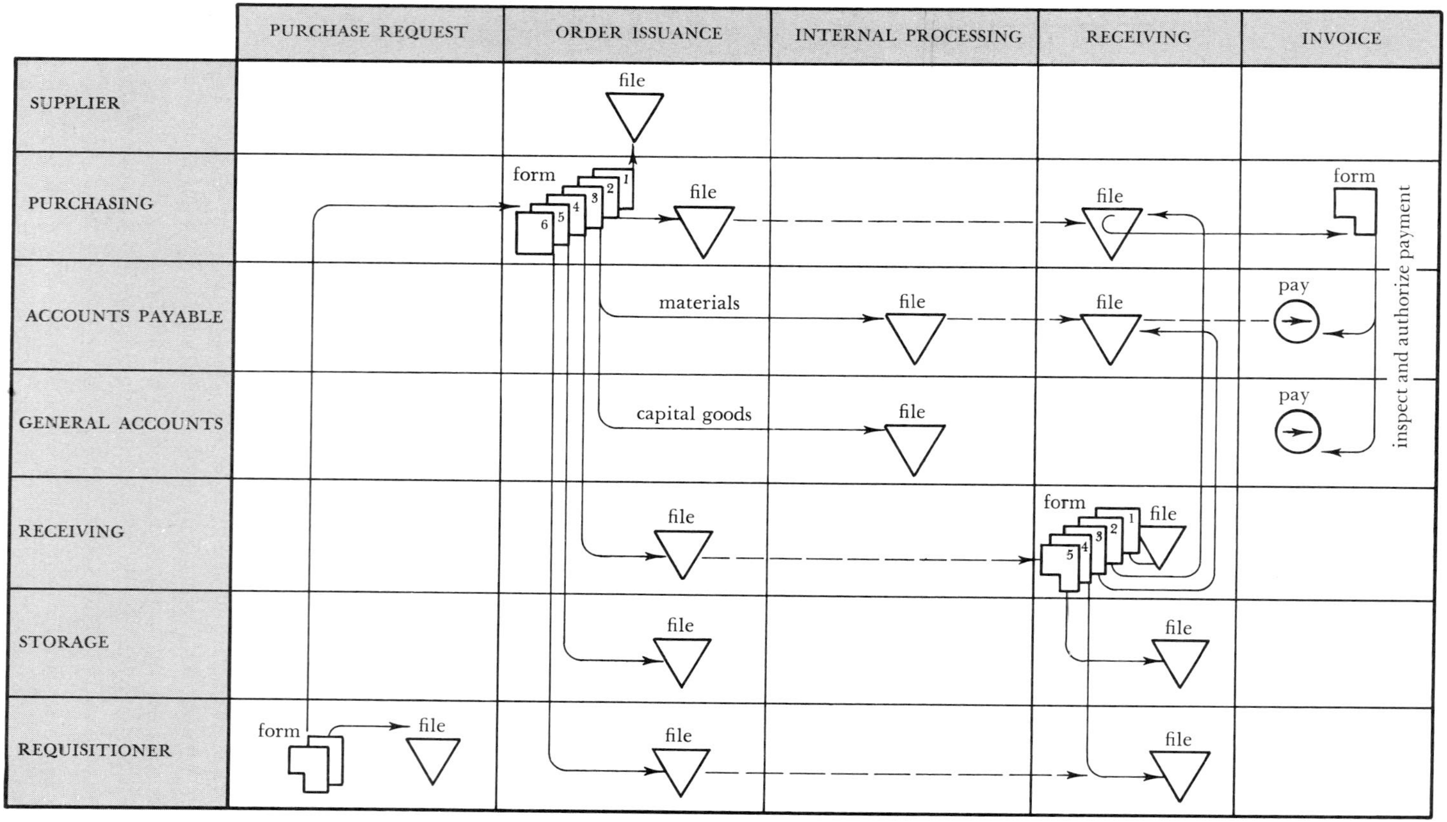

Figure 13–5 Purchasing information flow

propriate for the tasks they are to perform. In essence, this analysis is a series of questions: Could a less expensive replacement be found that would perform the required task? Are other less costly materials available that would be adequate? Are the supplier's prices reasonable? Can product redesign reduce the cost?

Purchasing can ask these questions, but it cannot supply the answers. If purchasing locates alternatives that can be bought on better terms than the original request, the alternatives are referred to the requisitioner. The originator of the request must make the final decision on changing a product or a supplier (if a supplier is specified in the requisition).

Substantial savings can result from value analysis, and firms that have used this approach cite many success stories. Since the requisitioner knows that his purchase requests will be reviewed, he is more likely to scrutinize his own demands from a purchasing point of view. As a rule, requisitioners are resentful if purchasing finds cheaper materials or a cheaper method of doing their job, since this tends to reflect on their performance. Where purchasing has succeeded in doing this in the past, the requisitioner is more likely to search for the least costly approach before submitting his request. In this fashion, value analysis spreads throughout the company, and frequently engineering specifications and tolerances are relaxed as areas of excessive precision are discovered and costly nonstandard parts are replaced by standard items.

Even where value analysis is conducted by the requisitioner, the purchasing department has an important part to play. Its knowledge of suppliers and of the competitive price levels are essential ingredients in wise purchasing decisions. Thus, ideally, the requisitioner should concentrate his analysis on the technical aspects of the materials, and purchasing should concentrate its analysis on the market situation.

The government has recognized the savings that can result by applying the value-analysis technique to the procurement of military hardware. To encourage its application, incentive clauses pertaining to value analysis have been written into most defense contracts. The savings from such programs are split by the government and the contractor on some predetermined basis, say, 90 percent to the government and 10 percent to the contractor. Some recent contracts awarded by the government have gone one step further and made value-analysis programs mandatory. In fact, one criterion now used in awarding a contract is the soundness and potential savings of the value-analysis program developed and proposed for the particular project.

Product specifications After deciding what to buy, there is an additional problem in many purchasing cycles—describing specifications for the product to be purchased. The requisitioner may ask for a product that does not fit the standards accepted in that area or that does not lend itself to a simple catalog description. In these cases an engineering drawing may be able to specify the product. But if this is not sufficient, an additional written description including all of the pertinent information about the qualities desired in the product will be required. This should include such factors as hardness, finish, composition, strength, moisture content, and weight.

If written specifications are required, they may be prepared by either purchasing or engineering. When standards obtained from outside agencies[1] can be included in the specifications, purchasing usually writes the specifications. But when they must be written without reference to a set of industry standards, specifications are usually drawn up by the engineering department. Purchasing will assist in the task, however, since it must understand the specifications of the item in order to purchase it.

Once the specifications have been formulated, purchasing often has the option of buying the item by brand name or by the specifications. Many firms manufacture products that are listed both by brand names and by written specifications. By establishing brand names for his products, a manufacturer hopes to create a differentiation between his products and similar ones made by his competitors. If large quantities are needed, buying by specifications is normally cheaper, whereas for small quantities brand-name purchases are often more economical. In virtually all cases, however, brand-name products will at least meet the minimum specifications whereas special orders may not.[2]

Supplier selection The next step in the purchasing sequence is the very heart of the purchasing activity—selecting the suppliers with whom orders will be placed for materials needed. This step is actually the culmination of a series of prior steps. First, the purchasing agent must determine who the potential suppliers are for a particular item or family of items. Information of this type may be amassed from salesmen, manufacturer's representatives, buyer's guides, trade journals, inspection tours, and from the experience and specific knowledge of the buyer. Compiling a list of the companies that can make the needed item is only a starting point, however. The relative proficiency of each one must be assessed. How well does each supplier measure up in terms of price, quality, and delivery? By the same token, only the suppliers who are able to meet satisfactory performance standards should be considered for possible orders. Most purchasing departments compile a list of acceptable suppliers (called the *approved supplier list*) for each class of item purchased. The advantage of such a list is that when a requisition is received the process of choosing the supplier is simplified. The purchasing department has only to select a few likely candidates from the list, contact them, and make its choice on the basis of comparative quotations of price and delivery. The development of approved supplier lists is a cumulative process, of course. When an item that has never been purchased before is requisitioned, it triggers the activities required to establish an approved

[1] Many functional areas have sets of descriptions for this purpose; the National Bureau of Standards publishes a great variety of industrial standards. Many specialized functional areas have their own standards; for example, the Society of Automotive Engineers publishes standards for oil, gas, and machine fittings for many types of motors.

[2] The problem of brand-name purchasing as opposed to specification purchasing is especially prevalent in drugs. Doctors have the option of prescribing by generic characteristics (specifications) or by brand name. Purchases by generic name are usually cheaper, and there is some argument as to whether there are really any differences in quality.

supplier list for that type of item. These lists are also cumulative from another point of view. Purchasing agents are continually scanning the marketplace in search of potential new suppliers to add to the approved list for the items that they buy regularly. This is done to ensure that when an order is placed with a supplier on the approved list, the firm has actually considered all of the best sources.

Once a supplier is added to the approved list, continued monitoring and evaluation of his performance are necessary and should be based upon actual results. This means that the purchasing department must rely on accounting, receiving, inspection,[3] and production for pertinent information on the materials bought. This information should go to purchasing as part of an established procedure so that purchasing can develop a performance appraisal for each supplier. The supplier's card in the approved list should indicate his current, relative performance in such areas as price, quality, service, and delivery. These data will guide the purchasing agent in sometimes choosing a reliable supplier with perhaps slightly higher prices over a more economical one who does not meet delivery dates—possibly a very important factor. Late deliveries can close an entire plant or shut down an assembly line, thus raising production costs enormously. On the other hand, if allowable lead time is more than adequate, some tardiness in delivery may be considered inexpensive and tolerable; the purchasing agent would then place the order with the lowest priced supplier despite any past records of late deliveries. The same reasoning applies to the quality of the purchase; inferior material may mean rework and rejects, which in turn raise production costs. Where the price differential is great enough, however, relatively poor quality material may be bought, even though it means more rework and more rejects, if the overall cost will be lower. This decision will have to be made jointly by production and purchasing, however. If poor material is purchased, production schedules may have to be altered, and modifications in labor and machine demands may have to be introduced to compensate for the increased number of rejects. This is another illustration of the interaction between purchasing and the other production activities. Thus, in determining the "best buy" for the firm, price is important, but the decision can be made only after such factors as quality, reliability, service, and delivery are also evaluated.

Supplier evaluation should be a continuous operation, because poor suppliers can improve and highly efficient suppliers can become careless. For this reason, many firms require that the purchasing agent submit monthly evaluation reports for all, or perhaps a sample, of the suppliers dealt with. When sampling techniques are used, top management usually stipulates that every supplier be evaluated at least once or twice a year. After these evaluations, suppliers whose performance is slipping are formally warned by letter of the specific reasons for the buying firm's dissatisfaction. If the suppliers' performance remains poor, they are dropped from the approved list and receive no new purchase orders.

In addition to the evaluation of suppliers on the existing list, companies often

---

[3] Sampling techniques are normally applied in the inspection of incoming materials.

insist that the purchasing agent submit periodically studies and evaluations of possible new sources of supply. These reports are designed to stimulate the search for better suppliers. Another common requirement is that the approved list contain suppliers from all geographic areas of the country, or that the list of approved suppliers include representatives from all sizes of business—from the large multiplant company down to the one-man business.

Some firms also have a policy limiting the percentage of business that can be given to any one supplier on the approved list. This is done to encourage competition and to avoid making the firm too dependent on any single supplier; many companies insist upon a minimum of three or four active sources for all material inputs used. Such a policy can be implemented by order splitting or by simply staggering the orders, and it serves to protect the firm against default by the suppliers due to strike, flood, or fire.

Purchasing Transactions

After a supplier has been selected for a particular order, the type of purchase procedure to be used must be determined. All purchasing transactions can be grouped into four basic categories according to type of purchase—items used continuously, large one-time orders, small-value purchases, and normal purchases not falling within any of the first three categories.

Production items used continuously   In handling items that are used continuously during the production process and for which there is a fairly predictable need, the purchasing agent tries to avoid using individual purchase orders. Instead, a *blanket-purchase order* is written. Such a contract will leave the actual delivery dates open, and it may or may not specify the quantity to be purchased and the price to be paid. If it does not specify the price, the one in effect on the date of the individual order is charged. Notification of delivery dates and desired size of shipments is sent to the supplier by the firm's production department. Purchasing is not involved in placing individual orders, but it does negotiate the basic contract, thus materially reducing both the cost and the time required to place and process an order.

While this type of contract is generally used for a homogeneous product such as sheet steel, it may be extended to cover a variety of products. For example, a contract may be made with a supplier for a specified quantity of small electric motors. Under the terms of this kind of contract, the purchaser usually places requisitions for many different types and sizes of motors and agrees to allow sufficient lead time for delivery. In return for this commitment, the purchaser is granted a discount based upon the dollar volume of his total annual purchase. Occasionally, a series of discount percentages are negotiated for ascending ranges of purchase dollar volumes. In either case, orders placed during the year are treated as partial releases that may be applied against the original contract. The price paid by the purchaser for each order is the list price before the discount deduction. This practice is designed to protect the supplier against the possibility that the order volume stipulated in the contract may not be reached. Then, at the end of the year, the volume of orders is totaled, and the discount, if any, is calculated and applied to the entire year's purchases. The size of such a discount can be substantial. Because the cost of materials obtained during the year is charged to operations at list prices, the discount has been compared to "found money" since it contributes directly to increased profits by many purchasers.

Blanket orders of this type are often split among two or more suppliers in order to protect the purchaser against any delays in the delivery of materials arising from problems at any one supplier's plant. There is usually a high degree of cooperation between the purchaser and supplier on this type of contract; some purchasers even go so far as to integrate their entire purchasing procedure with the production setup of their supplier. Some railroads, for example, order maintenance parts on an open contract by means of a punched card that is processed through their own purchasing systems and their supplier's production system. Because these two systems have been specifically designed to coordinate with one another, considerable money has been saved by both companies.

Probably the chief advantage of annual contracts is that they bring the company's top purchasing and negotiating skill to bear on a substantial portion of the year's purchases.[4] It also makes the releasing of orders during the year a routine operation that can be delegated to lower echelon personnel, thus conserving the time of the purchasing agent and his staff for more important duties, such as supplier evaluation.

From the supplier's point of view, the advantage of annual contracts is that long-term commitments produce increased stability in operations and in profit levels. Production runs can be increased to obtain lower manufacturing costs, and the selling and advertising expenses usually associated with the order volume stipulated in the contract can be minimized. These factors provide economic justification for the discount.[5]

Large one-time orders In the purchase of special machinery and other unique types of capital goods, a large portion of the cost arises from efforts to determine the specifications of the product. Many months of planning may be involved. Therefore, the seller will often submit contracts for the product that include the cost of the design work.

A firm with this type of purchase to make may negotiate with several suppliers, or it may work with only one; the contract may be on a fixed fee or a cost-plus basis, depending upon the situation. The distinguishing feature of this type of contract is that it is negotiated on a one-time basis.[6]

---

[4] It should be mentioned that a compromise approach is often followed whereby annual contracts are limited to a percentage such as 60 percent of yearly purchases for a particular item. The remaining volume is allotted to many firms, large and small, of wide geographic dispersion. This allocation avoids too much dependence on one supplier and encourages competition. Furthermore, if the results with one firm are not satisfactory, the annual contract can be negotiated with another—one that has proved its performance during the past year.

[5] Under the Robinson-Patman Act, quantity discounts must be based on real economies attained by the supplier.

[6] These contracts will be discussed more completely under Defense Contracting.

Small-value purchases   At the opposite end of the spectrum from the large one-time purchase are the low-cost items that are used infrequently. Typically, it costs a firm from $20 to $30 to process a purchase order, and in many firms the amount is even higher. If the needed item can be bought for less than this, use of the normal purchasing routine becomes highly uneconomical. To reduce the cost of purchasing these inexpensive items, many firms authorize direct petty-cash purchases or establish open orders with suppliers. Open orders are authorizations for departments, such as production, to purchase infrequently used low-cost items directly from a supplier. The supplier then bills the firm periodically for what has been ordered.

Notice that here again the purchasing department does none of the actual buying; it simply negotiates the contractual conditions and monitors the system to make sure that the conditions are properly applied.

Normal purchasing routine   All purchases that do not fit into one of the three categories mentioned above are considered part of the normal purchasing routine. The purchasing department processes the buying of the products requisitioned by other departments in the firm. Upon receipt of a requisition, purchasing places the order with a supplier and oversees the status of the order. For repeat orders it may return to the same supplier or it may survey the field for a new source. Notice that in this capacity the purchasing department coordinates a purchase request and does the actual buying; this general procedure is shown in Figure 13–4.

Defense contracting   In conclusion, one important highly specialized area of purchasing should be mentioned—government defense contracting. In recent years, defense contracts have ranged in the billions.

Single contracts of $1 billion or more that are to be spent over several years are not rare. Whatever the size of the contract, however, the procedure is the same: the government normally awards it to one company, which then becomes the *prime contractor*. Prime contractors in turn may subcontract portions of the contract which they themselves cannot or do not choose to produce. Except for minor limitations, prime contractors are free to subcontract as they wish. In effect, these prime contractors become purchasers of enormous quantities of materials. Since they assume responsibility for the work of the subcontractors (including the quality of the product and its delivery, and the subcontractors' compliance with government regulations regarding profits, wage regulations, work hours, and fair employment), an imposing work load is placed on the prime contractors' purchasing departments. These departments are responsible not only for awarding the subcontracts but also for monitoring all aspects of the subcontractors' activities. Because of the highly technical nature of most defense products, this means that purchasing must work closely with quality inspection and engineering personnel. Accordingly, many large defense contractors expand their purchasing departments to include specialists in production and industrial engineering who work directly with the subcontractors, often at their plants, to iron out technical production problems.

Defense contracts may be either negotiated or bid. Early in the 1960s most contracts were negotiated, but by 1964 the balance had shifted toward bid contracts. Even in bid contracts, however, there is a great deal of negotiation. Since many contracts are for the construction of products not yet in existence, it is virtually impossible to predict all aspects of the contract. Very often, unforeseen events occur that force the parties to renegotiate the contract. The rash of large cost overruns on weapons contracts clearly indicates the amount of renegotiation.

Most contracts are let after *two-stage bidding.* In the first stage, the bidders present their *technical proposals,* including proposed designs and summaries of available facilities and personnel. These technical proposals are then evaluated, and the few firms that meet the requirements are asked to furnish *cost bids;* the contract is then awarded to the lowest bidder.

The government's main objective in defense contracting is to obtain the needed equipment at the lowest possible cost while allowing a reasonable profit for the prime contractor. The government defines as reasonable a 7 percent profit for production and a 10 percent profit for research. Actually the prime contractor's profit is much greater than this because his profit margin extends to those portions of the contract performed by subcontractors and because much of the capital equipment used in fulfilling the contract is government owned. In short, the actual profit earned is high enough to ensure that profits from defense contracts are fully competitive with nondefense activities.

Purchasing Policy

As previously indicated, purchasing is far more than order taking and order placing. Purchasing agents play an active role in many related areas, such as production, and their decisions have a significant impact on these areas.

Make-or-Buy Decisions

To illustrate the interaction between purchasing decisions and production, let us consider the so-called make-or-buy decision.

Whether to manufacture a component or to buy it is an ever-present problem that has far-reaching implications throughout the manufacturing process. The relationship is circular; production is affected by this decision, which in turn is influenced by the requirements of the production process. Theoretically, a firm can purchase any or all of the parts that go into its output of goods and services, and, conversely, any part that is purchased can be manufactured. Where such decisions involve capital investments that commit the firm over long periods of time, they are normally treated as questions of *vertical integration.* Only in cases that require little or no capital outlay and that bind the firm for only a short period of time is the term "make or buy" used.

Make-or-buy decisions depend partly on the dollar costs and partly on the intangible costs involved. With respect to the first factor, the objective is to determine which alternative is least costly. Basically this process requires a comparison between the cost of making a unit and the cost of purchasing one. For items that are presently being made, for example, the potential purchase price would be compared with the potential reduction in costs if production of this item were halted.

Although in theory all components can be made or purchased, in practice some material inputs are always purchased. Internal production of certain items may require special skills or processes that are essentially alien to a particular firm. For this reason, most electronic companies making portable radios purchase the plastic cases that cover them. Another factor discouraging the internal manufacture of an item is the capital investment required. A firm may decide that the "opportunity costs" are too high or, in other words, that the returns would be greater if the needed capital were applied to other investment opportunities. Considerations of this sort prompt the electronics manufacturers mentioned above to purchase the transistors required for their portable radios. Lastly, and perhaps most obvious, is the fact that the firm may not be able to manufacture the items economically in the quantities required. In any of these instances, however, if the purchase volume of any particular component goes high enough, the firm may alter its policy and begin to manufacture the component. A periodic review of make-or-buy decisions is vital to determine if any change in the volume or production process warrants a change in the situation. Some tire companies which, for example, used to purchase synthetic cord for their tires now manufacture the cord themselves. Automobile manufacturers, on the other hand, have found that it does not pay to manufacture tires even though large quantities of them are used.[7]

Other factors complicate the make-or-buy decision, however, since measurable costs are only part of the economic considerations. The manager is also concerned with intangible costs such as employment levels, work loads, and production schedules. Firms often make parts that could be purchased for less simply to keep their labor force occupied or to keep production processes in operation. Conversely, some firms purchase parts that could be made for less simply to maintain supply lines in order to ensure their future availability. Quantities of certain components that are presently being made internally are occasionally purchased externally because they can be obtained faster. This is frequently done to prevent work stoppages due to an absence of the component; in the long run it is cheaper to buy the parts (even though they are being manufactured internally for less) rather than have the production process stop. Similarly, when the work load is unusually high, some work may be "sent out" to obviate the need for hiring more labor or buying more machines than are normally needed. This practice is common in process areas such as heat-treating, painting, and special machining.[8]

Purchasing executives must work closely with production executives in arriv-

---

[7] The Ford Motor Company tried for a time to make some of its own tires but soon discontinued the practice because it did not pay.

[8] The make-or-buy decision extends to process operations as well as to the purchase of finished objects.

ing at make-or-buy decisions; it is impossible to make such decisions intelligently without weighing all relevant factors, since the results of these decisions will influence the entire production process.

Centralized or Decentralized Purchasing

In determining the most efficient method of purchasing, the management of any firm must choose between centralized and decentralized methods. The problem grows more acute as the firm becomes larger and more complex. A multi-plant, decentralized firm usually has a centralized purchasing department in the headquarters building, far removed from the individual plants. Such a purchasing arrangement allows for the procurement of goods in great quantities because of the pooling of individual plant orders. The small number of orders placed and the large size of each order make reductions possible in purchase prices and operating costs. The usual procedure is to pool individual plant demands, draw up a contract for the entire amount, and notify suppliers that the firm will accept bids for the contract. Purchased in this fashion, the price for a barrel of oil might be 10 percent less than what individual plants could obtain.

Another advantage of centralized purchasing is that it permits greater specialization among the firm's buyers. This, in turn, should lead to better buying and greater standardization of material inputs; it also enables top management to exercise closer control over these activities. Vertical specialization, called the *exception principle* of purchasing, is also possible. Not only can buyers be assigned to the purchase of narrow ranges, or families, of items, but they can be assigned authority to place orders measured by the dollar value of each requisition. In this fashion, routine, low-dollar-value requisitions can be processed by low-rank clerks in the purchasing department. The important, high-dollar-value "exceptional" requisitions can thus be referred directly to higher organizational levels where personnel presumably possesses correspondingly higher purchasing skills. The purchasing agent and his top subordinates can then devote most of their time to dealing with the really important requisitions. Reserving the best skills for the "most important buys" is not always feasible when the purchasing function is decentralized.

There are disadvantages to centralized purchasing, however. It tends to be slow, rigid and rule-bound, and very costly for low-value purchases. In addition, centralized purchasing departments are seldom able to take advantage of local conditions or to keep closely attuned to individual plant needs and inventory conditions.[9] This failing is particularly evident in follow-up actions required because of material defects, short shipments, and missed shipping dates.

In view of these limitations, most companies employ a mixture of techniques drawn from both centralized and decentralized purchasing arrangements. Those

---

[9] Computers have been making inroads in this area, however. The naval aviation supply records are centrally located for the entire United States, and therefore all purchases are centrally made. Many companies with computers and improved communications networks (for example, Westinghouse Electric Corporation) are also moving in this direction.

items requiring large expenses, high-level control, substantial quantity discounts, or special purchasing knowledge are handled centrally by the top men in the purchasing department; all other purchases are made locally. Our discussion applies with equal force to smaller single-plant firms. Most smaller companies also have centralized purchasing departments that handle the majority of material inputs bought. Where advantages can be obtained from decentralized arrangements (such as departmental purchasing), however, purchasing is partially decentralized.

Purchasing Approaches

The analytical methods used to determine order quantities are covered in the next two chapters. For the moment let us confine our discussion to general policy questions on the procurement of materials and simply say that decisions on order quantities are a function of the price and the time of the purchase. When prices are lower than expected, companies tend to stockpile an item; when prices are above expectations, companies tend to purchase only immediate needs.

There are four main purchasing policies followed in production firms with respect to time and price factors: hand-to-mouth buying, averaging down, forward buying, and speculative buying.[10]

Hand-to-mouth buying   In following a hand-to-mouth buying policy, items are purchased only to meet short-term requirements; the purchase of materials that are not immediately needed is deferred.

A hand-to-mouth policy is normally instituted when (1) prices are above average and are expected to fall, (2) prices are in the process of falling, or (3) there is uncertainty over prices or company requirements. The chief objective of the policy is to minimize the inventory losses that would otherwise result from falling prices; this is best achieved by keeping the inventory levels as low as possible. There is a certain amount of risk involved in such a policy, of course. If prices rise instead of falling, the cost to the firm of buying materials for future needs will also rise.

Averaging down   Averaging down on the market is a term describing the purchase of a portion of a firm's requirements at the moment when the market dips sharply in the course of a gradual price change. In many industries, prices rarely rise or decline evenly; instead they tend to follow a saw-toothed pattern such as that shown in Figure 13–6. The policy of averaging down tries to take advantage of price dips as they occur; if followed successfully, it should result in material prices that are lower than the market average for the period. It should be noted, however, that this approach is advisable only when the demand for the item is definite and when there is a good chance that prices will change.

Forward buying   When the purchaser forecasts his future needs and purchases the required goods in economic quantities to meet those needs, he is

---

[10] There is a notable similarity between these policies for the purchase of physical goods and policies followed in the stock and commodity markets.

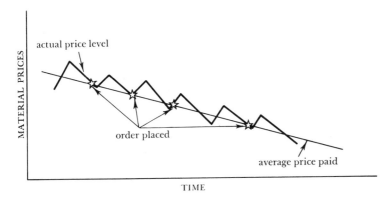

Figure 13–6   Averaging down on the market

following a policy of forward buying.[11] This approach is often used when prices are relatively stable over time or when only moderate price increases can be anticipated; quantities beyond immediate needs are bought in order to take advantage of economical large-volume purchases. If prices are expected to rise somewhat, material costs can obviously be reduced by buying in bulk before the rise.

Speculative buying   In speculative buying, quantities greater than usual are purchased in order to profit from rising prices. Here the objective is not only to have materials available for production but also to earn profits by buying cheap and selling dear. Speculation necessarily involves the risk of losses due to faulty judgment or to unexpected events that cause the price to remain stable or drop.

The magnitude of potential losses or gains and the nature of the risks involved in this type of speculation are such that these buying decisions are normally made at the highest company level. Some firms, such as egg wholesalers, make most of their profits in this fashion. In this type of industry, the chief executive is likely to spend most of his time as the firm's purchasing agent, and his ability to handle speculative purchasing is the major factor influencing the firm's profit picture. In a production-oriented company, however, speculative purchasing is not normally a function of the purchasing department; but when speculative opportunities arise, purchasing may alert top management to the fact. Of course, hand-to-mouth buying, averaging down on the market, and forward buying can all be considered speculation in the broad sense of the term. Each of these policies is an attempt to adapt purchasing to anticipated future price movements. But the main distinction between these three policies and truly speculative buying, as we have defined it, lies in the intent. Speculative buying seeks to make a positive profit by purchasing materials in anticipation of price rises; the other three approaches are more defensive in their orientation and seek to prevent or minimize losses that may occur because of unfavorable price movements.

---

[11] Most of the discussion on inventory in this and the next two chapters concerns this type of purchasing.

Special cases of speculative purchasing arise from time to time in manufacturing companies when they buy material inputs in quantities far beyond their ordinary purchasing needs. Such purchases are not aimed at making profits, however, but are designed to protect the firm against an anticipated stoppage in the lines of supply. A strike threat at a supplier's plant can trigger this type of action. If the stoppage does not occur, however, the firm may lose money because of the increased carrying costs of a large stockpile of material.

Reciprocal buying As the name implies, reciprocal buying agreements specify that one firm will purchase items from another firm and vice versa. It is difficult to set a hard and fast rule as to the advisability of such agreements. In many industries such as chemicals, where firms are said "to take in each other's wash," reciprocal buying is a common practice. Strong support for such agreements is often voiced because of the stability they create in sales and operations. Most purchasing agents are opposed to them, however, because of the rigidity and inflexibility such agreements impose on the purchasing process. It is argued that freedom in supplier selection and price negotiation is mandatory if the purchasing agent is expected to buy materials on the most favorable terms. Thus, it is crucial that top management weigh all the advantages and disadvantages of reciprocal buying agreements before entering into them. It is the purchasing agent's responsibility to present as clearly as possible the firm's material acquisition costs both with and without reciprocal buying agreements. In the final analysis, however, the specifics of a particular case, and not some principle, will determine whether a firm has such agreements.

Local buying To enhance their public image, some firms adopt a policy of local buying and play an active role in the affairs of the community. These decisions are most frequently followed by firms in small towns where the degree of industrialization and the general level of economic activity are relatively low. There is definite social merit in a decision to contribute to the stimulation of local business by buying needed materials from local suppliers. It should be recognized, however, that, like reciprocal purchasing, a policy of local buying restricts the ability of the purchasing agent to obtain the best buy for the firm; it places a damper on attempts to shop around for the best source. Here again it is necessary to weigh carefully the pluses and minuses of local buying, and each decision must reflect the specifics of a particular case.

The Inventory Problem

One of the major functions of materials management is to see that the right amount of input materials are available for the production process when they are needed. In order to do this, a firm must ordinarily stock, or inventory, the input materials. The question is: How much inventory should be held? If there is too little, the production process may stop because of a lack of raw material.

On the other hand, management does not want to carry too much inventory; surplus inventories are often termed the "graveyard" of American business and are thought to be one of the principal causes of business failure. The importance of avoiding surplus inventories is partially due to the increasing risk of obsolescence—the inevitable by-product of a highly competitive economy where the innovation rate has been steadily increasing. The risk of obsolescence is accentuated by a simultaneous increase in competition from such factors as the growing economies of large-scale operations and the high speed of communications and transportation, which together have literally transformed the United States into a single marketplace. In such an environment it is important that a firm remain flexible, and inventory, by its very nature, represents a tying-up of funds. Funds invested in material supplies or finished products are temporarily unavailable for other purposes. Thus, unnecessarily large inventories can introduce inflexibility and rigidity into a firm's operations; the unavailability of these funds may necessitate missed investment opportunities and possibly serious losses.

A broad but useful definition of *inventory* might therefore be: *an idle resource of any kind that possesses economic value.* Now let us examine inventory management in terms of flows of input into the inventory and withdrawals, or outputs, from it.

The basic inventory problem faced by any manufacturing firm is deciding on the appropriate quantity of resources to hold "idle in inventory" in order to maximize profits for the firm as a whole. Inventories are primarily composed of physical goods, but firms may also stockpile managerial and technical personnel, information, cash, production equipment, and building facilities.

Changes in the inventory levels of one asset will influence the firm's ability to hold inventories of other assets; capital tied up in finished goods, for example, cannot be used to purchase new equipment or raw materials. Conversely, an insufficient inventory of raw materials may cause an increase in the inventory of production equipment, as represented by idle production facilities. A slow-moving inventory will necessitate a larger amount of warehouse facilities, whereas a high turnover rate will reduce the extent of warehouse facilities required.

There are many different types of inventory problems, and they arise at all stages of the production process. In this chapter we are concerned primarily with the problems of raw materials and finished goods inventories. The principles underlying effective management of these inventories are generally applicable to other types of inventories.

The task of determining economic inventory levels faces all businesses at nearly every step in the production process. In the purchasing department the problem is to determine how much raw material to maintain, or how much to buy at a given time to take advantage of quantity discounts and to protect against the costs of holding the material. In the production area the question becomes one of determining how much process inventory to maintain for the separate successive stages of production. Similarly, the distribution function must establish what amount of finished goods should be maintained, and at what locations, to avoid running out of stock and incurring lost sales.

It is common practice to build up small inventories between phases of the production process to avoid chain-reaction stoppages. At top, rotary brushes are stored in roller boxes prior to a flat press operation (the finished product appears in the lower left foreground). At bottom, finished and partially finished machinery components are stored in pallet racks.

The Functions of Inventory

Many businessmen view inventories in an entirely negative sense, looking upon them as necessary evils that no one has been able to eliminate altogether but that should be kept at the lowest possible levels. A more positive view, however, is that inventory is an investment that should be held to a level consistent with the effective achievement of the purposes for which it was created. In other words, an inventory should meet the same criteria that are applied to other capital investments. Thus the earnings, the savings, and the intangible factors that may be expected to result from an investment in inventory should be balanced against the purchase price and maintenance expense of the investment. Before acquiring production equipment, for example, the expected savings in labor and material and the probable impact on working conditions should be compared with all the costs of the investment. Similarly, in the case of raw materials inventories, the cost of maintaining them must be compared with the savings that may be expected from a reduction in labor and machine costs (available material reduces the possibility of production stoppages); and management must also consider intangible factors such as the goodwill that may be produced by prompt and reliable deliveries.

One important reason why some businessmen have an exceedingly negative attitude toward inventories is that they apparently do not have an adequate understanding of the functions of inventories in a typical firm. Essentially, inventories are used to decouple, or separate, successive stages in the production and distribution process and also as a means of speculation.

Decoupling Production Stages

The most common use of inventories is for decoupling. Imagine, for example, two successive steps in a production process. If the first step should break down, and if there were no inventory between the stages, then the second would also be forced to shut down. To avoid such a waste, it is normal practice to build up small inventories between production stages in order to decouple the activities. The same reasoning applies to the relation between the production process and the distribution system. Finished goods inventories are used in part to insulate distribution from changes or breakdowns in production, thereby permitting an undisturbed flow of output to customers. Inventories thus enable the various stages in the production process and in the distribution system to operate more independently and economically than would otherwise be the case. To some extent, all the functions of inventory, with the exception of speculation, are simply extensions of this decoupling action, as we shall see in a moment.

Inventories facilitate intermittent production   Most manufacturing companies use the same facilities to make more than one type of product. The demand for any firm's product is rarely sufficient to justify single-product plants. Even huge oil refineries turn out a variety of chemical products in addition to oil and gasoline. Some plants, such as those in the hardware business, turn out literally thousands of different products from the same equipment; production runs are established for a given product and a stock sufficient to last until the next scheduled run is turned out. When this quantity of output is reached, the equipment is retooled and rescheduled for another product. Operations of this nature, featuring planned intervals in the manufacture of the firm's products, are labeled "intermittent production" processes because various products are made intermittently in lots and batches.

Here, the essential function of the stock, or inventory, is to coordinate demand and supply so that production can be accomplished economically. Separate and special machines are not required for each product, and the amount of each to be produced can be determined in an economic fashion.

Inventories cushion supply–demand dislocations   Another special case of decoupling is the separation of supply and demand. Predictions of the demand for products normally differ from the actual demand because of unforeseen factors and errors in estimation. Short-term fluctuations typically occur at random and thus preclude a direct matching of demand to supply. To cushion the effects of these random factors and to ensure a continuous flow of materials to the distribution system, firms normally maintain finished goods inventories. The size of these stocks is determined by the magnitude of the dislocations between supply and demand.

Inventories stabilize employment and production   Many industries are subject to seasonal or periodical fluctuations in the demand for their product. In order to maintain an adequate supply of skilled labor and to stabilize employment patterns in general, companies try to maintain production at a relatively consistent level by building up finished goods inventories during periods of low demand. A related example may be found in the research and development operations of some firms. During periods when contracts are not forthcoming, these firms maintain or stockpile their managerial and technical research talent in order to stabilize employment and lower dislocation costs. It is not customary to consider underutilized manpower as an inventory, but it certainly fits our broad definition—an idle resource awaiting demand. Furthermore, the decision process that determines the quantity of manpower held and the length of time it is held is substantially the same as the process that determines what level of material stocks will be maintained.

Firms use inventories to cushion their production facilities from all fluctuations in demand by maintaining an average level of output. Most firms do not equip themselves for peak or trough operations; if they were equipped for peak operations, there would be idle facilities much of the year, whereas if they planned for trough operations their ability to expand would be hampered. Thus, many firms concentrate on meeting total yearly demand by producing at a constant rate all year long. This enables them to utilize production facilities as efficiently as possible. During periods of low demand, more will be produced than needed and inventories will build up; the opposite will occur during periods of peak demand.

Inventories service customers Another important function of inventories is to ensure that products will be available in the marketplace in sufficient quantities so that customers will not have to wait for delivery. Using inventories in this way supports the sales effort significantly by enhancing the marketability of the product. Since the delivery date is a prime consideration in purchasing many products, the maintenance of inventory for rapid delivery will help sales considerably. In this respect, inventory acts as a kind of advertising and can be considered a similar type of investment. In many situations the product literally advertises itself by being available for the customer to see and perhaps examine, and the cost of this advertising is the expense of maintaining inventories at the point of sale.

Perhaps an extreme example of this use of inventory is the stock of goods used in the support of "impulse buying." Most retail stores make use of inventory displays to capture sales that the buyer had no intention of making before he saw the display.

The Speculative Motive

In volatile markets, such as commodities, speculation on inventories has become an accepted procedure. Firms in this market attempt to accumulate inventories at prices below what they feel they will be able to sell the commodities for in the future. To a lesser degree, the same practice is followed by manufacturing companies; steel purchases typically go up just before and during labor–management negotiations, for example. Part of the increased volume is bought in order to protect the purchasers against stoppages in the flow of materials, but part is also purchased for purely speculative motives. Purchasers may reason, for example, that one result of labor–management negotiations will be higher prices and that, as a consequence, they will profit by purchasing materials in bulk now at the lower price. Food processing is another area in which inventory price speculation plays an important role. In all of these areas, the ability of management to predict price fluctuations will often quite literally make the difference between profit and loss.

Although speculation is undoubtedly important in some industries, it is a highly specialized subject that does not properly fall within the domain of a text on production management.

Questions and Problems

1. Under what conditions would you consider purchasing to be a major business function that should report directly to the top echelon in an organization?
2. What are the advantages of centralized and decentralized purchasing, respectively?
3. What is meant by materials management? Why has this concept come into use in many companies?
4. What problems are created by a divided materials management in a firm?

5. What is value analysis? Who should carry it out?
6. What problems are involved in product specification?
7. What types of purchase contracts are used? Why is there such a variety? Be specific.
8. How does the make-or-buy policy of a company influence purchasing?
9. What is vertical integration?
10. What is averaging down? hand-to-mouth buying? forward buying? speculative buying?
11. Discuss the conditions under which you would (a) do forward buying, and (b) use only a few suppliers as sources of purchased material.
12. Do purchasing policies requiring written specifications, splitting of purchase orders, and reciprocity result in a narrow source of supply for purchased articles?
13. Must a purchasing director split orders or place an order with more than one supplier in order to get a competitive price?
14. The make-or-buy decision is a critical one. Evaluate an operating policy that provides for the purchase of all products, subassemblies, components, etc., that can be obtained at a price lower than the cost of internal manufacture.
15. A company that manufactures fifteen different sizes of tin cans is reviewing its policies regarding inventories and purchasing. What policies should the firm follow during a period of rising costs and prices and a declining or stable volume of sales?
16. "When a decision regarding possible backward vertical integration is made, the most significant factor to be considered is the contribution ratio." Discuss.
17. The Rodeo Distributing Company has opened a chain of drive-in hamburger stands along the East Coast. Their operations stress volume because the usual fare—hamburgers, hot dogs, prepackaged sandwiches, sodas, milkshakes, and soft ice cream—is offered for sale at low prices. Hamburgers and prepackaged sandwiches are made in the company plant located near Allentown, Pennsylvania.

The major items that the company purchases include ground meat, luncheon meats and cheeses, hot dogs, and various rolls and sandwich breads. Annual contracts have been negotiated with two large meat firms and three large bakeries for the procurement of these items. Milk is purchased from a local diary under an agreement that says that the company will take the dairy's entire annual production at the rates set by the state milk board. These rates vary by season and by the quality of milk.

Flavoring agents such as vanilla, chocolate, fruit syrups for ice cream, and other similar items are obtained from specialty houses. Each stand makes its own purchases and there is no company-wide policy, despite the fact that the prices for these items have proved to be highly volatile.

Operating supplies such as napkins, cartons, straws, and cups are also purchased locally. The company policy on these items restricts the inventory level to one week's supply or less since the delivery cycle for these items is one or two days. Each stand also handles soda and auxiliary food items such as ketchup and mustard on an individual basis.

The company recently signed a contract with a paper goods manufacturer to supply hamburger sandwiches and other products to the cafeterias operated in all of its plants. The company wishes to enter industrial distribution. The paper goods manufacturer now offers to furnish the company all the cups, plates, napkins, and other paper items it needs. Also, a newly formed bakery has offered to supply bread and rolls at a significant savings over the prices now paid for these items.

    (a) Develop a policy statement to govern each class of item the company now purchases.

    (b) There is a growing sentiment among the stand managers that more purchasing responsibility should be transferred to them. Do you advocate greater decentralization of this function?

18. Does reciprocal purchasing raise any ethical questions?
19. What are the advantages of centralized and decentralized purchasing to
    (a) A single hospital with fifteen requisitioning departments?
    (b) A group of eight regional hospitals?
20. Some chain food stores use a combination of centralized and decentralized purchasing for their grocery items, while in others purchasing is totally centralized. What items are likely to be purchased on a decentralized basis in the chains that allow it? Why would these items not be purchased centrally?
21. Indicate the various reasons why manufacturing organizations carry inventories, listing as many as you can. Why don't companies carry the largest inventories they have room to store?
22. In what way can inventories help to reduce cost? to increase costs?
23. "The only reason a firm carries inventory is to separate stages in the production and marketing cycles." Comment on this statement.
24. In examining the inventory planning and control system of a small firm (such as a garment manufacturer), there is apt to be relatively little in the way of formal procedure.
    (a) What are the important problems in inventory planning and control?
    (b) How is the absence of formal procedures dealing with these problems to be explained?
25. Why are inventories inevitable and subject to selection, choice, and manipulation?
26. "Minimum inventory should be the principal objective of production planning and procurement because this objective, if achieved, would provide the greatest operating profits." Discuss.

References

Aljian, G. W., *Purchasing Handbook,* 2nd ed., McGraw-Hill, New York, 1966.

Ammer, D. S., *Materials Management,* rev. ed., Irwin, Homewood, Ill., 1968.

Anyon, G. J., *Managing an Integrated Purchasing Process,* Holt, Rinehart and Winston, New York, 1963.

American Society of Tool and Manufacturing Engineers (ASTME), *Value Engineering in Manufacturing,* Prentice-Hall, Englewood Cliffs, N.J., 1967.

Cady, E. L., *Industrial Purchasing,* Wiley, New York, 1945.

Colton, R. R., *Industrial Purchasing: Principles and Practices,* Charles E. Merrill, Columbus, Ohio, 1962.

England, W. B., *Procurement,* 4th ed., Irwin, Homewood, Ill., 1962.

Hayes, F. A., and Renard, G. A., *Evaluating Purchasing Performance,* Research Study No. 66, American Management Assocation, New York, 1966.

Hodges, H. G., *Procurement—The Modern Science of Purchasing,* Harper and Row, New York, 1961.

MacNiece, E. H., *Production Forecasting, Planning and Control,* 3rd ed., Wiley, New York, 1961.

McElhiney, P. T., and Cook, R. I. (eds.), *The Logistics of Materials Management: Readings in Modern Purchasing,* Houghton Mifflin, Boston, Mass., 1969.

Miles, L. D., *Techniques of Value Analysis and Engineering,* McGraw-Hill, New York, 1961.

O'Brien, J. J. (ed.), *Scheduling Handbook,* McGraw-Hill, New York, 1969.

Westing, J. H., and Fine, I. V., *Industrial Purchasing,* 2nd ed., Wiley, New York, 1961.

Demand Forecasts

14

To gain further insight into the role of inventory in production management, we must examine its functions in the total production system. Inventory control is but one aspect of production planning and scheduling and must be integrated into the overall production system; it must also be closely coordinated with the company's financial and operating plans and policy structure.

Figure 14–1 illustrates a generalized view of a production system. The starting point in the system is the long-range market forecast, which is used to determine the optimum capacity of production facilities, the type of sales programs needed, the capital requirements, and the size of the labor force required. These decisions, in turn, influence inventory policy, since they determine the type of production process employed, the amount of funds available for inventory, the amount of storage facilities available, and the distribution system to be used.

Other company operating policies also affect inventories. The Scott Paper Company, for example, has a policy that attempts to minimize fluctuations in the company's employment level; thus, it must frame its inventory policy in a different light than a company without such a policy. Increasing pressure for steady employment levels has drastically changed the inventory policies of the automobile makers, too. In the past, when the costs of layoffs were low, auto companies tended to gear the level of their production more closely to actual demand. When demand went up, more workers were hired; when demand went down, workers were laid off. In this fashion the risks of inventory overage and

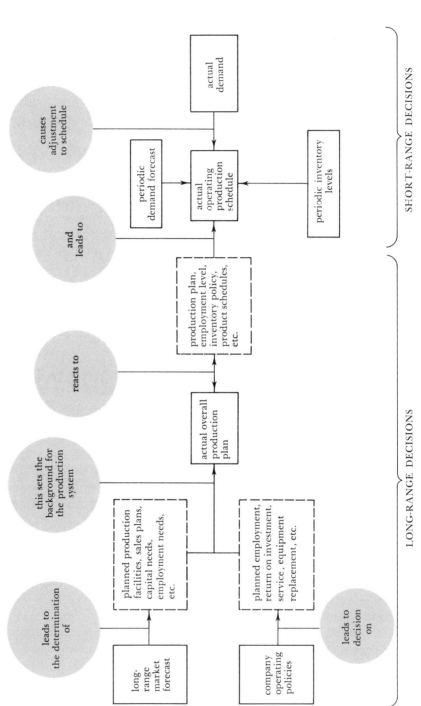

Figure 14–1 Generalized production system

inventory stockouts were held to a minimum. But now the cost of layoffs has increased, due perhaps to a Supplemental Unemployment Benefits Plan;[1] as a consequence, many manufacturers try to stabilize their employment level by "regularizing" production activity, and this has radically changed their inventory policy.

Thus, the overall production plan must be based on general company policies and the facilities available. Once this framework has been established, individual product manufacturing levels, employment levels by skills, and equipment and inventory levels can be determined. The starting point for all of these decisions is the product demand forecast for a specified period. This projected demand is examined in light of the current inventory level and the factors affecting production efficiency, and a new optimum level of product output is selected; then production schedules are planned.

Once production has started according to new schedules, the system must be constantly monitored. Actual production will rarely meet scheduled production exactly and, by the same token, does not normally match the demand forecasts precisely. Thus, to maintain an efficient operation, periodic short-term forecasts of demand are made, inventory levels are checked, and adjusted production schedules are formulated.

From this brief description of the production process, it can be seen that inventory management is but one phase of the overall system. A poor job of demand forecasting will lead to an ineffective production plan and to an inventory that is too large or too small. In the same sense, production activities that do not operate according to plan can bring about undesirable inventory conditions. In essence, it is the accuracy of forecasting that determines the success or failure of inventory management; therefore, for the remainder of this chapter, we will examine the process of making forecasts. This discussion should not be taken to mean, however, that production managers formulate demand forecasts. In fact, as a general rule, the sales, or marketing, department and occasionally the market research department is responsible for the performance of this function. Recently, such departments as operations research and management engineering have been called upon by more and more firms to help formulate demand forecasts, but this is still an exception to the rule. In any case, wherever demand forecasts are made, they are of vital interest to inventory management and to production management in general.[2]

Forecasting

Demand forecasts may be derived by means of a sophisticated analysis, or they may be the result of intuition. They may be hidden in the operating process, or they may be planned parts of the system. Whatever the case, forecasts play an

[1] Under this plan companies establish pools of money from which workers who are temporarily laid off are paid.

[2] Demand forecasts are needed for many management tasks. They are discussed at this point in the text because they are an intimate part of any inventory system. They will be mentioned again in most of the subsequent chapters of the text.

important role in inventory management; the question is not whether a forecast should or should not be made but rather if it will be suited to the task at hand. If a forecast is to be usable by production, it must meet the following conditions:

1. *The forecast must define expected demand in physical units.*
2. *The forecast should also include an indication of the probable variation around the expected demand, although, admittedly, such information is often very difficult to develop.*
3. *The forecast should be available in time to schedule all tasks required to achieve the necessary output.*
4. *The forecast must be made repeatedly during future periods to permit the necessary adjustments in production.*
5. *Finally, the forecast must be reliable because forecasting errors can cost considerable amounts of money.* Too large an inventory raises handling costs and increases the likelihood that the goods in stock will become obsolete. Too small an inventory inevitably leads to increased production costs.

No matter what method is used in making a forecast, however, some error will creep in; therefore, it is essential that inventory control systems be sufficiently flexible and responsive to change. Planning must provide for the accommodation of errors in the forecasts. The fact that any forecast will include errors should not lead management to take a "do nothing" attitude; in inventory control, "playing it by ear" would only mean that sound management policies for inventory did not exist.

The Forecasting Dilemma

Every manager who uses forecasts in planning operations faces one very fundamental dilemma, which can be expressed in the following two quotations:[3]

> *You can never plan the future by the past.*
> —EDMUND BURKE

> *I know of no way of judging the future but by the past.*
> —PATRICK HENRY

Both views are correct to a degree; the problem is to decide what weight should be given to each in any particular situation. The demand for output is uncertain and is caused by many factors. If management knew and completely understood the interactions between the factors that influence demand and those that influence production, it would be possible to build a precise predictive model. Even on a highly planned production line, however, the factors determining real output are not totally understood; breakdowns still occur, and inventories still fluctuate. Forecasts of demand, of course, are even less reliable. Nevertheless, even though the causal factors of demand are unknown, management can still create approaches that approximate reality.

---

[3] R. G. Brown, *Statistical Forecasting for Inventory Control* (New York: McGraw-Hill, 1959), p. 1.

What is Forecasting?

Forecasting may be defined as a technique for translating past experience into predictions of things to come. It requires making estimates of the magnitude and significance, both relative and absolute, of forces that will influence future operating conditions. Since the fundamental purpose of inventory management is to match resources with anticipated needs, the quality of forecasts makes a crucial difference. In this chapter we will examine the logic behind some of the many systematic approaches that have been found applicable to forecasting. Before embarking on this discussion, however, it is important to note that, in practice, forecasting is often very unsystematic and unscientific; intuition and hunch are still important forecasting tools. Indeed, the forecasting approaches employed by some managers appear to be little more than stargazing. These unstructured methods persist, however, because on occasion they have unaccountably produced predictions of high accuracy. It is impossible to teach intuition, but happily this is unnecessary since the systematic approaches in use today yield high probabilities of success in forecasting.

The Form of the Forecast

The form that a forecast takes will vary according to the use that is to be made of it. A total dollar volume estimate of demand may be sufficient for the sales department, but a total dollar amount will be of little use to production. In order to schedule labor, machine, and materials requirements, production must know the physical quantity of each product that will be required. Thus, forecasts designed for production use must be in physical units or in a form that may readily be translated into physical units.

Forecast time factors   The time span covered by any given forecast also depends on the use to which it will be put. Forecasts for the purchase of a new plant or new equipment must cover several years, whereas demand forecasts for planning future requirements in raw materials inventory, finished goods stocks, and employment may cover a week or only a day. Thus, it follows that firms must make a series of forecasts and that they must continually make new forecasts.

Forecast reliability   Forecasting is by definition an estimation of future prospects based upon incomplete evidence; therefore, it cannot be completely accurate. The application of forecasts must be tempered by the knowledge that deviations will exist. This will be true regardless of how complicated or precise the statistical methods used, but good procedures can reduce the magnitude of these deviations. Thus, good forecasts usually include not only the best estimate of the forecaster but also an estimate of the magnitude of likely deviations as a guide to the comparative reliability of the forecast. In order to set safety stocks, for example, inventory control must know the range of deviations that pertain to the forecast it is using. So it is in other types of planning, too.

Deviation is usually determined by first developing the best single estimate and then establishing limits above and below that indicate the range of deviations expected. The projected range of deviations can be determined intuitively by examining the actual historical deviations from period to period or by studying the accuracy of past estimates and then developing a statistical distribution of deviations. Each of these methods will be discussed after the common forecasting approaches have been analyzed.

Forecasting Approaches

Forecasting is a tricky and relatively experimental process. There are many different methods in use, and the appropriate one for a particular situation depends upon the nature of the firm, the products manufactured, the skills available, the information system in use, and the philosophy of management. Some forecasting techniques are routine and highly systematized; for example, the method used to forecast the heating oil needed by an oil distributor's customers. The distributor calculates the number of degree days that have elapsed since a user's tank was last filled. Degree days are a measure of cold and hence of the use of heating oil. To calculate degree days, the low and high temperatures during a day are added and then divided by 2, producing the average temperature. The average is then subtracted from a standard temperature, and the difference is the number of degree days. When the number of degree days since the user's tank was last filled reaches a certain figure, the tank is filled. This forecasting procedure is simple and can be followed in a mechanical fashion with little thought or intuition. Other approaches for gauging product demand in the face of dynamic competition from similar and substitute products are of necessity less systematized and generally more intuitive.

Executive Opinion and Educated Guess

One of the most widely used and influential forecasting techniques is the simple utilization of the opinions and intuition of management. There are varous methods of gathering these data. One way is to start at the top of a firm and ask each chief executive to make an independent estimate. Then, after these individual estimates are reviewed and discussed, they are converted by group judgment into a company estimate. Another approach is to start at the bottom and ask individual salesmen to make estimates of their customer demand. These estimates can then be reviewed and consolidated at each successively higher organizational level until a company consensus is worked out. Company budgets, which are forecasts of capital needs, are generally produced in this fashion.

There are various advantages to the "bottom-up" approach. First, it is not difficult to understand and use. Second, since virtually no specialized skills or tools are required, the cost is relatively low. Third, it makes direct use of the knowledge of all the people who work for the company, and this collective knowledge can be invaluable. Salesmen, who have close contact with customers, are an excellent source of information on the influence of advertising on sales. The fourth positive aspect of this approach is that the mere number of reviews is likely to preclude any far-fetched estimates and thus improve the accuracy of the forecast.

On the negative side, however, it should be rememberd that opinions and intuition are highly subjective. Personal estimates may be biased by the temperament of the individual, by his prejudices regarding past performances, or by opportunism. These estimates may also be biased because businessmen tend to give a disproportionate consideration to the most recent events. Thus, in a business downturn the future is apt to seem bleak, whereas in an upturn it seems rosy. This incomplete perspective is often termed the "weatherman's forecast"—an assumption that what is happening today will continue tomorrow.

One of the shortcomings in the bottom-up process is that individual opinion within the company is not given equal weight. The final estimate, although it has come through all the organizational channels, usually reflects the opinion of only one or two men at the top. This may or may not be bad, but it is not the result intended by the design of the system. Furthermore, the time required to process the review from stage to stage may be quite lengthy, which often precludes its use in periods when quick decisions are needed. The bottom-up approach is often used in combination with other techniques, however, to enable operating managers to participate in forecasting and to verify the findings of the other techniques.

Statistical Methods

Basically, all statistical approaches to forecasting project historical information into the future. This leads to the conclusion that the validity of the forecast depends upon the extent to which the past is representative of the future.[4]

When statistical methods are used, a specialist or a team of specialists is usually called upon to develop a statistical forecast, and then line executives adjust it according to their own predictions of future environmental changes. In this fashion, management feels that it is not blindly accepting the statistical information but rather enhancing it. To blend statistics and executive predictions most effectively, of course, management must have a basic understanding of the statistical procedures that are used, including their assumptions and their strengths and weaknesses.

Correlation analysis   One common statistical method of forecasting is called *correlation analysis*. This is simply the process of relating sales to other indices of economic activity, and it has long been used by businessmen. Some of the typical indices used for this purpose are railroad car loadings, new construction starts, automobile sales, the Index of Industrial Production (Federal Reserve Board), and the Gross National Product.

The ideal index is one describing a related activity that necessarily precedes

[4] This is just another way of expressing the dilemma noted at the beginning of our discussion on forecasting.

the activity to be forecast. This is termed a *leading time series*.[5] Statistics of new-car sales, for example, provide automobile-replacement-part manufacturers with a reliable guide to future demand. Similarly, the number of construction contracts let and construction starts are accurate guides for producers of building materials. Where such a relationship exists, the forecaster can readily obtain the information and utilize it while it is still timely. He must be sure that all of the pertinent known factors are considered, however. An increase in construction starts and contracts let may, by itself, be deceiving; a further breakdown into the type and location of the projects is usually required before an accurate picture can emerge.

If an index is to be useful, of course, it must come from a reliable source that furnishes frequent and up-to-date reporting. Moreover, there should be a *direct causal effect* between the index and the activity being analyzed. Certainly there is a causal relationship between new-car sales and the sale of auto replacement parts. But there are many things that have a noncausal correlation: the number of stork nests in Denmark was once found to have a high correlation with the number of births in Copenhagen![6] And there is a high correlation between the amount of money bet at the Kentucky Derby and the Gross National Product of the United States.[7] Such correlations are merely chance, however, and any conclusions based on such data are merely guesswork.

In the hands of experienced analysts, properly correlated relationships can be valuable indicators. In fact, many companies have found them to be the most reliable means available for forecasting.

There are two major steps in the development of a forecast using correlation analysis:

1. Construction of a curve that describes the relationship between the variables—a regression line.
2. Evaluation of how well the regression line describes the relationship between the variables—correlation.

In describing these steps, we will use simple linear correlation. This type of correlation analysis deals with the linear relationship between two variables. Correlation can also be used with nonlinear relationships and can handle more than two variables (multiple correlation).[8]

To illustrate the approach, consider the case of Modular Corporation, which sells metal cyclone fencing in a local area. Over time, the company has found that the volume of fencing sold is dependent on the amount of money earned (payroll) in its area. The figures for Modular's sales and the area's payroll for the years 1964–1971 are presented in Table 14–1.

---

[5] A time series is simply the history of an activity over time.

[6] G. U. Yule, "Why Do We Sometimes Get Nonsense Correlations Between Time Series," *Journal of the Royal Statistical Society,* Vol. 89, 1926, pp. 1–64.

[7] "Hot Tip," *Fortune,* August, 1958.

[8] We will use only simple linear correlation since it enables us to present the principles involved without having to confuse the issues with large amounts of calculations.

Table 14–1 Modular Corporation sales
and local payroll amounts

Year	Y *Sales* (in hundred thousands)	X *Local Payroll* (in hundred millions)
1964	6.10	1.36
1965	6.25	1.50
1966	6.40	1.62
1967	6.50	1.75
1968	6.64	1.82
1969	6.71	1.93
1970	6.80	2.02
1971	6.91	2.09

REGRESSION LINES These figures are plotted in Figure 14–2, with Modular's sales as a function of local payroll. In some instances, a freehand trend line such as the dashed line in Figure 14–2 may be all that is required to establish the sought-for relationship. In others, a less subjective trend line that can be statistically tested is desirable.

In those cases where two variables are present and where a straight line appears to fit the points (as in Figure 14–2), a least squares regression line is generally fitted. A least squares regression line is that line which comes closest to touching all of the points. Its name derives from the fact that the sum of the squares of the vertical distances between the line and the actual values is smaller than for any other straight line. A least squares regression line has another interesting property—the sum of the vertical distances from the actual values to the regression line is zero.

A least squares regression line is developed from the equation for a straight line,

$$Y = a + bX$$

In this equation, the dependent variable is Y. In our example, Y represents the amount of Modular's sales and X represents the independent variable, local payroll. The value of a gives the value of Y when $X = 0$. The coefficient b indicates the amount of change in Y for each unit change in X and is therefore equal to the slope of the line. b is called the *regression coefficient*. The properties of the least squares line can now be expressed as

1. The sum of the deviations of the observed Y values from the Y values of the regression line, Y_T, is zero:

$$\Sigma(Y - Y_T) = 0$$

2. The sum of the squares of the deviations of the observed Y values from the Y values of the regression line, Y_T, is a minimum:

$$\Sigma(Y - Y_T)^2 = \text{a minimum}$$

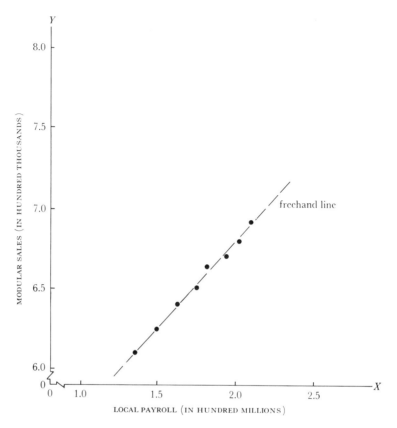

Figure 14–2 Scatter diagram of Modular Corporation sales as a function of local payroll

To fit a least squares line we must find the values for a and b that satisfy these properties.

THE NORMAL EQUATIONS   The a and b values that fit these properties are found through the use of the normal equations.[9]

$$\Sigma Y = Na + b\Sigma X$$

and

$$\Sigma XY = a\Sigma X + b\Sigma X^2$$

In these equations N equals the number of pairs of X, Y points. For Modular Corporation, $N = 8$. The X and Y values are the paired values for the independent and dependent variables.

SOLVING FOR a AND b To get the a and b values, we must solve the normal equations. To do this we need to find the values of ΣY, ΣX, ΣXY, and ΣX^2.

[9] The derivation of these equations can be found in the statistical references at the end of the chapter.

Table 14–2 Calculation of values for least squares regression line

Year	Y Modular Sales (in hundred thousands)	X Local Payroll (in hundred millions)	X^2	XY
1964	6.10	1.36	1.85	8.29
1965	6.25	1.50	2.25	9.37
1966	6.40	1.62	2.62	10.37
1967	6.50	1.75	3.06	11.38
1968	6.64	1.82	3.32	12.09
1969	6.71	1.93	3.73	12.93
1970	6.80	2.02	4.08	13.72
1971	6.91	2.09	4.37	14.45
	$\Sigma Y = 52.31$	$\Sigma X = 14.09$	$\Sigma X^2 = 25.28$	$\Sigma XY = 92.60$

These summations are developed tabularly in Table 14–2, which gives us the values

$$\Sigma Y = 52.31 \qquad \Sigma X = 14.09$$

$$\Sigma X^2 = 25.28 \qquad \Sigma XY = 92.60$$

Substituting these values into the normal equations yields

$$52.31 = 8a + 14.09b$$

$$92.60 = 14.09a + 25.28b$$

Solving the two equations simultaneously, we find

$$a = 4.71$$

$$b = 1.04$$

so that

$$Y_T = 4.71 + 1.04X$$

Given a forecast of $220 million for the 1972 payroll, our estimate for the sales in 1972 is[10]

$$Y_T = 4.71 + (1.04 \times 2.2)$$

$$= 6.99$$

THE VALUE OF THE ESTIMATE   The question that now arises is, Just how good is our sales estimate? This is a function of two conditions. First, how well does the regression line explain past variations? Second, will the past relationships hold true in the future? The second question must be handled subjectively, but a measure of the first can be developed statistically. This can be done by determining how much of the past variation in sales (Y) was attributable to the variations in payroll (X).

The total variation for the dependent variable Y is the sum of the variations

[10] On our freehand regression line, the sales value for a payroll of 2.2 was 7.01.

between the actual Y values and the mean of the Y values, $\overline{Y}$. Mathematically, this is $\Sigma(Y - \overline{Y})$.[11] The variation for a single value of Y is shown in Figure 14–3, where it is the vertical distance between $\overline{Y}$ and Y. The total variation has two components—explained and unexplained variations.

Explained variation is the variation explained by the regression line. It is computed as $\Sigma(Y_T - \overline{Y})$, where Y_T is the fitted Y value of the regression line. In Figure 14–3, the variation for the point Y is the vertical distance between Y_T and $\overline{Y}$.[12]

The unexplained variation is shown in Figure 14–3 as $Y - Y_T$. If the regression line passed through all of the actual values—that is, if it fit perfectly, there would be no unexplained variation.

COEFFICIENT OF DETERMINATION   With this background, we can proceed with the development of measures of goodness of fit. The ratio of the sum of the squares of the unexplained variation to the total variation,

$$\frac{\Sigma(Y - Y_T)^2}{\Sigma(Y - \overline{Y})^2}$$

gives the proportion of the total variation not explained by the regression line. One minus this proportion, then, is the proportion of the total variation that is explained by the regression line. This proportion,

$$1 - \frac{\Sigma(Y - Y_T)^2}{\Sigma(Y - \overline{Y})^2} \qquad \left[1 - \frac{\text{Unexplained variation}}{\text{Total variation}}\right]$$

is called the *coefficient of determination*.

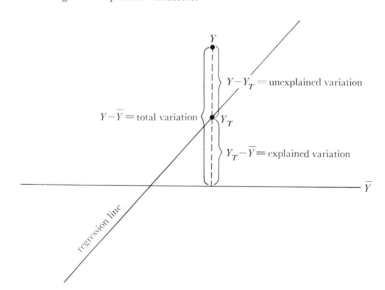

Figure 14–3   Correlation variations for a single point

[11] $\overline{Y} = \dfrac{\Sigma Y}{N}$

[12] Notice that if the slope of the regression line was 0 (i.e., $b = 0$), the line would be horizontal and none of the variation in Y would be explained.

Taple 14–3 Calculation of coefficient of correlation

Year	Y Modular Sales (in hundred thousands)	X Local Payroll (in hundred millions)	Y_T Fitted Trend Values	$(Y - Y_T)^2$	$(Y - \bar{Y})^2$
1964	6.10	1.36	6.12	0.0004	0.1936
1965	6.25	1.50	6.27	0.0004	0.0841
1966	6.40	1.62	6.39	0.0001	0.0196
1967	6.50	1.75	6.53	0.0009	0.0016
1968	6.64	1.82	6.60	0.0016	0.0100
1969	6.71	1.93	6.72	0.0001	0.0289
1970	6.80	2.02	6.81	0.0001	0.0676
1971	6.91	2.09	6.89	0.0004	0.1369
	$\Sigma Y = 52.31$	$\Sigma X = 14.09$		$\Sigma = 0.0040$	$\Sigma = 0.5423$

$$\bar{Y} = \frac{\Sigma Y}{N} = \frac{52.31}{8} = 6.54$$

$$r = \sqrt{1 - \frac{\Sigma(Y - Y_T)^2/(N - 2)}{\Sigma(Y - Y)^2/(N - 1)}} = \sqrt{1 - \frac{0.0040/6}{0.5423/7}} = \sqrt{1 - 0.0085}$$

$$= 0.99$$

COEFFICIENT OF CORRELATION   In practice, the square root of the coefficient of determination, the *coefficient of correlation*,

$$r = \sqrt{1 - \frac{\Sigma(Y - Y_T)^2}{\Sigma(Y - \bar{Y})^2}}$$

is used most because of the ease with which it furnishes an indication of the amount of explained variation. The coefficient of correlation can range between $+1$ and -1. When $r = 1$, the regression line passes through all of the actual values and all of the variation is explained. When $r = 0$, none of the variation in the dependent variable is explained by the regression line. Negative r values indicate inverse correlations.

For small samples,[13] r can be calculated from the expression

$$r = \frac{\Sigma(Y - Y_T)^2/(N - 2)}{\Sigma(Y - \bar{Y})^2/(N - 1)}$$

Values to solve for r for our example are given in Table 14–3. These calculations show a high correlation between sales and payroll, since $r = 0.99$. Squaring r to get the coefficient of determination, we find that $(0.99)^2$ or 98 percent of the variation in the dependent variable (sales) is explained by the regression line.

[13] In most instances, samples below 20 are regarded as small. Where the sample size is large, r can be calculated more directly by

$$r = \frac{N\Sigma XY - (\Sigma X)(\Sigma Y)}{\sqrt{N\Sigma X^2 - (\Sigma X)^2}\sqrt{N\Sigma Y^2 - (\Sigma Y)^2}}$$

CONFIDENCE LIMITS   How confident can we be that the correlation was not due to chance alone? In other words, how often would we expect to find this degree of correlation due only to chance? We realize that if we took a large sample our faith in the measure would increase, but how great a sample would we need, for example, to be 95 percent confident that our correlation did not result from chance alone? This question can be answered by Table 14–4, which gives values of r and N for the 95, 98, and 99 percent confidence levels. For sample size N, the value given for r must be exceeded if we are to be confident of the correlation.

For our example, $N = 8$ and $r = 0.99$. Table 14–4 indicates that for $N = 8$, we must exceed an r value of 0.834 to be at the 99 percent confidence level. Since our r value exceeds this, we can be highly confident that the correlation was not due to chance alone.

CAUSE AND EFFECT   Before we quickly accept the correlation, we must do some subjective evaluation. As stated earlier, a high correlation does not in itself establish a cause-and-effect relationship. It may occur because another factor is influencing both the independent and dependent variables. As an example, the prices of automobiles and replacement parts correlate very closely. However, this is due to other factors, primarily the cost of steel and labor. The field of forecasting is full of serious misuses of correlation that have led to serious forecasting errors. Where causal relationships have been developed, however, correlation analysis has rewarded its users handsomely.

In our example, if we are content that a causal relationship exists, the high correlation value would lead us to accept the regression line forecast of next year's sales.

Table 14–4   Values of N and R for selected confidence levels

N	*95 percent*	*98 percent*	*99 percent*
5	0.878	0.934	0.959
6	0.811	0.882	0.917
7	0.754	0.833	0.874
8	0.707	0.789	0.834
9	0.666	0.750	0.797
10	0.632	0.715	0.765
15	0.514	0.592	0.641
20	0.444	0.515	0.561
30	0.361	0.427	0.463
40	0.312	0.369	0.403
50	0.279	0.330	0.361
60	0.254	0.295	0.330
70	0.235	0.273	0.306
80	0.220	0.256	0.287
90	0.205	0.242	0.269
100	0.197	0.231	0.256

Time Series Analysis

In many industries, reliable leading time series are unavailable. Furthermore, short-run forecasts are required in many phases of production where the timing and rapidity of operations preclude the use of correlation techniques.

One of the most successful methods of making short-run forecasts is to extrapolate past historical demand. This is often done, for example, to make short-term adjustments in inventory or production levels. Since this approach depends on the projection of the past into the future, it has recognizable dangers. The best way to avoid the dangers is to have a thorough knowledge of what is involved in extrapolating a time series.

A time series is a history of the values of a variable over time. The forecast value, Y, for any time period is a function of four factors:

$$Y = T \times C \times S \times R$$

where T = underlying long-term trend. This is the pattern of change that exists over considerable periods of time.

C = cyclical variations. These are the wavelike fluctuations in the series due to general business conditions. The wave pattern does not necessarily repeat itself and is generally not the same for all industries or companies within an industry. Each product, company, and industry is affected differently by the general business activity.

S = seasonal variations. These are the changes that occur because of seasonal patterns. The patterns are normally repetitive.

R = residual or irregular variations. These are the variations that are not explained by T, C, or S. They are chance variations that normally cannot be forecast and are consequently a thorn in a forecaster's life.

The type of time series analysis that is used depends primarily on the nature of the data and the form of forecast required. In some cases, yearly or monthly forecasts that are projections of the underlying trend (with the S, R, and C factors removed) are needed. In others, the seasonal or cyclical pattern is what is wanted. We will concern ourselves with forecasting long-term trend, because this will develop the required understanding of time series forecasts.

Forecasting methodology The starting point in developing a trend forecast is to plot the data. The plot does not have to be extremely precise; what we are looking for is the general pattern of the data. The pattern will help in the determination of the best approach.

Figure 14–4 is a plot of the yearly sales of Argo Corporation. The data appear to follow a straight line. Management could draw a freehand line or fit a least squares trend line; either method would remove the C, S, and R components of the series, leaving the trend.

LINEAR LEAST SQUARES TREND A least squares trend line for a time series

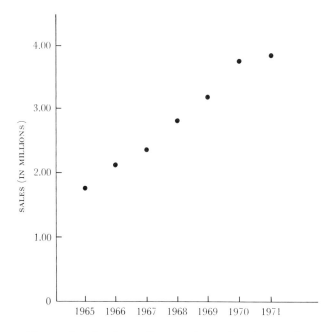

Figure 14–4   Argo Corporation sales time series

is calculated in much the same fashion in which the regression line was calculated for correlation. The only difference is that the X value is the number
of time periods from the base time period rather than the value of the independent variable. Since X equals the number of periods from the base year, the
calculations can be shortened by selecting the base year in the middle of the
time stream. Then $\Sigma X = 0$ and the other figures are easily calculated.

Table 14–5   Argo Corporation—linear least squares calculations

Year	Y Sales (in millions)	X Years from Base Year	X^2	XY	Y_T
1965	1.76	−3	9	−5.28	1.73
1966	2.12	−2	4	−4.24	2.10
1967	2.35	−1	1	−2.35	2.46
1968[a]	2.80	0	0	0	2.83
1969	3.20	1	1	3.20	3.20
1970	3.75	2	4	7.50	3.57
1971	3.80	3	9	11.40	3.93
	$\Sigma Y = 19.78$	$\Sigma X = 0$	$\Sigma X^2 = 28$	$\Sigma XY = 10.23$	

$$Y_T = 2.83 + .365X$$

[a] 1968 is chosen as the base year.

The calculations for a least squares trend line for Argo Corporation are presented in Table 14–5. From the normal equations,

$$\Sigma Y = Na + b\Sigma X \qquad\qquad 19.78 = 7a$$

$$\Sigma XY = a\Sigma X + b\Sigma X^2 \qquad\qquad 10.23 = 28b$$

Solving for a and b yields the trend line equation

$$Y_T = 2.83 + .365X$$

The forecast for 1972 is therefore

$$Y_T = 2.83 + .365(4)$$

$$= 4.29 \text{ million}$$

NONLINEAR TREND   The most commonly used trend lines are straight lines. This is due to the fact that generally they logically fit the data as well as the more complicated curves do. In addition, the calculation process for a straight line is relatively simple.

In some instances, however, straight lines will not do. A straight line implies that the trend will grow or decrease by a uniform amount each period. Some series do not grow this way. Money invested at compound interest, for example, grows at a uniform percentage rate, not by a uniform increment. This type of growth is exponential and would thus logically best be fit by an exponential curve. Some companies have developed computer programs that test series with various curves to see which fits best.

EXPONENTIAL LEAST SQUARES LINE   Nonlinear smooth curves are fit to time series by the same approach that is used for straight lines. To illustrate, we will fit an exponential curve to the Argo data.

The general equation for a curve of the exponential form is

$$Y = ab^x$$

This indicates that Y changes at the constant rate of b each time period. To fit a least squares curve we change the general equation to its logarithmic form

$$\log Y = \log a + x \log b$$

The corresponding normal equations are

$$\Sigma(\log Y) = N(\log a) + \Sigma x(\log b)$$

$$\Sigma(x \log Y) = \Sigma x(\log a) + \Sigma x^2(\log b)$$

These equations can be solved once we know $\Sigma(\log Y)$, Σx, $\Sigma(x \log Y)$, and Σx^2. This is done in Table 14–6. Since $\Sigma x = 0$, the normal equations become

$$\log a = \frac{\Sigma(\log Y)}{N} \quad \text{and} \quad \log b = \frac{\Sigma(x \log Y)}{\Sigma x^2}$$

Table 14–6 Argo sales and exponential least squares calculations

Year	Y Sales (in millions)	X	X²	log Y	x log Y	Y_T
1965	1.76	−3	9	.24551	−.73653	1.82
1966	2.12	−2	4	.32634	−.65268	2.08
1967	2.35	−1	1	.37107	−.37107	2.38
1968[a]	2.80	0	0	.44716	0	2.73
1969	3.20	1	1	.50515	.50515	3.11
1970	3.75	2	4	.57403	1.14806	3.57
1971	3.80	3	9	.57978	1.73934	4.08
	$\Sigma Y = 19.78$	$\Sigma x = 0$	$\Sigma X^2 = 28$	3.04904	1.63227	

$$\Sigma(\log Y) = 3.04904$$

$$\Sigma(x \log Y) = 1.63227$$

$$\log Y_T = 0.43556 + 0.05829x$$

$$Y_T = 2.73(1.1436)^x$$

[a] Base year = 1968.

Substituting the values from Table 14–6, we obtain

$$\log a = \frac{3.04904}{7} = 0.43556$$

$$\log b = \frac{1.63227}{28} = 0.05829$$

Taking the antilogs of log a and log b, we find that

$$a = 2.73 \text{ million}$$

$$b = 1.1436, \text{ an increase of } 14\% \text{ each period}$$

The trend equation can be stated in two ways

$$\log Y = 0.43556 + 0.05829x$$

or

$$Y = 2.73(1.1436)^x$$

The forecast for 1972 is 4.66 million.

In comparing the values from the straight line and the exponential curve, we find that in the early years both seem to do well. In the later years, however, the exponential overstates the sales at an increasing rate. This would lead a manager, unless he was optimistic, to select the linear trend line.

Moving Averages

Another way to determine a trend is to utilize the statistical technique of *simple moving averages*. Averages themselves are a common method of improving the accuracy of estimates. When making precise physical measurements, it is customary to take several measurements of a particular item and average them to determine the measurement of that item. In other words, the average is the best estimate since the averaging process effectively removes the random measurement errors.[14]

If one assumes that the market demand forces will remain constant over time, then the average of periodic measures of demand should be the best estimate of future demand. Furthermore, following this line of reasoning, the more periods included in the measurement the more accurate the estimate. In reality, however, we know that market forces do not remain constant. Therefore, a compromise between an average based on a great number of periods and an average based on only one or two periods is used to eliminate past data that are no longer relevant and yet retain sufficient data to produce reliable results. Thus, a period varying from six months to a year is usually used.

A six-month moving average is simply the sum of the demand during the past six months divided by 6. As each month passes, its data are added to the sum of the previous five months' data, and the earliest month is dropped off. In short, the moving average is a measure of trends during the previous six months and serves as an estimate of the next value in the series, which is the next month's demand.

Moving averages tend to smooth out short-term irregular and seasonal fluctuations in a series. If there is a temporary surge in the series, the average will increase by $1/N$ (or $1/6$ for a six-month moving average) of the surge. This increase will continue to be recorded in the average for N months. Thus, the larger the number of months in the average (N), the smaller the overall increase.[15]

Consider, for example, the demand for bedroom suites experienced by a small furniture manufacturer from January to June. Table 14–7 shows the total number of suites sold each month during the period. Using a simple moving average, the sales forecast for the next month would be 89 units. The smoothing effect of the moving average approach is evident when this figure is compared with the number for each month in the series. When July's demand is known, it can be added to the sum of the demand and January's value dropped off.

There is one major flaw in the simple moving average, which can be illustrated by rearranging the data presented in Table 14–7. Table 14–8 shows that the simple moving average would yield a projected sales volume of 89 units for both series. It is obvious from the data, however, that this figure understates the demand for bedroom suites in one case and in the other overstates it. The cause of this distortion is the smoothing factor built into a simple moving average, which makes the average lag behind trends. By obscuring marked short-term trends of this sort, a moving average can do the company a serious disservice.

Weighted moving averages Because of this flaw in simple moving average analysis, adjustments are usually applied to make the technique more responsive

---

[14] If a measurement *bias* exists, averaging will not remove it because, by definition, a bias will appear in all the values averaged and therefore in the result.

[15] The same principle applies for a sudden decline in the series, with the average decreasing by $1/N$ of the decline.

Table 14–7 ABC Furniture Manufacturing Company—
six-month demand schedule for bedroom suites

Month	Number of Bedroom Suites Sold
January	65
February	93
March	85
April	105
May	71
June	115
	$D = 534$

$$\text{MA (moving average)} = \frac{\Sigma D}{N} = \frac{534}{6} = 89 \text{ suites per month}$$

where ΣD = sum of demand values
       N = number of demand values in sum

Table 14–8 ABC Furniture Manufacturing Company—
rearranged six-month demand schedule
for bedroom suites

Month	Arrangement 1	Arrangement 2
January	65	115
February	71	105
March	85	93
April	93	85
May	105	71
June	115	65

to trends. One such adjustment is the addition of a version of the method of least squares. This modification weights the data of individual months so that the most recent ones receive the highest weights. Since months are weighted positively and negatively in terms of their distance from the middle of the series, an odd number of months is normally used to avoid fractions.

To illustrate this approach, let us examine the data shown in Table 14–9, which represent the sales volume of the same ABC Furniture Manufacturing Company for dining-room suites for each month of a seven-month period.

A simple moving average forecast for this period would be $(\Sigma D)/N = 266/7 = 38$ suites. It can be seen at a glance, however, that this figure does not reflect the trend of the data; therefore, we apply an adjustment factor.[16] This

[16] The adjustment factor is actually a numerical value for the slope of the regression, or "least squares," line, which runs through the midpoint of the series, in this case the April figure.

Table 14–9 ABC Furniture Manufacturing Company—weighted moving average data for dining-room suites

Month	Number of Dining-Room Suites Sold	Weighting Factor	Weighted[a] Demand	Square of Weight Factor
January	20	−3	−60	9
February	24	−2	−48	4
March	30	−1	−30	1
April	34	0	0	0
May	45	1	45	1
June	52	2	104	4
July	61	3	183	9
	$\Sigma D = 266$		$\Sigma WD = 194$	$\Sigma SW = 28$

[a] The weighted demand is obtained by multiplying the sales for each month by the appropriate weighting factor. Thus, for January the demand of 20 suites is multiplied by the weighting factor −3 to produce the weighted demand −60.

factor is calculated by dividing the sum of the weighted demands by the sum of the squares of the weighting factors. Thus, for the data in Table 14–9, the slope of the line is

$$S \text{ (slope)} = \frac{\Sigma \text{ WD (weighted demand)}}{\Sigma \text{ SW (squared weights)}} = \frac{194}{28} = 6.9$$

Now we can calculate the expected sales in any month as follows:

$$\text{ED (expected demand)} = \frac{\Sigma D \text{ (demand)}}{N \text{ (number of months)}} + S(N_i)$$

where N_i = number of months from the base month (April, in this case)

Thus, sales for August, which is four months from April, will be

$$\text{ED} = \frac{\Sigma D}{N} + S(N_i)$$

$$= 38 + (6.9)(4)$$

$$= 65.6$$

Graphically, the relationship of average demand to adjusted average demand for the data in Table 14–9 is illustrated in Figure 14–5. The superior correlation between the weighted average and the actual demand can readily be seen.[17]

The calculations required in making a forecast with adjusted moving average data may be expressed in a series of formulas. Notice that the process helps to minimize the sum of the squares of the errors between the actual demand and

---

[17] Since the trend line is assumed to be a straight line, this method will not be satisfactory for nonlinear trends. In such cases, second and higher degree curves must be used. For short-range forecasts, however, a straight line is usually satisfactory.

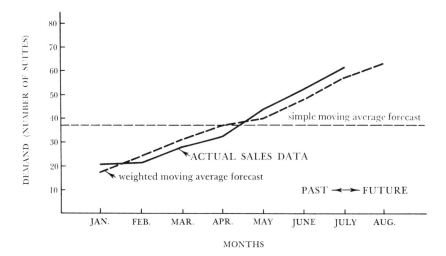

Figure 14–5 ABC Furniture Manufacturing Company—adjusted and unadjusted moving average demand forecasts

the computed line. The slope of the regression line represents the estimated magnitude of the trend.

If D_n = demand during period n
   D = total demand
   N = number of periods

then the total demand may be calculated as follows:

$$D = \sum_{n=1}^{N} D_n$$

We have already said that the average demand (AD) is obtained from the expression

$$AD = \frac{D}{N}$$

The weighted average demand can be expressed by the general equation

$$\Sigma\, WD = \frac{N-1}{2}\, D_n + \frac{N-3}{2}\, D_{n-1} + \frac{N-5}{2}\, D_{n-2} + \cdots$$

$$+ \frac{N - (2N - 1)}{2}\, D_{n-N+1}$$

Using the same nomenclature, the formula for the sum of the squares of the weights is

$$\Sigma\, SW = \left(\frac{N-1}{2}\right)^2 + \left(\frac{N-3}{2}\right)^2 + \left(\frac{N-5}{2}\right)^2 + \cdots + \left[\frac{N - (2N - 1)}{2}\right]^2$$

The slope (S) of the trend, or regression line, that may be applied to these data is the ratio of the weighted average demand to the sum of the squares of the weights:

$$S = \frac{\Sigma\ WD}{\Sigma\ SW}$$

All of these formulas may then be combined into the following formula for the demand forecast for any month:

$$ED = \frac{D}{N} + S(N_i)$$

where N_i = number of periods from the center or base period

Moving averages, both simple and weighted, have many characteristics that make them valuable forecasting tools. They effectively smooth out abrupt fluctuations in the demand pattern and thus provide stable estimates of demand. The stability of their response to change can be adjusted by altering the number of periods included in the average.

The major problems in using moving averages are the necessity of keeping extensive records of past data and the difficulty of changing the rate of response.

Simple exponential weighting Another approach, designed to overcome the limitations of moving averages, is called exponential weighting. It does away with the necessity of keeping extensive records of past data and permits the rate of response to be easily adjusted. As with other moving averages, it is able to screen out irregularities in the demand pattern.

The fundamental concept of exponential weighting is quite simple. The new estimate of average demand is equal to the old estimate adjusted by a fraction of the difference between the old estimate and the actual demand:

$$\text{New estimate} = \left(\begin{array}{c}\text{Old est. of latest}\\ \text{actual demand}\end{array}\right) + K\left(\begin{array}{c}\text{Latest actual}\\ \text{demand}\end{array} - \begin{array}{c}\text{Old est. of latest}\\ \text{actual demand}\end{array}\right)$$

The factor K is called a smoothing constant; it can be changed to adjust the formula's rate of response to current data, as we will discuss in a moment.

To facilitate its use, the equation is generally rearranged to read

$$\text{New forecast} = K\left(\begin{array}{c}\text{Latest actual}\\ \text{demand}\end{array}\right) + (1 - K)\left(\begin{array}{c}\text{Old estimate of latest}\\ \text{actual demand}\end{array}\right)$$

A forecast made in this fashion is a form of moving average. Each new forecast represents the sum of the previous weighted forecasts. This may be expressed algebraically when

d_0 = actual demand during the last time period
d_1 = actual demand during the period before the last
d_2 = actual demand during the second period before the last
K = a smoothing constant ranging between 0 and 1

Thus, the formula for estimating the new average demand becomes

$$\text{New forecast} = (1 - K)d_0 + (1 - K)Kd_1 + (1 - K)K^2d_2 + \cdots + (1 - K)K^n d_n$$

Notice that the terms further removed from the present in time carry less and less value, since the number $(1 - K)K^n$ becomes smaller as n increases; thus, greater weight is automatically given to current periods.

Adjusted exponential weighting This simple form of exponential weighting has its disadvantages, however. Like the simple moving average, it does not track trends in demand very well. Nevertheless, exponential weighting is relatively easy to adjust for trends, by calculating the current trend. The current trend is equal to the difference between the average demand for the latest two periods:

$$\text{Current trend} = \left(\begin{array}{c}\text{Average demand}\\\text{for the last period}\end{array}\right) - \left(\begin{array}{c}\text{Average demand for}\\\text{the period before last}\end{array}\right)$$

The average trend adjustment may then be calculated in the same fashion as the new estimate of average demand:

$$\text{New average trend} = K\left(\begin{array}{c}\text{Current trend}\\\text{adjustment}\end{array}\right) + (1 - K)\left(\begin{array}{c}\text{Old trend}\\\text{adjustment}\end{array}\right)$$

The next step is to combine this formula with the projected average demand in order to derive a forecast that is adjusted for trend.

The following formula corrects the simple exponential average for trend effects, just as the least squares correction adjusted the simple moving average for trend effects.

$$\text{New forecast demand} = \left(\begin{array}{c}\text{New average}\\\text{demand}\end{array}\right) + \frac{1 - K}{K}\left(\begin{array}{c}\text{New average}\\\text{trend}\end{array}\right)$$

The results obtained by this method depend to a great extent on the value selected for the smoothing constant K. If K is valued above 0.5, the estimated demand will tend to correlate with the actual demand fairly well because the time series data are so highly interrelated. This relationship can be seen from the equations: a high value for K gives greater weight to current values than to past ones. Conversely, a low value for K gives greater weight to past values than to current ones. Thus, it follows that for cyclical data a low-value K will yield the most accurate forecast, whereas high-value K will be best for data in which a trend is thought to exist.

An example may help to clarify this discussion. Let us return for a moment to the ABC Furniture Manufacturing Company. Suppose this company wishes to improve the demand forecasting shown in Table 14–9 by use of exponential smoothing. The first and most important question it must answer is What value of K will result in accurate demand projections for its dining-room suites? The most practical approach to resolving this question is a simple trial-and-error process. As data are accumulated, many values of K are employed, and the forecasts resulting from each K are checked against actual experience as it is recorded. In this way the most suitable K for the demand for dining-room suites may be determined. Even if this approach is not used, however, the value selected for K should be subject to periodic review so that significant shifts in demand can be taken into account.

Now, let us say that the ABC Company applied values of 0.1, 0.2, 0.3, 0.4, 0.5, and 0.6 for K and recorded the results for seven months as shown in Table 14–10. A value of 0.6 was selected as most accurate, based upon data for these first seven months. The firm arrived at this decision as follows. During the month of January, 20 dining-room suites were sold. Since no prior sales records were available, the figure for new average demand was 20. During February, 24 suites were sold; therefore the new average demand, using a K of 0.1, became

$$\text{New average demand} = K(\text{New demand}) + (1 - K)(\text{Old average})$$
$$= 0.1 \times 24 + 0.9 \times 20$$
$$= 20.4$$

The current trend was

$$\text{Current trend} = \text{New average} - \text{Old average}$$
$$= 20.4 - 20$$
$$= 0.4$$

Therefore, the new trend became[18]

$$\text{New trend} = K(\text{Current trend}) + (1 - K)(\text{Old trend})$$
$$= (0.1 \times 0.4) + (0.9 \times 0.0)$$
$$= 0.04$$

Then, combining the new average and the new trend, an expected demand was derived

$$\text{Expected demand} = \text{New average rate} + \frac{1 - K}{K}(\text{New trend})$$
$$= 20.4 + \left(\frac{1 - 0.1}{0.1}\right)0.04$$
$$= 20.8$$

Continuing this process, the company was able to compile the data shown in Table 14–10.

By comparing the actual sales shown in the "demand" column with the "next period forecast" column, the company found that low-value K's tend to track the trends slowly but that fluctuations in actual demand are heavily modified, thus producing a steady forecast.

The firm then tested the results with successively higher values of K, as shown in Table 14–10. Clearly, a value of 0.6 provides the most accurate forecast.

---

[18] The second term reduces to zero because there was no old trend information.

Table 14–10   Demand forecast data with exponential weighting

Month	Demand	New Average	Current Trend	New Trend	Next Period Forecast
		K = 0.1			
January	20	20	0	0	20
February	24	20.4	.4	.04	20.8
March	30	21.4	1.0	.14	22.7
April	34	22.7	1.3	.26	35.1
May	45	24.9	2.2	.45	29.0
June	52	27.6	2.7	.67	33.6
July	61	30.8	3.2	.92	39.1
		K = 0.2			
January	20	20	0	0	20
February	24	20.8	.8	.16	21.4
March	30	22.6	1.8	.49	24.6
April	34	24.9	2.3	.85	28.3
May	45	28.9	4.0	1.48	34.8
June	52	33.5	4.6	2.10	41.9
July	61	39.0	5.5	2.78	50.1
		K = 0.3			
January	20	20	0	0	20
February	24	21.2	1.2	.36	22.0
March	30	23.8	2.6	1.03	26.2
April	34	26.9	3.1	1.65	30.8
May	45	32.3	5.4	2.77	38.8
June	52	38.2	5.9	3.71	46.9
July	61	45.0	6.8	4.64	55.8
		K = 0.4			
January	20	20	0	0	20
February	24	21.6	1.6	.64	22.5
March	30	25.0	3.4	1.74	27.6
April	34	28.6	3.6	2.48	32.3
May	45	35.2	6.6	4.13	41.4
June	52	41.9	6.7	5.16	49.6
July	61	49.5	7.6	6.14	58.7
		K = 0.5			
January	20	20	0	0	20
February	24	22	2	1	23
March	30	26	4	2.5	28.5
April	34	30	4	3.25	33.2
May	45	37.5	7.5	5.37	42.9
June	52	44.7	7.2	6.28	51.0
July	61	52.8	8.1	7.19	60.0

(continued)

Table 14–10   (continued)

Month	Demand	New Average	Current Trend	New Trend	Next Period Forecast
			$K = 0.6$		
January	20	20	0	0	20
February	24	22.4	2.4	1.44	23.3
March	30	27.0	4.6	3.34	29.0
April	34	31.2	4.2	3.86	33.5
May	45	39.5	8.3	6.52	43.4
June	52	47.0	7.5	7.11	51.3
July	61	55.4	8.4	7.88	60.1

Other Means of Time Series Analysis

What has been presented does not exhaust the ways in which time series can be analyzed. Complex curves and series can be fit. Probability and cobweb models can be developed. What has been shown here is a reasonable picture of the field. The footnotes and the readings listed at the end of the chapter refer to publications where more sophisticated models can be found.

Estimates of Forecast Variations

We have said that if a business is to plan and control its inventory effectively, management should have an indication of the variations that can be expected for any forecast in addition to the forecast of average demand. For this reason, management needs probability measures of demand deviation; they are as vital to proper inventory control as the averages themselves. Averages alone can only provide an indication of the projected level of demand. But by knowing the level *plus* the range of possible deviation above and below this level, management can better select its inventory position.

There are many reasons for variation in demand; some are beyond the control of management and must be accepted as they are. All variations may be classified in one of two general categories: those that are due to random factors and have no pattern, and those that have a pattern. For firms that have seasonal or cyclical sales patterns, for example, the forecasting procedure must be adjusted to allow for these factors in the estimate of average demand. But other demand variations for which no pattern can be found are considered to be random.

Now, let us consider how to forecast the range of random variations. Instead of discussing all of the various techniques available, let us simply examine two typical examples. The first is the variability in a simple moving average forecast and the second is the variability in a least squares adjusted moving average forecast and least squares regression line.

Variations in a simple moving average   Let us look again at the demand schedule in Table 14–7, where the sales of bedroom suites in successive months amounted to 65, 93, 85, 105, 71, and 115. The moving average, you will recall, was 89. Thus, assuming that there is no trend and that causal factors remain stable, the forecast of sales for the average following month is 89 bedroom suites. How accurate is this prediction? The management will want to know the probable error of this forecast, and the best way to determine it is to apply statistical methods to the data available.

The best estimate of the probable error in this average forecast is the *standard deviation* of the forecast; the formula for computing it in this case is[19]

$$S_x = \sqrt{\frac{\Sigma(x - \bar{x})^2}{n - 1}}$$

where x = individual monthly demands
$\bar{x}$ = average demand
n = number of periods included

Hence, in terms of the data in Table 14–7, we have

$$S_x = \sqrt{\frac{(65 - 89)^2 + (93 - 89)^2 + (85 - 89)^2 + \cdots + (115 - 89)^2}{6 - 1}}$$

$$= 19.3 \text{ units}$$

Once a value has been determined for the standard deviation, it is possible to establish the probable limits of variation around the average forecast figure. To derive this figure, however, management must first determine how often it wishes its estimate of actual demand to fall within the limits set. If management wishes the actual figure to fall within the estimated limits 95 times out of 100, it will add two standard deviations to both sides of the average. Thus, in our example the upper limit would be $89 + 2(19.3)$, or 127.6, and the lower limit $89 - 2(19.3)$, or 50.4. If management would like to be correct 99.7 times out of 100, it must add three standard deviations to both sides of the average figure.[20]

If there are no changes in demand, this measure of variation will not have to be calculated again; the same average forecast and forecast of variation can be used. If there are changes in demand, however, a new moving average and a new range of variations must be worked out; the calculations followed in the example must be repeated.

Variations in a least squares adjusted moving average and least squares regression line[21]   Statistical methods can also be employed to estimate standard deviation ranges for random variations in cases where least squares adjusted moving averages or regression lines are developed to forecast demand. To illustrate this approach, consider the sales data for dining-room suites presented in

[19] The underlying assumption here is that the normal distribution can be applied without introducing significant errors.
[20] These values come from the normal distribution.
[21] The method is the same for both cases.

Table 14–9. The demand during successive months is listed as 20, 24, 30, 34, 45, 52, and 61. Using the method of least squares, a trend line was plotted for this demand, whereby the estimate for any month was 38 + 6.9 times the number of periods from the middle month.[22] The dispersion of the actual demand points about this line is assumed to be due to random movements. To measure the variation that exists around the trend line, the following formula is used:

$$S_{xt} = \sqrt{\frac{\Sigma(X - X_t)^2}{n - 2}}$$

where S_{xt} = standard error of estimate
  X = demand for a period
  X_t = estimated demand for a period from the trend line
  n = number of demand periods

$$S_{xt} = \sqrt{\frac{(20 - 17.3)^2 + (24 - 24.2)^2 + (30 - 31.1)^2 + \cdots + (61 - 58.7)^2}{7 - 2}}$$

$$= \sqrt{\frac{29.88}{5}}$$

$$= 2.44$$

The S_{xt} figure here is similar to the S_x figure calculated in the previous example except that the limits are drawn about a regression line and not about an average demand. The figure 2.44 can be used to establish probable limits for the variation in estimated demand for dining-room suites for the next month.[23]

Forecast Information Needs

The validity of any forecasting method depends to a great degree on the accuracy and timeliness of the information on which the forecast is made. This is particularly true for statistical methods, because the results are simply extrapolations of past data. Therefore, the sooner accurate information on past demand periods can be made available, the better the forecast will be.

Information concepts and information systems have recently become the subjects of increasing study by business and government. With accurate and timely information it is possible to gear inventory variations quite closely to fluctuations in real demand. Hence, an important aspect of the design of an inventory system is the information network that furnishes data on which inventory decisions are made. This interaction between the operating system and the information system can be found in all aspects of production within a company.

[22] This line with the equation $y = 38 + 6.9t$ passes through the middle month of the series, which is zero weighted.

[23] Control charts to check the forecasts can be developed. This approach will be discussed in the quality control chapters. For an explanation of control charts used for forecasting, see Riggs, J. L., *Production Systems*, Wiley, New York, 1970.

Questions and Problems

1. How does sales forecasting relate to inventory control?
2. What are the requirements of a sales forecast for inventory control?
3. "An accurate sales forecast is the secret to successful day-to-day scheduling or production." Comment on this statement.
4. Management has been described as the art of compromise. What is the nature of the compromise that applies to forecasting and inventory control?
5. What is the essence of time series analysis?
6. How do moving averages smooth short-term fluctuations in a series?
7. What are the advantages and limitations of exponential weighting?
8. What limits the use of simple moving averages and exponential weightings?
9. The monthly sales volume in dollars for the Beta Company last year was as follows:

January	$210,000	July	$384,600
February	248,600	August	361,100
March	305,700	September	373,900
April	408,100	October	424,400
May	373,800	November	289,400
June	365,800	December	201,200

Its product sold for $20 through June and for $25 for the rest of the year.
   (a) Using a simple moving average, plot the forecast sales volume for the next six months.
   (b) Will a weighted moving average lead to better forecasts? Why?
   (c) Calculate and plot the weighted moving average forecasts.

10. The Delta Company's forecast sales (in units) for this year are as follows:

January	4,000	July	10,000
February	4,000	August	10,000
March	5,000	September	8,000
April	6,000	October	5,000
May	7,000	November	4,000
June	7,000	December	4,000

   (a) Using a simple exponential weighting, develop the forecast for the next month.
   (b) Do the same with an adjusted exponential weighting.
   (c) What adjustment factor did you use? Why?

11. What types of variations in forecasts do the moving averages and exponential weighting consider? What type of variation is not considered?
   (a) What is the best measure of the probable error in a forecast?
   (b) Using this measure, establish limits of variation for Problem 9 for simple and adjusted moving average forecasts.

12. Which are better for inventory control, dollar or quantity forecasts?
13. Product A is in its period of rapid sales expansion. "For purposes of forecasting the short-run demand for this product, the use of a weighted moving average would be most meaningful." Discuss.

14. What effect do the following have on work force costs and inventory costs?
    (a) A high reaction adjustment rate in revising actual to forecasted sales.
    (b) A short review period for making such adjustments.
15. Assume that you are the administrator of a hospital and have been called upon to forecast the need for beds during the next five years. How would you go about preparing the forecasting?
16. The monthly history of automobile accidents for a particular city is shown below

January	500	July	487
February	508	August	495
March	494	September	515
April	481	October	470
May	498	November	490
June	485	December	510

   (a) Fit a linear trend line to the data and develop a forecast for January.
   (b) What is the coefficient of correlation, and what does it mean?
   (c) Fit a nonlinear trend line to the data and develop a January forecast.
   (d) Using a six-month moving average, develop a forecast for January.
   (e) Determine a forecast for January using exponential smoothing.
   (f) Compare the various forecasts. Which do you feel is best? Why?
17. The monthly demand for a product is listed below.
   (a) Prepare forecasts using three different forecasting approaches.
   (b) Why did you select the methods you used?
   (c) Which method gives the best forecast? Why?

MONTH	1970	1971	1972	1973
January	45	83	133	163
February	86	61	104	120
March	84	107	158	125
April	60	93	113	131
May	93	129	105	85
June	91	105	119	144
July	114	81	83	139
August	97	99	123	93
September	77	76	117	159
October	89	93	73	154
November	48	111	148	168
December	95	54	133	142

References

Acton, F. S., *Analysis of Straight-Line Data,* Wiley, New York, 1959; paperback edition, Dover, New York, 1966.

Bratt, E. C., *Business Cycles and Forecasting,* 5th ed., Irwin, Homewood, Ill., 1961.

Brown, R. G., *Smoothing, Forecasting and Prediction of Discrete Time Series,* Prentice-Hall, Englewood Cliffs, N.J., 1963.

Brown, R. G., *Statistical Forecasting for Inventory Control,* McGraw-Hill, New York, 1959.

Ezekiel, M., and Fox, K. A., *Methods of Correlation and Regression Analysis,* 3rd ed., Wiley, New York, 1959.

Frank, R. E., Kiehn, A., and Massey, W., *Quantitative Techniques in Marketing Analysis,* Irwin, Homewood, Ill., 1962.

Lapin, L. L., *Statistics for Modern Business Decisions,* Harcourt Brace Jovanovich, New York, 1973.

L'Esperance, W. L., *Modern Statistics for Business and Economics,* Macmillan, New York, 1971.

Williams, E. J., *Regression Analysis,* Wiley, New York, 1959.

Winters, P., "Forecasting Sales by Exponentially Weighted Moving Averages," *Management Sciences,* Vol. 6, No. 3, April 1960, pp. 324–342.

Wonnacott, T., and Wonnacott, R., *Introductory Statistics for Business and Economics,* Wiley, New York, 1972.

15

Inventory Control Systems

In the preceding chapters we examined various types of inventory problems and looked briefly at how the sales forecast, the most important source of data for inventory management, is made. In this chapter we will consider some of the common solutions to these inventory problems and the theories on which these solutions or control systems are based.

Inventory Costs in the Purchase of Goods

To analyze and solve inventory problems, management must deal with the various costs associated with inventories. Let us consider initially the costs that arise in attaining and maintaining inventories of *purchased* goods such as raw materials needed for production and finished goods stocked for sale.

Procurement Costs

The most obvious costs are those involved in the acquistion of the inventory, including the expense of such clerical operations as filing and reviewing the requisitions, processing the purchase orders, checking the incoming vouchers, and paying the bills. The important feature of these costs is that they are "one-time costs" and therefore may be treated like fixed costs. The larger the order quantity, the smaller these costs become on a per-unit basis because the entire expense of the order is spread over more items.

This economy factor encourages buyers to place a few large orders rather than many small ones, and they receive further encouragement by the trade practice of *quantity discounts*. Firms that purchase materials in large quantities are usually able to obtain a reduction in the unit price of the items. These quantity discounts presumably reflect cost reductions to the supplier in the form of lower handling, shipping, clerical, or manufacturing costs.[1]

Inventory Carrying Costs

The second major category of costs are those associated with carrying the inventory itself such as capital costs, handling and storage costs, spoilage and shortage costs, insurance and tax payments, and systems costs.

Capital costs   As with any other asset, inventories require capital investment. Funds allocated to inventories are not available for other uses; therefore, the opportunity cost is determined by the alternative use to which the funds could be put. If the firm has alternative uses for the capital that would return 8 percent, for example, then the capital cost of the inventory is 8 percent.

Handling and storage costs   The facilities required to store an inventory produce costs such as rent, heat, and light. Often storage facilities are available and have no alternative use; in that case, the costs of storage are fixed and do not vary with the inventory level. Beyond a given amount of inventory, however, these costs will begin to increase as more items are put in stock. At the point when storage costs begin to rise, they begin to influence decisions on the optimum inventory level.

The same considerations apply to handling costs. Normally, these are fixed. On occasion, however, special cases arise in which the per-unit handling costs fluctuate with the size of the inventory. This may occur because of overcrowding, which restricts mobility, because of inefficient stocking, or because less desirable warehouse space is used.

Spoilage and shortage costs   Many products deteriorate over time in storage. The precise nature of the deterioration varies from product to product, but whatever the cause, it represents a reduction in the company's assets and, as such, is a cost of holding inventories. This is termed the *spoilage cost*.

A common type of spoilage cost occurs when stock is left in inventory after the demand for the product has vanished. This can occur with varying degrees of severity. At one extreme, the cost is the sum of all further expenses required for carrying the unsalable item when the demand ceases. A classic example of this situation is the Christmas trees that are still unsold after the holiday season; they have virtually no further economic value, and their full purchase cost must be written off as a loss. This danger is shared by most forms of perishable in-

---

[1] Most such discounts are subject to legal restraints to ensure that the discounts are in fact due to scale economies and not simply the result of the economic strength of the purchaser. To guard against such monopolistic practices, the law requires all buyers to be offered the same discount opportunities and the discounts to be offered within reasonable reach of all customers.

ventory. In less extreme cases, such as women's fashion items, the value of the inventory may drop substantially at the end of the season, but some residual value can be recouped by selling the items at reduced prices.

Another type of spoilage cost occurs when products deteriorate physically in storage. Food products, for example, spoil when they are stored too long. Consequently, the value of the inventory is reduced by the amount of spoilage. Furthermore, since the quantity of available inventory is reduced, shortages and possible stockout costs may be incurred.

There are many other ways in which inventories may shrink and spoilage costs arise. In retail department stores, for example, reductions in inventory due to pilferage vary from 2 to 10 percent per year, which can represent a significant cost to the firm. Poor record-keeping, breakage, and loss can also cause expensive shortages.

Insurance and taxes Because inventories often represent a significant investment of a firm's capital, conservative management practice calls for insurance protection. Naturally, the cost of this insurance will vary according to the size and the value of the inventory. The same is true of taxes. Some states levy inventory taxes, for example, on various dates throughout the year; the more inventory a firm has on hand on those dates, the higher their tax bill will be. Where such taxes are in effect, prudent inventory management may dictate periodic reductions in inventory to coincide with the dates on which the assessments are made.

Systems costs One final type of inventory holding costs remains to be discussed—those associated with the administration of the inventory system in use, such as information-gathering costs, supervision costs, physical-stock-checking costs, and record-keeping-equipment costs. It is difficult to determine whether these expenses will be high or low except by making a comparison among actual inventory systems.

Many firms have found, for example, that on low-cost items it is less expensive and more efficient to do away with strict accountability; this is true for small hardware items that are usually stocked without separate records for each unit. Conversely, expensive items are checked thoroughly by use of individual records. Obviously, the cost of this approach is substantially below that required for maintaining strict accountability on all items.

Stockout Costs

A company also experiences a cost, called a *stockout cost,* if its supply of goods runs out before the demand for the product is satisfied. There are two types of stockouts. The first occurs if an item is not available for sale or to meet the production schedule but can be obtained through an emergency procedure. In this case the customer or production department receives the goods, but the supplier incurs the added cost of making them available quickly so that the sale will not be lost or the production line stopped.

In the case of finished goods, if an item is not available and cannot be obtained by emergency procedures, the seller has lost a sale. Often he loses more than that. At first glance this type of stockout cost might appear to be simply the loss of profit that would have resulted from the sale. On closer inspection, however, it becomes apparent that the customer's goodwill may have been lost, too. If the customer goes to a competitor for the item, he may continue going there in the future. Clearly, this cost is difficult to assess, but it is often considered to be a large sum. Some firms feel so strongly about avoiding this type of cost that they offer the customer substitutes of greater value than the item requested, or they may purchase the item from a competitor themselves and furnish it to the customer at a loss.

When an item is not available to the production department, it may mean that an entire production line must be shut down. If this happens, idle labor and machine costs as well as start-up and shutdown costs will be incurred. Both of these costs are generally easier to calculate than those of a lost sale.

Inventory Costs in the Supply of Goods

Up to this point in the discussion we have considered only the inventory costs of purchasing goods. Suppliers of goods also have inventory costs. Production managers must not only control their purchased-goods inventories to meet the demand at the input side of the production process, they must also control their inventory of work-in-process and finished goods to meet the demand at the output side. Many of the expenses of building and maintaining inventories of purchased goods are the same as those required for finished goods, such as holding costs and stockout costs. Other inventory costs, while they are not the same, are directly parallel; setup costs, for instance, are to the supplier what procurement costs are to the purchaser.

Setup Costs

Costs incurred by the supplier at the start of a production run in setting up the equipment or adjusting it to manufacture the product are termed *setup costs*. They also include the clerical costs arising from expediting, scheduling, and producing the shop order and from preparing the necessary shipping documents. For a given production method, these costs are relatively fixed, so that the unit cost of the setup drops as the size of the production lot increases. These savings are exactly comparable to those of the purchaser with respect to procurement costs. In fact, one reason for discounts to the purchaser on large orders is the lower setup costs of the supplier.

Production Costs

Some inventory costs faced by the supplier do not exist in the purchase of goods: overtime costs, labor-turnover costs (hiring, training, and layoff), and material start-up costs. Production management must also cope with these.

Overtime costs   Overtime costs may at times be a significant factor in determining inventory policy, and changes in overtime costs may sometimes be the result of inventory policy. Firms that try to keep finished-goods inventories at minimum levels may wind up with sudden spurts of overtime production when the item is needed to meet demand quickly. Conversely, a desire to avoid overtime operations may dictate periodic production for inventory during regular work hours.

Hiring, training, and layoff costs   Because the direct and indirect costs of hiring, training, and layoff are considerable, a firm may decide to produce temporarily for inventory rather than incur these added labor expenses. The direct costs of hiring include advertising, interviewing, testing, training, and the clerical operations that support each activity. The indirect costs are often found in the decreased efficiency of operations during the training period. If it becomes necessary to lay off workers, the direct costs will include increased unemployment insurance payments, separation pay, and the associated clerical activities. Indirect costs can accrue from a reduction in employee morale with its resultant decrease in productivity. Moreover, valued employees may be fearful about the security of their own jobs and leave the organization for other employment.

Material start-up costs   In most cases, material costs are constant per unit of production output, regardless of the number of units produced. On occasion, however, the number of units of output that do not meet specifications at the start of a new operation is greater than during the remainder of the production run. This happens frequently in the manufacture of precision gears, where the exacting specifications of the product demand top performance from both man and machine. Until the worker develops the skill needed to meet the specifications consistently, he must follow a sort of trial-and-error procedure that results in a high number of rejects at the beginning. Consequently, if a product is manufactured intermittently in small lots to avoid a large inventory, the total number of rejects will be higher because of the increased number of start-ups than if long production runs were utilized. In short, the added material costs of many short production runs and small inventories should be balanced against the cost of maintaining a larger inventory.

Inventory Models

Now that we have discussed inventory costs, let us see how production managers attack the problem of deciding how many units of a given item should be purchased or produced for stock at a given time.[2] Large-quantity purchases enable management to reduce the order-placing costs incurred in a given period. Buying in bulk also makes it possible to take advantage of quantity discounts and lower handling and shipping costs. On the other hand, the purchase of large

[2] The following discussion will consider the problem first in terms of purchases and then in terms of production; the logic is the same in both cases. By changing *purchase* to *produce* and *order cost* to *setup cost,* the analysis is adapted to production.

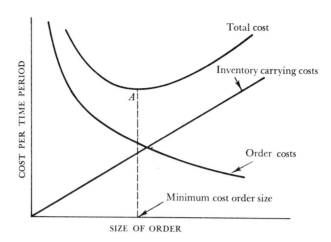

Figure 15–1 Order size–cost relationships

amounts of materials at one time raises the inventory carrying charges because of the increased size of the average inventory maintained.

Therefore, the inventory manager must weigh probable reductions in order costs against probable increases in inventory carrying costs in determining optimum purchase quantities. The relationship between these costs is shown graphically in Figure 15–1. Here we see that since order-placing costs are largely independent of the size of the order, these costs go down as the order size is increased because fewer orders are placed. Meanwhile, however, inventory costs increase as the size of the order grows.

To illustrate the relationship between these costs, let us consider the case of a plumbing-supply house that sells approximately 1,000 pipe valves of a given size and type each year, with little variation in monthly sales volume. If this firm orders valves from the manufacturer in quantities of 100, both the maximum inventory level and the average stock of goods on hand during the year will be lower than if the order size were 500. As a consequence, inventory costs such as storage, insurance, and interest, which vary directly with inventory level, will be lower. On the other hand, ordering 100 valves at a time means that ten orders must be placed, whereas only two orders are needed for an order size of 500. Since there are economies that pertain to large orders such as quantity discounts, lower order-placing costs, and lower receiving costs, a balance must be struck between inventory carrying and ordering costs. In short, the most economical order size for this firm, which will result in a minimum total annual inventory cost, will reflect a "compromise," or accommodation, between the two cost patterns. This compromise occurs at the lowest point on the total cost curve (*A*) shown in Figure 15–1.

Economic Lot and Order Quantities

As a starting point for our analysis of inventory control systems, let us examine some models that illustrate how economic order size is determined.

Suppose that a manufacturer estimates that he will need 18,000 transistors of a particular type over the period of a 200 work-day year, or 90 transistors per day, in order to maintain the daily production rate that his output requirements dictate.

Let us designate the variable costs associated with obtaining the transistor as follows:[3]

C_1 = cost of holding one unit of inventory for one unit of time ($0.10 per unit per year)
C_3 = ordering cost ($100 per order)

From our previous discussion we know that management now faces two major decisions:

1. How often should transistors be ordered?
2. How large should each order be?

For the sake of convenience, let us also assume that

D = total demand (18,000 units per year)
t = time interval between orders
T = total period (one year)
Q = order quantity

Figure 15–2 is a graphic presentation of the basic elements of this inventory example. It is assumed in this simplified model that orders are placed at fixed periodic intervals equal to t and that the materials ordered are instantaneously received. The amount ordered is designated as Q, which is equal to the rate of usage multiplied by the interval between orders. The average inventory held throughout the year would be $Q/2$, as illustrated by the dashed line; therefore, the cost of holding the inventory is $C_1(Q/2)$. Since the number of orders to be placed in a year is D/Q, the yearly ordering costs are $C_3(D/Q)$. We can compute total annual inventory cost by simply adding these two expressions:

$$\text{Total cost} = C = \frac{C_3 D}{Q} + \frac{C_1 Q}{2} \quad \leftarrow \text{total cost}$$

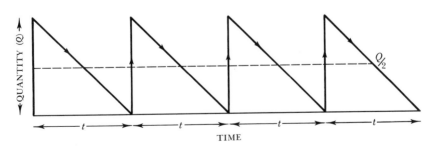

Figure 15–2 A graphic inventory model

[3] C_2 is generally reserved for stockout costs.

$FLS = economic$ $lot\ size$

Since C (total cost) is a function of Q (the order size), standard techniques of calculus can be used to determine what size Q will result in a minimum C. The technique is to differentiate C with respect to Q and then to equate the resulting mathematical expression, or derivative, to zero. Solution of this equation will provide the desired definition of Q. Differentiating C with respect to Q, we have

$$\frac{dC}{dQ} = -\frac{C_3 D}{Q^2} + \frac{C_1}{2}$$

How often to order

$$\frac{\text{Demand p/y}}{\text{EOQ}}$$

Then, equating this derivative with zero, we have

$$0 = -\frac{C_3 D}{Q^2} + \frac{C_1}{2}$$

And working out the solution for Q gives

$$Q = \sqrt{\frac{2 C_3 D}{C_1}}$$

Now, by applying this equation to the data in our example, we can obtain the most economical order quantity.[4]

$$Q = \sqrt{\frac{2(\text{Purchase cost} \times \text{demand})}{\text{carrying cost}}}$$

$$Q = \sqrt{\frac{2 \times 100 \times 18,000}{0.10}}$$

Carrying costs? exclusive per unit cost of purchasing cos carrying charges.

$$= \sqrt{36,000,000}$$

$$= 6,000 \text{ units}$$

Thus, we are able to derive the number of orders per year:

$$\frac{D}{Q} = \frac{18,000}{6,000} = 3$$

As a result, we find that the time between orders will be four months, or 66.6 work days. By substituting these values in the total cost equation, the minimum inventory cost is

$$C = 100 \times 3 + \frac{\$0.10 \times 6,000}{2} = \$600$$

Limitations of the basic model   The economic order quantity model and its equations are relatively easy to understand and apply. Ordinarily this is highly desirable, but here it seems to have led to many misapplications and poor results. Apparently managers have lost sight of the assumptions underlying the model and, because of its simplicity, have used it indiscriminately to answer all types of inventory problems. As a consequence, countless errors have been made, and the losses incurred, although by nature "hidden," must have been substantial. It is important, therefore, to review the assumptions upon which the economic

---

[4] This formula for determining the economic order quantity, or the economic lot size, was first worked out by F. W. Harris in 1915 and is still used for certain inventory problems.

order quantity model is based; with reference to the one shown in Figure 15–2, the assumptions are:

1. *Demand.* It is assumed that the demand for the period is precisely known and, furthermore, that the usage rate is constant.
2. *Acquisition.* It is assumed that depletion of the inventory results in an instantaneous placement of the replenishment order and that the materials ordered are received and available for use at that very same instant.
3. *Costs.* It is assumed that material costs, or prices, are constant regardless of quantity ordered. Inventory carrying costs such as insurance, storage, and interest are also assumed to be constant and independent of inventory level. In addition, order-placing costs are treated as a constant for the period without regard to the size or value of the order, and outage costs are assumed to be infinite.

In practice, inventory situations that meet such rigorous specifications are rare indeed. There are, however, enough situations that are sufficiently close to warrant some limited application of this basic model, such as inventories of standard items that have a relatively small dollar value and are used in large amounts— for example, stationery, office and factory supplies, and common hardware items. The demand for such items can be predicted quite accurately by an experienced purchasing agent. In addition, ordering and pickup can be easily and quickly accomplished; often all that is required is a phone call or a trip to a local store or warehouse. Finally, the outage cost of these items, measured in frustration, delay, and embarrassment, far exceeds their value.

Another very practical reason for using the basic model for these items is that their low dollar value doesn't warrant the use of more sophisticated inventory models. "Error costs" are usually relatively small and insignificant within the context of the cost profile of the purchasing firm. As a consequence, management is generally satisfied with the approximate results that the basic model can provide quickly and inexpensively.

Uses of the basic model　In applying the basic inventory model, many companies utilize various procedures and techniques designed to minimize the time and cost of calculations and thus permit rapid determination of proper order quantities. *Order tables* and *nomographs* are among the most common techniques used for this purpose.

ORDER TABLES　Firms that stock standard, low-cost items find it profitable to use order tables, one of which is shown in Table 15–1. These tables stipulate optimum order quantities of various demand rates and order costs. The quantities listed are based upon estimated and fixed order-placing costs and warehousing costs, which are usually shown either as a percentage of the purchase cost or as fixed sums that vary according to the type of item and the size of the order.

To illustrate how an order table is used, imagine a company that allows its branch offices to purchase stationery items directly from an office-supply firm on open account. The home office wants its branches to purchase these items in economic order quantities. It costs \$15 to process an order. Inventory costs for stationery items are \$0.10. To simplify the order-writing process, the company develops an order table with demand expressed in dollars instead of in units. This is done for two reasons: (1) stationery is normally ordered in this fashion, and (2) this method underscores the actual cost of purchasing the item.

To calculate the economic order quantity when the demand is expressed in dollars, the formula may be modified as follows:

$$Q = \sqrt{\frac{2C_3 \times \text{Yearly usage in dollars}}{C_1}}$$

For items such as stationery, where it is more convenient to visualize demand on a monthly rather than a yearly basis, a further change can be made in the formula:

$$Q = \sqrt{\frac{12 \text{ (months)} \times 2C_3 \times \text{Monthly usage in dollars}}{C_1}}$$

Applying this modified equation to our example, we have

$$Q = \sqrt{\frac{12 \times 2 \times 15 \times \text{Monthly usage in dollars}}{\$0.10}}$$

or

$$Q = 60\sqrt{\text{Monthly usage in dollars}}$$

In this fashion a table, such as Table 15–1, can be calculated for various demand rates. The user matches the projected need for the item in dollars (the left-hand column) with the opposite column to see how much of the item should be ordered. The same table can be used, of course, for all items and classes of items that have the same carrying costs and ordering costs. By the same token, a family of such tables can easily be developed for various carrying and ordering cost patterns.

Table 15–1   Stationery items order-cost table[a]

Monthly Use (in dollars)	Order Quantity (in units)
1	60
2	85
5	134
10	189
20	269
50	424
100	600
200	850

[a] Order cost = \$15; holding cost = \$0.10.

NOMOGRAPHS   Another common labor-saving method that is widely used to facilitate application of the basic inventory model is the nomograph. Many kinds of nomographs are currently in use.[5] To illustrate the basic concept of this technique, let us consider a typical nomograph as shown in Figure 15–3. When this chart is used to calculate the economic order quantity, a line must first be drawn connecting the order cost with the quantity used per year.[6] Then this line is continued until it crosses the reference line. From this point another line is drawn to the cost of holding the item in the far right column. Where this line crosses the "quantity to order" column gives us our answer. If the ordering cost were $20, if 3,000 units were used per year, and if the cost of holding one unit for one year were $5, lines would be drawn on a nomograph as shown in Figure 15–3. The economic order quantity in this case would thus be about 1,200 units.

Although it is somewhat more difficult to use this type of nomograph than to use order tables, it is simpler and quicker than calculating each order quantity separately. Furthermore, one nomograph can be used for calculations at varying demand rates, ordering costs, and holding costs.

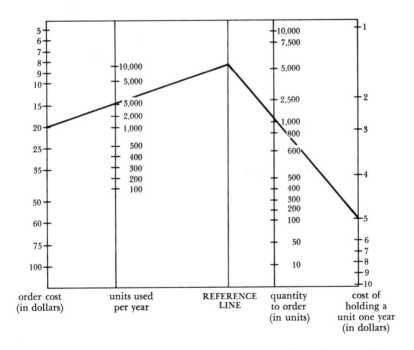

Figure 15–3   Nomograph for selecting economic order quantity

[5] The construction of various types of nomographs for inventory purposes is discussed in W. E. Welch, *Tested Scientific Inventory Control* (Greenwich, Conn.: Management Publishing Corp., 1956).

[6] This nomograph may also be presented in terms of units per month in demand and order quantity. It could just as easily have been prepared in terms of dollars, however, or with a different time base.

Adaptations of the basic model   Some of the rigorous assumptions implicit in the basic economic order quantity model can be modified and relaxed to broaden its area of application. In the following discussion, the assumptions regarding reorder time, replenishment cycle, and constant prices (no price discounts) will be modified in an attempt to make the model conform more closely with actual inventory dynamics.

REORDER TIME   One of the most serious limitations of the basic model is its assumption of instantaneous replacement of inventory. The number of situations in which instantaneous replacement is feasible are rare indeed. If, however, the materials being ordered have a fixed lead time for delivery, and if all ordered materials arrive at the same time, the fundamental concepts of the basic inventory model apply with no change. All that is necessary is to determine the point at which the order for new stock should be issued each period; this point may be specified in terms of the quantity of remaining inventory or as a point in time. Suppose, for example, that in our previous transistor example 10 work days of lead time are required before an order can be filled. This means that 10 times the daily usage of transistors ($10 \times 90 = 900$) must be in stock when the order is placed, or that the order must be placed $66.6 - 10 = 56.6$ days after receipt of the previous order. Figure 15–4 illustrates graphically how the reorder-point technique applies to the basic economic order quantity model.

For deterministic models of this sort, where the demand is known and constant and where there are no variations in supply, the time period between orders is equal to t, or the length of time that the materials ordered will remain in stock. Since the demand and supply factors are known, periodic orders can be scheduled and placed without a daily monitoring of the inventory level. Periodic monitoring of inventory is required, however, to determine if the rate of demand (as reflected in the depletion rate) has changed; when such changes do occur, the inventory control plan can be redesigned accordingly.

NONINSTANTANEOUS REPLACEMENT   To show how the basic inventory model can be adapted to conditions of noninstantaneous replacement, let us shift for a moment from the inventory problem of the purchaser to the inventory problem of the producer, that is, from economic order quantity to economic lot size.[7]

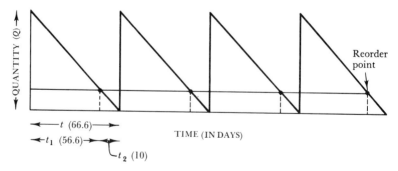

Figure 15–4   An inventory model with fixed reorder points

[7] This is the amount of output to be produced in one production run.

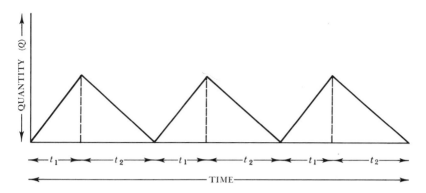

Figure 15–5 An inventory model showing noninstantaneous replacement

In determining the economic lot size for production activities, management is often faced with situations in which inventory replenishment takes place gradually over a period of time. This is the case, for example, when a firm utilizes intermittent production techniques for their various products. In these cases, a production run for a given product may last several hours, several days, several weeks, or several months, and goods are added to inventory as they are produced during the course of the run. Since goods are also being withdrawn to meet demand requirements during this period, we have a situation like the one illustrated in Figure 15–5.

Here, inventory is added during t_1 in each cycle, while items are being withdrawn from inventory to meet demand during the total time period $(t_1 + t_2)$. Suppose, for example, that a manufacturer wins a contract to supply parts to a purchaser at the rate of 250 per day and that he can produce 500 parts per day. Assuming for the moment that it is most economical for him to produce parts in 5,000-unit lots, it would take him ten days to produce a lot. Meanwhile, he must also service the customer during the ten days; therefore, at the end of the production period he would have in stock $5,000 - 10(250) = 2,500$ parts. He could then supply the user for ten more days before he would have to start production again.

To develop a formula for this type of model, enabling the manufacturer to know what economic lot size to produce, we will have to introduce a new concept to the basic model—the rate of arrival of items to stock (P). In order to build up an inventory, it is obvious that factor P must be greater than D, the rate of usage or demand.

To produce a lot, or an economic quantity of goods, takes time:

$$t_1 = \frac{Q}{P}$$

During the period t_1, the inventory will rise by the difference

$$P - D$$

At the end of the production period (t_1), the inventory will be at a maximum and equal to

$$(P - D)t_1$$

The average inventory during the entire period $t_1 + t_2$, including buildup and depletion, will be

$$\frac{(P - D)t_1}{2}$$

Substituting Q/P for t_1, we get

$$\frac{(P - D)Q}{2P}$$

Thus, the total cost of holding this inventory is

$$C = \frac{C_3 D}{Q} + C_1 \left[\frac{(P - D)Q}{2P} \right]$$

This cost equation may be simplified as follows:

$$C = \frac{C_3 D}{Q} + \frac{C_1 Q}{2} \left(1 - \frac{D}{P} \right)$$

The same techniques of calculus, which involve differentiating C with respect to Q, equating the derivative obtained with zero, and solving the resulting equation (which we previously applied to the basic model), can be used here to determine the "parameters of Q" that will minimize the total cost (C). The performance of these mathematical operations yields the following equation for Q:[8]

$$Q = \sqrt{\frac{2 C_3 D}{C_1 (1 - D/P)}}$$

To illustrate the use of this formula and to compare it with the equation for the basic model, let us return for a moment to the example introduced earlier in the chapter. Here, it will be recalled, the manufacturer needed 90 transistors a day in order to meet his output requirements. Now, let us suppose that instead of purchasing these items, the manufacturer decides to make them. He translates the necessary data into the symbols of the equation as follows:

$C_3 = \$100$ (here, setup costs, not order costs)
$C_1 = \$0.10$ per unit per year
$D = 18,000$ units at a rate of 90 per day
$P = 600$ units per day, or 120,000 per year

Since the manufacturer wishes to know what economic lot size to produce, he starts with the equation:

$$Q = \sqrt{\frac{2 C_3 D}{C_1 (1 - D/P)}}$$

[8] When applying this equation, care must be taken to ensure that the cost of holding inventory (C_1), the demand (D), and the production rate (P) are expressed in consistent terms.

Then, substituting the actual figures, he gets[9]

$$Q = \sqrt{\frac{2 \times 100 \times 18,000}{0.10(1 - 18,000/120,000)}}$$

$$= 6,500+ \text{ units}$$

The same approach used here for one product's economic lot size can be applied to production processes in which multiple items are made on the same equipment. The mathematics is essentially the same. The smaller the size of the run for various products, the greater the setup costs will be. On the other hand, the longer the run, the greater the inventory and hence the greater the holding costs will be.

Scheduling difficulties stemming from such factors as a lack of capacity, peak loads, and machine breakdowns may make the production of economic lot sizes inadvisable. This would be the case, for example, if producing lot sizes for some items precludes the possibility of meeting the demand for all items. Also, there is an additional cost that arises here—the cost of lost sales opportunities. If this cost is high, it will outweigh whatever savings might accrue from producing items in economic lot sizes. Therefore, before attempting economic-lot-size production, one must determine if the required scheduling will be consistent with the demand for all products.

QUANTITY DISCOUNTS   The basic model also assumes that the price of an item is fixed, regardless of the size of an order. In reality, however, discounts on large-quantity purchases are quite common. The buyer can also reduce his shipping and handling costs by purchasing or producing for inventory in volume. In deciding whether or not to take advantage of these discounts, however, the manager must remember that as the size of his inventory increases, so will the costs of handling and storing that inventory.

Thus we can establish the general guideline that management should take advantage of discounts only if the additional inventory costs are less than the savings from the discounts. To illustrate, let us return to the basic economic-order-quantity formula:

$$Q = \sqrt{\frac{2C_3 D}{C_1}}$$

C_1, as we have said earlier, is the cost of carrying a unit in inventory for a given period of time. It is composed of interest, handling, and deterioration costs and can be expressed as i (the interest rate) times c_1 (the purchase price of the item). Thus, the formula becomes

$$Q = \sqrt{\frac{2C_3 D}{i(c_1)}}$$

[9] Notice that the value for Q is larger than the value for A in the instantaneous replacement example (6,500 versus 6,000). Since C_1 is reduced by $(1 - D/P)$ in this equation, the Q calculated in this fashion will always be greater than the Q calculated for instantaneous replacement.

We also know that with quantity discounts the cost per item is smaller than it would be without the discount; therefore,

$$c_{1d} \text{ (price with discount)} < c_1 \text{ (price without discount)}$$

It is apparent from the formula that a reduction in price c_1 will raise the economic order quantity. But an increase in Q will, in turn, raise the inventory carrying costs. Thus, to be economically sound, the reduction in price must yield savings at least equal to this rise in inventory carrying costs. Therefore, to evaluate the savings that will accrue from a particular quantity discount, we can apply a simple test that may be expressed mathematically. If we compare the purchase savings $D(c_1 - c_{1d})$ with the added inventory carrying costs

$$\frac{Q_d \times ic_{1d}}{2} - \frac{Q \times ic_1}{2}$$

and if

$$D(c_1 - c_{1d}) > \left(\frac{Q_d \times ic_{1d}}{2} - \frac{Q \times ic_1}{2} \right)$$

then it may pay to take advantage of the discount. It should be noted that the optimum level at which to take a discount is attained when Q is made just large enough to obtain the lower price. In other words, when the minimum order size necessary to get the discount is used, the firm is maximizing the savings it can earn by large-volume purchases and minimizing the corresponding increase in inventory carrying costs.

There is one more important factor to be considered in deciding whether or not to take the discount, and that is the risk of carrying extra inventory. Suppose, for example, that without the discount a firm would carry an average of two months' inventory but that with it they would carry six months'. Clearly, if the savings accrued from the discount were minimal, it would not pay to take the discount unless demand were extremely stable. The reason, of course, is the risk factor. Although it is comparatively simple to add the element of risk (R) to the equation, as shown below, it is not so easy to determine how large R should be.

Savings > Added inventory carrying costs + Added risk factor

$$D(c_1 - c_{1d}) > \frac{Q_d \times ic_{1d}}{2} - \frac{Q \times ic_1}{2} + R$$

Obviously, the answer will have a strong bearing on whether or not a discount should be pursued yet, unfortunately, there is no easy way of accurately gauging the magnitude of risk. Many approaches are employed, most of which use historical data pertaining to the industry and the item as well as the experienced judgment of the inventory manager.

Aggregate Inventory Concepts

In practice, inventories are made up of a large number of items. A manufacturer may stock 50 to 100 or more varieties of screws. The screws may differ in length, diameter, thread, material, and type (wood, metal, 'self-tapping). As another example, retail clothing stores carry socks in many sizes, colors, lengths, materials, and weaves.

ABC Inventory Analysis

The cost of collecting the required data and calculating an inventory policy for each item can be extremely high. For some items, the cost of developing the economic policy may be greater than the cost savings from its use. Companies therefore rarely study every inventory item in the detail necessary to formulate a special inventory policy for each one. Instead, inventory items are divided into three classes generally known as A, B, and C. This division reflects the concept that it is uneconomical to spend the same effort on all items. Some items represent inconsequential amounts of money, while others involve large sums. As in most activities, a small part of the total inventory makes up the greater part of the total investment.[10]

The division of inventory items into these three classes is termed ABC inventory analysis. The A group of items encompasses the highest dollar value items, the B group the middle dollar value, and the C group the least. The typical ABC breakdown is shown in Figure 15-6. Class A, which represents only 25 percent of the total volume of items, accounts for over 75 percent of the total dollar value. The opposite relationship holds for class C, where 50 percent of the total number of items accounts for only about 5 percent of the total dollar value.

Since the savings that can be obtained are a function of the dollar volume involved, it is clear that more attention should be paid to the A items than to the others.[11] The information necessary to pursue a selective ABC inventory policy

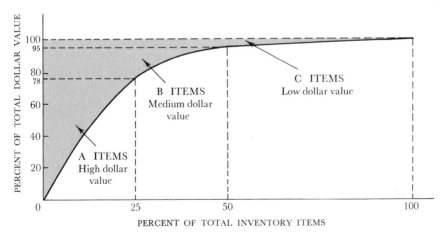

Figure 15–6 Typical ABC inventory breakdown

[10] This concept is known as the Pareto principle after the Italian economist Vilfredo Pareto. It simply states that a small part of any total activity accounts for the major portion of the total value involved in the activity.

[11] The same pattern was explained in the discussion of work methods. Those areas where the greatest opportunity for savings existed were attacked first.

is easy to obtain. High-dollar items are treated first and most carefully.

An example of the treatment that would be given the three divisions is:

A items: Economic order quantities are carefully calculated for each item. The usage rates and the procurement costs are reviewed continually with each order. Tight inventory control is maintained.

B items: Economic order quantities are developed and reviewed periodically —every 3, 6, or 12 months. Normal inventory control is exercised.

C items: Specific economic order quantity calculations are not made. Rough tables are used, or quantities that will suffice for long periods—a year or more—are ordered. Inventories are checked physically once every six months or every year to determine if new orders should be placed.

Aggregate Resource Limitations

A second factor that deters a firm from calculating an economic order quantity for each item and stocking accordingly is the limitation of the firm's resources. Companies frequently cannot carry the amount of inventory that the economic order quantity would require because they do not have enough money to invest in inventory or do not have the space required to store it. When this occurs, the theoretical inventory values must be modified.

We will illustrate this by considering a company that has allocated an average of $4,000 for inventory. The order costs are $64 per order, and the carrying costs are 20 percent of the item cost per year. The calculations for the economic order quantity and the average investment are shown in Table 15–2.

The difficulty is that in order to purchase according to the economic order quantity, an average investment of $5,020 will be needed. The company must therefore make an adjustment to its inventory policy. One way this can be done

Table 15–2 Average investment required for economic order quantities (EOQ)

Item	Purchase Price	Requirements per Year	Economic Order Quantity	Average Quantity in Stock	Average Investment
1	$4.00	2,000	565	282.5	$1,130
2	$1.00	4,000	1,600	800	800
3	$8.00	3,000	490	245	1,960
4	$2.00	4,000	1,130	565	1,130
					$5,020

C_1 = carrying costs = 20 percent of purchase price per year
C_3 = order costs = $64 per order

Sample EOQ calculations for item 1:

$$Q = \sqrt{\frac{2C_3 D}{C_1}} = \sqrt{\frac{2 \times 64 \times 2000}{.20 \times 4.00}} = 565$$

Table 15–3 Adjusted inventory investment and order size

Item	Adjusted Investment	Adjusted Order Size
1	$ 900	450
2	640	1,380
3	1,560	390
4	900	900

is to carry an average inventory dollar value for each item that is a proportion of the value calculated from the economic order quantities.[12] The proportion is set by the ratio of the money available for inventory to the amount established by the quantity formulation. As an example, for item 1, the average dollar inventory would be

$$\left(\frac{\$4,000}{\$5,020}\right)1,130 = \$900$$

The order quantity for item 1 would then be

$$\frac{900 \times 2}{400} = 450 \text{ units}$$

The values for the other items are shown in Table 15–3.

Adjustments for other restrictions can be developed in like fashion.[13]

A General Evaluation of the Economic Order Quantity

So far we have considered the specific advantages and limitations of the basic economic order quantity or economic lot size model. Now, let us step back and take a look at the relative merits of this model in a larger perspective.

We have seen how the model's usefulness can be increased by introducing various modifications of its underlying assumptions. If it is thus made more realistic, the model can be applied effectively to a greater variety of inventory problems. The most widespread use of the basic model continues to be in the management of large inventories of standard low-cost items, where it seems to be put to best advantage.

Nonetheless, this model does have other potential applications. First, it can provide an excellent background against which to demonstrate the interactions between various inventory factors because, as a simple model, it facilitates the pinpointing of changes caused by variation in any of the factors. Second, it can clarify some basic principles that apply to all inventory situations, the most important of which is that order quantities are directly related not to demand but

---

[12] The rationale for this adjustment is developed in Miller, D. W., and Starr, M. K., *Inventory Control: Theory and Practice*, Prentice-Hall, Englewood Cliffs, N.J., 1962, pp. 93–164.

[13] Miller and Starr, *loc. cit.*

rather to the *square root of demand*. Thus, assuming constant ordering and carrying costs, a doubling of demand will not require a doubling of inventory; rather, as demand increases, less inventory will be required per unit of demand. Another principle that we may derive from the model is that the total costs are relatively insensitive to changes in order quantities. This is evident from the nature of the total cost curve in Figure 15–1. Because of the general flatness of this U-shaped curve, most of the gain that could be achieved by balancing the opposing costs is attainable when order sizes are within the extensive flat region. This point becomes particularly important when considering probabilistic demand. Here, the theory is that it is not necessary to be totally accurate in order to develop a good inventory policy and that approximate measures are often adequate.

Inventory Models with Uncertainty

As we have indicated, the practical application of inventory models requiring a known demand factor is limited. In most instances there is uncertainty in both the demand and supply functions, and the source of this uncertainty, whether known or unknown, cannot be removed.

Safety Stock

To cope with the problems of uncertainty, many inventory systems incorporate "safety stocks"—additional inventory to reduce the problem of stockouts, whether caused by increased demand or late delivery. Safety stocks are thus reserved for emergencies. It is common practice to exclude safety-stock inventory when determining reorder quantities or when timing the reorders. This fact, it should be noted, necessarily leads to sub-optimization; thus, the solutions worked out are not optimal but are "good approximations"[14] of the best answers. The problem is to strike a balance between the cost of holding extra inventory and the estimated cost of an outage.

Figure 15–7 illustrates how the need for safety stock can arise from an unexpected volume of demand or from variations in delivery time. We can see that during period t_1 both the demand and the delivery cycle were as expected. In this instance, safety stock was not required. During time period t_2, however, the demand was greater than expected and the delivery cycle shorter. The short delivery cycle was not enough to offset the increased demand, though, and so safety stock was needed. Finally, in period t_3 the demand was average, but since the delivery cycle was extended, safety stock was needed again.

In determining safety-stock levels, management must undertake the following:

1. It must arrive at a figure for average demand and the typical degree of variation above and below the average. This necessitates a statistical dis-

---

[14] This point will be considered at greater length later in this chapter.

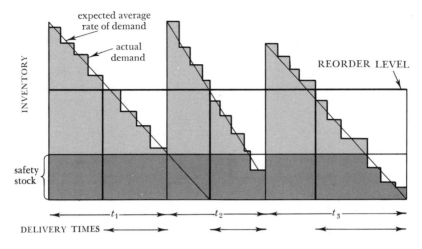

Figure 15–7   Inventory model with safety stock

tribution of demand data. Methods for obtaining this type of information were discussed in Chapter 14.

2. It must compute the average delivery, or lead, time and the statistical distribution of expected variations.
3. It must establish a policy regarding stockouts, or, as it is often termed, a "service policy." In so doing, management defines the degree to which it wants to be certain that outages do not occur. Such a policy will specify the desired level of customer service on the basis of an analysis of the costs involved in not supplying this service.

Stockout Costs

In order for management to determine what level of safety stock to maintain, it must attempt to measure the cost of a stockout. There are many kinds of stockout costs. One is simply the loss of profit from a lost sale; another may also involve a loss of customer goodwill, which can entail the loss of future sales as well. In fact, the disappointed customer may spread his discontent to other customers, further reducing future sales. Stockout costs in manufacturing may include losses due to idle machines and idle labor, as well as the subsequent expediting costs incurred to minimize the delay. In short, because of the complexity of these costs, it is virtually impossible to measure them. Yet, some estimation must be made for the purpose of determining the level of safety stock. The most practical approach to this dilemma is to supply management with estimates of the inventories required, including safety stock, to support various service policies. This will facilitate the establishment of a service policy based upon the comparative specifics of probable outages, as measured against various inventory levels and investment.

To illustrate this approach, consider the case of a central warehouse that furnishes products to a chain of supermarkets. As a rule, one week elapses between the placing of a requisition and the receipt of the items ordered by a store, and company policy calls for each store to place a weekly order for all required items. The quantity of each item requested is standardized at the level of average weekly demand. Within this policy framework, each store manager is charged with the responsibility for developing inventory policies and levels for each item in his supermarket. One way the manager can do this is to begin by accumulating weekly sales figures for each brand of produce during the past year. Data of this sort have been tabulated for Brand A in Table 15–4, showing the number of weeks during the past year that the demand for Brand A reached various quantity levels. Using these data, the cumulative distribution can be graphed, as in Figure 15–8, which shows the percentage probability for any week during the year when demand can be expected to exceed a particular level.[15] From this type of graph the reader can directly obtain the probability percentages for different demand levels.

In this particular example, the average weekly demand is 400 units; accordingly, this quantity might be established as the weekly order size for a supermarket. The graph shows, however, that if a safety stock is not set up, the store may expect to run out of Brand A about 50 percent of the time; such a service record would certainly not be acceptable to a supermarket. Suppose, instead, that management establishes the policy "that a store must not experience an outage more than 10 percent of the time." Glancing again at Figure 15–8, we see that a weekly inventory level of 650 units of Brand A would be required to conform with this policy. Thus the safety stock would have to be $650 - 400$

Table 15–4   Weekly demand for Brand A

Demand Quantity (in units)	Number of Weeks Demand Occurred
901–1,000	0
801–900	2
701–800	2
601–700	4
501–600	8.
401–500	10
301–400	20
201–300	4
101–200	2
1–100	0

[15] The implicit assumption here is that the demand in the following year will be approximately the same as that in the year studied. Conceivably, management could apply a percentage adjustment to reflect an anticipated increase or decrease in the demand for the particular product. Whether such an adjustment (and its magnitude) is necessary could be assessed by means of the forecasting techniques discussed in Chapter 14.

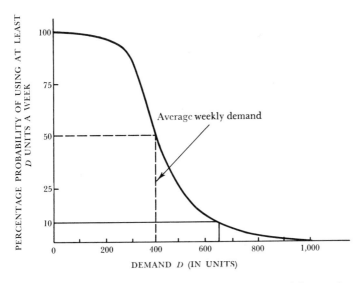

Figure 15–8 Cumulative distribution of demand by weeks

(the average order quantity), or 250 units. If management goes one step further and sets up a service policy specifying that a store must never be out of stock, the store would be forced to stock a weekly inventory of 900 units, of which 500 units would represent the safety stock. Information of this nature may be presented to management in tabular form; Table 15–5, for example, summarizes the data in Figure 15–8.

A policy of maintaining enough safety stock to prevent all stockouts is generally not economical. The principle of diminishing returns applies to safety stocks; as the desired degree of protection against outages rises, the required safety-stock levels increase precipitously, thereby yielding progressively smaller returns on inventory investment. Thus, most firms consider a "reasonable" number of stockouts acceptable because of the high cost of trying to eliminate them altogether.

Table 15–5 Safety-stock levels for various service policies

Percent of Weeks in Which Stockouts Will Occur	Safety Stock Required (in units)	Weekly Order Quantity
0	500	400 (in all cases)
5	430	
10	250	
20	150	
30	100	
40	50	
50	0	

Under typical operating conditions, then, the level of safety stock will be lower than what is needed for the projected maximum demand rate; instead, a "reasonable" inventory level will be set. Determination of this level will depend upon the demand forecast and the shape of the probability curve derived from that forecast; it will also depend upon management's decision regarding what constitutes a "reasonable" number of outages—in other words, upon the firm's service policy.

Inventory Systems

We can now proceed to analyze the systems that managements use to control inventories. Basically there are just two types of inventory systems, although both have numerous variations. One is termed the "fixed-order-size system"; a fixed quantity of goods is ordered whenever inventory dips below a predetermined level. The time between orders varies with the demand rates, but the size of the order remains constant. In practice, fixed-order-size systems are generally called *perpetual inventory systems,* since up-to-date records of the inventory's status are kept. Each time items are withdrawn from or added to the inventory, the records are updated to reflect the new status. This posting operation may be done manually on inventory record cards or, as is increasingly the case, through remote input terminals to a computer file. In general, only class A and B inventories are maintained in this fashion.

The "two-bin system," an application of the fixed-order-size approach, is one of the oldest inventory systems in use. For illustration, imagine that all material of a given type is placed in two large bins. When the first is empty, the second is put into use and a replacement order for a fixed amount is dispatched immediately. When the new material arrives, it is placed in the empty bin and the process continues. Simple versions of this system are often applied to the storage of manufacturing items such as nuts, screws, and washers.

In the second basic type, the fixed-order-interval system, periodic reviews of inventories are made, at which time they are restored to some predetermined optimum level. No running records of daily inventory activity are kept. The status of the inventory is known only at the time of the review, which may take place weekly, monthly, quarterly, or yearly. Because of this, inventory systems of this type are commonly called *periodic inventory systems.* Such systems are generally used for class B or C inventories or in instances where the large number of items precludes the updating of each inventory transaction, such as in supermarkets, retail stores, and many warehousing situations.

Fixed-Order-Size Periodic Inventory Systems

To illustrate how the two systems differ in operation, let us reexamine our earlier example illustrating economic order quantities of transistors, where we said that

$$D = 18{,}000 \text{ units per year}$$

$$Q = 6{,}000 \text{ units per order (from the EOQ formula)}$$

$$\text{Usage} = 90 \text{ per day}$$

ROP = reorder point

Now let us assume that

$$\text{Delivery (lead) time} = 20 \text{ work days}$$

$$\text{Work days per year} = 200$$

By a simple computation we know that the 6,000 units will last 6,000/90, or 66.6, days. Since the delivery time is 20 days, management will have to reorder when 20×90, or 1,800, units remain in stock; this is the reorder point. Let us also assume that there is a safety-stock level. (We will discuss the factors influencing safety stock after the basic concepts of the two systems have been explained.)

Now, under the first system, we would begin by monitoring the inventory until it reached 1,800 units. When it reached this level, the firm would place an order for another 6,000 units, and, assuming that demand remained constant, the order would arrive just as the safety-stock level was reached. Once again there would be 6,000 units in addition to the safety stock in inventory. If demand were uncertain, however, the inventory level would range above or below 6,000, depending on whether or not the safety stock were used; this is illustrated in Figure 15–9. In the first order cycle, demand was just as predicted, and so the reorder point was reached after 46.6 days and no safety stock was used. In the second cycle, demand was greater than predicted, and so the reorder point was reached in 40 days and some safety stock was used.

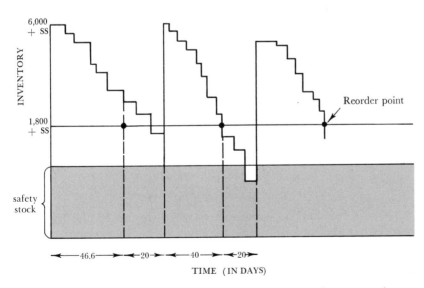

Figure 15–9 Fixed-order-size inventory system under uncertainty

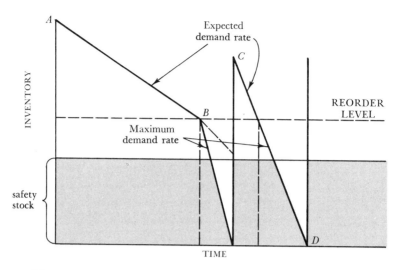

Figure 15–10 Fixed-order-size safety stock relationships

Safety stock The amount of safety stock required in a perpetual inventory system is determined solely by the amount of stock needed to guard against a stockout during the delivery time. If the amount of safety stock added to the normal inventory on hand is greater than the maximum amount sold during the delivery time, then the chances are excellent that no shortage will result. In Figure 15–10, for example, the demand proceeded at an expected pace from point *A* to point *B*. At point *B* an order was entered for the fixed order quantity. Then, in the interval from *B* to *C* and from *C* to *D*, demand rose to maximum levels. Since the safety stock plus the inventory that remained when the order was placed were equal to maximum demand, no stockout occurred. Instead, all that happened was that orders were placed at an increasing rate.

Fixed-Order-Interval Periodic Inventory Systems

To illustrate how periodic inventory systems work, we will use the same data:

$$D = 18,000 \text{ units per year}$$
$$Q = 6,000 \text{ units per order}$$
$$\text{Usage} = 90 \text{ per day}$$
$$\text{Delivery (lead) time} = 20 \text{ work days}$$

Now let us assume that the manufacturer wishes to control the transistors as part of a regular fixed-order-interval inventory system. The inventory is reviewed and new orders are placed 66.6 − 20, or 46.6, days after the cycle initially begins. Thereafter, new orders are placed every 66.6 days. The quantity ordered each time will be equal to the difference between the amount of inventory at the time the order is placed and the desired maximum inventory, plus the expected usage (or sales) during the delivery time, minus any orders placed but not yet received:

Order quantity = (Q − Present inventory) + Usage during delivery time

− Back orders + Safety stock

For example, if demand remains at the expected level:

Order quantity = $[6,000 − (20 \times 90)] + (20 \times 90)$ + Safety stock

= 6,000 + Safety stock

In this case, the moment the new order arrives, the inventory would stand at 6,000 units plus the safety stock. In short, where demand is linear and known, the fixed-order-interval and the fixed-order-size systems yield the same results.

When demand varies, however, this is not so. Consider the pattern shown in Figure 15–11, which is the same demand data used to illustrate the fixed-order size example in Figure 15–9. The first period of 66.6 days is identical in both because the demand was as expected. When demand rose sharply during the next 66.6 days, however, the results were different. In the fixed-order-interval system, the inventory is checked every 66.6 days; the difference between the maximum desired inventory of 6,000 plus safety stock and the stock on hand is noted, and the projected demand during the delivery time (the next 20 days) is calculated at the latest demand rate. If the new demand rate continues in the next period, as it does in Figure 15–11, the inventory will be replenished until it reaches the maximum desired level of 6,000 units plus safety stock.

A major difficulty with this approach is that it will cause inventory levels to fluctuate violently if management "overcorrects" in estimating demand changes.

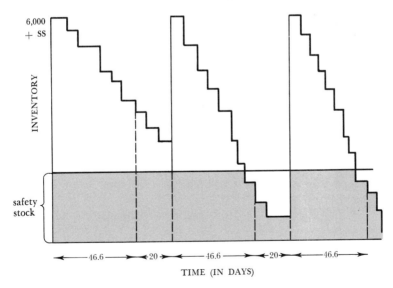

Figure 15–11   Fixed-order-interval inventory system under uncertainty

This typically occurs when random fluctuations are mistaken for permanent changes in demand. For example, imagine a system, using a monthly review of inventory, that correctly estimates average demand at 50 units a month. One month, because of random factors, there could conceivably be a demand for 70 units. According to the system, 70 units would be reordered to get the inventory back to where it was, and an additional amount above the 70 would be ordered to take care of demand expected during the delivery time. This extra amount would be calculated at the new, 70 units a month, demand rate. Again, because of random factors, demand in the next month might be only 35 units. A considerable overstocking would therefore exist, and management might cut its maximum inventory level to compensate for it.[16] Since extreme fluctuations may arise, it is important to make certain that demand has actually shifted before changing demand rates and thus maximum inventory levels.

Safety stock   We have said that in fixed-order-size systems safety stock is needed only to cover the demand during the delivery time. In fixed-order-interval systems this is not true. Here, the safety stock must be sufficient to guard against stockouts during both delivery time and normal inventory activity, as is demonstrated in Figure 15–12. Here it can be seen that during the first inventory cycle, the normal demand rate existed for the order period t_1, and so enough inventory was ordered to meet that demand. At that point, however, demand increased to its maximum level and continued at that rate throughout the entire next cycle. By the time the second order interval t_1 had elapsed, the safety stock

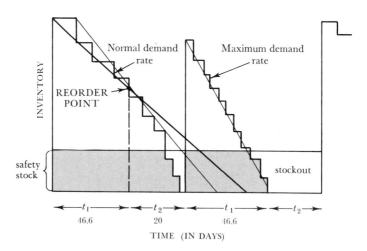

Figure 15–12   Fixed order interval with safety stock

[16] It should be noted that the severity of these fluctuations can be eased by using such techniques as weighted moving averages or exponential smoothing to forecast the demand for the next period. These techniques were discussed in Chapter 14. The fluctuations discussed are typical of servomechanisms, which continually hunt and never settle down to an equilibrium point. If the right objective function is developed and used, however, the oscillations can be avoided or minimized.

was fully depleted, and so no stock was available during the delivery time t_2. Although this is an extreme case, it illustrates that, with the same service policy, larger safety stocks are required for fixed-order-interval systems than for fixed-order-size systems. With the same demand pattern and the same amount of safety stock, there were no stockouts in the fixed-order-size system.

Safety-stock calculation So far we have discussed safety stock reorder points and order quantity as if these factors were determined independently. The order quantity, as we have said, is arrived at by considering the carrying costs, the reorder costs, and the average demand forecast, while the safety stock is determined by the length of the delivery time and its variations, the variations in the demand forecast, and the service policy. Thus, the total inventory has been defined as the sum of the two components

$$I = \frac{Q}{2} + S$$

where S = safety stock
Q = order quantity

Close analysis will reveal, however, that these elements are not entirely independent, although the degree of interaction is often negligible. Where the order size is fixed, the size itself will determine how often stockouts will be encountered; with the safety stock fixed, the larger the order, the less frequently the firm will have a stockout, but the probability of service will be high. With smaller quantities ordered and a fixed safety stock, the chance of stockouts increases and the probability of service decreases. Most advanced works in the field of inventory present various approaches that include this interaction in the analyses.[17]

At this point we can discuss briefly the mathematical formula for determining safety stocks in a fixed-order-size system. To simplify the problem, we will assume that delivery time is constant, that demand is relatively stable between periods, and that variations in demand within a period are distributed normally. In this hypothetical situation, the cost of holding safety stock would have to be minimized by reference to the formula:[18]

$$C = \frac{C_3 D}{Q} + \frac{C_1 Q}{2} + C_1 S_D P \sqrt{t}$$

where S_D = standard deviation of the demand variations within a period
t = delivery (lead) time
P = standard normal deviate, giving a desired probability of being out of stock each time inventory reaches a minimum

P is a function of the order quantity, the level of safety stock, and the level of

---

[17] See R. B. Fetter and W. C. Dalleck, *Decision Models for Inventory Management* (Homewood, Ill.: Irwin, 1961); T. M. Whitin, *The Theory of Inventory Management* (Princeton, N.J.: Princeton University Press, 1953); and Miller and Starr, *op. cit.*

[18] For the fixed-order-interval case, the equation is the same except for $\sqrt{t}$, which becomes $\sqrt{t} + r$, where r = order interval.

service desired. Because of this interaction, the cost equation becomes extremely difficult to state, and thus it is difficult to minimize cost even in this simplified case.

If we allowed the delivery time to vary and demand to change between periods, as they do in real life, the problem would become even more complex. Furthermore, if you consider the great variety of items in a normal inventory, you can visualize the tremendous amount of work required to determine optimal solutions. Because of this, approximate solutions to the problem are generally followed.

Safety stock may be determined in a wide variety of expedient ways. We will discuss four methods, which are representative but by no means exclusive.

DEMAND PERCENTAGE   This method was explained in the discussion of stock-out costs. First a plot of the cumulative demand, as shown in Figure 15–8, is developed. Then management must decide what percent of stockouts is bearable, and the demand associated with this level of stockouts is found from the distribution. In Figure 15–8, a 10 percent level of stockout was acceptable to management. The demand associated with this was 650 units. If the average order time were 3 weeks, then the reorder point would be 1,950 units (3×650). Since the average usage is 400 units per week, 750 units ($3 \times 650 - 3 \times 400$) of safety stock would be held.

CONSERVATIVE METHOD   In this method, safety stock is the difference between the largest usage that ever occurred and the average usage, multiplied by the longest delivery time.

$$SS = (\text{Largest usage} - \text{Average usage})(\text{Longest delivery time})$$

This method yields a tremendous safety stock. It almost guarantees no stockouts, but the cost of carrying the extra safety stock is great. It would be used only when an item is indispensable—the cost of a stockout infinite.

PERCENT OF AVERAGE DEMAND   This method develops a safety stock by multiplying the average usage by a percentage factor, which is usually between 25 and 50 percent. Returning once more to Figure 15–8, we find that the average demand was 400 units. If we assume an average delivery time of 3 weeks, the safety stock for a 25 percent factor would be (400×3) ($.25$) = 300 units.

SQUARE ROOT OF LEAD TIME   Inventory studies have shown that delivery time does not very often vary by more than its square root. This means that the safety stock has to protect only during this time period. Thus, for our example,

$$SS = 400 \times \sqrt{3} = 690 \text{ units}$$

Management is responsible for the selection of the approach for calculating safety stock. The aim is to find a method that fits a particular case and balances the risk of stockouts with the carrying costs and the cost of calculation.

Where a demand history exists, the demand percentage method has the firmest foundation. Where no demand history exists, the percentage of the expected demand generally serves well until a demand pattern can be developed.

Comparison of the Periodic and Perpetual Inventory Systems

The two systems are both designed to control inventories in the face of uncertainty. Whether one or the other is employed in a particular instance depends upon the nature of the items stocked, the type of controls needed, and the nature of the source of supply.

The fixed-order-size system is well suited for managing inventories of low-value items, since it permits looser control. Items of this sort are usually bought in large quantities relative to their use and can be readily obtained from the supplier at any time. They can be controlled by a simple two-bin process without a large investment in record-keeping. Perpetual inventories also lend themselves to the stocking of high-cost items that can be purchased at any time. These items are controlled by continuous posting to inventory records. In this way the status of the high-cost items can be closely watched. This is costly, however, for inventories with a large number of items, since the clerical costs are high; yet, with the use of computers, such costs can be reduced. The broader application of perpetual inventory records made feasible by computers will in turn result in closer control of inventories.

The fixed-order-interval system lends itself to inventories that consist of a large number of products because the clerical cost of periodic evaluation is substantially below that required for perpetual recording. This system is also well suited for items whose availability may be limited because of the suppliers' demand for periodic orders so that they can plan their production runs economically. In order to use the fixed-order-interval system, however, higher safety stocks must be maintained.

A Sample Inventory Problem

To help tie together the preceding discussion of inventory management, a typical inventory problem will now be presented and analyzed. Table 15–6 shows various quantities of a small electric motor that a firm uses in manufacturing its product. These motors are purchased from a supply house that stocks them in large quantities, so they are readily available. Delivery is good; the motors are delivered punctually five days after an order is issued. All of the firm's other

Table 15–6 Motor-demand history

Month	Demand
1	90
2	110
3	102
4	103
5	95
6	106
	606

purchasing is done on a fixed-order-size basis, with perpetual inventory records kept on each item. Up until now, the motors have been ordered by the engineering department since they were being used only in small quantities. Because the number needed has risen, however, management wants to incorporate the motors into its normal inventory system to improve control. Since management believes that past demand is a good reflection of future demand (at least for the coming year), it anticipates no problem in doing this.

The first step in designing a probabilistic inventory system is to forecast the demand pattern and its variations. From the data given in Table 15–6, for example, we can see that the average expected demand is 606/6, or 101 motors per month. The amount of variation in the demand will be considered in the design of a safety-stock level. Once the average demand pattern has been determined, the economic order quantity and the appropriate level of safety stock can be calculated. These are determined separately according to the approximate methods discussed earlier.

To determine the order quantity, we must first examine the cost pattern. In this case, if we know that the order cost is $10 per order and the cost of carrying one unit for a year is about $0.60 per unit, we can determine the order quantity by means of the following formula:

$$Q = \sqrt{\frac{2C_3 D}{C_1}}$$

$$= \sqrt{\frac{2 \times 10 \times 1200}{0.60}}$$

$$= 200 \text{ units}$$

Then, on the assumption that the average work month contains 20 days, we can say that average daily usage is 101/20, or 5 units per day. Thus, the average expected usage during the delivery time is 5 × 5, or 25 units. Accordingly, the reorder point may be set at 200 − 175, or 25 units.

As it will be recalled, the fixed-order-size system only requires enough safety stock to protect the firm against stockouts during the delivery time. Suppose in this case that management wishes to be 95 percent certain that no stockouts will occur since the motor is part of an expensive unit that cannot be assembled without it. Referring to the demand pattern for daily usage during the past six months shown in Table 15–7, we can construct a graph relating the percentage probability for any given day when demand can be expected to exceed a certain level, as shown in Figure 15–13.

In Figure 15–13, a line drawn from the 5 percent point on the vertical axis intersects demand at 8 units. This tells us that 95 percent of the time demand was less than 8 units per day. Accordingly, to be 95 percent certain that no stockouts will occur during the delivery time, the firm should have a total of 5 × 8, or 40 units on hand. Since regular inventory, which is geared to normal usage, consists of 25 units during the delivery time, 15 units of safety stock will be required to meet this level of service. The maximum inventory on hand at

Table 15–7 Daily-demand history

Number of Days Demand Occurred	Demand Quantity (in units)
7	3
33	4
40	5
30	6
3	7
3	8
2	9
1	10

the start of the period is the economic order quantity (Q) + safety stock, or 215 units. The average inventory is $200/2 + 15$, or 115 units. This inventory situation is illustrated graphically in Figure 15–14.

The final step is to monitor this system continually to determine if the demand pattern has changed. One simple method of doing this is to use control charts. In this case, for example, the expected average monthly demand was 101 units, with a standard deviation equal to 7.3 units.[19] We would expect, in accordance with statistical probability theory, that 95 percent of the monthly demand would fall within the range of the average demand plus or minus two standard deviations, or, in this case, $101 \pm 2(7.3)$. Management could establish control charts with these limits and plot the monthly demand as it occurs. Control charts facilitate the spotting of a trend, and if the demand falls outside the

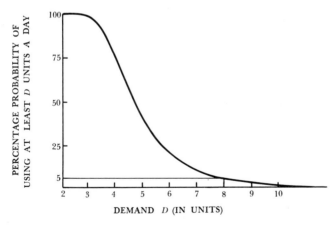

Figure 15–13 Cumulative distribution of demand by day

[19] To calculate standard deviation, as discussed in Chapter 14,

$$S = \sqrt{\frac{\Sigma(D - \bar{D})^2}{n - 1}} = \sqrt{\frac{268}{5}} = 7.3 \text{ units}$$

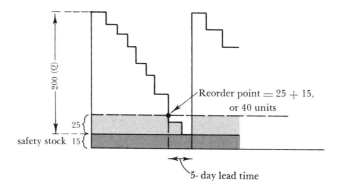

Figure 15-14 Hypothetical inventory model

charts' limits, management can be alerted to the necessity of reevaluating demand estimates.[20]

The Overall Inventory Problem

In the development of a comprehensive inventory system, one must consider much more than formulas for determining economic order quantities, production lot sizes, and inventory levels. One must also think of the means and costs required to obtain the necessary information to run the system. Precise, highly mathematical inventory techniques are of little use unless the information to feed into the models is available and at a "reasonable" cost. Inventory systems that necessitate high data-processing costs in the determination of economic inventory levels may well be uneconomical in the larger perspective. Inventory systems that select approximate, reasonable inventory levels and have low data-processing costs are often preferable.

Following this reasoning, the designer of an inventory system must consider all aspects of the system and not just the inventory model. For this purpose, an inventory system can be divided into six areas.

1. The decision models used to determine stock levels, safety stock, order points, and quantities.
2. The methods used to record inventory information, including periodic or perpetual monitoring, physical checking to determine discrepancies between inventory records and actual stock, and communication throughout an organization with respect to inventory.
3. The methods used to determine such inventory costs as stockout, ordering, and carrying costs.
4. The methods used to develop demand forecasts and variations, and delivery forecasts and variations.

---

[20] Sometimes monthly demand will not give a sufficiently accurate indication of demand changes, and so control charts can be designed on a daily or weekly basis. This requires more plotting, however, and raises the cost of control.

5. The feedback system used to report exception information.
6. The methods used to store and handle inventory.

A breakdown in any one of these areas can undermine the efficiency of the entire system. In this chapter and in Chapter 14, we have concentrated on areas 1, 3, and 4 because these problem areas are peculiar to inventory. Since the other areas pertain as well to other phases of business, they are discussed in detail in other chapters.

Questions and Problems

1. State what you believe should be the main determinants of inventory levels for a company. How far would you go in controlling these levels?
2. Describe the technique of determining economic lot size. What are the limitations of this technique?
3. What inventory costs must be considered for purchased goods? What inventory costs must be taken into account for manufactured products?
4. Under what circumstances should a company consider order points and economic order quantities? Are there limitations in applying these concepts?
5. Discuss why the safety-stock level to operate at a given level of customer service is actually related to the economic lot size, even though they are usually calculated independently.
6. Discuss the following statements:
    (a) The economic manufacturing lot size is not a valid concept because it produces a suboptimal solution to the total production program decision.
    (b) The economic lot size attempts to minimize manufacturing costs by relating the size of the lot to setup and shop order-handling costs.
    (c) The order point is determined by a quantity of material that protects a company against the costs of material depletion arising from unforeseen changes in lead time, transportation delays, etc.
    (d) Under the two-bin system of inventory control, the replenishment quantity depends upon lead time.
    (e) A fixed-order-interval system will generally be the most effective approach to inventory management in cases where there are great fluctuations in lead cycles.
7. "Under the order-point method of inventory control, the protective reserve consisting of lead time coverage and safety factor should be adjusted to give protection against changes in the lead time and the anticipated demand or usage." Discuss.
8. An electronics assembly company carries an inventory of 20,000 different items used in the assemblies it produces.
    (a) What would be your reaction if you discovered that each item in the company's inventory was managed by the "reorder cycle" method?
    (b) Would you expect to find any safety stock components of inventory?
    (c) In your opinion, should any attention be paid to the recalculation of expected demand for inventory items as actual usage data are obtained? (Assume that the company keeps up-to-date records on usage.)
9. How do practical inventory control systems take account of uncertainties in demand? in lead time? in production rates?

10. What is a reorder point and how can it be determined?
11. Can minimum, maximum, and economic lot size controls be used in the same plant?
12. Based on the following data, is a lot of 1,000, 3,000, 6,000, or 12,000 units the most economical to manufacture?

Setup cost	$3.00
Value	$0.04 per unit
Carrying costs	20 percent of value of average inventory per year
Storage costs	$0.03 per unit per year
Consumption	12,000 units per year
Minimum stock on hand at any time	1,000 units

Assume that there is a steady annual consumption. Compute the average inventory with the following formula:

$$\text{Average inventory} = \frac{\text{Minimum inventory} + \text{Maximum inventory}}{2}$$

13. The Suzy Corporation uses a certain material at an even rate throughout the year. Its annual usage of the material is 12,000 pounds. In the past it has purchased the material in equal monthly installments, at a price of $1.00 per pound, but the supplier has offered a 5 percent quantity discount if the corporation will purchase the material in equal semiannual installments. The corporation maintains a minimum stock of the material of 500 pounds. The Suzy Corporation has estimated that its order costs are $20.00 per order, its storage cost $0.10 per pound, and its carrying costs 20 percent of the value of the inventory.
    (a) Should the Suzy Corporation take advantage of this offer? Show in logical fashion the calculations on which your decision is based.
    (b) Suppose the corporation decided to go into an order-point inventory control system. If it determined that it wished to continue with a reserve stock of 500 pounds, that it would order in quantities of 5,000 pounds, and that approximately one month was needed from order to delivery, compute (1) the order point, (2) the minimum inventory, and (3) the maximum inventory.
14. You have been asked to set up order-point inventory control for a certain raw material that is used in the manufacture of fountain pens. Usage of this part has been relatively constant at 500 units per day and 120,000 units per year. The part can usually be obtained on one day's notice, although occasionally deliveries have been delayed for longer periods of time. The present cost of the part is $1.00 per unit. Order costs are estimated at $30.00, storage costs at $0.05 per unit per year, and carrying costs at 20 percent per year. Shutdown costs are estimated at $300 per day in those operations affected by a stockout of this part. A survey of past records indicates that a reserve stock of 2,000 units would probably result in three days of shutdown for lack of parts during the year, but a reserve of 5,000 units would probably reduce shutdowns to one day per year. The present purchasing practice has been to order in quantities of 10,000.
    (a) What is the proper amount of reserve stock?
    (b) What is the proper order point?

(c) One of your suppliers offers you a quantity discount of $0.03 per unit if you will purchase the part in quantities of 20,000 units. Should this offer be taken?

15. The management of a furniture factory has decided to manufacture certain parts of a table in lots of 130 pieces. Would you recommend that this lot size be used? Base your answer on the accompanying formula applied to the following data:

Production	4,000 pieces per month
Usage	140 pieces per month
Cost per piece	$2.40
Setup and preparatory costs	$3.00
Carrying costs	20 percent per year
Safety factor	40 pieces
Storage charge per piece	$0.25 per year

The formula for the economic lot size is

$$X = \sqrt{\frac{24MA + IAS}{\left(IC + 2T\right)\left(1 + \frac{M}{P}\right)}}$$

where X = economic lot size
  P = number of pieces actually produced per month
  M = average number of pieces used per month
  C = cost per part including material, labor, and overhead, but not setup cost
  A = cost of set up and all other preparation costs chargeable to the lot
  I = annual carrying cost, including interest, taxes, and insurance
  S = safety factor (the number of pieces in stock when a new lot arrives)
  T = storage charge per unit per year

16. The RST Company has the following cost structure for ordering and inventorying its product:

Cost of processing an order	$15.00
Carrying costs	20 percent
Storage costs	$0.10 per unit per year
Usage	10,000 units per year
Minimum inventory	500 units
Purchase cost in lots of 1,000	$10.00
in lots of 2,000	$9.90
in lots of 5,000	$9.75
Number of working days	250
Delivery time	2 weeks

(a) Determine the economic order quantity.
(b) What is the order point?

17. As inventory control manager of the Omega Company, determine from the following data the proper (a) order point, (b) maximum inventory level, and (c) minimum inventory level for raw material A. Show all computations clearly.

Usage	100 units per day
Carrying costs	20 percent

Work days	20 per month
Storage costs	$0.02 per unit per month
Cost of placing order	$5.00
Reserve stock	500 units
Delivery time	5 days
Purchase cost in lots of 1,000	$10.00
in lots of 2,000	$9.80

You suspect that the price of A is going to drop sharply in the near future. Consequently, you have informed the control clerk to notify you when raw material A reaches the order point, as you are going on a hand-to-mouth ordering policy.
  (a) Assuming the above facts, what is the smallest quantity you can safely order at this point?
  (b) Choose an economic ordering quantity.
18. The Municipal Hospital uses a disposable item in its surgical procedure. The item comes from a local source. A fixed-order quantity inventory system is used. The carrying costs are $0.40 per unit/year, lead time for orders is 7 days, order costs are $25.00 per order, and yearly usage is 3,600 units. The demand has the following pattern

USAGE/DAY	NUMBER OF OCCURRENCES
7 or less	3
8	9
9	165
10	168
11	12
12	4
13 or more	3

What would the order quantity, reorder point, and minimum inventory level be if safety stock is determined by
  (a) Demand percentage
  (b) Conservative method
  (c) Percent of average demand
  (d) Square root of lead time
19. Why are inventories commonly broken into A, B, and C classes? Does this breakdown negate the principles of inventory control that have been put forth in this chapter?

References

Barrett, D. A., *Automatic Inventory Control Techniques,* International Publications Service, New York, 1969.

Brown, R. G., *Decision Rules for Inventory Management,* Holt, Rinehart and Winston, New York, 1967.

Buchan, J., and Koenigsberg, E., *Scientific Inventory Management,* Prentice-Hall, Englewood Cliffs, N.J., 1963.

Buffa, E. S., *Production-Inventory Systems: Planning and Control,* Irwin, Homewood, Ill., 1968.

Fetter, R. B., and Dalleck, W. C., *Decision Models for Inventory Management,* Irwin, Homewood, Ill., 1961.

Greene, J. H., *Production and Inventory Control Handbook,* McGraw-Hill, New York, 1970.

Hadley, G., and Whitin, T. M., *Analysis of Inventory Systems,* Prentice-Hall, Englewood Cliffs, N.J., 1963.

Killeen, L. M., *Techniques of Inventory Management,* American Management Association, New York, 1969.

Magee, J. F., and Boodman, D. M., *Production Planning and Inventory Control,* 2nd ed., McGraw-Hill, New York, 1967.

Naddor, E., *Inventory Systems,* Wiley, New York, 1966.

Plossl, G., and Wright, O., *Production and Inventory Control,* Prentice-Hall, Englewood Cliffs, N.J., 1967.

Starr, M. K., and Miller, D. W., *Inventory Control: Theory and Practice,* Prentice-Hall, Englewood Cliffs, N.J., 1962.

Wagner, H. M., *Statistical Management of Inventory Systems,* Wiley, New York, 1962.

Whitin, T. M., *The Theory of Inventory Management,* Greenwood Press, Westport, Conn., 1957.

III

Production Process

In Part II the task of obtaining the inputs to the conversion or production process was discussed. In the remaining chapters, the design, direction, maintenance, and control of the production process will be analyzed.

The design of the production process is treated chronologically. First the problem of plant location—finding a site for the process—is considered. Once the site has been selected, the plant must be set up or "laid out." Hence, the second design chapter deals with the aspects of plant layout. Finally, the flow of material (materials handling) through the plant must be planned and coordinated with the production activity. A discussion of the materials handling system completes the analysis of the design of the production facility.

The next group of chapters treats the direction, maintenance, and control of the production process itself. Chapter 19 covers the preproduction planning that is necessary before the process can be activated. Chapter 20 treats all of the activities in the production process that must be coordinated and controlled so that the output is delivered to the customer according to a predetermined schedule. The problems of maintaining the production process itself (maintenance analysis) are analyzed in Chapter 21, and the book concludes with two chapters on how quality and cost control are established and maintained in the production process.

16

Plant Location Analysis

The basic objective in designing any production process is the establishment of an effective capability for the manufacture and delivery of a firm's product line. In the preceding chapters we discussed the inputs to the production process. Once the input decisions have been made, the task facing management is how to design and operate a system that will be both competitive and profitable. Operating costs are affected by many factors; in this connection, we have already discussed the importance of managerial decisions concerning labor, materials, and capital resources. Of equal significance are decisions affecting the plant's physical capacity such as plant layout, materials handling, maintenance, and the planning and control of production operations and quality levels. Each of these factors will be treated independently in the chapters that follow. In this chapter we will concentrate on the decision processes that management follows in selecting locations for production plants.

Location[1]

The physical factors associated with the location of a firm can have a significant impact on the firm's operations and cost structure. In an established company, problems connected with location can arise in many ways. As its sales force opens up new markets for its products, a firm may wonder where to locate added capacity in order to service the markets most effectively. Shifts in the market

[1] The analysis that follows is confined to production facilities, but it is equally applicable to all location problems; for example, warehouses, stores, service facilities, and offices.

structure can also bring about a relocation of facilities. Another reason for moving may be the depletion of resources. The recent decline in importance of the
Pittsburgh area as a site for heavy industry can be attributed, among other factors, to the burning up of available bituminous coal. The petroleum industry is
confronted with this problem on an even larger scale; increasing emphasis on
foreign crude oil sources is raising costs for inland refineries that were formerly
well located in terms of sources of crude oil. In other industries, changes in the
nature and costs of transportation may make the present plant sites uncompetitive. A rise in labor costs or overhead expenses, such as power, can also force
management to think of relocation. There are a host of indirect factors such as
schools, union activity, and housing that can lead management to look for other
locations on occasion.

For a new enterprise, the question of location is naturally of primary importance. A poorly chosen site may doom the firm from the outset. With no
existing facilities to tie it down, management is free to evaluate numerous alternatives in terms of physical, competitive, and indirect factors in order to select
an optimal site. No location is so good that it will guarantee success, but some
are poor enough to ensure failure.

The high degree of decentralization in many industries is an indication that
there are many good locations for most industries. In the great majority of cases,
no one place is uniquely superior to all others. Improved transportation facilities
and communications media have enlarged the marketplace that can be served from
a given plant site. "Local sales advantages" have steadily decreased in importance
as a location factor. For similar reasons, proximity to sources of raw materials—
once the dominant factor in the steel industry, for example—has also decreased
in importance; as a consequence, there has been considerable geographical dispersion within individual industries. Figure 16–1 shows the present location of
individual plants in the steel industry, which has usually been considered to be
an industry concentrated in only a few areas of the country. Twenty-nine states
have plants that produce steel. In the electronics industry there are plants in
New England, the Middle Atlantic states, the Midwest, the South, and the Far
West. Many other industries—those producing furniture, shoes, and chemicals,
for example—are similarly widespread.

In short, there are many good locations, and it is exceedingly difficult to rank
one above another. Is IBM at Endicott, New York, better situated than Sperry
Rand at Philadelphia? Is Xerox in California in a better location than National
Cash Register at Dayton? It is difficult to substantiate any preference. Thus, the
task of site selection is fundamentally one of finding a *good* location. Just to
accomplish this much is a significant achievement.

Dynamics of Location Analysis

The location decision continually faces the management of a firm. The fact
that a firm may have stayed at its present site for a long period of time does not
mean that its location was not considered during that period. As in the stock

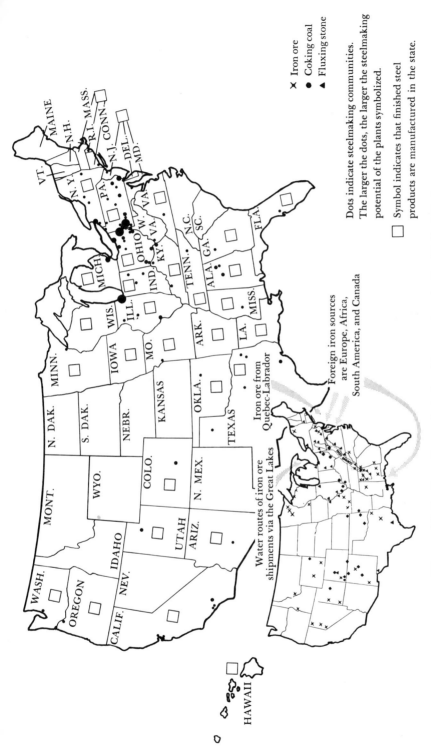

Figure 16–1 Locations of steelmaking centers in the United States

SOURCE: U.S. Department of the Interior, Bureau of Mines, and Geological Survey.

✕ Iron ore
● Coking coal
▲ Fluxing stone

Dots indicate steelmaking communities. The larger the dots, the larger the steelmaking potential of the plants symbolized.

☐ Symbol indicates that finished steel products are manufactured in the state.

Water routes of iron ore shipments via the Great Lakes

Iron ore from Quebec-Labrador

Foreign iron sources are Europe, Africa, South America, and Canada

market, there is always the choice of "staying put" or of relocating. At various times, when factors affected by location become relatively more important, management gives serious thought to the possibility of relocating; at other times these factors are obscured by more pressing problems.

When confronted with rising sales and shifting markets, the average firm usually has the following alternatives:

1. *Not to expand and to allow the growth in business to go to competitors.*
2. *Not to expand but to subcontract the overage and thus attempt to keep business.*
3. *Expand where presently located.*
4. *Maintain the present location but build new facilities at various other places.*
5. *Abandon the present location and relocate all facilities.*

Any company that has remained at a given site for some time has had to weigh these alternatives, for no location will remain competitive indefinitely. At present, methods of transportation and their costs are undergoing radical changes and are causing many firms to move. The opening of the St. Lawrence Seaway, for example, sharply increased the desirability of situating import and export industries in the North Central states. Similarly, the desirability of a south-central location has been enhanced by the relatively cheap power available from the government-sponsored TVA. The Pacific Northwest, in more recent years, has also benefited from government power projects. Both of these areas have attracted aluminum and other industries that have high power requirements. When the management of a firm decides against relocating, it is balancing the possible extra profit to be gained by moving against the savings in effort and capital that would result from remaining at the present site. Only when the advantages of relocation far outweigh the "rationalized savings," or "psychic profit," of remaining will a move normally occur.

Measurement of Locational Factors

In evaluating location alternatives, two different types of information must be considered. One encompasses the locational factors that can be measured on a cost, or quantitative, basis. The other includes the factors that *cannot* be measured in terms of dollars but only on a qualitative basis. The techniques for evaluating the quantitative and qualitative factors will now be analyzed, and then they will be applied to particular types of location problems.

Quantitative Factors in Location Analysis

The objective of location analysis is to maximize a company's profit. Since, with respect to location, maximum profits occur when costs are minimized, location analysis normally focuses on minimizing the *total* costs of operation. This analysis assumes that some costs will be higher in one location than in another, but it ensures that *all* relevant costs will be taken into consideration.

For purposes of analysis, total costs are divided into operating (or variable) costs and fixed costs. The operating costs relevant to location analysis can, in turn, be subdivided into (1) the cost of obtaining the inputs for production, (2) the cost of converting the inputs to outputs, and (3) the cost of distributing the final product. These specific cost elements affect location decisions in all industries, but their relative importance is subject to wide variation from industry to industry, depending largely upon the nature of the product being manufactured and the technology employed. Although it is difficult to make meaningful generalizations about these cost elements, a few axiomatic observations may prove helpful. In cases where the ratio of product (or raw material) weight or volume to its value is high, greater emphasis tends to be placed upon transportation costs as a determinant of location. Witness the tendency to situate brick, cement, and glass factories near a source of the needed raw material. These industries service a relatively small market area for the same reason. Distributors of lumber and other bulky building supplies tend to follow suit because the awkward size of their products also raises transportation costs. In the automobile industry, assembly plants are located near the various marketplaces because of the competitive need to keep transportation costs down to manageable proportions. This factor assumes even greater relative importance in industries where the initial processing results in a decrease of weight and volume. Since it is economical to reduce as much as possible the distance that raw materials must travel, steel mills, metallic smelters, and wood and pulp mills are situated near their respective raw materials. Similarly, in the aluminum industry, processing plants that reduce bauxite (imported from the Caribbean area) to alumina are found along the Gulf coast of the United States. Here, the transformation of bauxite reduces its weight and volume by about half. Since water transportation is generally the cheapest mode, many of these industries are situated at seaports and along major rivers. Interestingly enough, iron ores from Venezuela and other foreign sources can be shipped to steel mills in Detroit, Gary, and elsewhere in the Midwest at costs that are competitive with domestic ores because of the opening of the St. Lawrence Seaway, which permits direct delivery by boat.

Generalizing further, if the production process requires an unusual amount of electric power, this cost can be a decisive factor in location decisions. Cases in point are the aluminum reduction mills, which transform alumina to aluminum. These plants are found in the Pacific Northwest and in the TVA area, where power is cheap and abundant. For the same reason, Alcoa located one of its plants in the Hudson Bay area, where the company generates its own electrical power. Because water is a significant element in the processing of paper, petroleum, and chemicals, sites along rivers are characteristic of these industries. In a different case, where the production process requires highly skilled and intelligent workers, as in the research-oriented electronics and aerospace industries, the availability of high-skilled labor becomes the crucial location factor; in those industries it is also important that firms be located in or near communities that have good colleges and research centers for the employees and good schools for their children. Thus, it is not surprising that these industries have clustered around the prominent universities and research centers in Massachusetts, California, and Pennsylvania.

One should not assume that the cost structure, or the relative importance of the various cost elements, remains constant within an industry. Wide variations are encountered when the potential costs at different possible sites are compared, but each firm must be concerned with the net advantage—all cost elements considered—of each specific site. To illustrate, let us consider the decision process for evaluating relative labor costs.

The fact that wage rates in one area may be considerably lower than elsewhere does not mean that firms should rush to locate their plants there. There may be important reasons why that area would not be the optimum location. When the labor component of operating costs is evaluated, wage levels per se are not the basic factor; rather, the labor unit cost, or labor productivity, is the crucial factor. This is what really determines the advantages or disadvantages of particular sites in terms of the labor force. The American industrial system is based upon high wage rates and high productivity, which result in low labor costs per unit. In contrast, foreign industry has typically relied upon low wage rates and has tolerated low productivity.[2] This very condition makes American industry competitive with foreign industry. Now the question arises: Can a producer move to a low-wage-level area and, through the erection of efficient plants, obtain the advantages of *both* high productivity and a low wage level? Because they believed they could, many American firms have considered overseas sites for their manufacturing plants. Relocation in labor-rich, underindustrialized sections of the United States, such as the state of Mississippi, has been prompted by the same motive; however, such a decision is more complex than it might seem. A possible advantage in labor costs may be offset by disadvantages in other factors; fuel, power, taxes, transportation, credit, capital equipment, and other expenses may outweigh the labor advantage. In industries such as oil and chemicals, which have a huge investment in capital equipment, labor costs represent only a small percentage of the total costs; therefore, the nonlabor costs tend to be more important in a location decision. On the other hand, in the garment, textile, and other "labor-intensive" industries, labor costs are a high percentage of total costs; therefore it is generally to the advantage of these industries to locate in low-wage areas. In sum, each industry must evaluate the relative importance of the various cost factors to determine which site would be most advantageous. Any company is apt to find itself in dire straits, however, if it bases its location decision upon any single cost factor, instead of considering the total cost picture.

Break-even analysis   One useful way of assessing the interaction between variable operating costs and fixed costs in deciding upon a location is to make

---

[2] The increase in productivity of foreign plants together with their lower labor costs has in recent years been one of the main reasons the United States has shifted from a country that exports more than it imports to one that imports more than it exports.

a "location break-even" analysis. The break-even chart, a traditional management tool, attempts to show graphically the interrelationships among production volume, cost structure, and sales volume. As such, the chart can be used to depict the effect of changing production volumes on the operating costs and profits that pertain to alternate possible plant sites. By enabling management to consider the relative economic feasibility of alternate sites at different operating volumes, break-even analysis sharpens the precision with which location decisions can be made.

To construct a break-even chart for location analysis, the volume in physical units is plotted along the horizontal (X) axis and the cost in dollars is plotted along the vertical (Y) axis. The sales revenue is assumed to be independent of the plant site, since it is believed that company products and markets will be largely unaffected by this factor. The line representing total costs is a composite of fixed and variable costs. Fixed costs are plotted first; for limited areas of production near full capacity, they may be represented by a horizontal line. Variable costs are plotted beginning at the point of intersection of the fixed cost line and the Y axis. The slope of the variable cost line reflects the behavior of costs that vary with the level of output.

The general form of a typical location break-even chart is shown in Figure 16–2. Figure 16–3, on the other hand, illustrates a hypothetical break-even analysis for five possible locations. Table 16–1 lists the cost breakdown for those five locations. Notice that only the costs that are considered relevant have been included in the analysis, which means that they are significant and that they differ from one site to the next, thus providing a basis for decision making.

Of particular interest in Figure 16–3 is the fact that the total cost lines for the various sites intersect, indicating that the advantage of each site is not absolute but will vary according to the level of output. Sites that possess certain advantages at one level of output lose them at another level. For example, sites

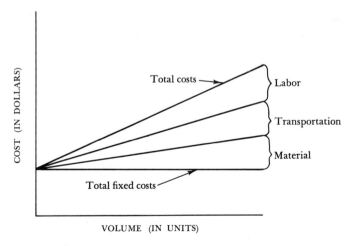

Figure 16–2 General form of a location break-even chart

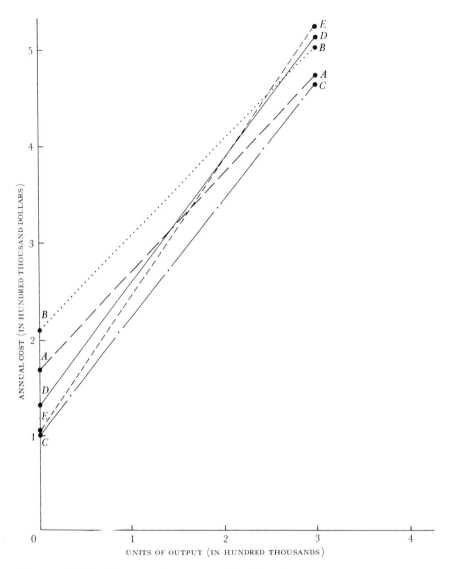

Figure 16–3 Comparative cost relationships for locations in Table 16–1

that are attractive because of the low fixed costs they would provide may, at high volumes of output, become quite expensive because of operating costs. Therefore, in comparing cost factors, it is crucial that the same level of output volume be used, or else the comparison will have little value. In determining this output volume, management faces the difficult task of deciding what relative weight to assign to forecast sales expansion. Should the output volume used in comparing possible sites be the present level of operations? Or should the comparative feasibility of the alternate sites be based upon the sales volume expected

Table 16-1 Comparative costs for five possible locations[a]

	Site A	Site B	Site C	Site D	Site E
Material (per unit)	$ 0.34	$ 0.32	$ 0.48	$ 0.42	$ 0.49
Transportation (per unit)	0.32	0.30	0.36	0.40	0.47
Electric power[b]	30,000.00	48,000.00	67,000.00	35,000.00	72,600.00
Taxes (per year)	110,000.00	138,000.00	4,500.00	80,000.00	5,700.00
Labor (per unit)	0.40	0.36	0.41	0.43	0.44
Water[b]	6,000.00	4,900.00	11,000.00	2,900.00	6,600.00
Insurance (per year)	12,000.00	18,000.00	13,500.00	12,700.00	14,200.00

[a] All other costs, such as land and buildings, are assumed to be equal for all alternatives.
[b] Estimated cost per year at average level of output. In these calculations, electric power and water are treated as relevant fixed costs.

in two, three, or even five years? This problem is particularly acute when a production facility for a new product is being constructed because a poor estimate of operating volume can lead to the construction of a plant that is too small or too large or perhaps in an unfavorable location. Poor estimates of volume can also have a severe impact on operating costs. There is no easy solution to this problem, but most businessmen seem to prefer to discount the reliability of future sales estimates and base their evaluation upon operating volumes predicted for the immediate period. Industry and product characteristics could, of course, alter this approach, but for most businesses it seems to be consistent with their conservative judgment.

Location cost-summary chart An alternate approach to the comparative evaluation of the cost data for possible sites is the construction of a location cost-summary chart. On such a chart, relevant operating cost elements that are affected by location appear in a vertical column at the left; here again, expenses that are independent of the site are not included. The alternate sites under consideration are listed across the top of the chart. Next, an appropriate unit of production such as a ton of steel, a box of candy, or a television set is chosen. Then, assuming a projected volume of output, costs per unit of production for each cost element listed are determined for each of the possible locations. When all of the unit costs under each site are added together, they yield a composite site cost that can be used to determine the relative net cost advantage or disadvantage for each of the alternatives. A location cost-summary chart appears in Table 16-2. The chief advantage of this type of analysis is its clarity of presentation and comprehensibility. The analysis is limited, however, in that it fails to consider all the factors that can influence a choice of location.[3] For example, the summary chart is unable to reflect in a meaningful fashion the impact of changes in the firm's level of operation. Fixed costs per unit are determined for

[3] Here, as in the break-even analysis, intangibles that may be of decisive importance are not considered. A separate analysis is required for these intangibles, as we shall discuss in a moment.

Table 16–2   Location cost-summary chart

	Site A	Site B	Site C	Site D
Power	$0.030	$0.040	$0.030	$0.040
Labor	0.130	0.150	0.120	0.110
Material	0.080	0.060	0.070	0.080
Taxes	0.001	0.0015	0.001	0.001
Water	0.001	0.001	0.001	0.001
Insurance	0.010	0.012	0.014	0.011
Transportation	0.020	0.030	0.035	0.025
Total composite site cost	$0.272	$0.2945	$0.271	$0.258

only one volume, and possible future changes in cost structure—that is, in the ratio of fixed to variable costs, which can be critical in a comparative evaluation—are not specified. Consequently, care must be taken in interpreting these charts lest they be used improperly.

Qualitative Factors in Location Analysis

In searching for the optimum plant site, management must also consider relevant factors to which cost values cannot be assigned; these are usually termed *intangibles*. Break-even analysis and cost-per-unit summaries do not provide a means for gauging intangibles, yet they can be extremely significant in location decisions. The lack of good schools in an area, for example, may make it difficult to obtain skilled personnel. Other important intangibles are

1. Labor supply
2. Union activity
3. Labor skills available
4. Community attitudes toward company activities
5. Local transportation facilities
6. Recreation
7. Community growth potential
8. Universities, colleges, and research centers
9. Community tax status

To evaluate the relative importance of factors of this type, a noncost evaluation system can be used. Although, of necessity, this is a highly subjective technique, a structured analysis is usually more precise than unstructured managerial judgment. One of the methods used is termed *qualitative factor analysis*.

Qualitative factor analysis[4]   The first step in this method is to develop a list of factors that cannot be evaluated monetarily but are nonetheless considered important in a location. These factors are then ranked in order of their relative

[4] This approach is quite similar to the methods used in job evaluation.

importance, or else they are assigned point values that reflect their respective merits.

A simple ranking technique will suffice for enterprises that wish to examine the importance of noncost factors in a systematic fashion but do not feel it necessary to undertake a more complicated procedure. Although the results of a simple ranking analysis may not be as precise as a more complex point system, it is certainly better than to neglect the noncost factors altogether. Companies that prefer a more extensive analysis are likely to find simple ranking inadequate for their purpose because it does not provide a breakdown of the factors used by the rater in his evaluation; therefore, simple ranking tends to be more subjective than the point system.

The point-rating system does have this breakdown. There are shortcomings in obtaining a rating in points for each factor, of course, but the method offers the distinct advantage of providing the best means now available for evaluating the noncost factors at various alternative sites. There are three steps in designing a point-rating system. The first (as we have mentioned) is to make a list of all the important intangibles associated with a location; it should be a comprehensive list.

The next step is to develop a scale for each intangible based on a qualitative measure of that factor; it should ordinarily be composed of descriptive phrases to which points are affixed. In Table 16–3, one of the factors to be evaluated is

Table 16–3 Point-rating scale of noncost factors

	Points
Research climate (sufficient educational facilities and research organizations to attract research personnel)	
No schools or laboratories exist	0
A few low-quality facilities exist	50
Good industrial laboratories exist, but no educational facilities	100
Good educational facilities exist, but no industrial facilities	150
Good educational and industrial facilities exist	200
Excellent facilities and future possibilities	250
Production labor pool (availability of semiskilled production workers)	
Unavailable	0
Available in limited numbers at premium wages	20
Available in sufficient numbers for the present but not for the future	40
Available in sufficient numbers for the present and the future	60
An abundance of extremely skilled workers	80
Community attitudes (desire for and acceptance of the company's activities)	
Violently opposed to company activities	0
Will accept grudgingly	25
Cooperative	50
Cooperative and helpful to a high degree	75

the availability of semiskilled labor; its scale ranges from "unavailable" to "an abundance of extremely skilled workers." The points associated with this scale range from 0 to 80.

The third step is to weight the factors themselves. If their relative importance is thought to vary, the more important ones may be given several times the weight of the least significant one. If, for example, the availability of a large labor pool is considered to be more important than local recreation facilities, it may be assigned a point value three or four times as great. In Table 16–3, "research climate" is weighted to show that it is more than three times (250/80) as important as the "production labor pool." If the factors are all considered equal, however, no weighting function is required.

After the factors have been weighted, the table is complete and ready for use. To utilize such a table for the selection of the best plant site, management must first establish the minimum degree of availability that it considers mandatory for each factor. For example, under "research climate," management may decide that no site should be considered that does not have at least "good educational facilities." This same procedure is followed for all other factors; any sites that do not satisfy these initial conditions can be omitted immediately. The remaining locations are then evaluated factor by factor and assigned the appropriate number of points at each stage. Following this, the points are totaled for each site, and the one with the highest point value is considered the best (in terms of noncost factors).

The location that appears most attractive on a noncost basis can then be compared with the one selected on a cost basis. If the two answers agree, the final selection is made; if they disagree, however, management must make a subjective choice between the two. In such cases, the location with the superior cost rating will normally prevail unless the noncost factor rating of the minimum cost alternative was extremely poor.

The chief criticism of these two methods of evaluating noncost factors concerns the subjectivity associated with both the initial weighting of the factors and the selection of the proper factor rating to describe a particular location. Of necessity, the breakdown of a factor into qualitative degrees is done very roughly, making it difficult to select the rating, or qualitative degree, most descriptive of a characteristic of a location. Despite these limitations, point-rating scales are the only real substitute for unstructured subjective analysis of noncost factors; this partially explains why there is a heavy reliance on cost factors in the location-decision process.

The Location-Decision Process

The Decision Process for a Single Plant[5]

The location-decision process has three stages. The first requires an evaluation of various geographic areas and the selection of an optimum area using the techniques described above. The region selected is often large enough to include all

---

[5] *Single plant* is used to denote the fact that a product is to be produced at only one site.

points with a 50- or 100-mile radius of the specific site (perhaps a city or town) that was used in the location analysis. For all intents and purposes, all points within this circle are thought to have approximately the same advantages over other points outside the circle.

Within each region there is usually a choice of an urban, rural, or suburban site. Even in the highly populated New York area, rural and suburban sites can be found within 10 to 15 miles of the city. Thus, at the second stage, relative merits of these different types of localities must be assessed; Table 16–4 summarizes the advantages normally attributed to each. The relative importance of the factors listed will, of course, vary from industry to industry, depending primarily upon the product made and the technology used. The weighting of these factors and the decision process itself are often subjective.

Finally, at the third stage, the actual site itself must be found. The availability of sufficient land to build on or a suitable building to lease will be the determining factor. When appraising a particular site, management will usually consider loading facilities, transportation facilities for materials and for workers, the amount of room available for expansion and parking, and other local con-

Table 16–4   Comparative advantages among urban,
rural, and suburban plant locations

Advantages of urban sites
1. Better transportation systems for raw materials, labor, and finished goods
2. Larger labor supply (variety and quantity of skills)
3. Complementary related industries (source of materials, labor skills, and services such as IBM)
4. Larger local market (industrial and retail consumers)
5. Greater ease of finance (institutions available and practices developed)
6. Municipal services (streets, police, fire, power, sewers)
7. Business services (data processing, C.P.A.'s, consultants, etc.)
8. Industry and business-oriented civic attitudes

Advantages of rural sites
1. More plentiful process water (from streams, lakes, watersheds)
2. Cheaper land (expansion, parking)
3. Lower taxes
4. Fewer restrictive ordinances
5. Improved labor stability (less mobility, less competition, lower wages)
6. Recreation close by (hunting, fishing, etc.)

Advantages of suburban sites
1. Compromise (can simultaneously benefit to a degree from both sets of advantages)
2. Planned industrial parks (excellent industrial space)
3. Larger land availability (lower taxes and fewer restrictive ordinances than in urban area)
4. Labor skills, finances, related industries, and local markets are nearly comparable to urban sites

---

ditions. While we have discussed the process of selecting a plant site in a sequential pattern, in reality there is a great deal of overlap between the three stages, each having a bearing on the decisions made in the others.

Making a complete location analysis can be quite expensive, particularly if data must be gathered for many alternative sites. Fortunately, many local agencies are willing to provide these data free of charge. Groups that can be called on for this purpose include local and state chambers of commerce, power companies, railroads, and industrial development commissions set up by various levels of government. Admittedly, these agencies are promotion-minded and will champion their respective localities. However, they can and will, if specifically requested, furnish much useful data at little or no cost. An astute management will "interpret" this information in the proper perspective for making its decision.

The Multiplant Location-Decision Process

Where more than one plant is involved in supplying a given marketing area, the location decision becomes more complex. Comparisons between single alternative locations cannot be made; instead, each new alternative site must be compared within the framework of the entire network. Thus, the range of analysis includes the network of existing plant sites and the new proposed sites. The objective is to select a new location that will minimize the cost of the entire network. This complex problem lends itself to solution by linear programing methods.

As an example, let us consider a hypothetical company—Metals, Inc., which makes automotive parts that are used in the assembly of automobiles. At present, the company has three plants, one in Cleveland, one in Denver, and one in Philadelphia. These plants supply four automobile assembly plants: in Oakland, Gary, Houston, and Newark. Of late, the output from the company's plants has not been able to keep pace with its orders. As a result, the company has decided to build a new plant to expand its productive capacity. It is considering San Francisco and Atlanta as possible sites; both appear to be excellent choices in terms of noncost factors.

The production costs and output requirements for each of the existing plants are shown in Table 16–5, together with the estimated production costs of the two new proposed locations. Transportation costs from all these plants to the assembly plants are shown in Table 16–6. The question facing Metals, Inc. is: Which proposed plant site will yield the lowest cost to the enterprise as a whole? A simple comparison of production costs would indicate that Atlanta was best, because its unit production cost is $0.49 whereas at San Francisco it is $0.53. Atlanta may not, however, be the optimum location from the point of view of the entire company system. The interactions between the proposed sites and the existing ones must be considered. Consequently, the total costs that the entire system would incur if the new plant were located in Atlanta must be compared with those incurred for a San Francisco location before a decision can be reached. Let us assume, for the sake of simplicity, that each of the existing

Table 16–5 Demand and production data

Assembly Plant	Assembly Plant Requirements (in units per month)	Production Plant	Normal Production Loads (in units per month)	Unit Production Costs
Oakland	9,000	Denver	6,000	$0.48
Gary	10,000	Philadelphia	14,000	0.50
Houston	12,000	Cleveland	15,000	0.52
Newark	15,000	Total	35,000	
Total	46,000			

Required from new plant: 46,000 − 35,000 = 11,000 units per month

Estimated Unit Production Costs	
Atlanta	$0.49
San Francisco	0.53

plants—in Cleveland, Denver, and Philadelphia—will continue to produce the same volume of output, so that the production costs of these facilities will not be affected by the site decision. Therefore, we may exclude these costs from our analysis as irrelevant. The systems costs that *are* affected by the choice of a new plant location are primarily the transportation costs. The choice of a site will determine which plants, including the new one, will ship what quantities of goods to the company's different assembly plants. This means that management must determine for each of the proposed locations which distribution assignment would result in minimum transportation costs. If these transportation costs are then calculated for both San Francisco and Atlanta, a comparison of these figures would reveal which site would be optimal from the point of view of system transportation costs. The only other relevant costs for this analysis are the production costs at the alternative plants themselves. When system transportation costs and estimated production costs are totaled for each site, the lower sum will indicate which one would optimize the profits of the system.

Table 16–6 Transportation costs

	From				
To	Cleveland	Denver	Philadelphia	San Francisco	Atlanta
Gary	$0.25	$0.35	$0.36	$0.60	$0.35
Houston	0.55	0.30	0.45	0.38	0.30
Newark	0.40	0.50	0.26	0.65	0.41
Oakland	0.60	0.40	0.66	0.27	0.50

The decision approach outlined above depends upon the ability of management to match plant capacities and assembly plant demands in a manner that will minimize transportation costs. This problem is typical of those problems that can be solved by use of a transportation method of linear programing. To do so, a network such as the one illustrated in Figure 16–4 (for San Francisco) is constructed, using the production sites and capacities as headings for the vertical columns and the assembly plant sites and demands as headings for the horizontal rows. The applicable transportation costs are then placed in the corner of each square. Thus, in Figure 16–4, we see that it costs $0.35 to ship one unit of output from Denver to Gary. These transportation costs may be used as a basis for matching capacities and demands. Notice that in the example the total capacity of the four plants is equal to the total demand of the four assembly plants. When the assignment process is complete, there is full utilization of production capacity and full satisfaction of sales demand. In actual situations this may not be so, however, and slack variables representing alternative demand and capacity data must be introduced to make the solution sufficiently flexible.

To determine the minimum transportation costs for the system, we can begin by assigning the production output to the assembly plants in an arbitrary fashion. Starting in the upper left-hand corner (the northwest corner), we can assign 10,000 units of Cleveland's output to Gary as shown in Figure 16–5. This satisfies the demand at the Gary assembly plant. Cleveland still has 5,000 (15,000 − 10,000) units of production to be allocated, and these are sent to

From / To		Cleveland (C)	Denver (D)	Philadelphia (P)	Atlanta (a)	Demand (in thousands of units)
Gary (y)		$.25	$.35	$.36	$.35	10
Houston (H)		$.55	$.30	$.45	$.30	12
Newark (n)		$.40	$.50	$.26	$.41	15
Oakland (O)		$.60	$.40	$.66	$.50	9
Capacity (in thousands of units)		15	6	14	11	46

Figure 16–4   Basic transportation network

From / To	Cleveland (C)	Denver (D)	Philadelphia (P)	San Francisco (S)	Demand (in thousands of units)
Gary (G)	$.25 10	$.35	$.36	$.60	10
Houston (H)	$.55 5	$.30 6	$.45 1	$.38	12
Newark (N)	$.40	$.50	$.26 13	$.65 2	15
Oakland (O)	$.60	$.40	$.66 9	$.27 9	9
Capacity (in thousands of units)	15	6	14	11	46

Figure 16–5 The initial, or northwest, solution

Houston. Houston's demand is 12,000 units; since 5,000 have been satisfied by Cleveland, 7,000 are still needed. Denver can ship 6,000 and Philadelphia 1,000 units. Following through in this fashion, Philadelphia ships its remaining 13,000 units of output to Newark, and San Francisco ships 2,000 units to Newark and 9,000 to Oakland. The transportation costs for this solution are shown in Table 16–7.

Table 16–7 Transportation costs of the initial solution

Cleveland to Gary	$10,000 \times \$0.25 = \$\ 2,500$
Cleveland to Houston	$5,000 \times 0.55 = 2,750$
Denver to Houston	$6,000 \times 0.30 = 1,800$
Philadelphia to Houston	$1,000 \times 0.45 = 450$
Philadelphia to Newark	$13,000 \times 0.26 = 3,380$
San Francisco to Newark	$2,000 \times 0.65 = 1,300$
San Francisco to Oakland	$9,000 \times 0.27 = \underline{2,430}$
	$\$14,610$

Is this particular solution the least costly? We can determine this by seeing if the costs can be reduced by shifting allocations to the empty squares. To illustrate this process, let us take the first empty square in the second vertical column DG (Denver–Gary). Any changes that we make must conform to the restrictions of the available plant outputs and assembly plant demands. If we shift one unit from CG to DG and one unit from DH to CH, as shown in Figure 16–6, we will meet this restriction. This change would not, however, be advantageous since it would be shifting from lower to higher cost squares. By adding a unit to DG and CH and subtracting one from DH and CG, we add $0.35 + $0.55 = $0.90 and subtract $0.25 + $0.30 = $0.55; in sum, we are adding $0.90 − $0.55 = $0.35 to our costs.

All of the empty squares should be tested to see if shifting allocations to them will result in lower total transportation costs. The empty squares should be tested in sequence starting with the first one in the first vertical column and proceeding down the column. Then, empty squares in the second column should be checked and the process continued until all have been tested. The shifts do not have to be made in a rectangular pattern; there should be a closed path starting with the empty square and returning to it, with right angle turns at squares that have allocations. Squares can be skipped, but no diagonal movement is allowable. The square being tested is assigned a (+) value since an allocation is added to it, and alternate (−) and (+) values are assigned to the other squares around the path. Only one closed path is available for each empty square.

Following this procedure for the empty squares in Figure 16–6, our calculations and decisions are shown in Table 16–8. Since it is advantageous to shift some of the allocation to square SH, the change is made and the new matrix is shown in Figure 16–7.

| From / To | Plants | | | | Demand |
	Cleveland (C)	Denver (D)	Philadelphia (P)	San Francisco (S)	(in thousands of units)
Gary (Y)	$.25 10 (−) →	$.35 (+)	$.36	$.60	10
Houston (H)	$.55 5 (+) ←	$.30 6 (−)	$.45 1	$.38	12
Newark (N)	$.40	$.50	$.26 13	$.65 2	15
Oakland (O)	$.60	$.40	$.66	$.27 9	9
Capacity (in thousands of units)	15	6	14	11	46

Figure 16–6 Evaluation of empty square DG

Table 16-8 Summary: Evaluation of empty squares to test proposed allocation plan for San Francisco

Tested Square	Path	Cost Change	Action
CN	CN → CH → PH → CN	+$0.40 − $0.55 + $0.45 − $0.26 = +$0.04	No change
CO	CO → CH → PH → PN → SN → SO → CO	+$0.60 − $0.55 + $0.45 − $0.26 + $0.65 − $0.27 = +$0.62	No change
DG	DG → DH → CH → CG → DG	+$0.35 − $0.30 + $0.55 − $0.25 = +$0.35	No change
DN	DN → DH → PH → PN → DN	+$0.50 − $0.30 + $0.45 − $0.26 = +$0.39	No change
DO	DO → DH → PH → PN → SN → SO → DO	+$0.40 − $0.30 + $0.45 − $0.26 + $0.65 − $0.27 = +$0.67	No change
PG	PG → PH → CH → CG → PP	+$0.36 − $0.45 + $0.55 − $0.25 = +$0.21	No change
PO	PO → PN → SN → SO → PO	+$0.66 − $0.26 + $0.65 − $0.27 = +$0.78	No change
SG	SG → SN → PN → PH → CH → CG → SG	+$0.60 − $0.65 + $0.26 − $0.45 + $0.55 − $0.25 = +$0.06	No change
SH	SH → SN → PN → PH → SN	+$0.38 − $0.65 + $0.26 − $0.45 = −$0.46	Change allocation

Table 16-9 Summary: Evaluation of empty squares to test proposed allocation plan for Atlanta

Tested Square	Path	Cost Change	Action
CO	CO → CH → SH → SO → CO	+$0.60 − $0.55 + $0.38 − $0.27 = +$0.16	No change
DG	DG → DH → CH → CG → DG	+$0.35 − $0.30 + $0.55 − $0.25 = +$0.35	No change
DN	DN → CN → DH → DN	+$0.50 − $0.40 + $0.55 − $0.30 = +$0.35	No change
DO	DO → DH → SH → SO → DO	+$0.40 − $0.30 + $0.38 − $0.27 = +$0.21	No change
PG	PG → PN → CN → CG → PG	+$0.36 − $0.26 + $0.40 − $0.25 = +$0.25	No change
PH	PH → PN → CN → CH → PH	+$0.45 − $0.26 + $0.40 − $0.55 = +$0.04	No change
PO	PO → PN → CN → CH → SH → SO → PO	+$0.66 − $0.26 + $0.40 − $0.55 + $0.38 − $0.27 = +$0.36	No change
SG	SG → SH → CH → CG → SG	+$0.60 − $0.38 + $0.55 − $0.25 = +$0.52	No change
SN	SN → GN → GH → SH → SN	+$0.65 − $0.40 + $0.55 − $0.38 = +$0.42	No change

Figure 16–7 Allocation reflecting shift to square SH

Having finished one iteration through the matrix, we must proceed as before and test the new allocations to see if they are the best. The allocations in Figure 16–7 are not the best; as shown below, a favorable allocation can be made for square CN.

Tested Square	Path	Cost Change	Action
CN	CN→CH→SH→SN→CN	$0.40 − $0.55 + $0.38 − $0.65 = − $0.42	Change allocation

The new allocation reflecting this change in CN is shown in Figure 16–8. Continuing as before, we test the empty squares as indicated in Table 16–9. Since no changes can be made, Figure 16–8 thus reflects the best possible allocation. The transportation costs for this matrix and the production costs for the San Francisco site are shown in Table 16–10.

In a like fashion, the transportation costs for the Atlanta site can be determined; the best allocations are shown in Figure 16–9. Notice that since the transportation costs from Atlanta differ from those of San Francisco, the allocations are also different.

The transportation costs of the Atlanta site and its production costs are shown in Table 16–11. It can be seen that San Francisco is the better site, since its total cost is $370 ($19,930 − $19,560) less than Atlanta's; this is true even in spite of the lower production costs at Atlanta.

| From \ To | Plants | | | | Demand (in thousands of units) |
	Cleveland (C)	Denver (D)	Philadelphia (P)	San Francisco (S)	
Gary (G)	$.25 — 10	$.35	$.36	$.60	10
Houston (H)	$.55 — 4	$.30 — 6	$.45	$.38 — 2	12
Newark (N)	$.40 — 1	$.50	$.26 — 14	$.65	15
Oakland (O)	$.60	$.40	$.66	$.27 — 9	9
Capacity (in thousands of units)	15	6	14	11	46

Figure 16–8 Allocation reflecting shift to square CN

This is a highly simplified problem, but it does demonstrate what factors must be considered in multiplant location decisions and what analytical tools are available.

| From \ To | Plants | | | | Demand (in thousands of units) |
	Cleveland (C)	Denver (D)	Philadelphia (P)	Atlanta (A)	
Gary (G)	$.25 — 10	$.35	$.36	$.35	10
Houston (H)	$.55	$.30 — 1	$.45	$.30 — 11	12
Newark (N)	$.40 — 1	$.50	$.26 — 14	$.41	15
Oakland (O)	$.60 — 4	$.40 — 5	$.66	$.50	9
Capacity (in thousands of units)	15	6	14	11	46

Figure 16–9 Best allocation for the Atlanta site

Table 16–10   Minimum cost networks for the San Francisco site

Transportation costs			
Cleveland to Gary	$10,000 \times \$0.25 =$	\$ 2,500
Cleveland to Houston	$4,000 \times 0.55 =$	2,200
Denver to Houston	$6,000 \times 0.30 =$	1,800
Cleveland to Newark	$1,000 \times 0.40 =$	400
Philadelphia to Newark	$14,000 \times 0.26 =$	3,640
San Francisco to Houston	$2,000 \times 0.38 =$	760
San Francisco to Oakland	$9,000 \times 0.27 =$	2,430
		$13,730
Production costs	$11,000 \times \$0.53 =$	\$ 5,830
Total relevant cost		$19,560

Table 16–11   Minimum cost networks for the Atlanta site

Transportation costs			
Cleveland to Gary	$10,000 \times \$0.25 =$	\$ 2,500
Denver to Houston	$1,000 \times 0.30 =$	300
Cleveland to Newark	$1,000 \times 0.40 =$	400
Cleveland to Oakland	$4,000 \times 0.60 =$	2,400
Denver to Oakland	$5,000 \times 0.40 =$	2,000
Philadelphia to Newark	$14,000 \times 0.26 =$	3,640
Atlanta to Houston	$11,000 \times 0.30 =$	3,300
		$14,540
Production costs	$11,000 \times \$0.49 =$	\$ 5,390
Total relevant cost		$19,930

Current Location Trends

There seems to be a definite trend in recent years toward increased decentralization in business locations. More and more firms are setting up branch operations rather than expanding activities at existing sites. Industries that used to be highly centralized are now spreading throughout the country. This trend is accentuated by the development of a number of large national markets, all of which are expanding and shifting locations. One indication of this fact is that the population center of the United States has gradually been moving from the East to the Midwest. Another contributing factor is the increasing number of rural and urban communities that are trying to attract industry by offering such inducements as tax concessions, free land and buildings, and assurances of a favorable community climate. The rapid development of business communities in Puerto Rico and Florida attest to this fact. Suburban areas are luring industry

Keystone Industrial Park, located near Scranton, Pennsylvania, illustrates the trend to locate plants in rural industrial parks. These parks benefit from their closeness to highway networks, sources of labor, and desirable residential areas.

away from large cities with lower cost land, lower taxes, and better living conditions that offer access to the cultural facilities and other advantages of the urban centers. Suburban industrial parks are becoming increasingly popular because they offer lots of land for expansion, sufficient parking space, and many other intangible assets, all at a reasonable price. More and more communities are seeking to protect their income from the declining fortunes of specific industries by using low tax rates to attract new and growing industries. Industries in those areas benefit from this trend, too, because they enjoy greater freedom and flexibility in future relocation decisions; they can feel free to move since their decision will not have a disruptive effect on the community's economy, as would be the case if there were only one major industry in the area.

The diversity of business locations is not confined to the continental United States. The possibility of building plants in Puerto Rico, Alaska, Hawaii, or foreign countries is increasingly being considered. Foreign markets, notably in Europe, are expanding rapidly. As the underdeveloped countries of Africa, Asia, and South America mature, they too will represent significant markets. Foreign areas can generally offer abundant, low-cost, unskilled labor and relatively cheap local materials, but skilled labor is often difficult to find. In fact, there is a definite shortage of many skills in Europe, which keeps wage rates high. Low capital supply and high capital costs are universal problems in foreign countries. Productivity levels tend to be lower than those in the United States, and, as in this country, competent management is at a premium. Generalizations of this sort are, of course, unsatisfactory to the manager who wishes to evaluate a possible foreign site for his business, but reliable data are often difficult to obtain. However, in the past ten years, companies locating in countries such as Taiwan, Korea, and others with pools of low-cost labor have been able to train workers for highly skilled jobs. Firms located in those countries have thus benefited from efficient plants and low-cost production labor. As such, they have been able to offset the transportation costs to the United States and compete aggressively in our markets.

At present, the regions in the United States that seem to be attracting most of the new plant sites are the South, the Southwest, and the Pacific Coast states. Corresponding population shifts have occurred, and there has been a development of academic, research, and community institutions in those regions, both of which seem to indicate that this trend will continue. Because of the availability of low-cost land in those areas, there is a definite trend toward the construction of one-story buildings. These can house efficient layouts, thus permitting smooth work flows and low materials-handling costs because of eliminating the multiflow movement of materials. Furthermore, new construction materials and techniques make it relatively inexpensive to construct attractive buildings of this type.

It is comforting to realize, however, that there are many good sites available for a firm; witness the success of companies that have remained where they started or have moved to certain areas simply because of the highly subjective decisions of their chief executives. Location decisions in one successful multi-plant firm actually depend, in the final analysis, on their proximity to good fishing areas! The wide diversity in location among successful firms in the same industry further attests to the large number of good ones; thus, the key objective really seems to be to avoid a poor location, and the techniques described in this chapter are useful tools for this purpose.

Questions and Problems

1. What is the purpose of location analysis?
2. How important is a plant's location to its profitability?
3. List and explain three important advantages and three important disadvantages to a corporation if it were to build a new factory for manufacturing television sets in a small town, say, in east central Pennsylvania, rather than adding to its main plant in Philadelphia.
4. How often does the question of plant location arise? List the principal situations.
5. What kinds of data are needed to analyze alternate sites within a given general area?
6. Dunn is a small town in a Southern state located near another small town in that state. Interested groups in the community are eager to further Dunn's economic development and have succeeded in making available an industrial park for the location of new industries. Low tax rates, low assessments, and attractive financing plans for plant construction are offered as inducements to new industries. The climate is ideal. What advice would you give to a small manufacturer of electronic devices who is seriously considering the community's interesting offer? He will employ approximately 40 men and women.

7. "Plant location is a recurring problem involving business survival." Evaluate this statement.
8. Does the use of a transportation model represent the most meaningful and realistic approach available to management when a plant location decision must be made?
9. Why is the multiplant location problem more complicated than the single-plant problem?
10. How can break-even analysis be used in selecting a new plant site?
11. In 1962 the newly formed XYZ Corporation built a plant in Newark, N.J. The selection of Newark was the result of an intensive location analysis. XYZ is now faced with the need to expand and has decided to build another plant to make the same product, utilizing the same production process. One XYZ executive wants to use the same location approach for the new plant as was used for the successful Newark plant. Another disagrees.

   Should the same procedure be followed? If you believe so, why? If not, why not?
12. The Omega Company maintains branch warehouses in Philadelphia, Chicago, St. Louis, and San Francisco.

   The company's products are currently made in three factories, which are situated in Pittsburgh, Detroit, and Denver. Because of a sharp increase in demand, the company is no longer able to satisfy the market requirements with its existing three plants. Consequently, the company plans to build a fourth manufacturing facility. Two cities—Houston and Indianapolis—are being considered. On the basis of the data presented in the following tables, recommend which plant site should be selected.

TRANSPORTATION COSTS (IN DOLLARS PER UNIT) TO

FROM	Philadelphia	Chicago	St. Louis	San Francisco
Pittsburgh	$0.30	$0.40	$0.35	$0.75
Detroit	0.50	0.25	0.45	0.70
Denver	0.60	0.55	0.40	0.40
Houston	0.65	0.50	0.35	0.45
Indianapolis	0.45	0.20	0.25	0.65

MONTHLY REQUIREMENTS		MONTHLY PRODUCTION CAPACITY	
Warehouse	Number of units	Plant	Number of units
Philadelphia	18,000	Pittsburgh	20,000
Chicago	14,000	Detroit	15,000
St. Louis	12,000	Denver	14,000
San Francisco	20,000	New plant	15,000
Total	64,000	Total	64,000

ESTIMATED PRODUCTION COSTS
(IN DOLLARS PER UNIT)

Houston	$0.42
Indianapolis	0.38

What other studies would you recommend prior to making a final decision?

13. How can the qualitative factors in location analysis be evaluated systematically?
14. The Allied Company, a manufacturer of glue, must give up its plant in downtown Philadelphia because of the historical redevelopment of the area. As a possible new plant site, this company is considering Pittsburgh and Atlanta. It also has plants in Denver, Houston, and St. Louis, and its warehouses are maintained in Baltimore, Chicago, Dallas, and San Francisco.

The following data have been obtained from company forecasts and records:

DEMAND DATA

Warehouse	Units per month
Baltimore	17,000
Chicago	22,000
Dallas	20,000
San Francisco	18,000
Total	77,000

PRODUCTION DATA

Plant	Units per month	Unit production costs
Denver	14,000	$0.62
Houston	24,000	0.60
St. Louis	23,000	0.60
Total	61,000	

NEW PLANT

Site	Production	Unit production costs
Pittsburgh	16,000	$0.58
Atlanta	16,000	0.56

TRANSPORTATION COSTS (IN DOLLARS PER UNIT) FROM

TO	Denver	Houston	St. Louis	Pittsburgh	Atlanta
Baltimore	$0.50	$0.45	$0.32	$0.12	$0.20
Chicago	0.35	0.40	0.28	0.22	0.30
Dallas	0.35	0.10	0.38	0.45	0.28
San Francisco	0.40	0.30	0.42	0.55	0.50

Which of the two sites would you recommend? Use the transportation model to support your position.

15. Is a plant location decision likely to be an example of merely meeting minimum requirements as opposed to optimizing?
16. The TM Machine Company has decided to construct a new plant with a capacity of 8,000 units per month. The number of sites under construction has been reduced to two—Asbury Park, N.J. and Cambridge, Ohio. A study of pro-

duction and transportation costs for the Cambridge location revealed that the selection of this site would have the following results:

Cost of production (8,000 units)	$60,000
Minimum total cost of transportation of the company's product to its markets (monthly)	14,000
Cambridge total	$74,000

The following data pertain to the Asbury Park location:

MONTHLY DEMAND DATA			MONTHLY PRODUCTION CAPACITY	
Warehouse	Number of units		Plant	Number of units
New York	8,000		Hartford, Conn.	8,000
Philadelphia	6,000		Harrisburg, Pa.	10,000
Boston	5,000		Asbury Park, N.J.	8,000
Providence	4,000		Total	26,000
Utica	3,000			
Total	26,000			

	TRANSPORTATION COSTS (IN DOLLARS PER UNIT) TO				
FROM	New York	Philadelphia	Boston	Providence	Utica
Hartford, Conn.	$0.40	$0.60	$0.50	$0.30	$0.65
Harrisburg, Pa.	0.65	0.50	0.80	0.55	0.70
Asbury Park, N.J.	0.25	0.30	0.60	0.70	0.55

If the monthly production cost at the Asbury Park plant were $64,000, which location would be best from a cost point of view?

17. The major problem in business decision making is to emphasize and identify the alternatives. Is this a real problem in plant location decisions?

18. Select three factors that are generally considered in locating a new plant. Explain how they might be applied differently in locating the plant of a single-plant company and one of the plants of a multiplant company.

19. "The noncost factor approach in the location of a plant is the most realistic and meaningful one available to management." Discuss.

References

Armour, G. C., and Buffa, E. S., "A Heuristic Algorithm and Computer Simulation Approach to the Relative Location of Facilities," *Management Science,* Vol. 9, No. 2, Jan. 1963.

Basic Industrial Location Factors, U.S. Department of Commerce, Washington, D.C., 1946.

Dillon, J. D., "The Geographical Distribution of Production in Multiple Plant Operations," *Management Science,* Vol. 2, No. 4, July 1956.

Francis, R. L., "On the Location of Multiple New Facilities with Respect to Existing Facilities," *The Journal of Industrial Engineering,* Vol. 15, No. 2, March–April 1964.

Greenhut, M. L., *Plant Location in Theory and Practice,* Univ. of North Carolina Press, Chapel Hill, N.C., 1956.

Isard, W., *Location and Space Economy: A General Theory Relating to Industrial Location, Market Areas, Land Use, Trade, and Urban Structure,* MIT Press, Cambridge, Mass., 1956.

Maynard, H. B., *Handbook of Modern Manufacturing Management,* McGraw-Hill, New York, 1970.

Mayer, R. R., *Production Management,* 2nd ed., McGraw-Hill, New York, 1968.

"Production Costs Here and Abroad," *Studies in Business Economics,* National Industrial Conference Board, New York, 1958.

"Techniques of Plant Location," *Studies in Business Policy,* No. 61, National Industrial Conference Board, New York, 1953.

Timms, H. L., and Pohlen, M. F., *The Production in Business,* 3rd ed., Irwin, Homewood, Ill., 1970.

Yaseen, L., *Plant Location,* American Research Council, Larchmont, N.Y., 1960.

17

Plant Layout Analysis

After the location for a new plant has been decided upon, the buildings must be designed and the facilities "laid out" within the buildings. The layout of production facilities, their maintenance, and the manner in which materials are moved from one facility to another constitute the master plan, which coordinates all aspects of the production system. The company's buildings, floor space, departments, processing equipment, parts, manufacturing methods, service facilities, and labor must be integrated into a smoothly functioning system. The basic objective, of course, is to create a production system that can meet the capacity and quality requirements of the firm in the most economic manner possible.[1]

Layout

Layout problems are common to all enterprises. A retailer must arrange his counters and display his merchandise upon them with the customer in mind. An office manager must position desks, tables, and office equipment in a manner that will facilitate the flow of work. Manufacturers must position machinery so as to achieve a smooth flow of products through their factories.

Because of the broad scope of the task, layouts for an entire company are usually reviewed by all of its departments. Layouts must facilitate the physical

---

[1] In the design of a production plant, the layout and materials handling problems must be considered at the same time. Since this is not feasible for teaching purposes, separate chapters are devoted to these topics.

coordination of the various departments and functions. Whatever volume of output is selected as the most economical production capacity, in terms of sales requirements, will determine the amount of investment in land, buildings, machinery, labor, and equipment. This optimum capacity figure also dictates the pattern of the work-in-process flow and materially affects the cost of labor, supplies, maintenance, and overhead. In short, the layout decision is the crucial point at which sales, finance, engineering, and production must be coordinated in order to have a physically integrated production system.

The Dynamics of Layout

Because of the dynamic nature of the U.S. economy, the layout of an integrated production system must be flexible enough to permit future changes brought about by production technology, changes in product design, or changes in product mix. In a sense, of course, *all* layouts are flexible; they can all be changed at a price. A *truly* flexible layout, however, is one that can be changed at minimum cost.

A layout is of necessity a compromise between many factors. It remains efficient as long as there is no substantial change in the rate of production, the technology of production, or the final product. When there are significant changes in any of these factors, however, there should be a corresponding change in the layout. Most of these changes will be minor; basic large-scale changes are relatively infrequent. To keep a layout efficient requires continuous review, however, and each small change plays an important role in minimizing costs.

In short, the layout task is quite complex not only because of the magnitude of the problem, but also because almost all of the relevant factors are highly interdependent. The type of production process used affects the materials handling system; the type of labor used affects the production process; the requirements for flexibility affect the type of machinery used. Because of the scope and interaction involved, there is no general approach to an optimal solution; instead, the design of a layout is largely an experienced art. Here we can only cite various rules, principles, and approaches that have proved valuable in the past.

It would seem that the development of a good layout depends upon a series of previously made decisions on location, capacity, facilities, manufacturing method, product mix, and a multitude of less basic, but nevertheless important, factors such as the position of equipment, the flow of materials, and materials handling. Some of these factors are so important that they are discussed in separate chapters. Thus, plant location, work measurement, methods study, and production control are treated separately. In this chapter we are limiting our discussion to the determination of the amount of equipment needed to meet the production schedule and the physical positioning of this equipment within the plant.

Capacity

In considering the layout of a new plant or in redesigning an old one, basic managerial decisions must be made about the required product output levels and the operation of the plant. Policies must be established on working hours, the number of shifts, and the use of overtime. Once all of these decisions have been made, management has a frame of reference for evaluating all subsequent questions on capacity.

The concepts of external and internal balance are two basic criteria often used to determine capacity level. *External balance* is defined as the matching of plant capacity to projected sales demand, whereas *internal balance* is defined as the balancing of internal operations to eliminate production bottlenecks and yet produce the desired output. Application of these criteria leads to the matching of production capability at each step of the manufacturing process.

External balance In assessing external balance, the manager seeks to equate productive capacity with the expected level of demand. Total sales volume in physical units is not an acceptable measure of demand for this purpose, since there may be seasonal or cyclical variations. Similarly, total demand in dollars is usually unsatisfactory because when a company manufactures mixed products, dollar demand does not indicate how much of each will be required for the total production level of the facility. What the manager needs to know in order to determine the overall output capacity is the weekly or monthly demand for the various products in physical units.

There are three commonly accepted methods of achieving external balance:

1. To design the facility to meet peak demand. Production levels can be set at the expected peak of actual demand. This would permit the maintenance of minimum inventories, since the production facility could then keep pace with even the largest sales demands. The use of equipment and labor would be subject to wide fluctuations, however, since at all levels below peak production there would be idle capacity. This approach guarantees the satisfaction of demand, but its basic inefficiencies create problems.

2. To design the physical facility to meet some intermediate level of output, such as average demand. When production levels are fixed at average demand, the objective is to establish a steady production rate that will just satisfy the normal annual demand for the firm's products. In this way, the benefits of a stable work force and full utilization of facilities can be enjoyed. Using this approach, however, means that it will be necessary to accumulate and maintain inventories to meet the sales demand of peak periods. Indeed, large seasonal or cyclical demand variations may make such an approach difficult or perhaps impractical to implement if the costs of maintaining inventories begin to exceed the gains derived from regular production.

3. To design the physical facility to meet the low point in demand. Labor and equipment utilization would be highest if the production levels were geared to the lowest level of demand. Furthermore, there would be little fluctuation in the level of activity, and inventory levels would be at a minimum. Management faces the problem of whether to allow the excess of demand over production to fall to competitors or to subcontract this amount. The latter approach is the basis for "tapered vertical integration," which is practiced by many companies. Enough steel is produced at the Ford Motor Company to meet minimal company needs, for example, and the remaining steel is purchased. In this fashion, Ford can maintain full use of its steel-production capacity even during business troughs. Another common application of this approach is in restaurants and theaters, which scale their operations to a "minimum demand" and allow the overflow to go to competitors.

Several other factors must be weighed in the external balance decision process. One is the time factor. Should the external balance be aimed at the present or at the future market? What elements of the production system are essential now, and what elements can be added with growth? In making allowance for future market demand, it is common practice to buy enough equipment to meet the present demand and provide space to accommodate additional equipment that may be needed in the future. Thus, the current overhead costs attributable to future requirements can be minimized, while still making arrangements for future capacity needs. Failure to plan for future expansion may ultimately cost the firm unnecessary time and money; moreover, the additional space may not be available when it is needed. In short, some future overhead costs probably must be borne by present operations.

Another factor to consider is the capital requirements of alternative capacity decisions. The amount of investment needed to obtain a given capacity depends upon the amount of subcontracting done and the number of shifts during which the facilities are worked. Thus, a basic policy designed to keep the plant in full operation by establishing a low production level and subcontracting overages removes the danger of having costly idle capacity when conditions become acute—for example, when sales fall off. Conversely, the inflexibility of this approach can have an adverse impact on profits. Nonetheless, because this policy does reduce the investment outlay and results in a high utilization of facilities, it is used in many industries.

Finally, there is the problem of deciding how many shifts will produce the best results for a firm. When a plant is in operation for more than one shift, production costs will not be the same for all. Per-unit labor costs will usually rise because shift premiums of up to 15 percent are common. Supervision and other overhead costs also increase. Finally, it has been found that in many industries, such as the electronics and aerospace industries, the productivity levels of a second and third shift are significantly below that of the primary shift because of poorer supervision. This fact tends to accentuate the cost impact of a shift differential in labor base rates. Actually, the answer to the problem of whether additional shifts may be profitable is normally determined by the degree of capitalization in the industry. Industries with heavy capital investment in equipment per worker typically utilize multiple shifts in order to reduce the investment burden. The gains they derive from full utilization of capital facilities is far greater than the costs of relatively inefficient labor. Where capital investment per worker is moderate or low, industries may find that the wage premium and added overhead costs will make additional shifts economically unfeasible; therefore, they may increase the size of their plants.

What approach to external balance will prove most profitable for a particular company? This is difficult to answer since there are so many interrelated factors involved. It is not merely a matter of minimizing the costs of labor turnover, plant investment, or inventory; it requires that the costs and revenues of each alternative be balanced over a period of time. This is a problem of major economic significance involving the entire firm. At present, methods are available only for examining various specific aspects of the problem, but an acceptable overall approach is still lacking.

Internal balance   Internal balance is the equalization of capacities in successive stages of the production process. Once the decision on overall capacity, or external balance, has been made, the problem is simply to provide the correct capacity at each stage of the process so that the production flow is balanced. Thus, for example, when four stages of production are used successively and the first requires twice as much operating time as the second, four times as much as the third, and twice as much as the fourth, simple arithmetic indicates that the ratio of facilities needed to balance the output will be $4:2:1:2$. That is, four stations of step 1 are required, two of step 2, one of step 3, and two of step 4; this simple example is illustrated in Table 17–1.

Table 17–1   Internal balance analysis

Operation Number and Name	Relative Standard Times for Each Operation	Number of Machines Required to Achieve Internal Balance
1. Turret lathe	4.0	4
2. Milling machine	2.0	2
3. Drill press	1.0	1
4. Shear	2.0	2

Situations that are this simple are rare, however. The machines used normally do not have the exact capacity required to provide perfect balancing. The output volume set for the plant as a whole by the external balance decision would generally necessitate fractional quantities of machines if the desired output were to be obtained precisely. The same problem is encountered when attempting to balance work loads on production lines that are mechanically paced. Perfect balance would require the work loads of all workers to be precisely equal, yet this arrangement is extremely difficult to maintain. If the output at any position along the line is below what is needed to match the output of previous stages, a bottleneck will result. On the other hand, if the line is paced to meet the slowest output along the line, costly capacity will remain idle part of every day. This dilemma is one of the most difficult problems to be resolved in the design of automated production processes.

The task of achieving internal balance becomes more complex when many products are manufactured on the same equipment. If the equipment is used to make only one or two products, the calculations for determining how many machines are needed are *relatively* simple. Thus, if 6,000 stampings per shift are needed to meet anticipated demand and the equipment produces 1,600 stampings per shift, then four machines are required. If the production process is complex, "shrinkage," or "yield," may be a significant factor. Shrinkage, or yield, is a generic term for rejects or defective parts. In the simple stamping operation cited above, conceivably a 2 or 3 percent reject rate could apply. Thus, in order to obtain 6,000 good stampings, a lot of 6,120 or 6,180 would have to be processed to allow for rejects. The number of stamping machines needed to produce 6,000 good units would have to be calculated in terms of 6,120 or 6,180 units. In this case, four machines would still provide sufficient capacity, but in more complex operations this might not be so. In such cases, if the shrinkage calculation increases the number of machines required, then the feasibility of trying to reduce the percentage of rejects made, thereby lowering the additional investment required, should be considered.

If small fractions of machines are required in order to achieve balance, overtime or subcontracting are often employed instead of investing in additional machinery. Although this conserves capital and reduces floor space requirements, it does place an added burden on the production planning and control function.

Where a variety of products are manufactured on the same equipment, the task of estimating how much equipment will be needed is much more difficult because of the time required to change from one product to another. This period is usually termed the *setup* or *starting* time. The problem is further complicated if the demand pattern shifts over time, as it does with seasonal products. Many managers tackle this problem by calculating the production quantity and economic lot size of each product per period. If determined in this fashion, the quantity of equipment (capacity) estimated should be capable of turning out the total of all required outputs with allowance for associated setup times. The reason for this is that, as previously discussed, the amount of equipment required to turn out a specified volume of output is a function of the task standard time and the hours of work. To minimize the capital investment required to achieve internal balance under such circumstances, the scheduled hours of work may be varied at successive stages of production. Machines at a bottleneck position may be operated ten or twelve hours a day, for example, to match the output from machines at other positions in an eight-hour day. Additional storage space must be provided in such cases to hold the larger amount of work-in-process inventories that are created. This added cost as well as the extra expense of overtime operations can be justified, however, if the machine investment costs are high or if the product demand is unstable or declining.

In performing internal balance calculations, it is important that actual experience be used as the basis for computation rather than projected theoretical output levels. Output levels in a plant are seldom precisely equal to the calculated standard output. Workers may produce above or below the standard. Consequently, when experience data on actual output levels are available, they should be used.

Internal and external balance   The internal and external balance goals are not independent of each other; they interact in the decision process. To illustrate their interaction, consider the most common measure of equipment utilization in use today, which is variously called the *capacity measure,* the *use measure,* or the *plant efficiency factor.* In essence, it is the ratio of actual output to theoretical capacity.

$$\text{Plant efficiency} = \frac{\text{Actual use}}{\text{Theoretical use}}$$

To apply this simple ratio, it is necessary to select a physical unit with which to measure capacity. Industries that manufacture a homogeneous product family such as tires, books, or automobiles can use the product unit. Where the product is less homogeneous, other simple measures such as tons of steel per day may be used. In cases of extreme diversity—say, a job shop—any measure couched in terms of finished product would be useless; therefore, available hours by class of machines are used.

Once the unit is selected, efficiency can be easily measured by using the ratio given above. Because of breakdowns, preventive maintenance, schedule delays, outages, operator problems, and other inefficiencies, the theoretical limit of 100 percent is rarely achieved. In industry the range normally varies between 50 and 95 percent.

The firm's capacity factor is directly related to both the internal and external balance decisions, as well as to such other factors as the maintenance policy. For the moment, let us confine ourselves to a consideration of the interaction of the internal and external balance decisions as they affect capacity. If the firm's external balance decision is to operate its machines to meet peak demand, the capacity factor will be low. If its decision is to meet minimum demand, the factor will be high. Some production processes require special machines that are idle much of the time but are necessary for internal balance. In these cases, the use measure will be low, but the total plant may be operating at a high level of efficiency.

In a factory, the use factor is frequently employed as a control device. Trend lines for the ratio are plotted for each section on the basis of available figures. Negative slopes, representing falling efficiency, indicate the need for corrective action to reduce idleness resulting from maintenance problems, breakdowns, and other delays. Targets may be set for future use levels so that management may measure the effectiveness of devices designed to promote better utilization of facilities. If underutilization is the result of overcapacity and not operating inefficiencies, a company will often bid for subcontracted work at prices as low as the break-even cost level in order to cover its fixed costs.

As a further example of the interaction between internal and external balance, consider the operation of a petroleum cracking plant, where internal balance is a prime concern. In order to be efficient, the process must be operated at a pace that will balance the production capacities of the various stages. External balance is important in determining the multiples of production units that will be employed.

In short, the two facets of the capacity decision—external and internal balance—are highly interrelated and must be taken into account; the importance of each varies according to the particular process used.

Facility Types

Before closing this discussion of capacity, brief mention must be made of a problem of growing significance, namely, the type of equipment that a firm will employ as a matter of policy. At the root of this problem lies that frequently heard and frequently misused word—*automation*. A firm's management must continually reevaluate the ratio of capital to labor used in its production process. If management increases the ratio by substituting capital in the form of machines for labor, can it boost its profits? Given today's rapidly advancing technology and high labor costs, the introduction of equipment that increases the normal productivity of labor or reduces the labor skills required (and therefore the wage rates) is often a profitable move.

In general, the level of labor effort, skills, and wage rates decline as one moves from manual to automatic machinery, as is indicated in Table 17–2. Labor productivity, on the other hand, invariably increases as the production process becomes more automated, resulting in reduced labor unit costs. Offsetting these savings, however, are higher investment, supervisory, training, and maintenance costs. Since highly automated equipment tends to be quite specialized, it is exceedingly vulnerable to shifts in demand. In industries where sudden shifts are characteristic, therefore, automated equipment can quickly become obsolete or useless. Manual machines, on the other hand, tend to be general purpose in nature; because they are more flexible, they have a more lasting usefulness. But a firm's decision about whether or not to automate is complicated by factors other than cost. Its management must also weigh the impact of automation on the size of the work force, since reductions are a natural consequence of higher labor productivity. The pressures of labor unions and the community itself are important factors in this consideration. The introduction of labor-

Table 17–2   The relationship of labor requirements and machine characteristics

Machine Type	Description	Level of Labor Effort
A	Manually operated	Machines require constant attention. High-skilled labor is needed.
B	Semiautomatic	Operator loads and unloads for each cycle. Less-skilled labor is needed than for A.
C	Automatic	Operator loads for many cycles; he unloads and reloads later. Labor skill requirements are low.
D	Automated	Self-correction; feedback control. Labor attention required is minimal.

A machine assembly bay illustrates a typical plant floor layout for a job-shop operation.

saving equipment should always be carefully planned and a·compromise established between the interests of the company in lowering costs and the interests of the work force and the community in promoting job security. Retraining for other jobs, transfer to other company plants, and severance pay are among the devices that have been successfully used to soften the blow to workers when a production process becomes automated.

Classes of Layouts

In general, there are three classes of layouts: process layout, product layout, and fixed material layout. We will examine each of these in turn.

Process Layout

A process layout is one in which equipment with similar functions are grouped together. Figure 17–1 is a simplified model of a typical process layout. Notice that activities are organized into a group of work centers. This type of layout is

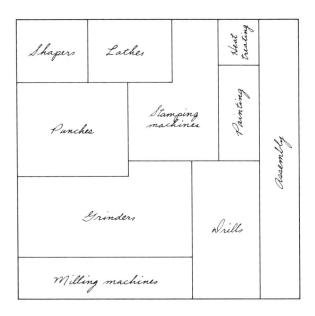

Figure 17–1   Process layout in a fabricating plant

a natural result of specialization. It is used when the expected volume of output is not great enough to warrant specialized production facilities, so that the same facilities are used to manufacture a wide variety of products. The quantity of any particular item produced is usually low in such cases, although the total output may be exceedingly large. Under these conditions, process layout will allow the greatest possible operating flexibility.

Product Layout

In contrast to process layout, product layout is suited to manufacturing processes that have a single output. Here the equipment is arranged in the same sequence as the operations required for manufacturing the product. This approach is, of course, the familiar production line, a simplified version of which appears in Figure 17–2. This type of layout is used where the planned output volume is large enough to support a specialized layout, but because it is so specialized, a product layout is extremely inflexible. Thus, to be more specific, it is used only when there is (1) high-volume output, (2) certainty of product specifications, and (3) relatively stable product demand.

Fixed Material Layout

The third type is the fixed material layout. Here the material itself does not move; instead, the processes and input materials are brought to the final product area. Two factors dictate the need for this type of layout. If a product is extremely large or heavy, it may be more practical to leave it in a fixed position

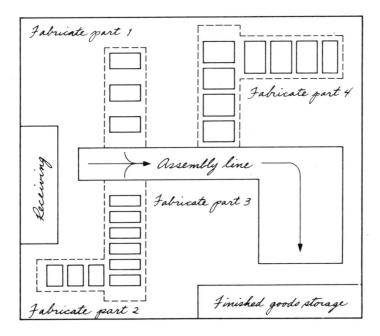

Figure 17–2 Product layout in a fabrication and assembly plant

and work on it there. A second reason for using the fixed material layout is an extremely low volume of output. Below a certain level of output, the savings that would accrue from a more specialized production line are minimal. One obvious example of this situation is in the production of missiles and aircraft; the shipbuilding and housing industries are other examples. Since the fixed material layout is highly specialized and confined to a few industries, we mention it only in passing; the remainder of the chapter will be devoted to the two common methods of organizing a production line—product and process layout.

Layout Construction

The most common way of "making a layout" is by means of two- or three-dimensional scale replicas of the types of machines involved. The usual procedure is to make a scale drawing of the available floor space showing the location of columns; electrical outlets; power, water, and gas lines; elevators; rest rooms; and other significant physical features. A layout plan is then created by positioning the machine replicas, drawn or built to the same scale, on the floor plan. The plan is then examined critically with respect to work flow, floor space utilization, and availability of service facilities such as tool sheds and stockrooms. Alternative plans are created by rearranging the replicas, and then a comparative evaluation is made. The most efficient floor plan can serve as a model for the actual installation or rearrangement of the machines. The plan can later be used as a starting point for replanning the layout when shifts in product mix or production levels or the introduction of new machines warrant it.

Although there are no hard and fast rules or procedures for the design of a layout, experience indicates that a consideration of aisle and storage space, the sites of columns and windows, and the location of power, gas, and water lines is commonly omitted during planning. Fortunately, check lists that will alert the layout planner to these and other important factors are readily available in production and industrial engineering handbooks.

It should be noted that the layout design has an impact on other functional areas of the firm. The basic building block in the construction of a layout is the individual work station. Sufficient space must be furnished so that the operator may move freely and do his work; the grouping of individual work stations results in the layout. If the workplace layout is poorly planned, space is wasted and worker performance is impaired. The planner's design of efficient layouts for each work station in the minimum space is actually a phase of labor simplification. Once the layout is designed, it becomes part of the standard practice for a particular operation and thus provides a basis for establishing the task output standards that will be used to determine the number of machines required to achieve internal balance. In short, as we have said before, there is a strong interrelationship between layout planning and other decision areas such as labor measurement and labor simplification.

Comparison of Layout Classes

The glamour associated with automation has led to the belief that efficient production can be achieved only by means of product-line layout. Often this is not the case, however. The most efficient type of layout for a particular firm is the one that is best able to match the objectives and restrictions of its production process. There are advantages and disadvantages to both process and product layout. In process layout, equipment is arranged in a flexible pattern so that it can be used efficiently on diverse products. In product layout, on the other hand, if a piece of equipment is needed for only a moment in several locations, each location must have its own machine; this results in a perhaps unnecessarily high investment in equipment. Furthermore, if a machine breaks down in a process layout, only that operation is affected, whereas the whole production line may be bottlenecked in a product-line layout. A disadvantage of process layout is that it complicates the tasks of scheduling, routing, and the adequate allocation of costs to a greater extent than product layout, largely because each order must be treated separately. Materials handling costs are also higher since there is no set pattern of movement; inefficiencies creep in, too, because considerable backtracking is often necessary. Because the flow of goods through the firm is relatively slow, work-in-process inventories are high. Inspection costs also tend to be greater because skilled inspectors are needed to review the many different products and operations, and labor costs are generally higher for substantially the same reason.

Product layouts do offer an important advantage in that they make the use of

This large bakery in Los Angeles uses a continuous process layout to move its products through the preparation, baking, and packaging processes.

automatic equipment feasible as long as the tasks are repetitive and can be divided into simple operations. Materials handling is simplified also, since fixed routes may be established for the material and the total distance to be traveled is less. On the other hand, the output rate is relatively fixed so that a drop in the scheduled volume can result in an expensive underutilization of the entire line. For this reason, sufficient volume to ensure continuous full utilization of the line is often cited as a *sine qua non* of product layout. This type of layout also makes it difficult to increase the daily output level; the only practical ways of doing so are by using overtime or multishift operation, and both of these alternatives create cost control problems. In addition, product layouts are highly vulnerable to bottlenecks and stoppages since work-in-process inventory between operations is small. Design changes in product are more costly and time consuming. Finally, although direct labor costs are normally low because semiskilled labor can quickly be trained to perform the repetitive tasks, the indirect labor costs are high. A whole corps of designers, setup men, repairmen, and methods engineers are required to keep the operation running smoothly.

The Layout Compromise

In view of the advantages and disadvantages just discussed, most layouts combine product and process layouts. Relatively few conform entirely to either of the two approaches we have examined. In general, assembly operations tend to use some variety of product layout, and fabrication tends to use some form of process layout. In the final analysis, however, the characteristics of the production process itself should determine the specific blend of these two approaches used in any given firm.

We will now examine some of the specific problems that pertain to process and product layouts. These problems are encountered in designing a plant no matter what blend of the two approaches is used.

An Analysis of Process Layout Problems

In a process layout, the performance of many different operations in varying sequences at perhaps many different work centers is required. Therefore, the cost of moving the material from operation to operation will vary (all other factors like weight, volume, and quantities being equal) according to the location of the various work areas. In this type of layout, materials for a particular job move as a lot from one work station to another; when work on a lot is finished at one station, the lot is moved to the next where succeeding work is to be performed. This is true in both factory and office operations.

Moving materials from one location to another has two types of costs: the so-called "pick up and put down" costs and the cost of travel between operations. Pick up and put down costs are generally fixed regardless of how far the material has to travel, whereas travel costs usually vary with the distance traveled. It follows, therefore, that the most efficient process layout minimizes the travel costs. Thus, management will seek this goal in its calculations:

$$\text{Travel costs} = \sum_{i} \sum_{j} N_{ij} \times D_{ij}$$

where N_{ij} = number of loads between departments i and j
            D_{ij} = distance between departments i and j

If the number of work centers is small, the minimum travel distance can be determined simply by trial and error. To illustrate, we may reverse the familiar example of determining the optimal routing plan for the traveling salesman. Suppose that we hold his path (sequence of operations) constant and change the location of the cities (machine centers) that he visits in an effort to reduce the total distance traveled. Let us further suppose that there are many salesmen (orders) who must visit the cities (machine centers) and that the importance of each salesman (order) as measured by the number of trips (load) also varies. Clearly, the objective is to arrange the cities (machine centers) so that the total distance traveled on all the trips (loads) by all the salesmen (orders) is at a minimum.

A further example may help clarify the approach. Suppose the ABC Company utilizes a process layout. There are nine work centers, which we will call A through I, involved in the manufacture of this company's products. To obtain a layout that will minimize the distance traveled, it is necessary first to record the way material moves from one work station to another during production cycles. Figure 17–3 is a grid showing the number of loads that must be trans-

	A	B	C	D	E	F	G	H	I
A		20				80		20	
B			20	90	10				
C									100
D			50		40				
E			30					20	20
F							10	70	
G		10							
H		90			20				
I									

Figure 17–3   ABC Company materials movement data

ported between the stations listed during one production cycle. Here we see, for example, that 20 lots travel from Station A to Station B as 90 lots travel from B to D. The data required to make such a chart are obtained from the order routing sheets and from the projected quantity of each item that will be produced during the period for which the layout will apply.

At present, the ABC Company is using the layout shown in Figure 17–4.

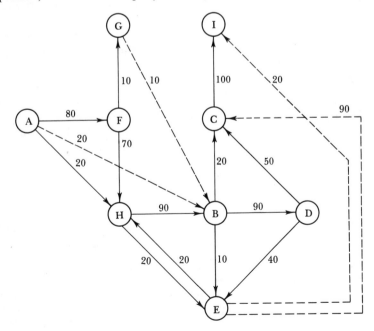

Figure 17–4   Current ABC Company layout

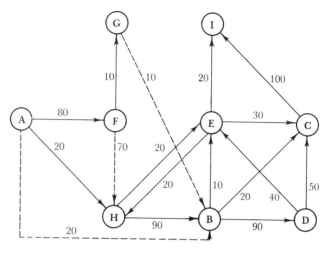

Figure 17–5 First iteration

Work stations are indicated by circles, and the connecting lines are labeled to indicate the number of lots that move between them. Movements to adjacent centers are shown by solid lines, and movements to nonadjacent ones by dotted lines. The best layout is clearly the one that minimizes movements among nonadjacent centers.

The ABC Company developed this particular layout by placing Station B, the work center with the greatest activity measured in loads moved (trips), at the center of the floor and then positioning around B the stations to which B sends lots, with their connecting stations placed adjacent to them where possible. This layout has four inefficient nonadjacent moves, from Station G to B, 10 lots; from E to I, 20 lots; from E to C, 90 lots; and from A to B, 20 lots. In all, 140 lots are transported to nonadjacent stations.

In following the criterion established above for the best layout, the planner might rearrange the B, C, D, and E complex as shown in Figure 17–5. Here the nonadjacent transfers are only from G to B and from A to B, for a total of 30 lots. Carrying this process of rearrangement[2] a step further, a final solution is shown in Figure 17–6.

In our example, the number of work stations is small, but with a more realistic number of stations and considerable interaction resulting from many types of products, the problem becomes quite complex. For example, with only six work stations there are 6 factorial, or 720, different possible arrangements. Manual trial-and-error methods can be used for simple problems, but where the range

[2] Layout analysis of this sort, whether performed on paper or by computer, is applicable to both service and office operations. Banks and insurance companies, in particular, have effectively reduced interoffice travel costs with this approach. By careful selection of location sites, they have also reduced the time it takes workers to reach their offices, which is comparable to the minimization of materials movement in the manufacturing field.

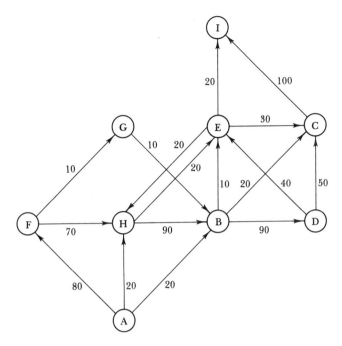

Figure 17-6 Final solution

of alternatives becomes more complex, computers must be programed to carry out the interaction decision process and arrive at a solution.

After determining the best arrangement of work stations, a preliminary floor plan should be developed that reflects the characteristics of the site. An estimate of the total floor area required can be obtained by multiplying the number of machines (or desks) in each work area by the floor space required by each machine (or desk). Then, using a common rule of thumb, this space is multiplied by 3 or 4 to allow for aisle and storage space, and the result is the total area required per station.

On the basis of this information, a block diagram may be drawn that reflects the space requirements of the work centers in their ideal arrangement, as has been done in Figure 17-7. This block diagram must then be adjusted until its dimensions conform with those of the site itself. If the available space is rectangular and the layout irregular, as in Figure 17-7, then the shapes and sizes of the work areas must be varied a bit to fit the rectangle; Figure 17-8 shows the adjusted block diagram.

Because this adjusted block diagram is merely a general layout, it is necessary to put in the specifics. Aisle space, machine location, workplace layout, service area, and materials-handling equipment must be indicated. This is done by a simple trial-and-error arrangement of two- and three-dimensional models, and the insertion of these details usually necessitates further minor compromises within the block diagram.

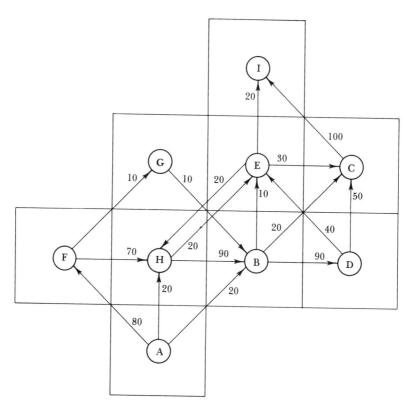

Figure 17–7 Initial block diagram

An Analysis of Product Layout Problems

Materials normally move by unit in a product-line layout instead of by lot, as in a process layout. Each unit proceeds sequentially through the work stations. In order for a production line to be efficient, therefore, the work load at each station must be adjusted so that the output at each is nearly equal. Thus, in product-line layout, the output rate is determined by the output of the slowest operation, but the rate of the entire line, of course, must be sufficient to meet the desired total volume.

The task of balancing a line, or equalizing the output of the positions, is easy to describe but rather difficult to perform. The basic balancing operation is the transference of work elements from operations with low output to operations with high output, the objective being to equalize the production capability of each operation. In this fashion "delay losses" due to the underutilization of men and machines may be minimized and costs lowered. In assembly or office operations, where the main ingredient is human labor, task elements may be added or subtracted rather easily. Where machine operations play a large role at a work station, as in fabrication, it is difficult to divide jobs into transferable elements.

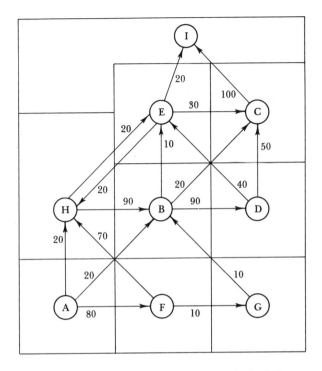

Figure 17–8   Block diagram adjusted to fit building space

Thus, firms are often faced with the problem of trying to integrate a machine with a high rate of output for a task that cannot be subdivided into parts within a process that has a slower rate of output in general. For this reason, balancing a fabrication line is generally much more difficult than balancing an assembly line. This is less true in newly designed processes that employ automated machinery, because it is often possible to divide machine operations into such minute elements that the fabrication operation can be balanced as easily as the assembly operation.

To balance a line, it is necessary to have reliable time data for the smallest possible independent work elements. If elements are to be transferable, adequate time standards must exist; the sequence of operations must also be known. For example, if a surface has to be milled before it can be drilled and tapped, the sequence is fixed. If in another operation the order in which joints are soldered doesn't matter, the sequence is flexible. Knowledge of whether the sequence of work elements is fixed or flexible is important because it serves as a guide in determining which elements are transferable and which are not.[3]

[3] The term *precedence* denotes a sequential relationship that is unalterable. Because it specifies that certain operations must be performed before others in the manufacturing process, precedence can restrict the designers' freedom in rearranging work elements to balance a line.

Table 17–3   Hub fabrication operating time data

Operation	Machine	Standard Production Time (in minutes)
1. Drill 5/8″ hole	Four-spindle drill press	1.304
2. Ream 0.685″ hole	Special drill press	.343
3. Center both ends	Centering machine	.240
4. Rough turn	Lathe	.923
5. Finish turn	Lathe	.353
6. Face to length	Drill press	.111
7. Drill 5/32″ hole	Drill press	.300
8. Drill 47/64″ hole	Four-spindle drill press	.240
9. Ream 9.749″ hole	Drill press	.133
10. Spotface	Drill press	.133
11. Countersink	Drill press	.074
12. Close 3/4″ thread	Threading machine	.400
13. Mill keyway	Hand miller	.120
14. Final inspection	Operator	1.200

Two examples will demonstrate the balancing problems involved in product-line layouts. The first is the fabrication of flanged hubs in an automobile plant. The hubs are the only output of the department in which they are made. To meet the production schedule, 4,000 units must be produced during each eight-hour shift. Table 17–3 lists the operations performed, the equipment used, and the standard output per operation per shift. The sequence of operations is fixed. The rate of output is set by the equipment, since all operations are "machine paced."

The problem is to balance the line at the required output of 4,000 units per shift. To meet that level, one unit must be produced every 0.120 minute. If this is done, it can be seen from the production times required for the various operations listed in Table 17–3 that many operations will need more than one machine. Table 17–4 lists the number of machines that will be required at each operation if the production line is to meet the 4,000-unit output level. In addition, it shows the number of units that could be produced by each operator or machine per shift. From this list it is clear that some pieces of equipment will be idle a considerable part of the day while others will be worked steadily. The hand miller at operation 13 will operate constantly, for example, whereas each threading machine at operation 12 will be idle one-sixth of the time because its pace is limited below capacity by the operations that precede it, specifically, operations 3 and 8. This enforced idleness results from the fact that the elements of the various tasks cannot be divided because of the limitations of the equipment and the setup requirements.

Another example of enforced idleness occurs at operations 9 and 10. Both are performed on drill presses, and since both take a little longer than 0.120

Table 17–4 Hub fabrication machine requirements

Operation	Output per Machine if Operated Continuously (in units)	Number of Machines Required
1	368	11
2	1,400	3
3	2,000	2
4	520	8
5	1,360	3
6	4,320	1
7	1,600	3
8	2,000	2
9	3,600	2
10	3,600	2
11	6,480	1
12	1,200	4
13	4,000	1
14	400	10

minute to perform, two machines are required at each position, resulting in much idle machine time. If the tasks could be divided into smaller elements so that one tiny step could be transferred to another operation, one of the two additional machines would not be needed; however, this is impossible. Thus, losses are inevitable in this case due to delays and underutilization of equipment; a perfect balance is not attainable because of constraints inherent in the process.

Now let us examine a second example of balancing problems—the manufacture of a vibrator. This is a subassembly unit that goes into some automobile radios to convert direct current to alternating current. Here, the production process is essentially an assembly cycle, which means that the elements of work are typically smaller and can more readily be adjusted.

Figure 17–9 depicts the parts to be assembled. A quick glance at this sketch will reveal the sequencing restrictions inherent in the operation. In assembling the vibrator, the gasket must be placed on the vibrator, the vibrator placed in the can, and the flanges crimped. To attach the vibrator socket to the chassis, the socket must be positioned on the chassis; the screws, nuts, and lockwashers positioned and engaged; and finally, the screws tightened. To attach the vibrator to the chassis, the vibrator must be inserted in the socket, the vibrator pins bent (crimped) to hold the vibrator to the socket, and the wire leads soldered to the pins. Notice that there is no sequence restriction on assembling the vibrator or the socket; either can precede the other, or they can be done simultaneously. Similarly, the crimping and screw tightening do not have to be performed in any fixed sequence.

The sequence requirements of this assembly operation are presented in Table

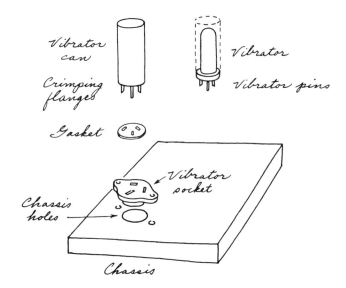

Figure 17–9 Vibrator assembly

Table 17–5 Vibrator assembly sequence

Element	Description	Elements That Must Previously Have Been Completed	Time Required to Perform Elements (in minutes)
a	Position vibrator socket on chassis		0.02
b_1	Position nut and lockwasher, and engage screw	a	0.03
b_2	Position nut and lockwasher, and engage screw	a	0.03
c_1	Tighten screw	ab_1	0.015
c_2	Tighten screw	ab_2	0.015
d	Position gasket on vibrator base		0.01
e	Insert vibrator in can	d	0.01
f_1	Crimp can flanges	de	0.018
f_2	Crimp can flanges	de	0.018
f_3	Crimp can flanges	de	0.018
g	Insert vibrator in socket	abdef	0.02
h_1	Crimp vibrator flange to socket	abdefg	0.02
h_2	Crimp vibrator flange to socket	abdefg	0.02
h_3	Crimp vibrator flange to socket	abdefg	0.02
i_1	Solder lead to vibrator	$abdefgh_1$	0.018
i_2	Solder lead to vibrator (restricted opening)	$abdefgh_2$	0.028
i_3	Solder lead to vibrator (restricted opening)	$abdefgh_3$	0.028
		Total time	0.338

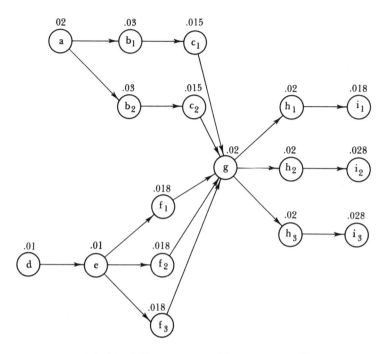

Figure 17-10   Vibrator assembly sequence diagram

17-5, which divides the operation into its smallest elements, gives the time required to complete each element, and indicates what completed tasks are a
prerequisite for the element. Where no work must be done prior to the performance of any element—where, in other words, precedence does not exist—
sequencing is of no import. The information presented as it is in Table 17-5
makes it difficult to develop a sequencing solution. We may, however, construct
a chart using this information that will aid our analysis. This type of chart,
shown in Figure 17-10, presents the sequence requirements and the time needed
to perform each operation in a form not unlike the flow charts used in PERT
analysis. With the data laid out this way we can proceed to balance the line,
provided we know the output level required. In this case, let us suppose that an
assembly must come off of the line every 0.06 minute.

Given this restriction, we can now group the elements at work stations in such
a way that the total activity at any station does not take longer than 0.06 minute
to perform. Since it takes a total of 0.338 minute to perform all elements of the
task, and the maximum time needed per position is 0.06 minute, it is clear that
there must be 0.338/0.06, or six, work stations in the process. Assuming that
production proceeds at a rate of one unit every 0.06 minute, more than six stations will be inefficient for producing the desired quantity and less than six will
not satisfy the demand.

Figure 17-11 illustrates one solution to the problem within these restrictions.
The solution was arrived at by manual trial and error, or what was previously

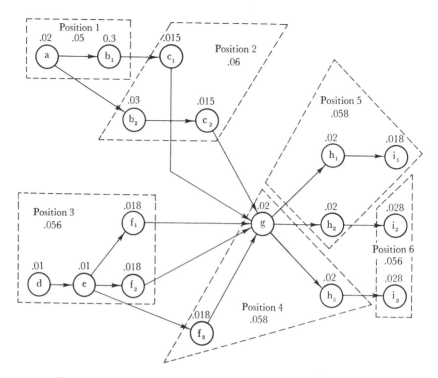

Figure 17–11 Vibrator assembly—one feasible solution

called "pencil and paper simulation." Since the problem was simple, this approach was useful. In large-scale problems, computers offer the only practical means of balancing the line; however, they use the same basic procedure.

Work-in-Process Inventories

When complete balance cannot be obtained on a production line, work-in-process inventory will tend to build up between a fast operation and a succeeding slow one within the line. Conversely, a fast operation that follows a slow one will frequently run out of material. Sooner or later, the fast operations will have to be shut down or the slow ones will have to be worked overtime in order to maintain an efficient flow of materials through the process.

To decouple operations, small inventories must be built up within the line periodically. Where banks of inventory exist between stations, small failures in individual work stations will not cripple the entire line; the work-in-process inventory can fill the gap temporarily until the station is repaired. Secondly, if there are small inventories between stations in machine-paced lines, the operator is not under pressure to complete an operation just so the next operator will have work to perform. Since the time it takes a worker to perform an operation is not constant but varies around the standard time, operators sometimes take more than the standard time to finish their work. When that happens, and there is no work-in-process inventory, succeeding operators have to wait for material or receive incomplete units. Tests conducted on paced production lines with and without work-in-process inventory indicate that lines with inventory banks produce more on the average. Having such banks between stations raises the inventory cost of the operation, however, so the additional earnings must be balanced against the higher costs.

Service Considerations

In addition to the direct production process, numerous service functions must be considered in preparing a plant layout. The fact that these functions do not have a tangible output sometimes leads managers of firms to ignore their layout to a large extent. Receiving, warehousing, shipping, and rest rooms are vital functions that affect the operations of a firm in important ways, however, and their physical location and area needs merit equally careful consideration in the layout process.

The service activities of a firm may be divided into three main categories: employee services, process services, and physical services. We will examine only the first two; the third is outside the scope of this text because it is primarily concerned with the plant itself[4] and not with the production process.

Employee Services

The most common employee services in industry are cafeterias, rest rooms, and medical facilities. The techniques of process layout discussed earlier apply in determining the best location and size of these services. Notice that in this case the movement involves people, so that the cost is reflected in the amount of time these people are away from their jobs. Once this simple fact is realized, many methods of minimizing these costs will spring to mind. One obvious example is the use of roving coffee dispensers in large office buildings. These dispensers minimize the costly employee travel time required during the coffee break. The specific approach taken depends, of course, on the nature of the employee service. Cafeterias may be designed for maximum speed and minimum cost in exactly the same way as a production line. Note that for service functions, the least travel time is not necessarily the decisive locational determinant, however. Medical facilities should be situated primarily in terms of space and accessibility. Low noise levels, efficient space utilization, minimum aisle traffic, and many other factors are quite important in these locational decisions.

Process Services

Firms also require space for process services, including storerooms for raw material and finished goods; receiving, shipping, and warehousing facilities; and

---

[4] This category includes heating, parking, building repairs, janitorial services, and many others.

room to perform maintenance work on the production equipment. Process services are of two classes. The first, which include receiving and warehousing, participate directly in the material flow pattern. In product layouts, these services are comparatively easy to establish, since the flow of material is obvious from the position of the production line itself. In process layout, however, these activities must be considered as important elements in the original formulation of the layout.

Deciding how much space to allocate for these services is a much more difficult matter, however. Since the inflow of material usually fluctuates over time, a receiving area can be designed to accommodate peak volume, average volume, or any other volume desired. To select an appropriate volume, the costs and advantages of each capacity must be balanced and a minimum obtained. Decisions of this sort lend themselves to solution by queuing models.[5]

The second class of process services does not affect the flow of materials through the firm but influences the cost pattern of the operations instead. Such services include tool cribs and maintenance facilities. Their location is important largely because of employee time spent going to and from the facility; thus, they may be studied in the same way as a process layout.[6]

Nonmanufacturing Industries

Although our discussion of layout techniques has concentrated largely upon manufacturing plants, these principles are directly applicable to offices and consumer-oriented industries such as restaurants, cafeterias, department stores, and supermarkets. One of the reasons our discussion has been oriented toward manufacturing is that examples are so plentiful here. As the emphasis in our national economy shifts toward service industries, however, the techniques that originated in manufacturing will be gradually adopted there. As consumer-oriented establishments grow, there will be increased attention placed upon the cost-cutting and output-raising approaches that have been so successfully used in manufacturing.

Questions and Problems

1. Differentiate among job-shop, intermittent, and continuous production. What is the distinction between a process and a product layout?
2. Define the concepts of internal and external balance in plant layout. Is the conceptual distinction between the two applicable to product and process layouts? to factories, banks, and retail stores?
3. What makes the task of balancing a line difficult in practice?
4. "The impetus for designing a new plant layout is frequently a low profit margin,

---

[5] Queuing, or waiting line models, will be discussed in the next two chapters.

[6] This suggestion highlights the fact that in designing a product layout, the procedure used to design a process layout must still be followed since the production process is only one of the activities that must be considered in the overall layout.

but this result is less likely to happen in economically depressed times than in good." Evaluate this statement.

What other factors can provide such an impetus?

5. For what production capacity should a new plant layout be designed?

6. How can you tell a poor layout when you see one?

7. In process layout problems, what criteria (note the *plural*) might you consider in assessing various layout arrangements?

8. A well-known electric equipment manufacturer recently tried a rather unique layout in a new plant. Instead of having centralized storage areas, all incoming materials were stored at the point of first use. Among the principal savings anticipated was a reduction in the cost of paper work and supervision needed to maintain proper inventories.

Write a brief defense or rebuttal of this unique plan. Indicate what effect the layout of the plant—product or process—would have on the feasibility of the plan.

9. In what context does the problem of line balance occur, and how is it solved?

10. Assume that you have been asked to balance a production line where the sequence of operations is not fixed and the individual tasks can be combined in various ways. Production must be equal to 2,000 units per shift, and the sum of all the individual task times is 2.00 minutes.

   (a) What is the minimum number of work stations required, and what is the resulting percentage of idle time?

   (b) What factors might compel you to have more than this minimum number, and hence more than the minimum amount of idle time?

11. Compare the use of shop basic data as an aid in determining the shop layout and the use of office basic data in determing the office layout.

12. A machine shop has five jobs to produce and five machines, any one of which can do any of the jobs, but at differing costs. The jobs must be assigned for simultaneous production, each job being assigned to one machine.

   (a) Determine the *lowest cost assignment* on the basis of the following total direct cost data:

	MACHINE				
JOB	1	2	3	4	5
A	$430	$440	$465	$480	$490
B	320	340	350	375	380
C	295	300	330	320	320
D	270	290	310	275	280
E	245	240	265	280	250

   (b) How might this problem be considered a responsibility of the plant layout function?

13. Evaluate the following statements:

   (a) When a firm is manufacturing a large variety of low-volume products, it is more likely to utilize a product-oriented grouping of machines and general-purpose equipment and to have a reasonably good internal balance.

   (b) The least costly layout for a firm is always one that avoids back-tracking, uses a straight-line flow of work, and locates each operation near others that are most closely related to it.

(c) The use of product-line layout makes it unnecessary to route and schedule the manufacture of a company's products in a formal way.

(d) If a company is manufacturing a small volume of any one product, it is most likely to consider general-purpose equipment and a product-oriented layout.

14. In an industrial economy, how important is a proper plant layout? Why? In an upward economic swing, is proper plant layout more or less important than during a downward swing?

15. A committee is to be formed to plan a new layout. How would you justify the inclusion of a member from the industrial relations department?

16. What implications for plant layout are there in the apparent tendency toward increased mechanization? What differences would you anticipate in plant layouts in China as compared with the United States?

17. Assume the existence of a production line situation where all of the operations listed below cannot be further subdivided (or combined) and the sequence is fixed as shown. Each operation is performed at a separate work station.

(a) If 1,000 units of production are required for each 8-hour shift, how many work stations will be needed for each operation?

(b) What is the average percentage of idle time for the entire production process, assuming that this is the only job performed in the plant and workers must be paid for the entire shift?

(c) What would you have to do to increase production to 1,200 units per shift? To decrease it to 800 units per shift? Would the percentage of idle time increase or decrease under each of these conditions?

| | STANDARD PRODUCTION |
OPERATION	TIME (IN MINUTES)
1	1.20
2	0.80
3	1.00
4	2.40
5	0.40
6	3.00
7	1.20

18. A single-product company wants to produce 2,000 units per day. The product is made in batches of 100 units, and four operations are required. The materials handling (movement) time between operations is 10 minutes per batch. The machines are set up once a day. The operating data are as follows:

	OPERATION 1 (LATHE)	OPERATION 2 (MILLING)	OPERATION 3 (GRINDING)	OPERATION 4 (ASSEMBLY)
Setup (minutes)	20	5	15	0
Teardown (minutes)	15	5	10	0
Operate (minutes per unit)	6	4	8	2

How many of each type of machine (lathe, milling, and grinding) would you recommend purchasing to meet this production requirement?

19. The following operation process chart pertains to the manufacture of books:

Operation 1	Print
Operation 2	Fold and trim
Operation 3	Sew (sewing machine)
Operation 4	Make covers
Operation 5	Assemble covers (fabricating press)

As indicated, operation 3 is performed on a sewing machine and operation 5 on a fabricating press. If the standard times for these operations are 3.0 minutes and 2.0 minutes, respectively, determine how many of each of these machines will be necessary to support the production of 4,200 books daily.

References

Apple, J. M., *Plant Layout and Materials Handling,* 2nd ed., Ronald Press, New York, 1963.

Arcus, A. L., "COMSOAL: A Computer Method for Sequencing Operations for Assembly Lines," in E. S. Buffa (ed.), *Readings in Production Operations Management,* Wiley, New York, 1966.

Immer, J. R., *Layout Planning Techniques,* McGraw-Hill, New York, 1950.

Ireson, W. G., *Factory Planning and Plant Layout,* Prentice-Hall, Englewood Cliffs, N.J., 1952.

Mallick, R. W., and Gaudreau, A. T., *Plant Layout,* Wiley, New York, 1951.

Moore, J. M., *Plant Layout and Design,* Macmillan, New York, New York, 1962.

Reed, R., Jr., *Plant Layout,* Irwin, Homewood, Ill., 1961.

Shubin, J. A., and Madeheim, H., *Plant Layout: Developing and Improving Manufacturing Plants,* Prentice-Hall, Englewood Cliffs, N.J., 1951.

Timms, H. L., *The Production Function in Business,* Irwin, Homewood, Ill., 1970.

Vergin, R. C., and Rodgers, J. D., "An Algorithm and Computational Procedure for Locating Economic Facilities," *Management Science,* Vol. 13, No. 6, Feb. 1967.

Vollmann, T. E., and Buffa, E. S., "The Facilities Layout Problem in Perspective," *Management Science,* Vol. 12, No. 10, June 1966.

Wilson, R. C., "A Review of Facility Design Models," *The Journal of Industrial Engineering,* Vol. XV, No. 3, May–June 1964.

18

Materials Handling Systems

As discussed at the beginning of Chapter 17, the design and operation of a production plant requires, in addition to the layout of the physical production facilities, the development of a materials handling system to move the materials from one stage of production to another. Materials handling includes moving, packaging, and storing all the materials used by the firm. In companies that manufacture or assemble products, raw materials must be moved from an incoming means of transportation through receiving, inspection, production, and finished-goods storage to the marketing distribution system. In retailing, the sequence is much the same: goods must be moved from receiving through inspection and display and finally on to the customer. In addition, these firms and other activities such as hospitals must develop means of moving their customers through their facilities. Service industries such as insurance and banking have comparable channels for the movement of documents and clients. Some industries like trucking, airlines, and railroads specialize entirely in materials handling.

It may be well to emphasize that, except for the transportation industries, the task of materials handling is not an end in itself, but one aspect of the overall production process. Therefore, the production process has a strong influence on the type of system used in the loading, unloading, and storing of materials. In addition, the handling system is judged partly by how well it services the production process.

Materials handling activities in the production process are by nature costly and in turn add little to the value of the product. Virtually all of the material movements in a manufacturing process are nonproductive in that the form of the product is not changed.

516

Estimates of the actual costs of materials handling vary, as might be expected, with the nature of the business. They do, however, serve as a rough measure of the importance of the process. When considered in relation to labor costs in manufacturing, materials handling costs vary from 10 to 50 percent of the total labor costs; the most common estimate given is 25 percent. Another way of estimating materials handling costs is to consider what percentage of indirect costs they represent. Here the most quoted estimate is 80 percent, with the dispersion around this figure being quite small.

In view of the magnitude of these costs, it is little wonder that a great deal of effort is expended to develop new and better materials handling systems. New types of materials handling equipment are continually being developed. In fact, the pace of the technology in this field has advanced so fast that some have termed it "revolutionary." Today, equipment performs a vast number of tasks that were formerly done manually; this new equipment has greatly increased productivity and flexibility, too. A quick tour through almost any enterprise from a brokerage house to an automobile plant would convince anyone of the high degree of mechanization now prevalent in the materials handling function. A comparison of the costs of materials handling before the present mechanization and now would also show that, in general, major savings have been achieved through mechanization.

When technological breakthroughs in materials handling equipment occur, large savings can usually be realized. Between major technological changes, this is not the case, however; the substitution of one type of mechanical equipment for another does not save a firm as much as the initial mechanization. As a consequence, managers have become increasingly concerned with the operating efficiency of their systems. New equipment is still purchased, of course, if it will lead to savings, but management realizes that as the state of technology advances, significant savings from the introduction of newer equipment are harder to attain. Thus, when forklift trucks were first introduced, the materials handling savings were often impressive; only rarely can these savings be matched by the modernization of these trucks, however. The same principle of diminishing returns applies to increasing the speed of commercial aircraft; many airlines have found that modest increases in aircraft speed only permit insignificant reductions in overall travel time. Therefore, airline managers have tended to concentrate in recent years on ways of speeding up the boarding and deplaning procedures.

Before we proceed further with this discussion of the methods available for coping with materials handling problems, let us briefly mention the many types of equipment that are available in this field.

Materials Handling Equipment

Numerous technical and trade journals describe materials handling equipment in depth. Accordingly, we will confine ourselves here to a brief description of the broad characteristics of this equipment.

Equipment Classes

There are many ways in which materials handling equipment can be classified; one is according to its characteristic movements.

Major Classes of Movement	Examples
Fixed path	Conveyors, hoists, lifts, cranes
Variable path	Tractors, trucks, railway, aircraft and water carriers

Each type of equipment must be suited to particular movement requirements. Clearly, the design of a materials handling system depends upon two sets of decision criteria: the characteristics of the different pieces of equipment and the specifics of the production process. There are three principal determinants of the movement requirements for any given process:

1. *The nature of the material to be moved*
2. *The path over which the material is moved*
3. *The volume of material moved*

The materials to be moved may be liquid, gas, or solid in nature and they may be of varying sizes and weights; accordingly, the handling equipment must be suitably designed. In the electronics industry, for example, conveyor surfaces with "high adhesion" are used to move delicate miniature components along an assembly line. This same approach is followed in the movement of large fragile materials such as ceramics and glassware. Among the factors that must be considered for the route over which the materials move are the length of the path, the number of turns and the turn radii, the vertical elevations, and the flexibility of movement required.

The type of materials handling system used also depends upon the amount of material to be moved. Generally, where the volume is relatively small and, consequently, usage of the system is light, the installation of a sophisticated, expensive system would not be considered justified. Where constant use is envisioned, however, the added expense of special handling accessories specifically designed for the unique characteristics of the particular production process could be justified by the savings they would permit. Comparisons between alternative methods of movement must include all cost factors. If use of a particular type of equipment would reduce breakage, this should be considered in its favor. If one method requires more floor space than another, this should be evaluated negatively.

Variable versus Fixed Movement Equipment

To a large extent, the choice between variable or fixed movement equipment is dictated by the type of production layout employed. In general, variable path equipment is best suited to process layouts, whereas fixed path equipment is usually more appropriate for product layouts; there are some exceptions to this generalization, of course. Since fixed path equipment is stationary, it is best

Materials movement devices facilitate the sorting of pistons for automobile engines according to minute differences in weight and size.

utilized when the material flow is continuous and permanent in direction, as it is in product layout. On the other hand, since variable path equipment moves materials in separate lots, it is more flexible; this makes it suitable for process layouts where diverse paths must be followed for different batches of material. Clearly, variable path equipment is more economical for process layout. Where large quantities of materials follow the same path, however, fixed path equipment is more economical; moreover, it obviates the need to tag materials since they cannot go astray once they are put on the fixed path.

Fixed Movement Equipment

The most common type of fixed path equipment is conveyors. They are utilized in most large production layouts; in fact, some automobile assembly plants have over 25 miles of conveyors. The chief types of conveyors are designated "gravity," "endless chain," "belt," "pneumatic," "pipeline," "screw," and "vibrating." Conveyors may be located overhead, at work level, on the floor, or

(Left) Teflon-coated conveyor belts move these rolls through the baking ovens. The Teflon coating keeps the rolls from sticking and facilitates the cleaning of the belts. (Below) Conveyor systems move these vinegar bottles through the filling, capping, inspection, and packaging functions in a continuous process.

in any combination of these levels. They can be used simply to move materials or they may also serve as work stations and as storage areas for work-in-process inventory.

Gravity conveyor   As the name implies, gravity conveyors rely on nature for their driving force; roller, wheel, and chute conveyors fall into this category. They are used primarily to move materials and are a relatively inexpensive type of conveyor as a rule, although for some applications, such as in moving grain, they can be quite expensive. Compared with other types, gravity conveyors are highly flexible and transportable and are well suited to variable paths. Movement is restricted, however, to routes that involve some degree of vertical fall.

Endless chain conveyors   These conveyors are usually driven by an electric motor and, as a consequence, are usually more expensive than gravity conveyors. They have several important advantages, however. These conveyors can move materials up as well as down, and the progress of the materials can be closely controlled. In addition, special carrying devices and containers can be attached to the chain. Frequently, production tasks such as dip painting, cleaning, and washing may be performed as the conveyor moves. Finally, by varying the speed of the conveyor at different points, or by building loops into it, work-in-process inventory may be stored between operating stages.

Belt conveyors   Belt conveyors are also driven by electric motors. The belts are usually made of some flexible material such as rubber. However, special belts are used in many industries. In the baking industry, for example, Teflon-coated metal is utilized to prevent sticking. The belt passes over rollers, which normally create a trough in the center of the belt where the materials are concentrated. Conveyors of this sort are used mainly for transporting bulky materials. Baggage is moved from the ground to the baggage compartments of airplanes and ships by conveyor belts; they are also used to move ores and coal from the mine face to work areas. Stock brokerage firms and insurance companies even use them to route papers to various parts of their buildings. When work is to be performed, however, the material must be taken from the belt and later replaced when the work is completed.

Other conveyor equipment   Pipelines are often employed for moving liquids and gases such as gasoline and natural gas. Pneumatic tubes are used in some firms for the rapid dissemination of internal communications. Pneumatic tubes are also used by the U.S. Post Office in certain cities.

Screw conveyors have been successfully used to lift materials in both grain elevators and food-processing firms. Vibrating conveyors are also found in the food-processing industry to move delicate foods in steady streams without damage.

Miscellaneous fixed path equipment   Other types of fixed path equipment are also in use, of course. Probably the most common are cranes, a large variety of which are found in industry. Overhead bridge cranes are commonly employed in factories where large, heavy pieces of equipment such as electrical transformers, generators, and power regulators are manufactured. These cranes ride on parallel overhead rails and are usually designed so that they can service any place in the work area of the plant.

Another common type of crane, which is designed for outside work, is the gantry crane. It moves in limited areas on wheels, providing its own superstructure, and is chiefly used for such tasks as moving lumber and loading and unloading in railroad freight yards. Large cranes of this sort must be disassembled if they are to be moved from one location to another, however—that is their main limitation.

Another prevalent type of fixed path equipment is elevators and lifts, which are used to raise everything from materials to workers. Since moving materials on this type of equipment is quite costly, however, the modern trend is to construct one-story plants, thus eliminating the need to raise and lower materials between floors.

Variable Path Equipment

Virtually all variable path equipment in use today is, in essence, some form of truck. Various types of trucks have been developed to meet specific product and process needs; the equipment is tailored basically to fit the load weight, the travel distance, and the frequency of movement. Truck bodies have been designed for the movement of liquids, scrap, finished goods, and even groceries. When the loads are not too heavy and the hauls are short, manual equipment (usually some form of dolly) may be used. However, when the load size and weight and the distances to be traveled are great, powered equipment is used. Today, most industrial trucks are powered. They are generally equipped with forks or platforms that can be raised or lowered to facilitate the movement and storage of materials, and for this reason the loads are generally placed on pallets or skids.

Design of a Materials Handling System

When to Start a Study

As we mentioned previously, materials handling systems must be closely integrated with the plant layout. Many different combinations of equipment could be used to achieve this purpose. In order to move materials at minimum cost, the alternative equipment and materials handling systems must be carefully evaluated long before installation. In addition, the system that is installed must be reviewed periodically to ensure that it is, and will continue to be, as effective as possible.

The rapid changes in materials handling technology can make an existing approach obsolete and noncompetitive. The introduction of forklift trucks revolutionized warehousing, for example. By the same token, the introduction of a new product or a shift in output within a product line may call for a reassessment of handling facilities. The same would be true if the production system itself changed because of the installation of new production processes or if there were a new layout of existing facilities.

There are also other, less dramatic, indications of a need to reevaluate handling practices. An increase in production delays, as evidenced by lower machine utilization and greater idle labor time, or a rise in material breakage or spoilage rates are danger signals. Such inefficient practices as transferring materials from one container to another can be symptomatic of major handling problems. In short, many factors may make it desirable to have a systems audit in materials handling.

What to Consider in a Study

A rough check list of factors to consider during an audit or in the initial design of a materials handling system has been developed. It is the result of considerable experimentation and experience and may serve as a rough guide in analyzing a materials handling problem; it should be used with care, however.

1. Eliminate all handling as far as possible.
2. Maintain a simple line of flow, avoiding changes of direction.
3. Maintain a steady rate of material flow.
4. Mechanize handling wherever economically feasible.
5. Accommodate the largest work load possible.
6. Use gravity feeds wherever possible.
7. Minimize travel distance.
8. Use flexible equipment wherever possible.
9. Move materials as rapidly as possible.
10. Relieve production processes and workers of handling operations.

How to Conduct a Study

What must be moved   The initial step in the design of a materials handling system or in an audit of an existing system is to determine what materials must be transported or stored. This may be accomplished by preparing a list of all end products, subassemblies, components, and raw materials involved in the production process.

When and how much must be moved   The next questions to answer are: When will the move take place and how much will be moved? To determine this, the production forecast for end products must be extended until it is possible to estimate the total amount of subassemblies, components, and raw materials that must be moved. Then the average daily movement required to meet the production forecast is determined.

At this point we know what is to be moved, when it is to be moved, and how much is to be moved. Now we must determine the nature of the move to be made and how it is to be done. For this purpose we must turn to the flow-process charts for each item; they list all of the storage and movement requirements for the items. Next, by using layout blueprints and visiting the production floor itself, we can calculate the distances required for each move.

With this information in hand, we can design a materials handling process chart that will summarize the movement of each production item. Table 18–1 is a partially complete materials handling process chart describing materials movements in the production of a metal bracket. It shows all of the information that has been collected to date, including the daily production quantity, the type of handling operation, the distance to be traveled, and the number of moves required daily.

Some columns on the chart are empty because information regarding the time required for moving, the type of carrier, and the method of transportation has not yet been gathered. The reason for this is that no method has yet been selected for moving the materials; all efforts to date have been devoted to determining what has to be done, not to how it will be done.

Movement times   In order to evaluate alternative equipment, the manager must know the movement time of each. Once these times are known, the amount of each type of transport equipment that would be needed can be calculated and the costs of the different methods compared. In any materials handling operation, four distinct stages may be identified:

1. Load
2. Transport loaded
3. Unload
4. Transport unloaded

To obtain time standards for these operations, the manager can use direct time studies or synthetic time systems. Where power equipment is used, the necessary time data can generally be obtained from the equipment manufacturer. For example, if a forklift truck is to be used in a loading operation that involves obtaining a loaded pallet from a stack of pallets and moving it to another station,

Table 18–1   ABC Company—materials handling process chart (partially complete)
            Part name: Bracket   Daily production quantity: 3,000

Handling Description	Move	Store	Distance to Be Traveled (in feet)	Number of Daily Moves	Time (in minutes)	Carrier	Transportation
To shear	X		50	2			
Await shear open		X					
Await move to drill press		X					
To drill press	X		40	4			

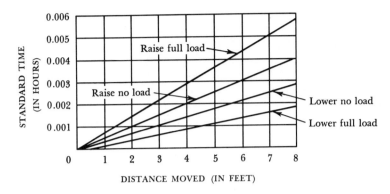

Figure 18–1 Forklift truck raise and lower times

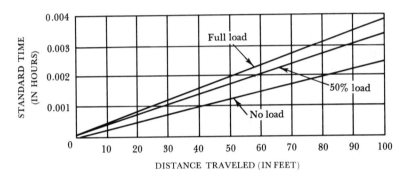

Figure 18–2 Forklift truck travel times

the times can be computed readily from a table such as the one shown in Figure 18–1. Here we can see that it takes 0.003 hour to raise the fork unloaded to a pallet 6 feet from the ground and 0.0013 hour to lower it loaded so that the truck can move.

The times required for a forklift truck to travel at varying load capacities can be obtained in the same manner from Figure 18–2; comparable travel time charts are available from equipment manufacturers.

After time standards are determined for the loading, movement, and unloading operations, the standard time for moving one load can be calculated by simply adding the times for each of the component operations.[1] Once the time per load is known, it can be multiplied by the number of daily loads to yield the time per day. When these calculations are completed for all jobs and for all of the various alternative equipment systems, the materials handling process chart may be completed, as shown in Table 18–2. Then the only task remaining is to

[1] If allowances are to be added, that is done in the same manner as that described for labor measurement.

Table 18–2 ABC Company—materials handling process chart

Part name: Bracket   Daily production quantity: 3,000

Handling Description	*Move* ⇨	*Store* ▽	*Distance to Be Traveled* (in feet)	*Number of Daily Moves*	*Time* (in minutes)	*Carrier*	*Transportation*
To shear	X		50	2	10	Pallet	Forklift
Await shear open		X				Pallet	
Await move to drill press		X				Tote bin	
To drill press	X		40	4	5	Tote bin	Pallet jack

compute the daily work loads for the various types of equipment used in each materials handling system and to compare them in terms of equipment needs and, hence, costs.

How much equipment is needed The amount of each type of equipment needed to support planned production levels can be calculated, in the simplest case, as follows:

$$\text{Number of machines} = \frac{\text{Daily load (in hours)}}{\text{Working hours}}$$

This simple formula overlooks the fact that the machines may not be operative for an entire day, however. It also assumes that there will never be a time during the day when the machines may be needed in two places at the same time. Some allowance may be made for these problems in an approximate way by specifying a *utilization factor* for each type of equipment. Thus, a utilization factor of 60 percent indicates that the equipment would be expected to be used only 60 percent of the day.

$$\text{Number of machines} = \frac{\text{Daily load (in hours)}}{\text{Working hours} \times \text{Utilization factor}}$$

We now have a built-in safety factor providing for machine downtime, but it does not allow directly for the fact that the equipment may be needed in several places simultaneously during the day; it makes the allowance indirectly by making more machines available.

Estimating the number of machines required often means a consideration of complex interacting factors. Frequently the manager will want to take into account the distribution of machine breakdown characteristics, or of calls for transport equipment, or of service times. He may also want to consider the cost of not performing the move when requested. When management wishes to include all of these factors in its analysis, queuing techniques often prove useful in developing a solution.

Queuing or Waiting Line Analysis

A great number of queuing problems exist in business. Production materials wait to be processed, customers wait at supermarket checkout counters, letters wait to be answered, hospital patients wait for tests and x-rays. In some instances, the cost of waiting is less than the cost of additional service facilities to eliminate the waiting. In others, the cost of waiting far exceeds the cost of additional facilities. The aim of queuing analysis is to provide a means to evaluate the alternatives and thus lead to optimal decisions.

The basic concepts and language of queuing theory are quite simple. A *customer* is an individual, machine, or activity that requires servicing. The *service* is performed by a service facility. Service facilities that can handle only one customer at a time are termed *single-channel service facilities*. Those that can handle more than one customer at a time are called *multichannel service facilities*. Waiting lines, or *queues,* are formed by customers who are waiting for service. Single-channel and multichannel facilities are illustrated diagramatically in Figure 18–3.

Customers arrive at the service facility according to a pattern, or *arrival distribution*. The distribution can vary greatly. It can be random, constant, peaked at particular times, or fit a theoretical distribution such as the Poisson distribution.

The time that it takes to service customers also fits a pattern. Automated tasks, such as filling soda bottles, have a constant service rate. This, however, is not the general case. In a more typical situation, the service time varies from customer to customer. The time to check out a shopper at a supermarket, for example, varies according to the number of items, the speed of the checker, the arrangement of the items, and the speed of payment.

Another consideration in a queuing problem is the manner in which customers are selected for servicing. This selection process is termed *queue discipline*. The

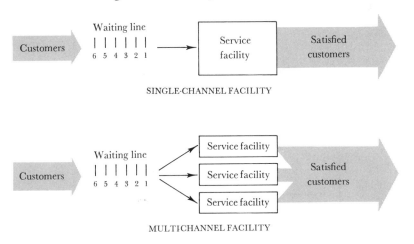

SINGLE-CHANNEL FACILITY

MULTICHANNEL FACILITY

Figure 18–3 Single- and multichannel service facilities

most common discipline is first in first out (FIFO). In some inventory applications, last in first out (LIFO) methods are used. Other disciplines employed are random and priority. Computer operating systems make extensive use of priority systems to select jobs from their queues.

Queuing models   Queuing models can be classified as illustrated in Table 18–3. Four different classes of queuing models are enumerated: single-channel single-phase, single-channel multiphase, multichannel single-phase, and multichannel multiphase. Within these four classes, numerous different models can exist, because the arrival and service distributions and the queue disciplines can all vary. The mathematical complexity of multiphase models is beyond the scope of this text. We will therefore consider only single-phase models with single and multiple channels. Even these models, as will be shown, can become mathematically overwhelming. For simplicity, therefore, we will treat only a subclass of these models characterized by:

1. *An arrival distribution that is Poisson.*   A Poisson distribution implies (a) that an arrival can occur at any time and (b) that the probability that

Table 18–3   Classes of queuing models

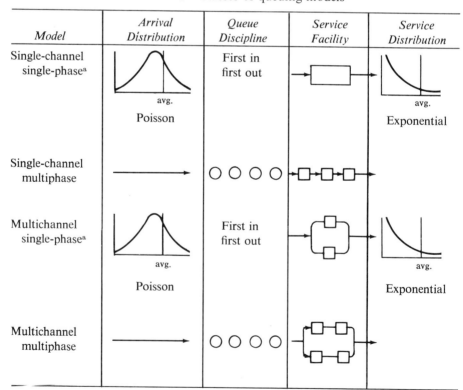

Model	Arrival Distribution	Queue Discipline	Service Facility	Service Distribution
Single-channel single-phase[a]	avg. Poisson	First in first out		avg. Exponential
Single-channel multiphase		O O O O		
Multichannel single-phase[a]	avg. Poisson	First in first out		avg. Exponential
Multichannel multiphase		O O O O		

[a] Models meeting these conditions will be analyzed in the succeeding pages.

the arrival will occur at any time is the same regardless of what occurred before or during the length of the waiting line. These conditions closely fit the case of equipment breakdowns in a large production facility.

2. *A queuing discipline of first in first out (FIFO).* A further condition is that once a customer is in the queue he will not leave.

3. *An average rate of service faster than the average rate of arrivals.* Queuing analysis cannot cope with a situation where the average rate of arrivals is greater than the average rate of service. In such cases, the queue will continuously increase. Such a condition is unstable and cannot exist for any length of time.

4. *An exponential service distribution.* This type of distribution covers most maintenance and toll-booth types of service facilities. As can be seen from the graph of this distribution in Table 18–3, there is a high probability that the service time will be shorter than average. Sometimes, however, long service times will occur.

5. *An infinite number of customers.* In reality, virtually no situations meet this condition. However, where the number of customers is large, or where customers can return after servicing, the error in results is small enough to be tolerated. This assumption simplifies the model a great deal.

6. *There is no limitation on the size of the queue.*

Before proceeding to develop queuing equations embodying these conditions and illustrating their use in selected problems, an important caution should be noted. Not every queuing problem meets these conditions. Forcing them on problems they do not fit may lead to disastrous results. Like other mathematical models, queuing models must accurately fit the real world situation to which they are applied if the results are to be of any value.

Queuing equations In order to solve queuing problems, we generally need to calculate values for the following factors:

P_0: the probability of an arrival not having to wait for service; that is, the probability that there are no other customers being serviced or waiting

L_q: the average number of customers waiting for service (in the queue)

L: the average number of customers in the system (in the queue or being serviced)

W: the average time in the system (waiting time and service time)

W_q: the average waiting time before service (in the queue)

Given the conditions stated previously, the equations for these values are those presented in Table 18–4. In these equations,

A = average number of arrivals per unit of time
S = average number of units serviced per unit of time at a service channel
N = number of service channels

Table 18–4   Queuing equations[a] for single-phase service

Single-Channel	*Multichannel*
$P_0 = 1 - \dfrac{A}{S}$	$P_0 = \dfrac{1}{\displaystyle\sum_{n=0}^{N-1} \dfrac{1}{n!}\left(\dfrac{A}{S}\right)^n + \dfrac{1}{N!}\left(\dfrac{A}{S}\right)^N \left(\dfrac{NS}{NS-A}\right)}$
$L_q = \dfrac{A^2}{S(S-A)}$	$L_q = \dfrac{(A/S)^{N+1}}{(N-1)!(N-A/S)^2} \times P_0$
$L = \dfrac{A}{S-A}$	$L = L_q + \dfrac{A}{S}$
$W = \dfrac{1}{S-A}$	$W = \dfrac{L}{A}$
$W_q = \dfrac{A}{S(S-A)}$	$W_q = \dfrac{L_q}{A}$

[a] These equations are for the assumptions listed on pages 528–529.

Single-channel problem   Let us consider a set of problems with which we can illustrate the use of queuing models. We will proceed from a fairly simple case to one of considerable complexity.

Suppose we analyze the materials movement problem of a raw materials stockroom that receives orders from individual machine operators located in various plant operating departments. At present, when the orders are received, the material is loaded onto a hand truck and pushed to the appropriate location. Orders come to the stockroom at an average rate of four per hour with a Poisson distribution. Deliveries are made on a first come, first serve basis at an average rate of five per hour distributed exponentially. The machine operators are idle while they are waiting for delivery of the material. Their pay is $5 per hour.

The company is considering replacing the hand truck with a new forklift truck, which will be run by the current operator of the hand truck. Tests indicate that the forklift truck can deliver an average of nine orders per hour. The truck will require an incremental cash investment of $8,000 and will necessitate added yearly maintenance and operating costs of $1,500. The company would like to make the switch if it can recoup its investment in two years. Since the order will be serviced by only one truck, we have a single-channel problem, as shown in Figure 18–4.

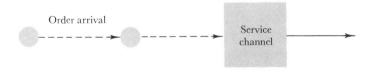

Figure 18–4   Single-channel diagram

SOLUTION   From the equations of Table 18–4, we can find the average number of orders in the system at any time for the hand truck:

$$L = \frac{A}{S - A} = \frac{4}{5 - 4} = 4 \text{ orders}$$

Since each order represents one machine operator, machine operator cost in idle time is

$$4 \times \$5/\text{hour} = \$20 \text{ per hour}$$

For the forklift truck, the average number of orders in the system is

$$L = \frac{A}{S - A} = \frac{4}{9 - 4} = 0.8 \text{ order}$$

and therefore

$$\text{Idle operator cost} = 0.8 \times \$5/\text{hour} = \$4 \text{ per hour}$$

Hourly savings using the forklift truck in place of the hand truck is $16.

If a switch is made to the forklift truck during the normal 40-hour week, $40 \times 16 = \$640$ will be saved. Over a 50-week year, $32,000 will be saved. This clearly will repay the $8,000 cost of the forklift and the $1,500 of maintenance and operating costs within the company's limit of two years.

Multichannel Problem 1   Let us consider that our plant has grown. Additional activities have been added, and the requests for material have increased to nine per hour.

Management is considering two alternatives to gain increased servicing capability. Each will have the same annual costs. One approach calls for redesigning the present stockroom to achieve easier access to the materials. In addition, two more stockroom clerks would be hired to collect the material for the orders and have them ready for the truck. In this way, the truck's idle time can be cut and more deliveries made. Tests indicate that an average of 17 deliveries per hour can be serviced in this fashion.

The alternative approach is to add another truck at the present facility. This would increase the service capability, but because of loading problems, each truck will average only eight orders per hour. This alternative involves more than one channel and is diagramed in Figure 18–5.

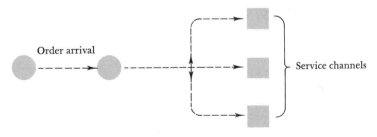

Figure 18–5   Multiple service channel diagram

SINGLE-CHANNEL SOLUTIONS   At first glance, the question might be asked, Why not let things stay as they are? The arrival time is nine per hour and the service rate is nine per hour; shouldn't the present system work? No, it will not. One of the limitations of queuing models is that the arrival rate must be greater than the service rate. The reason for this can now be shown mathematically.

In the present system, the time an order waits in the queue is

$$W_q = \frac{A}{S(S-A)} = \frac{9}{9(9-9)} = \frac{9}{0}$$

While mathematically this is indeterminate, conceptually it approaches infinity. This means that the waiting line will continue to increase, as will the time to service a request.

SOLVING THE IMPROVED SINGLE-CHANNEL MODEL   Since we cannot leave the system as it is, let us investigate the plan to redo the present stockroom and add additional clerks. The values for A and S are

$$A = 9, \quad S = 17$$

The probability of not having to wait for service is

$$P_0 = 1 - \frac{A}{S} = 1 - \frac{9}{17} = 0.47$$

The average number of orders in the system at any time is

$$L = \frac{A}{S-A} = \frac{9}{17-9} = 1.12 \text{ orders}$$

The average time it takes to service an order is

$$W = \frac{1}{S-A} = \frac{1}{17-9} = 0.125 \text{ hour}$$

SOLVING THE MULTICHANNEL ALTERNATIVE   For the alternative of adding another truck to the present stockroom, we have

$$A = 9, \quad N = 2, \quad S = 8$$

The probability of not having to wait for service is

$$P_0 = \cfrac{1}{\displaystyle\sum_{n=0}^{N-1} \frac{1}{n!}\left(\frac{A}{S}\right)^n + \frac{1}{N!}\left(\frac{A}{S}\right)^N \left(\frac{NS}{NS-A}\right)}$$

$$= \cfrac{1}{\left[\displaystyle\sum_{n=0}^{1} \frac{1}{n!}\left(\frac{9}{8}\right)^n\right] + \frac{1}{2!}\left(\frac{9}{8}\right)^2 \left(\frac{2 \times 8}{(2 \times 8)-9}\right)}$$

$$\sum_{n=0}^{1} \frac{1}{n!}\left(\frac{9}{8}\right)^n = 1 + \frac{9}{8} = 2.12$$

$$\frac{1}{2!}\left(\frac{9}{8}\right)^{2}\left(\frac{2\times 8}{(2\times 8)-9}\right) = 1.44$$

$$P_0 = \frac{1}{2.12 + 1.44} = 0.28$$

The average number of orders in the system is

$$L = L_q + \frac{A}{S}$$

$$L_q = \frac{(A/S)^{N+1}}{(N-1)!(N-A/S)^{2}} \times P_0 = \frac{(9/8)^{2+1}}{(2-1)!(2-9/8)^{2}} \times 0.28$$

$$= .52$$

$$L = .52 + 9/8 = 1.64$$

The average time it takes to service an order is

$$W = \frac{L}{A} = \frac{L_q + \dfrac{A}{S}}{A} = \frac{L_q}{A} + \frac{1}{S}$$

$$= \frac{.52}{9} + \frac{1}{8} = .185 \text{ hour}$$

COMPARISON OF ALTERNATIVES We can now evaluate the two alternatives by comparing the average number of orders in the system and the average time it takes to service an order. In both instances, the two-truck alternative is inferior. The improved stockroom with one truck will fill the orders faster, thus requiring less waiting and idle time.

Multichannel Problem 2 For the final problem, let us assume that we now must expand the capacity of our single stockroom. To do this, management has decided to use additional forklift trucks. The problem is to decide how many trucks must be available to provide satisfactory service. Satisfactory service has been defined as that service at which the probability of an arriving order having to wait more than 30 minutes before service begins will be less than 0.20 on the average. In short, when orders arrive, they must wait in a queue if all trucks are busy. Management wants to keep this wait to a tolerable level.

For this problem, to keep the calculations as simple as possible, we will let the arrival rate $A = 4$ per hour and the service rate $S = 2$ per hour. All of the earlier conditions, Poisson arrival distribution, exponential service distribution, and FIFO queue discipline still hold.

THE ANALYTICAL APPROACH The probability that the system will be completely idle at various intervals during the day is

$$P_0 = \frac{1}{\displaystyle\sum_{n=0}^{N-1} \frac{1}{n!}\left(\frac{A}{S}\right)^{n} + \frac{1}{N!}\left(\frac{A}{S}\right)^{N}\left(\frac{NS}{NS-A}\right)}$$

Now suppose we guess, on the basis of past experience, that three forklift trucks are needed. With $A = 4, S = 2, N = 3$, the formula becomes

$$P_0 = \frac{1}{\left[\sum\limits_{n=0}^{2} \frac{1}{n!}\left(\frac{4}{2}\right)^n\right] + \left[\frac{1}{3!}\left(\frac{4}{2}\right)^3\left(\frac{3 \times 2}{(3 \times 2) - 4}\right)\right]}$$

We calculate

$$\left[\sum\limits_{n=0}^{2} \frac{1}{n!}\left(\frac{4}{2}\right)^n\right] = 1 + 2 + 2 = 5$$

and

$$\left[\frac{1}{3!}\left(\frac{4}{2}\right)^3\left(\frac{3 \times 2}{(3 \times 2) - 4}\right)\right] = \frac{1}{6} \times 8 \times \frac{6}{2} = 4$$

Therefore,

$$P_0 = \frac{1}{9}$$

The probability that an arriving order will have to wait—that is, that there will be at least as many requests on hand as there are trucks—is

$$P_{>0} = \frac{S(A/S)^N}{(N-1)!(NS-A)}P_0$$

For three trucks this becomes

$$P_{>0} = \frac{2(4/2)^3}{2![(3 \times 2) - 4]} \times \frac{1}{9}$$

$$= \frac{2 \times 8}{2 \times 2} \times \frac{1}{9} = \frac{4}{9}$$

The probability that a request for a truck will take longer than time t to service is

$$P_{>t} = e^{-NSt(1-A/NS)} \times P_{>0}$$

$$= e^{-3 \times 2 \times 0.5[1 - 4/(3 \times 2)]} \times \frac{4}{9}$$

$$= e^{-3 \times 1/3} \times \frac{4}{9}$$

$$= \frac{1}{2.72} \times \frac{4}{9} = 0.163$$

Therefore, three trucks will meet our criteria, since the probability that any order will have to wait more than one-half hour is 0.163, which is less than the 0.20 limit we arbitrarily selected.

In the interests of economy, the next question to ask is: Will two trucks be adequate? If we use two trucks, the average rate of service will be $N \times S = 2 \times 2$, or 4, and we know that orders also arrive at this rate. From our discussion of queuing, we know that the service rate must be greater than the arrival rate or the queue will simply continue to grow. Therefore, it is clear that two trucks will not suffice. We can again show mathematically that the queue will continue to grow since the probability that the system will be completely idle for two trucks is

$$P_0 = \frac{1}{\sum\limits_{n=0}^{1} \frac{1}{n!} \left(\frac{A}{S}\right)^n + \frac{1}{N!} \left(\frac{A}{S}\right)^N \left(\frac{NS}{NS - A}\right)}$$

Evaluating the last term in the denominator, we get

$$\frac{NS}{NS - A} = \frac{2 \times 2}{(2 \times 2) - 4} = \frac{4}{0}$$

If we accept $4/0$ as approaching infinity as a limit, the probability that the queue will ever be empty ($P_0 = 1/\infty$) approaches zero as a limit. In other words, the probability that both trucks will be idle is zero, which simply means that the queue will never disappear.

QUEUING BY SIMULATION   As can be seen, the analytical or mathematical approach to this multichannel problem is more complex than in the earlier examples. As queuing problems increase in complexity, it becomes impractical if not impossible to solve them mathematically. We can, however, approximate a solution through simulation. To illustrate, let us develop a solution for this problem using simulation.

The first step is to generate the arrival and service distributions. The arrival distribution is Poisson, with an average rate of four per hour or one every 15 minutes. This distribution may be developed from the equation

$$T = 15 \ln (1/y)$$

where y takes random values between 0 and 1. Twenty-five arrival times have been generated in this manner and are shown in column (2) of Table 18–5.

Service times can be generated mathematically in similar fashion and are listed in column (4).

Another way to obtain these times is to take random samples of the actual times between arrivals and the times required to service a request. This approach eliminates the need to make assumptions about the distributions since actual historical times are used.

To simulate the queuing process, the arrivals are related to a starting point in order to provide a time sequence for the arrival of requests. Thus, order 1 arrives 9 minutes after the work day starts and order 2, 22 minutes after the same starting point. Service times for each order are also listed.

Simulation begins as order 1 is assigned to truck A when it arrives, 9 minutes after the day begins. The work is completed at 26 minutes. Order 2 arrives at 22 minutes. Truck A is occupied so the order is placed on truck B. Order 3 is taken by truck C since both A and B are working. Until order 7 arrives, there is always a truck available when the orders come in. When order 7 arrives 75 minutes after work begins, however, truck A is unavailable until 106 minutes,

Table 18-5 Monte Carlo queuing simulation—three forklift trucks (A, B, C)

(1) Arrival Number	(2) Arrival Times Measured from Previous Arrival (in minutes)	(3) Arrival Times Measured from Starting Period (in minutes)	(4) Service Times (in minutes)	(5) Truck Performing Work	(6) Time Work Starts (in minutes from 0)	(7) Time Service Completed (in minutes from 0)	(8) Waiting Time (in minutes)
1	9	9	17	A	9	26	0
2	13	22	8	B	22	30	0
3	1	23	24	C	23	54	0
4	32	55	51	A	55	106	0
5	1	56	26	B	56	82	0
6	17	73	13	C	73	86	0
7	2	75	36	B	82	118	7
8	9	84	99	C	86	185	2
9	24	108	5	A	108	113	0
10	92	200	10	A	200	210	0
11	7	207	48	B	207	255	0
12	9	216	33	C	216	249	0
13	18	234	85	A	234	319	0
14	13	247	52	C	249	301	2
15	17	264	40	B	264	304	0
16	2	266	16	C	301	317	35
17	4	270	3	B	304	307	37
18	20	290	4	B	307	311	17
19	13	303	69	B	311	380	8
20	10	313	6	C	317	323	4
21	25	338	65	A	338	393	0
22	5	343	11	C	343	354	0
23	3	346	26	C	354	380	8
24	2	348	22	C	380	402	32
25	19	367	46	B	380	426	13

B until 82 minutes, and C until 86 minutes. Therefore order 7 must wait 7 minutes until B is available to service it.

Following this procedure, the simulation was completed for twenty-five orders. It was found that three orders, numbers 16, 17, and 24 had to wait longer than 30 minutes. Thus, on the basis of this brief simulation, the probability that an order will have to wait more than one-half hour may be expressed as $3/25 = 0.12$. When we computed the probability mathematically, the answer was 0.163; the disparity is largely due to the small number of orders used in our simulation model. In practice, considerably more than twenty-five orders would have to be processed to yield a reliable answer. This could be done on a computer, which could simulate thousands of days of orders in only a few minutes.

Table 18–6 lists the simulation calculations for our hypothetical problem assuming that there are two trucks. Notice that once the queue starts to build up at order 13 it continues; the service rate never catches up to the arrivals. This same result was forecast by the mathematical analysis.

The Selection of a Materials Handling System

Once the optimum amount and type of equipment have been selected for each materials handling system, the final step in the process—selection of a particular system—can be made.

One method of making this decision is first to determine which systems meet the plant's handling needs. For example, in the queuing problem any type of equipment that could move the material so that the probability of waiting for service longer than 30 minutes would be less than 0.20 would meet the stated handling needs. Once all of the feasible equipment systems have been identified, they can be evaluated economically by using the methods presented in the chapters on capital allocation. The equipment that is most economical would then be selected for the plant.

Operating Effectiveness

It is difficult to assess the effectiveness of a materials handling system; absolute measures are hard to invent and even harder to apply. Management is usually forced to control performance indirectly by comparing expenditures for materials handling with operating costs and more specifically with the direct costs of manufacturing operations. For this purpose, materials handling costs may be accumulated and compared with other direct labor costs or with the total value of products manufactured at factory-cost level. This formula provides some index of materials handling effectiveness:

$$\text{MHI} = \frac{\text{Materials handling operating costs}}{\text{Total factory direct labor costs}}$$

$$\text{MHI} = \frac{\text{Materials handling operating costs}}{\text{Factory cost of products manufactured}}$$

Table 18–6 Monte Carlo queuing simulation—two trucks (A, B)

(1) Arrival Number	(2) Arrival Times Measured from Previous Arrival (in minutes)	(3) Arrival Times Measured from Starting Period (in minutes)	(4) Service Times (in minutes)	(5) Truck Performing Work	(6) Time Work Starts (in minutes from 0)	(7) Time Service Completed (in minutes from 0)	(8) Waiting Time (in minutes)
1	9	9	17	A	9	26	0
2	13	22	8	B	22	30	0
3	1	23	24	A	26	50	3
4	32	55	51	A	55	106	0
5	1	56	26	B	56	82	0
6	17	73	13	B	82	95	9
7	2	75	36	B	95	131	20
8	9	84	99	A	106	183	22
9	24	108	5	B	131	136	23
10	92	200	10	A	200	210	0
11	7	207	48	B	207	255	0
12	9	216	33	A	216	249	0
13	18	234	85	A	249	334	15
14	13	247	52	B	255	307	8
15	17	264	40	B	307	347	43
16	2	266	16	A	334	350	68
17	4	270	3	B	347	350	77
18	20	290	4	A	350	354	60
19	13	303	69	B	350	419	47
20	10	313	6	A	354	360	41
21	25	338	55	A	360	415	22
22	5	343	11	A	415	426	72
23	3	346	26	B	419	445	73
24	2	348	22	A	426	446	78
25	19	367	46	B			

In the steel industry this approach has been successfully employed with a slight modification. The MHI is calculated by comparing materials handling operating costs to "tons of steel shipped." Many other modifications are feasible. By keeping record of the index value over time, shifts in handling costs can be spotted and, if warranted, a materials handling audit instituted.

Questions and Problems

1. What are the major classes of materials handling equipment?
2. Can materials handling costs easily be determined?
3. What are the principal factors in deciding what pieces of transport equipment should be selected for a given process?
4. Evaluate the following statements:
   (a) Conveyors are more or less automatically associated with mass production, but an examination of the many types of conveyors indicates that they have rather special uses.
   (b) The ideal materials handling system can be achieved only if a product-oriented analysis is made.
   (c) The best measure of the effectiveness of a materials handling system is the materials handling cost per unit of product shipped.
5. A plant manager has the problem of moving 120 pallet loadings a distance of 500 feet. He is trying to decide whether to use one forklift truck to do the job or one forklift truck plus a tractor and six trailers. Each trailer carries a single pallet load. Both the tractor and the forklift truck travel 250 feet per minute. The time required to load or unload a forklift truck is 20 seconds. The time it takes to load or unload a single trailer using the forklift is one minute. Labor costs are $2.40 per hour. Which method would you recommend? Discuss fully.
6. Assume that you are a planner for a major oil company, which has recently purchased a piece of land at a major intersection in a large city. You have just completed a course in queuing theory and have been asked to design a new gasoline station for the site, emphasizing such factors as the optimum number of gas pumps to install, their layout, the number of men required to staff the station, and the design of the parking apron. There are two other gas stations (competing oil companies) located at the same intersection, and your company has another gas station less than a mile away.

   In your answer discuss the system factors and characteristics that will affect your design decisions, the data you will require, and the operating characteristics of the station you want to consider—that is, your objectives in designing the system.
7. What indicators show when a materials handling system should be reevaluated?
8. What steps should be taken in studying materials handling?
9. Can materials handling be studied independently of layout and maintenance?
10. What is queuing theory? To what types of problems is it applicable?
11. What data are needed in queuing analysis?
12. Why must the service rate be greater than the arrival rate in queuing problems?

13. What are the limits to solving queuing problems mathematically? Does simulation overcome these limitations?

14. Give an example of each of the different queuing models shown in Table 18–3. For instance, a supermarket checkout system fits the multichannel single-phase model.

15. How are simulation models different from mathematical models?

16. A company uses a forklift to move materials throughout its plant. Orders for using the truck arrive at an average rate of 6 per hour according to a Poisson distribution. Two types of trucks are on the market. One is slow and will handle orders exponentially, at the rate of 8 per hour at a cost of $6 an hour. The other is fast, handling orders exponentially at the rate of 12 per hour at a cost of $10 an hour. Which truck should be bought? To arrive at your decision, use both a mathematical model and simulation. Do the results agree?

17. A company has a messenger service through which messengers are supposed to pick up mail every hour. The time the messengers actually arrive varies from the scheduled time in a normal fashion, with a standard deviation of 12 minutes. Mail is put into the pick-up bin according to a Poisson distribution, with the average rate of arrival of 4 per hour. How long is the average waiting time for mail before it is picked up? Solve this problem by simulation.

18. A taxi company receives an average of 20 calls an hour distributed according to a Poisson distribution. The company has 7 cabs. The average time to service a call and pick up and deliver a customer is 10 minutes and fits an exponential distribution.

    (a) What is the probability that a taxi is idle?

    (b) On the average, how many customers are waiting?

    (c) On the average, how many customers are in the system—waiting and being serviced?

    (d) What is the average waiting time?

    (e) What is the average time in the system?

19. For the situation in problem 18, it is estimated that the company makes a profit of $0.10 per minute of trip time. The cost to operate a taxi is $4.00 per hour. Should the company add another cab to its fleet?

20. Products arrive at the final inspection station of a plant according to the following distribution:

TIME BETWEEN ARRIVALS	FREQUENCY
1.5	2
3.0	8
4.5	12
6.0	21
7.5	20
9.0	12
10.5	11
12.0	8
13.5	5
15.0	1
	100

The time it takes to inspect the product is:

SERVICE TIME	FREQUENCY
1.5	10
3.0	23
4.5	34
6.0	21
7.5	9
9.0	3
	100

Using a simulation technique, determine the average amount of waiting time.

References

Ackoff, R. L., and Sasieni, M. W., *Fundamentals of Operations Research,* Wiley, New York, 1968.

Apple, J. M., *Plant Layout and Materials Handling,* 2nd ed., Ronald Press, New York, 1963.

Bolz, H. A., and Hagemann, G. E., *Materials Handling Handbook,* Ronald Press, New York, 1958.

Boot, J. C., and Cox, E. B., *Statistical Analysis for Managerial Decisions,* McGraw-Hill, New York, 1970.

Chorafas, D. N., *Systems and Simulation,* Academic Press, New York, 1965.

Fetter, R. B., and Galliher, H. T., "Waiting-Line Models in Materials Handling," *Journal of Industrial Engineering,* Vol. 9, No. 3, May–June 1958.

Gordon, G., *System Simulation,* Prentice-Hall, Englewood Cliffs, N.J., 1969.

Haynes, D. O., *Materials Handling Equipment,* Chilton, Philadelphia, Pa., 1957.

Immer, J. R., *Materials Handling,* McGraw-Hill, New York, 1953.

Meier, R. C., *et al., Simulation in Business and Economics,* Prentice-Hall, Englewood Cliffs, N.J., 1969.

Morris, W. T., *Analysis for Materials Handling Management,* Irwin, Homewood, Ill., 1962.

Panico, J. A., *Queuing Theory: A Study of Waiting Lines for Business, Economics and Science,* Prentice-Hall, Englewood Cliffs, N.J., 1969.

Riggs, J. L., *Economic Decision Models for Engineers and Managers,* McGraw-Hill, New York, 1968.

Schmidt, J. W., *et al., Simulation and Analysis of Industrial Systems,* Irwin, Homewood, Ill., 1970.

Stocker, H. E., *Materials Handling,* 2nd ed., Prentice-Hall, Englewood Cliffs, N.J., 1951.

19

Production Planning and Control I: Preproduction Planning

The primary concern of production planning and control is the delivery of products to customers or to inventory stocks according to some predetermined schedule. All the activities in the manufacturing cycle must be planned, coordinated, and controlled to achieve this objective. From a long-range point of view (usually from five to ten years in the future), production planning largely deals with plant construction and location and with product-line design and development. In plans projected over a two- to five-year period, capital-equipment budgeting and plant capacity and layout are the principal concern. Finally, short-range planning (from several months to a year), focuses on such areas as inventory goals and labor budgets. Because production planning and control normally refers to short-range activities, we will concentrate on that aspect in this section. Accordingly, we will discuss the issues and problems that arise in the planned utilization of the labor force, materials, and physical facilities that are required for manufacturing products in accordance with the objectives of the firm.

The particular variety of production planning and control system used in any given instance and the scope of that system are primarily determined by policy decisions on the following:

1. *Whether to make or buy the product*
2. *Whether manufacturing will be intermittent or continuous*
3. *Whether manufacturing will be for stock or for order*
4. *What size the production order will be*
5. *Where the repair work will be done*

Together, these policy decisions define the manufacturing environment and constitute the working boundaries for production plans. Because of their importance, we will discuss each separately in the pages that follow. It is important to remember, however, that these policy decisions are in fact mutually interdependent.

The Production Environment

The Make-or-Buy Decision

Deciding whether a given product or part should be made in the plant or bought from another firm is a fundamental part of the production planning process. It is sometimes thought that this is simply a function of dollars and cents—that management is solely interested in obtaining items at the lowest cost and will therefore manufacture only those that have an internal cost advantage. In reality, however, many other factors enter into the decision. If, for example, the firm does not have the capability of making the particular item and cannot acquire the capability quickly or economically, the short-run decision is easily made—to buy. This should be recognized as simply a short-run decision, however. Long-range production planning might indicate that it would be advisable to acquire a plant and facilities for internal manufacture because of the long-range prospect of expanded sales, or because of anticipated cost, quality, or delivery difficulties in the continued purchase of the particular item. It was for reasons such as these that RCA and General Electric decided to manufacture transistors and other semiconductors themselves. For items that can be either purchased or manufactured, cost is of course an important factor, but the need to *control* quality and delivery can be equally significant.

The level of production activity also has a strong bearing on the make-or-buy decision. When the work load is high and plant capacity is being utilized to the maximum, there is a greater tendency to purchase items; indeed, the lack of available capacity can make such decisions mandatory. Emergencies stemming from machine breakdowns and rush orders can also dictate an increased level of component purchasing. When the work load is down, on the other hand, and idle capacity exists, there is no longer any pressure deterring a company from manufacturing the products and parts internally, but a blanket decision to manufacture wherever possible in those cases is clearly not sound. The additional costs incurred could aggravate the financial impact of the decline in sales that initially caused the low plant work load. Many firms solve this problem by establishing a cost differential of 10 to 15 percent as a cutoff point so that where the gain from procurement is greater than the differential, and the quality and delivery are favorable, the item will not be manufactured.[1]

---

[1] The size of the differential can be adjusted to fit the degree of emergency. Some companies employ a differential of over 10 percent because they feel that whenever possible items should be made rather than bought.

One can better understand why such a standard is used by calculating the costs of manufacturing a product or component internally. These costs may be broadly divided into material, direct labor, and overhead costs. Overhead costs remain relatively fixed despite changes in production levels so that when the work load is down there are fewer products to absorb these costs. Therefore, as long as the contribution to overhead from manufacturing a product exceeds the savings that could be gained by purchasing it elsewhere, the firm will usually benefit from internal manufacture. Hence, it is not surprising to find that companies with high overhead, or fixed, costs normally attempt to keep their production facilities fully employed at all times, whereas companies with low fixed costs are more prone to purchase items elsewhere. In addition, internal production helps stabilize the work force and minimizes the labor turnover costs associated with periodic layoffs. A stable work load also makes it easier to keep supervisory personnel.

The make-or-buy decision is not an irrevocable one; in fact, it should be reviewed periodically for each particular item. Nonetheless, the decision does have a potent short-term impact because it defines the task of the firm's manufacturing department. The list of items to be manufactured internally is arrived at by a series of make-or-buy decisions covering the company's product line from the top down.

Figure 19–1 illustrates this procedure. Here, for example, an automobile manufacturer may be trying to decide whether to make car radios himself or buy them from a supplier. As shown in the diagram, he may compromise and decide to buy 20 percent of his radios and manufacture the other 80 percent. Having made this decision, he must then choose what proportion of the assemblies and subassemblies needed for producing radios to manufacture himself and what proportion to buy. This, in turn, must be followed by separate make-or-buy decisions for each of the components of the assemblies and subassemblies. The total manufacturing task of the plant is indicated by the shaded area in Figure 19–1. The objective of production planning and control is to manufacture all of the items specified in the proper quantities and at the right time.

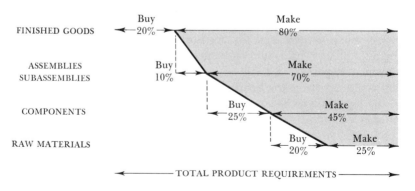

Figure 19–1   Product-line "sourcing": from the top down

Intermittent or Continuous Production

The second environmental factor that affects production planning and control is the type of production process employed, which in turn is largely dependent upon the characteristics of the product. In a very general sense, there are two basic manufacturing systems: continuous and intermittent.[2] Using continuous manufacturing, the product configuration and manufacturing methods are theoretically frozen at the beginning of the production run, and standard products are turned out at a relatively constant rate through the established production pipeline. Automobiles, refrigerators, and radios are generally made in this fashion, for example. In contrast, the level of manufacturing activity is subject to wide fluctuations when the intermittent approach is followed. The product configuration and manufacturing methods employed are also subject to change as required. Machine shops and job order specialty shops commonly employ the intermittent manufacturing approach.

In practice there are few instances of purely continuous or purely intermittent manufacturing operations in industry. Most companies strike some compromise between these extremes. Certain general characteristics can be listed, however, that will help us define the extreme toward which a company's production may be inclined.

Characteristics of Continuous Manufacturing

1. Large-volume production of standardized products is a common feature.
2. Specialized machines are generally employed, usually within the framework of a product-line layout.
3. Fixed path equipment such as cranes and conveyors are a common mode of materials handling.
4. Semiskilled and unskilled laborers are often adequate; consequently, labor costs are relatively low.

Characteristics of Intermittent Manufacturing

1. The company generally manufactures a wide variety of products; for the majority of items, sales volumes and consequently production order sizes are small in relation to total output.
2. General-purpose production machines are normally utilized, and process layout is favored.
3. Materials handling equipment is typically of the varied path type such as hand trucks and forklift trucks.
4. Relatively high-cost, skilled labor is needed to turn out the various quantities and types of products.

The manufacturing approach employed governs to a large extent the nature of the production planning and control function, which must be tailored to fit the

---

[2] Many writers and practitioners substitute the term *repetitive* for continuous and *nonrepetitive* for intermittent.

characteristics of the manufacturing operation. *Serialized control* is generally used if manufacturing is continuous; *order control* is used if it is intermittent. In both cases the objectives of planning and control and the activities it performs are substantially the same. There is one important difference, however. Intermittent manufacturing places a greater burden on the production planning and control activity. Consequently, by studying the problems of planning and control for an intermittent manufacturing operation, we will be better able to dissect and analyze production control in general. Thus, although our discussion will be oriented toward intermittent manufacture, or order control, it is important to remember that the same issues and problems arise in the serial control of a continuous manufacturing operation.

Production for Stock or Order

Another factor that affects the selection of a production planning and control system is the question of whether goods will be produced for stock or for order. The key factor here is the firm's policy regarding the time that can be allowed to elapse between receiving a customer's order and filling his order. Simply stated, Will customers have their orders filled immediately from stock or will they have to wait until the desired products can be made? A decision can be reached only after a carefully weighing of such factors as the value of the product, the nature of the production process and cycle, the demand for the product, the service expectations of the customer, the practices of competitive firms, and the custom of the industry. By producing for order, all inventory levels—including raw materials, work-in-process, and finished goods inventories—can be minimized; therefore, investment in inventory will also be minimized. This can result in a significant reduction in working capital requirements, and it can remove to a large extent such common inventory risks as obsolescence and deterioration.

On the other hand, from a production planning and control point of view, making to order can pose some serious problems. Each order must be processed individually through the production system, which means that the materials that will be needed must be determined separately each time, and a bill of materials developed, reviewed, and "sourced." Orders must then be generated and instructions delivered to the purchasing and production departments. Support activities such as industrial engineering must be scheduled separately for each order, and the order itself must be scheduled in relation to other orders for the production sections and the specific machines. The efficient performance of these tasks for each order demands a high degree of coordination and much follow-up work.

Other problems associated with making to order arise from the wide shifts in the level of activity that normally accompany this approach. Planning for the work force is difficult; some of the time it is necessary to lay off part of the labor force whereas at other times it is necessary to work the existing force overtime. This lack of stability inflates labor costs and tends to reduce plant productivity.

It also increases the difficulty of maintaining satisfactory levels of workmanship quality.

To help reduce the problems of manufacturing for order, a compromise approach is frequently taken whereby companies produce standard components and subassemblies for inventory and then draw upon these stocks of semifinished goods when orders are received. Although this device helps stabilize operations, it raises inventory investments and risks; accordingly, a balance of some sort must be struck between these two approaches.

The inherent advantages of manufacturing for stock, including short service cycles and manufacturing stability, constitute the problems of making for order. Similarly, the problems of manufacturing for stock, such as higher inventory investment and risk, comprise the advantages of making for order. An additional advantage of making for stock is that it is suited to both intermittent and continuous manufacturing, whereas making for order is suited only to an intermittent production.

The effectiveness of a policy of producing for stock depends to a large extent upon the accuracy of sales forecasts. When fairly reliable forecasts are possible, production runs can be regulated by economic-lot-size analysis, which is not normally possible when products are made for order.

The influence of changing demand To understand how changes in demand can influence production for stock, let us consider a company with a seasonal demand pattern. The company makes a sales forecast at the beginning of the year, which spells out monthly requirements as shown in Table 19–1. The first column shows the expected sales for the month, and the next column lists the cumulative expected sales. The third column indicates the level of inventory

Table 19–1 Projected sales and needed safety stocks (in units)

Month	(1) Expected Sales	(2) Cumulative Sales Forecast	(3) Safety Stock Inventory Required[a]	(4) Cumulative Production Requirements
January	600	600	300	550
February	400	1,000	250	900
March	300	1,300	210	1,160
April	400	1,700	250	1,600
May	600	2,300	300	2,250
June	900	3,200	350	3,200
July	1,100	4,300	400	4,350
August	1,200	5,500	420	5,570
September	1,300	6,800	440	6,890
October	1,200	8,000	420	8,070
November	1,100	9,100	400	9,150
December	900	10,000	350	10,000

[a] An opening inventory of 350 units is assumed, and the average safety stock is 340 units.

reserves required as safety stock, and the last column gives the total amount that must be produced by the end of each month. Sales of 600 units are forecast for January, for example; the inventory level is 350, and 300 units are allocated to safety stock. Therefore, 50 units are available to meet demand. Subtracting 50 from the total demand of 600, we have a total production requirement of 550 units. For February the figures would then be

$$550 \qquad + \qquad 400 \qquad - \qquad 50 \qquad = \qquad 900$$

| (January total pro- duction required) | (new forecast demand) | (reduction in safety stock) | (total production required) |

Thus, the cumulative sales requirements, less the opening inventory, constitute the "demand" placed upon the plant for finished products.

Table 19–2 summarizes the available production capacity expressed in working days.

The objective of production planning and control is, of course, to design the most efficient way of meeting these requirements. Figure 19–2 contrasts two methods of achieving this objective. The first approach calls for a steady rate of production, which would yield just enough (10,000 units) to meet the year's requirements so that at year's end the inventory balance would be zero.[3] As is shown in the diagram, this plan would create large inventories during the earlier months; the exact amount of these projected end-of-month inventories is shown in Table 19–3.[4] The average monthly inventory is 1,035 units; when 340 units

Table 19–2   The summarized available production
capacity expressed in working days

| | Production Days | |
Month	Month	Cumulative
January	22	22
February	19	41
March	21	62
April	21	83
May	22	105
June	20	125
July	12[a]	137
August	22	159
September	20	179
October	23	202
November	19	221
December	19	240

[a] In July there is a two-week shutdown for vacations.

[3] Implicit in this statement is the assumption that actual sales and production will be exactly equal to the quantities forecast.

[4] The end-of-month inventory represents the difference between the cumulative number of units manufactured and the cumulative number of units sold.

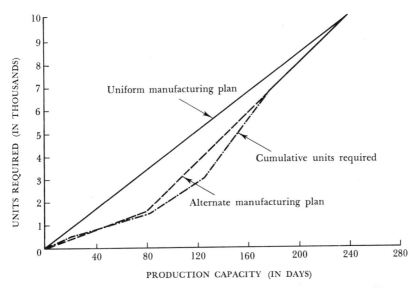

Figure 19–2 Cumulative sales requirements and alternate manufacturing plans

of average safety stock is added, we have a total average inventory of 1,375 units.

There are many other possible production plans. The one shown as a broken line in Figure 19–2 calls for a low manufacturing rate of 20 units per day for the first 80 working days followed later in the year by a daily rate of approximately 53 units. This approach greatly reduces the average inventory level during the year, but it requires a greater productive capacity than the steady rate of production examined earlier. In the latter, a production capacity of approximately 42 units per day is needed, whereas the former requires a productive

Table 19–3 Projected end-of-month inventories for the steady production rate example

Month	Units in Inventory	Month	Units in Inventory
January	374	July	1,404
February	822	August	1,108
March	1,444	September	628
April	1,880	October	414
May	2,160	November	132
June	2,050	December	0
	Average monthly inventory	1,035	
	Average inventory reserve	340	
	Total average inventory	1,375	

capacity of 53 units per day. In addition, the sharp shift from a daily production rate of 20 to 53 units may be accompanied by the added costs associated with a fluctuating labor force. Indeed, in any given situation the savings made by lower inventories must be balanced against these other expenses. In this balancing process it is important to weigh the specifics of the situation; for example, the need for "far greater capacity" can mean facilities acquisitions, a multishift operation, or a varying utilization of existing machinery.

In practice, several manufacturing plans would be projected, and for each one calculations of expected operating characteristics would be made. Then the approach with the lowest overall cost that met the product's demand pattern would be selected.

Determining the Production Order Size

The size of production orders influences the choice of a production planning and control system in much the same fashion as the choice of producing for stock or for order. The particular size of the production order depends upon many factors. If the product is made to order, the customer controls the size of the order since the quantity contracted for must be supplied. In some instances, management is able to combine orders from several customers into a single production run; where this is possible, production runs may be able to approximate economic lot sizes. But the degree to which management can combine orders depends on the timing and the similarity of the products; the decisive factor will be management's ability to meet established delivery schedules. For this reason, one way to increase the ability to merge orders is to offer a delivery date that will add positive slack to the production schedule. Delivery time must still be competitive, however, and the possibility of losing orders because of late delivery limits the amount of slack that can be added in this fashion. Another approach that is sometimes employed is to offer the customer a lower price if he will accept a later delivery date, but this is a risky technique. It can prove costly if additional orders that could be combined with the original order are not received; in that case, the original order must be filled by itself with the added production costs.

In contrast, when units are produced for stock, there are two principal ways of selecting the order size. Judgment, intuition, and experience in the form of rules of thumb and other empirical standards is one method; it is both timely and inexpensive. The economy may be illusory, however, since large losses can result from poorly chosen production lot sizes.

The second approach to lot size determination requires the use of mathematical formulas and models. These economic-lot-size models cannot be used blindly but must be modified to reflect the operating characteristics of the particular firm. In essence, however, these formulas are simply a more precise approach to solving the problem of balancing insufficient production against excessive production in order to minimize the overall costs of production, inventory, and loss of goodwill.

The results obtained from inventory formulas must be tempered to accommodate seasonal variations in demand and the availability of plant capacity. If the work load is low, for example, considerable idle capacity exists, and a larger production than economic lot size may be needed to stabilize the manufacturing activity. If the work load is high, on the other hand, production runs of the economic lot size may mean that some products will not be ready in time to meet their delivery dates; therefore, lots smaller than economic lot size may be produced. In short, the assumptions and accuracy limitations of the mathematical approaches and the imperfections of the data make these approaches just aids to management decision making, not "automatic deciders."

The Location of Repair Work

The final factor that affects the environment of production planning and control is the manner in which work is done on faulty production output. Nearly all firms find it necessary to do at least some repair work on their output; to appreciate the impact of this work on the planning and control of production, it may be divided into three categories:

1. The repair of products that are found defective during the manufacturing cycle
2. The repair of products that develop defects during the warranty period[5]
3. The repair of products that have developed defects because of normal wear and tear by the customer

Let us first consider the last two categories. Defects of this sort are often corrected by facilities outside of the plant. Field servicemen may visit the customer's site, as in the electronic computer and powerhouse equipment industries, for example, or field service depots may be established, as in the television and electrical appliance fields. Often independent companies are set up as authorized service representatives for the products of the manufacturer, who then pays these agents for all warranty repairs. In other industries, however, repairs are normally made at the plant where the item was manufactured, as for example, in the precision photographic industry. Two reasons for making repairs at the manufacturing plant are the need for special facilities, tools, or labor skills and the need for repair parts that cannot be economically maintained at many depots. For industries that make repairs at the manufacturing plant, the problems are essentially the same as those for industries that discover defects during the production process.

For repairs necessitated by defects found during the manufacturing cycle, the problem is whether these units should be run through the regular production sequence or taken off the line and repaired in a separate department. If they are run through the production pipeline, many serious problems can arise—for example, how much capacity at each stage of the production cycle should be left available for this work? In the design and operation of production facilities, it is difficult to predict the number of units that will require repair and what the work

---

[5] Defects that occur during the warranty period are the company's responsibility to repair; in category 3 the cost of repair is borne by the user.

will be. As a result, the work load necessitated by repairs is difficult to schedule within the regular production process. Improper scheduling can 'lead to idle facilities and idle labor or to lengthy repair cycles and dissatisfied customers; therefore, to avoid such scheduling problems many firms have set up special repair departments. This technique has been successfully used in the automobile, electronics, and aerospace industries. A separate repair department has another advantage to recommend it. Because frequently it takes greater skill to diagnose and correct defects than it took to make the item originally, trade unions have been successful in getting repair occupations recognized in labor contracts. The fact that such occupations now exist with separate work jurisdictions makes it mandatory that separate employees be assigned to repair activities—a factor that by itself often leads to the creation of separate departments.

Where the duplication of facilities necessitated by a separate repair department is too costly, repair work is frequently performed on the existing equipment during the night shift. Some companies establish skeleton second and third shifts to do this work. These crews also act as a hedge against peak loads and rush orders.

Preproduction Activities

Having now described in general terms the factors that influence the selection of a production planning and control system, we will turn to the activities that comprise the manufacturing cycle and analyze the problems of planning and controlling them. Manufacturing activities fall naturally into two categories: preproduction and production. Preproduction activities, as the name implies, consist of all functions that must be performed before the start of production. Their objective is to ensure that all of the resources needed for production are available at the right time and in sufficient quantities. In contrast, production activities deal with the conversion of these input resources into the desired final product.

The preproduction phase of the manufacturing cycle can be divided into seven stages: authorization and master scheduling, engineering release, breakdown and ordering, procurement, in-plant services, receiving and inspection, and the accumulation of materials. These are presented in their most typical sequence in the following list:

> *The Preproduction Functions of the Manufacturing Cycle*
> Authorization and master scheduling
> Engineering release
> Breakdown and ordering
> Procurement cycle
> In-plant services
>   Industrial engineering
>   Tools and fixtures
>   Quality control
> Receiving and inspection
> Accumulation of materials

Authorization and Master Scheduling

Authorization It is axiomatic that no production work should be undertaken without proper authorization. This requires the establishment of "recognized sources" of authority for making and communicating order decisions. The decision regarding what will be manufactured and in what time sequence affects all of the firm's major functions—sales, finance, engineering, and manufacturing. Hence, it is important that order decisions reflect the best thinking of the key managers from each of the participating functional areas of the firm, supported by data on such factors as inventory levels, financial resources, demand forecasts, and production costs.

To achieve the necessary coordination, some firms establish "production authorization" committees with representatives from each of the major departments. Other firms prefer to vest the decision-making authority in one individual and rely on his ability to coordinate the various aspects of the problem. In either case work orders, often referred to as DTW's (directives to work), are issued; they spell out what products are to be manufactured and in what quantities. The DTW is circulated to all participating departments and constitutes an authorization to spend money and allocate men and facilities for manufacturing the product.

Production master schedule The DTW also tells when the final product is scheduled for delivery to the customer, including the starting date and weekly or monthly production rate. This information is used to create a production master schedule. Table 19–4 lists part of a manufacturing firm's master schedule, which shows the quantities of finished goods the plant must deliver to the warehouse each month. Since the master schedule is the foundation for planning and controlling all manufacturing activities, all production orders should be routed through the central decision agency so that every order can be incorporated in the schedule. This procedure also permits order points and economic lot sizes to be reviewed so that these may be adjusted, if necessary, in light of changes in demand forecasts, the projected plant work load, or the production process.

Developing a master schedule is a two-stage process. First, previously authorized production programs are reviewed in light of the most recent production, sales, and delivery data, and adjustments in the master schedule are made when necessary. Second, the feasibility of authorizing new production programs is

Table 19–4 A portion of the master schedule for the
ABC Manufacturing Company

Product (desk model)	*Month 197–*											
	J	F	M	A	M	J	J	A	S	O	N	D
A	45	30					30	30	30	30		
B				75	75	75					75	75
C		25	25	25					25	25	25	
D				60	70	70						40
E	100	100	75					100	100	100	100	

evaluated in view of the firm's prior commitments. New production programs are authorized for two basic reasons: to meet a customer's order or to readjust an inventory position.

Adjustments to scheduled production Review of the current status of authorized production programs is designed to pick up significant deviations from the master plan. Such deviations occur either because production has not been according to plan or because the demand for the product has been greater or less than expected; in either case, an adjustment in the master schedule is called for. The following information should be used in deciding whether to revise a master schedule:

$$I_p = \text{planned inventory level}$$
$$I_a = \text{actual inventory level}$$
$$D_p = \text{cumulative planned deliveries}$$
$$D_a = \text{actual deliveries}$$
$$P_1, P_2, \cdots, P_N = \text{planned monthly production rate}$$
$$F_1, F_2, \cdots, F_N = \text{original monthly sales forecast}$$
$$RF_1, RF_2, \cdots, RF_N = \text{revised monthly sales forecast}$$

When all of this information is available, master schedule adjustments can be made according to a mathematical approach such as the following:

$$\Delta P_2 = K \times [(I_p - I_a) + (D_p - D_a)$$

| (change in production for second month) | (adjustment factor) | (difference between planned and actual inventory) | (difference between planned and actual delivery) |

$$+ (RF_2 + RF_3 + \cdots + RF_N - F_2 - F_3 - \cdots - F_N)]$$

(difference between original and new sales projections)

$$NP_2 = P_2 + \Delta P_2$$

| (new production planned for second month) | (original production planned for second month) | (change in production for second month) |

This formula states that the production rate for the following period has been adjusted to reflect deviations from the original plan that have occurred in the inventory level, cumulative production, and projected sales. K acts to temper the amount of the adjustment. K values range between 0.0 and 1.0. If K is close to 1.0, the production rate will be highly responsive to changes; smaller values of K make the production rate less sensitive to deviations from the plan, and therefore they result in a more stable manufacturing operation. The value of K that is applicable to each situation is determined by testing and by trial and error.

It should be noted that this formula makes the implicit assumption that the production rate can be altered instantaneously—in this case, during the following month. Often this is not true, however, since it may take one month to alter the production rate, for example; hence, it becomes necessary to express the formula in terms of changing the production rate for future periods. Thus, although we would like to alter the production rate for the following period (the second month), we cannot make a change until the third month. To accommodate this factor the formula must be expanded.

The new production rate (NP_2) from the original formula cannot be met, because the production rate set by the original master schedule cannot be changed in time. What we need to determine is the difference between the desired and the actual production during the second month. This difference can be found in the formula:

$$NP_2 = P_2 + K[(I_p - I_a) + (D_p - D_a) + (RF_2 + RF_3 + \cdots + RF_N$$
$$- F_2 - F_3 - \cdots - F_N)]$$

With this value for NP_2, the original formula can be modified to

$$\Delta P_3 = K[(NP_2 - P_2) + (I_p - I_a) + (D_p - D_a)$$
$$+ (RF_3 + RF_4 + \cdots + RF_N - F_3 - F_4 - \cdots - F_N)]$$

where $NP_2 - P_2$ = difference between desired and actual production during the second month

The scheduling of new production Once the production rates for items already on the master schedule have been adjusted, management can begin to schedule new production. The principal criteria for authorizing production and for placing items on the master schedule (whether production is to order or for inventory) are the lead time required to begin production, the date when the product will be needed, and the load on the production facilities. The demands created by all three factors must be satisfied. If, for example, the delivery date promised on a sales order is six months away, and it takes two months to obtain raw materials and set up the production line for the item and another two months (once production is started) to meet the order, then without even considering the production load, management might be expected to defer authorizing production for this item for a month or two. If production is slack now, however, or will be at a peak five months from now, it might schedule the product immediately.

The Gantt chart Of the many techniques employed to support this type of planning, the oldest and probably still the most frequently used is the Gantt chart.[6] This chart is relatively inexpensive and can be easily and effectively used for planning purposes. It provides the planner with a critical insight into the interrelationships among the specific activities within an entire process. Even the most complicated production plans can be presented clearly on a chart, which makes it an excellent communication device; understanding and interpreting a chart is relatively easy and, what is more, it can be done accurately and consistently by all informed observers.

Essentially a Gantt chart is a device for depicting a work plan in terms of

[6] The use of charts in planning and controlling plant activities stems from the work of Henry L. Gantt, and the charts are still referred to as "Gantt charts" in honor of their originator.

Production engineers use a Gantt-type wall chart to schedule production runs on their machines.

time and for showing the progress of the work in relation to the plan. This chart may be adapted to any type of manufacturing process and any activity within that process. There are three basic varieties of Gantt charts:

1. Load charts
2. Record charts
3. Program process charts

By helping the planner to visualize the relationship between what is done and what is planned, all Gantt charts pinpoint potential and actual problems in time for corrective action to be taken.

LOAD CHARTS[7]   The purpose of load charts is to show the work assignments that have been made to a plant, a department, or a group of men or machines. Work is typically measured in units of time, hours, days, or weeks. Therefore, what is recorded is the amount of time that the work will take, and not the particular item being manufactured or the nature of the task. The chart presents the hours, days, or weeks when the facilities are scheduled to be used; in addition,

[7] Over the years there have evolved a standard format and construction technique for preparing the charts which facilitate both their preparation and interpretation. This standard format will be used throughout the discussion.

it also indicates the cumulative work load, indicating for the time period selected the proportion of total capacity that has been assigned.

A typical load chart for a turret lathe department is shown in Figure 19–3. The light lines indicate the work scheduled on each type of machine. The work is measured in "elapsed hours," or the amount of time it would take if all the lathes of that particular type were put on the job. Thus, during the week of October 5, lathe EL1 is scheduled to be operated 80 percent of the time. Since there is only one machine in this category, there will be only 32 hours of work. During the same period, lathes EL2 will be busy 75 percent of the time; since there are eight machines of this type available, this means there will be 240 hours of work.

The heavy lines opposite each type of lathe reflect the cumulative work load that has been assigned to all machines in that category; by glancing at these lines the manager can immediately compare available capacity with utilization. The heavy line at the top of the chart reflects the cumulative work load of the entire lathe department. It indicates that if the total work could be distributed evenly to all the lathes, the department would have only 16.5 days of work assigned to it.

According to the standard notations used on Gantt charts of all types and as shown in Figure 19–4, the ▼ symbol at the beginning of October in Figure 19–3 merely indicates that the chart was begun at that time. When the same symbol appears again below October 5, it simply means that data were added to the chart at that time.

The load chart is a valuable tool for scheduling. In considering whether an item can be produced in sufficient quantity by a given date, the manager has merely to glance at the chart to see whether or not the facilities needed for production are available. As time passes, of course, the chart is constantly updated to reflect added loads. Thus, during periods of peak or heavy loads the data on the chart can help determine:

1. The assignment of priorities to future orders and whether to subcontract or refuse orders
2. When to utilize overtime or multishift operations
3. When to consider the acquisition of additional men or equipment to provide needed capacity

Conversely, when the work load is slack, Gantt load charts can help the manufacturer decide:

1. What types of orders and work are needed to keep men and machines busy
2. When to reduce the level of the work force

Load charts are also useful in assessing the feasibility of future plans. Since the charts provide a permanent record of the success of past plans, they can help the manager gain an insight into the probable success of proposed ones.[8]

---

[8] Load charts are used most frequently in manufacturing operations, but they could easily be used in other fields as well. For example, a computer programing group could use Gantt load charts to plan and control the amount of work assigned to each analyst.

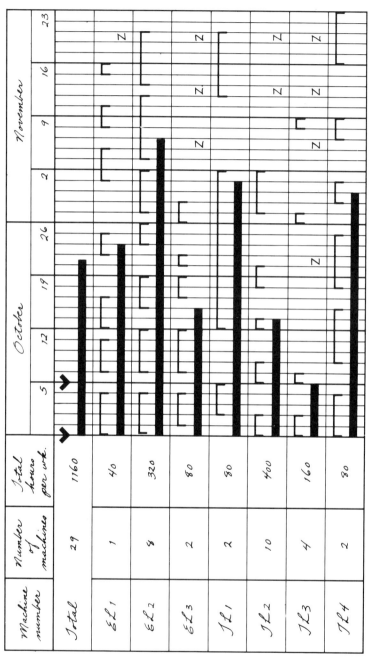

Figure 19–3 Gantt load chart for the ABC Company turret lathe department

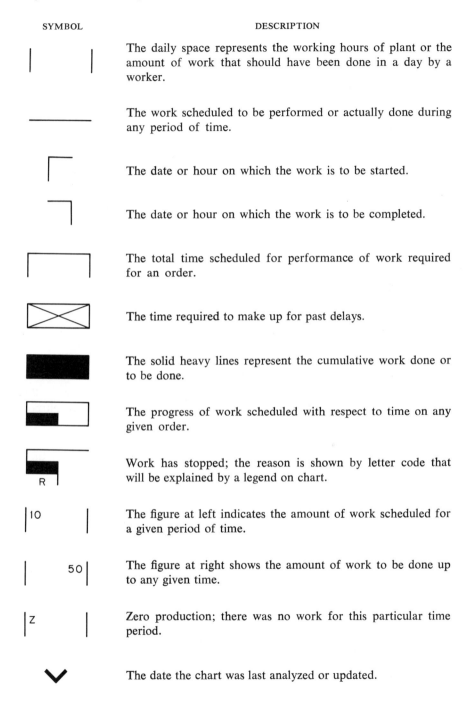

SYMBOL   DESCRIPTION

The daily space represents the working hours of plant or the amount of work that should have been done in a day by a worker.

The work scheduled to be performed or actually done during any period of time.

The date or hour on which the work is to be started.

The date or hour on which the work is to be completed.

The total time scheduled for performance of work required for an order.

The time required to make up for past delays.

The solid heavy lines represent the cumulative work done or to be done.

The progress of work scheduled with respect to time on any given order.

Work has stopped; the reason is shown by letter code that will be explained by a legend on chart.

The figure at left indicates the amount of work scheduled for a given period of time.

The figure at right shows the amount of work to be done up to any given time.

Zero production; there was no work for this particular time period.

The date the chart was last analyzed or updated.

Figure 19–4   Symbolic notation for Gantt charts

RECORD CHARTS   As another type of Gantt chart, record charts are primarily a reporting device. For each activity plotted, they show the actual operating times; if a machine is idle, the reason is specified. In addition, the charts indicate whether or not the tasks assigned to each activity have been accomplished and if not, the reasons for the delay. These data alert management to problem areas as they develop and thus facilitate prompt corrective action.

A sample record chart summarizing the accomplishments of the men in the same turret lathe department during a typical work week appears in Figure 19–5. Each man is expected to do eight hours of assigned tasks during a day. Thus, the light line measures in hours the work actually performed during the day, and the heavy line measures in hours each man's cumulative performance for the week. From the chart it can be seen that Brown did only six hours of work on Monday. The letter T that appears in the last Monday square indicates that tool trouble was the cause of the delay. Repairs again delayed this worker on Tuesday, hence the symbol R in Tuesday's squares. Rhoads, however, has no excuse for his low output; he appears to be too slow to achieve the normal production rate expected.

For each foreman and group leader, it is customary to show by heavy lines the cumulative average performance of all men reporting to him.[9] The men reporting to group leader Smith, for example, averaged 37.5 production hours for the 48-hour work week. Those reporting to Winters, the other group leader, averaged 38 hours. Overall, the men in foreman Jones's department averaged 37.75 hours of productive work.

PROGRAM PROGRESS CHARTS   This final type of Gantt chart shows the sequence of tasks necessary to achieve a specific objective. The basic purpose of program progress charts is to show the time and sequential relationships among the activities within a production plan, and therefore they attack the same problem as PERT does. Typically, this type of chart is used in planning the preproduction activities of a specific manufacturing program and the movement of an order or lot through the various production stages.

In this chart the light line denotes the planned amount of time required for the performance of each activity or operation. The sequence and interrelationships among tasks is evident immediately because of the use of time for the horizontal axis. A heavy line denotes the actual performance. If these charts are kept up to date, management can keep in constant touch with a program's status. Reasons for delays, when they occur, are indicated. By examining these problems in terms of the overall program objective, management should be able to take the necessary remedial action to help keep the program on schedule.

Figure 19–6 illustrates a preproduction plan. In this case, the preproduction cycle extends over a period of twenty weeks. Since the Model 3A clock has been manufactured before, relatively short cycles of two weeks each have been planned for engineering release and for breakdown and ordering. Purchasing is

---

[9] Again it should be noted that, although this example was taken from the production phase of a manufacturing process, this chart can be applied to all manufacturing and to many nonmanufacturing activities as well.

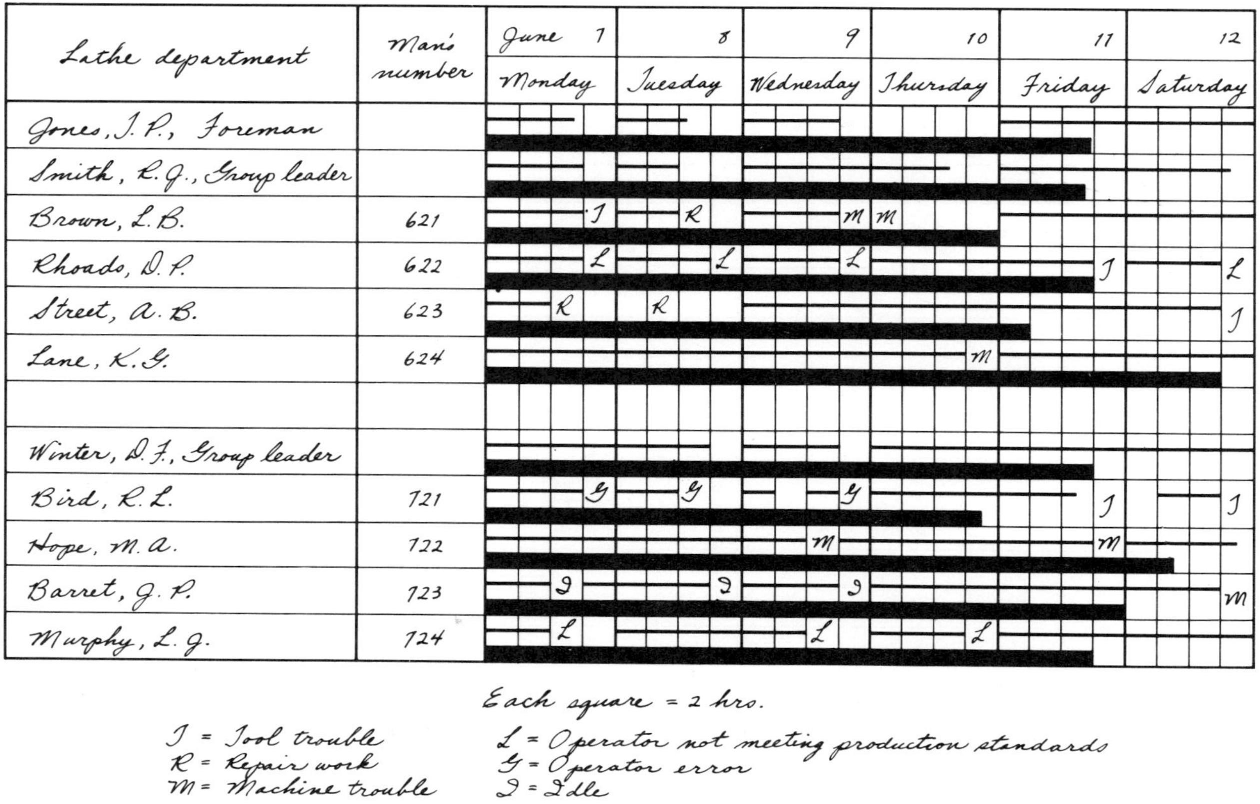

Lathe department	Man's number	June 1 Monday	Tuesday	Wednesday	Thursday	Friday	12 Saturday
Jones, J.P., Foreman							
Smith, L.G., Group leader							
Brown, L.B.	621	J	R	M	M		
Rhoda, O.P.	622	L	L	L			L
Steet, A.B.	623	R	R				J
Lane, K.L.	624				M		
Winter, D.F., Group leader							
Bird, R.L.	721	E	E	E			J
Hope, M.A.	722			M		M	
Barret, G.P.	723	E	E	E			M
Murphy, L.G.	724	L		L		L	

Each square = 2 hrs.

J = Tool trouble
R = Repair work
M = Machine trouble
L = Operator not meeting production standards
E = Operator error
I = Idle

Figure 19–5 Gantt man record chart for the ABC Company turret lathe department

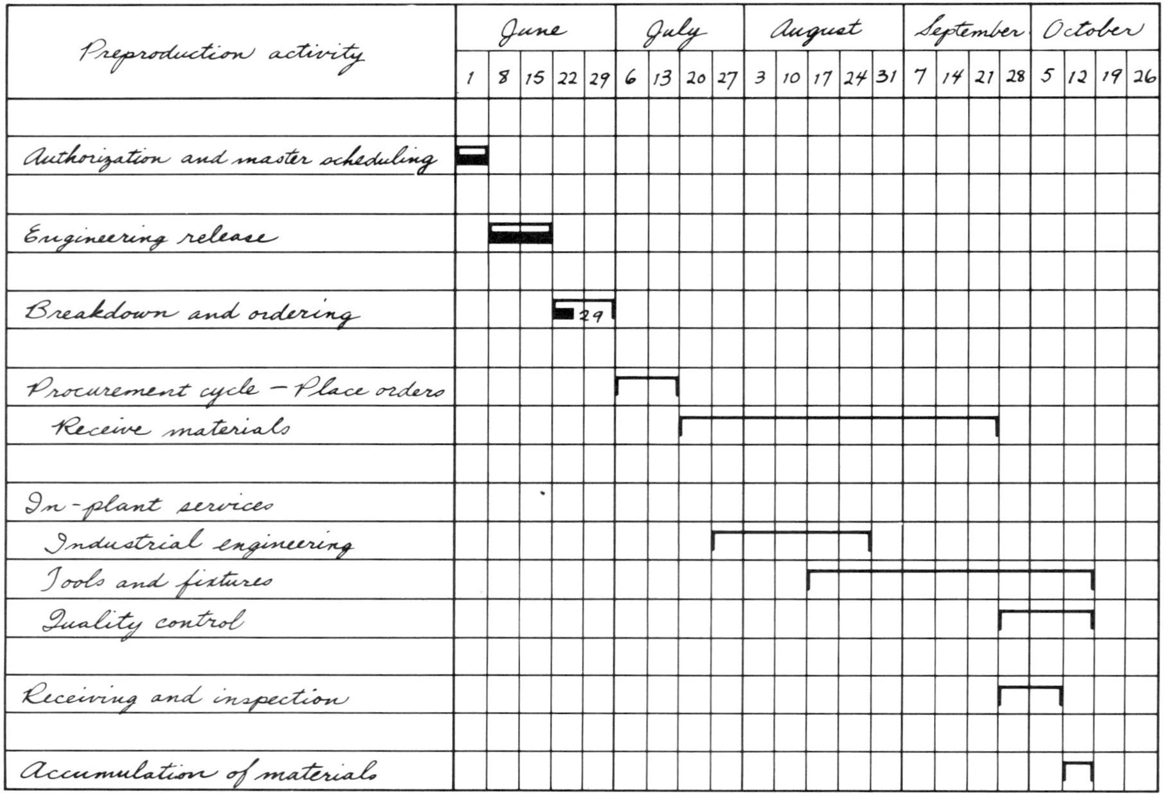

Preproduction activity

June | July | August | September | October
1 8 15 22 29 | 6 13 20 27 | 3 10 17 24 31 | 7 14 21 28 | 5 12 19 26

Authorization and master scheduling

Engineering release

Breakdown and ordering

Procurement cycle – Place orders

Receive materials

In-plant service

Industrial engineering

Tools and fixtures

Quality control

Receiving and inspection

Accumulation of material

Figure 19-6 Gantt progress chart—preproduction plan for the ABC Company—manufacture of 100 Model 3A clocks

the element in the cycle that requires the most time. To ensure that the deadlines are met, periodic performance reviews are usually conducted, often on a weekly basis. During these reviews the chart is updated to reflect actual performance, and any corrective action that seems necessary is planned. In the diagram, for example, manufacturing authorization and engineering release were completed on time, but the breakdown and ordering task was behind schedule. Number 29 indicates that on June 29th, when the chart was last updated, only about one-third of breakdown and ordering had been completed. This situation warrants investigation.

GANTT CHARTS: A CRITIQUE Gantt charts have proved to be excellent aids during the initial planning of manufacturing operations. However, they tend to become confusing once an activity has started and an attempt is made to show changes in the schedule. The result is inevitably a badly cluttered presentation, even when a multicolor scheme is used to designate changes in the plan.[10] As a rule, the amount of confusion and misinterpretation increase perceptively with each replanning cycle.

For these reasons, Gantt charts are now used principally for planning and recording purposes; rescheduling generally means issuing a new chart. There are mechanical Gantt charts in use that employ colored strings, pegs, and cards; to some extent these modifications have solved the replanning problem. On one of these mechanical Gantt charts, it is possible to display simultaneously a complete job history—original plans, actual performance, and revised schedules. There are many commercial variations of the mechanical Gantt chart, but the two most popular are termed the Productro Board and the Schedugraph.

For planning purposes, program progress Gantt charts have another limitation. Many of the problems facing management are extremely complex, and planning alternatives with these charts can be quite time-consuming. Furthermore, the charting technique does not indicate which alternative is the best or which is even capable of achieving the goal. Planning with Gantt charts is a trial-and-error procedure, largely because there is no way to match costs with the various phases of a program or with the program as a whole. For simple problems, such as planning the operations of the turret lathe department, however, these limitations are not serious; the low cost and simplicity of the charts make them an excellent tool for such purposes. For large and complex problems, however, the charts' limitations are serious; fortunately, new planning and scheduling devices such as PERT can now overcome these shortcomings.

Engineering Release

The issuance of a DTW and the release of the master schedule trigger a chain of preproduction activities, which will only be outlined briefly at this point since

---

[10] It should be noted in this regard that using several colors, such as green and red, to denote sequential changes in schedules, etc., has proved to be far superior to using a single-color record. Even with multicolor charts, however, there is cluttering and an increased likelihood of misinterpretation.

they were treated in detail earlier. The basic purpose of all of these activities is to prepare for the actual production of the item.

The first step is to check the engineering aspects of the manufacturing process to see if all the information that engineering must furnish to production is up to date and accurate. Assuming that the product specifications have already been decided upon, the specific manufacturing information for which engineering is responsible can be checked, including a list of the materials needed to produce one unit of the item,[11] the blueprints for all parts and assemblies, the procedural instructions for manufacturing, and finally the testing and inspection of the parts and the finished item. When these data have been reviewed and found satisfactory, an engineering release is issued for the product; this is the starting signal for the next preproduction step, breakdown and ordering.[12]

For products that have been previously manufactured, the engineering review should consume comparatively little time and effort. Errors in the engineering information should have been found the hard way during the earlier production programs and corrected at that time. Where products have been updated or new models introduced, the review should be focused on the new parts and the interfaces between the new and old elements.

Brand new products normally require a much more intensive review. It is an unwise economy to limit the engineering review on new products, since inadequate attention can result in far greater costs later on in terms of reworking the product or having idle facilities. Where the preproduction time must be minimized, the product is often reviewed piecemeal—by sections of subsystems; each piece is processed through the rest of preproduction as soon as it is released by engineering. Although this approach complicates the planning and control function, it can save time, which may be of crucial importance. Suppose, for example, that there were a strong demand for a brand new product and that there were a race with the firm's competitors. By treating the sections as though they were finished products, subsystems could be started through the manufacturing process before the design of the entire product system was completed. Such "crash programs," as they are called, involve great risks, however. An error that is detected late in the engineering review may mean that all of the completed units, as well as all those in process at the time, may have to be reworked.

Breakdown and Ordering

After the engineering release has been issued to production control, the required materials must be ordered. Before this can be done, however, the make-or-buy decisions must be made. As a general rule, this task is necessary only for new products and new models of old products. Where there has been little change in the product since it was last manufactured, the old decisions need only be reviewed.

[11] This is termed a *unit bill of materials.*
[12] This important step should be formalized by the issuance of a standard document, which is often termed an *engineering notice* or *engineering letter.*

When all the make-or-buy decisions have been made or reviewed, a complete bill of materials must be prepared from the unit bill of materials furnished by engineering. Assuming that the engineering information is complete, this preparation is merely a simple multiplication process; the number of items to be made is multiplied by the number of components in each item. In the event that a unit bill of materials is not available, management must go back to the engineering blueprints to develop one; as soon as one is obtained, ordering can begin.

The ordering process consists of issuing *purchase requisitions* for units that will be purchased and *labor cards* for units that will be made internally; both documents give a detailed description of the item involved and specify the quantity desired.

Another important aspect of breakdown and ordering is the "engineering changes" that occur after manufacturing has started; this is particularly true of new models and new products whose design flaws may not have become apparent until then. Similarly, customer reaction to the first units of a new product may make it apparent that further changes are necessary. Altering an item that is already in production requires a high degree of planning, coordination, and follow-up to minimize the costs and time needed to make the change; it may mean manufacturing or procuring new materials or modifying existing components. Furthermore, obsolete and irreparable items must be scrapped and sold. In short, to introduce engineering changes with a minimum of disruption and confusion requires careful handling, and it is a real test for the production control group.

Procurement Cycle

Requisitions for all items to be purchased are forwarded from production control to the purchasing department, where they are transformed into purchase orders that bear the contractual terms for price and delivery. Periodic follow-ups are then made to ensure that suppliers meet the delivery dates stipulated in the order. If the suppliers have any questions about performance features, tolerances, or other specifications, they are answered by the purchasing department.

In-Plant Services

Between the issuance of the DTW and the final accumulation of materials before production begins, a number of support activities take place to prepare the plant for the new production run. The principal ones are industrial engineering, facilities planning, tools and fixtures control, and quality control. Industrial engineering is responsible for the design of the overall manufacturing process, including the specific methods of operation and the design of the work stations. Ideally, this work should be accomplished during the final stage of the innovation cycle, as the pilot manufacturing run takes place. But any work remaining must now be completed. Labor time standards for each of the operations must also be developed. These tasks largely constitute a review, of course, if the particular product has been previously manufactured.

The labor standards and the projected monthly production rate taken from the master schedule are used for facilities planning. The number of machines and work places required for each operation in the run are determined, the necessary tools and fixtures in the right quantities are acquired, and suitable layout and materials handling systems are designed.

Just as production planning and control has the final word on the production plan, so quality control must develop an inspection plan to check on work-in-process. Inspection points and procedures must be established or reviewed (as the case may be), and the facilities needed to support this system must be obtained and built into the production process.

Receiving and Inspection

While these preproduction tasks are going on, some of the material inputs will begin to arrive. Both the quantity and the quality of these shipments must be measured to make certain that the right materials were received. Partial quantity deliveries are common, but they indicate the need for follow-up action to ensure that the suppliers ship the rest of the order on schedule. Quality discrepancies are generally a more serious problem. If the deviations are minor, the item may often be used as it is. If the defects are serious, however, or if time is short, some or all of the units made have to be fixed at the buyer's plant. This work can be done either by the firm's personnel or by representatives of the supplier, depending upon the agreement between the two parties. When time permits, the supplier will probably prefer to have the defective items shipped back to his own plant or service depot for correction, because this is generally the least expensive alternative. In every case, however, quality deviations are a sensitive problem, and all decisions and subsequent communication with the suppliers should be conducted through the purchasing agent, for he will have to negotiate with them the question of who will pay for the repair work.[13]

Accumulation of Materials

All satisfactory material inputs are then forwarded to the stockroom; a review of the stockroom records will indicate when all the materials have been received and are available for production. This review procedure will normally start between two weeks and one month before the scheduled beginning of production. The actual availability of materials and the estimated date for the receipt of any items that are missing will enable management to decide whether or not to start the production run as scheduled. Ideally, all required materials should be on hand before starting production, but operations often begin when a few items are still missing and their delivery is expected momentarily. The missing items might not be needed until the end of the run, for example, and there is no harm in starting as long as the items are received by the time they are needed. Fur-

---

[13] Experience indicates that ambiguous or fallacious information furnished to suppliers on blueprints, etc., is often largely responsible for quality deviations; hence the need to proceed with tact.

thermore, early starts of this nature can help raise the plant work load to the desired level, and it can save time. These advantages can be of great importance to a firm at various times.

The final accumulation of materials should be timed to coincide with the completion of all the necessary in-plant service functions described earlier in this chapter. Thus, the receiving of all material inputs should indicate a total state of readiness and signal a formal close to the preproduction phase of the manufacturing cycle.

Preproduction Planning

The effective performance of preproduction activities is a crucial factor in the success of a production run. As in so many other functional areas, effectiveness depends on a proper balance between cost and the time required to perform the tasks involved. The length of the production cycle has a direct impact on order intervals and sizes and on inventory levels. In many industries, preproduction activities consume more than half the total production time; in the electronics and electrical machinery industries, for example, preproduction time can comprise as much as 70 percent of the manufacturing cycle. Unduly long cycles increase the cost of running a business and cut into company profits, largely by increasing the investment in work-in-process and finished goods inventories. In contrast, short production cycles can lead to a larger "return on investment," which is a popular measure of managerial and company achievement. Long production cycles are also undesirable because of uncompetitive delivery dates, which can literally ruin a firm's prospects for "to order" business. On the other hand, efforts to achieve a short production cycle can also hurt the firm if they result in either preproduction or production costs that are too high and uncompetitive. Here again a balance must be struck to achieve a reasonable use of resources, men, and facilities. The proper assignment of resources and the sequencing of preproduction tasks with a minimum of backtracking and lost time will lead to minimum production cycles and costs.

Questions and Problems

1. What is the primary function of production planning and control?
2. What are the major problems in production planning and control?
3. What factors influence the make-or-buy decision? Who should make this decision?
4. How is labor turnover related to make or buy?
5. Does the production system in a given plant have any implications for production planning and control? Specifically, how does the type of manufacturing (that is, continuous or intermittent) affect production planning and control? Explain and give examples.
6. The basic functions of production control may be defined as routing, scheduling, dispatching, and control. How would each of these be affected by a decision to

buy rather than make subassemblies? How would they be affected by a change from manufacturing for stock to manufacturing to order?

7. What is the difference between the amount of development cost in production for stock and production to order?

8. The XYZ Company has made a forecast of its sales for the coming year. The product it manufactures costs $10 per unit. Inventory carrying costs are estimated at 20 percent a year, and storage costs are estimated at $0.10 per unit per year.

FORECAST (IN UNITS)

January	200	July	700
February	300	August	600
March	500	September	500
April	700	October	300
May	900	November	300
June	800	December	200

(a) Show *graphically* the impact of a decision to produce at a uniform rate throughout the year on the inventory of finished goods.

(b) Assuming that the company has no reserve stock, how much inventory must it have on hand January 1 to carry out the above policy?

(c) By varying its production between 400 units and 600 units, the company can reduce its maximum inventory to 800 units during the peak month. Assuming that the costs of variable operation for the year are $1,200, should the company produce at a variable rate or should it produce at a uniform rate?

9. "The general sales forecast is developed on a dollar basis for either the entire line of products or for the different product groups." If this is the company's practice, what limitations does this place on the activities of production control? Because of these limitations, should production control develop its own sales estimates?

10. Analyze the statement, "Scheduling decisions are, in part, an attempt to reduce the time for production runs to an optimum level in order to give greater service and maintain greater turnover. One way in which this may be done is to carry optimum amounts of inventories."

11. Three production policies are being considered by the management of a company that makes mechanical pencils and pens:

   (1) A production schedule based on annual monthly average of sales.
   (2) A production schedule based on semiannual monthly average of sales.
   (3) A production schedule based on quarterly monthly average of sales.

The estimated monthly sales volume in dollars for the year 197— was as follows:

January	$210,000	July	$384,600
February	248,600	August	361,100
March	305,700	September	373,900
April	408,100	October	424,400
May	373,800	November	289,400
June	365,800	December	201,200

The inventory on hand January 1 was $180,000.

(a) Compute the monthly sales average for the year.

    (b) Compute the monthly sales averages for the first six months and the last six months.

    (c) Compute the monthly sales averages for each quarter beginning with January.

    (d) Plot the forecast sales curve.

    (e) Plot the inventory transfers required for each program (three diagrams).

    (f) Compute the inventory requirements of each program.

    (g) In deciding what policy to recommend, balance the financial requirements of inventories against the costs and difficulties of changing the size of the productive personnel. Compute the inventory carrying costs at the annual rate of 15 percent of the inventory's value. Consider as unimportant any changes in production that range from 1 to 8 percent.

Which policy would you recommend?

12. The Baker Company is a highly mechanized manufacturer of assembled metal products. It utilizes special-purpose equipment, a product layout, and conveyorized materials handling. Its projected sales forecast (in units) for the last six months of 197— is as follows:

July	30,000	October	70,000
August	40,000	November	90,000
September	50,000	December	80,000

The Baker Company wants to know whether it should produce during the last six months of the year at an even rate, or at different rates based on quarterly averages of sales during the third and fourth quarters, respectively.

13. Given the following data, in what size lots should the Able Company produce radio parts?

Annual volume	18,000 units
Rate of usage	Steady
Cost of issuing each manufacturing order	$5.00
Material cost	$0.80 per unit
Labor cost	$0.15 per unit
Overhead cost	150 percent of direct labor cost
Taxes and insurance	4 percent of the annual amortized value of plant and equipment
Interest on investment	10 percent of the annual amortized value of plant and equipment

14. What preproduction activities are required in production planning and control?

15. Describe the major characteristics of Gantt charts, and tell what they indicate and where they may be used.

16. Compare the use of Gantt charts with network analysis in scheduling the tasks required in planning and controlling the forthcoming workload of a company.

17. Use a Gantt chart to schedule your major activities for a day. Update the chart at specified times during the day.

18. A company has four orders that it wishes to schedule through its production process. Each order must go through three different departments in order: De-

partment A, then Department B, then Department C. The following table gives the number of days each job takes in each department. Job 100, for example, needs 6 days in Department A, 5 in Department B, and 7 in Department C.

DEPT.	JOBS			
	100	105	108	112
A	6	4	8	2
B	5	2	9	3
C	7	2	5	2

(a) Use a Gantt layout chart to determine the best schedule—the one taking the least total time—for the work.

(b) How much open time does each department have in your answer to (a)?

(c) Would your task become more difficult with 10 departments and 20 jobs? What does this indicate about the scheduling task?

19. The president of a company wants to determine how orders for three new products will affect the company production before he accepts the orders. He has asked you to prepare Gantt charts for

(1) a master schedule

(2) machine loads

(3) progress on the orders

The orders call for delivery of 70 units of each product each month for a year. The products are made up of the following parts:

PRODUCT	PARTS
A	A1, A2, A3
B	B1, B2, B3
C	C1, C2

Three departments are involved in production of the parts. Each part moves through the departments according to the following sequence. The sequence cannot be changed.

PART	OPERATIONS SEQUENCE
A1	$1 \to 2 \to 3$
A2	$3 \to 2 \to 1$
B1	$2 \to 2 \to 3$
B2	$2 \to 2 \to 1$
B3	$2 \to 3 \to 2$
C1	$1 \to 1 \to 3$
C2	$3 \to 1 \to 1$

The parts all take the same amount of time to produce in each department, although the capacities of the departments are different. A load chart for the departments has been kept through January since some work is in progress (see Figure 19–7). It indicates the work already scheduled and the department capacities.

To meet the president's request, prepare a production program for the year starting in January and develop the machine loading through March.

Dept	Machine	Capacity per day	January 1	8	15	22	29	February 5	12	19	26	March 5	12	19	26
								Week beginning							
1	20	70		▬											
1	21	35				▬		▬							
2	8	65					▬								
2	9	30	▬												
2	10	25			▬		▬								
3	2	80	▬												
3	5	20		▬			▬								

Figure 19-7

References

Bock, R. H., and Holstein, W. K., *Production Planning and Control: Text and Readings,* Charles E. Merrill, Columbus, Ohio, 1963.

Buffa, E. S., *Production-Inventory Systems: Planning and Control,* Irwin, Homewood, Ill., 1968.

Clark, W., *The Gantt Chart, A Working Tool of Management,* 3rd ed., Pitman, London, 1952.

Conway, R. W., Maxwell, W. L., and Miller, L. W., *The Theory of Scheduling,* Addison-Wesley, Reading, Mass., 1967.

Gavett, J. W., *Production and Operations Management,* Harcourt Brace Jovanovich, New York, 1968.

Greene, J. H., *Production and Inventory Control Handbook,* McGraw-Hill, New York, 1970.

Hoffmann, T. R., *Production: Management and Manufacturing Systems,* Wadsworth, Belmont, Calif., 1967.

Holt, C. C., *et al., Planning Production, Inventories and Work Force,* Prentice-Hall, Englewood Cliffs, N.J., 1960.

Hopeman, R. J., *Production: Concepts-Analysis-Control,* 2nd ed., Charles E. Merrill, Columbus, Ohio, 1970.

Magee, J. F., and Boodman, D. M., *Production Planning and Inventory Control,* 2nd ed., McGraw-Hill, New York, 1967.

Muth, J. F., and Thompson, G. E., *Industrial Scheduling,* Prentice-Hall, Englewood Cliffs, N.J., 1963.

Niland, P., *Production Planning, Scheduling, and Inventory Control,* Macmillan, New York, 1970.

O'Brien, J. J. (ed.), *Scheduling Handbook,* McGraw-Hill, New York, 1969.

Rago, L. J., *Production Analysis and Control,* International Textbook, Scranton, Pa., 1963.

Ramlow, D. H., and Wall, E. H., *Production Planning and Control,* Prentice-Hall, Englewood Cliffs, N.J., 1967.

Zeyher, L., *Production Manager's Desk Book,* Prentice-Hall, Englewood Cliffs, N.J., 1969.

20 *Production Planning and Control II: The Production Process*

The decision to start production is normally made after completion of all pre-production activities, which include the following:

1. Industrial engineering. A manufacturing process must have been established. Detailed work methods or standard practices must have been designed for each operation in the process. Labor output standards must have been formulated and the workplaces must have been arranged so that materials and tools can be "stocked" to support the operator's activities. Instructors must be on hand to help the assigned workers learn their respective tasks.

2. Tools and test equipment. Arrangement of physical facilities must have been completed, and the layout plan must be in effect. All necessary machines and test equipment, including tools and fixtures, must be ready for use.

3. Quality control. Inspection and test procedures to assure conformance with the product specifications must have been prepared, including statistical quality control plans. Positions for the performance of the operations must have been integrated into the work flow and layout, and all necessary instruments and gauges must have been checked and must be available.

4. Manpower. Workers with the proper skills must be on hand in the proper quantities, and the line supervisors must be ready to direct the manufacturing of the product.

In addition to the completion of these tasks, a detailed plan of all production activities is needed before production itself can begin; preparing this detailed plan is a responsibility of the production planning and control function. This task is often referred to as *supplementary planning* because it supplements the master schedule that establishes the overall production goal in terms of the quantity of finished goods and the delivery dates to be met. Supplementary plans deal with both planning and control. In the planning portion the order is "routed" and "scheduled," which simply means that the product's path through the production process is defined, and the average time required for performing the work along the established route is projected.

In the control portion of the supplementary plan, the process is "activated" and "monitored"; action is taken to ensure that the product moves along its route according to schedule, and the progress of each product or order is periodically checked and corrective action planned whenever deviations occur.

Now let us examine the activities in the supplementary planning phase of production planning and control in more detail.

Routing

We have defined routing as the function that determines the path that each internally manufactured order will take through the production plant. It prescribes the sequence of operations that will transform the input materials into the desired end products. The concept of routing is most widely used in factories, but it may also be applied in other areas of business. For example, sales managers have found it to be a useful means of scheduling sales calls on customers in a more effective sequence.

In a manufacturing plant, the routing of an order is generally spelled out on a route sheet, an example of which is shown in Figure 20–1. Notice that there is a great similarity between this sheet and the operation process chart discussed earlier. This is not surprising when we consider that the methods analysis that provides information for the operation process chart is also the source for preparing the route sheet; in fact, many companies use the same form for both purposes. A route sheet contains a complete description of the item to be manufactured, including (in this case) the name of the product, its identifying symbol, and its blueprint number. In addition, for each operation required to produce the fastener, the setup time and standard operation times are provided. These data are useful for scheduling purposes, as we shall see later in this chapter. The route sheet also specifies what machines can be used to perform each operation, including alternate machines where feasible. Thus, in Figure 20–1, for example, operation 1 can be performed on either machine PA-17 or PC-16. Such information is extremely valuable to the manager in meeting emergencies and preventing bottlenecks; with such data in hand he may expand the capacity needed to achieve internal balance by making use of more than one type of machine for an operation. Such flexibility is extremely useful, particularly when the plant work load is at a high level.

ABC Manufacturing Company
Route Sheet

Symbol P6A3	Draw. No. 62271-3	Date: 6-22	Prepared by J. C. Brown
Description: Heavy-duty fastener			Remarks
Economic lot size 15000	Material: CRS .083"		

Time per piece (min.)	Setup time per lot (min.)	Operation No.	Operation Description	Machine assignment	Operation	Transportation	Inspection
			Material accumulation—on hand				
0.5	10	1	Blank and file	PA-17, PC-16			
1.0	12	2	Form and stamp	PD-19, PB-32, PS-12			
			Delivered to P.S.				
1.0	15	3	Pierce	DP-1, KP-9			
3.5	25	4	Straddle mill-shakleway	MM-2, EM-4			
5.0	1.0	5	Tumble in sawdust	T-2			
2.0	3.0	6	Deburr top	G-1, G-9			
2.5	15	11	Ebony black high-gloss finish	X-11			
			Deliver to finished goods				

Figure 20–1 ABC Manufacturing Company—route sheet: heavy-duty fastener

Machine Breakpoints

Specifying alternative machines on the supplementary plan is also valuable from another point of view. Different machines usually have different operation-cost characteristics. Therefore, unit production costs, which vary with volume, will probably not be the same for all alternatives, given a certain production volume. This means that for any specified production quantity there will be a most economical, or "best," machine for performing each operation. The critical volumes at which economical manufacturing shifts from one machine to the next are called *machine breakpoints*. In preparing a route sheet, machine breakpoint studies are also performed and attached to it. This enables the planner to utilize the lowest cost machines for the volumes needed wherever possible. A simple example will illustrate how such breakpoints are established.

In Figure 20–1 we see that operation 2 can be performed on three different machines: PD-19, PB-32, or PS-12. To determine the production volume at which it would be economically best to use each of the machines, the applicable costs are first classified as fixed or variable, as in Table 20–1. Fixed costs in this context are largely setup and tooling costs; they are "fixed" in the sense that they are performed only once during a production run, regardless of the size of the run. Setup costs are typically the most important of this group. Variable costs

Table 20–1   Cost classification

Machine	Fixed Costs	Variable Costs per Unit
PD-19	$ 8.00	$0.25
PB-32	40.00	0.15
PS-12	80.00	0.07

include labor, materials, power, and other costs that vary with volume; of these, labor and material costs are generally the most important. Now we can develop a simple linear equation relating machine costs to the production volume.

$$TC = FC + (VC \times V)$$

where TC = total costs
        FC = fixed costs
        VC = variable costs per unit
        V = production volume

Substituting values for the three alternatives of operation 2, we have

$$TC_{PD-19} = \$8.00 + \$0.25V$$

$$TC_{PB-32} = \$40.00 + \$0.15V$$

$$TC_{PS-12} = \$80.00 + \$0.07V$$

To obtain a machine breakpoint, we must solve two of the equations simultaneously for V. Thus, the breakpoint for PD-19 and PB-32 is found by solving:

$$\$8.00 + \$0.25V = \$40.00 + \$0.15V$$

$$V = 320 \text{ units}$$

The breakpoints between PD-19 and PS-12 and between PB-32 and PS-12 may be obtained in a similar fashion. This breakpoint analysis can be shown graphically by plotting the total cost lines for each machine as in Figure 20–2. The figure reveals that, assuming all three machines are available when the operation is to be performed, PD-19 should be used for production runs up to a volume of 319, that PB-32 should be used for production runs between 320 and 499, and that PS-12 should be employed when production quantities equal or exceed 500.

Routing Precedence

Another useful piece of information that should appear on the route sheet is called *precedence*. The path given on the route sheet should be the best, or optimum, sequence for the required operations. In most cases the item can be manufactured with varying degrees of effectiveness using any number of possible sequences. This fact becomes significant when the level of production activity varies widely from one machine or department to another. A choice of alternative sequences makes it possible to avoid bottlenecks and fill in areas of low

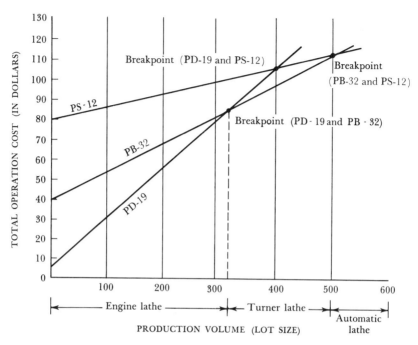

Figure 20–2 ABC Manufacturing Company—breakpoint analysis for route
sheet P6A3, operation 2

activity at minimal cost. In addition, using an alternate route may be the only
way to meet the target delivery date if the work loads of some of the machines
in the best sequence are already heavy.

There are limits, however, to the extent to which work loads may be balanced
or stabilized by changing the sequence of operations, and these limits are defined
by precedence. The nature of the product and production process used make it
mandatory that certain operations be performed before others. Precedence relationships are frequently presented graphically, as in Figure 20–3, which describes those found in the manufacture of the heavy-duty fastener of Figure
20–1. Notice how closely this type of diagram resembles a PERT network. It
can be seen that operation 2 must follow operation 1, but that operation 2 may
be followed by either operation 6 or operation 3. As long as the precedence relationships are followed, any sequence of operations may be scheduled that will
help to stabilize plant work loads.

Routing Follow-up

In Figure 20–1, notice that columns entitled "Operation," "Transportation,"
and "Inspection" are provided for follow-up purposes. Experience may indicate
that certain specific machines and routes are far more desirable than others. Such
discoveries may occur because there was a lack of "total" knowledge when the

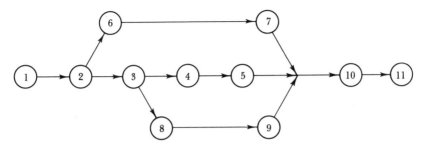

Figure 20–3 ABC Manufacturing Company—precedence diagram: heavy-duty fastener

original route sheet was prepared or simply because the original planning was inferior. In any case, preferable machines and routes should be noted to guide future scheduling of a product and to help evaluate the performance of the routing personnel.

Scheduling

Normal Scheduling

Scheduling, the second step in supplementary planning, means the determination of when and where each operation in the production process will be done. This information is usually recorded on what is called the *order,* or *lot, schedule,* which frequently takes the form of a Gantt progress chart as illustrated in Figure 20–4. This chart shows how the operations for manufacturing a lot of 500

Order schedule			500 brackets — model no. 42693							
Operation Description	Operation number	Department number	Date							
			4/1	4/2	4/3	4/4	4/5	4/8	4/9	
Shear to size	1	(6) Brake	⌐⌐							
Drill holes	2	(4) Press		⌐⌐						
Bend to form	3	(6) Brake			⌐					
Inspection	100	(25) Inspect					⌐			
Paint per spec.	4	(15) Finish						⌐		
Final inspection	101	(25) Inspect							⌐	
									To stock	

Figure 20–4 ABC Manufacturing Company—order, or lot, schedule

brackets have been assigned among the departments of the ABC Manufacturing Company.

Since the company utilizes a process-type layout, the schedule must specify when the work will be ready for each department and when it must be completed. Thus, we see that department 6 will receive the bracket material on April 1 and that it should complete its operations and deliver the lot to department 4 by noon of the next day.

A progress chart records the timing of work movements between departments, but within each department a priority must be established among the many jobs waiting to be completed. The Gantt load chart is the planning tool commonly used to determine the order in which jobs are started so that production schedules can be met as efficiently as possible.

Delivery Date Problems

The most common type of delivery date problem is not having enough time to use normal production scheduling. When operations are scheduled normally (as shown in Figure 20–4), they can be performed in sequence on the most economical machines. The length of the production cycle reflects the standard operating times for the individual tasks. For example, using the sequence in Figure 20–4 (which is based on standard times), a projected time of 6.8 days will be needed to produce 500 brackets. Conceivably, a production cycle of this length may not be satisfactory, especially if the start of production had been delayed for some reason, say, for example, the tardy delivery of raw materials. Therefore, some means must be used to accelerate this production.

Dovetail scheduling   One way of accomplishing this objective is to employ *dovetail scheduling,* which simply means that the order is divided into sublots, each of which is processed separately through the plant. Thus, in our bracket example, the order of 500 units might be broken into five sublots of 100 units each. This would mean that work on operation 2 could begin after only 100 units had been produced at operation 1, rather than having to wait for the completion of all 500 units. Similarly, when the first 100 units were through operation 2, operation 3 could begin. Several operations could thus be performed simultaneously, thereby substantially reducing the total production time.

If carried to its limit, dovetailing would mean individual movement of each unit through the production process or, in fact, establishment of a product layout in place of a process layout; this is obviously impractical. The time saved by dovetailing must therefore be balanced against the added costs of materials handling, paper work, and control. The greater the number of sublots, the more time is saved, but also the more added costs are incurred.

Another limitation is that dovetailing itself is not quite so simple to achieve as this explanation may suggest. To illustrate the difficulties involved, let us schedule the dovetailed production of the 500 brackets. Figure 20–5 depicts the new dovetail schedule, which requires only 4.25 days instead of the original 6.8 days. The dovetailing of operation 2 with operation 1 presents no problem be-

Order schedule			500 brackets - model no. 426J3						
Operation Description	Operation number	Department number	Date						
			4/1	4/2	4/3	4/4	4/5	4/8	4/9
Shear to size	1	(6) Brake	▭	▭					
Drill holes	2	(4) Press	▭	▭					
Bend to form	3	(6) Brake		▭					
Inspection	100	(25) Inspect			▭				
Paint per spec	4	(15) Finish				▭			
Final inspection	101	(25) Inspect				▭	▭		
									To stock

Figure 20–5 ABC Manufacturing Company—order, or lot, schedule: dovetail scheduling

cause the second step takes longer than the first. Therefore, the press department will still be working on the initial 100 units when the second 100 arrive from operation 1. Thus, continuity of production can be maintained at both operations. However, operation 3 takes less time than operation 2. Hence, if each sublot from operation 2 were worked on when it arrived, operation 3 would run out of work before the next batch arrived; this would mean either idle capacity at operation 3 or, should the equipment be used on other orders during the waiting period, additional setup costs. The solution to this problem is to delay the start of operation 3 until there is a sufficient backlog of work, so that continuous production can be scheduled. In other words, operation 3 should be timed to start so that sublots 1 to 4 will be completed at the precise moment when the last sublot arrives from operation 2. This type of problem is quite common; it occurs whenever the time needed to perform one operation is shorter than that needed to perform the operation immediately preceding it. Notice in our example that the problem occurs again in dovetailing inspection 101.

Split routing scheduling Another way of acclerating the production process is *split routing*, whereby the performance of one operation is assigned to more than one machine. Often, machines listed as alternate facilities on the routing sheet are employed. Here, too, added costs are incurred, of course, including the expense of additional machine setups, paper work, and control. Moreover, when alternate machines are employed, variable costs are also increased because less economical machines are being used.

Overtime and multiple-shift scheduling One final method of accelerating the production output is by using overtime or multiple-shift operations. Overtime is generally thought of as a short-run solution, whereas multiple-shift operations, by their nature, are typically reserved for the solution of problems of longer duration. Nonetheless, as we mentioned previously, some companies maintain a token second shift for the sole purpose of handling emergencies.

Before using any of these accelerating devices, the planner must be sure to balance the relative value of the time saved against the added costs.

Work-Load Problems

We have also indicated that a large backlog of work can bring about a conflict between normal production cycles and promised delivery dates. Before discussing this type of problem, it should be pointed out that heavy work loads can result in positive benefits as well as problems. One benefit is the use of "combined routing" in making up schedules. This technique can be employed when the same operation must be performed on items in more than one lot or order. There will be significant savings if the schedules can be arranged so that with a single setup the common operation may be performed without interruption on all items from the many orders. Combined routing is the most economical way to accomplish an operation since the setup costs are minimized and the output per machine is maximized. As might be expected, however, combined routing has certain limitations: it can raise the work-in-process inventory costs, and it requires more careful timing of the orders.

Scheduling Practices

The major scheduling problem that arises when work loads are high is the assignment of priorities among the various jobs. It is often necessary for some orders to wait while others are being processed.[1] Since the number of orders to be processed has already been decided, the subsequent problem is to determine their sequence. The assignment of priorities to jobs is a difficult task, and many valid criteria could be used, including:

1. Meeting promised delivery dates, or the need to replenish inventory
2. The maximization of profit
3. The minimization of production costs

At times these criteria may be compatible, but not always. For example, a policy of meeting all delivery dates without fail may raise production costs well above the level that would prevail if a few of them were missed.

It is, of course, up to the firm to decide what priorities will be assigned to given projects. In the next few pages we will examine the scheduling problems that typically accompany various types of priority systems.

The run-out approach   One simple approach to production scheduling is the "run-out priority system"; it is most applicable to production that is geared to

---

[1] This situation may be caused by poor master scheduling, that is, by accepting too many orders.

inventory levels. It is demand-oriented and seeks to minimize stockouts by granting highest priority to items most in danger of running out.

The first step is to calculate the run-out time for each product under consideration. To do this, the total current inventory, defined as inventory in the warehouse and items currently in production on orders already received, is determined. Then a forecast of future monthly usage is developed. Finally, the number of months that may elapse before the total inventory will run out is calculated by subtracting the monthly forecasts from the total inventory. As a result, orders for products with the shortest run-out time are processed first. To improve the effectiveness of this procedure, products may also be assigned weights that reflect their relative financial or strategic importance to the firm. After the run-out times for all products have been calculated, the weights are reviewed, and any products that are heavily weighted and have, say, less than two months until run-out time are given a top priority rating. Orders for these products would be processed first, regardless of the run-out times of others.

The run-out time approach has two principal scheduling advantages. First, it is an easy, inexpensive, and fast way to assign priorities and schedule production. Second, it minimizes stockouts and thus helps to improve the service the company can give its customers. On the negative side, however, the run-out time approach is only suited to production that is geared to inventory levels. Moreover, it ignores inventory costs; consequently, it is uneconomical for companies that are anxious to minimize those costs.

The graphic solution to meet the profit criterion Another criterion for assigning priority is profit; this means that when capacity is scarce it should be used to manufacture items that will yield the greatest return to the firm. This decision rule is easily stated and widely accepted by business executives, but implementing it is often far from easy. In comparatively simple cases a graphic solution to the problem will suffice. In more complex cases, however, some type of linear programing must be used; the simplex approach discussed in Chapter 6 is probably the most widespread. Notice the similarity between determining what products should be made in order to maximize profits and this type of scheduling problem. The basic difference is that product-line determination is the decision on what orders should be taken, whereas scheduling is the decision on what sequence should be followed.

To explain further some of the methods used to assign priorities and schedule projects using the profit criterion, let us examine several typical approaches. One makes use of a graphic solution, as the following simple problem will illustrate.

The XYZ Manufacturing Company makes two types of metal clips. Sales have been brisk in recent months and now there is a backlog of orders. Furthermore, sales forecasts indicate that demand will continue to outstrip production unless the company moves to a new and larger plant. The production process for each model consists of three operations—stamping, forming, and painting. Table 20–2 summarizes the standard operating times required to perform these tasks on each model. The total available capacity in minutes of operating time is also given for

Table 20-2   Standard operating times for clip production

Metal Clips	Operation—Standard Times (in minutes)		
	Stamping	Forming	Painting
Model A	0.4	0.6	0.4
Model B	0.8	0.2	0.4
Total daily capacity	1,440	1,440	1,920

each type of machine. Thus, for example, both the stamping machine and the forming machine can be run for 1,440 minutes a day.

Our objective is to schedule the stamping, forming, and painting operations in such a way that profits are maximized.[2] This problem may be plotted and solved graphically as in Figure 20-6. Here we see that the number of Model A clips manufactured may be measured along the vertical axis on the graph and the number of Model B clips manufactured along the horizontal axis. First, we assume that the entire productive capacity is devoted to manufacturing Model A and so we determine the total number of units that could be made at each stage of the process if that were so. Then we assume that only Model B will be

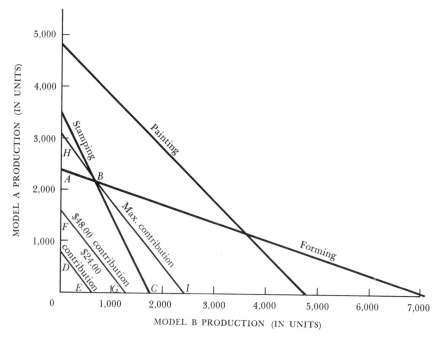

Figure 20-6   XYZ Manufacturing Company—graphical solution to the machine assignment problem for producing Model A and Model B clips

---

[2] It is assumed that maximum profits will result when the contribution from the plant is maximized.

made and again determine the number of units that could be produced for each operation. The results are then marked off on the appropriate axes. Thus, if only Model A were produced at the stamping operation, the daily output would be 3,600;[3] if only Model B were produced, the total would be 1,800. A line drawn diagonally between these points, therefore, will define all possible divisions of stamping time capacity between the two models, assuming that the total capacity available is used. For example, if equal amounts of stamping capacity were assigned to each model, the daily production would be 1,800 Model A's and 900 Model B's. This line does not necessarily depict the actual stamping activity, however; since it is possible to operate at less than full capacity, production can be at some lower point, between the line and the origin (0). However, it is *not* possible to exceed the line and operate at a higher point farther from the origin; the maximum possible output of the stamping process is defined by this line.

This principle also applies to the capacity lines for the painting and forming operations; actual production must be within the capability of *all* operations. It would be impractical, therefore, to paint 4,800 Model A clips daily (even if there were enough painting capacity to do so) because only 2,400 Model A clips can be processed daily by the forming machines. A valid production plan must consider the limitations of each of the production operations. Expressed graphically, this simply means that output must be within the area bounded by the origin, *A, B,* and *C.* In this case there is considerable imbalance among the capacities of the three production processes; painting has much more capacity than the other two; this suggests that any further expansion of facilities should first take place in the stamping and forming operations.

So far we have concentrated on the restrictions imposed by production technology, but to obtain an optimum production schedule it is also necessary to consider economic factors. Models A and B contribute $0.03 per unit and $0.04 per unit, respectively, to expenses. This information may be used to construct lines of "constant contribution" as follows. Assume for the moment that our objective is to obtain a total contribution of $24.00 from each day's output of clips. If the total contribution were to be obtained from Model A, we would have to manufacture 24.00/0.03, or 800 units. If the manufacture of Model B were expected to furnish the entire sum, we would have to turn out 24.00/0.04, or 600 units. The line drawn between these two extremes (labeled *DE* in Figure 20–6) is termed a *constant contribution line;* it defines all production possibilities that could yield a total daily contribution of $24.00. A line representing a constant contribution of $48.00 (*FG*) is parallel to *DE* and twice as far from the origin because the contribution per unit of the two models is constant. For this reason, an optimum production plan may be determined by the constant contribution line that is farthest from the origin yet still within production capability of the plant; in Figure 20–6 it is the area 0*ABC.* In our example, the maximum contribution is obtained when a constant contribution line (*HBI*) is

---

[3] This is found by dividing the available capacity (1,440) by the time to produce a unit (0.4).

drawn through the optimum operating point (B); the production plan, therefore, should call for 2,150 units of Model A and 725 units of Model B, given by the coordinates of B. This combined output will yield a maximum total contribution of about \$93.50 per day.

The principal advantage of the graphic method is the ease with which it may be understood and applied. On the basis of data shown on this type of graph, a production plan can be quickly and inexpensively formulated. The major weakness of this approach is that it can only be used for relatively simple problems. Introducing more products and processes would make the approach impractical; simply introducing a third production process would require a three-dimensional chart, for example, which is certainly less easy to use and understand. Charts for four or more products are not at all feasible because it would be impossible to identify the applicable axis.

Linear programing to meet the profit criterion   Another way of attacking the same sequencing problem is to use some type of linear programing. This method can handle many products and processes, but as the number of products and processes increases, manual solution becomes impractical and the analyst is forced to use a computer. Where scheduling must be done on a daily basis or as inexpensively as possible, the need for a computer may limit the applicability of this approach.

Solving this scheduling problem by linear programing follows the procedure described in Chapter 6. The problem is to maximize the contribution subject to the constraints of the production process; thus, the revenue equation is

$$R = 0.03X_1 + 0.04X_2$$

where $X_1 =$ number of units of Model A produced
        $X_2 =$ number of units of Model B produced

The production constraints are

$$0.4X_1 + 0.8X_2 \leq 1{,}440, \qquad \text{for stamping}$$
$$0.6X_1 + 0.2X_2 \leq 1{,}440 \qquad \text{for forming}$$
$$0.4X_1 + 0.4X_2 \leq 1{,}920 \qquad \text{for painting}$$

Using the simplex method, the first step is to introduce the slack variables X_3, X_4, and X_5. X_3 represents the unused stamping capacity, X_4 the unused forming capacity, and X_5 the unused painting capacity. The constraints become

$$0.4X_1 + 0.8X_2 + X_3 + 0 \ \ + 0 \ \ \ = 1{,}440$$
$$0.6X_1 + 0.2X_2 + 0 \ \ + X_4 + 0 \ \ \ = 1{,}440$$
$$0.4X_1 + 0.4X_2 + 0 \ \ + 0 \ \ + X_5 = 1{,}920$$

Putting the equations into the simplex tableau, we have

X_1	X_2	X_3	X_4	X_5		
0.4	0.8	1	0	0	1,440	S
0.6	0.2	0	1	0	1,440	F
0.4	0.4	0	0	1	1,920	P
-0.03	-0.04	0	0	0	0	R

Solving the equations according to the method explained in Chapter 6, we move through three tableaux to

X_1	X_2	X_3	X_4	X_5		
0	1	1.5	-1	0	720	X_2
1	0	-0.5	2	0	2,160	X_1
0	0	-0.4	-0.4	1	768	P
0	0	0.045	0.02	0	93.60	R

The optimum production plan according to this tableau would call for an output of 2,160 units of Model A and 720 units of Model B, which together would yield a daily contribution of $93.60. Notice that these values vary slightly from those obtained in the graphic approach. The values from the programing solution represent a true optimum with slightly more contribution than that obtained in the graphic approach.[4]

We also learn from the tableau that the painting facility has 768 minutes of idle machine capacity. This information was also available from the graphic approach and, as mentioned earlier, it is valuable for planning plant expansions or in considering whether to manufacture additional products.

The index approach to minimizing production costs   Management frequently faces the problem of how to schedule a great number of orders to achieve the lowest production cost. In addition, the time and money available for solving this problem are very often limited; a satisfactory answer must be found quickly so that the work can be processed. Under these circumstances, approximation techniques are often employed, which means that the solutions derived are not optimum. Nonetheless, to the experienced production planner they can be valuable and effective tools. The *index method* is one such technique; its major advantage is that it permits a rapid, inexpensive solution to machine-assignment problems. For this reason it is ideally suited to job-shop operations, as the following example will demonstrate.

The DEF Manufacturing Company, a small job shop, has orders for four products that it must make during June on three available machines. The size of each order is as follows:

Order	Number of Pieces
1	40
2	15
3	30
4	50

The standard time needed to manufacture one unit of product on each of the machines is shown in Table 20–3 together with the total number of machine hours that will be available during June. In essence, the index method compares

[4] Actually, the graph yields a true optimum also, but it is impossible to read with sufficient precision.

Table 20–3 Standard operating time for job-shop orders
(in hours)

	Machine A	Machine B	Machine C
Order 1	2.0	0.5	1.5
2	4.0	3.0	3.5
3	2.5	1.5	1.0
4			2.5
Available capacity	160	50	130

per-unit machine production times for each order, on the assumption that the machine with the lowest production time will turn out the item at least cost. In the typical job shop, where the same worker may be assigned to several different machines and the base rates of the men are approximately the same, this technique is especially useful.[5]

The index itself is a measure of the unnecessary cost incurred when a machine other than the one offering the lowest cost is employed on a particular order; it is derived from the following formula:

$$\text{Index number for Machine X} = \frac{\left(\begin{array}{c}\text{Standard time to produce}\\ \text{one unit on}\\ \text{Machine X}\end{array}\right) - \left(\begin{array}{c}\text{Standard time to produce}\\ \text{one unit on the machine}\\ \text{with the lowest}\\ \text{standard time}\end{array}\right)}{\text{Standard time to produce one unit on the machine}\\ \text{with the lowest standard time}}$$

The index values for the alternative facilities available for manufacturing product 1 of the DEF Company are

$$\text{Index}_A = \frac{2.0 - 0.5}{0.5} = 3.0$$

$$\text{Index}_B = \frac{0.5 - 0.5}{0.5} = 0.0$$

$$\text{Index}_C = \frac{1.5 - 0.5}{0.5} = 2.0$$

The index number for the machine with the lowest standard time (in this case Machine B) will always be zero. The larger the index number for a given machine, the greater the cost of using that machine. Thus, in this case it would be more economical to use Machine B than C, but even Machine C would be preferable to Machine A.

Index numbers can be calculated in a similar fashion for all the orders. Once this is done they are placed on an order assignment chart, an example of which appears in Table 20–4. The chart initially contains the index numbers and the

[5] The material cost for the item will probably be the same regardless of machine employed, and the overhead is generally a fixed percentage of direct labor hours or dollars. Thus, the total unit cost for any order is determined primarily by its labor cost.

Table 20–4   DEF Manufacturing Company order assignment chart

Order	Machine A		Machine B		Machine C	
	Hours per order	*Index number*	*Hours per order*	*Index number*	*Hours per order*	*Index number*
1	80	3.0	⟨20⟩	0.0	60	2.0
2	⟨60⟩	0.3	45	0.0	52.5	0.16
3	⟨75⟩	1.5	45	0.5	30	0.0
4					⟨125⟩	0.0
Available capacity	160		50		130	
Utilization	135 (85%)		20 (40%)		125 (96%)	

number of hours required to complete each order for each machine, and it also gives the available machine capacity.

Applying the data on the chart so that jobs are scheduled on the machines with the smallest index number, we see that order 1 should be assigned to Machine B, which has an index of 0. We would also like to assign order 2 to Machine B for the same reason, but glancing at the capacity figures we note that the machine cannot handle both orders during the same time period. Accordingly, order 2 will be shifted to another machine because that move is less costly to the firm than if order 1 were moved. To measure the loss incurred by this shift, we measure the difference between doing the work on Machine B and on the next best machine. For order 1 this difference is between an index of 0 on Machine B and 2.0 on Machine C; for order 2 it is between 0 on B and 0.16 on C. Further examination of the chart reveals, however, that moving order 2 to the next best alternative, Machine C, is impossible since order 4 can only be made on Machine C and will utilize practically all of its available hours. Since order 4 must be assigned to Machine C, therefore, order 2 must be shifted to the third alternative, Machine A. Another comparison of order 1 and order 2 should now be made in terms of this altered situation. The comparative index number for Machine A for order 1 is 3.0 and for order 2 is 0.3; this indicates that it is still best to shift order 2 to Machine A and not to Machine B.

Following the same procedure, order 3 should ideally be manufactured on Machine C also, but there is not enough capacity. The next best alternative, Machine B, cannot handle both orders either, so order 3 must be assigned to Machine A. Before drawing up the final production plan, however, we should consider the feasibility of shifting order 1 from Machine B to Machine A and order 3 from Machine A to Machine B. A check confirms the fact that order 3 should indeed be assigned to Machine A because $1.5 - 0.5$ is less than $3.0 - 0.0$.

When the final assignments are made, they are indicated on the order assignment chart by circling the appropriate production hours per order. Order 1 is to be made on Machine B, orders 2 and 3 on Machine A, and order 4 on Machine C.

These assignments can still be improved, however. As scheduled, Machine B has 30 hours of idle capacity; it is also the most efficient machine to process order 2. Suppose that 30 hours of work (2/3 of work required on order 2) were done on Machine B and the remaining 1/3 on Machine A? This would entail two machine setups for one order; both Machines A and B would have to be set up to perform the work on order 2. Therefore, the question is whether it would be cheaper to set up both machines and gain the benefit of operating efficiency, or to run only Machine A and save the setup cost. This question illustrates a deficiency in the index method; fixed costs, like setup costs, which do not vary with the quantity of output, are not considered. Accordingly, where these costs are large, the index method does not yield valid answers.

Apart from this limitation, however, the index method does provide good machine assignments quickly and cheaply, particularly after the scheduler has mastered the method of obtaining the best configuration on the order assignment chart.

The transportation approach to maximum profit or minimum costs   When a more precise solution to the least costly machine assignment is necessary, the transportation method of linear programing can be employed. This approach has the advantage that maximum profit (or minimum cost) can be introduced as a constraint in developing the solution. When the problem has many dimensions in terms of products and machines, computers are frequently used.

To illustrate the transportation method, let us consider an example. The GHI Manufacturing Company wishes to assign existing orders to available machines in such a way as to achieve maximum utilization and maximum total contribution. The relevant data may be summarized as follows:

Orders to be processed

Order Number	Quantity (in units)
100	240
101	150
102	360
103	420

Standard output per hour per machine

Order Number	Units of Production		
	Machine A	Machine B	Machine C
100	5	6	10
101	6	10	15
102	20	8	15
103	14	6	20

Estimated unit production costs

Order Number	Cost per Piece		
	Machine A	*Machine B*	*Machine C*
100	$2.00	$1.75	$1.50
101	1.80	1.30	1.20
102	0.50	0.70	1.20
103	0.60	0.30	0.80

Available machine capacity

Machine	*Hours*
A	24
B	40
C	36

Estimated unit prices

Order Number	*Price per Unit*
100	$3.00
101	2.00
102	1.60
103	0.90

The first step in reaching a solution is to establish a common unit for meas-uring available capacities and planned work loads. Again, this is done by means of index numbers. The common unit is called *equivalant standard hours* (ESH). Since our objective is to assign orders to machines, the index numbers indicate the relative production capabilities of the alternate machines. Here, however, the most efficient machine is assigned an index of 1.0. The index numbers for the other machines are then obtained by comparing their respective average rates of production for all orders with that of the most efficient machine. Thus, in our example, the average rates of production are

$$\text{Machine A} = \frac{5 + 6 + 20 + 14}{4} = 11.25$$

$$\text{Machine B} = \frac{6 + 10 + 8 + 6}{4} = 7.5$$

$$\text{Machine C} = \frac{10 + 15 + 15 + 20}{4} = 15$$

The most efficient machine is Machine C; therefore we assign it an index num-ber of 1.0. The index numbers for Machines A and B then become fractions.

$$\text{Index number}_A = \frac{11.25}{15} = 0.75$$

$$\text{Index number}_B = \frac{7.5}{15} = 0.5$$

Once the index numbers have been established, the hours of machine capacity and the work load can be converted to equivalent standard hours (ESH) by multiplying the hours available at each machine by its index number, thus giving us the machine capacity in ESH:

Machine	Index Number	Available Hours	Capacity ESH
A	0.75	24	18
B	0.50	40	20
C	1.0	36	36

The work load that pertains to each order is converted to ESH by dividing the quantity of each order by the production rate of the standard Machine C:

Order Number	Quantity	Production Rate on Machine C	Work Load ESH
100	240	10	24
101	150	15	10
102	360	15	24
103	420	20	21

Finally, the contribution per ESH for each order on each machine must be computed. This is done by first determining the contribution per unit on each machine for each order. The unit contribution per machine for an order is equal to the difference between the product's estimated selling price and the cost of producing it on the machine. These figures are then multiplied by the production rate of the standard machine. For example, the calculations that were made for the unit contribution per machine for order 100 are shown below.

Order Number	Estimated Unit Sale Price	Machine	Unit Production Cost	Unit Contribution
100	$3.00	A	$2.00	$1.00
100	3.00	B	1.75	1.25
100	3.00	C	1.50	1.50

To obtain the machine contribution in terms of ESH, the unit contributions are then multiplied by the production rate of the most efficient machine.

Order Number	Machine	Unit Contribution	Standard Production Rate on Machine C	Contribution per ESH
100	A	$1.00	10	$10.00
100	B	1.25	10	12.50
100	C	1.50	10	15.00

The contributions per ESH for all orders are shown in the following summary.

Order Number	Machine A	Machine B	Machine C
100	$10.00	$12.50	$15.00
101	3.00	10.50	12.00
102	16.50	13.50	6.00
103	6.00	12.00	2.00

Once these values are determined, we can proceed to the transportation model since all of the required data are now expressed in the same terms. The work load, the capacity, and the contribution are shown in terms of ESH. A transportation matrix of the type previously discussed in Chapter 16 can be constructed for solving the problem. The initial matrix is shown in Figure 20–7. Here the orders are listed vertically and the machines horizontally. A slack variable for machine capacity is introduced to represent the difference between the work load and the capacity; for purposes of this type of transportation analysis, the two quantities must be equal. Since, in this case, the work load is equal to 79, but the machine capacity is only 74, an imaginary machine, X, with a work load of 5 is introduced. The contributions per ESH are then entered in the appropriate blocks of the matrix, and the matrix is ready for solution. Here we have assumed that the contribution for the imaginary Machine X is $1.00, but the particular value used in this case does not matter as long as it is the same for all orders.

Order no	Machine a	B	C	X	Total work load (ESH)
100	$10.00	$12.50	$15.00	$1.00	24
101	$3.00	$10.50	$12.00	$1.00	10
102	$16.50	$13.50	$6.00	$1.00	24
103	$6.00	$12.00	$2.00	$1.00	21
Total machine Capacity (ESH)	18	20	36	5	79 / 79

Figure 20–7 GHI Manufacturing Company—initial matrix for machine assignment

Order no	Machine a	B	C	X	Total work load (ESH)
100	$10.00	$12.50	$15.00 24	$1.00	24
101	$3.00	$10.50	$12.00 10	$1.00	10
102	$16.50 18	$13.50	$6.00 2	$1.00 4	24
103	$6.00	$12.00 20	$2.00	$1.00 1	21
Total machine Capacity (ESH)	18	20	36	5	79 / 79

Figure 20–8 GHI Manufacturing Company—transportation model solution of machine-assignment problem

The matrix is then solved; the final solution is shown in Figure 20–8, which assigns orders as follows:

Order Number	Machine	ESH per Machine
100	C	24
101	C	10
102	A	18
	C	2
	X	4
103	B	20
	X	1

We know that the work load exceeds the capacity by 5 hours, so we are not surprised to find 5 hours of work assigned to the imaginary Machine X. In practice, this work could be subcontracted or produced with overtime labor.

The total contribution that would be achieved by this solution is the sum of the contribution of each machine (the contribution per ESH multiplied by the number of ESH assigned to the machine).

Order Number	Machine Assignment	ESH	Contribution per ESH	Total Contribution
100	C	24	$15.00	$ 360.00
101	C	10	12.00	120.00
102	A	18	16.50	297.00
	C	2	6.00	12.00
103	B	20	12.00	240.00
				$1,029.00

It is important to note that, like the approximation index method, the transportation approach does not take setup costs into consideration.[6] Order 102, for example, is run on both Machines A and C, which entails two setups. Whether this is, in fact, more economical than doing the entire job on Machine A is ignored in this solution; the same is true of fixed costs.

Simulation in Scheduling

The approaches to scheduling we have discussed so far give some indication of the amount of effort and research that have been devoted to determining the best sequence for processing orders through a plant. Under different circumstances, delivery dates, production loads, and production capacities, these approaches have led to the development of scheduling procedures and rules that have proved useful and successful. The validity of these procedures and rules, whether they are based on intuition and judgment or on quantitative methods, rests ultimately upon management's ability to forecast production rates, ordering distributions, machine breakdowns, and needed production times. The value of producation schedules depends, in the final analysis, on the accuracy of these forecasts.

In practice, an exact production schedule can seldom, if ever, be achieved because of the many variations in material flows and machine operations (including machine breakdowns, absenteeism, spoilage, rework, emergency orders, and differences in worker performance) that are encountered in a typical factory. All of these variations complicate the task of predicting precisely when operations and orders will be completed; the problem is further aggravated by the steadily increasing complexity of production systems.

As a consequence, management wants to know how effective the present scheduling rules are and how actual experience can be used to develop more effective rules. Answers to these fundamental queries are now being sought by means of simulation. It is possible to program in a computer mathematical and logical models of production facilities that are designed to duplicate actual factory operations. Assumptions about the factory operations can be simplified if the programmed or computer solutions would otherwise be too complex or costly. One method of simplifying a model, for example, is to assume that there is no split routing, or that there is no rescheduling because of priority routing. Generally, however, such factors as absenteeism, machine breakdowns, and rejection of parts are included in the models by using actual distributions gleaned from past data or by making assumptions about the nature of the distributions.

Once the computer model has been built and tested, various scheduling rules can be simulated. Management can thus test the effectiveness of its scheduling concepts and select those which seem to yield the best results. As with all simulations, the "best" rule tested may or may not be the optimum one. The reason is simply that in simulation a particular rule can be evaluated only in terms of the others tested; a rule that was not tested may actually be better.

---

[6] Setup costs are nonlinear.

Now, to demonstrate the usefulness of simulation in scheduling, let us describe briefly a simulation that was used to develop and test scheduling concepts in the machine shop of a large electronics equipment manufacturer.

The first step was to program a computer model of the production facilities. It was tested by comparing its detailed results with those obtained in the factory when the same scheduling procedures were used. The deviations between the computer's predictions, based on production standards, and the actual outcome were analyzed for individual machines and groups of machines to determine if the computer model was accurately predicting breakdowns and other factors that result in nonstandard operations. Once management was satisfied that the computer model was sufficiently accurate, the next phase began.

For six months, factory operations continued to be scheduled as before. At the same time, however, the orders were scheduled on the computer's simulated factory according to two new sets of rules.

During this time, factory performance data were meticulously gathered so that the results from the computer simulation could be compared with actual operations. As a result of this comparison, the scheduling rules employed by the company were modified; in fact, management felt that the improvement was so significant that the model was updated periodically to try out possible new scheduling rules.

Probably the most significant contribution of the model is the fact that new scheduling rules may be tested before being applied. Since the computer can examine the activity of a simulated factory for an entire year in a matter of minutes (if the model is accurate), the new rules can be quickly, fairly, and inexpensively evaluated. Older methods all required new techniques to be tried out in the plant, which can be very costly; this factor often discouraged experimentation. Another discouraging factor was that prior to the development of good management-information systems, historical data could not be obtained and used in developing new scheduling rules. For this reason, the effectiveness of new rules could not readily be measured by actual production results.

To help evaluate the relative effectiveness of alternate sets of scheduling rules, computer programs have been expanded to incorporate a technique for analyzing and measuring results; among the criteria most frequently applied are:

1. *Job completion.*   The percentage of orders, or lots, completed on time and the variance with the completion percentages.
2. *Inventory carrying costs.*   A measure of the inventory costs of the various scheduling rules, including both finished and work-in-process inventory.
3. *Utilization.*   The percentage utilization of available machines and manpower.
4. *Flexibility.*   The ability to deal effectively with the vagaries of production life in terms of meeting delivery dates under varying order and flow conditions.

The initial applications of simulation to scheduling problems have been quite successful, particularly in areas where older scheduling techniques have failed.

Thus, it seems likely that the use of simulation will increase. Model building is becoming increasingly common as more and more computers become available at lower cost. Properly used, the technique can provide a means for developing and introducing scheduling rules with a minimum of error and cost. Its major limitation at present is the fact that workable models have not yet been developed that contain all of the complexity of the actual production processes. The ability to build increasingly complex models, however, is growing rapidly, and this promises to make simulation suitable for an expanding number of situations.

Scheduling—An Overall View

Many different approaches to assigning production facilities to specific orders, or lots, have been discussed. It is impossible to state categorically that one method is better than another in all cases. It is management's task to select the one or several that will yield satisfactory results for the established scheduling criteria.

Activating

After the production schedule has been designed, it must be put into operation; this task is termed *activating*, and it can literally make or break a production process. Functionally speaking, it is on the dividing line between production planning and production control. In a planning sense, it involves accumulating all of the resources needed for each step of the production process for every order. Everything needed to support work on an order must be available, including materials, tools, fixtures, instruction sheets, and shop drawings. The importance of having everything on hand at the proper time cannot be overstated; the greatest single cause of idleness is delays resulting from the late arrival of production materials.

Activating also includes a control function. The progress of operations and orders must be monitored so that delays and shop problems can be spotted and remedied as quickly as possible by changes in routes and production assignments so that the shop is kept running with a minimum of disturbance and lost time.

Activating is typically performed by a dispatcher who, as his title implies, is in charge of sending orders through the factory. Normally, there are many dispatchers in a plant, each one with jurisdiction over the operations performed by specific departments or machine groups. The dispatcher usually has expediters working under him who are generally assigned to oversee specific orders or lots. They report progress, particularly any delays or problems, and put into effect any modified plans that may have been developed by the dispatcher. Many of their activities may seem mundane at first glance. For example, they may have to check with the receiving department to see if certain needed parts have arrived, which may require physical inspection of the packages on the receiving dock. If the parts are there, the expediters may speed them through receiving and inspection, if need be, by carrying them to the production floor. Their job is to speed up the flow of materials wherever necessary and, in general, to overcome shortcomings in the production plan in order to avoid changes in production schedules. These troubleshooters are a built-in safety valve for overcoming planning and operating deficiencies and as such are a vital part of most production systems.

In many industries and companies, the job of moving parts and solving production problems for a group of products is too large a task for one man. This is particularly true where product designs are subject to frequent change or where new products are often introduced on a crash basis; in such cases the timing may not permit a thorough check to be made of the production process prior to the start of production. Similarly, the nature of the product may be such that some of the detailed specifications can only be completed after some production experience is available. Finally, the product may be at a stage of development where refinements and modifications should be introduced as soon as they occur; this often occurs in the aerospace and electronics industries where production problems frequently require consultation with the design and development groups. Top-level attention is often needed to decide when product modifications will begin. It may be decided, for example, that the best course is to make some of the products the old way and gradually shift to the new product design on a carefully planned minimum disruption basis. In short, in many industries there is a real need for a full-time problem solver for each product. The name given to such troubleshooters may be "production coordinator," "administrator," or, as is becoming more popular, "product manager." The use of product managers to oversee the progress of particular items is not always restricted to their production phase; many firms, particularly in the defense industry, ask product managers to oversee a product·from the beginning of its design until it is shipped to the customer.

Monitoring

The final stage of production planning and control involves monitoring the production system to provide the required information for control of operations. In order to make the adjustments needed to ensure the closest possible conformance with the master delivery schedule, management must have a steady flow of information about the status of orders and the reasons for any deviations from plans. This feedback, as it is called, helps management take corrective action and, in addition, aids in the development of future plans.

Management uses a number of different approaches to monitor production systems and obtain the necessary control information. The monitoring aspects of the dispatcher's job have already been described; here data are largely gathered on an ad hoc, personal basis—no formal system is used. Similarly, the individual expediters generally gather status information as required; in fact, they normally receive their information from the complaints of people in production.[7]

---

[7] This is sometimes scathingly referred to as a "squeaky wheel system"; the problem arises, then the expediter reacts.

Production problems have far-reaching effects, not only in production but also in other departments such as sales or engineering. Often, management cannot afford to wait for complaints before gathering data about production problems. The type of control exercised by expediters is not always adequate because solutions to major production problems should reflect the overall interests of the company, not merely what is expedient at the moment. A formal information-gathering system and decision-making procedure is needed.

Line of Balance

We will now examine one particular approach for gathering production information for control purposes. This technique was developed as a control system for complex programs involving the interrelationship of many operations. It is called the line of balance (LOB) approach and was designed at the request of the U.S. Department of Defense for controlling certain government contracts.[8] Many companies that have used LOB report that they have found it to be an excellent system and thus they have extended it to commercial operations. Briefly, the technique may be described as an updated application of Gantt charting to complex projects.[9] It is particularly suited to production programs that involve the simultaneous manufacture of subassemblies that are later consolidated into a final product. The LOB technique may be divided into four major stages:

1. The objective
2. The program plan
3. The program progress
4. The line of balance

The objective   This first stage seeks to match performance with the objectives of the production program. The first step is to plot on a graph the time when each unit in the program is scheduled to be developed (see Figure 20–9). The horizontal axis represents the delivery time and is usually measured in months; the vertical axis represents the cumulative number of units that are both scheduled to be delivered and actually delivered. A line called a *schedule curve* is then drawn to indicate how many units should be delivered by a particular date. Thus, in Figure 20–9 we see that by the end of September, 50 units have been scheduled. As time progresses, an *actual delivery line* is added to the chart, indicating the actual number of units delivered to that date. Here, for example, at the end of May, five units have been delivered.

The program plan   The second stage of LOB depicts the key operations to be performed and the length of time before the final operation when each must be completed. The *program plan* is thus said to measure lead time; it is constructed by selecting from the manufacturing process those activities that are

---

[8] The U.S. Department of the Navy, in particular, requested companies to use the line of balance.

[9] This is also true of the original PERT techniques.

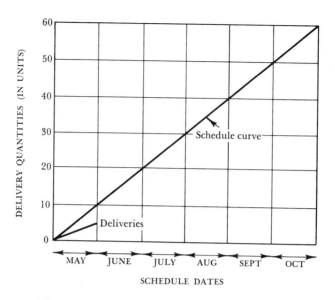

Figure 20-9   Objective chart (cumulative)

critical in terms of meeting the schedule. They are then arranged according to a time sequence, with the completion of an activity labeled a *control point*. The program plan for our example is shown in Figure 20–10; here we note six major control points:

1. The internal fabrication of parts for subassembly B
2. The purchase of parts for subassembly A
3. The purchase of parts for subassembly B
4. The completion of subassembly A
5. The completion of subassembly B
6. Final assembly

The longest lead time for any subassembly component thus becomes the overall lead time for that subassemply. In our case, the control points show, for ex-

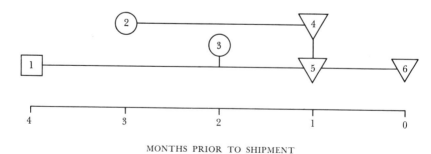

MONTHS PRIOR TO SHIPMENT

Figure 20-10   Program plan

ample, that the parts for subassembly B must be available four months before the unit into which they are built is completed and that the last purchased part for the same unit must be available two months before that time.

The program progress This stage of the LOB control system is concerned with the quantities of materials and subassemblies that are available at the activity points on the program (production) plan at specific times. The program progress chart in Figure 20–11 is essentially a graphic representation of a physical inventory taken at the various control points. Notice that this is not strictly a numerical count, for if two units of the same subassembly are required at the final assembly stage, the inventory count for that point would be the total number of completed subassemblies divided by 2. On the chart, the horizontal axis represents the numbered control points depicted in the program (production) plan, and the vertical axis represents a cumulative quantity scale. The chart tells us that at this time the material needed for 45 completed products has been fabricated and has passed control point 1. It also indicates that purchased material sufficient for 30 units of subassembly B is available.

The line of balance All of the information necessary for preparing a line of balance is gathered by means of the foregoing charts. The data must now be structured so that they may be analyzed from a larger perspective; this is done by striking a *line of balance* across the progress chart to show the quantities required at each control point to support the delivery schedule.

The line of balance is derived as follows: first, the three charts are placed on one sheet of paper; the objective chart is placed to the left of the progress chart, and the program plan is placed below the progress chart (as shown in Figure

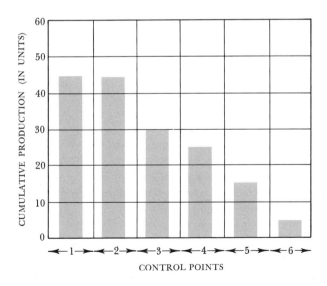

Figure 20–11 Progress chart

20–12). Next, a vertical line is drawn on the objective chart corresponding to the date of the study. In Figure 20–12 the study date is. shown by a heavy line at the end of May, which extends below the objective chart. From the extension of the study date line, horizontal lines are drawn for each production activity. The length of these lines represents the lead time of the activity in months. For example, the purchase of parts for subassembly B (activity 3) must be completed two months before a final unit can be finished. Consequently, the lead time line for activity 3 extends two months from the study date. Following the same procedure, the lead time lines for the other activities are drawn. The next step is to draw a heavy vertical line from the end of each lead time line up to the schedule curve. The point at which a lead time line meets the schedule curve tells how many units of production must be available at that control point to meet the schedule. Thus we see, for example, that at control point 3, purchase parts for 30 units of subassembly B should be on hand if the schedule is to be met.

Now the manager can ask whether the units available at the control points will be sufficient to meet the scheduled demands. To determine this, heavy horizontal dashed lines are drawn from the intersecting points on the schedule curve to the corresponding activity bar on the progress chart. These lines are joined to form a stairstep curve, called a *line of balance*. Examination of the line of balance will reveal the overall "health" of the schedule. Notice, for example, that activity 6 is off schedule; ten units are needed but only five are completed. The problem is to determine the cause of this lag; to do this the manager refers to the program plan. Starting with activity 6, he works along the network and examines the effect of each activity on the overall process. The completion of activity 6 is dependent upon activities 4 and 5, for example. The line of balance curve indicates that activity 4 is ahead of schedule but that activity 5 is behind; therefore, the bottleneck must precede activity 5. Activity 5 depends upon activities 1, 2, and 3. The line of balance curve shows that activity 2 is ahead of schedule, 3 is on schedule, but 1 is behind. It is now obvious that some action is required to accelerate deliveries from the fabrication area; if this is not possible, the schedule will have to be extended.

Line of Balance: A Critique

The line of balance approach falls between the PERT and Gantt charts in relative complexity; it is simpler than PERT but more complicated than Gantt charts. The same relationship also exists with respect to the cost of applying the system; therefore, the line of balance approach is well suited to production operations with only moderate control costs.

The major contribution of LOB is that it formalizes the recording and analysis of data. This is a distinct aid, since, by institutionalizing the LOB system, management can establish a production monitoring and control procedure that is reliable and readily followed.

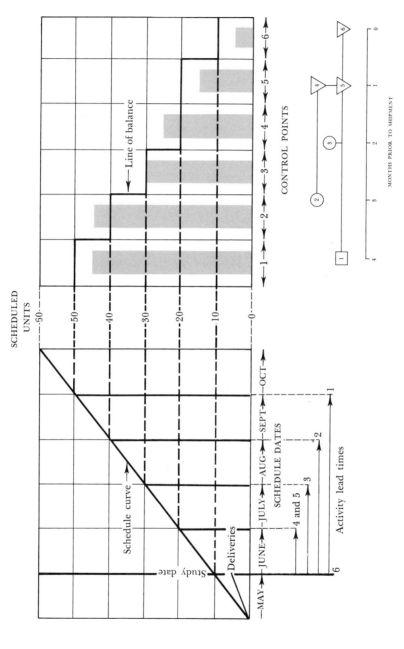

Figure 20–12 Line of balance

Table 20–5   Overall production planning and control

Preproduction Activities	*Production Activities*
Authorization and master scheduling	Supplementary planning
Engineering release	Routing
Breakdown and ordering	Scheduling
Procurement cycle	Activating
In-plant services	Monitoring
Industrial engineering	
Tools and fixtures	
Quality control	
Receiving and inspection	
Accumulation of materials	

←─────────────────────*Time*─────────────────────→

An Overview

We can now construct an outline of the overall production planning and control task as shown in Table 20–5. Here we see that the process is divided into two major areas: preproduction and production activities. Each of these in turn is divided into subactivities. The four production subactivities—routing, scheduling, activating, and monitoring—were discussed in this chapter; preproduction activities were discussed in Chapter 19. Overall, the production planning and control function may be viewed as the nervous system of a factory. As such, it issues directives that govern the actions of the entire plant. The actions taken by each section of the company are reported along information channels. This information is then measured and evaluated and thus provides a basis for formulating new directives.

A quick summary of the paper work issued by production planning and control to synchronize production activities will give one an idea of the vital communications role it plays. From the moment an order is authorized until the moment a delivery ticket is issued confirming the arrival of finished goods in the warehouse, the forms listed below provide data for planning and control.

Production Planning and Control Summary of Major Documents

1. Master delivery schedule
   (a) This schedule represents the delivery objectives of the factory operation.
2. Preproduction schedule
   (a) This schedule synchronizes the performance of all preproduction activities (industrial engineering, purchasing, etc.).
3. Breakdown and ordering
   (a) Issue *requisitions* for all purchased materials and supplies.
   (b) Issue *labor cards* ordering the proper quantity of labor to perform all necessary operations.

(c) Issue *tool requisitions* both for making new tools and repairing existing ones

(d) Issue *unit bill of materials list* (or simply a list of materials ordered) for use as a reference to check the availability of material resources.

4. Production cycle

(a) Issue *order schedule* for each lot or order.

(b) Issue *load charts* for each department, machine, and man in the plant. Preparation of the order schedule and batting orders rests upon development of *route sheets* that include *precedence diagrams* and *breakpoint analysis charts*.

(c) Issue *record charts* summarizing the actual performance and utilization of men, machines, and departments.

(d) Issue *job tickets* that are attached to each order or lot and depict the route to be followed.

(e) Issue *move tickets* that indicate how (materials handling equipment, etc.) each lot is to be moved between operations.

(f) Issue *delivery record* that indicates the quantities of finished goods to be delivered to the warehouse each week.

The number of documents needed to move an order through the manufacturing cycle is truly staggering; in addition, these documents must be widely distributed. The DTW, for example, gives information useful to almost all sections of a company; likewise, copies of the master delivery schedule, the preproduction schedule, and all production cycle documents are sent to all departments that participate either directly or indirectly in the production process. The payroll department needs the list of operations performed and the labor cards in order to record wages earned. Finance and accounting needs to know what departments will contribute to the manufacture of a particular product or shop order. In short, the demand for information issued by the product planning and control function is almost insatiable; in addition, it must be timely and accurate. With such requirements it is not surprising that many companies are now using computers to process the information. The role assigned to the computer in different industries varies widely, but breakdown and ordering is almost always the first area to be computerized because it is typically a routine and repetitive operation and accounts for the greatest volume of data. As previously discussed, however, the computer can be used with equal success for planning work loads and scheduling orders.

Questions and Problems

1. What is routing?
2. What is the relationship between routing and machine break-even points?
3. Your company has decided to add a new item to its product line and believes it can sell 10,000 units per year at a constant rate throughout the year. Either

Machine X or Machine Y, both of which you have available, can be used to make the item. After considerable investigation, you discover the following facts:

	MACHINE X	MACHINE Y
Direct labor costs per unit	$0.75	$0.50
Direct material costs per unit	0.50	0.50
Setup cost per lot	0.25	0.80

The overhead costs are 100 percent of direct labor costs. The inventory carrying costs, exclusive of capital charges, is calculated to be $0.10 per unit per year. The company is in an expanding business and needs to estimate a 20 percent opportunity cost on any invested capital.

Which machine should you use and why?

4. The Acme Gasket Company manufactures a wide assortment of gaskets. No gasket is produced in lot quantities that exceed the normal sales requirements for six months. Model 218 has an average annual sales requirement of 800 units and can be produced by four different methods whose cost conditions are outlined as follows:

	METHOD 1	METHOD 2	METHOD 3	METHOD 4
Unit variable cost	$ 4.00	$ 4.00	$ 3.75	$ 3.50
Setup costs	40.00	45.00	60.00	60.00
Other fixed costs	80.00	80.00	300.00	300.00

(a) Under normal conditions, which method would be used to produce Model 218 gasket?

(b) Suppose each of the machines would otherwise stand idle if it was not used in the production of this gasket. Which method should be used?

5. Compute the break-even point in the production of a steel lid by each of the following two processes:

	SPINNING MACHINE	PRESS
Unit labor cost	$ 0.06	$ 0.02
Unit variable overhead	0.038	0.0075
Total fixed overhead	11.50	225.00

6. Compute the break-even point in the production of a steel can by each of the following three means:

	WELDING	MACHINING	STAMPING
Unit labor cost	$ 0.50	$ 0.45	$ 0.04
Unit variable overhead	0.28	0.21	0.07
Total fixed overhead	67.00	87.00	612.00

7. What are the requirements for good scheduling in a mass production, flow-type operation? in a custom or job shop?

8. The Acme Company has received an urgent order for 4,000 gaskets of a special nature, none of which it has in inventory. These gaskets are produced by a method that uses four sequential operations, the times for which are as follows:

$$\begin{array}{lll}
\text{Operation} & 1 & 0.40 \text{ min. per piece} \\
& 2 & 1.20 \text{ min. per piece} \\
& 3 & 0.60 \text{ min. per piece} \\
& 4 & 0.90 \text{ min. per piece}
\end{array}$$

(a) Based strictly on the data given above, how much time may be saved by subdividing the lot into batches of 1,000 and using dovetail scheduling? Determine *graphically* the time necessary for dovetailing.

(b) What other factors should be taken into consideration before the customer is given a delivery date?

9. The technique of linear programing has been used increasingly in production problems. Is it equally useful in all of the chief problem areas of production planning and control? Explain.

10. The Argo Company is a manufacturer of children's wagons. It has just received an order for 2,000 wagons. Delivery must be made in 60 days. Fortunately, all materials are on hand and can be obtained from the stockroom on one day's notice. The body is formed in the stamping department, which has a capacity of 250 per day. From there it goes to the welding department where mounting brackets are welded on; the output from this department is 400 per day. Wheels are fabricated and assembled in a special wheel department, where two operations are involved—forming and molding (putting the rubber tread on). The first operation can produce 800 wheels per day while the latter can produce 1,000 per day. After molding, the wheels are heat treated for one day. The handle and axles are processed separately in the lathe department. The production rates are 300 and 800 per day, respectively. The packing and shipping department can handle 300 wagons per day.

Prepare a schedule for processing this order. Because the factory work load is high, it is requested that the start of work on this order be delayed until the latest possible date. (Note: The work must be put through in batches. It is against company policy to work overtime of any kind.)

11. The ABC Company has received an order to make 4,500 golf carts, which require one step on a turret lathe. The production control department wants to know how many machine-hours should be scheduled in the lathe department for the order. As the analyst, you go to the lathe department and gather the following direct time study data:

		ELEMENTS			
1	2	3	4	5	
0.07	0.15	0.27	0.42	0.53	
0.60	0.69	0.81	0.96	0.08	
0.14	0.22	0.42	0.57	0.68	CYCLES
0.76	0.83	0.95	0.10	0.20	
0.27	0.35	0.47	0.62	0.73	

(a) The worker is pace rated at 110 percent and there is a job difficulty factor of 5 percent.

(b) The allowance for personal time and irregular occurrences totals 40 minutes.

(c) The base rate for a machinist is $3.00 per hour.

(d) The union–management contract states that an average worker on incentive will earn 125 percent bonus if he works at a normal pace.

Prepare a report for the production control department, indicating how many machine-hours the lathe department should schedule for the golf cart order.

12. A plastics manufacturer has been operating as a job shop, making a wide variety of products to customer order. He recently received an order to manufacture a large volume of television cabinets for a national manufacturer and will erect a new plant for this purpose near his old plant. Show specifically the differences in routing and scheduling as carried out between the old and new plants.

13. Department 100 of the Gamma Company is a finishing section. For the month of March, the department was budgeted to finish 3,000 pieces of equipment at a total direct labor cost of $7,500. However, the actual expenses incurred during the month were $9,200. The plant manager was quite upset at what he calls the gross inefficiency of this department. At his request you investigate this problem and turn up the following additional information.

(a) The actual number of pieces processed through the department was 3,800.
(b) A new finishing process was introduced at the beginning of March.
(c) As of March 1, all employees in the department received an increase in base rate from $2.00 per hour to $2.10 per hour; this increase was provided for in the union–management contract but overlooked in preparing the budget.

Prepare an evaluation of this department's performance during March. Discuss briefly the problem areas that should be explored before remedial action is developed.

14. What is the purpose of the line of balance technique? How is it performed?
15. Where does production control get the necessary authority to order production?
16. Why can't exact production schedules be developed in practice?
17. What part does computer simulation play in scheduling?
18. How can the transportation and simplex methods of linear programing be used in production scheduling and routing?
19. The Rapid Mower Company has set its production schedule to produce 6,000 units of a new mower model in the next 40 weeks. They are using the line-of-balance approach for production control.

The steps in the production program are shown and described in Figure 20–13.

The production schedule calls for 150 units to be completed in each of the 40 weeks. At the end of 15 weeks the progress report shows the following progress at each step:

STEP	UNITS	STEP	UNITS
1	2,800	8	2,050
2	2,510	9	1,853
3	2,510	10	1,705
4	2,105	11	1,575
5	2,224	12	1,450
6	2,135	13	1,390
7	1,975		

(a) Construct a line of balance for the current status of the program.

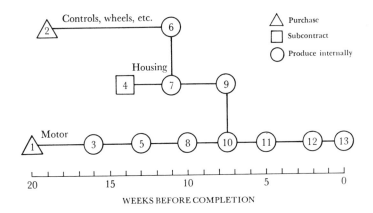

Controls, wheels, etc.

Purchase
Subcontract
Produce internally

Housing

Motor

WEEKS BEFORE COMPLETION

20   15   10   5   0

Figure 20–13

1 Purchase motor units
2 Purchase controls, wheels, blades, and other small parts
3 Assemble motor units
4 Cast motor housing
5 Add motor mounts
6 Complete wheel and control subassembly

7 Assemble wheels and controls to motor housing
8 Paint motor subassembly
9 Paint housing subassembly
10 Assemble motor, housing, and blade
11 Add trim
12 Inspect
13 Package

(b) What are the most critical events? Is the program in balance or are some items out of balance?
20. Does the line of balance method make use of "management by exception"?

References

Buffa, E. S., *Production-Inventory Systems: Planning and Control,* Irwin, Homewood, Ill., 1968.

Clark, W., *The Gantt Chart, A Working Tool of Management,* 3rd ed., Pitman, London, 1952.

Department of the Navy, *Line of Balance Technology,* Office of Naval Materiel, U.S. Government Printing Office, Washington, D.C., 1962.

Di Roccaferrera, G. M., *Introduction to Linear Programming Processes,* South-Western, Cincinnati, Ohio, 1967.

Gavett, J. W., *Production and Operations Management,* Harcourt Brace Jovanovich, New York, 1968.

Goldfarb, N., and Kaiser, W. N. (eds.), *Gantt Charts and Statistical Quality Control,* Hofstra, Hempstead, N.Y., 1964.

Greene, J. H., *Production and Inventory Control Handbook,* McGraw-Hill, New York, 1970.

Hopeman, R., *Production: Concepts-Analysis-Control,* 2d ed., Charles E. Merrill, Columbus, Ohio, 1971.

Iannone, A. L., *Management Program Planning and Control with PERT, MOST and LOB*, Prentice-Hall, Englewood Cliffs, N.J., 1967.

Meier, R. C., *et al., Simulation in Business and Economics*, Prentice-Hall, Englewood Cliffs, N.J., 1969.

Niland, P., *Production Planning, Scheduling, and Inventory Control*, Macmillan, New York, 1970.

Riggs, J. L., *Production Systems Planning, Analysis and Control*, Wiley, New York, 1970.

Robertson, D. C., *Project Planning and Control: Simplified Critical Path Analysis*, CRC Press, Cleveland, Ohio, 1967.

Schmidt, J. W., *et al., Simulation and Analysis of Industrial Systems*, Irwin, Homewood, Ill., 1970.

Timms, H. L., and Pohlen, M. F., *The Production Function in Business*, 3rd ed., Irwin, Homewood, Ill., 1970.

Wiest, J. D., and Levy, F. K., *A Management Guide to PERT/CPM*, Prentice-Hall, Englewood Cliffs, N.J., 1969.

21

Maintenance Analysis

Since modern production plants are highly mechanized, the maintenance of production facilities must be considered both in operating and in designing the plant. Machine failures have far-reaching effects and may result in thousands of man-hours of idle time or even in a complete shutdown of the plant. Similarly, in an office, the failure of a computer or a punch card system can completely halt all operations.

It is not surprising to find, therefore, that plant managers have been attaching more importance to preventing such breakdowns in recent years. The trend toward mechanization and automation has greatly increased the investment in capital goods; to obtain an adequate return on the investment, a high level of utilization is required, which means that the equipment must be kept in operating condition. The extent to which this objective is achieved depends largely upon the maintenance policy.

The Concept of Maintenance

Broadly defined, the term *maintenance* embraces all the activities involved in keeping an entire production system or specific equipment within the system in working order. In this sense of the word, a firm's maintenance policy may be said to delimit the degree of reliability considered essential in its production process. *Reliability* is defined operationally as the certainty or probability that a production system or a piece of equipment will function properly for a reasonable time after it is put into use. The policy objective, from management's point of view, is simply to minimize the total cost of maintaining an acceptable level of equipment reliability. There are numerous interrelated methods of maintaining and improving this reliability. One way is to improve the engineering design. In fields where safety is paramount, parts are often "overdesigned" to ensure that there will be practically no chance of a breakdown. For this reason, bridges are normally constructed to carry more than three times their expected maximum load. Engineering designs featuring easily replaceable elements are frequently used to reduce downtime and maintenance costs. The extent to which design can be utilized to raise reliability is limited by cost. Ideally, therefore, an economic balance should be struck between increased design and manufacturing costs and the estimated improvement in reliability.

A second way to maintain and improve reliability is the management of in-plant inventory levels. If relatively high work-in-process inventories are maintained between successive stages of the production process, these stages can be decoupled so that a breakdown in one will not stop the entire process until the between-stages inventories are depleted. Here, again, the advantage of insulation against the impact of breakdowns means increased costs—in this case, carrying additional in-plant inventory—and so these two factors must be traded off against each other in figuring out the optimum size for between-stages inventory.

Neither of these two indirect approaches to reliability will be treated in this chapter. The design approach is considered in the discussion on product reliability in Chapter 5, and the decoupling of successive production stages is basically an inventory problem of the sort discussed in Chapters 14 and 15. The impact of decoupling on operations was previously considered in terms of its effect on capacity and layout decisions in Chapter 17, and its effect on production schedules in Chapter 19. In this chapter we will examine three direct approaches to the achievement of satisfactory equipment reliability:

1. The use of preventive maintenance to minimize breakdowns, including inspection and operating procedures that prevent delay and system or equipment failures.
2. The establishment of a repair facility.
3. The use of parallel paths of production so that breakdowns will not paralyze the entire production system.

The fewer the number of breakdowns, the more efficiently a firm will operate. The frequency and severity of breakdowns can often be reduced if preventive measures such as oiling, greasing, and overhauling the equipment periodically are taken. Preventive maintenance costs money, however, and constitutes an investment that is worthy of attention.

When equipment failures occur, the departments affected would understandably like them to be fixed at once. Management, however, must think first of operating the firm at the lowest possible total cost and this objective may militate against immediate repair. Thus, a maintenance policy should strike a balance between preventive and repair maintenance that will be consistent with *satisfactory* reliability; this can be an extremely difficult task.

Preventive Maintenance

There are two aspects of preventive maintenance. The first, which can be termed *routine maintenance,* is aimed at preventing wear and deterioration and involves such activities as oiling, cleaning, and collecting scrap and other wastes. The principal function of management in this field is to make sure that routine maintenance is properly done according to a definite time schedule prepared for each piece of equipment on the basis of company experience and the manufacturer's suggestions. In addition, the lubricant and lubrication procedure must be prescribed and then responsibility for its performance assigned. These duties should be given to the equipment operator wherever feasible. If the maintenance routine is simple, this is the most economical approach. If special skills are required, however, or if the management–union contract work rules prevent the operator from doing the work himself, then the duty must be assigned to the maintenance department, or, as it is sometimes termed, the plant engineering function. For control purposes, a card is usually attached to each piece of equipment listing its particular maintenance schedule; as each job is completed, the date is filled in on the card. This procedure makes it possible to assign to departmental supervisors the responsibility for the routine care of equipment within their departments. Periodic checking of equipment maintenance cards is all that is usually required.

Being a nonglamorous field, routine maintenance does not often receive the attention it deserves, but it is an extremely important function. Management should stress this point by requiring periodic reports from operating supervisors and by conducting periodic audits. Positive recognition in the form of a letter of commendation, given when established maintenance routines are performed over a period of time without a miss, can also be quite effective. On the other hand, when maintenance is not performed according to schedule, some form of disciplinary action is in order. Where a plant engineering department is in charge of maintenance, the production supervisors should be requested to report poor performance by that department. In this way, the data needed to identify and correct maintenance problems may be made available for action by management.

The second aspect of preventive maintenance is *inspection.* Periodic inspection will often detect the need for repairs or replacements well in advance of actual breakdowns. Proper automobile maintenance includes periodic inspection of tires, generators, cooling and ignition systems, and any parts that show wear, for example. This inspection is normally conducted when the car is lubricated; regular inspection can materially reduce the chance of major breakdowns and increase the reliability of the car.

Breakdown Maintenance

Experience indicates that no matter how much time is spent on preventive maintenance, breakdowns will still occur. Therefore, some provision must be made for the facility that will be available for the repair of equipment that has failed.

This repair facility need not be an internal operation. In many cases it is more economical to hire outside specialists for the job. The repair of automobiles and trucks, typewriters and other office machines, and computers is usually handled this way, for example. Indeed, many manufacturers and producers of services insist on providing the necessary maintenance support for the equipment they sell. Often the nature of the skills required or the infrequency of usage make reliance upon outside maintenance facilities the most economical approach.

It is often neither necessary nor economically desirable to make a repair the instant a failure occurs. Operations can sometimes be safely continued at a reduced level despite a minor failure. Often repairs can be scheduled to achieve well-planned utilization of maintenance facilities, thus permitting reductions in the cost of those facilities.

The maintenance of redundant, or standby, facilities in a production system is another way of reducing the impact of machine failures. It also increases the investment in equipment, however, and the costs of extra floor space such as rent, building depreciation, heat, light, and so on. If the standby equipment is less efficient than the regular equipment (this is often the case because obsolescent machines are frequently used for this purpose), the costs incurred because of the temporary reduction in efficiency must also be taken into consideration.

Breakdown costs   There are two types of breakdown maintenance costs. The first is the cost of repairing the facility, such as the cost of labor, parts, and other items needed to restore the equipment to operating condition. The second type of cost is that chargeable to the consequences of the breakdown, including idle labor costs, overtime required to catch up to the scheduled output, loss of good will through failure to meet schedules, medical costs, and others that are a direct result of the breakdown. Often, this second type of cost is many times more significant than the actual repair costs.

Relationships between Preventive Maintenance and Breakdown Maintenance

The typical relationship between preventive maintenance and breakdown maintenance is illustrated in Figure 21–1. Up to a point, as the cost of preventive maintenance is increased, the total maintenance cost will decrease. This occurs because an increase in preventive maintenance will typically result in a proportionally greater decrease in repair costs, thus lowering the total cost curve. At some point the decrease in breakdown maintenance costs will be less than the increase in preventive maintenance costs, and thus increased preventive maintenance expenditures will raise the total cost curve.

The exact interaction of these cost factors is, of course, dependent upon the particular equipment used. In examining problems of this sort, management wants to know what combination of the two maintenance costs will result in the lowest total costs. An optimum combination usually sets an acceptable level of breakdowns since management's aim in designing a preventive maintenance

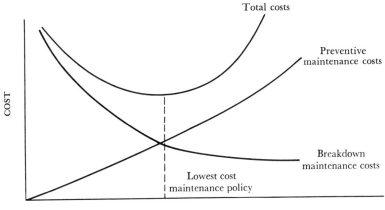

Figure 21–1 Maintenance economics

policy or a breakdown repair policy is not to minimize either cost but to keep the total costs at a minimum, as indicated in Figure 21–1.

Minimizing Total Maintenance Costs

The problem of minimizing the total maintenance costs can be divided into three parts and treated separately, although in reality all three are highly interrelated. The first is how to determine the best relationship between preventive and breakdown maintenance. The second is how to determine the level of repair work or replacement of defective components that is appropriate when a failure occurs or is anticipated. Finally, the third is how to determine the optimum size of the maintenance staff.

The remainder of this chapter will be devoted to an analysis of the problems associated with these three aspects of maintenance.

Balancing Preventive Maintenance and Breakdown Maintenance

Breakdown Distributions

Before a maintenance program can be designed for a specific piece of equipment, management must try to estimate the probable frequency of breakdown for that piece. If it were possible to predict accurately when a machine was about to fail, preventive maintenance could easily be scheduled just before the breakdown; in reality, such a prediction rarely ever occurs. For this reason, management keeps records of equipment performance or obtains them from manufacturers or other users; keeping such records is an important part of the maintenance function. From these data it is possible to construct some type of

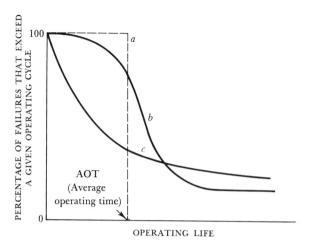

Figure 21–2 Hypothetical breakdown distributions

breakdown distribution that will show the frequency with which a certain kind of machine breaks down over a given time period. Figure 21–2 shows three hypothetical distribution curves.

The dotted line *a* represents a piece of equipment with a constant operating cycle. According to the figure, this equipment is expected to operate for an average time (to AOT) and then fail. Once it has been repaired, it will again operate to AOT without failure. According to our hypothetical distribution, 100 percent of the time the machine will operate after repair until AOT. Knowing this, it would be simple to design an appropriate maintenance policy for this equipment; just prior to AOT, maintenance would be performed. Assuming that this maintenance was timed properly, breakdown costs could be successfully avoided for the life of the equipment.

In practice, breakdown distributions take various shapes depending upon the peculiarities of the particular equipment. A simple machine might have a curve such as *b* in Figure 21–2, which indicates that the majority of the failures occur near the average operating time (AOT), with a few failures at either extreme. A more complex machine with a large number of parts might have a curve such as *c,* reflecting the likelihood that the failure of any of the components will result in a breakdown of the entire machine. The number of failures occurring near AOT are substantially less than for curve *b* because more variables mean that more failures will occur at the extremes.

The closer an actual curve approaches the hypothetical vertical *a*, the more accurately management will be able to forecast the occurrence of breakdowns. Fairly correct forecasting permits a better maintenance policy, since inspections and repair efforts can be consistently scheduled just before the actual breakdowns. This in turn leads to a greater assurance of equipment reliability and also to a maximum return for a minimum expenditure of maintenance dollars. The more concave the distribution curve is, the more difficult it becomes to make accurate forecasts of when breakdowns will occur and thus to schedule maintenance "immediately before" anticipated breakdowns. A concave distribution curve makes it unlikely that maintenance efforts will be timed to coincide with actual breakdowns; therefore, the operating stability of a complex machine will probably be far lower than it is on a simpler machine with an inverted S-shaped curve such as *b* in Figure 21–2. On complex equipment, "action breakdowns" are likely to occur frequently, and the costs of preventive and repair maintenance will be high.

Time and Cost Relationships

Before the information from breakdown distributions can be used to develop a maintenance policy, several factors must be considered. First, there is the relationship between the time and costs required for preventive maintenance and those required to repair breakdowns. If preventive maintenance takes as much time as breakdown repairs and if the costs are approximately the same, there may be no advantage in preventive maintenance. In that situation, a minimum of maintenance time will be spent if the company simply waits until the breakdowns occur. A case in point might be an operation that is run continuously because of the cost of shutting the equipment down. Often, however, preventive maintenance can be performed while the system is normally inoperative, such as during lunch periods or off-shifts, and it would be advantageous to do so.

Closely related to the time factor in considering repair costs is the question of downtime and its associated costs. Breakdown costs can be quite high in an automated process or where labor costs are high; in those cases the maintenance policy should stress preventive maintenance. This would be true even if the cost of preventive maintenance were greater than the breakdown repair costs, provided preventive maintenance could be performed during scheduled downtime. In this fashion, the advantage of operating stability would offset the added maintenance expense. If preventive maintenance cannot be performed during scheduled downtime, waiting for a breakdown may still be the best choice; as a general rule, however, high downtime costs enhance the value of preventive maintenance.

This same line of reasoning can be used to decide the optimum size of repair crews. When downtime costs are high, large crews become more attractive if all other maintenance factors are equal. This aspect of the problem will be discussed in more detail later in this chapter.

The use of breakdown distribution analysis does not guarantee the correct answers, but it helps to isolate the important factors that should be considered in designing a preventive maintenance program.

Repair Alternatives

When preventive maintenance or breakdown repairs are being performed, the question often arises of how much repair work should be done. In many instances, parts that have not yet failed are replaced because the added cost of the extra work is small once the maintenance task has begun. Consider, for example, an automobile motor. If it becomes necessary to replace a piston ring in the engine, it may pay to replace all piston rings, bearings, and other internal parts at the same time; the additional work involved is small in comparison with the cost of disassembling the motor. If the parts were not replaced and subsequently failed, the repair costs would be inordinately high because the motor would once again have to be disassembled.

Management faces many maintenance problems of this sort. To illustrate one, let us consider the maintenance of four transistors mounted on an electronic subassembly. There are many alternative repair policies that management could follow when a failure occurs.

1. Replace only the bad transistor.
2. Replace all transistors.
3. Replace the bad transistor and all others that have operated longer than the average expected life.
4. Replace the bad transistor and all others that are within 10 percent of the average expected life. (This is simply a variation of the preceding alternative and gives some indication of the great number of possibilities present.)

These four policies are by no means all of the possible alternatives; they simply indicate the type of policies that could be formulated. The problem is to determine which alternative represents the lowest total cost. In order to evaluate the first alternative—replacing only the defective transistor—the manager must make a forecast of successive transistor failures over the operating life of the equipment. By multiplying the number of expected failures by the average cost of replacement, an estimate of the total cost of this alternative can be made.

To evaluate the second alternative—replacing all of the transistors when one fails—the manager must predict when the first transistor in the subassembly may be expected to fail. At that point all transistors are replaced and the process is repeated. The total cost is estimated by multiplying the number of failures by the cost of replacing all transistors each time.

For the third and fourth alternatives, the cost evaluation problem is more complex. Like the second approach, a prediction of when the first failure will occur is required in both of these cases. The defective transistor is replaced together with any others that have operated more than the standard time. A forecast must then be made as to when the next failure will occur, at which time the defective transistor and all others past the average expected lifetime will be replaced. This procedure is repeated until the estimated life expectancy of the equipment is covered. Both of these alternatives require that a record of each transistor's operating time be maintained. In effect, policies 3 and 4 are combinations of policies 1 and 2.

One way to evaluate the various repair alternatives is to simulate the occurrence of transistor failures and to calculate the costs associated with those policies.[1] To do this, a model must be constructed that will generate data com-

---

[1] It should be noted that this process merely indicates the lowest cost alternative among those selected by the experimenter; it does not indicate the optimum solution.

parable to the real-life situation; for this purpose we will develop a Monte Carlo simulation model for the transistor problem. This method is called a "Monte Carlo simulation" because random numbers are used to generate data. Monte Carlo is, of course, a place for roulette, a random game.

Example of a Monte Carlo Simulation Model

In order to build this type of model, management must obtain accurate cost and failure data; for our example the standard times required to do repair work are given in Table 21–1.[2]
The costs associated with these operations are

$$\text{Downtime cost} = \$6.00 \text{ per minute}$$

$$\text{Transistor cost} = \$5.00 \text{ each}$$

$$\text{Repairman's wage} = \$4.00 \text{ per hour}$$

Transistor failure data are shown in Figure 21–3, which is a historical record of 2,000 transistor failures arranged as a frequency distribution; these data are also tabulated in the first two columns of Table 21–2. It is assumed that a sample as large as this is representative. Using these data on failures, management wants to build a simulation model with which to test the following three alternative replacement policies:

1. Replace only the bad transistor.
2. Replace all transistors when one fails.
3. Replace the bad transistor and all others that have been in operation more than 900 hours.

Table 21–1 Standard times for repair work

	Minute(s)
Remove subassembly and insert standby unit	1
Disassemble subassembly	2.5
Replace 1 transistor(s)	1
2	2
3	3
4	4
Assemble subassembly	2.5
Remove standby unit and replace subassembly	1
Total time to replace 1 transistor(s)	8
2	9
3	10
4	11

[2] The times given are assumed to be constant. To assume that replacement times vary would significantly complicate the work, and the more accurate results would differ very little in the long run.

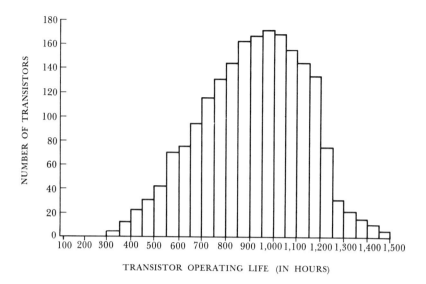

Figure 21–3 Frequency distribution

The company is currently following the first policy,[3] which entails replacing the entire subassembly with a standby unit whenever a failure takes place. Then the bad transistor is replaced and the original subassembly is returned to its place in the computer.

The Simulation Process

The first step in simulating the costs of transistor replacement is to project the occurrence of transistor failures. First the analyst must calculate the cumulative number of failures, as shown in the third column of Table 21–2. These figures tell him, for example, that 16 out of 2,000 transistors failed within 399 hours of operation. These figures are then converted into percentages; thus $16/2,000 \times 100$, or 0.8 percent of the transistors failed within 399 hours and 1.9 percent within 499 hours. The cumulative failure frequency percentages are then plotted, as in Figure 21–4.[4] In effect, the analyst is converting the past history of transistor failures into a cumulative probability distribution; it can therefore readily be seen that of the 2,000 transistor failures, 53.5 percent occurred within 949 hours of operating time. If the historical data are indeed representative of transistor failures, it is probable that future ones will take place with the same relative frequency; thus, we have a model.

Having determined the probable frequency of transistor failures, the analyst

[3] Simulation of costs generated while already operating under a given policy provides a chance to compare simulated results with past history. If the simulated results are similar to those that have actually occurred, then it is reasonable to continue the simulation experiment.

[4] The cumulative frequency distribution is, in effect, a "crystal ball" that gives the analyst a picture of how events in the future would appear if they were ordered in the same manner as the distribution.

Table 21-2 Transistor operating life (in hours)

Hours	Number of Failures	Cumulative Number of Failures	Cumulative Percentage of Failures
0–300	4		
300–349	0	4	0.2
350–399	12	16	0.8
400–449	22	38	1.9
450–499	31	69	3.5
500–549	43	112	5.6
550–599	70	182	9.1
600–649	76	258	12.9
650–699	93	351	17.5
700–749	116	467	23.3
750–799	131	598	29.9
800–849	143	741	37.0
850–899	162	903	45.1
900–949	167	1,070	53.5
950–999	172	1,242	62.1
1,000–1,049	169	1,411	70.5
1,050–1,099	156	1,567	78.3
1,100–1,149	144	1,711	85.5
1,150–1,199	133	1,844	92.2
1,200–1,249	74	1,918	95.9
1,250–1,299	31	1,949	97.4
1,300–1,349	21	1,970	98.5
1,350–1,399	15	1,985	99.2
1,400–1,449	10	1,995	99.7
1,450–1,499	5	2,000	100.0
1,500–1,559	0		
	2,000		

now wants to simulate them. To do so he must select data from the model in such a way that each item has an equal probability of being selected. This may be accomplished by selecting two-digit numbers from tables of random numbers. Using each number to represent a probability of failure, the analyst locates that number on the cumulative percent axis of Figure 21–4 and draws a line across to the smooth curve; at the point of intersection he drops a perpendicular to the horizontal axis and records the hour at which this failure took place. For example, random number 39 (representing 39 percent) intersects the curve at about 840 hours. In a like fashion, he can generate a series of random numbers and the hours at which their associated failures took place. In this way he will have simulated failure times that correspond to the long-run frequency of the actual failures.

Simulating maintenance costs under the first approach To simulate the policy of replacing only the defective transistors (the policy currently being followed

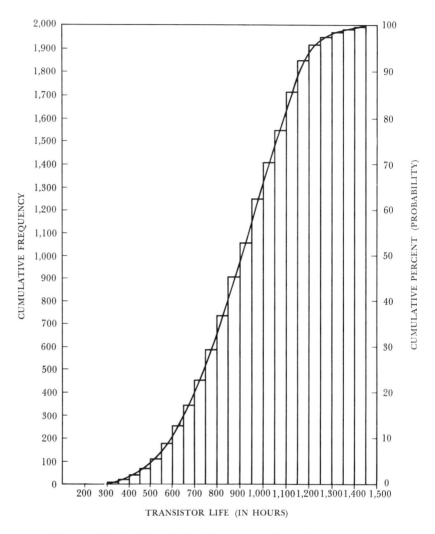

Figure 21–4 Cumulative frequency of transistor failures

by the company in our example), a simulated failure history must be generated for each of our four transistor positions. Table 21–3 shows how this may be done. For the first transistor position, the first random number is 39, as just described, corresponding to a failure time of 840 hours. The next random number, 77, is applied to the second transistor position; according to Figure 21–4, failure occurs after 1,060 hours. In this way, failure times are developed for all transistors assigned in turn to the four transistor positions. The cumulative operating history for each position is obtained by successively totaling the failure times for that position; this is also shown in Table 21–3. Thus, for the first position, the initial failure occurs at 840 hours and the next at 1,010 hours; chrono-

Table 21-3 Selected transistor failures (times) from cumulative distribution

First Transistor Position			Second Transistor Position			Third Transistor Position			Fourth Transistor Position		
Random number	Failure time	Cumulative failure time	Random number	Failure time	Cumulative failure time	Random number	Failure time	Cumulative failure time	Random number	Failure time	Cumulative failure time
39	840	840	77	1,060	1,060	01	350	350	98	1,300	1,300
69	1,010	1,850	88	1,140	2,200	63	980	1,330	22	710	2,010
94	1,190	3,040	94	1,190	3,390	80	1,095	2,425	72	1,030	3,040
58	950	3,990	22	710	4,100	14	630	3,055	53	920	3,960
29	770	4,760	55	930	5,030	23	720	3,775	07	540	4,500
29	770	5,530	51	910	5,940	59	955	4,730	66	990	5,490
50	900	6,430	30	775	6,715	82	1,110	5,840	53	920	6,410
80	1,095	7,525	70	1,020	7,735	70	1,020	6,860	61	970	7,380
31	785	8,310	21	700	8,435	48	890	7,750	56	940	8,320
38	830	9,140	19	680	9,115	46	875	8,625	41	850	9,170

logically, therefore, the second failure takes place after 840 + 1,010, or 1,850, hours of operation. Similarly, if the next failure time recorded is 1,190, then in terms of operating time, this failure is assumed to take place at 1,850 + 1,190 hours, or after 3,040 hours of operating time.

In simulating this type of problem, it is useful to show the tabulated material in graphic form; Figure 21–5, therefore, presents transistor failures during a 6,000-hour period for the three policies being evaluated. The 6,000 hours corresponds to one year of typical three-shift operation for the system.

To calculate the costs associated with a given policy, the analyst counts the number of replacements made and determines the full cost of those replacements. Since twenty-five replacements of one transistor are necessary under the first policy, its maintenance costs may be calculated as follows:

Transistor cost = $25 \times \$5.00 = \$125.00$
Cost of replacing transistors
   Replacement time = 25×8 = 200 minutes,
    or 3.3 hours
   Repairman's wages = $3.3 \times \$4.00 = \quad 13.20$
Downtime cost[5] = $(25 \times 2)(\$6.00) = \quad 300.00$

$$\overline{\hphantom{xxxxx}}$$
$$\$438.20$$

Simulating maintenance costs under the second approach   Since the second policy calls for the replacement of all transistors when one fails, the transistors must be treated in groups of four. The first group of transistors would fail at their respective positions at 840, 1,060, 350, and 1,300 hours. The first failure would occur at the third position at 350 hours; at that time all transistors would be replaced and a new group of four installed. Their respective failure times are 1,010, 1,140, 980, and 710. Thus the failure is at the fourth position after 710 hours. Chronologically this would be after 350 + 710, or 1060 hours of operation. This process is repeated for 6,000 operating hours; the figures are presented in Table 21–4 and shown graphically in Figure 21–5.

Under this policy it is necessary to replace all four transistors eight different times, and the cost of doing this is

Transistor cost = $(8 \times 4)(\$5.00) = \$160.00$
Cost of replacing transistors
   Replacement time = 8×11
    = 88 minutes

Repairman's wages = $\dfrac{88 \times \$4.00}{60} = \quad 5.90$

Downtime cost = $(8 \times 2)(\$6.00) = \quad 96.00$

$$\overline{\hphantom{xxxxx}}$$
$$\$261.90$$

[5] For each replacement, there are only two minutes of downtime cost. It takes one minute to remove the defective unit and insert a standby unit. It takes another minute to remove the standby unit and replace the repaired unit.

Table 21-4   Data for determining transistor replacements—second policy

Transistor Lives Shown Four at a Time				Lowest Time	Position Number	Operating Hours at Which All Transistors Are Replaced
1	*2*	*3*	*4*			
840	1,060	350	1,300	350	3	350
1,010	1,140	980	710	710	4	1,060
1,190	1,190	1,905	1,030	1,030	4	2,090
950	710	630	920	630	3	2,720
770	930	720	540	540	4	3,260
770	910	955	990	770	1	4,030
900	775	1,110	920	775	2	4,805
1,095	1,020	1,020	970	970	4	5,775
785	700	890	940	700	2	6,475
830	680	875	850	680	2	7,155

Simulating maintenance costs under the third approach   The third approach, which involves replacing the transistor that has failed and all others that have been in operation for longer than 900 hours, is more difficult to simulate. From the randomly selected transistor lives given in Table 21–4, notice that the first transistor failure (transistor 3) occurs after 350 hours of simulated operating time. At this time all other transistors have functioned only 350 hours; since this is less than 900 hours, therefore, only transistor 3 must be replaced. Transistors 1, 2, and 4 have 490, 710, and 950 hours of life remaining, respectively. The new transistor at the third position has 980 hours of life remaining. The next transistor failure occurs at 840 hours, when transistor 1 must be replaced. At this point, transistors 2 and 4 have accumulated 840 hours of operating time, but since this is less than 900 hours they are not replaced; neither is the new transistor at the third position, which has accumulated 490 hours of operating time out of an expected life of 980 hours.

Continuing with the simulation process, the next transistor fails at 1,060 hours (No. 2). The status of the other three transistors is as follows:

Transistor	Operating Time (in hours)	Life Remaining (in hours)
1	1,060 − 840 = 220	1,010 − 220 = 790
3	1,060 − 350 = 710	980 − (1,060 − 350) = 270
4	1,060 − 0 = 1,060	1,300 − 1,060 = 240

Although each of these transistors has life remaining, the operating time of No. 4 exceeds the 900-hour average operating time, and so it is replaced. Thus, at 1,060 operating hours, all original transistors have been replaced, and the status of the subassembly is as follows:

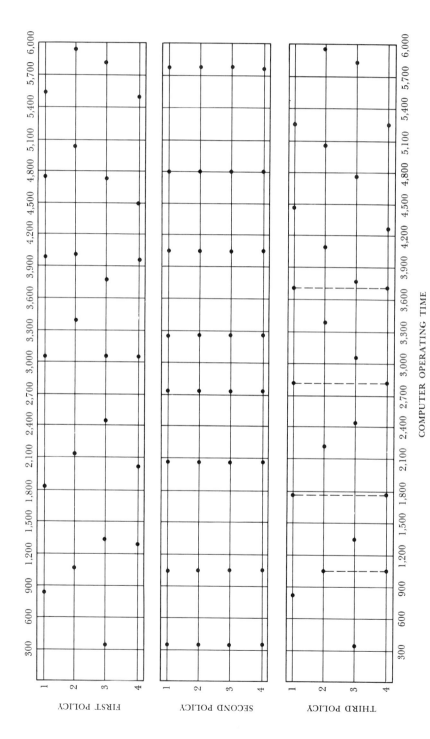

Figure 21–5 Replacement times for transistors under three alternative policies

Transistor	Operating Time (in hours)	Life Remaining (in hours)
1	220	790
2	0	1,140
3	710	270
4	0	710

Table 21–5 carries these calculations out over a period of 6,000 simulated hours of operating time, and the replacements are plotted in Figure 21–5.

Under this third policy, twenty-one maintenance periods occur; seventeen require replacement of only one transistor and four require replacement of two transistors. The costs of following this policy are given in Table 21–6.

Comparison of Maintenance Policies

Now that the three policies have been simulated, their operating costs can be compared; they are $438.20, $261.90, and $388.47, respectively. On this basis, the second policy appears to be the best. Because in our example we simulated only one trial for each policy, chance factors could easily alter the results significantly. Consequently, in an actual case, each policy would be simulated many times and an average operating cost would be calculated, thus making the selection of random numbers more representative.

Simulation thus makes it possible to evaluate various maintenance policies in terms of their predicted operating costs. Because the costs forecast are not real costs, the final policy decision should also reflect the assumptions made and such factors as the size of the maintenance crew and the availability of required repair skills that were not part of the simulation model.

Crew Size Considerations

To this point we have discussed the amount of preventive maintenance and the amount of repair work that must be done. The final aspect of maintenance problems—the size of the maintenance staff—will now be considered.

Since the skills required for maintenance work are often quite specialized, the problem of determining the optimum size of a maintenance staff is complicated. It is more a matter of deciding how much of each particular skill is required than of simply figuring out the number of workers needed. More specifically, management must decide whether the company needs a particular maintenance skill on its staff or whether it can simply purchase the service from a specialist, say, the manufacturer. Balancing these factors to determine the proper economic size is essentially the familiar inventory type of problem. The possibility of employing a large maintenance staff and thus reducing the cost of failures must be weighed against having a small staff and paying a higher price for failures. Inefficiencies exist in both cases; the problem is to minimize inefficiency and its associated costs. In general, the larger the maintenance staff, the higher the cost

Table 21-5 Calculations for transistor replacements—third policy (replace bad transistors and all those exceeding 900 hours)

Elapsed Time at Which Replacement Occurs	Time Expired Since Last Replacement	Transistors Replaced 1	2	3	4	First Position Operating time	Life remaining	Second Position Operating time	Life remaining	Third Position Operating time	Life remaining	Fourth Position Operating time	Life remaining
0						0	840	0	1,060	0	350	0	1,300
350	350			x		350	490	350	710	0	980	350	950
840	490	x				0	1,010	840	220	490	490	840	460
1,060	220		x			220	790	0	1,140	710	270	1,060	240
					x							0	710
1,330	270			x		490	520	270	870	0	1,095	270	440
1,770	440				x	930	80	710	430	440	655	0	1,030
		x				0	1,190						
2,200	430		x			430	760	0	1,190	870	225	430	600
2,425	225			x		655	535	225	965	0	630	655	375

2,800	375	×	1,030	150	600	590	375	255	0	920
3,055	255	×	255	695	855	335	0	720	255	665
3,390	335	×	590	360	0	710	335	385	590	330
3,720	330	×	920	770	330	380	665	55	0	540
3,775	55	×	55	715	385	325	0	955	55	485
4,100	325	×	380	390	0	930	325	630	380	160
4,260	160	×	540	230	160	770	485	470	0	990
4,490	230	×	0	770	390	540	715	240	230	760
4,720	240	×	240	530	630	300	0	1,110	470	520
5,020	300	×	540	230	0	910	300	810	770	220
5,240	220	×	760	10	220	690	520	590	0	920
5,250	10	×	0	900	230	680	530	580	10	910
5,830	580	×	580	320	810	100	0	1,020	590	330
5,930	100	×	680	220	0	775	100	920	690	230
6,150	220	×	0	1,095	220	555	320	770	910	10

970

Table 21–6   Costs of following the third policy

Transistor cost =	$25 \times \$5.00 = \$125.00$
Cost of replacing	
17 single transistors =	$\dfrac{17 \times 8 \times \$4.00}{60} = 9.07$
4 double transistors =	$\dfrac{4 \times 9 \times \$4.00}{60} = 2.40$
Downtime cost =	$(21 \times 2)\ \$6.00 = 252.00$
	$\$388.47$

of wages will be and the greater the probability will be of the staff having periods of time with no maintenance work to perform. When a breakdown occurs, however, there is a greater probability that a large staff will be available to repair it quickly, thus minimizing the consequences of the failure. With a small staff, on the other hand, it is entirely possible that they will be fully occupied and even that there will be a backlog of repair jobs; crew costs will be low, but the adverse consequences of a failure will be heightened. In any case the optimum crew size for a firm should balance the crew cost with the cost of waiting for repairs. This is shown in Figure 21–6.

Waiting-Line Approach

Determining the optimum crew size can be approached by applying queuing theory, which was introduced in Chapter 18. To understand this, let us consider the following situation in which management is interested in determining the optimum maintenance crew size for servicing its machines. The machines break down at an average rate of three per hour. The breakdowns are distributed in such a manner that they can be considered to fit a Poisson distribution. Downtime costs the company $25 per hour per machine, and each maintenance worker gets $4.00 an hour. One worker can service machines at an average rate of five

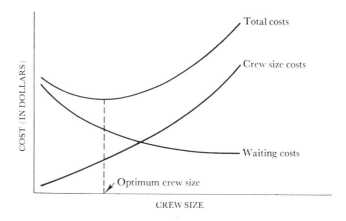

Figure 21–6   Crew size and waiting costs

per hour distributed exponentially, two workers can service seven per hour distributed exponentially, and a team of three workers can do eight per hour distributed exponentially.

In this case, the problem is one of the simpler types of waiting-line problems. Repeating the conditions:

1. The input is distributed according to a Poisson distribution.
2. The repairs are handled at a single place—first in, first out—with no unit leaving until it is repaired.
3. The output rates follow an exponential distribution.

Using the single-channel, single-phase equations from Chapter 18, the proportion of arrivals that will have to wait is equal to A/S, where A = average number of arrivals per unit of time and S = average number of units serviced per unit of time.

By the same token, the proportion of time during which arrivals will not have to wait for service is

$$P_0 = 1 - \frac{A}{S}$$

The average time a machine spends awaiting repair and being repaired is

$$W = \frac{1}{S - A}$$

And the average number of units waiting to be serviced and being serviced is

$$L = \frac{A}{S - A}$$

With these simple equations, the problem can easily be solved; one simply needs to calculate the total cost for each crew size and select the crew with the lowest total cost.

We begin with one man working alone; his salary is $4.00 per hour. The average total cost of downtime per hour is the product of the average number of units in the repair system and the hourly cost of downtime. The average number of machines in the repair system may be derived from

$$L = \frac{A}{S - A} = \frac{3}{5 - 3} = 1.5 \text{ machines}$$

The hourly cost for machine downtime is $25; therefore, the average total downtime cost per hour is

$$\$25 \times 1.5 \text{ machines} = \$37.50$$

Thus, the total cost per hour for one repair man is $37.50 + $4.00, or $41.50.

For the two-man team, we simply repeat the procedure. The average number of machines in the system is

$$L = \frac{A}{S - A} = \frac{3}{7 - 3} = 0.75 \text{ machine}$$

The average total downtime cost per hour is

$$\$25 \times 0.75 \text{ machine} = \$18.75$$

Therefore, the total cost per hour is $\$18.75 + \$8.00$, or $\$26.75$.

For the three-man team, we follow the same procedure again. The average number of machines in the system is

$$L = \frac{A}{S - A} = \frac{3}{8 - 3} = 0.6 \text{ machine}$$

The downtime cost per hour is

$$\$25 \times 0.6 \text{ machine} = \$15.00$$

Thus, the total cost per hour is $\$15.00 + \$12.00$, or $\$27.00$. On the basis of this analysis, it is clear that the two-man maintenance team is the most economical.

In practice, the analyst usually plots a graph of the results obtained when various team sizes are inserted into a mathematical format, such as the one shown in Figure 21–7. In our simple illustration, a graph is unnecessary, but in more complex situations where the numbers are larger, plotting values on a graph often helps the analyst determine the optimum size for a maintenance team.

Limitations to the mathematical approach   Application of the waiting-line approach, as exemplified in our sample situation above, appears to be quite simple, but in reality it is quite complex. The basic concepts of waiting-line theory are rather straightforward, but the approach itself is not easily applied

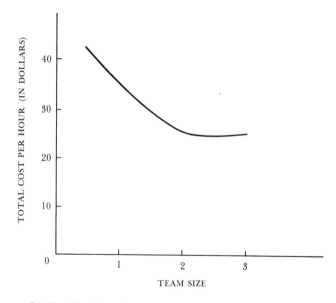

Figure 21–7   Total maintenance cost as a function of team size

because of the complexities of the probabilities associated with the arrival of units for service and the availability of service. It is often quite difficult to determine the distribution of the arrival of units for service. In addition, the equation describing the arrivals can be a rather complex mathematical expression. In our illustration using the Poisson distribution, the "universe" from which the breakdowns could occur was assumed to be infinite; unfortunately, however, this is rarely the case. For finite universes, it is very difficult to set up general equations to solve a particular problem at hand; each problem must be treated as a special case, usually involving complicated mathematics. A further difficulty arises when considering service time. In our example, we also assumed that there was only one channel of service. In practice, however, the number of channels varies, thus complicating determination of the distribution of service times and the distribution of calls for service. In short, multichannel operations make it more difficult to construct a valid model. This point was clearly illustrated in Chapter 18.

The simulation approach In practice, there are many complicated maintenance problems involving waiting lines that cannot be solved mathematically. This may be the result of (1) the inability to describe service and arrival distributions mathematically; (2) the great complexity of works whereby, even if the distributions could be described mathematically, they could not be manipulated for a decision; or (3) the great cost of the manipulation.

In many of these cases, solutions have been derived by simulation. Generalized simulation programs for waiting-line networks are gradually coming into use as a decision aid in the layout of production facilities and to help set up guidelines for operating these facilities. Special computer languages have also been developed to deal with problems of this sort.

Learning Curves

Another factor entering into the determination of optimum crew size is the change in output that results from learning the associated tasks. Until quite recently, little thought was given to the improvement in performance that comes about through repeated performance of the same task, although it is common to most manual activities. Group or team, as well as individual, output improves with learning, and this increased productivity naturally reduces the time required to complete a task. The graphical representation of the relationship between output and learning is called a *learning curve*.

The current use of learning curves is a result of the interest shown in them by the airframe industry. A research study commissioned by the Department of Defense to look at the learning process involved in the production of various airframes showed that while different airplanes had different production times, the rate of improvement resulting from learning was substantially the same for all planes. The 80 percent learning curve found to fit the situation was subsequently found to fit many other production activities also, including electronic assembly, automatic machine operations, ship construction, and other assembly tasks. In fact, the 80 percent curve fit so many activities that it was carried over to many situations without determining if it was valid for each situation and thus probably has been used in some instances erroneously.

Developing a learning curve   An 80 percent learning curve denotes that the accumulated average time used to produce twice as many units is 80 percent of the average time required to produce the initial units. Each time the output is doubled, a 20 percent improvement in time will take place. As as example, consider a maintenance crew that takes 100 hours to overhaul a particular piece of production equipment for the first time. If the output is doubled and two units are overhauled, the accumulated average time per unit will be 80 percent times 100 hours = 80 hours. Since this is an average time per unit, the total time will be 2 × 80 = 160 hours. If production were doubled from two to four units, the average time per unit would be 80 percent of the previous average, or .80 × 80 hours = 64 hours.

This process can be seen in Table 21–6, where the sample calculations are provided for production of 2, 4, and 8 units. The figures for production lots up to 256 are also shown. Note that the greatest reduction of time takes place during the beginning production and tapers off gradually as the number of units produced rises. This condition is presented graphically in Figure 21–8. The rate of production changes dramatically at first and then tapers off to a limit where added production will not materially change the rate.

Learning curve equations   The shape of the curve in Figure 21–8 suggests that a learning curve is a form of an exponential curve. Furthermore, the inverse relationship of cumulative units produced and cumulative average man-hours per unit denotes that the curve has a negative exponent.

Table 21–6   Production times for an 80 percent learning curve

(1) Units	(2) *Average Man-Hours per Unit*	(3) *Production Time* (1) × (2)
1	100.0	100.0
2	$\dfrac{2 \times 100 \times .80}{2} = 80.0$	160.0
4	$\dfrac{4 \times 80 \times .80}{4} = 64.0$	256.0
8	$\dfrac{8 \times 64 \times .80}{8} = 51.2$	409.6
16	40.9	653.4
32	32.8	1048.6
64	26.2	1677.4
128	20.9	2684.2
256	16.7	4295.7

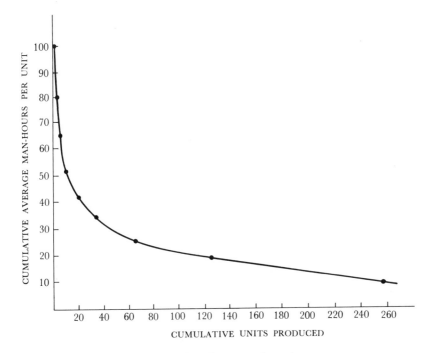

Figure 21–8 An 80 percent learning curve

The equation for this type of curve is

$$Y = aN^{-b}$$

where Y = cumulative average time per unit
   a = time required to produce the first unit
   N = number of units produced
   $-b$ = exponent of the curve

To simplify manual calculation, the equation can be restated as[6]

$$\log Y = \log a + (-b) \log N$$

In this equation, $-b$ is the slope of the logarithmic line and is a constant. Finding the slope of a learning curve greatly simplifies the calculation of the total time required to produce a given number of units of output. Table 21–7 has b values for learning curves between 65 and 95 percent. Tables of b values are usually available; however, let us explore how the slope may be calculated if a table is not available. The equation

$$\log Y = \log a + (-b) \log N$$

[6] The logarithm of the product of two numbers, such as a and N, is the sum of their logarithms, and the logarithm of their quotient is the difference of their logarithms. The logarithm of a number raised to a power, such as N^{-b}, is the product of the exponent times the logarithm of the number, or $-b \log N$. For computer calculation, the original equation can be used.

Table 21–7 Learning curve values

Learning Curve	Slope b	1 − b
95%	.074	.926
90%	.152	.848
85%	.234	.766
80%	.322	.678
75%	.415	.585
70%	.515	.485
65%	.624	.376

can be solved for b as follows:

$$b \log N = \log a - \log Y$$

$$b = \frac{\log a - \log Y}{\log N}$$

In our example, for an 80 percent curve and an output of two units, $Y = 80$.[7]

$$b = \frac{\log (100) - \log (80)}{\log (2)}$$

$$= \frac{2.00 - 1.9031}{0.3010}$$

$$= 0.3219, \text{ or } 0.322$$

This value agrees with Table 21–7.

Determination of total man-hours Once the b values are known for a learning curve, it is relatively simple to determine the total time requirements for a given level of production. For example, suppose management has decided to overhaul all of the production equipment in a section of the plant where there are 65 machines in all. Past experience on similar equipment indicates that a learning curve of 80 percent fits. The maintenance crew required 130 hours to overhaul the first unit. Management now wants to know how long it will take to overhaul the 65 machines.

$$\log Y = \log a + (-b) \log N$$
$$= \log (130) + (-0.322) \log (65)$$
$$= 2.1139 - (0.322 \times 1.8129)$$
$$= 2.1139 - 0.5837$$
$$= 1.5302$$

$$Y = \text{antilog } (1.5302)$$
$$= 33.90 \text{ hours per machine}$$

The total time for the 65 machines would be

$$\text{Total time} = 65 \times 33.90$$
$$= 2,203.5 \text{ hours}$$

[7] See Table 21–6.

Notice that if management had merely multiplied the time it took to do the first unit (130 hours) by the number of machines (65), they would have overstated the time needed for the repairs by [(65 × 130) − 2,203.5] or 6,246.5 hours. This is not an insignificant error.

Unit time   Before leaving learning curve calculations, let us develop one additional concept—the time required to produce a single unit without including the time for all of the output that has gone before it. The time required to produce the *n*th unit may be found from the equation[8]

$$Y_n = (1 - b)Y$$

where *b* is again the slope of the learning curve and *Y* is the average time to produce the preceding *n*−1 units.

To illustrate the use of Y_n let us return to the previous example. Halfway through the overhaul, management considered overhauling five other machines in another section of the plant. They wanted to know the maximum time it would take to overhaul each of these units.

The time to overhaul the first of these five (the 66th machine) would be

$$Y_{66} = (1 - b)Y$$

From Table 21–6, (1 − *b*) for an 80 percent learning curve is 0.678; therefore,

$$Y_{66} = 0.678 \times 33.90$$
$$= 22.98 \text{ hours}$$

Since learning will reduce the time for the other four machines, the maximum time to overhaul each machine will be 22.98 hours.

Uses of learning curves   To this point we have shown the use of learning curves to develop the input for production scheduling and for estimating production costs. Although the examples have all been from maintenance, all areas of management require this type of information if they are to operate effectively. The influence that learning has on production time is readily apparent in the examples.

The most obvious area of learning takes place in the hand and assembly op-

---

[8] This equation is derived as follows:

$$\text{Total time} = T = aN^{-b} \times N$$
$$= aN^{-b+1}$$
$$= aN^{1-b}$$

Taking the first derivative,

$$\frac{dT}{dN} = (1 - b)aN^{-b}$$

$$Y_n = (1 - b)aN^{-b}$$

Since $aN^{-b} = Y$,

$$Y_n = (1 - b)Y$$

erations that make up direct labor costs.[9] Indirect costs, too, may be expected to be influenced. Fewer rejects, less waste, and the need for less supervision should occur as operators become more skilled. For these reasons, indirect costs should also fall with learning.

As noted previously, learning curves can also be used for areas other than production scheduling. One important use is in planning capital expenditures. To illustrate this, let us recall the concept of the break-even chart presented in Chapter 6, where variable costs—chiefly labor and material—were taken as fixed per unit of output and plotted as a straight line. From our discussion of learning, we would expect these costs to drop per unit of output during the later stages of production. The same thing should happen to fixed costs, since supervision, which is generally part of fixed costs, should decline with learning. The overall effect on the break-even chart is shown in Figure 21–9. Notice that less capital will be required than if no learning had taken place, since the break-even point will be reached at a lower level of output. Further profits will be influenced greatly for the same reason.

Learning curves are conceptually simple and are relatively easy to apply. Because of this, they can give their user a false sense of accuracy. Often output will follow the learning pattern for a period of time and then suddenly change materially. Methods changes, inconsistencies in material or labor, changes in

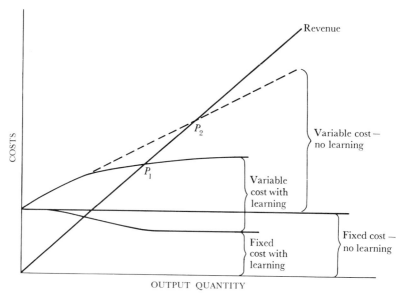

Figure 21–9   Break-even chart with learning

[9] In the discussion of time studies, special emphasis was placed on the requirement that operators to be timed to develop standards should be well trained and should have worked on the task long enough to have gained from learning. If this is not the case, it is obvious from this discussion that the standards developed will be inaccurate and, in time study terms, "too loose."

models, and improved management will all influence output. It is very difficult to isolate the cause-and-effect relationship of each of these with output. Learning curves therefore are not totally scientific—a large amount of empiricism is involved. However, this does not make learning curves good or bad. If we accept that they are not infallible and are not totally predictive, we will find that they are an effective tool for many management decisions.

Maintenance Information

Before leaving maintenance, we should consider the question of the availability of the data needed to plan and operate an effective maintenance activity. Throughout this discussion of the problems and approaches in the area of maintenance, the existence of satisfactory maintenance records has been taken for granted. Without information from these records, it would be impossible to solve almost any serious maintenance problem. No estimate of breakdown distributions would be available; no insight regarding either the expected lives of the equipment or the critical parts to repair would be possible. Without information from these records, management can only guess at an optimal maintenance program.

The data have other uses, too. Information on machine-part failures often suggests modifications in design or in inspection routines. If preventive maintenance concentrates on high-failure areas, the effectiveness of the entire process can often be significantly improved. Furthermore, high-failure data, if forwarded to the manufacturer, may lead to a better product with improved operating characteristics and reliability. A classic example of the value of such information is found in the history of commercial airlines. Investigations of airplane crashes, equipment failures, and flight and maintenance records have furnished a wealth of valuable information that has helped airline managers design better maintenance inspection and repair routines; it has also helped manufacturers improve the design and manufacture of the airplanes. Improved data regarding breakdowns would be extremely useful to the production planning and control departments of most enterprises. In short, information on equipment life, operating characteristics, and annual maintenance costs is an important part of the comparative evaluation that leads to the final choice of a machine.

Maintenance records can also assist in allocating total maintenance costs among departments requesting service. Distribution of these charges on the basis of use-frequency or hours is usually the most equitable approach. Such records pinpoint areas of high maintenance cost and therefore stimulate investigations. Perhaps closer supervision or better work methods could reduce the need for service and, therefore, the cost. The performance-measuring role is two-sided. The department being serviced is encouraged to balk at unreasonable charges under this type of system, which often helps to highlight an underutilization of maintenance crews and facilities. However, maintenance must be recognized for what it is—an expensive yet necessary activity. Idle maintenance time will inevitably occur and must be reported as such. If the maintenance crew is in fact the optimum size, there will still be periodic underutilization; it is part of the price of maintenance, which should be recognized by all levels of management. Only if this fact is recognized can accurate reporting be fostered and sound data be provided for the purposes mentioned earlier.

In designing any maintenance program, the first step is to determine what information must be collected. Then a procedure that includes both reporting responsibility and the timing and format of the reporting should be developed and implemented. Experience indicates that close managerial follow-up is necessary to ensure the timely receipt of accurate and complete data.

Questions and Problems

1. Explain why maintenance is inherently inefficient. What steps can be taken to minimize this inefficiency? Does built-in inefficiency pertain only to the function of maintenance work in operating an enterprise?
2. What are the general responsibilities of a maintenance department?
3. Characterize the kinds of costs that are associated with machine breakdowns.
4. What is a preventive maintenance program? What steps would be necessary to initiate such a program?
5. If it takes as long to perform preventive maintenance as it does to repair a piece of equipment, is there any advantage to preventive maintenance?
6. Under what general conditions is preventive maintenance appropriate for a *single* machine?
7. How does the supervision of maintenance workers differ from the supervision of those who work on the product? Can *practical* standards of performance be established for maintenance men?
8. Often there is specialization within the maintenance department. What is the effect of this specialization on the size of the maintenance group?
9. Explain how simulation might be helpful in managing the maintenance function of a manufacturing enterprise. What role would Monte Carlo play in analyzing the situation?
10. Discuss preventive maintenance as a concomitant of modern automated production systems.
11. Evaluate the following statements:
    (a) One area that does not lend itself to compromise is preventive maintenance: money spent on preventive maintenance is always a good investment as long as potential equipment failures can be eliminated.
    (b) A sound preventive maintenance program will always reduce the total cost of operating equipment.
12. The Epsilon Company wants to know what repair policy to pursue for three identical components used in a generator. The cost data are as follows:

Wage rate	$ 3.00 per hour
Component cost	$ 5.00 per unit
Downtime cost	$10.00 per unit

It takes six man-hours to replace a single component and an additional three hours for any other component replaced at the same time. The repair alternatives facing the company are

(a) Replace each component as it fails.

(b) Replace all three components when any one fails.

(c) Replace each component as it fails plus all those in operation over 450 hours.

The simulated service lines of the components are as follows:

	C_1	C_2	C_3
S_1 (hours)	350	480	440
S_2	480	400	250
S_3	670	610	620
S_4	460	320	500
S_5	560	520	350
S_6	220	410	770
S_7	600	770	930
S_8	900	330	530
S_9	440	910	470
S_{10}	390	470	790

13. The Federal Aviation Agency requires that two engine parts of a DC-7 be replaced at 400 hours and 600 hours, respectively. The former part costs $10.00 and the installation cost is $20.00. The latter part costs $7.00 with an identical installation cost. If the two parts are installed together, the combined installation cost is $25.00.

The Leaping Lion Airways is faced with two alternatives: first to replace each part at the required time or, second, to replace both parts together whenever one has to be replaced.

(a) *For a cycle of 3,600 hours,* show clearly the respective costs of each alternative, indicating which one is preferred.

(b) In the typical factory situation, deciding upon an appropriate repair policy is much more complicated. What factors are important in a factory situation that do not pertain to the airplane problem?

14. The Alpha Company has an automated process for manufacturing its highly specialized line of products. It is currently formulating a maintenance policy for three control motors that regulate the process. Simulation of the anticipated use to be made of the control motors produced the following table describing the expected life of these motors.

MOTOR 1 (IN HOURS)	MOTOR 2 (IN HOURS)	MOTOR 3 (IN HOURS)
300	250	275
400	350	325
350	375	400
425	300	425
325	400	250

Assume that the following cost data pertain:

Downtime cost	$15.00 per hour
Time to replace 1 motor	6 hours
Time to replace 2 motors	8 hours
Time to replace 3 motors	10 hours
Motor cost	$20.00 each
Labor cost	$ 4.00 per hour

Recommend a maintenance policy based upon the following two alternatives:
(a) Replace each motor when it fails.
(b) Replace each motor when it fails, as well as all others that have been in use 300 or more hours.

15. How large should the maintenance crew be to repair a bank of machines if each maintenance worker gets $5.00 per hour; machine downtime costs the company $20.00 per hour; the average number of arrivals per hour is 4, and they are distributed according to a Poisson distribution; and the average rate of service is 6 per hour distributed exponentially?

16. Is it true that under certain circumstances a policy of preventive maintenance would not be advisable for a company? In such circumstances, would there be any possible means of getting comparatively quick "feedback" of machine performance so as to minimize downtime?

17. A metal-working factory has 40 lathes, each of which can work on any of the firm's products. There is enough work to keep the 40 machines busy. When a machine is being repaired, the loss in production is $500 per day. On the average, five machines undergo repair each day. The breakdowns occur according to a Poisson distribution. The company has room for additional lathes; each additional lathe will cost the firm $50 a day.

How many additional machines should the company obtain to minimize the downtime cost?

18. The XYZ Insurance Company has a print shop that prints all of its forms and documents. Machine maintenance has been poor, and management is reviewing the maintenance policies. The equipment averages three breakdowns a week, which follow a Poisson distribution. Each breakdown costs the company $150 in lost production and waiting costs.

Three alternative maintenance plans are being considered. They all assume an exponential service distribution. Which of the three is the most economical?
(a) A single repairman who can average 4 repairs a week and whose salary is $200 per week.
(b) A repairman and a helper who together can average 6 repairs a week at a salary cost of $300 per week.
(c) Two repairmen who together can average 8 repairs a week at a salary cost of $400 per week.

19. What is meant by an 85 percent learning rate?

20. Are support activities affected by learning? What would be the effect on the support activities of an actual learning rate of 70 percent as opposed to a planned rate of 90 percent?

21. How would learning rates influence your decision to produce to stock or to produce to order?

22. With a learning rate of 90 percent, it took 50 hours to produce 10 units. How long should it take to produce 40 units?

23. In reviewing its production records, a company found it took 100 hours to produce 10 units. It took 80 hours to produce the next 15 units, or overall 180 hours to produce 25 units. The company is planning a large production order and wants to know what the learning rate is so that it can properly schedule the work.

24. A group of assembly workers have been producing output according to the formula

$$Y = aN^{-0.20}$$

(a) What is the learning rate (that is, the rate for $b = 0.20$)?

(b) If it takes a man 10 hours to produce his first unit of output, how long will it take him to produce 4 units?

(c) How many units will he produce in 80 hours?

References

Andress, F. J., "The Learning Curve as a Production Tool," *Harvard Business Review*, Jan.–Feb., 1954.

Barish, N. N., *Economic Analysis for Engineering and Managerial Decision Making*, McGraw-Hill, New York, 1962.

Blanchard, B. B., Jr., and Lowery, E. E., *Maintainability: Principles and Practices*, McGraw-Hill, New York, 1969.

Bovaird, R. L., "Characteristics of Optional Maintenance Policies," *Management Science*, Vol. 7, No. 3, April 1961.

Bowman, E. H., and Fetter, R. B., *Analysis for Productions and Operations Management*, 3rd ed., Irwin, Homewood, Ill., 1968.

Cox, D. R., and Smith, W. L., *Queues*, Barnes and Noble, New York, 1961.

Goldman, A. S., and Slattery, T. B., *Maintainability: A Major Element of System Effectiveness*, Wiley, New York, 1964.

Hughes, R. C., and Golem, H. G., *Production Efficiency Curve and its Application*, Arts and Crafts Press, San Diego, Calif., 1944.

Jordan, R. B., "Learning How to Use the Learning Curve," *NAA Bulletin*, Sec. 2., Jan. 1958.

Morris, W. T., *Analysis for Materials Handling Management*, Irwin, Homewood, Ill., 1962.

Parsons, G. W. S., "The 80% Learning Curve," *Modern Machine Shop*, March 1960.

Quinn, J. D., "The Real Goal of Maintenance Engineering," *Factory*, Vol. 121, No. 6, June 1963.

Takacs, L., *Introduction to the Theory of Queues*, Oxford Univ. Press, London, 1962.

Turban, E., "The Use of Mathematical Models in Maintenance," *Management Science*, Vol. 13, No. 6, Feb. 1967.

22

Quality Control Systems

It is important that a production process meet the quantity goals established in the production schedule, but it is of equal importance that the output meet quality specifications as well. Manufacturing quality assurance is the job of trying to achieve a quality product during the production cycle.

Manufacturing Quality Assurance

To manufacture products of the desired quality, control over their quality must be exercised throughout production and its associated functions, including production planning, procurement, and distribution (as shown in Figure 22–1). Quality considerations are present in every aspect of the production cycle—from the purchase of the raw materials to the delivery of the product to the customer.

Quality Assurance within the Organization

In most manufacturing firms the monitoring of the quality level—quality assurance—is usually assigned to a staff group that reports to top management. Organizationally this group is commonly referred to as quality control. The authority that quality control exercises varies according to the relative difficulty of controlling quality and to management's assessment of the consequences of circulating defective products. In industries as diverse as missile production and

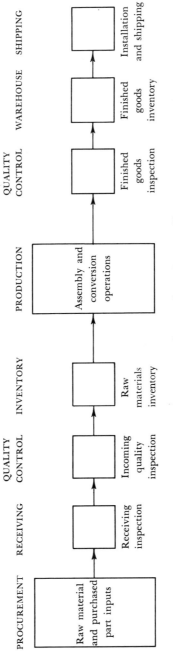

Figure 22–1 The scope of manufacturing quality assurance

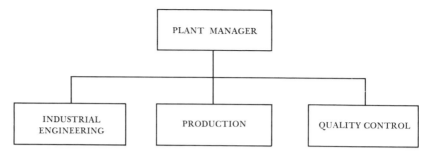

Figure 22–2 Typical quality control–production relationship

the preparation of baby foods, quality control sometimes has authority to stop production, and it may even have authority to dictate corrective measures.

Granting quality control this authority can create organizational problems. The line manager is responsible for the quantity and quality of the output from his department, but he is deprived of the authority to determine how the product is to be made if quality control can dictate corrective measures. To avoid an imbalance between authority and responsibility, most firms do not give quality control this much authority. Instead, it is usually permitted only to *recommend* corrective action or the closing of a production line, and the decision itself is left to the head of production since he is responsible for the output. Should the heads of production and quality control disagree, the decision is passed up to the next higher level of management.

The organization structure used to implement this approach is shown in Figure 22–2. The head of production is responsible to the plant manager for the production output. He must meet both the quantity and quality standards that are established. Quality control acts as a control for the plant manager by monitoring the output to see that it meets quality standards. If it does not, quality control can reject the output. Since quality control is independent of the head of production, it should not be swayed by the pressure of meeting production schedules into passing output that is not up to quality standards. When disagreements over the quality of the output arise, they are passed to the plant manager for resolution.

The Task of Manufacturing Quality Assurance

In performing its monitoring function, quality control must decide the amount and type of inspection and control required to ensure achievement of the specifications economically.

It is important to note that monitoring involves more than just inspection. The emphasis in inspection is on the quality of past production. The inspectors measure the critical characteristics of the product and compare these measurements with a standard. Any output that does not meet the standard is removed from the process. Notice that no corrective action designed to preclude future defective parts is inherent in the inspection process.

Inspection of product is a constant factor on this multiline conveyor belt

Quality assurance has a broader function than this; it includes determining where, when, and how many products to inspect; if there are more rejects than expected, quality assurance must locate the defects in the production system and recommend corrective action. Thus, quality assurance is concerned with the quality of both past and future production.

The Economics of Quality Assurance

There are three types of costs that interact in quality assurance.

1. *Preventive costs.* These costs are incurred in attempting to prevent failures, such as in the area of production planning, employee training, incoming goods inspection, and the design of production systems.
2. *Inspection costs.* These costs are incurred in measuring a firm's output against quality standards. Costs of this sort consist primarily of inspection and testing activities.
3. *Failure costs.* These costs are the direct result of defective items. They include not only the expense of reworking and scrapping, but also (in the area of customer goodwill) the deterioration of the company's reputation and image and the loss of future sales to competitors.

There are various estimates of how the overall expense of quality assurance may be divided among these three categories. One frequently quoted breakdown assigns 70 percent of the costs of quality to failures, about 25 percent to inspection, and only 5 percent to preventive activities. These figures are rather startling; they indicate that the largest expense by far is the failure cost and that the second largest amount is spent attempting to stop defects from reaching the customer. In contrast, very little is spent in trying to prevent product defects from occurring in the first place.

Any approach in which a disproportionately large amount of money is devoted to correcting past mistakes is likely to be ineffective and, what is worse, self-perpetuating. As an example, consider what happens when this approach is followed. When the level of rejects produced rises, the failure costs also rise. To combat this, management increases inspection activities, which, of course, raises the inspection costs. We know that inspection cannot eliminate defective products altogether but only prevent most of them from reaching the customer. Even with the best inspection operations, however, some defective products will reach the customer. As a result, failure costs remain high, and inspection costs in turn are also high. Moreover, production costs likewise are up because of the level of rejects. Consequently, management has little money to work with in the preventive area, and so the quality program (under these conditions) can only be ineffective.

Ironically, the indicated remedy for the excessive cost of quality control is to increase, *not* decrease, the funds allocated to prevention. Additional funds should be spent on reliability, process control, and quality engineering in order to reduce the number of defects produced, which in turn would reduce inspection and failure costs.

In Chapter 5 we examined the concept of reliability engineering, and throughout the book we have analyzed the design of production systems. To complete the picture of quality assurance, there remains only the control of quality in the production process—the subject of this chapter.

Production Quality Assurance

There are essentially two ways of controlling the quality of production. The first is to control the quality level of output by inspecting to make sure that, on the average, no more than a predetermined maximum level of defects are allowed to pass. In practice, this is most often done by the technique of acceptance sampling. In the second method, control is exerted over the production process itself, thus permitting adjustments and corrections to be made before the defect occurs. This type of control is generally implemented by means of statistical control charts. Briefly, control charts are designed to prevent deviations from the acceptable norm before they occur in volume, whereas acceptance sampling is designed to control the quality level passing the inspection point. After we have discussed the economics of quality control, we will examine acceptance sampling and control charts more closely.

The Level of Quality Needed

Generally, the more control that is exerted throughout the production process, the fewer the defects that will be produced and passed by inspection. The costs of control and the costs of manufacturing and distributing a defective product offset each other to a degree.

Typical control and failure cost curves are plotted in Figure 22–3. The total quality cost curve also appears at the top of the graph. As we have seen in other applications of this technique in earlier chapters, the most profitable operating point is where total costs are lowest, not where there are no rejects. A firm can generally earn a greater profit by allowing the shipment of a certain minimum level of defects than by striving for the elimination of all defects. When added control is exerted to lower the level of previously undetected rejects, total costs go up. On the other hand, if control is cut back too far and more than the optimal level of rejects are shipped, total costs will also go up. In many cases this optimal level of producer control is made a condition of the purchase contract and is therefore subject to negotiation. The user can reduce his acceptance-testing costs and avoid the inconvenience and expense of receiving and using defective materials if the producer has a high level of control in manufacturing the product. This control, of course, raises the production costs and is often included, after negotiation, as an item in the purchase contract. Alternatively, the producer may offer a price concession for accepting untested goods or pay the

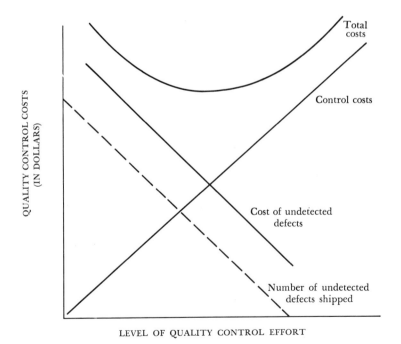

Figure 22–3 Control costs and undetected defects costs

user directly for performing output tests. This is done in the electronics industry, for example, where testing a subassembly or component sometimes requires the acquisition, and perhaps one-time use, of expensive test equipment. For certain products, only testing within an overall system can provide a meaningful answer to their acceptability. This type of testing is often used when a small producer, who has neither the facilities, funds, nor skilled personnel to conduct tests, sells to a large corporation such as GE, RCA, or Westinghouse.

As we have said before, regardless of the level of control imposed, some defective products will slip by to the customer; human and mechanical errors inevitably prevent the achievement of 100 percent quality output. This raises the question of what level of rejects is acceptable.[1]

Acceptable Quality Level

If we could secure the type of information needed to construct cost curves of the type shown in Figure 22–3, there would be no problem in setting an acceptable quality level (AQL); the AQL would simply be the level associated with the lowest total costs. However, this type of information is almost always unobtainable. In many instances the control cost curve can be determined, but the undetected defect cost curve can virtually never be known. Therefore, in practice, the AQL is generally set by judgment and expressed as a percentage of allowable defects. As could be expected, the AQL varies according to the pressures for quality. If subsequent production operations are costly, or if a defective item could cause great danger or harm to a customer, a low AQL will be established. On the other hand, if later production stages are not costly and the dangers to a customer are minimal, the AQL will be high. Thus, for example, pharmaceutical firms normally operate with very low AQL's, whereas nail producers operate with high AQL's.

Acceptance Sampling

Since one phase of management's efforts to achieve an acceptable quality level involves an assessment of the quality of past output, some type of inspection procedure is needed. For example, a firm is generally concerned about the quality of raw materials it purchases because defective materials will lower the quality of its output; therefore, most firms inspect incoming purchased materials. A firm also wants to ensure that its own output meets quality standards, so it establishes final inspection points. Inspections are also made between stages of a production process wherever it is deemed economically advantageous to do so.

Where to Inspect

One of the first decisions that must be made in any inspection procedure is where in the production process to inspect. This is essentially a technological and economic decision. As an example, consider the control problems of a six-

---

[1] Another aspect of this question will be considered when producer's and consumer's risks are discussed later in this chapter.

step production process whose characteristics are shown in Table 22–1. If no inspection is made between stages, and there is only a final inspection, the cost of producing the rejects is as listed in Table 22–2. Management now wants to know if it should inspect between production steps as well, and if so, at what points, considering the fact that the cost of an inspector is $200 per week and that 100 percent inspection is planned.

Even a quick glance at Table 22–2 shows that some inspection between stages would be economically sound. The question is: At what point would the inspection be most beneficial? This requires calculation of the between-stages costs. At Step 5, for example, we note that 100 rejects are passed on to Step 6; the cost of working them at Step 6 is $100 \times (\$8.00 - \$7.00) = \$100$. Clearly, it would not be economically sound to place an inspector costing $200 a week at that point. The same is not true between Steps 4 and 5, however, because the cost of working the 300 rejects produced at Stage 4 includes the cost at Step 6 as well as that at Step 5:

$$300 \times (\$7.00 - \$6.40) = \$180.00 \text{ for Stage 5}$$
$$300 \times (\$8.00 - \$7.00) = \$300.00 \text{ for Stage 6}$$
$$\text{Total} \quad \$480.00$$

Therefore, it would be profitable to inspect between Steps 4 and 5.

Table 22–1   Characteristics of a sample six-step production process

			Steps			
	1	*2*	*3*	*4*	*5*	*6*
Expected additional rejects (new rejects produced)	800	600	30	300	100	100
Product costs per unit through the step	$4.00	$4.40	$5.40	$6.40	$7.00	$8.00

Table 22–2   Weekly failure costs without intermediate inspection (only final inspection is performed)

Step	Number of Rejects		Failure Cost per Unit		Totals
1·	800	×	($8.00 − $4.00)	=	$3,200
2	600	×	($8.00 − $4.40)	=	2,160
3	30	×	($8.00 − $5.40)	=	78
4	300	×	($8.00 − $6.40)	=	480
5	100	×	($8.00 − $7.00)	=	100
					$6,018

Final inspection takes care of Step 6

Following this procedure, other points of inspection could also be established. This example is greatly oversimplified, but it illustrates that the decision of where to inspect is largely economic, based upon a comparison of inspection versus noninspection costs. The technological aspect of the decision is reflected in the costs of reworking defective items.

How to Inspect

In the example, we said that 100 percent inspection was planned, but it has several limitations. For one thing, it is the most expensive approach; every unit of output must be inspected. There is the cost of inspection personnel as well as the expense of setting up many inspection stations and maintaining the equipment used. Secondly, 100 percent inspection is clearly impossible in cases where the inspection is destructive or harmful to the product, as for example, to photographic film. The most important limitation of this approach is that it cannot give a 100 percent guarantee that only items that meet the quality standards will be shipped; human and mechanical errors inevitably creep in. Particularly where the number of units to be inspected is large, inspectors are apt to overlook defects as a result of boredom or the monotony of the task, or just because of simple human errors.

These limitations of 100 percent inspection gave rise to the concept of acceptance sampling whereby, in its simplest form, the quality of a certain number of products of the same type is measured by drawing a random sample from the lot. The sample is tested; then the entire lot is either accepted or rejected on the basis of the quality of the sample. Rejected lots may then be inspected 100 percent.

Acceptance sampling has several significant advantages: it reduces inspection costs; it is the only possible test procedure when testing is destructive; it reduces the number of rejects in products that are damaged by excess handling; and it actually raises the output quality above that provided by 100 percent inspection where inspection is monotonous.

On the other hand, since the judgment is based on a sample, there is always a risk of making an error by accepting a bad lot or rejecting a good lot. Generally this risk is no greater than in 100 percent inspection, however, and it is often less because greater care is normally exerted in sampling than in 100 percent inspection.

Acceptance Sampling Plans

There are many types of acceptance sampling plans. Some call for one sample from a lot; others employ double or multiple sampling from a single lot. The plans also differ in the way the items in the sample are measured. Some items are measured exactly (*variable sampling*), while others are simply measured to determine if they are, or are not, acceptable (*attribute sampling*).

Attribute Sampling

In acceptance sampling for attributes, parts are simply categorized as either good or no good. This type of sampling is well suited for such products as light bulbs, which either do or do not operate, or for glass plate, which is or is not cracked. Attribute sampling can be extended to other types of products by developing limits and accepting only those items whose characteristics fall within the limits.

In the ball bearing industry, for example, the diameters of the spherical bearings are checked by passing the bearing through two holes. Bearings that are too large to pass through the first hole (maximum acceptable diameter) are rejected, and bearings that pass through the second hole (minimum acceptable diameter) are also rejected. A good bearing goes through the first hole but is blocked by the second and will roll laterally into the "OK" box.

Attribute sampling, like all acceptance sampling plans, requires a definition of good and bad lots before sampling can proceed.

Operating Characteristic Curves

The producer and the consumer may well have different criteria for distinguishing a "good" lot from a "bad" lot. Naturally, the consumer would like the entire lot to be free of defects, but normally this is not economically feasible. Consequently, some level of defects that is mutually acceptable to the consumer and producer must be decided upon.

In order to determine precisely if a lot meets a quality standard, a firm must undertake a 100 percent inspection. Neglecting inspection errors, 100 percent inspection will show the exact percentage of the product that is defective. In order to find out if the whole lot is acceptable, the actual percentage of defectives is simply compared with the acceptance level, and then the lot is either accepted or rejected.

In the extreme case of 100 percent inspection with no inspection errors, the probability of accepting a bad lot is 0 and the probability of accepting a good lot is 100 percent.[2] This situation is illustrated graphically in Figure 22–4: up to the acceptable percentage level of defects in a lot, the probability of accepting the lot is 100 percent; past the acceptable level of defects, the probability of accepting the lot is 0. A curve showing the probability of acceptance for different quantities of defects is termed the *operating characteristics* (OC) *curve.* OC curves describe acceptance sampling plans according to the probability of accepting lots with various levels of defects. The OC curve for 100 percent inspection with no inspection errors is, of course, the ideal curve since there is no producer's or consumer's risk.

[2] In sampling, accepting a bad lot is termed a *consumer's risk,* whereas rejecting a lot with fewer defectives than the standard is termed a *producer's risk.*

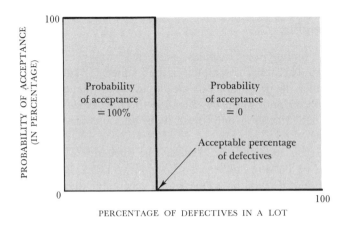

Figure 22–4   Probability curve for 100 percent inspection
with no inspection errors

OC Curve Specification

In order to appraise the effectiveness of a sampling plan for less than 100 percent inspection, two conditions must be specified: the size of the sample (n) and the allowable number of defectives in the sample before the lot is rejected (c). For every set of n and c values, a family of curves can be drawn. For any particular set of n and c values, the OC curve shows how well the sampling plan is able to differentiate between good and bad lots; a typical OC curve is shown in Figure 22–5. It is drawn for a sampling plan where the sample size (n) is 10 and the allowable number of rejects per sample (c) is 1. The curve shows the probability at which this measure will accept lots with different percentages of defects. Thus, we see that lots having a 10 percent level of defectives are deemed acceptable about 75 percent of the time. Stated in another way, the probability of finding up to 1 defective unit in a random sample of 10 is 75 percent. The probability of finding more than 1 defective unit in this same sample is 25 percent. If the percentage of defectives in the lots were 20 percent, the probability of accepting the lot would fall to 33⅓ percent and the probability of rejecting it would rise to 66⅔ percent. These figures indicate that the sampling plan is a good one because if the actual quality is good, there is a high probability of acceptance, and if the actual quality is bad, there is a high probability of rejection.

If all other factors are held constant, the ability of a sampling plan to differentiate between good and bad lots depends upon the size of the sample. For example, Figure 22–6 presents three OC curves, each having the same proportion between the allowable number of defects and the sample size but each having a different sample size. As the size of the sample increases, notice that the OC curve becomes steeper, reflecting the fact that it is more discriminating. All three plans discriminate satisfactorily—that is, they are approximately equal in

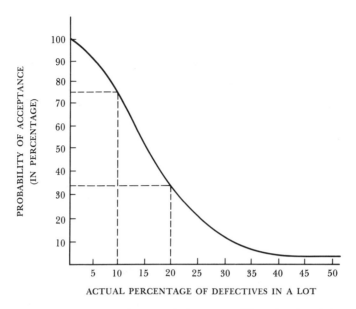

Figure 22–5 Operating characteristics curve [Sample size (n) = 10; acceptable number of defectives per lot (c) = 1]

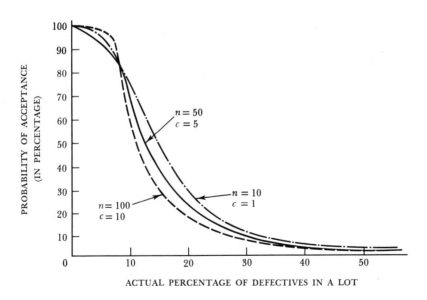

Figure 22–6 OC curves with n and c equal to a constant

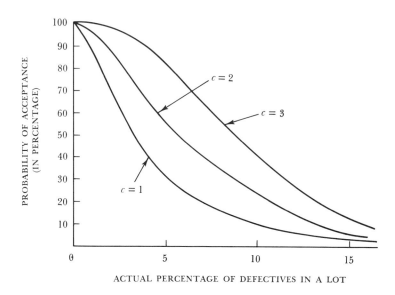

Figure 22–7 OC curves for $n = 50$ with various c levels

effectiveness—up to about 10 percent defectives. At this point, the curves cross each other, indicating that from that point on, plans with larger sample sizes are much more effective. With lots containing 15 percent defectives, the sample size of 100 will accept the lot only 30 percent of the time, whereas the sample size of 10 will accept the lot over 50 percent of the time.

As could be expected, if the sample size is held constant and the acceptable number of defects in the sample is allowed to increase, the sampling plan will become less discriminating. Figure 22–7 shows three OC curves, each of which has the same sample size of 50. The allowable number of defectives varies from 1 to 3, however. Notice that for a lot in which the actual defect rate is 5 percent, the OC curve with $c = 1$ will accept it 30 percent of the time, the OC curve with $c = 2$ will accept it 55 percent of the time, and the OC curve with $c = 3$ will accept it 83 percent of the time. Thus, an increase in the size of the acceptance number shifts the OC curve away from the origin, but the shape and slope of the curve remain relatively the same; only the level of the curve is changed. The lower the acceptance number, the more discriminating the approach becomes.

Economics of Sampling Plans

As explained earlier, an OC curve that could discriminate perfectly between good and bad lots would have a pattern like the one shown in Figure 22–4. However, the only sampling plan that could have this type of curve is the impossible one of 100 percent inspection with no errors. The merit of any potential sampling plan, therefore, depends upon the relationship between sampling costs and the risk of accepting a bad lot or rejecting a good one. We have pointed out the two basic ways of making a sampling plan more discriminating: to increase the size of the sample (which raises sampling costs) or to lower the number of allowable defects (which increases the probability of rejecting a good lot and thus raises production costs). On the other hand, a more discriminating sampling plan will lower the probability of passing a defective item, which will reduce the failure costs associated with the plan. Therefore, the best sampling plan can only be the one that results in the lowest total cost. To justify 100 percent sampling, there must be a great danger in passing a bad lot. Conversely, to justify no inspection, the consumer's risk must be small in relation to the cost of inspection. The usual case falls between these two extremes, with enough consumer's and producer's risk to warrant some degree of sampling inspection.

The Design of a Sampling Plan

There are various ways of controlling the amount of consumer's and producer's risk in a sampling plan. One common method is to design an OC curve that will pass through the two points that indicate the maximum acceptable producer's and consumer's risks. Before such a curve may be constructed, however, two proportions must be established.

The first is the acceptable quality level (AQL), or the highest percentage of

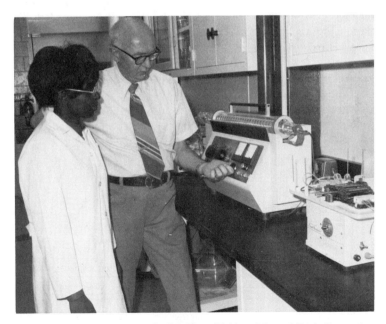

Photo Courtesy of Jell-O/Dover Division of General Foods Corporation

In the food-processing industry, training technicians in the use of sophisticated equipment is an essential in Quality Control.

defective units that is *clearly* acceptable to the purchasing firm. Thus, although a firm might like to have no more than 2 percent of defective units in any purchased lot (its AQL), it will often accept lots with a higher percentage of defects. But at some higher level of defects the lot will definitely become unacceptable to the purchasing firm; this point is often referred to as "the buyer's rebellion point." Beyond this level it is assumed that the buyer will take strong action, such as returning the lots to the manufacturer. In our example, let us say that the firm will not accept lots in which over 20 percent of the units are defective. This rebellion point is termed the *lot tolerance percent defectives* (LTPD) and serves as the dividing line between acceptable and unacceptable lots. Thus, in our example, the AQL and LTPD indicate that the firm is "indifferent" in varying degrees of intensity to lots in which between 2 and 20 percent of the units are defective.

If both sides are to reap the economic advantages of acceptance sampling, the customer must be willing to accept some risk that lots containing a percentage of defectives higher than the 20 percent LTPD will be accepted, and the producer must be willing to assume some risk that lots in which there is a percentage of defectives lower than the 2 percent AQL will be rejected. Limits to these risks are normally established in the sampling plan. Frequently used limits for α errors (producer's risk) and for β errors (consumer's risk) are 5 and 10 percent, respectively. This means, in theory, that no more than 5 percent of the lots with fewer defectives than the AQL will be rejected and that no more than 10 percent of the lots with greater than the LTPD will be accepted. This theoretical relationship among α, β, AQL, and LTPD is shown graphically in Figure 22–8. The practical task in making an actual sampling plan is to design an OC

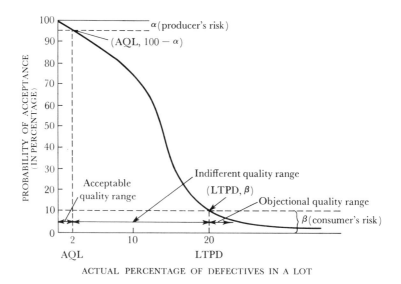

Figure 22–8 General relationships of an OC curve

curve that fits the values chosen for α, β, AQL, and LTPD. In our example the OC curve must meet the following conditions:

$$AQL = 2 \text{ percent}$$
$$LTPD = 20 \text{ percent}$$
$$\alpha = 5 \text{ percent}$$
$$\beta = 10 \text{ percent}$$

Therefore, the OC curve must pass through the points (AQL, 100 percent $-\ \alpha$) and (LTPD, β). The assumption is made, however, that any of the family of curves that passes through these two points is acceptable.[3]

Finding an OC curve that passes through the established points requires, in practice, a trial-and-error approach. Various sets of n and c values must be selected, and the OC curves they describe must be tested. Suppose, for example, that we wish to find an OC curve that passes through the points established in our example; we must determine the values for the sample size (n) and the acceptance number (c) so that the OC curve will pass through those points.

To begin with, we must assume an arbitrary sample size and an arbitrary acceptance number; then the probabilities of accepting lots with AQL and LTPD are figured out.[4] Once calculated, these values are compared with 100 percent $-\ \alpha$ and with β to see if they are the same. Usually they are not, and so another set of n and c values must be selected and the process repeated. Ultimately, a set of n and c values will be found in which the probability of accepting a lot with AQL defectives is equal to 100 percent $-\ \alpha$, or 95 percent, and the probability of accepting a lot with LTPD is equal to β, or 10 percent.

An iterative process of this sort is not difficult, but it is time-consuming. Fortunately, standard tables and charts are available that materially reduce the amount of work required to find a set of n and c values that meet the limits set by α, β, AQL, and LTPD values.[5]

Average Outgoing Quality

One way to upgrade the quality of the *outgoing* product and still minimize the amount of inspection required is to perform 100 percent inspection on lots that do not meet the standard established by the sampling plan. Any items in the

---

[3] As will be seen, fitting a curve to two points is fairly complicated; fitting a curve to more points would be uneconomical.

[4] The values for the probability of acceptance of a lot are calculated from the general equation of the OC curve. This equation is an expansion of the binomial where an infinite size lot is assumed and

$$p = \text{percentage of defectives}$$
$$p_c = \text{probability of a sample containing } c \text{ defectives}$$
$$= (C_c^n)\, p^c (1-p)^{n-c}$$

This equation is solved for p_c when $p = $ AQL and $p = $ LTPD, with various values of n and c.

[5] For example, see J. M. Cameron, "Tables for Constructing and for Computing the OC Characteristics of Single-Sampling Plans," *Industrial Quality Control*, July 1952, or H. F. Dodge and H. G. Romig, *Sampling Inspection Tables*, 2nd ed. (New York: Wiley, 1959).

lot that are found to be defective are then replaced with good units. When this type of sampling plan is followed, the average outgoing quality (AOQ) of shipments cannot exceed a specified maximum percentage of defectives.

The average outgoing quality is calculated in the following fashion. For any particular sampling plan, there is a fixed probability of accepting a lot with a given percentage of defectives. In the situation depicted in Figure 22–9, for example, 73 percent of the lots in which 10 percent of the units were defective would be accepted. Therefore, the average number of defectives per lot that would be accepted when the incoming lots have 10 percent defectives is 0.73 × (0.10 × the remaining number of units in the lot). The remaining number of units must be used since the defectives in the sample would be rejected. In Figure 22–9 the lot size is 100 and the sample size is 10. Thus, in every inspected lot with 10 percent defectives, an average number of 0.73 × [0.10(100 − 10)] = 6.57 defective units would pass through inspection. Since this lot contains 100 units, we could say that 6.57 percent of the accepted lot would be defective on the average. Thus, in general terms, the equation for average outgoing quality is

$$\text{AOQ (a percentage figure)} = \frac{\text{Average number of defectives} \times 100}{\text{Lot size}}$$

$$= \frac{P_D \times P_A(N - n)}{N}$$

where P_D = percentage of defectives in a lot
  P_A = probability of accepting a lot with P_D defectives
  N = lot size
  n = sample size

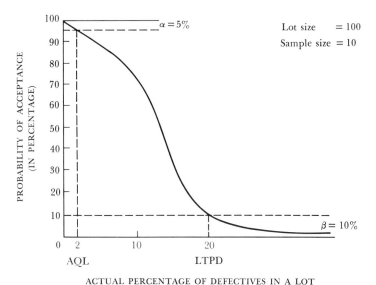

ACTUAL PERCENTAGE OF DEFECTIVES IN A LOT

Figure 22–9 Specific sampling plan—OC curve

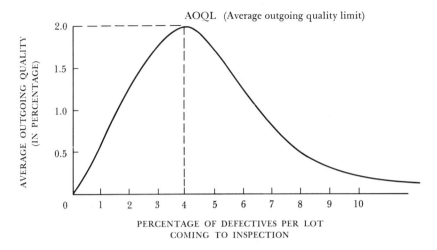

Figure 22–10 A sample AOQ curve

We can now calculate an AOQ curve for any given sampling plan, showing the average outgoing quality level for any incoming level of defectives permitted by the plan. To draw the curve, the AOQ values for different levels of incoming quality are calculated and plotted, with each AOQ value being a point on the AOQ curve.

A typical AOQ curve is shown in Figure 22–10. Notice that the curve has a limiting value for the average outgoing quality, which is called the AOQL; in Figure 22–10 it is 2 percent. The limiting value in an AOQ curve is determined by a particular sampling plan; the shape of the curve, however, remains consistent from plan to plan.

When good lots come to inspection (in the case of Figure 22–10 this includes lots with up to 4 percent defectives per lot), there is a high probability that they will be accepted; defectives that happen to be in these lots are also accepted. When the percentage of defectives in an inspected lot surpasses the acceptable limit, there is an increased probability that the lot will be rejected. When a lot is rejected, it is subjected to 100 percent inspection; any rejects are replaced, and so the number of defectives passed is reduced. Therefore, as the quality of the lots coming to inspection becomes worse, the AOQ improves.

Sampling plans designed in this fashion have a built-in maximum limit for the average outgoing percentage level of defectives, which means that the AOQ can never exceed the AOQL regardless of the quality level coming to inspection. The level of the AOQL depends upon the sampling plan, which in turn is affected by management's concept of the consequences of accepting a bad unit. The amount of 100 percent inspection necessary to maintain the AOQ is established by the plan itself. When lots are good, most of them are accepted by sampling and little inspection is done. When lots are bad, more of them are rejected and the amount of 100 percent inspection increases.[6]

Multiple or Sequential Sampling

Another way to reduce the amount of inspection required to maintain an average outgoing level is to use a multiple, or sequential, sampling plan. In this type of plan, more than one sample is usually taken from a lot, and the individual sample sizes are smaller than those needed for the same discrimination in single sampling. As we shall see, this approach reduces the total amount of sampling that is required to maintain an AOQ level.

One variety of multiple sampling is double sampling, in which an initial sample is taken and the number of defective units in the sample (c) is determined. This number is then compared with an acceptance number (c_1), and if the number of defective units is equal to or less than c_1, the lot is accepted. If the number of defectives is greater than c_1, however, it is compared with a larger acceptance number (c_2). If c is greater than c_2, the lot is rejected and subjected to 100 percent inspection. If the number of defectives (c) is between c_1 and c_2, another sample of the same size as the original is drawn from the lot. The defectives in the new sample are added to the ones in the original sample and the total number is compared with c_2; if it greater, the lot is rejected.

This type of sampling plan is depicted graphically in Figure 22–11. In lot 1, the number of rejects is equal to or less than c_1; therefore it is accepted. Lot 2 has more rejects than c_2 and is rejected. Samples from lots 3 and 4 initially had more rejects than c_1 but less than c_2. Additional samples were taken, and lot 3 was rejected and lot 4 was accepted.

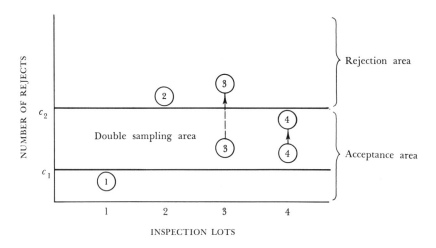

Figure 22–11   Double sampling

---

[6] This causes some complications in scheduling the sampling personnel.

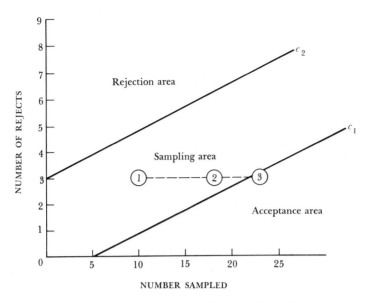

Figure 22–12   A sequential sampling plan

Thus, if the incoming quality is good, only an initial sample is required. Since this is typically a smaller sample than is used in single sampling, the overall sampling costs are usually lower; the larger the lot size, the greater will be the savings that will accrue from the use of double sampling.

The basic advantages of double sampling can be extended by taking sequential samples. Under this plan, samples are initially drawn from a lot as in double sampling. After inspecting the initial sample, the lot is either accepted or rejected, or another sample is drawn. More samples are taken as needed until the lot is either accepted or rejected. Figure 22–12 is a graphic presentation of a sequential sampling plan. Here we see that an initial sample of ten is drawn. If there are more than five defective units, the lot is rejected; if there is one or none at all, the lot is accepted. If there is more than one but less than five defective units in the lot, a further sample is drawn. The size of the second and subsequent samples can be quite small without sacrificing accuracy; they can even be as small as one. As a consequence, sequential sampling can reduce sampling costs even more than double sampling. In the example shown in Figure 22–12, three defects were found in the first sample, so a second sample of eight units was taken. No additional defects were found in the second sample. Nonetheless, the combined number of defectives still fell in the continued sampling area, but when a third sample of five was taken, the lot was finally accepted.

A sequential sampling plan, like the single sampling plan, is described by its α, β, LTPD, and AQL limits. Published charts and tables for OC curves for multiple sampling plans are also available.[7]

[7] H. F. Dodge and H. G. Romig, *Sampling Inspection Tables,* 2nd ed. (New York: Wiley, 1959), Appendix 5.

Variable Sampling

Many products have characteristics that can actually be measured rather than simply labeled as good or bad. Such characteristics include weight, dimensions, strength, and heat. In variable sampling, the underlying distribution generally used is the normal distribution, while in attribute sampling the binomial distribution is used. This difference in measurement and frequency distribution naturally alters the relationship between n, c, α, β, AQL, and LTPD.

In variable sampling the cost of inspecting an item is greater than in attribute sampling. The critical characteristic is not merely assessed on a "go–no go" basis; actual measurement is required. Offsetting the added inspection costs per unit, however, is the fact that in variable sampling fewer items have to be sampled to obtain the same degree of discrimination. Stated another way, for the same sampling discrimination, fewer samples must be drawn in variable sampling than in attribute sampling. Consequently, variable sampling may be less costly than attribute sampling. The chance of this happening increases as the sample sizes increase. To obtain the same level of discrimination obtained by an attribute sample size of ten requires a variable sample of about seven. This is a reduction of sample size of 30 percent. With an attribute sample size of 100, the variable sample can be over 50 percent less.[8]

There is one major limitation of variable sampling. Every critical characteristic of a product must have its own sampling plan. Thus, for products with multiple critical characteristics, inspection costs may skyrocket. If attribute sampling is employed, a single plan for the whole product can be designed.

Conceptual Aspects

Conceptually, the same ideas hold for variable sampling as for attribute sampling. The ability of a plan to discriminate is still shown by its OC curve. To determine the correct OC curve for a particular case, the same α, β, AQL, and LTPD points must be satisfied. A well-designed variable sampling plan can assure the same AOQ as an attribute plan, and sequential sampling is also applicable to variable sampling; the only difference between the two approaches is in the distributions used.

Control Charts

One important application of statistical sampling techniques is the control chart, which has been used as an instrument for controlling production output since 1924.[9] The charts may be used to measure both attributes and variable characteristics of products and to indicate when a process is under control and when it is moving out of control. If the process seems to be moving out of control, the

---

[8] A. H. Bowker and H. P. Goode, *Sampling Inspection by Variables* (New York: McGraw-Hill, 1952), p. 33.

[9] W. A. Shewhart, *Economic Control of Quality of Manufactured Product* (Princeton, N.J.: Van Nostrand, 1931).

charts also provide a measure of the likelihood of it actually going out of control. This capability makes the control chart a useful tool for preventing deviations.

Product variations that occur during the production process are attributable either to chance or to various assignable factors, or to both. Very little can be done to reduce chance variations except to change the process or to remove the rejects by acceptance sampling. However, variations that are due to specific causes such as differences in workers, machines, and raw materials can be controlled. If this is done, the system is said to be in a state of statistical control. One way to impose statistical control on a system is to use statistical control charts. Note that the use of such charts is designed to prevent deviations and not, as in acceptance sampling, to find them after they occur.

The Concept behind Control Charts

To illustrate the mechanics of control charts, let us imagine a production step in which steel rods are cut. A tolerance of ±0.06 inch is allowed in the length of the rods. Many lots of the rods have been produced that meet these tolerances, but suddenly a lot appears with lengths over the tolerance limits. Intuitively, we recognize that something unusual has taken place. The cutting tool may be worn, the material defective, or the operator performing incorrectly. The variation in output is too great to be attributed to normal variation; some specific cause seems to be responsible.

Usual, or chance, variations are expressed on control charts in the form of control limits. Variations that fall within these limits are generally attributed to unassignable causes or chance factors. Variations that fall outside these limits suggest, therefore, assignable causes. Accordingly, when there are variations beyond the limits, the process is considered to be out of control and in need of corrective action.

Figure 22–13 presents a simplified control chart. The majority of cut steel rods fall within the limits and require no investigation since their variation in

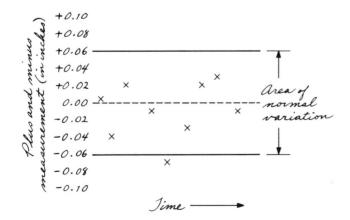

Figure 22–13   A sample control chart for cutting steel rods

measurement is assumed to be due to chance. The one rod outside the limits merits investigation. If an identifiable cause (such as tool slippage or wear) is noticed, it must be corrected; otherwise the process will soon be out of control despite the fact that, with only one exception, the output has been within acceptable limits. Sometimes no assignable cause for the defective part may be found; in that case the defect may possibly have been caused by chance variation. The persistence of nonassignable defects, however, indicates that the process is out of control but that the cause has not yet been isolated.

The Use of Control Charts

The same basic approach to control charts is used for both attribute and variable sampling; however, the method of calculating the control limits is different. The steps usually taken in developing and using control charts are as follows:

1. The characteristics that are to be controlled are selected, and the method of measurement is determined.
2. The output of the process is sampled.
3. On the basis of the samples, control limits are calculated.
4. The limits are checked to see if they are economically feasible.
5. The limits are then placed on a chart, and the characteristics of the samples are plotted.
6. Where variations occur outside the limits, corrective action is taken.

If the production process is under control, approximately 50 percent of the lots should fall on either side of the chart's center line. If consecutive lots all begin to fall on the high side or on the low side, or if the lots are consistently at points just inside an outside limit, the process may be out of control or tending in that direction. In such cases, corrective action should be initiated to preclude the manufacture of reject lots.

Another important service of quality assurance that is too frequently overlooked is the testing of how well the capability of a machine or process matches the task specifications or tolerance limits assigned to it. Such tests can be performed easily and effectively since the necessary data are obtained while designing the control chart.

Let us return for a moment to our example of the cutting operation on steel rods where the given specification was a tolerance of ±0.06 inch. In setting up a control chart, the natural variability of the process must be determined in order to fix the control limits. Three possible ranges of variability are shown in Figure 22–14. Here we see that the variability of process A is well suited for cutting steel rods; in fact, this is the process previously described and shown in Figure 22–13. Process B is capable of satisfying tighter and more exacting tolerances than those of the steel rods; therefore, it is "too good" for this task since the ability to hold tight tolerances or display little natural variability is often reflected in the initial cost of a machine and in the cost of a highly skilled operator to run the machine.

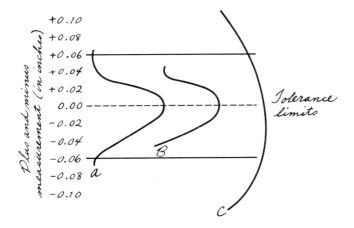

Figure 22–14   Choice of process for cutting steel rods

On the other hand, since the variability of process C is so great, the machine "in control" would not produce satisfactory rods; therefore, another process should be utilized. If this is not possible, however, it will be necessary to inspect the output 100 percent and live with a high reject rate, but the cost of such an approach can be considerable if a large number of rods is to be made.

Thus, control charts, as their name implies, are useful tools for monitoring a production process. They can determine whether it is in or out of control and whether it is performing according to its natural capability. They do not, however, directly measure the quality, or "dimension," of the finished product.

Control Charts for Variables

Control charts for variables are generally based on the normal distribution, and they are most frequently designed for samples of means rather than for individual measurements. The main reason for designing charts for samples of means is that even when an actual distribution is skewed, the sampling distribution of the mean of a series of random samples approaches normality. This, in essence, is the central limits theory of statistics, which states that where large samples are taken, the means of the samples tend to be distributed normally about the mean of those means, as depicted graphically in Figure 22–15. This figure shows that while the distribution of individual measurements of the diameters of a casting is skewed, the distribution of the mean diameter of a sample of size 25 is essentially normal.

Two characteristics of normal distribution are used in developing variable control charts: measures of central tendency and measures of spread or variability. For control chart purposes, the most common measure of central tendency is the arithmetic average—the mean. The spread is normally measured by the standard deviation; however, the range, R (which is equal to the difference between the largest and the smallest measurements in a sample), is frequently

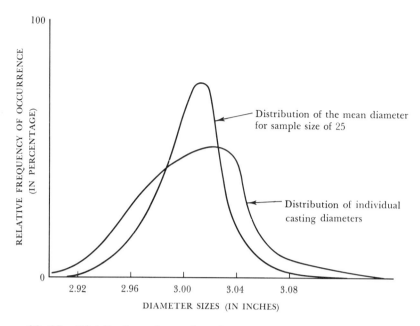

Figure 22–15 Distribution of samples of means and individual measurements

employed instead because it is easy to use in calculations for control chart work.

The variations in the mean and in the range must both be considered in deciding if a process is under control. There are thus two general conditions that could cause sample statistics to fall outside the control limits. One is a shifting condition that would make the mean move, with the range remaining constant. If, for example, a drill becomes worn, the means taken of sample outputs would be less than with a good drill, but the range would probably remain stable. The other condition is a stable mean and a changing range. If the bearings on the drill become worn, the drill would rove, forcing the range to become greater, yet the mean could conceivably stay well within the limits. In some instances, both conditions may take place concurrently; these variations are depicted graphically in Figure 22–16.

In constructing control charts, the average sample values for both the mean and the range are calculated. Upper and lower control limits of ± 3 standard deviations are established about the average mean value and the average range value. (The 3 standard deviation limits are selected since experience has proved them to be the most economical.)

$$\text{Mean} \begin{cases} \text{Upper limit} = \bar{\bar{x}} + 3\sigma_{\bar{x}} \\ \text{Center} \quad\quad = \bar{\bar{x}} \\ \text{Lower limit} = \bar{\bar{x}} - 3\sigma_{\bar{x}} \end{cases}$$

$$\text{Range} \begin{cases} \text{Upper limit} = \bar{\bar{R}} + 3\sigma_{\bar{R}} \\ \text{Center} \quad\quad = \bar{\bar{R}} \\ \text{Lower limit} = \bar{\bar{R}} - 3\sigma_{\bar{R}} \end{cases}$$

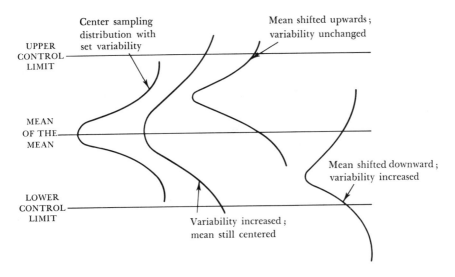

UPPER CONTROL LIMIT

Center sampling distribution with set variability

Mean shifted upwards; variability unchanged

MEAN OF THE MEAN

Mean shifted downward; variability increased

LOWER CONTROL LIMIT

Variability increased; mean still centered

Figure 22–16 Changes in means and variability

Once the control limits have been computed statistically, one must check to see if they are economically feasible. If the variation they represent is less than that needed to meet the specifications, the limits are normally satisfactory. If, however, the usual variation shown by the control limits is greater than that desired in the specification, further examination is called for. Is it cheaper to improve the process or to accept the number of rejects that will be produced? If the process can be improved cheaply, the control limits are not satisfactory; but if the cost of improving the process is greater than the cost of the rejects, the limits are satisfactory.

An application of variable control charts To illustrate the construction of variable control charts, let us consider a process designed to produce rods to a specified length of 3 ± 0.006 inches. A machine is set up, and production is started at the rate of 150 units per hour. From the first 300 rods produced, 25 samples of 5 are selected at random; then the mean and range are calculated for each sample. For the first one, the rods measure

$$
\begin{array}{r}
2.998 \\
3.004 \\
3.003 \\
2.997 \\
3.005 \\
\hline
15.007
\end{array}
$$

$$\bar{x} = \frac{15.007}{5} = 3.0012 \text{ inches}$$

$$\bar{R} = 3.005 - 2.997 = 0.008 \text{ inch}$$

From the means and ranges for the individual samples we can now calculate an overall mean and range; these are simply the averages for the sampling distributions of means and ranges

$$\bar{\bar{x}} = \frac{\text{Sum of the sample means}}{\text{Number of samples}} = \frac{75.0400}{25} = 3.0016 \text{ inches}$$

$$\bar{\bar{R}} = \frac{\text{Sum of the sample ranges}}{\text{Number of samples}} = \frac{0.1075}{25} = 0.0043 \text{ inch}$$

The next step is to calculate the standard deviations of the sampling distributions of means and ranges, since it is on the basis of these values that control limits are set. The standard deviations can be calculated using the general formula for them.[10] To simplify the process, tables of values are available that can be substituted in the following revised formulas to give results that closely approximate those obtained by actually calculating the standard deviations.

$$\text{Mean} \begin{cases} \text{Upper limit} = \bar{\bar{x}} + A\bar{\bar{R}} \\ \text{Center} \quad\quad = \bar{\bar{x}} \\ \text{Lower limit} = \bar{\bar{x}} - A\bar{\bar{R}} \end{cases}$$

$$\text{Range} \begin{cases} \text{Upper limit} = B\bar{\bar{R}} \\ \text{Center} \quad\quad = \bar{\bar{R}} \\ \text{Lower limit} = C\bar{\bar{R}} \end{cases}$$

Substituting for the values of A, B, and C from Table 22–3 and those calculated for $\bar{\bar{R}}$ and $\bar{\bar{x}}$, we can determine the control limits. From the table we see that for the sample size of 5, $A = 0.577$, $B = 2.114$, and $C = 0.00$; therefore:

$$\text{Mean} \begin{cases} \text{Upper limit} = 3.0016 + (0.577 \times 0.0043) = 3.004 \\ \text{Center} \quad\quad\quad\quad\quad\quad\quad\quad\quad\quad\quad = 3.0016 \\ \text{Lower limit} = 3.0016 - (0.577 \times 0.0043) = 2.9992 \end{cases}$$

$$\text{Range} \begin{cases} \text{Upper limit} = 2.114 \times 0.0043 \quad\quad\quad = 0.0091 \\ \text{Center} \quad\quad\quad\quad\quad\quad\quad\quad\quad\quad\quad = 0.0043 \\ \text{Lower limit} = 0.00 \times 0.0043 \quad\quad\quad\quad = 0.000 \end{cases}$$

With these values the charts in Figure 22–17 can be constructed. Since the 3 standard deviation limits were used, we would expect 99.73 percent of all sample mean and range values to fall within the limits. We may therefore assume that if a value falls outside them, it is due to some assignable cause requiring corrective action. Further, since the control limits are smaller than the specifications for cutting the rod, they are acceptable. Although, in theory, one may statistically calculate the number of times during actual production when samples should be taken from the output, in practice the frequency of inspection is normally based on judgment. Judgment, in turn, is influenced by such factors as the availability

---

[10] This was done in Chapter 5, where confidence limits were set for forecasts.

Table 22–3 Sample factors for computing control limits[a]

Sample Size n	Mean Factor A	Range Factor B	Range Factor C
2	1.880	3.268	0.00
3	1.023	2.574	0.00
4	.729	2.282	0.00
5	.577	2.114	0.00
6	.483	2.004	0.00
7	.419	1.924	.076
8	.373	1.864	.136
9	.337	1.816	.184
10	.308	1.777	.223

[a] Adapted from A. V. Feigenbaum, *Total Quality Control* (New York: McGraw-Hill, 1961), p. 265.

of inspectors, the history of the quality of the process, the output rate, and the cost of producing rejects.

In our rod-cutting example, samples were taken and their means and ranges plotted. Notice that the range in sample 4 (Figure 22–17) was excessive and that corrective action was taken; in sample 6 the mean value was below the lower limit, which also called for corrective action. There doesn't seem to be a definable trend toward any of the control limits, however, which indicates that the process is basically under control.

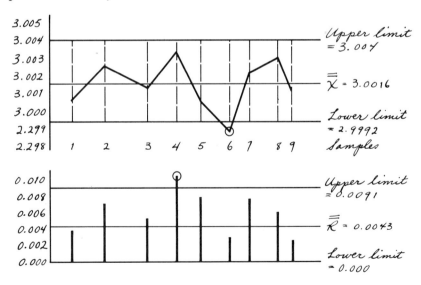

Figure 22–17 Variable control charts

Control Charts for Attributes

Control charts for attributes are based on the binomial distribution, in which the standard error of a proportion is equal to

$$\sigma_p = \sqrt{\frac{p(1-p)}{n}}$$

where p = number of rejects ÷ total observations
        n = size of the sample

Following the procedure outlined for variable control charts, the control limits are set at

$$\text{Upper limit} = \bar{p} + 3\sigma_p$$
$$\text{Center} = \bar{p}$$
$$\text{Lower limit} = \bar{p} - 3\sigma_p$$

No range of variation exists because the measurement is simply good or bad. Other than these differences, the procedure is the same as for variable control charts.

To illustrate how attribute control charts are applied, let us turn to Table 22–4, which lists the number of rejects found in 20 random samples of 50 observations taken during the first ten days of a job run. We wish to determine if

Table 22–4   Attribute sampling data

Lot Number	Number of Rejects	Fraction Defective
1	1	0.02
2	3	0.06
3	2	0.04
4	2	0.04
5	8	0.16
6	3	0.06
7	1	0.02
8	1	0.02
9	2	0.04
10	5	0.10
11	1	0.02
12	3	0.06
13	2	0.04
14	3	0.06
15	1	0.02
16	3	0.06
17	3	0.06
18	3	0.06
19	1	0.02
20	2	0.04
	$\Sigma = 50$	

the process is under control and also to establish appropriate control limits. First we calculate the fraction of defectives in each lot. Then we calculate the values for $\bar{p}$ and σ_p as follows:

$$\bar{p} = \frac{\text{Total number of defectives}}{\text{Number of observations}} = \frac{50}{50 \times 20} = 0.05$$

$$\sigma_p = \sqrt{\frac{0.05 \times 0.95}{50}} = 0.03$$

The upper and lower control limits are thus:

$$\text{Upper limit} = 0.05 + 3(0.03) = 0.14$$

$$\text{Lower limit} = 0.05 - 3(0.03) = 0.00$$

Using these limits we may construct a control chart such as the one shown in Figure 22–18. The proportion of defective units in each lot is plotted on the chart. Since the fraction in sample 5 is greater than the upper control limit, the reason for this is investigated. It is found that a new operator was placed on the job during the period of time when sample 5 was drawn and that the excess rate of defectives was produced during her initial work period. Since the cause of the excessive number of rejects was found and, presumably, remedied during the new operator's first few days, these figures should be omitted when calculating the control limits.

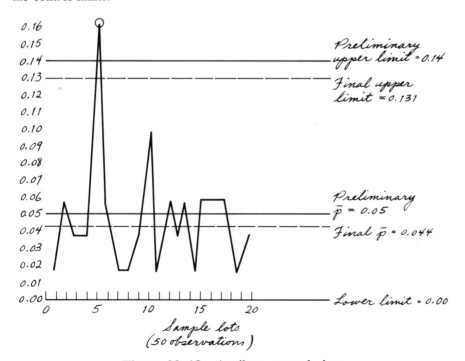

Figure 22–18 Attribute control chart

The control limits are thus recalculated omitting sample 5, giving us:

$$\bar{p} = \frac{42}{50 \times 19} = 0.044$$

$$\sigma_p = \sqrt{\frac{0.044 \times 0.956}{50}} = 0.029$$

Upper limit $= 0.044 + 3(0.029) = 0.131$

Lower limit $= 0.044 - 3(0.029) = 0.00$

The new limits are plotted in Figure 22–18. Since none of the samples (except 5) fall outside of the new limits, we know that the process is under control and that the control limits can be used as standards.

Questions and Problems

1. In what basic ways can the quality of outgoing products be controlled?
2. Describe what is meant by alpha and beta errors (producer's and consumer's risks) in quality control work.

   Consider manufacturing companies in various industries that are interested in quality inspection of finished goods before shipment to customers. Name at least one industry that should be interested in protection against alpha errors and state why, and one that should be more concerned about beta errors and why.
3. What determines an acceptable quality level?
4. What does the term *quality* connote in production activities?
5. What is an OC curve? What information can be learned from an OC curve?
6. What effect on the OC curve does an increase in sample size have? Are OC curves that are more discriminating better than those that are less discriminating?
7. What are AQL, LTPD, α, β? What relationships do they have with each other and to the OC curve?
8. When should single, double, and sequential sampling be used? What economic considerations govern their selection?
9. Given the following data, would it be economical to place an inspector after operation 1 if the next inspection point came after operation 5? If the next inspection point were after operation 3?

   Inspectors receive $1.50 per hour.
   Standard lot size is 200 units (each lot passes through the sequence of operations).

	OPERATION				
	1	2	3	4	5
Rejections traceable to each operation (percent)	8.0	0.2	0.6	1.2	0.6
Inspection time per piece (in minutes)	4.0	0.5	3.5	5.0	2.0
Cumulative material labor and factory overhead per piece	$1.50	$1.84	$2.76	$3.44	$3.72

10. The Titan Stamping Works wants to reduce inspection costs by decreasing the number of inspection operations from six to three. The company has decided that one of the three inspection operations will be a final inspection, and it asks your advice on where to locate the remaining two operations. A study of inspection records and cost data shows the following:

	OPERATION					
	1	2	3	4	5	6
Number of defects per week	200	50	80	125	40	10
Cumulative manufac- turing costs	$5.00	$5.25	$7.50	$9.50	$10.00	$12.50

   (a) Assuming that inspection costs will not vary from operation to operation, where would you place the remaining inspection operations?
   (b) What other suggestions do you have for reducing the cost of maintaining quality standards?

11. Suppose you know that the output of one of your suppliers typically has a certain percentage of defectives. What action, if any, should you take?

12. Under what circumstances is a formal statistical quality control program justified? What would be the most important content of such a program?

13. Indicate whether each of the following statements on statistical quality control is *true* or *false* and why.
   (a) An acceptable lot under random sampling techniques is one that of necessity has some defective units.
   (b) The "representativeness" of a sample is in direct proportion to the size of the sample.
   (c) The limits on the statistical control chart should preferably be determined with reference to economic rather than standard statistical considerations.
   (d) The statistical control chart and acceptance sampling are aimed at different objectives, although both involve sampling.
   (e) The acceptance quality level completely defines the conditions so that the sample size can be statistically determined.

14. In quality control, compare the procedure for controlling attributes with that for controlling variables.

15. How can both consumer's and producer's risks be reduced in a sampling procedure?

16. In a certain manufacturing situation, management wants to be "sure" of accepting lots that are 5 percent or less defective and wants to be "sure" of rejecting lots that are 10 percent or more defective. A sampling plan has been devised to take a sample of five items and reject the lot if any defective items are found in the sample.
   (a) Calculate the alpha and beta errors in this plan; that is, how "sure" can management be that the criteria will be met?
   (b) Sketch the operating characteristic curve.
   (c) Does this seem like a good sampling plan, given management's objectives? Why? If it is not a good plan, describe how it could be improved.

17. What is the concept behind the use of control charts?

18. How does the control-chart approach differ for attributes and variables?

19. Why must the variations in the mean and range both be evaluated in order to know if a process is under control?
20. Develop an OC curve for a single sampling lot inspection plant where $n = 100$ and $c = 4$. If $\alpha = 0.10$ and $\beta = 0.10$ for this OC curve, what are the LTPD and AQL values?
21. A firm desires to keep its consumer's and producer's risks to 0.05 each with an AQL of 0.02 and a LTDP of 0.10. What size sample should be taken, and how many defectives are allowable in the sample before the lot is rejected?
22. If a sample has $n = 100$, $c = 2$, $\alpha = 0.05$, and $\beta = 0.10$, what are the AQL and LTPD values?
23. Develop a control chart for the following data. The sample size is 100.

Sample Number	1	2	3	4	5	6	7	8	9	10	11	12	13	14	15	16
Number of Rejects	2	1	0	2	1	4	2	1	3	5	7	6	8	3	1	2

Is the process under control? What control limits should be used for future production?

24. From the following data, determine
   (a) the control limits and center line for the mean of the sample $\bar{\bar{x}}$.
   (b) the control limits and center line for the range $\bar{\bar{R}}$.

Sample size $= 4$

SAMPLE	x_1	x_2	x_3	x_4
1	0.702	0.708	0.690	0.695
2	0.718	0.709	0.698	0.719
3	0.699	0.688	0.697	0.701
4	0.702	0.714	0.698	0.697
5	0.700	0.693	0.691	0.702
6	0.724	0.708	0.704	0.679
7	0.717.	0.713	0.705	0.712
8	0.698	0.700	0.689	0.704
9	0.708	0.696	0.728	0.685
10	0.689	0.678	0.687	0.682

References

Bowker, A. H., and Lieberman, G. J., *Engineering Statistics*, Prentice-Hall, Englewood Cliffs, N.J., 1959.

Caplen, R. H., *A Practical Approach to Quality Control*, Auerbach Publishers, Princeton, N.J., 1969.

Dodge, H. F., and Romig, H. G., *Sampling Inspection Tables*, 2nd ed., Wiley, New York, 1959.

Duncan, A. J., *Quality Control and Industrial Statistics*, 3rd ed., Irwin, Homewood, Ill., 1965.

Enrick, N. L., *Quality Control and Reliability*, Textile Book Service, Metuchen, N.J., 1969.

Feigenbaum, A. V., *Total Quality Control*, McGraw-Hill, New York, 1961.

Fetter, R. B., *The Quality Control System*, Irwin, Homewood, Ill., 1967.

Gilmore, H. L., and Schwartz, H. C., *Integrated Product Testing and Evaluation*, Wiley, New York, 1969.

Goldfarb, N., and Kaiser, W. N. (eds.), *Gantt Charts and Statistical Quality Control*, Hofstra, Hempstead, N.Y., 1964.

Grant, E. L., *Statistical Quality Control*, 3rd ed., McGraw-Hill, New York, 1964.

Hagan, J. T., *A Management Role for Quality Control*, American Management Association, New York, 1968.

Hansen, B. L., *Quality Control: Theory and Applications*, Prentice-Hall, Englewood Cliffs, N.J., 1963.

Kirkpatrick, E. G., *Quality Control for Managers and Engineers*, Wiley, New York, 1970.

Landers, R. R., *Reliability and Product Assurance*, Prentice-Hall, Englewood Cliffs, N.J., 1963.

Military Standard Sampling Procedures and Tables for Inspection by Attributes, MIL-STD-105C, Govt. Printing Office, Washington, D.C., July 1961.

Military Standard Sampling Procedures and Tables for Inspection by Variables for Percent Defective, MIL-STD-414, Govt. Printing Office, Washington, D.C., June 1957.

Smith, C. S., *Quality and Reliability: An Integrated Approach*, Pitman, New York, 1969.

Wetherill, G. B., *Sampling, Inspection, and Quality Control*, Barnes and Noble, New York, 1969.

23

The Firm *as a* Cost System

Introduction

"The name of the game is business and we keep score with money." Although some might take issue with this business adage, arguing that business should not be called a "game" since in many ways it is something less than "fair" or "sporting," none would deny that money is used "to keep score." It is the universal common denominator that pervades all functions and activities of a firm. The company's "annual score" is expressed in dollars and is broken down into such significant categories as sales revenue, profit, asset value, and net worth. Various ratios are also used for this purpose, and they too are expressed in dollars—for example, return on investment, the ratio of sales to average inventory (turnover ratio), the ratio of current assets to current liabilities (current ratio), and sales dollar analysis. How good the score is for any year may be assessed by comparing its dollar figures with those of other years.

Trends are another useful barometer of the company's managerial performance; these include changes in sales, profits, return on investment, and net worth. But trends must be appraised in the light of other factors. How do the company's operating specifics compare with the average for the economy or with the industry as a whole? General economy and industry data are usually readily accessible; relevant figures can be obtained from trade associations, from independent research companies' publications such as *Dun's Review & Modern Industry,* *Moody's Industrial Manual,* and *Standard & Poor's Corporation Records,* and from government agencies such as the Bureau of Labor Statistics and the Economic Research Service. An apparent trend may also be the result of a nonrecurring phenomenon such as the sale of a product line or the company's buildings and grounds, an unusual government contract, or the receipt of a special order to replenish the stock of a customer who has suffered a disaster. Many factors have to be considered in measuring the performance of a firm, but in the final analysis they are all expressed in dollars.

As can be seen in Figure 23–1, revenues are output-oriented; they stem principally (excluding special sales of product lines and buildings) from the sale of company products. The economic competitiveness of marketplaces varies, and some large companies are able to exert considerable influence over prices and market conditions. For the typical firm, however, the market demand generally establishes prices, product configuration, and delivery (quantities and time) targets; it has very little control over these factors. Thus, at the risk of oversimplifying, we can say that costs are principally input- and process-oriented. Other costs can also be important, such as those incurred in financial planning, legal advice, selling, advertising, and sales promotion, all of which are associated with distribution. Since our discussion is oriented toward manufacturing, however, we will ignore these other costs, noting only that many of the concepts, problems, and decision approaches we have already discussed can be applied to these areas with equal effectiveness. The factors that affect the cost of labor, rent, heat, and materials exist, to a large extent, within the four walls of the firm, and consequently they are subject to much greater managerial control than revenue. It is primarily for this reason that businessmen are typically so concerned with costs. If sufficiently low costs can be achieved, prices can be reduced, thus bringing about larger sales volumes; or, if prices are held constant, low costs can result in increased profits. Another stimulus to cost control and reduction is the real or potential price cutting of competitors, which can adversely affect company operations.

We can now identify two principal uses for costs: price setting and the planning and control of operations. As indicated, price setting involves more than an examination of company costs; it also depends upon marketplace factors such as quantity–price relationships (called *demand characteristics*), government regulations, and the actions of competitors. Because these factors are necessarily

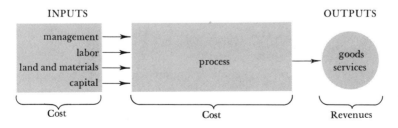

Figure 23–1   Model of a firm

beyond the scope of this text, our discussion on pricing will only deal with how the required cost data are furnished. We will also examine how cost data facilitate the planning and control of operations. Planning and controlling are but two of the five managerial functions identified earlier in the book. The others—organizing, assembling resources, and directing—also make considerable use of cost data. The decisions made in all five categories of management are affected by cost considerations and in turn help to determine the cost of the firm. Whether his responsibility is broad or narrow, the manager needs cost data to help him identify and resolve problems so that the firm can operate. This textbook has largely dealt with the problems encountered in managing the production of the firm. Cost data help relate production management functions to enterprise functions so that the company can perform in an effective, synchronized manner. Let us consider a few examples of the cohesive function of cost data.[1]

Planning

Major planning decisions include product line, plant location, production lot sizes, and inventory levels. Evaluation of a product line requires a consideration of manufacturing costs and the contribution of each item. The funding of the necessary design and development expenses must also be studied if changes are to be made in existing products or if new products are to be developed. Similarly, the objective of a plant location study is to select a plant site that will yield competitive operating costs, and an optimal production lot size is calculated by balancing paper-work and setup costs with storage and carrying costs. The same is true for the establishment of inventory levels, which also involves balancing utilization and idleness costs, for example, with the production lot size determinants.

Organizing

An organization structure delineates, among other things, responsibility for performing different activities within the firm. The structure also provides a basis for planning and controlling the costs that arise in performing those activities. For example, managers are held responsible for doing their assigned work as efficiently as possible at minimum cost. Also, the organizational decision regarding the use of product-line or process layout is approached by evaluating the costs of initial investment and those of such factors as floor space, heat, and light.

Assembling Resources

All of the activities involved in creating a manufacturing process and operating it by means of labor, materials, and supervision use cost data. An economy study

---

[1] The reader should note that the examples that follow have been selected to demonstrate the linking function provided by costs. We do not want to convey the impression that costs are the only consideration in the production areas mentioned here or even to state that costs are most important. Rather, we describe the role of cost as merely a contributing factor whose importance will vary from industry to industry and firm to firm.

will guide the selection of machines by comparing the cost of acquisition, labor, maintenance, insurance, and taxes. The development and selection of work methods will reflect the necessary setup and labor costs. The purchasing agent will use value analysis to compare costs in terms of discounts and substitutions, and his determination of the economic purchase order size is substantially the same cost-balancing method used in establishing optimal production quantities.

Directing

Directing a manufacturing process also necessitates many cost-oriented decisions. The operability of facilities depends upon the firm's maintenance policy, which is determined by evaluating such factors as repair, crew size, and overtime costs and then balancing them. Peak loads may make it necessary to consider multiple-shift or overtime operations or the subcontracting of work. The assignment of workers to specific tasks means a consideration of various labor cost factors such as the expense of job training and the base rates. Further operating restrictions imposed by a union–management contract can also be evaluated in terms of their impact on operating costs.

Controlling

The objectives of production are, to state them simply, to deliver at the right time a product with the desired quality, in the right quantity, and produced at the minimum cost. So important is the need to monitor and evaluate actual performance against preestablished standards that significant functional areas usually carry the word "control" in their titles; a few examples are the financial, production, inventory, and quality control departments. One could generalize and say that the achievement of minimum cost is the basic criterion in assessing performance in all functional areas of a firm. This in turn means that cost control must be exercised throughout the organization; therefore, it may be useful at this point to describe the elements of an effective control mechanism.

As we can see from the summary shown in Table 23–1, control is basically a comparison of actual performance with planned (or "standard") performance. When results fail to measure up to expectations, the trouble spots can quickly be identified so that corrective action may be taken. Formulating corrective action is facilitated by variance analysis, which helps to identify "causes" and "effects."

The use of cost data for control purposes is a three-step process:

1. *Setting of cost standards.* This includes a consideration of how to categorize items (such as departments) or expense factors (such as material and labor) into controllable groups. Then a method for establishing realistic performance standards must be devised.
2. *Comparison of actual versus standard.* Performance standards must be explained to the operators, and responsibility must be assigned for collecting actual cost data, which will be compared with the standard and reported to the appropriate manager in the manner prescribed by the firm's

Table 23–1   The planning–controlling cycle

Planning	*Controlling*	*Controlling*	*Planning*
Setting of performance standard	Comparing actual performance to standard	Variance identification analysis and evaluation	Developing corrective action

management information system. Particular attention should be paid to the format of reporting to see that the presentation is precisely tailored to the needs of the responsible executive and that it is timely, complete, and accurate. The design of the system must specify all details of the information flow from the raw data through accumulation, processing, storage, and delivery to the manager.

3. *Interpretation and use of cost information.*   Once reported, comparative cost data must be studied and interpreted by the manager. The analysis of any variances that may appear must be directed toward creating a basis for remedial action, if required.

This chapter will be concerned with the setting of cost standards and the interpretation of control data.

The Setting of Cost Control Standards

Introduction[2]

We are concerned here with determining the costs of manufacturing a product or operating a department or a plant. To do so, we must accumulate and summarize data on costs attributable to the particular *cost center*—product, department, or plant—in which we are interested.

For each cost center, costs are grouped into *cost elements* such as rent, direct labor, direct material, electricity, or insurance. When detailed data are required, elements can be divided into subelements. For example, rent may be broken into subelements pertaining to individual buildings or facilities in an area; insurance can be divided into types such as fire, theft, or inventory insurance; and direct labor costs can be broken down to show those pertaining to different occupations or skills.

In order that data can be presented in units that facilitate management planning and control, costs are usually stated in terms of a time dimension. To illustrate, if one examines the costs of operating a plant for a week, a month, a quarter, or a year, the time period becomes a significant boundary for comparisons and analyses and makes it easier to prescribe action. It is important that

---

[2] It is not within the scope of this text to provide a detailed and comprehensive treatment of cost accounting. Rather, our intention is to present a managerial overview of the field. The definitions presented have been pieced together with the aim of brevity and simplicity. Greater rigor can be obtained by consulting an accounting textbook.

standard time intervals be established for all cost elements and cost centers so that cost data can be accumulated, processed, and reported in a meaningful way.

Another obvious but important point that should be stressed is that the company's accounting records, which delineate cost elements and subelements, should be designed so that they are purpose-oriented. Since the main reason for keeping records is to provide data for management planning and control, the detail introduced should reflect the nature of the firm's operations. Thus, the records of a hotel should be quite specific with regard to building services such as heat, electricity, and janitorial services, whereas a small company that leases its space could simply lump all of these factors together as "rent." The point is simple but significant: the detail should reflect what management needs to know; it should also reflect managerial rank and responsibility. An assembly department is the most significant unit of the firm to the responsible superintendent, so he should be provided with specific information regarding its labor and material. To the company president the costs of this same department may be totaled and presented in aggregate form as an element in a plant summary report. It is important to note that the president can get detailed information if it is desired. The cost accounting system of most companies can, therefore, be visualized as a hierarchy of cost centers, elements, and subelements designed to satisfy effectively and efficiently management's need for cost data from the top to the bottom of the organization.

The term *cost standard* had been defined in various ways, many of which are couched in apparently complex and sophisticated terms. For our purposes, however, a simple working-level definition seems most appropriate. To production management, a cost standard specifies what the managers of the firm feel a cost element or the expenses of a cost center *should* be under prescribed operating conditions. These standards indicate how much should be spent for rent, heat, and direct labor during a certain period, or in order to make a specified quantity of products. A cost standard might indicate, for example, that the labor cost per unit for a ball bearing is $0.030. This is what the ball bearings should cost if the operating conditions—that is, the process and methods, materials, labor skills, and lot size assumed in the formulation of the standard—do in fact exist in actual production. Thus, the operating manager views the cost standard as an indication of "normal," or 100 percent efficiency. If the standard is surpassed, however, and the actual cost of the aforementioned ball bearing is only $0.026 per unit, the assumption is that efficiency of performance is greater than 100 percent—in this case $0.030/$0.026, or approximately 115 percent. Conversely, if the actual costs had risen to $0.035 per ball bearing, the initial interpretation would be that operating efficiency has fallen to $0.030/$0.035, or approximately 86 percent. Before a value judgment of actual performance can be made, of course, there must be a detailed study of any changes that may have taken place in other factors affecting performance; we shall consider this in more detail later when we discuss variance analysis.

Implicit in this discussion of cost standards for control purposes is the fact that these standards are also used for planning purposes. Since they represent desired normal costs or expectations, these standards provide a natural basis for establishing working capital requirements and preparing various operating budgets, as we shall discuss further.

Approaches to Cost Standards

Three principal approaches are used to set up cost standards in industry today:

1. Historical cost standards
2. Estimated cost standards
3. Standard cost standards

In the historical approach, experience in the form of previous "actual costs" provides the basis for determining the cost standard. Actual historical data of this sort can be methodically accumulated in carefully kept company records, often in considerable detail. For example, a furniture manufacturing company might accumulate actual labor costs for producing its dinette sets so that the subelements of cutting, forming, gluing, and finishing can be identified for tables and chairs. These data might then be used as a standard for planning and controlling the operation of each of these activities. On the other hand, the same company could accumulate gross figures only, and plan and control its operations on the basis of the overall cost per dinette set. If the company were very small and did not have very much in the way of formal accounting practices, the source of sales experience data might be the memory of the company's executives. This is not as far-fetched as it might seem, since many small machine shops follow this practice; they keep records only in aggregate terms and often cannot accurately assign costs to specific orders or products. In such situations, memory data, which are subject to all the failings of inaccuracy and lack of detail, constitute the only available basis for establishing cost standards used for pricing as well as planning and controlling plant operations. Clearly, the detailed data accumulated in the first case would provide a better basis for planning and controlling the manufacture of dinette sets than the latter approaches.

All historical approaches have one common basic failing as cost standards—they indicate what each cost *was,* not what it *should* be, which, of course, is the fundamental purpose of a standard. Even if nothing has changed and the historical data are directly relevant, management will still be unable to assess accurately the efficiency of performance. For this reason, many companies assign improvement targets when employing historical data. For example, the furniture company could strive to reduce the labor cost of dinette sets recorded in the previous production lot by 5 or 10 percent. It is hoped that in this way an improvement trend can be initiated and maintained. But this device merely circumvents the fundamental question of 100 percent efficiency or normal expectancy. Indeed, the feasibility of the cost-reduction target established is not directly assessable. An unrealistic target can be unfair to the work force, and the response may be grievances, unionization, or even a strike.

Often the weaknesses of historical cost standards are compounded because conditions change. The design of the dinette set may be altered, for example, and even a small change in styling or materials will invalidate historical data. Production methods and tools may be improved and labor base rates increased. If we are concerned with the total costs, changes in taxes, insurance, rent, heat, and executive salaries (to mention only a few) could also have an impact on the validity of historical cost data.

Clearly, all of these problems are compounded if the degree of rigor in data accumulation declines. Gross records and memory data reduce even further the usefulness of historical standards for purposes of control and improvement trend analysis. However, a heavy investment designed to ensure the accumulation of complete, accurate, and detailed experience data is not really the solution. "Three-decimal-place" data accuracy cannot overcome the basic failings of historical standards: the fact that they deal with actual rather than ideal costs and that they are unable to cope with changes in operating conditions.

Estimated Cost Standards

One way to overcome the weakness of historical cost standards is to formulate estimated costs. Using this approach, management tries to estimate what costs should be and what they will be over a particular period or for a particular production lot. Although the concept of 100 percent efficiency is useful, management must forecast actual as well as ideal costs. Management would agree that 100 percent efficiency should be attained and even surpassed if possible, but it is of more immediate importance to know what the costs will be at present levels of operating efficiency. Overoptimistic estimates can produce cost overruns and operating losses; if actual costs, reflecting present operating efficiency, are not competitive, a loss of business may result. It would be simply poor business to divorce a concern with efficiency from the development of realistic cost standards.

Historical data usually serve as a point of departure for setting estimated cost standards. Firms that employ this approach usually take pains to accumulate detailed experience data. Future conditions, including expected product design changes and new methods, are included in the analysis in an effort to extrapolate meaningful standards from actual past costs. Subjective assessments of the efficiency of various parts or predictions of improvements to come are developed so that "should" costs may be formulated. Although this process is subjective, it should not be immediately dismissed as worthless. Experienced estimators can formulate reasonably accurate assessments of efficiency. Because of their experience they have developed a "feel" for operations and costs that can be quite useful.

There is often justification for using intuitively estimated standards. When a company embarks on a new product venture, for example, information to support the development of standard costs is just not available. In other situations—say, an aerospace firm bidding on a government contract—time may not be avail-

able for the establishment of standard costs or the associated costs may be pro-
hibitive.

However, for companies that continuously manufacture standardized products,
estimated cost standards can be quite useful for planning and controlling their
operations. For those companies, methods and materials are apt to be comparatively fixed and the entire *modus operandi* well defined and understood. Therefore, experienced estimators can effectively assess efficiency levels and improvement trends to generate cost standards that are "reasonable" (meaning that the
error is comparatively small, perhaps about 5 or 10 percent). Such standards
may well satisfy management data needs for purposes of setting prices and labor
performance goals. If greater precision is required (as it is when management
seeks to plan closely and exercise tight control over its operations), the more
precise standard cost approach is used.

Standard Labor Costs

Underlying the formulation of standard costs is the concept of normal, or 100
percent, efficiency. Therefore, we will first define the word *normal* in terms of a
typical manufacturing company. At the risk of oversimplifying, we will then
divide all manufacturing costs per unit of product into three categories: direct
labor, direct material, and overhead. The treatment of these cost elements by the
standard cost approach will demonstrate the nature of this method and suggest
how standard costs can be developed for other cost centers such as plants or departments and for cost elements such as rent, heat, and supervision.

The starting point in the development of standard labor costs is to determine
how the product will be made. The overall process must be defined and a sound
method developed for each operation. Facilities, tools, and fixtures must be specified, and a standard method for performing each task must be established. The
workplace layout of materials and tools must also be detailed, as well as the
precise sequence of motions that will be followed by the operator. An appropriate labor measurement technique, say, direct time study or predetermined time
values, is then employed to measure the standard time ($\overline{T}$). If an incentive factor is used, an output standard time (T_o) will be developed, which will be the
basis for determining the standard labor cost when multiplied by the appropriate
labor base rate for each task or operation. Thus,

$$C_L = T_o \times \text{BR}$$

where C_L = standard direct labor cost per unit
           T_o = output standard time per unit
           BR = base rate of labor skill used

If there are many operations in the production process, this formula is modified
as follows:

$$C_L = \sum_{i=1}^{n} (T_{oi} \times \text{BR}_i)$$

where T_{oi} = output standard for operation i
   BR_i = base rate applicable to operation i
   n = number of operations in the process

To illustrate, let us consider the operations involved in the manufacture of table tops for the dinette sets that we discussed previously, namely, cutting, forming, and finishing. The relevant data are summarized in Table 23–2.

Table 23–2   Manufacturing summary: dinette table top

Operation	Output Standard per Unit (in minutes)	Labor Occupation Number	Base Rate (per hour)	$T_o \times BR$ (in percent)
1. Cutting	5.0	1047	$2.40	$\frac{5.0}{60} \times 2.40 = 0.20$
2. Forming	15.0	1050	3.00	$\frac{15}{60} \times 3.00 = 0.75$
3. Finishing	20.0	1051	3.30	$\frac{20}{60} \times 3.30 = 1.10$

$$C_L = \sum_{i=1}^{3} T_{oi} \times BR_i = 0.20 + 0.75 + 1.10$$
$$= \$2.05 \text{ per table top}$$

Standard Cost for Direct Material

The material content of a product depends upon its configuration. Decisions made regarding the product's form, features, and such operating characteristics as weight and strength will determine what kinds of materials will be used and in what quantities. Material quantity is also affected by the manufacturing process used since it will determine material shrinkage and losses due to spoilage or rejects. In the manufacture of round dinette table tops from square wooden boards, for example, the material content of the table tops is the wooden boards, yet the scraps produced in shaping the tops cannot be used. This is termed *shrinkage*. Calculations regarding the number of square feet of wood needed per table top must also reflect normal production losses due to splintering of the wood and workmanship errors. Here, a loss factor of perhaps 2 percent is added to cover the cost of wood purchased and ruined.

Determination of the material content of each product is a joint decision. Participating departments should include sales, design engineering, quality assurance, and reliability engineering. A satisfactory level of product effectiveness is sought through adjustments in material specifications and the elimination of redundant components. The capabilities of the process will be introduced by manufacturing personnel. An evaluation of the costs will be made in terms of specifications and tolerances for length, thickness, and tensile strength. The purchasing department will furnish information on available materials and components and their prices.

Value analysis, an activity undertaken by the purchasing department, will seek to match the right part or material with the purpose of the product. The final outcome of this group deliberation will be a unit bill of material (UBM) for the product. When the UBM is carefully priced for the optimal quantity of product, a standard material unit cost can be established. For the dinette table tops, the materials to be purchased would be expressed as "board feet of rock maple wood per unit." The standard cost for this material would be expressed as "16 square feet of Specification 1001 rock maple at $0.30 per square foot, or $4.80 per unit."

Estimation of the standard overhead cost per unit requires the following steps:

1. The operating volume or production rate for a specific period must be projected. Typically, this projection will take the form of "so many" units per year. In some instances, companies will attempt to develop standard overhead costs for smaller time periods, perhaps on a semiannual, quarterly, or even monthly basis. Usually, however, production rates are forecast annually.

2. For the same specified period, all overhead cost elements such as insurance, heat, light, power, building depreciation, and supervision are also projected. Historical data are used for this purpose, as well as cost quotations, which can be obtained from the suppliers of these services. As indicated in our earlier discussion of break-even analysis, many of the overhead costs are not fixed but are considered to be "semivariable" since their magnitude depends upon production volume. For this reason, as in break-even analysis, the usual approach is to project the magnitude of each cost element for two separate volumes that include the anticipated level of operation. The total overhead cost can then be summed up graphically as in Figure 23–2,

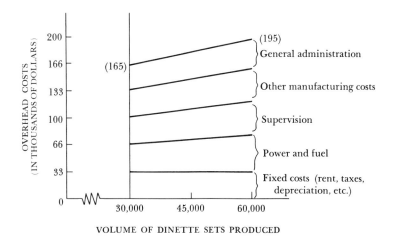

Figure 23–2   Graphic summation of overhead cost of the ABC Manufacturing Company cutting department. Overhead cost projection for year 197—

which depicts projections of the component operating costs incurred by the manufacturer of dinette sets. Here we see that the total overhead cost of manufacturing dinette sets varies from $165,000 for an annual volume of 30,000 units to $195,000 when 60,000 units are produced. Thus, at the anticipated volume of 45,000 sets, an overhead cost of $180,000 is projected, which would mean a standard overhead cost of $4.00 per set. Within the given volume range, these costs are assumed to vary in linear fashion as depicted, but this assumption is not technically correct since the mode of change associated with any given volume is subject to great variation. The supervision cost, for example, would follow a step pattern; each step upward in cost accompanying an increase in volume would reflect the need to add a supervisor. However, linear approximations prove satisfactory for cost assignment and control purposes where the objectives are to make realistic assignments of the overhead costs to the products manufactured and to provide a basis for evaluating the actual costs incurred so that cost estimating and control can be made more effective. In this respect experience has justified the linear approximation.

In Figure 23–3 the line 0C is significant because it indicates how the projected overhead costs will be assigned to the dinette sets produced. Such a line is commonly termed the *overhead liquidation line*, and its slope ($4.00 per set) is referred to as the *overhead liquidation rate*. At the projected volume of 45,000 units, the overhead cost assignment, or liquidation, is exactly equal to the projected overhead cost of $180,000. However, below this volume the liquidation of overhead lags behind the anticipated rate of incurring these costs; above the

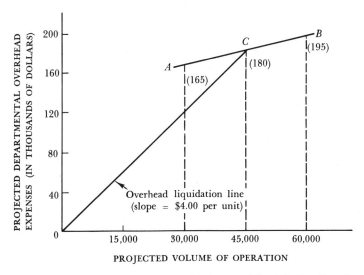

Figure 23–3 Overhead expense projection and liquidation line for the cutting department

critical volume, overliquidation will occur, assuming that the cost projections (line *AB*) are reasonably accurate, so that more costs will be liquidated than are actually incurred. The characteristics of the liquidation line and its significance for management will be discussed in greater depth in the remainder of this chapter.

Comparative Evaluation of Actual Costs

Standard manufacturing costs provide a basis for evaluating whether the results (that is, the products) delivered have been achieved at a reasonable cost. Initially, these standards are used for planning what costs *should* be incurred in a particular production program. They describe what manpower, materials, and other expenses should be expected, and operating effectiveness is measured simply by how the actual costs compare with these standards. Thus, the objective is not merely the gross measurement of efficiency but also the gaining of insights that will guide future planning and operations. By helping to identify and correct performance faults and, of equal importance, errors in planning and standards, modifications can be made for future manufacturing programs.

This process is frequently called *variance analysis*. It involves a detailed examination of those production operations pinpointed as trouble spots by a series of inclusive cost comparisons that link cost deviations (actual versus standard) to possible causes. To illustrate, let us return to the manufacturer of dinette sets. We will suppose that the operating records of the ABC Furniture Manufacturing Company have been carefully reviewed and that the actual cost data as summarized in Table 23–3 have been obtained from those records for the month and year ending December 197–. We will use the cost standards developed earlier as the basis for comparative analysis, and we will examine each of the major cost categories—labor, material, and overhead—separately.

Labor Variance Analysis

The cause of the labor variance of $1,092.30 experienced by finishing department No. 100 during December must be determined before corrective managerial action can be taken. There are three principal causes of labor variance: volume, rate, and efficiency. Volume variance arises when the actual operating level is different from the forecast operating volume that appears in the labor budget. In the case at hand, for example, the actual number of table tops finished could be larger than the 3,000 scheduled, which might explain why the actual labor expenditure was more than the budgeted, or standard, figure. If this were in fact the case, the standard cost would be modified to reflect the actual operating level, thereby facilitating a meaningful assessment of the production of table tops.

Similarly, the labor budget was prepared using a forecast labor, or base, rate —in this case $3.30 per hour. If the rate actually paid was more than this figure, a cost variance could result, so the standard budget should be modified to reflect the actual rate paid. It should be noted in passing that when forecasting errors

Table 23–3 ABC Furniture Manufacturing Company—
Summary of operating costs, December 197–

Labor
Finishing department No. 100 (job No. 365)

Schedule	3,000 table tops A-1 dinette set
Standard time per table top	20 minutes
Total labor hours required	1,000 hours
Labor assignment	
Inspection 1051, base rate	$3.30 per hour
Total labor budget	$3,300
Actual labor expenditure	$4,392.30
Total labor variance	($1,092.30)

Material
Job No. 365

Schedule	3,000 table tops A-1 dinette set
Standard material per table	16 square feet Grade A rock maple at $0.30 per square foot
Standard material cost per table	$4.80
Total materials budget for job	$14,400
Actual material cost	$15,246
Total material variance	($846)

Overhead
Cutting department No. 60 (the only function of this department is to make special oval table tops for Model A-1 dinette set)

Forecast production for year ending December 197–	45,000 table tops
Projected overhead costs allocated to this department	$180,500
Standard overhead liquidation	$4.00 per unit
Actual overhead expenses	$180,000

---

of this sort occur, the causes should be pinpointed so that future planning can be more realistic. This applies particularly to time and rate variances, where such errors should be few because of union–management contracts or the establishment of standard occupation descriptions and base rates.

The efficiency variance is generally more significant, for it compares the actual time recorded with the standard time given in the labor budget. If the plant was unable to meet the productivity level predicted, management must find out why; competitive pressures make it mandatory to have high plant efficiency. If the actual labor productivity is above or below normal, an investigation is in order. In either event, one should check to see if the standard was correct and accurately applied to the production procedures used.

Returning to our example, in order to find out the causes of the variance, the following information was obtained from the superintendent of the finishing department:

Finishing department No. 100 (job No. 365)

Actual number of units finished	3,300
Actual average time per unit	22 minutes
Actual base rate paid (second shift)	$3.63
Actual labor hours	1,210
Actual labor cost	1,210 hours × $3.63 per hour
	= $4,392.30

With this additional information, we can now assign a cause to the labor variance.

Volume variance (V_v) If we wish to know how much variance would have occurred if only the volume had changed and the base rate and standard time had been as budgeted, we may apply the formula

$$V_v = (V_{std} - V_{act}) \times \overline{T}_{std} \times BR_{std}$$

where V_v = volume variance
V_{std} = forecast or standard volume (number of units)
V_{act} = actual volume (or number) of units produced
$\overline{T}_{std}$ = forecast standard time
BR_{std} = forecast base rate

Substituting the data in this example, we get[3]

$$V_v = (3,000 - 3,300 \text{ units}) \times \frac{20}{60} \text{ hr. per unit} \times \$3.30 \text{ per hr.}$$

$$= -300 \times \frac{20}{60} \times \$3.30 = -\$330$$

These calculations mean that $330 of the total variance of $1,092.30 can be attributed to the fact that more table tops were made than had been anticipated. The responsibility for this portion of the variance belongs to the scheduling or forecasting functions, not to the finishing department.

Rate variance (V_r) If we wish to isolate that part of the variance that occurred because of a change in the base rate, we use the formula

$$V_r = (BR_{std} - BR_{act}) \times \overline{T}_{act} \times V_{act}$$

where V_r = rate variance
BR_{std} = forecast base rate
BR_{act} = actual base rate
$\overline{T}_{act}$ = actual mean time per table top
V_{act} = actual number of units produced

Substituting the relevant data from our example, we get

$$V_r = (\$3.30 - \$3.63) \times \frac{22}{60} \text{ hr. per unit} \times 3,300 \text{ units}$$

$$= -\$0.33 \times \frac{22}{60} \times 3,300$$

$$= -\$399.30$$

[3] A negative value for V_v means "loss variance."

These figures reveal that the base rate paid was larger than the one budgeted; there was thus a total negative variance of $729.30 as a result of poor forecasting of the quantity of table tops that would be made and the base rate that would be paid.

Efficiency variance (V_e) The remaining variance must then be due to "inefficiency." The efficiency variance is calculated using the following formula:

$$V_e = \bar{T}_{std} - \bar{T}_{act} \times BR_{std} \times V_{act}$$

Substituting in our data, we obtain

$$V_e = (20\text{--}22) \text{ min. per unit} \times \$3.30 \text{ per hr.} \times 3,300 \text{ units}$$

$$= -2 \times \frac{\$3.30}{60} \times 3,300 = -\$363$$

These figures indicate that the inability of the plant to achieve the anticipated productivity level was responsible for $363 of the total variance.

In calculating the labor rate and efficiency, a sticky problem arises when both are favorable (positive) or, as here, unfavorable (negative). Figure 23–4 helps to illustrate the computation of these variances. It can be seen that $363.00 has been assigned to labor efficiency and rate variances in each of the lightly shaded blocks. But an arbitrary rate is needed in order to assign the variance of $36.30 which lies in the heavily shaded area. The most commonly used approach is to assume that this is part of the rate variance, which is what we did in the example. It should be noted, however, that rate variance implies a forecasting error, whereas efficiency variance implies a factory performance problem; the inherent implications and responsibilities are quite different.

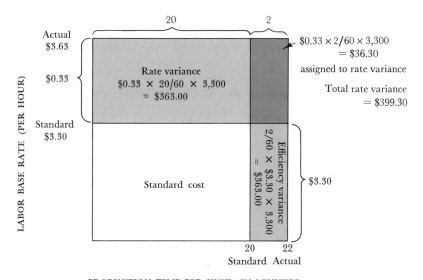

Figure 23–4   Calculation of labor efficiency and rate variances

The results of this variance analysis were summarized for management review as follows:

Finishing department No. 100 (job No. 365)   December 197–
Labor variance analysis

Variance Cause	Variance Amount
Volume	− $ 330.00
Rate	− 339.30
Efficiency	− 363.00
Total labor variance	− $1,092.30

Further review of this problem provided the following information:

1. An unexpected surge in Christmas sales made it necessary to produce the additional 300 sets. This fact will be considered when preparing the production forecast and schedule for the last quarter of the following year.
2. The Christmas surge affected the entire line of dinette sets offered by the firm. The heavy work load caused the finishing of these table tops to be assigned to the night shift, where a labor base rate differential of 10 percent is paid, which accounted for the rate variance. If the forecast calls for continuing the high level of plant activity, attention will be given to the possibility of increasing the plant's capacity by acquiring additional machines.
3. The night shift in the finishing department had been a token force to handle emergencies or rush orders. The heavy work load assigned made it necessary to hire new employees, which necessitated attendant training costs; this fact manifested itself in the department's inability to achieve the standard productivity levels.

It was concluded that the planning standards were satisfactory and could be used in the future, but that closer attention should be paid to scheduling so that night shift differentials and new employee training costs could be anticipated and minimized. Other factors that might also have caused labor variance included spoilage, quality, machine assignment, employee morale, use of overtime, and subcontracting.

Material Variance Analysis

In a similar fashion, it is possible to divide the total (negative) material variance of $846 encountered on job No. 365 into volume, rate, and efficiency components. An investigation of job No. 365 revealed the following significant data:

Job No. 365: Actual data

Actual price paid for Grade A rock maple was $0.28 per square foot
Actual usage was 16.5 square feet per unit
Volume as previously noted was 3,300 units

The formulas and figures used in computing the material variances will now be illustrated.

Volume variance (MV_v) As before, we ask how much variance would have occurred if only the volume had changed while the rate (price) and usage remained as forecast. The formula is

$$MV_v = (V_{std} - V_{act}) \times \bar{U}_{std} \times P_{std}$$

where U_{std} = forecast number of square feet of Grade A rock maple needed per table top

P_{std} = forecast price for Grade A rock maple (in dollars per square foot)

Substituting the relevant figures, we get

$$MV_v = (3,000 - 3,300) \times 16 \text{ sq. ft. per unit} \times \$0.30 \text{ per sq. ft.}$$
$$= -300 \times 16 \times \$0.30$$
$$= -\$1,440$$

We can see that the change in volume, if the standards are correct, should have produced a greater material variance than the $-\$846$ actually experienced. Unlike the labor situation above, the planning standards here were apparently surpassed by actual accomplishments.

Rate variance (MV_r) If we wish to find how much material variance occurred because of a change in rate—here, material price—we use the equation

$$MV_r = (\bar{P}_{std} - \bar{P}_{act}) \times \bar{U}_{act} \times V_{act}$$

where P_{act} = actual price paid for Grade A rock maple

$\bar{U}_{act}$ = actual number of square feet used per table top

Here, too, the convention of assigning a shaded area variance to the rate cause is followed, as depicted in Figure 23–4. Substituting the data from our example into the equation, we get

$$MV_r = (\$0.30 - \$0.28) \times 16.5 \times 3,300$$
$$= \$0.02 \times 16.5 \times 3,300$$
$$= \$1.089$$

This outcome suggests that the price concession obtained by the purchasing department had a substantial positive impact.

Efficiency variance (MV_e) Finally, the remaining variance is due to using more or less material per unit than planned. It is found by calculating

$$MV_e = (\bar{U}_{std} - \bar{U}_{act}) \times \bar{P}_{std} \times V_{act}$$

or

$$MV_e = (16 - 16.5) \times \$0.30 \times 3,300$$
$$= -\$495$$

The inability of the plant to maintain the planned material productivity level resulted in a negative variance of $495, which accounted for approximately 59 percent of the total loss incurred on this job.

The calculation of the rate (price) and efficiency component of the material variance is illustrated in Figure 23–5. For management review purposes, a material variance table was prepared:

Job No. 365: Material variance analysis

Variance Cause	Variance Amount
Volume	− $1,440
Rate	1,089
Efficiency	− 495
Total material variance	− $ 846

Further study concerning the possible causes of this problem revealed that:

1. The increased production schedule permitted the ordering of larger quantities of Grade A rock maple than had been predicted; therefore, an unexpected large-quantity price saving was enjoyed.
2. The assignment of job No. 365 to an inexperienced night shift caused heavier than usual spoilage and shrinkage rates, which resulted in an above-normal amount of maple being used on the average unit.
3. A surge in Christmas sales caused the increased quantity of tables to be scheduled, as previously noted.

Here, too, it was felt that the planning standards were satisfactory and that a trained work force could achieve them. The possibility of enjoying the lower rate for large-quantity purchases was noted. It was agreed that the forecast would be carefully reviewed in the future and that the lower price for maple would be incorporated into the standard if projected volumes seemed to justfy it. Other factors that might have influenced material variances included methods and processes, quality (repairs), and employee morale.

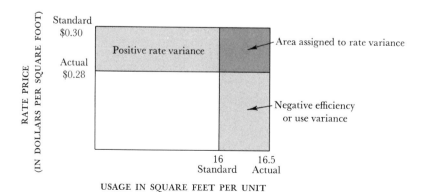

Figure 23–5   The computation of material variance due to rate and efficiency

Overhead Variance Analysis

To explain further how overhead variance is identified and then analyzed into its component parts, let us quickly review how an overhead liquidation rate is set. For the cutting department, for example, total overhead expenses were projected at the beginning of the year for two operating volumes—30,000 and 60,000 units. As in break-even analysis, a chart was drawn on which the two expense points, $165,000 and $195,000, determined the projected overhead expense line. In Figure 23–3 this line is designated AB. An estimated operating volume for the year was then forecast; in this case it was 45,000 sets. In the overhead expense line, point C corresponds to this estimated volume and indicates a projected overhead expense of $180,000. This figure now becomes the standard against which actual expenses will be measured. The line $0C$ is called the *overhead liquidation line,* and its slope, $4.00 per unit, is the rate at which overhead expenses will be liquidated against the units produced in the cutting department. In other words, each set passing through that department will be charged $4.00 of overhead expense. If 45,000 units are actually produced, then the projected $180,000 of overhead expense will be precisely allocated to the Model A-1 dinette sets as planned.

To support the analysis of overhead performance, the following additional information was obtained from the superintendent of the cutting department:

Cutting department No. 60: Operating data for year ending December 197–

Number of Model A-1 tables produced:	44,000
Actual overhead expenses assigned:	$180,000
Overhead expenses liquidated at $4.00 per unit:	$176,000
Overhead underliquidation (unfavorable variance):	($4,000)

It is now possible to analyze this variance into its component causes. For purposes of overhead variance analysis, there are two main categories of causes: volume and efficiency (or spending).

Volume variance (OHV_v) As before, the purpose of the volume variance is to isolate the portion of variance that occurred because the actual volume of operation deviated from the one forecast. The volume variance is found by using the equation

$$OHV_v = L \times V_{act} - [OH]_{act}^{std}$$

where $[OH]_{act}^{std}$ = the forecast (standard) expense for the actual volume
   L = overhead liquidation rate
   V_{act} = actual volume of units produced

The value of $[OH]_{act}^{std}$ must be obtained from the projection curve. It is the value along the line AB in Figure 23–6 that corresponds to 44,000 units, which is $179,000. Figure 23–6 gives a magnified view of that portion of Figure 23–3 which is in the immediate vicinity of the originally forecast volume of 45,000. The $[OH]_{act}^{std}$ can also be calculated from the original data. The overhead cost for 30,000 units of output is $165,000, while for 60,000 units it is $195,000.

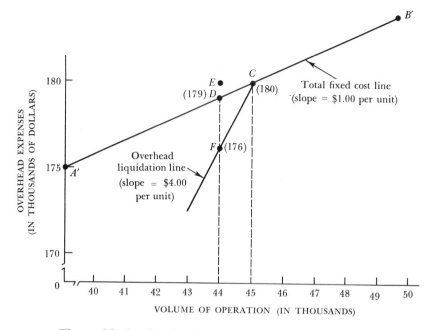

Figure 23–6   Overhead expenses—cutting department

Therefore, overhead costs increase at a rate of $1.00 per unit of output for production over 30,000 units. For 44,000 units the overhead cost is $165,000 + $(44,000 − 30,000) \times \$1.00 = \$179,000$. The calculation of OHV_v is thus:

$$OHV_v = (\$4.00 \times 44,000) - \$179,000$$
$$= \$176,000 - \$179,000 = -\$3,000$$

Point F in Figure 23–6 gives us the first term $(L \times V_{act})$ on the right-hand side of the equation, and DF represents the "volume variance." Because the actual volume was below the forecast one, decreases in both standard overhead expenses (line AB) and the overhead expenses liquidation (line $0C$) are to be expected; the rate used was based upon the forecast volume of 45,000 units and is only "right" for that level of operation. These decreases occur at different rates, however, as shown in the figure, and a volume variance is generated as a consequence.

Efficiency variance (OHV_e) The efficiency variance identifies the portion of the variance that occurred because actual expenses deviated from standard. It is simply the difference between the actual overhead expenses incurred and the "standard expenses" for the actual volume. The equation is:

$$OHV_e = [OH]^{std}_{act} - OH_{act}$$

where OH_{act} = actual overhead expenses assigned

Substituting the applicable data to this equation, we get

$$OHV_e = \$179{,}000 - \$180{,}000 = -\$1{,}000$$

In Figure 23–6, point E indicates that actual expenses of $\$180,000$ are incurred at an actual volume of 44,000. An overhead variance table can now be prepared for management's consideration.

Cutting department: Overhead variance analysis

Variance Cause	Variance Amount
Volume	$-\$3,000$
Efficiency	$- 1,000$
Total overhead variance	$-\$4,000$

In this case management's attention was focused principally on the efficiency variance for the cutting department viewed as a cost center. Subsequent investigation and analysis pinpointed as culprits the two cost elements power and rent, since the rate for each of these elements rose above the predicted levels. It was agreed that future estimation of standard overhead expense levels and therefore liquidation rates would reflect the higher rates.

Use of Costs Standards

The relationship of variance analysis to the planning and control of cost operations is depicted in Figure 23–7. It might be noted that three significant aspects of this relationship will influence the effectiveness of the management cycle: standards control, reporting format, and responsibility assignments.

Standards Control

Setting and maintaining cost standards is a major responsibility; the timeliness and accuracy of these standards must be the specific duty of a designated mana-

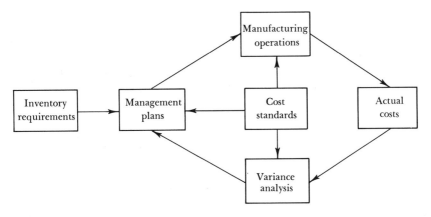

Figure 23–7   Planning and control of the cost of manufacturing operations

ger, such as the head of the industrial engineering department or the accounting department, since a system of periodic checking of processes and methods must be established. In addition, a chart of accounts specifying cost elements and cost centers must be clearly set forth. The accounting function must be set up to accumulate actual costs in a manner that will make available the categories of cost needed for variance analysis and other cost comparisons desired by management. For cost elements such as labor and materials, the necessary subcategories must be isolated for cost-reporting purposes. These subcategories should conform to the categories for which standards have been deemed necessary. For example, it is not uncommon to set labor standards for each operation in a process, and the collection of actual costs must accommodate this. Furthermore, a policy must also be formulated regarding inspection, repair, and test activities. Frequently a percentage of direct labor costs constitutes the standard for inspection and repair costs; this is the practice in the electronics and aerospace industries. In such situations, monitoring simply involves a comparison of actual expenditures with the predetermined amount allocated for these purposes. Wherever possible, standard test costs per unit are established and standard labor variance analysis techniques are applied. But in electronics, aerospace, and other dynamic process industries, tests are often unpredictable because of the need to diagnose and correct performance standards that are difficult to set and maintain. In those cases, monitoring is accomplished by simply comparing the actual costs with a historically derived percentage of direct labor.

Similarly, subcategories of materials such as supplies (hardware) or direct materials (metals, chemicals) can be established. Here too, policy decisions made by top operating management determine where standards will be set and consequently how actual costs will be accumulated.

In the area of overhead expenses, a major policy decision is the allocation of fixed company-wide expenses, such as plant protection and maintenance and executive salaries, to particular departments and products. When the production process results in joint products or by-products, this becomes a particularly difficult task. Frequently, firms settle for the best judgment of management. The problem is also complicated when, as in a job-lot shop, a single department makes a wide variety of items. A common solution to this latter problem is to allocate overhead expenses on the basis of the ratio of direct labor costs (or hours) to the number of process (machine) hours applied.

Reporting Format

The reporting of cost comparisons, including historical trends and operating variances, must be in a format that may be easily understood and easily used by management. Tabular summaries, bar and pie charts, and trend-line charts are among the formats most frequently used for this purpose. For variance analysis reporting, summary tables of the sort used here for the ABC Furniture Manufacturing Company example are typical. The format should include a section for summarizing the reasons for variance in order to facilitate the selection of corrective action. The three important responsibilities in this process are: design of the reporting format, preparation of reports, and analysis of variance causes. Each responsibility must be assigned to specific departments or specific individuals. (Some companies set up permanent or ad hoc committees or study teams to analyze specific variances such as machine-shop labor elements or departmental overhead liquidation.)

Responsibility Assignments

The need to make cost planning and control a definite responsibility within the manufacturing organization has already been stressed. Actually, however, it would be correct to say that it should be everyone's responsibility. Cost standards are generally established for the administrative units defined by the firm's organization chart. Each division, department, and often each identifiable subunit, such as a production center within a firm's manufacturing department, is established as a cost center. The cost standards for these units will comprise many cost elements emanating both from within (labor, salaries, materials, supplies) and from without (corporate assessment of executive salaries, interest on capital, plant expansion and renovations, heat, light, power). The term *budget* is often used to describe these standards. Indeed, the preparation of a cost center's budget is one of the principal applications of cost standards. A budget represents the planned expenses for operating the cost center over a specific period of time—generally a month, quarter, or year. Effectiveness is assessed by comparing the actual costs with the budget, both on a total basis and for specific cost elements. The latter analysis is important because cost elements outside the department are beyond the control of the departmental manager and he should not be held responsible for variances in those elements. A good measure of performance limits its assessment to those items that are controllable. This distinction is important; notice, for example, that in the sample budget form shown in Table 23–4, costs are labeled "controllable" and "noncontrollable." Control evaluations of this manager's performance are made only within the former category.

For product cost centers, as distinct from administrative cost centers, cost elements include costs associated with administrative cost centers such as production planning, industrial engineering, and assembly, each of which contributes a predetermined piece of the product cost. Since the "piece" is that portion of the costs applicable to the respective departments, control over costs in product cost centers is exercised indirectly by monitoring the performance of the administrative units themselves. If each department's cost is held within the standard and if the distribution of cost pieces to particular products is correct, then the planned product cost will be realized. The second "if" is critical. The distribution of departmental costs, particularly those incurred by service units such as quality control, among particular products should be reviewed periodically.

Table 23–4 Factory overhead

	Month		Year to Date	
	Actual	Budget	Actual	Budget
Direct Labor				
Expense Liquidation				
Net Overhead				
Percent of direct labor				
Expenditure variance—gain or loss				
Volume variance—gain or loss				
Salaries and Wages				
101 Supervision				
102 Office and clerical				
109 Inspection and test				
110 Stock handling				
112 Other labor				
115 Internal maintenance—labor				
119 Operating power equipment				
122 Taking of inventories				
125 Replacement of parts				
128 Overtime allowance—direct				
130 Overtime allowance—indirect				
132 Make-up payments				
134 Idle time				
136 Training				
138 Night work allowance				
140 Salaries redistributed				
Total Salaries and Wages				
Employee Service Expense				
Supplies and Other Expense				
201 Stationery and office supplies				
210 Shop supplies (202–210)				
215 Power supplies				
217 Gasoline				
228 Blueprints				
306 Telephone and telegraph				
307 Travel, other reimbursable expense				
312 Trucking and transportation				
317 Rearrangement of plant facilities				
330 Power				
350 Equipment rentals				
368 Scrap disposal credits				
370 Miscellaneous expense				
390 Expenses transferred from other depts.				
395 Expenses transferred between sections				
Total Supplies and Other Expense				
Maintenance				
235 Internal maintenance material				
403 Machinery and motors				
404 Electrical accessories				

Table 23–4 (continued)

	Month		Year to Date	
	Actual	Budget	Actual	Budget
405 Autos, trucks, and trailers				
406 Shop equipment, office furniture, and appliances				
407 Power plant facilities				
408 Buildings				
409 Outside facilities				
410 Elevators and escalators				
411 Test equipment				
412 Tools, jigs, dies, molds, fixtures				
413 U.S. Government owned facilities				
419 Preventive maintenance				
Total Maintenance				
Total Expense Controllable by Section				
Fixed and Assessed Charges				
501 Depreciation				
503 Taxes				
504 Insurance				
505 Building operation				
506 Rent purchased				
507 Specific cleaning				
508 Plant protection				
651 Sectional administration				
652 Manufacturing engineering				
653 Inspection				
654 Quality coordination				
655 Cost estimating				
661 Plant administration				
662 Plant engineering				
663 Assembly stockrooms				
666 Production control				
667 Mail service				
668 Material control				
671 Restaurant				
674 Financial				
675 Personnel				
681 Purchasing				
682 Purchased material inspection				
683 Receiving				
Total Fixed and Assessed Charges				
(Not Controllable by Section)				
Total Expense				
701 Expense credits				
728 Overtime premium transaction				
Total Expense Credits				
Net Overhead				
Assessed to other sections or underassessed				

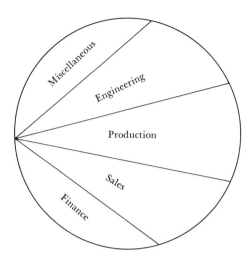

Figure 23–8 Partitioning of a firm's activities into primary activity groups

The Firm as a Cost System

The direct relationship between organizational responsibility and cost makes it possible to view the firm as a cost system. Figure 23–8 depicts the beginning of the organizational process in which the activities of the firm are divided into the primary categories: production, sales, engineering, finance, and miscellaneous. Then, in Figure 23–9, a more detailed breakdown is given in a typical organization chart for the production phase. For each administrative unit (or cost center), budgets are developed that reflect appropriate cost elements or total costs attributable to a cost center. At each higher level, the budget includes the costs of the lower cost centers. For example, the assembly department budget includes the (budgeted) costs of all production centers that feed it. Thus, it can be said that costs flow upward from the elements at the lowest levels and are accumulated and matched against elemental standards and unit budgets at various ascending levels to provide management with the planning–controlling data it needs. The arrows in Figure 23–9 represent the cost flow within the manufacturing system.

When the concept of a cost system is expanded to include the entire firm, the merging of budgets and costs, including the revenue budgets provided by the sales department, leads to company-wide profit and loss projections, break-even analysis, and sales-dollar analysis that will support top-level executive decisions.

Other Uses of Cost Standards

In addition to its use in profit and loss, break-even, and sales-dollar analyses, standard cost data can be used for deciding product contribution or inputs for economy studies and for formulating significant ratios such as the ratios of direct

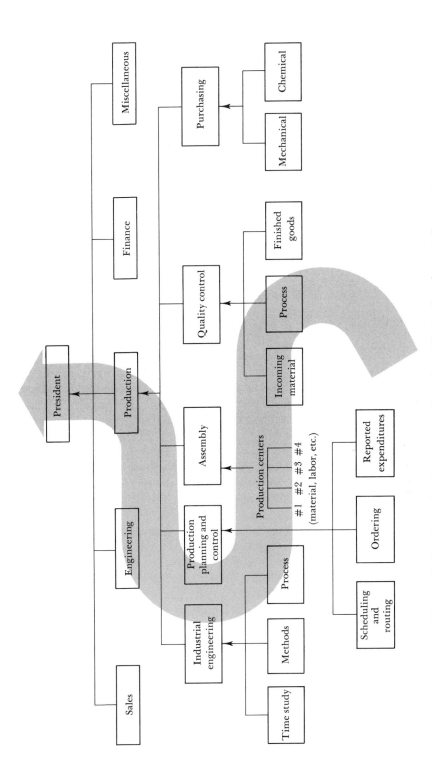

Figure 23–9 A production organization chart illustrating the cost flow pattern

to indirect labor, capital to labor, and material to labor. Trend lines for these ratios can show the changing nature of an industry. To illustrate, the growing importance, in percentage terms, of test labor in the electronic equipment manufacturing industry prompted most firms to invest in automatic plug-in testers. The failure of one firm in an industry to introduce labor-saving equipment would be reflected in a capital-to-labor ratio that was lower than the average. For example, many knitwear manufacturers in the North now realize that Southern mills have lost, in a relative sense, their previous labor base rates advantage and that these mills have maintained their competitive edge by introducing new materials and labor-saving devices; this fact is reflected in their operating characteristics. Indeed, the cost structure of textile yarn manufacturers as an industry has now come to resemble that of the chemical industry, which is "low labor intensive."

Cost Reduction Programs

The need to control operating costs and cut them wherever possible is widely recognized in our competitive economy. Industries that are "labor intensive" focus attention on work simplification drives or on acquiring labor-saving devices. This has been the approach in the garment and knitwear industries, for example. If material costs are dominant, as in the assembly of home appliances such as TV sets, management concentrates its efforts on improving buying practices or on introducing substitute materials. Highly capital-intensive industries tend to emphasize the maintenance of their plant loads by bidding for work at break-even prices, instituting around-the-clock operations (as in the paper and chemical industries), and developing expensive maintenance programs.

To be truly effective, cost reduction efforts should result in the lowering of the cost standard used for planning and control. Furthermore, since the savings are not realized until the lower costs are achieved, a mechanism such as a management committee is needed that can implement the indicated changes in operating techniques and material specifications. Goals are typically set for these programs in terms of reduced costs, say, a 10 percent decrease in repair costs. Experience indicates that such target setting, if the goals are realistic, is an important first step in successful cost-reduction programs. It is imperative that the targets do not merely represent wishful thinking, but rather that they reflect careful study and experienced judgment. As a rule, industrial engineers are assigned the task of setting labor cost targets and material cost reductions so that these targets will reflect the considered judgment of top purchasing and engineering personnel. At this point the use of teams or committees is advisable. Each team should be given definite areas and targets for study and each should have authority to make recommendations. Ideally, the team should be composed of representative talents from the functional areas that must cope with the problem. A team working on material cost reduction should have a member from purchasing, engineering, manufacturing, cost estimating, and quality control to ensure that the team will have all the skills needed to identify and evaluate available alternatives. Other skills that may prove necessary, such as industrial engineering, should be available on call. Time limits for meeting the target should also be set, and the savings achieved should be reported regularly. Teams that meet their targets should be rewarded and should receive wide recognition. RCA has successfully employed this team, target, and time approach; winning team members are given a weekend with their families at a luxury resort with all expenses paid. This program has paid handsome dividends for the company.

Another effective device in cost reduction programs is the suggestion box. Here, too, employees are usually rewarded financially for ideas that produce savings. Leading suggestions receive special recognition and gifts. The potential for cost savings is surprisingly great when a factory supervisory group and a work force are efficiency-conscious. Many companies provide work-simplification courses free in order to equip interested employees with tools that will help them improve their work methods. The Socony Mobil Oil Company is among the foremost advocates of this training. One important point that strongly influences the effectiveness of suggestion programs is the promptness and objectivity with which ideas are evaluated and rewards are calculated. For this reason, some large corporations maintain a separate department just to administer these programs.

An Overview of Cost Standards

The magnitude and flow of costs within a production system stem from activities that embrace functions such as purchasing, production planning, and control on the one hand, and problem areas such as inventory, productivity, and capital acquisition on the other. Indeed, these activities constitute an inventory of problem issues and factors that must be resolved so that the production system can be designed and operated effectively. This textbook is intended to assist the manager in the decision making required to direct the operation of the sum and parts that constitute a production system, and cost control is one of the most important aspects of that decision process.

Questions and Problems

1. Why are good cost records so important to the management of a manufacturing firm? Are they equally important to the management of a hospital?
2. How are cost data used in control?
3. How does a "standard cost" system relate to accounting conventions? Budgetary control?
4. What are the limitations of historical cost standards? Do estimated cost standards overcome these limitations?
5. How are standard costs and actual costs related?
6. What are *labor variances*? How can these variances occur?
7. What are *volume, rate, material,* and *efficiency variances*? Are there other types of cost variances? If so, what are they?

8. What role do cost standards play in budget setting?
9. What is the connection between organization structure and cost responsibility? Does this mean that a cost system is in fact a minor image of the organization structure?
10. Why are cost centers used in some firms?
11. How must the cost and information systems relate?
12. "The cost system is the major feedback system in a firm." Discuss.
13. What are the weaknesses in a cost-reduction program?
14. What are the measures of overall firm cost effectiveness; that is, how can a company's management be measured?
15. Is it possible to design a cost system for a firm independent of the firm's product, mode of operation, and organization?
16. Since the controller is normally in charge of a company's cost system, and since time studies set standards for the cost system, shouldn't time studies be part of the controller's function?

References

Anthony, R. N., *Management Accounting Principles*, rev. ed., Irwin, Homewood, Ill., 1970.

————, *Planning and Control Systems*, Harvard University Press, Cambridge, Mass., 1965.

Beyer, R., *Profitability Accounting for Planning and Control*, Ronald Press, New York, 1963.

Bruns, W. J., and De Coster, D. T., *Accounting and Its Behavioral Implications*, McGraw-Hill, New York, 1969.

Dearden, J., *Cost and Budget Analysis*, Prentice-Hall, Englewood Cliffs, N.J., 1962.

English, J. M. (ed.), *Cost Effectiveness: Economic Evaluation of Engineered Systems*, Wiley, New York, 1968.

Gordon, M. J., and Shillinglaw, G., *Accounting—A Management Approach*, 4th ed., Irwin, Homewood, Ill., 1969.

Grant, E. L., and Ireson, W. G., *Principles of Engineering Economy*, 5th ed., Ronald Press, New York, 1970.

Henrici, S. B., *Standard Costs for Manufacturing*, 3rd ed., McGraw-Hill, New York, 1963.

Horngren, C. T., *Cost Accounting—A Managerial Emphasis*, 2nd ed., Prentice-Hall, Englewood Cliffs, N.J., 1967.

Reynolds, A., and Coates, J., *Cost Control for Production Management*, Machinery Technical Books, New York, 1962.

Shillinglaw, G., *Cost Accounting—Analysis and Control*, rev. ed., Irwin, Homewood, Ill., 1967.

Stedry, A. R., *Budget Control and Cost Behavior*, Markham, Chicago, Ill., 1967.

Vatter, P., *Standards for Cost Analysis*, General Accounting Office, Washington, D.C., 1969.

Appendix

Glossary of PERT Terms   709

Table of Logarithms   711

Present Value of $1.00   713

Present Value of $1.00 Received Annually for x Years   714

Glossary of PERT Terms

ACTIVITY   A time-consuming operation required in the execution of a task. It is represented on a network or flow chart by an arrow. One *event* is separted from another by an *activity*. An activity cannot be started until its preceding event has been accomplished, and a succeeding event cannot be accomplished until the activity is complete.

ACTIVITY TIMES   Estimates of the elapsed time required to complete an activity in a specified manner. Three time estimates must be given for each activity: *most likely, optimistic,* and *pessimistic.*

ACTUAL DATE   The date on which the completion of an event is accomplished.

BEGINNING EVENT   That event which marks the beginning of the actual work constituting an activity.

CRITICAL PATH   That particular sequence of activities in a network comprising the most rigorous time constraint in the accomplishment of the end event; i.e., it is the most time-consuming path.

END EVENT   That event which signifies the completion of a network.

EVENT   A meaningful, specific accomplishment (physical or intellectual) in the program plan, which is recognizable at a particular instant in time. Events do not consume time or resources and are normally represented in the network by circles or rectangles.

EXPECTED ACTIVITY TIME (t_e) The mathematical most probable time, computed using the beta distribution, which incorporates the *optimistic* (a), *most likely* (m), and *pessimistic* (b) times.

$$t_e = \frac{a + 4m + b}{6}$$

EXPECTED TIME (T_E) A summation of the *expected times* $(t_e\text{'s})$ (measured from the initial event) of the activities preceding the event. It is expressed as a "calendar date" or time elapsed from the initial event, and it denotes the expected completion time. Where more than one activity precedes an event, the date used is the latest one.

LATEST TIME (T_L) The latest calendar date by which an event can be completed and still meet the schedule requirement of the end event.

MOST LIKELY TIME (*m*)   A probable time that (1) could reasonably be expected by the person best qualified to judge, and (2) would occur most often if the activity could be repeated numerous times under exactly the same conditions.

NEGATIVE SLACK   Slack time is *negative* when the expected date of an event, T_E, is later than the computed latest date, T_L. When a scheduled or desired date for the end event is required in computations, it becomes the T_L for the end event; thus, when the computed T_E is later than the scheduled date, slack time along the most critical path will be negative in value. Other paths may be either negative or positive when this condition exists.

NETWORK   A diagramatic representation of a program or project plan showing the sequence and interrelationship of significant finite events to achieve end objectives under planned resource applications and performance specifications. A network may be revised by adding or deleting events or activities as required during the life of a program or project.

OPTIMISTIC TIME (*a*)   A minimum time that (1) is experienced only when unusually good luck is experienced and (2) has no more than one chance in 100 of being realized.

PESSIMISTIC TIME (*b*)   A maximum time that (1) can occur only if unusually bad luck is experienced and (2) has only one chance in 100 of being realized. This time should reflect the possibility of an initial failure and a fresh start; it should not, however, be influenced by the possibility of strikes or "acts of God," such as floods or fires.

POSITIVE SLACK   Slack time is *positive* when the expected date, T_E, is earlier than the computed latest date, T_L. When a scheduled or desired date for the end event is required in computations, it becomes the T_L for the end event; thus when the computed expected date of the end event is earlier than the scheduled date, slack time along the most critical path will be positive in value.

PRECEDING EVENT (BEGINNING EVENT)   That event which marks the beginning of the actual work constituting an activity.

PROBABILITY (*P_r*)   The numerical value is derived from normal probability tables after calculating the quotient of scheduled date in weeks minus the expected date in weeks divided by the standard deviation of the event.

SCHEDULE DATE (T_S)   A predetermined calendar date designated by the program or contract and assigned to an event; it specifies a date for the planned accomplishment of that event.

SLACK TIME   The difference in time, when comparing the expected dates with the latest dates, required to complete the most critical path and each subcritical path, from the starting event to the end event, in the network. Slack time is $T_L - T_E$.

STANDARD DEVIATION OF AN ACTIVITY   A statistical measure of the uncertainty of establishing the expected time of an activity; it is computed from the formula $(b - a)/6$.

STANDARD DEVIATION OF AN EVENT   A statistical measure of the uncertainty associated with the achievement of the expected date for an event. It is calculated by computing the square root of the sum of the squares of the activity standard deviation on the most time-consuming path leading to a particular *event*.

VARIANCE (σ^2)   In *PERT*, variance for an activity is the square of the activity standard deviation. Variance of an event is the sum of the activity variances along the most time-consuming path leading to the particular event.

Table of logarithms

N	0	1	2	3	4	5	6	7	8	9	1	2	3	4	5	6	7	8	9
															Proportional Parts				
10	0000	0043	0086	0128	0170	0212	0253	0294	0334	0374	4	8	12	17	21	25	29	33	37
11	0414	0453	0492	0531	0569	0607	0645	0682	0719	0755	4	8	11	15	19	23	26	30	34
12	0792	0828	0864	0899	0934	0969	1004	1038	1072	1106	3	7	10	14	17	21	24	28	31
13	1139	1173	1206	1239	1271	1303	1335	1367	1399	1430	3	6	10	13	16	19	23	26	29
14	1461	1492	1523	1553	1584	1614	1644	1673	1703	1732	3	6	9	12	15	18	21	24	27
15	1761	1790	1818	1847	1875	1903	1931	1959	1987	2014	3	6	8	11	14	17	20	22	25
16	2041	2068	2095	2122	2148	2175	2201	2227	2253	2279	3	5	8	11	13	16	18	21	24
17	2304	2330	2355	2380	2405	2430	2455	2480	2504	2529	2	5	7	10	12	15	17	20	22
18	2553	2577	2601	2625	2648	2672	2695	2718	2742	2765	2	5	7	9	12	14	16	19	21
19	2788	2810	2833	2856	2878	2900	2923	2945	2967	2989	2	4	7	9	11	13	16	18	20
20	3010	3032	3054	3075	3096	3118	3139	3160	3181	3201	2	4	6	8	11	13	15	17	19
21	3222	3243	3263	3284	3304	3324	3345	3365	3385	3404	2	4	6	8	10	12	14	16	18
22	3424	3444	3464	3483	3502	3522	3541	3560	3579	3598	2	4	6	8	10	12	14	15	17
23	3617	3636	3655	3674	3692	3711	3729	3747	3766	3784	2	4	6	7	9	11	13	15	17
24	3802	3820	3838	3856	3874	3892	3909	3927	3945	3962	2	4	5	7	9	11	12	14	16
25	3979	3997	4014	4031	4048	4065	4082	4099	4116	4133	2	3	5	7	9	10	12	14	15
26	4150	4166	4183	4200	4216	4232	4249	4265	4281	4298	2	3	5	7	8	10	11	13	15
27	4314	4330	4346	4362	4378	4393	4409	4425	4440	4456	2	3	5	6	8	9	11	13	14
28	4472	4487	4502	4518	4533	4548	4564	4579	4594	4609	2	3	5	6	8	9	11	12	14
29	4624	4639	4654	4669	4683	4698	4713	4728	4742	4757	1	3	4	6	7	9	10	12	13
30	4771	4786	4800	4814	4829	4843	4857	4871	4886	4900	1	3	4	6	7	9	10	11	13
31	4914	4928	4942	4955	4969	4983	4997	5011	5024	5038	1	3	4	6	7	8	10	11	12
32	5051	5065	5079	5092	5105	5119	5132	5145	5159	5172	1	3	4	5	7	8	9	11	12
33	5185	5198	5211	5224	5237	5250	5263	5276	5289	5302	1	3	4	5	6	8	9	10	12
34	5315	5328	5340	5353	5366	5378	5391	5403	5416	5428	1	3	4	5	6	8	9	10	11
35	5441	5453	5465	5478	5490	5502	5514	5527	5539	5551	1	2	4	5	6	7	9	10	11
36	5563	5575	5587	5599	5611	5623	5635	5647	5658	5670	1	2	4	5	6	7	8	10	11
37	5682	5694	5705	5717	5729	5740	5752	5763	5775	5786	1	2	3	5	6	7	8	9	10
38	5798	5809	5821	5832	5843	5855	5866	5877	5888	5899	1	2	3	5	6	7	8	9	10
39	5911	5922	5933	5944	5955	5966	5977	5988	5999	6010	1	2	3	4	5	7	8	9	10
40	6021	6031	6042	6053	6064	6075	6085	6096	6107	6117	1	2	3	4	5	6	8	9	10
41	6128	6138	6149	6160	6170	6180	6191	6201	6212	6222	1	2	3	4	5	6	7	8	9
42	6232	6243	6253	6263	6274	6284	6294	6304	6314	6325	1	2	3	4	5	6	7	8	9
43	6335	6345	6355	6365	6375	6385	6395	6405	6415	6425	1	2	3	4	5	6	7	8	9
44	6435	6444	6454	6464	6474	6484	6493	6503	6513	6522	1	2	3	4	5	6	7	8	9
45	6532	6542	6551	6561	6571	6580	6590	6599	6609	6618	1	2	3	4	5	6	7	8	9
46	6628	6637	6646	6656	6665	6675	6684	6693	6702	6712	1	2	3	4	5	6	7	7	8
47	6721	6730	6739	6749	6758	6767	6776	6785	6794	6803	1	2	3	4	5	5	6	7	8
48	6812	6821	6830	6839	6848	6857	6866	6875	6884	6893	1	2	3	4	4	5	6	7	8
49	6902	6911	6920	6928	6937	6946	6955	6964	6972	6981	1	2	3	4	4	5	6	7	8
50	6990	6998	7007	7016	7024	7033	7042	7050	7059	7067	1	2	3	3	4	5	6	7	8
51	7076	7084	7093	7101	7110	7118	7126	7135	7143	7152	1	2	3	3	4	5	6	7	8
52	7160	7168	7177	7185	7193	7202	7210	7218	7226	7235	1	2	2	3	4	5	6	7	7
53	7243	7251	7259	7267	7275	7284	7292	7300	7308	7316	1	2	2	3	4	5	6	6	7
54	7324	7332	7340	7348	7356	7364	7372	7380	7388	7396	1	2	2	3	4	5	6	6	7
N	0	1	2	3	4	5	6	7	8	9	1	2	3	4	5	6	7	8	9

Table of logarithms (continued)

N	0	1	2	3	4	5	6	7	8	9	1	2	Proportional Parts 3	4	5	6	7	8	9
55	7404	7412	7419	7427	7435	7443	7451	7459	7466	7474	1	2	2	3	4	5	5	6	7
56	7482	7490	7497	7505	7513	7520	7528	7536	7543	7551	1	2	2	3	4	5	5	6	7
57	7559	7566	7574	7582	7589	7597	7604	7612	7619	7627	1	2	2	3	4	5	5	6	7
58	7634	7642	7649	7657	7664	7672	7679	7686	7694	7701	1	1	2	3	4	4	5	6	7
59	7709	7716	7723	7731	7738	7745	7752	7760	7767	7774	1	1	2	3	4	4	5	6	7
60	7782	7789	7796	7803	7810	7818	7825	7832	7839	7846	1	1	2	3	4	4	5	6	6
61	7853	7860	7868	7875	7882	7889	7896	7903	7910	7917	1	1	2	3	4	4	5	6	6
62	7924	7931	7938	7945	7952	7959	7966	7973	7980	7987	1	1	2	3	3	4	5	6	6
63	7993	8000	8007	8014	8021	8028	8035	8041	8048	8055	1	1	2	3	3	4	5	5	6
64	8062	8069	8075	8082	8089	8096	8102	8109	8116	8122	1	1	2	3	3	4	5	5	6
65	8129	8136	8142	8149	8156	8162	8169	8176	8182	8189	1	1	2	3	3	4	5	5	6
66	8195	8202	8209	8215	8222	8228	8235	8241	8248	8254	1	1	2	3	3	4	5	5	6
67	8261	8267	8274	8280	8287	8293	8299	8306	8312	8319	1	1	2	3	3	4	5	5	6
68	8325	8331	8338	8344	8351	8357	8363	8370	8376	8382	1	1	2	3	3	4	4	5	6
69	8388	8395	8401	8407	8414	8420	8426	8432	8439	8445	1	1	2	2	3	4	4	5	6
70	8451	8457	8463	8470	8476	8482	8488	8494	8500	8506	1	1	2	2	3	4	4	5	6
71	8513	8519	8525	8531	8537	8543	8549	8555	8561	8567	1	1	2	2	3	4	4	5	5
72	8573	8579	8585	8591	8597	8603	8609	8615	8621	8627	1	1	2	2	3	4	4	5	5
73	8633	8639	8645	8651	8657	8663	8669	8675	8681	8686	1	1	2	2	3	4	4	5	5
74	8692	8698	8704	8710	8716	8722	8727	8733	8739	8745	1	1	2	2	3	4	4	5	5
75	8751	8756	8762	8768	8774	8779	8785	8791	8797	8802	1	1	2	2	3	3	4	5	5
76	8808	8814	8820	8825	8831	8837	8842	8848	8854	8859	1	1	2	2	3	3	4	5	5
77	8865	8871	8876	8882	8887	8893	8899	8904	8910	8915	1	1	2	2	3	3	4	4	5
78	8921	8927	8932	8938	8943	8949	8954	8960	8965	8971	1	1	2	2	3	3	4	4	5
79	8976	8982	8987	8993	8998	9004	9009	9015	9020	9025	1	1	2	2	3	3	4	4	5
80	9031	9036	9042	9047	9053	9058	9063	9069	9074	9079	1	1	2	2	3	3	4	4	5
81	9085	9090	9096	9101	9106	9112	9117	9122	9128	9133	1	1	2	2	3	3	4	4	5
82	9138	9143	9149	9154	9159	9165	9170	9175	9180	9186	1	1	2	2	3	3	4	4	5
83	9191	9196	9201	9206	9212	9217	9222	9227	9232	9238	1	1	2	2	3	3	4	4	5
84	9243	9248	9253	9258	9263	9269	9274	9279	9284	9289	1	1	2	2	3	3	4	4	5
85	9294	9299	9304	9309	9315	9320	9325	9330	9335	9340	1	1	2	2	3	3	4	4	5
86	9345	9350	9355	9360	9365	9370	9375	9380	9385	9390	1	1	2	2	3	3	4	4	5
87	9395	9400	9405	9410	9415	9420	9425	9430	9435	9440	0	1	1	2	2	3	3	4	4
88	9445	9450	9455	9460	9465	9469	9474	9479	9484	9489	0	1	1	2	2	3	3	4	4
89	9494	9499	9504	9509	9513	9518	9523	9528	9533	9538	0	1	1	2	2	3	3	4	4
90	9542	9547	9552	9557	9562	9566	9571	9576	9581	9586	0	1	1	2	2	3	3	4	4
91	9590	9595	9600	9605	9609	9614	9619	9624	9628	9633	0	1	1	2	2	3	3	4	4
92	9638	9643	9647	9652	9657	9661	9666	9671	9675	9680	0	1	1	2	2	3	3	4	4
93	9685	9689	9694	9699	9703	9708	9713	9717	9722	9727	0	1	1	2	2	3	3	4	4
94	9731	9736	9741	9745	9750	9754	9759	9763	9768	9773	0	1	1	2	2	3	3	4	4
95	9777	9782	9786	9791	9795	9800	9805	9809	9814	9818	0	1	1	2	2	3	3	4	4
96	9823	9827	9832	9836	9841	9845	9850	9854	9859	9863	0	1	1	2	2	3	3	4	4
97	9868	9872	9877	9881	9886	9890	9894	9899	9903	9908	0	1	1	2	2	3	3	4	4
98	9912	9917	9921	9926	9930	9934	9939	9943	9948	9952	0	1	1	2	2	3	3	4	4
99	9956	9961	9965	9969	9974	9978	9983	9987	9991	9996	0	1	1	2	2	3	3	3	4
N	0	1	2	3	4	5	6	7	8	9	1	2	3	4	5	6	7	8	9

Present value of $1.00

Periods	2%	4%	6%	8%	10%	12%	14%	16%	18%	20%	22%	24%	26%	28%	30%	40%	50%
1	0.980	0.962	0.943	0.926	0.909	0.893	0.877	0.862	0.847	0.833	0.820	0.806	0.794	0.781	0.769	0.714	0.667
2	0.961	0.925	0.890	0.857	0.826	0.797	0.769	0.743	0.718	0.694	0.672	0.650	0.630	0.610	0.592	0.510	0.444
3	0.942	0.889	0.840	0.794	0.751	0.712	0.675	0.641	0.609	0.579	0.551	0.524	0.500	0.477	0.455	0.364	0.296
4	0.924	0.855	0.792	0.735	0.683	0.636	0.592	0.552	0.516	0.482	0.451	0.423	0.397	0.373	0.350	0.260	0.197
5	0.906	0.822	0.747	0.681	0.621	0.567	0.519	0.476	0.437	0.402	0.370	0.341	0.315	0.291	0.269	0.186	0.131
6	0.888	0.790	0.705	0.630	0.564	0.507	0.456	0.410	0.370	0.335	0.303	0.275	0.250	0.227	0.207	0.133	0.088
7	0.871	0.760	0.665	0.583	0.513	0.452	0.400	0.354	0.314	0.279	0.249	0.222	0.198	0.178	0.159	0.095	0.059
8	0.853	0.731	0.627	0.540	0.467	0.404	0.351	0.305	0.266	0.233	0.204	0.179	0.157	0.139	0.123	0.068	0.039
9	0.837	0.703	0.592	0.500	0.424	0.361	0.308	0.263	0.225	0.194	0.167	0.144	0.125	0.108	0.094	0.048	0.026
10	0.820	0.676	0.558	0.463	0.386	0.322	0.270	0.227	0.191	0.162	0.137	0.116	0.099	0.085	0.073	0.035	0.017
11	0.804	0.650	0.527	0.429	0.350	0.287	0.237	0.195	0.162	0.135	0.112	0.094	0.079	0.066	0.056	0.025	0.012
12	0.788	0.625	0.497	0.397	0.319	0.257	0.208	0.168	0.137	0.112	0.092	0.076	0.062	0.052	0.043	0.018	0.008
13	0.773	0.601	0.469	0.368	0.290	0.229	0.182	0.145	0.116	0.093	0.075	0.061	0.050	0.040	0.033	0.013	0.005
14	0.758	0.577	0.442	0.340	0.263	0.205	0.160	0.125	0.099	0.078	0.062	0.049	0.039	0.032	0.025	0.009	0.003
15	0.743	0.555	0.417	0.315	0.239	0.183	0.140	0.108	0.084	0.065	0.051	0.040	0.031	0.025	0.020	0.006	0.002
16	0.728	0.534	0.394	0.292	0.218	0.163	0.123	0.093	0.071	0.054	0.042	0.032	0.025	0.019	0.015	0.005	0.002
17	0.714	0.513	0.371	0.270	0.198	0.146	0.108	0.080	0.060	0.045	0.034	0.026	0.020	0.015	0.012	0.003	0.001
18	0.700	0.494	0.350	0.250	0.180	0.130	0.095	0.069	0.051	0.038	0.028	0.021	0.016	0.012	0.009	0.002	0.001
19	0.686	0.475	0.331	0.232	0.164	0.116	0.083	0.060	0.043	0.031	0.023	0.017	0.012	0.009	0.007	0.002	0.001
20	0.673	0.456	0.312	0.215	0.149	0.104	0.073	0.051	0.037	0.026	0.019	0.014	0.010	0.007	0.005	0.001	
21	0.660	0.439	0.294	0.199	0.135	0.093	0.064	0.044	0.031	0.022	0.015	0.011	0.008	0.006	0.004	0.001	
22	0.647	0.422	0.278	0.184	0.123	0.083	0.056	0.038	0.026	0.018	0.013	0.009	0.006	0.004	0.003	0.001	
23	0.634	0.406	0.262	0.170	0.112	0.074	0.049	0.033	0.022	0.015	0.010	0.007	0.005	0.003	0.002		
24	0.622	0.390	0.247	0.158	0.102	0.066	0.043	0.028	0.019	0.013	0.008	0.006	0.004	0.003	0.002		
25	0.610	0.375	0.233	0.146	0.092	0.059	0.038	0.024	0.016	0.010	0.007	0.005	0.003	0.002	0.001		
26	0.598	0.361	0.220	0.135	0.084	0.053	0.033	0.021	0.014	0.009	0.006	0.004	0.002	0.002	0.001		
27	0.586	0.347	0.207	0.125	0.076	0.047	0.029	0.018	0.011	0.007	0.005	0.003	0.002	0.001	0.001		
28	0.574	0.333	0.196	0.116	0.069	0.042	0.026	0.016	0.010	0.006	0.004	0.002	0.002	0.001	0.001		
29	0.563	0.321	0.185	0.107	0.063	0.037	0.022	0.014	0.008	0.005	0.003	0.002	0.001	0.001	0.001		
30	0.552	0.308	0.174	0.099	0.057	0.033	0.020	0.012	0.007	0.004	0.003	0.002	0.001	0.001			
40	0.453	0.208	0.097	0.046	0.022	0.011	0.005	0.003	0.001	0.001							
50	0.372	0.141	0.054	0.021	0.009	0.003	0.001	0.001									

Present value of $1.00 received annually for x years

Periods	2%	4%	6%	8%	10%	12%	14%	16%	18%	20%	22%	24%	25%	26%	28%	30%	40%	50%
1	0.930	0.962	0.943	0.926	0.909	0.893	0.877	0.862	0.847	0.833	0.820	0.806	0.800	0.794	0.781	0.769	0.714	0.667
2	1.942	1.886	1.833	1.783	1.736	1.690	1.647	1.605	1.566	1.528	1.492	1.457	1.440	1.424	1.392	1.361	1.224	1.111
3	2.884	2.775	2.673	2.577	2.487	2.402	2.322	2.246	2.174	2.106	2.042	1.981	1.952	1.923	1.868	1.816	1.589	1.407
4	3.808	3.630	3.465	3.312	3.170	3.037	2.914	2.798	2.690	2.589	2.494	2.404	2.362	2.320	2.241	2.166	1.849	1.605
5	4.713	4.452	4.212	3.993	3.791	3.605	3.433	3.274	3.127	2.991	2.864	2.745	2.689	2.635	2.532	2.436	2.035	1.737
6	5.601	5.242	4.917	4.623	4.355	4.111	3.889	3.685	3.498	3.326	3.167	3.020	2.951	2.885	2.759	2.643	2.168	1.824
7	6.472	6.002	5.582	5.206	4.868	4.564	4.288	4.039	3.812	3.605	3.416	3.242	3.161	3.083	2.937	2.802	2.263	1.883
8	7.325	6.733	6.210	5.747	5.335	4.968	4.639	4.344	4.078	3.837	3.619	3.421	3.329	3.241	3.076	2.925	2.331	1.922
9	8.162	7.435	6.802	6.247	5.759	5.328	4.946	4.607	4.303	4.031	3.786	3.566	3.463	3.366	3.184	3.019	2.379	1.948
10	8.983	8.111	7.360	6.710	6.145	5.650	5.216	4.833	4.494	4.192	3.923	3.682	3.571	3.465	3.269	3.092	2.414	1.965
11	9.787	8.760	7.887	7.139	6.495	5.988	5.453	5.029	4.656	4.327	4.035	3.776	3.656	3.544	3.335	3.147	2.438	1.977
12	10.575	9.385	8.384	7.536	6.814	6.194	5.660	5.197	4.793	4.439	4.127	3.851	3.725	3.606	3.387	3.190	2.456	1.985
13	11.343	9.986	8.853	7.904	7.103	6.424	5.842	5.342	4.910	4.533	4.203	3.912	3.780	3.656	3.427	3.223	2.468	1.990
14	12.106	10.563	9.295	8.244	7.367	6.628	6.002	5.468	5.008	4.611	4.265	3.962	3.824	3.695	3.459	3.249	2.477	1.993
15	12.849	11.118	9.712	8.559	7.606	6.811	6.142	5.575	5.092	4.675	4.315	4.001	3.859	3.726	3.483	3.268	2.484	1.995
16	13.578	11.652	10.106	8.851	7.824	6.974	6.265	5.669	5.162	4.730	4.357	4.033	3.887	3.751	3.503	3.283	2.489	1.997
17	14.292	12.166	10.477	9.122	8.022	7.120	6.373	5.749	5.222	4.775	4.391	4.059	3.910	3.771	3.518	3.295	2.492	1.998
18	14.992	12.659	10.828	9.372	8.201	7.250	6.467	5.818	5.273	4.812	4.419	4.080	3.928	3.786	3.529	3.304	2.494	1.999
19	15.678	13.134	11.158	9.604	8.365	7.366	6.550	5.877	5.316	4.844	4.442	4.097	3.942	3.799	3.539	3.311	2.496	1.999
20	16.351	13.590	11.470	9.818	8.514	7.469	6.623	5.929	5.353	4.870	4.460	4.110	3.954	3.808	3.546	3.316	2.497	1.999
21	17.011	14.029	11.764	10.017	8.649	7.562	6.687	5.973	5.384	4.891	4.476	4.121	3.963	3.816	3.551	3.320	2.498	2.000
22	17.658	14.451	12.042	10.201	8.772	7.645	6.743	6.011	5.410	4.909	4.488	4.130	3.970	3.822	3.556	3.323	2.498	2.000
23	18.292	14.857	12.303	10.371	8.883	7.718	6.792	6.044	5.432	4.925	4.499	4.137	3.976	3.827	3.559	3.325	2.499	2.000
24	18.914	15.247	12.550	10.529	8.985	7.784	6.835	6.073	5.451	4.937	4.507	4.143	3.981	3.831	3.562	3.327	2.499	2.000
25	19.523	15.622	12.783	10.675	9.077	7.843	6.873	6.097	5.467	4.948	4.514	4.147	3.985	3.834	3.564	3.329	2.499	2.000
26	20.121	15.983	13.003	10.810	9.161	7.896	6.906	6.118	5.480	4.956	4.520	4.151	3.988	3.837	3.566	3.330	2.500	2.000
27	20.707	16.330	13.211	10.935	9.237	7.943	6.935	6.136	5.492	4.964	4.524	4.154	3.990	3.839	3.567	3.331	2.500	2.000
28	21.281	16.663	13.406	11.051	9.307	7.984	6.961	6.152	5.502	4.970	4.528	4.157	3.992	3.840	3.568	3.331	2.500	2.000
29	21.844	16.984	13.591	11.158	9.370	8.022	6.983	6.166	5.510	4.975	4.531	4.159	3.994	3.841	3.569	3.332	2.500	2.000
30	22.396	17.292	13.765	11.258	9.427	8.055	7.003	6.177	5.517	4.979	4.534	4.160	3.995	3.842	3.569	3.332	2.500	2.000
40	27.355	19.793	15.046	11.925	9.779	8.244	7.105	6.234	5.548	4.997	4.544	4.166	3.999	3.846	3.571	3.333	2.500	2.000
50	31.424	21.482	15.762	12.234	9.915	8.304	7.133	6.246	5.554	4.999	4.545	4.167	4.000	3.846	3.571	3.333	2.500	2.000

Index

ABC inventory, 433–434
Acceptable quality level (AQL), 648, 655–657, 662
Acceptance sampling, attribute sampling, 650, 651
 inspection, 648–650
 sampling plans, 650
 variable sampling, 650
Acceptance theory of authority, 48
Accounting life, 197
Activating, 595–596
Aggregate inventory concepts, 432–433
Aggregate inventory limitations, 434
Alpha errors, 656–657, 661
Anatomical factors, 233–234
Anthropometric data, 235
Applied research, 89, 90
Arithmetic mean, 665
Attribute sampling, 651–661
Authorization, 553
Automation, 494
Average outgoing quality (AOQ), 657–660, 662
Average outgoing quality level (AOQL), 659, 662
Average value, 201, 205–209
Average (normal) worker, 286, 297–299
Averaging down, 374

Barth, Carl, 8
Basic data, 313–316
Behavioral system, 239
Beta errors, 656–657, 661
Binomial distribution, 670
Blanket purchase order, 368–369
Block diagram, 503
Book value, 193
Breakdown and ordering, 564–565
Breakdown costs, 612
Breakdown distributions, 613–616
Breakdown maintenance, 611–612, 612–613
Break-even charts, 150–153, 464–467
 fixed costs, 150

uses, 153
variable costs, 150
Bureau of Labor Statistics, 677

Capital acquisitions, 180
Capital demand curve, 182
Capital planning, 180
Capital recovery factor, 207
Capital rejection rate, 96, 184–187
 absolute return, 187
 fluctuating effective rates, 185–186
 long-term minimum rates, 186
 postponability, 187
 supply of funds, 187
Capital supply, external sources, 184
 internal sources, 183
Central tendency, 665
Coefficient of correlation, 387
Coefficient of determination, 396
Combined reliability, 140
Confidence limits, 398
Constant product failure rates, 138
Consumer's risk, 656–657
Continuous production, 545
Contribution ratio, 163–164
Control charts, 662–672
 for attributes, 670–672
 concepts, 663–664
 example for variables, 667–669
 use, 664–665
 for variables, 665–669
Controllable costs, 699
Correlation analysis, basic concept, 391–392
 coefficient of correlation, 387
 coefficient of determination, 396
 confidence limits, 398
 explained variation, 395–396
 normal equations, 394–395
 regression coefficient, 393
 regression line, 393–394
Cost budget accounts, 700–701
Cost center, 680
Cost effectiveness, 124
Cost elements, 680

Cost reduction program, 704
Costs and organizational relationships, 678–679
Cost standards, 679–680, 681–682
Cost standard systems, 697
Cost trends, 676–677
Cost variance analysis, 688–692
  efficiency variance, 691–692
  labor variance, 688–690
  rate variance, 690
  volume variance, 690
Current ratio, 676
Cyclegraph, 270

Decision making, background, 54–56
Decision theory, 56
Defense contracting, 370–371
Demand characteristics, 677
Demand forecasts, basic concept, 385–387
Departmentation, 37–38
  customer, 41
  functional, 40
  geographical, 41
  matrix, 43
  product, 40–41
  project, 42–43
Depreciation, 184, 194–196, 227
  declining-balance, 195–196
  straight-line, 194–195
  sum-of-digits, 196
Direct costs, 196
Directive to work (DTW), 553
Discounted cash flow, 201, 216–220
Discounted value, 190–191, 217, 218
Dovetail scheduling, 578–579
Dun's Review & Modern Industry, 676

Economic (or technological) life, 198, 214–215
Economic lot size, 422, 429–431, 547, 550
Economic order quantity models, basic model, 422–424
  general evaluation, 435
  limitations, 424–425
  nomographs, 427
  noninstantaneous replacement, 428–431
  order tables, 425–426
  quantity discounts, 431
  reorder time, 428
Economic Research Service, 677
Efficiency, 251–252

Employee selection, interviewing, 333
  recruiting, 333
  testing, 334–335
Engineering release, 563–564
Estimated cost standards, 683–684
Exception principle, 373
Expense streams, 191
Exponential distribution, 529

Failure rates (FR), 133, 136
Firm as a cost system, 702
Follow-the-leader decisions, 59
Forecasting, concept, 387–388
  definition, 389
  dilemma, 388
  form, 389
  reliability, 389
  time factors, 389
Forecasting methods, correlation analysis, 391–398
  educated guess, 390–399
  time series, 399–411
Forecast variation, least squares regression, 412–413
  simple moving average, 411–412
  weighted moving average, 412–413
Forward buying, 374–375
Functional authority, 46

Gantt, Henry L., 8, 555
Gantt charts, 555–563
Gantt chart symbols, 559
Gantt load charts, 556–558, 578
Gantt program progress charts, 560–563, 577
Gantt record charts, 560
Gilbreth, Frank and Lillian, 8

Hand-to-mouth buying, 374
Hiring, 336
Historical cost standards, 682–683
Human factors, 233

Income streams, 188–191, 215
Incremental costs, 193
Industrial engineering, 565–566
Infant mortality, 134
Innovation cycle, 88, 93
Inspection, 648–650
Interest costs, 196
Intermittent production, 545
Intuitive decision making, 57–58
Inventory, basic concept, 376–378
Inventory costs of purchased goods, carrying costs, 418–419, 423

Inventory costs of purchased goods
(*continued*)
   procurement costs, 417, 423
   production costs, 420–421
   setup costs, 420
   stockout costs, 419–420, 437–440
Inventory functions, 379–381
   decoupling, 379
   speculative, 381
Inventory models with uncertainty,
   426–440
Inventory systems, fixed order interval,
   442–444
   fixed order size, 440–442

Job analysis, 328–331
Job enlargement, 244–245
Job specifications, 331
Job standardization, 332

Labor productivity, 251
Labor standards, 285
   historical, 287–289
   predetermined, 308–318
   time study, 289–308
   work sampling, 318–324
Layout, basic concepts, 487–488
   dynamics, 488
   employee services, 511
   external balance, 489–491
   fixed material, 496
   internal balance, 491–492
   nonmanufacturing, 512
   process, 495–496
   process services, 511–512
   product, 496
Layout classes, comparisons of,
   498–499
Layout construction, 497–498
Leading time series, 392
Lead time, 363
Learning curves, 631–637
   average man-hours, 632–634
   equations, 632–635
   time to produce next unit, 635
   total man-hours, 634–635
   uses, 635–637
Least common multiple, 211
Left- and right-hand chart, 255, 273
Life expectancy, 133
Linear programing, 75, 168–177
   constant contribution line, 583
   graphic solution, 581–584
   inequalities, 169
   matrix, 169

objective function, 170
   profit maximization, 168–177
   sensitivity, 176
   shadow prices, 175
   simplex solution, 170–177, 584–585
   slack variables, 169
   transportation example, 588–593
Line authority, 46
Line of balance, 597–600
   balance, 600–601
   objective, 597
   program plan, 597–599
   program progress, 599
Location, foreign sites, 481–482
   multiple plants, 472–479
   physical factors, 459–462
   qualitative factors, 468
      factor analysis, 468–469
      point rating, 469–470
   quantitative factors, break-even
      analysis, 464–467
   cost factors, 462–464
   cost summary, 467–468
   labor costs and productivity, 464
   single plant, 470–472
   trends, 479–482
Location of repair work, 551–552
Long-range market forecast, 385
Lot tolerance percent defective
   (LTPD), 656–658, 661, 662

Machine breakpoints, 574–575
Machine life, 197
Make or buy, 371–373, 543–544
Maintenance concept, 609–611
Maintenance crew size, 625–631
Management, definition, 28–29
   by exception, 35
   span of control, 38–40
Management functions, 31
   assembling resources, 44–45
   controlling, 48–49
      timing, 50–51
      universality concept, 50
   directing, 46–47
      source of authority, 47
      types of authority, 46
   organizing, 37–43
   planning, 33–37
Management theory, behavioral, 30
   decision making, 30
   traditional, 29–30
Man–machine chart, 255, 273–276
Manufacturing quality assurance, 126

MAPI (Machinery and Allied Products Institute), 201, 220–227
 initial net investment, 222, 226
 next-year operating advantage, 221
 next-year tax adjustment, 222
 terminal net investment, 222, 226
 urgency rating, 221, 223, 227
Margin of safety (MS) ratio, 167
Market information, 147
Market research, 88, 93, 146–148
Master scheduling, 553–555
Material variance analysis, 692–695
 efficiency rate, 693
 volume, 693
Materials handling concepts, 516
Materials handling costs, 516–517
Materials handling design, model factors, 523–524
 movement times, 524–525
 quality of equipment, 526
 queuing (waiting line), 527–535
Materials handling effectiveness, 537–539
Materials handling equipment, 518–519
 fixed path, 520–521
 variable path, 522
Materials management, 357
 organization, 358–361
Mean time between failures (MTBF), 133, 137–140
Memomotion, 270
Methods Time Measurement (MTM), 311–312
Micromotion study, 267
Model building and testing, 72
Model limitations, 69
Models, analog, 64
 deterministic, 65
 iconic, 64
 mathematical, 65
 probabalistic, 66
 schematic, 62–63
 simulation, 66, 69
 verbal, 62
Monitoring, 596–601
Monte Carlo simulation, 617–625
Moody's Industrial Manual, 676
Motivation, 239–247
 achievement needs, 242
 need hierarchy, 243
 physiological needs, 242
 psychological needs, 242
 security needs, 242
 social needs, 242

Multiple-activity analysis, 255, 276–277
Multiple sampling, 660–662

Need satisfaction, 243–247
New product design, 90–91
Nomographs, 427
Noncontrollable costs, 699
Normal distribution, 665
Normal scheduling, 577–578

Overtime orders, 369
Operating characteristic (OC) curves, 651–654, 661, 662
Operations management, 2–3
Operator chart, 255
Opportunity costs, 196, 372
Optimization, 71
Overhead costs, 196
Overhead liquidation line, 687
Overhead liquidation rate, 687
Overhead variance analysis, 695–697
 efficiency, 696
 volume, 695

Participation, 245–247
Payback period, 201, 202–205
PERT, 78, 98–100
 activity path, 100, 103
 cost trade-off analysis, 107
 critical path, 107–108
 event, 100
 implementation, 108–110
 network, 100
 network time estimate, 101–103
 slack analysis, 105–107
PERT/COST, 78, 110–112
 budget report, 113
 cost outlook report, 115
 glossary of terms, 709–710
 manpower loading reports, 117
 project summary report, 113
 schedule outlook report, 115
Pilot run, 93
Plant capacity factor, 493
Plant efficiency factor, 493–494
Poisson distribution, 528
Predetermined time values, advantages and limitations, 312–313
 formula, 316–318
 installation, 310–311
 Methods Time Measurement (MTM), 311
 therbligs, 309, 313
Preproduction activities, 552

Present value, 190, 209–214, 217, 218
  average cost, 201, 212–214
  total cost, 201, 209–212
Present worth factor, 212
Preventive maintenance, 611, 612–613
Prime contractor, 371
Principles of motion economy, 263–266
Process chart, 257–259, 277
Process layout analysis, 500–504
Producer's risk, 656–657
Product configuration, 92
Product contribution, 162
Product derating, 142
Product design, production process, 94
  timing, 95
Product development costs, 148
Product diversification, 90
Product effectiveness, 130
  critical characteristics, 131
Product financial plans, 149
Product layout analysis, 504–509
Product line, 145
  balance, 160
  evaluation, 155
    economic feasibility, 148
    market research, 146
  simplification, 156–158
  standardization, 158–166
Product mortality, 136
Product reliability, 122–125
Product revenues, 148
Product safety margins, 141
Production, to order, 546–550
  for stock, 546–550
Production management, 1–3
  history, 7–8
Production order size, 550–551
Production problems, 82
  allocation, 74–75, 160–177, 472–479, 577–596
  competitive, 80–81, 88, 93, 146–148
  inventory, 73–74, 417–450, 509–510
  queuing, 76–77, 527–535
  replacement, 79–80, 201–228
  routing, 78–79, 500–504, 573–577
  search, 81, 254–279
  sequencing, 77–78, 98–118, 500–504, 504–509
Production systems, 20–22
Production variation, 126
Productivity, 251
Profit–volume analysis, 164–166
Purchasing, 356–357, 361–376, 565
  centralized/decentralized, 373

information, 363
profit specification, 365–366
purchasing cycle, 361, 565
supplies selection, 366–368
Pure research, 89–90

Quality assurance, 122–123, 644–664
Quality control economics, 645–646
  failure costs, 645
  inspection costs, 645
  preventive costs, 645
Quality control organization, 642–644
Quality factor relationships, 129
Quality level, 647–648
Quality in service, 128
Queuing, 76–77
  annual rate, 529
  arrival distribution, 527
  assumptions, 528–529
  equations, 529–530
  examples, 530–537, 625–631
  multichannel, 527, 531–535
  queue discipline, 527
  service distribution, 528
  service rate, 529
  simulation, 535–537
  single-channel, 527, 530–531

Rating factor, 298
Receiving, 358, 565
Reciprocal buying, 376
Redundancy, 142
Regression coefficient, 393
Regression line, 393–394
Relevant costs, 192–194
Reliability, definition, 132
  measures, 134
Reliability engineering, 125
Repair alternatives, 615–616
Resale or salvage value, 193, 215–216
Routing, 573–577
Routing follow-up, 576–577
Routing precedence, 575–576

S-shaped product-life curves, 95, 148
Safety stock, 436, 442, 444–445
  calculation, 445–446
Sales volume analysis, 161
Sample inventory problem, 447–449
Scalar principal, 46
Scheduling, index method, 585–588
Scheduling practices, graphic solution, 581–584
  index approach, 585–588
  run-out approach, 580

simplex example, 584–585
simulation, 593–595
transportation approach, 588–593
Scientific method, 60–62
Sequential sampling, 660–662
Setup time, 492
Shewhart, Walter, 8
SIMO chart, 311, 313, 315, 317
Simulation, 535–537, 593–595,
    617–625
Smoothing constant, 407–410
Speculative buying, 375
Split routing, 579
Staff authority, 46
Standard costs, 680–688
Standard cost standards, 684–688
    direct material, 685–688
    labor costs, 684–685
Standard cost variance analysis,
    688–697
Standard deviation, 412, 466
Standard error of estimate, 413
Standard error of a proportion, 670
*Standard and Poor's Corporation
    Records*, 676
Standard practice, 259
Suboptimization, 71, 252
Suggestion programs, 272
Sunk costs, 192–194
System, comprehensive model, 18–20
    control, 11–12
    conversion process, 10
    definition, 9
    environment, 12–13
    flow patterns, 9–11
    information flow, 13–14
    inputs, 10
    outputs, 10
    subsystem, 15–18
Systems approach, 9, 56, 60
Systems approach to decision making,
    decision process, 70
    definition, 70
    objective criteria, 71–72
    problem definition, 71

Tapered vertical integration, 489
Taylor, Frederick W., 7–8, 289, 356
Time series analysis, adjusted ex-
    ponential weighting, 408–410
    cyclical variations, 399
    exponential least squares line,
        401–402
    least square trend, 399–401

nonlinear trend, 401
residual or irregular variation, 399
seasonal variation, 399
simple exponential weighting,
    407–408
simple moving average, 402–403
trend, 399
weighted moving average, 403–407
Time study
    average observed times (AOT),
        292–297
    cycles, determining sample size of,
        296–297
    elements, 289–290
    fatigue allowances, 304
    irregular allowances, 304
    machine allowances, 305
    objective rating, 300–301
    personal time allowances, 303
    rating or leveling, 297
    select times (ST), 290–297, 301
    standard times, 306
    subjective rating, 299–300
Training, 335–336
Transportation LP model, 472–479
Trial-and-error decision making, 58–59
Two-stage bidding, 371

Unit bill of material (UBM), 686

Value analysis, 363–365
Variable sampling, 662
Vertical integration, 371

Wage incentives, 347–351
    high-task, 350–352
    low-task, 348–350
    measured day work, 350–351
    piece rate, 349
Wage and salary administration,
    337–352
    external balance, 338
    factor comparison, 340–342
    internal balance, 339
    occupation grading, 340
    point plans, 343–347
    ranking, 340
    red circle rates, 345
Waiting line. *See* Queuing
Work-in-process inventory, 509–510
Work methods, 250
    in clerical activities, 281–282
    developing new methods, 271
    installation, 280

Work methods (*continued*)
  INTER-work station, 254, 257, 277
  INTRA-work station, 254, 273
  management role, 281
  organizational aspects, 253
  problem analysis, 259–263
  selection of best methods, 272–279
Work sampling, 318–324
  accuracy, 319–323
  advantages and limitations, 323–324

element definition, 321
for output standards, 323
sample size, 319–321
to set allowances, 322
Working conditions, 234–238
  atmospheric, 238
  lighting, 236
  noise, 236–238
  safety, 238

1. A=6   cost = $6.00 p/h

S=5

Type A

1 machine $\frac{A}{S-A} = \frac{6}{8-6} = \frac{6}{5}$ = 3 machine

3 × $6.00 = $18.00

2 machines   A=6   cost = $12.00
S=16

$\frac{6}{16-6} = \frac{6}{10} = \frac{3}{5}$ = .6 machines

.60 × $12.00 = $7.20

3 machines   A=6   cost $18.00
S=24

$\frac{6}{24-6} = \frac{6}{18} = \frac{1}{3}$ = .33 machines

$\frac{1}{3}$ × $18.00 = $6.00

Type B   1 machine $\frac{A=6}{S=12}$ cost = $12.00

$\frac{6}{12-6} = \frac{6}{6}$ = 1 machine

1 × $10.00 = $10.00

2 machines   A=6   cost = $20.00
S=24

$\frac{6}{24-6} = \frac{6}{18} = \frac{1}{3}$ = .33 machines

$\frac{1}{3}$ × $20.00 = $6.67

3 machines   A=6   cost = $30.00
S=36

$\frac{6}{36-6} = \frac{6}{30} = \frac{1}{5}$ = .20 machines

.20 × $30.00 = $6.00

) If no waiting line is desired (less than 40%), 3 machine of type A has only .33 prob. of one unit waiting at a cost of $6.00.

2 machine of Type B has only .33 prob of one unit waiting at a cost of $6.6)

Therefore, to minimize cost, 3 machines of type A would be cheaper.

If 3 unit waiting is acceptable, 1 machine of Type A has 3 units waiting at a cost of $18.00. One machine of Type B has only one unit waiting at a cost of $10.00.

Therefore, to minimize cost and in their case # of units waiting, 1 machine of type A would be better, because A is only $6.00 per unit waiting, and B is $10.00.

$A = 6$

$S = 3$

$N = 4$

$$\sum_{n=0}^{3} \frac{1}{n!}\left(\frac{6}{3}\right)^{n} = 1 + 2 + 2 + \frac{4}{3} = \frac{15}{3} + \frac{4}{3} = \frac{19}{3}$$

$$\frac{1}{4!}\left(\frac{6}{3}\right)^{4}\left(\frac{4 \cdot 3}{4 \cdot 3 - 6}\right) = \frac{1}{24}(16)(2) = \frac{32}{24} = \frac{4}{3}$$

$$P_0 = \frac{1}{\frac{19}{3} + \frac{4}{3}} = \frac{1}{\frac{23}{3}} = \frac{3}{23}$$

$$P_{>0} = \frac{3\left(\frac{6}{3}\right)^{4}}{3!\,(12-6)} \cdot \frac{3}{23}$$

$$= \frac{48}{36} \cdot \frac{3}{23}$$

$$= \frac{4}{3} \cdot \frac{3}{23}$$

$$= \frac{4}{23}$$

$t = \frac{1}{3}hr.$ $e^{-2 \cdot 72}$

$$P_{>t} = e^{-4 \cdot 3 \cdot \frac{1}{3}\left(1 - \frac{1}{2}\right)} \cdot \frac{4}{23}$$

$$= e^{-2} \times \frac{4}{23}$$

$$= \frac{1}{(2.72)^{2}} \times \frac{4}{23}$$

$$= \frac{1}{7.40} \times \frac{4}{23}$$

$$= \frac{4}{170.2}$$

$$= .0235$$

$$
\begin{array}{r}
2 \cdot 72 \\
2 \cdot 72 \\
\hline
5\ 44 \\
19\ 0\ 4 \\
5\ 44 \\
\hline
7.3\ 9\ 8\ 4
\end{array}
$$

$$
\begin{array}{r}
7.40 \\
23 \\
\hline
2\ 2\ 2\ 0 \\
14\ 8\ 0 \\
\hline
1\ 7\ 0.2\ 0
\end{array}
$$

$$EOQ = \sqrt{\frac{2 C_3 D}{C_1}}$$

$$= \sqrt{\frac{2 \times 5 \times 18,000}{.10 \times 1.28}}$$

$$= \sqrt{140,625}$$

$$= 375$$

.80
.15
.225
.04
.06
___
1.275